W9-CTY-889

THE ENCYCLOPEDIA OF
Commercial Real Estate
Advice

How to Add Value When Buying, Selling, Repositioning, Developing, Financing, and Managing

TERRY PAINTER

WILEY

Copyright © 2021 by John Wiley & Sons, Inc. All rights reserved.

Published by John Wiley & Sons, Inc., Hoboken, New Jersey.
Published simultaneously in Canada.

No part of this publication may be reproduced, stored in a retrieval system, or transmitted in any form or by any means, electronic, mechanical, photocopying, recording, scanning, or otherwise, except as permitted under Section 107 or 108 of the 1976 United States Copyright Act, without either the prior written permission of the Publisher, or authorization through payment of the appropriate per-copy fee to the Copyright Clearance Center, Inc., 222 Rosewood Drive, Danvers, MA 01923, (978) 750-8400, fax (978) 646-8600, or on the Web at www.copyright.com. Requests to the Publisher for permission should be addressed to the Permissions Department, John Wiley & Sons, Inc., 111 River Street, Hoboken, NJ 07030, (201) 748-6011, fax (201) 748-6008, or online at http://www.wiley.com/go/permissions.

Limit of Liability/Disclaimer of Warranty: While the publisher and author have used their best efforts in preparing this book, they make no representations or warranties with respect to the accuracy or completeness of the contents of this book and specifically disclaim any implied warranties of merchantability or fitness for a particular purpose. No warranty may be created or extended by sales representatives or written sales materials. The advice and strategies contained herein may not be suitable for your situation. You should consult with a professional where appropriate. Neither the publisher nor author shall be liable for any loss of profit or any other commercial damages, including but not limited to special, incidental, consequential, or other damages.

For general information on our other products and services or for technical support, please contact our Customer Care Department within the United States at (800) 762-2974, outside the United States at (317) 572-3993 or fax (317) 572-4002.

Wiley publishes in a variety of print and electronic formats and by print-on-demand. Some material included with standard print versions of this book may not be included in e-books or in print-on-demand. If this book refers to media such as a CD or DVD that is not included in the version you purchased, you may download this material at http://booksupport.wiley.com. For more information about Wiley products, visit www.wiley.com.

Library of Congress Cataloging-in-Publication Data
Names: Painter, Terry, author.
Title: The encyclopedia of commercial real estate advice : how to add value
    when buying, selling, repositioning, developing, financing, and
    managing / Terry Painter.
Description: First Edition. | Hoboken : Wiley, 2020. | Includes index.
Identifiers: LCCN 2020029287 (print) | LCCN 2020029288 (ebook) | ISBN
    9781119629115 (cloth) | ISBN 9781119629153 (adobe pdf) | ISBN
    9781119629184 (epub)
Subjects: LCSH: Industrial real estate. | Commercial buildings. | Real
    estate investment. | Real estate business–Finance.
Classification: LCC HD1393.5 .P335 2020 (print) | LCC HD1393.5 (ebook) |
    DDC 333.33/87—dc23
LC record available at https://lccn.loc.gov/2020029287
LC ebook record available at https://lccn.loc.gov/2020029288

Cover Design and Illustration: Wiley

Printed in the United States of America

SKY10021106_091420

Dedicated to Bruce Allen Painter

1949–2019

My big brother, who stood by me through thick and thin.

And to my wife Margie, who provided the ideal conditions for writing this book, and to Max, who insisted, "Father, you have to write a book."

Contents

PART VI
Smart Strategies for Developing

PART VII
Smart Strategies for Financing

Encyclopedia Topics

ENCYCLOPEDIA TOPIC G
Development   **295**

ENCYCLOPEDIA TOPIC H
Financing   357

ENCYCLOPEDIA TOPIC I
Commercial Loan Programs   391

ENCYCLOPEDIA TOPIC J
Managing and Leasing   427

Foreword

For over 20 years, I've invested in commercial real estate in nearly every section of the United States and have taught thousands of everyday people how to successfully invest in large apartment buildings, shopping centers, office buildings, self-storage facilities, and so on.

When I first met Terry Painter in 2004, my commercial real estate business was experiencing out-of-control growth. I needed to talk to him about a 140-unit apartment complex we were purchasing in Dallas, Texas. We had just been within days of getting our financing approved when the lender, without warning, backed out. On that day and until today, I still wonder how a guy who's so intelligent can have such a witty sense of humor. Typically, people as sharp as Terry aren't very funny.

Well, to make a long story short, Terry is the smartest finance guy I ever met. But not just book-smart; Terry had gleaned his wisdom from the most valuable school one could attend—the School of Hard Knocks. He could virtually read through our deal's financial statements and share with us what the numbers truly meant from not only a rate of return perspective, but a human and emotional perspective. It was at that time that I started learning the importance of closely working with people who were smarter than me. Just to let you know, Terry came to the rescue on that Dallas deal and closed on a loan for us in 38 days with zero issues. Since then, he is the first person we call when a commercial loan is needed.

Some of the best deals our group got involved in were the ones Terry advised us to pass on. Sometimes the greatest value is exiting at the beginning a deal that could be a time bomb. And likewise, many deals that Terry advised us to move forward on were personally life-changing deals for us and many others. Terry was, and has always been, the smartest guy in the room. Period.

The Encyclopedia of Commercial Real Estate Advice is a serious, bottom-line book about making and modeling sound business decisions around buying and selling a commercial property. It covers raising money from investors, due diligence (most important in my opinion), developing from the ground up, repositioning a property to its highest and best use (my personal favorite), leasing and management, and of course, financing. It's probably the most useful, advanced real estate book I have ever read.

For Terry to pour his vast real-world knowledge and passion into this book is a true blessing to any reader or student of this great business called commercial real estate. Terry is more than just a great lender, though. His deep and practical command of the commercial lending world is more than just concepts. His advice is from years and years and hundreds of closed transactions all over the United States, helping investors (perhaps just like you!) reach lifetime financial targets and lifestyle goals. To me, and perhaps you, that's what life is about. My advice to readers is to get someone who's smarter than yourself on your team. That person is the author of this phenomenal book.

Peter Harris, best-selling author of *Commercial Real Estate Investing For Dummies*
CommercialRealEstateInvestingForDummies.com

Introduction

Congratulations! If you are reading this book, you are a very lucky person. If you are already investing in commercial real estate, thinking about it, or working in this field, you are a member of a very exclusive group. According to the IRS, less than 8% of all Americans who file tax returns get to invest in income property and under 3% own commercial investment real estate. And if you work in this industry like I do (I do commercial mortgages), well, I hope you think it's fun, as I do, and, might I add, never boring.

As an investor in commercial property, you get to wake up in the morning and say to yourself, "What can I do to this property to add value?" Maybe you have found a Class C minus apartment complex in an up-and-coming neighborhood. Yes, get rid of the slow-paying and no-paying renters, and the ones who have rusty bikes and junk on their patios. Then do about $4,500 per unit in cosmetic upgrades and the rents can be raised $100 per month. Just with those ideas you can be on your way to increasing the property value by 20% or more in five years. I know of no other investment opportunity that is designed like commercial real estate—one where you can choose the right property, add value, and be rewarded with a pay raise, increased equity, and amazing tax benefits.

Remember when you just had a day job? You only had one source of income—the paycheck. With commercial real estate, you get to have *four* sources of income: rental income, rental increases, appreciation, and depreciation. (I know, how can something appreciate and depreciate at the same time? Only in America.) Oh, but wait! There is actually a fifth one—leveraging your equity tax free into a larger, more profitable property by doing a cash-out refinance or a 1031 tax-deferred exchange. These are covered in detail in Chapter 5.

Is commercial real estate a better or safer investment than the stock market? Well, this is really comparing apples with oranges. Commercial real estate is slow moving. It just doesn't have wild swings from one day to the next like the ones stocks are known for. It is unlikely that you will ever lose 25% of your equity or, for that matter, gain 25% as stocks can over a year—or, even worse, experience a drop of 12% in one week as the Dow did on February 28, 2020, as fears of the COVID-19 crisis impacted the world.

Commercial property investment certainly has its risks, which are explained in detail in Chapter 1. One major risk is choosing a higher-risk property type. Unless you have experience and a nice chunk of cash, you might want to avoid hotels, retail, and office properties. Recessions consistently seem to give these properties heartburn. Oh, and I had better add Class C minus apartment complexes in blue-collar neighborhoods to this list. Boy, do they take a lot of mothering, complete with nagging tenants to be nice to each other and pay the rent. During the Great Recession and the coronavirus recession, these properties had the most slow-paying and no-paying tenants in the multifamily sector due to job loss. Class A, B, and C apartment buildings in good neighborhoods had a very low rate of default.

Recessions can actually offer a bonus when buying commercial property. Many of my clients can't wait for the next one. They have cash put aside to snatch distressed properties at a discount. Many of my experienced clients are careful to recession-proof their properties. Chapter 2 gives you 10 tested methods of doing this. Just one of them, structuring the property so that it can break even at 75% occupancy after paying all the expenses and the mortgage, can make your property bulletproof during a recession.

Actually, in my experience the highest risk is taking shortcuts on due diligence when buying, and getting married to a property who is not who you thought it was. To avoid falling into this trap, be sure to read Chapter 3, especially the 11 due diligence mistakes to avoid.

Unlike investing passively in stocks, investing in commercial real estate is a hands-on business. What causes stocks to go up and down is the performance of the companies they represent and the whims of investors buying and selling each day. Conversely, commercial real estate depends on your entrepreneurial skill. This is what I love the most about it and why I am writing this book, which is chock-full of solid, tested advice on how to make the right decisions and avoid pitfalls when buying, selling, repositioning, developing, financing, and managing commercial real estate.

When my editor, Richard Narramore, contacted me to see if I would be interested in writing this book, my first thought was—"sounds interesting." My next thought was: "Hey, wait a minute, this is my book." Why? Because for 23 years, I have lived and breathed commercial real estate. I have financed just about every type of commercial property—from memory-care facilities to a biodiesel plant—during every economic cycle. I know the pros and cons and the quirks of just about all of them. I know that a light-industrial complex will survive better than an office complex during tough economic times. That for the newbie, apartments are one of the easiest types of property to learn about, but that they can be alarmingly risky, since managing them is a bear. That self-storage is a much better investment for the beginner, as it is easy to manage and usually highly profitable at 85% occupancy, but that self-storage properties are difficult to buy. I have learned that owning a commercial property out of state quadruples the risk, and that if you do not have any working capital that's an even bigger risk. Did you know that smaller property management companies steal from the properties they manage more often than you would think? There are 11 very creative ways they do this, outlined in detail in Chapter 12.

I have taught seminars to new investors about how to choose the right commercial property, how to finance it, and how to recession-proof it. I have trained commercial realtors on how to avoid having their deals crash and burn after they have put over a hundred hours into them. I have assisted many of my clients in putting together financing proposals for repositioning all kinds of commercial properties. One of my deepest passions is working with developers—they are amazing people! They start out with an idea, which leads to finding the right piece of land. They then run some numbers. This leads to a design drawing. Next they mix in thousands of hours of work and a lot of brick and mortar. They then get to walk by the bustling property someday with their grandkids and say—"I built this!" Read Chapter 8 to find out if you have what it takes to be a developer.

At my companies, Business Loan Store and Apartment Loan Store, we finance all types of commercial real estate, but we are also advisory firms. I love assisting our clients with making the best decisions based on their long- and short-term financial goals. You would be surprised how many are sitting on the fence on what those goals are. What? You don't know yet if this is going to be a fix-and-flip or a long-term hold? From a lending perspective, my work is forensic in nature: looking under every rock, and sometimes bringing shock and awe to borrowers and their real estate brokers. "Oh, you didn't know that was hiding under there?" I love crunching the numbers: discarding the fiction and uncovering the facts. I do not get to fall in love with a property at first sight. But some of my clients do just that.

Some of the subjects covered in this book are why wealth grows faster using other people's money, how to value a property in 15 minutes, how to fake it until you make it when raising investors, why it might be better to do a cash-out refinance than selling, how to get the most bang for your buck when repositioning and developing, trade secrets on getting the best rate and terms on your commercial loan (lenders are not going to like that I have disclosed their secrets), and whether it's better to self-manage or to hire professional management.

THIS BOOK WILL SAVE YOU TIME AND MONEY

Many experts will tell you that anyone can begin investing in commercial real estate. If that were true, then everyone would be doing it. The problem is that commercial real estate is just not simple. Also, it takes a substantial amount of money.

On the other hand, if would-be investors only focused on how complicated it is and how much time it takes to do it properly, few would ever get started. The advice in this book is designed to save you time and money. Much of it comes from what I have learned from working on deals with highly experienced commercial real estate investors. But in the seminars I found myself taking on over the years, I am sure I've taught well over a hundred enthusiastic inexperienced investors, many of whom had found a great property to buy. Most in this group just didn't know how unlikely it would be for them to succeed. Most didn't even have enough cash to come close to covering the down payment. But they were so driven by a dream that I found myself joining them in their madness. Guiding these entrepreneurs, and helping them avoid hazards, has given me most of the material for this book.

HOW TO USE THIS BOOK

There are eight parts to this book, each representing a major topic. Each one starts out with informative chapters followed by an encyclopedia where you can look up individual subjects that interest you pertaining to the topic. Each encyclopedia subject is not just defined, but has sound nuts-and-bolts advice. With 336 encyclopedia subjects on just about everything from *A* to *Z* on commercial real estate, you can go back to the encyclopedia sections over time when you need a resource on a subject. As a bonus, there are 136 Time and Money Saving Tips spread throughout the chapters and encyclopedia sections. Commercial real estate terms that are in *italics* are included in the encyclopedia sections, where you can learn more about them.

Smart Strategies for Buying

Who Are You When Buying a Commercial Property?

It might seem strange for someone writing a book on commercial real estate advice to begin the first chapter by asking the reader "Who are you when buying a commercial property?" I am asking you this question because I have found it to be the most important question buyers of commercial real estate can ask themselves to save time and money.

Some of my buying clients clearly did not ask themselves this question. Many seemed to lack confidence. They spent so much time evaluating the wrong properties, and so many different types of properties, that I found myself spinning in circles with them and getting dizzy. Did they want to buy properties close to home or out of state? Properties that did not need any work, or those they could add value to? They couldn't make up their mind. For some, all the choices seemed to be too risky. They just could not decide on the level of risk they could live with. After bumping into endless walls, many found themselves quite miserable. Some just quit the process. Some made it through and actually closed on a property. But many of them ended up owning the wrong property in the wrong place at what turned out to be the wrong price.

And then I have had clients that clearly knew who they were and what they wanted from the beginning. Most of them were experienced. It seemed as though they were born to invest in real estate. I had fun working with investors in this group; we shared the love of the deal. They also bumped into lots of walls because that's what you do when you buy commercial investment property. But they had a blueprint to follow that kept them going in the right direction.

The goal of this chapter is to help you understand which category of investor you fall into, and how to determine the risk level of a commercial property you are interested in purchasing.

SEVEN TOP CHARACTER TRAITS OF EXPERIENCED COMMERCIAL REAL ESTATE INVESTORS

1. Are You Determined, Confident, and Unstoppable?

In 2005, an LAPD officer named Kelly Fabros called me for financing. She had taken a course called The Maui Millionaires and decided at the age of 32 that she was going to retire from the force. She was going to move on to becoming a millionaire through commercial real estate investments. Our first conversation went something like this:

"Hey Terry, I have found the perfect 164-unit apartment complex called Riverwalk Apartments in Wichita."

"How much is it, Kelly?"

"Six million eight hundred thousand."

To get people who are not qualified off the phone fast I always ask them two questions:

"How much do you have to put down?"

"One hundred and sixty thousand."

I then added, "And do you have experience owning a large apartment complex?"

She replied, "No, but I'm not concerned about that. I do own a home we rent out."

"I'm sorry," I told her, "you are just not qualified. Why don't you buy something you can afford and have the experience to run, like a fourplex?"

"You don't need to insult me," she answered, "Riverwalk is what I am looking for."

I went on, "I'm certainly not trying to insult you. It's just that you only have about two percent to put down and no experience."

Kelly very proudly told me, "That's not going to be a problem. I can find investors."

You would think that would be the end of it. Not at all. Kelly Fabros is the most determined and focused beginning commercial property investor I have ever worked with to this day. Her confidence and determination are unyielding. Through the course she had taken she had learned that if she found the right property for the right price she could raise investors to muster up the down payment, and that is exactly what she did. She brought in a high-powered executive from Intel, her parents, and a few other investors and had the down payment. Now she had my attention. I gave her an extensive due diligence list and she knocked off 100% of it enthusiastically. After crunching the numbers together, I told her that the property would not cash flow the 75% loan she wanted and that she would have to negotiate the price down to $6.3 million. "Okay, not a problem," she told me. And she did it. Kelly repeated this recipe many more times and did indeed become a millionaire.

I have come to recognize what I call the "Kelly factor" in other commercial property investors.

They just do not know they cannot do something that to others is so obviously out of their league. They don't have those thoughts of "Oh, no, what have I gotten myself into? What if everyone can tell that I'm just winging it?" Or "This is so much more than I can handle, I've had enough!" Instead, they see every roadblock as a challenge to find a solution for it. And then they knock down those roadblocks. If they don't know something, they learn what they need to know. If they don't have the down payment, their enthusiasm is so contagious that they have investors lining up to join them!

2. Can You Make the Right Choices at the Beginning?

Are you good at making choices at the beginning, or are you a wanderer? You really have two choices: is it more you to be proactive or reactive? As a buyer, are you more prone to start out knowing what you want and be in charge of finding a property that meets those objectives? Do you have the willpower to not detour much from those goals? Or is it more you to go with the flow—to start out in a direction that seems interesting and then veer from it because something completely different catches your eye?

For my client Janet, finding the right commercial property reminded her a lot of online dating. She had sold four rental homes and wanted to get into commercial property. She found a 24-unit apartment complex in her hometown of Syracuse, New York, offered at a 7% *cap rate*. This made it a good buy since properties of this quality were going for closer to a 6.5% cap. She thought that maybe she would do some cosmetic work on it, raise the rents, increase the value, and flip it. It started out with "Hey, I like your pics, let's meet up." Which led to "Thank goodness I didn't waste my time on that one—it has too many problems." And then her real estate broker showed her a small strip mall that had really good looks and a great upside—under-market rents. Janet hadn't thought of retail but got the feeling that this property just might have chemistry. The meetup went well. But then she looked at the rent roll. The tenants were indeed paying under-market rent, but it concerned her that most of the leases did not mature for two to three years. The realtor explained that this was why he had chosen the property for her: "It is such a good buy." She replied, "So, the property is overpriced now, but in two years it will be worth it?" When Janet finally got the financials the net operating income (NOI) did not match up with the cap rate. Now she was really mad because she felt she had been lied to.

So a friend told her that she really should try self-storage. She went on LoopNet—the largest online commercial property listing service in the United States. Janet found a self-storage facility in Chattanooga, Tennessee, offered at a 9% cap. During the flight over to see the property she was filled with excitement. On the ground, this turned to confusion when the listing agent told her that the current owners were managing it and living on-site and that there was a nice apartment for her to live in while she ran the business. Janet's intention was certainly not to move to Chattanooga and buy herself a job. And if she paid the estimated $24,000 per year to have someone else live there and manage the property, she would be buying it at a 6% cap and the property would be vastly overpriced. The listing agent had a remedy—a great price on a single-tenant property in town. The tenant was a day care center. Janet thought, okay, maybe this is the one.

Successful, proactive commercial property investors know who they are, what they are looking for, and where they are looking for it. They know exactly what their financial objectives are for the short term and the long term. These investors have a plan and they do not deviate much from it. It would not occur to them to see which way the wind blew that day and drift in that direction like Janet did. They are willing to look at dozens of properties to find the one that fits their plan. Proactive investors also know what type of commercial property fits their lifestyle and become experts in that type. These self-directed individuals know where they want to buy and whether they would be comfortable moving for a property that needs hands-on management. They know their minimum acceptable return on investment and maximum risk level and they stay within their comfort zone on both. Very importantly, they know if they can live with having partners or whether this will drive them crazy.

Proactive investors know whether they are looking for an opportunistic investment or a solid, stable one. They know what size market is best for them—*primary*, *secondary*, *tertiary*, or *very small* (see Encyclopedia Topic H, Financing). These investors know what their competition is and what they can do to outdo it. They have a budget for repairs and financing costs, and they stay with that. They likely already have a team together—the best real estate brokers, investors, general contractors, lenders, property managers, insurance agents, and attorneys. These entrepreneurs are able to see value-add strategies for a property that everyone else has missed. They only employ the most cost-effective ones and know how to estimate costs for these accurately (see Chapter 7 on repositioning). Most importantly, they only buy properties that fit most of their objectives. And the ones that don't—well, they just walk away (see *buyer's list of property objectives* in Encyclopedia Topic A, Buying).

3. Can You Walk Away—Even if You Are in Love with the Property?

This might seem like a no-brainer, but you would be surprised how often buyers find themselves falling head over heels for a property and then paying too much for it. In a seller's market, sometimes buyers are just tired of looking and settle for less than they should. First impressions can really get you in trouble.

My client Craig knew right away that he'd found the light-industrial complex he was looking for. All the signs told him that it was the right property. He told me, "There is so much synchronicity. The sellers have been so forthright in providing me with everything I asked for. I really hit it off with them over lunch and they were so transparent on sharing some repair items." But after investing a great deal of time in due diligence, the property was just not meeting his financial objectives. His realtor arranged a meeting with the listing agent and the sellers. Craig planned to show the sellers on paper that their numbers did not work at the price they were asking. The meeting did not go well—the sellers wouldn't budge. Craig's broker told him, "They know you want it—you should not have had lunch with them." Craig started thinking that he could make their price work and that he could recover the loss over time by adding value and raising rents. Fortunately he woke up the next morning and decided to walk away.

Buying the property for the right price is the single best action that you can take right out of the gate to increase your cash on cash return. A few years ago one of my borrowers fell madly in love with a brand new 64-unit apartment complex, which I'm sure was the nicest in Utah. It certainly was the most expensive. I could see why. It was breathtakingly beautiful, with granite countertops, Karastan carpets, and magnificent river views from every room. I told the borrower, "John, do you realize based on current cap rates and comparable sales on A Class multifamily that this property is only worth about 13 million and you have just offered 14.5 million for it?" "I don't care," he replied. "Terry, you have to help me get it." I argued, "It's not like you are going to be living there, and your friends will never likely see it. Find something that is priced below replacement costs like the last property you bought." "No," he replied. "I want this one!" Two months later we closed on the deal. That was after we showed the 13-million-dollar appraisal to the seller and he dropped the price by half a million. John still paid a million dollars more than it was worth.

It takes so much time and money to raise the net income of a commercial property compared to the time it takes to buy one for the right price. Just think about what John will have to do to make up the million dollars he overpaid. The property was new and did not need anything. Plus it was well managed and few, if any, expenses could be cut. That leaves raising rents, which were already at market. Let's say he could raise the rent of all 64 units by $100 per month. It would take 13 years for those rent increases to add up to a million dollars.

The bottom line is that no one starts out shopping for a commercial property with the objective of paying more than a property is worth. This only happens when there is an emotional attachment to a property for sale. Many of my clients have found a property with good looks and absolutely had to have it at first. But after doing their due diligence and recognizing that it was overpriced, most woke up and told themselves, "No, this doesn't fit my financial objectives. I'm going to pass on it."

4. Are You Willing to Become an Expert in a Commercial Property Type?

Thirty years ago my client Roger Allen, a professor in real estate and finance at Boise State University, kind of fell into the self-storage business. A student came to him with the idea of building a bunch of small garages on a vacant piece of land. He asked the youngster what in the world did he want to do that for and how he expected to do it if he did not have any money. Roger ended up financing the project and found himself in the self-storage business. Today he has 15 facilities and over 15,000 units. I told him that he had the equivalent of a doctorate in self-storage. Building a self-storage property from the ground up is one of the more risky commercial real estate investments. This is because there is usually a lot of competition and these properties take a lot of time to reach stabilized occupancy. But because Roger knows exactly how to evaluate the need for them, how to market them, and how to manage them, the risk is very low for him.

Lenders prefer to make loans to those who have experience in that property type. Many top-producing commercial real estate brokers specialize in just one type of property. CBRE Group will not allow its brokers to specialize in more than one type. Why? For exactly the same reason you do not find a physician who specializes in both radiology and orthopedics. Most types of commercial real estate really are that specialized. Yes, all types do have many of the same analytical components, such as rent rolls, operating expenses, and NOI—and let's not forget capitalization rates. But that's where the similarities end. Understanding how to lease and handle tenant improvements for an office property is very different from leasing and managing an industrial complex. So if banks and real estate agents have discovered that one can be more successful by specializing in one type of commercial property, does it not make sense for buyers of commercial real estate to do the same? It's not to say that once you master the quirks of one property type you cannot succeed at another. The point here is that when you get good at something and have mastered the learning curve, you can duplicate this repeatedly, saving time and money.

5. Are You Willing to Buy in Your Own Backyard?

Buying in your own backyard means being able to drive to the property you are interested in purchasing within an hour. If it takes much longer than that, you are just not as likely to check on the property very often.

It is interesting that Fannie Mae is reluctant to make a loan to would-be apartment building buyers if the property is in a state other than the one in which the borrower lives. During the Great Recession, almost all of Fannie's defaults came from this sector. Just about all the commercial property failures in my commercial finance business were from out-of-state borrowers too. So unless you visit the property often and have a hands-on approach to your out-of-the-area property, you could be quadrupling the risk of losing the property. When the property is in your own backyard, you can make surprise visits. You will know when the parking lot has trash on it, or if the lawn is turning brown. When you own a property locally you will be able to oversee leasing and maintenance at a level that just cannot be matched in a property that is far away. Just being able to drive by the property often and getting to know your tenants will give you a competitive advantage.

One of the main problems of buying out of state is that it can be difficult to know and understand the market you are buying in. A commercial property in another state that might appear to be a good buy if it were located in your backyard may be overpriced where it is. Also, it's always better to buy where your trusted team of professionals is expert, in a market you already know and live near. We are talking about your buyer's real estate broker, your local lender or commercial mortgage broker, your property manager, and your commercial real estate attorney.

I am an expert in many of the markets I lend in. But as a commercial mortgage banker who lends in all 50 states, I am at a disadvantage in that I just cannot have current, cutting-edge knowledge of all the markets we lend in. Often I have to rely on professionals who live and work in those markets or research companies for the data I need to evaluate a property and the competition. I think you will find yourself in the same situation if you purchase property in a market you are not familiar with. Most of my large commercial investors who own over $20 million in real estate invest in their own market first.

If you live in a very expensive area, such as San Francisco where commercial properties sell below a 5% cap, you can be handsomely rewarded for investing in a lower-priced, higher-cap-rate market such as Dallas, Texas, where you can still find quality commercial properties at an 8% cap. The majority of my California clients buy out of state. However, they know that they have to have excellent management and visit the property often to pull this off.

6. Do You Know What Value-Add Strategies You Ideally Want?

Mike Warren, the founder of AMJ Inc. in Gainesville, Florida, has purchased and repositioned over $400 million in commercial real estate. When he first looks at a property, he immediately starts looking for value-add strategies. He does this by what he calls "undoing restraints," or determining what can be done to undo a constraint that somebody else didn't find or could not act on. Mike knows that if he buys a property and does not improve it that it will not go up much in value.

Constraints can involve regulations, zoning changes, or making physical changes that can attract better-quality, higher-paying tenants.

Many of my clients get an intuitive rush of value-add ideas when they first find a property. And some even lie awake at night thinking about them. For some, this is the part of buying commercial real estate that is the most fun. Do you know your value-add strategies at the beginning? The least costly ones are operational and involve improving management: raising rents and lowering expenses. Cosmetic changes, like a new coat of paint or striping the parking lot, are moderately expensive. And construction changes, like replacing a roof or adding on more square footage, are very expensive. Go to Chapter 7 for much more detail on this subject.

Time and Money Saving Tip

Wouldn't it be much better to have the best value-add deals find you instead of you having to pound the pavement to find them? Just follow this recipe that one of my most successful real estate investors uses. Put it out to 10 or more real estate professionals (real estate brokers, commercial loan brokers, commercial property managers, and bankers) that you have the wherewithal to close on a specific type and size of commercial property. Let them all know that you will use them if they find you a deal. Tell them you are looking for a distressed seller who is motivated by bankruptcy, recession, divorce, bad health, death, or rehabilitation projects that have gone wrong. Then just relax and wait for the phone to ring.

7. Do You Know Your Acceptable Risk Level?

As already mentioned, the most important question to ask when buying commercial real estate is "Who are you?" The second most important question is probably: "Is it worth it to take these risks for the expected return on this investment?"

The real estate market has always gone up and down in cycles and always will. Boom periods can last from two to 10 years and are followed by recessions that can last from eight months to a year and a half. In the summer of 2007, many commercial real estate investors didn't know they were buying at the top of the market, as prices had continually gone up over a six-year bull market. By December of that year, the Great Recession was building momentum and prices started tumbling. This occurred on a bigger scale when in January of 2020 most investors, real estate brokers, and lenders of commercial real estate were preparing for another good year. After 10 years of a continual up market with property values soaring, most seemed to forget that recessions even existed.

Two months later, the United States and most of the world found itself freefalling into the coronavirus recession that history will likely remember along the lines of the Great Depression of 1929. During the seven-week period from March 26 through May 7, 2020, 33 million workers applied for unemployment benefits, raising the rate from 3.5% to 14.7%, according to the Bureau of Labor Statistics. Many of these workers could not pay their rent and their bosses could not pay theirs, either.

The coronavirus recession might be a one in a hundred-year event. No one knows for sure. The silver lining for commercial real estate buyers is that recessions turn seller's markets into buyer's markets and bring prices down, which brings up the question, "How do you know if prices have hit the bottom and you are getting the best price?" Sorry—you won't know where the bottom is until prices start going up again. So when is the best time to buy? Read on.

FOUR PHASES OF THE COMMERCIAL REAL ESTATE MARKET CYCLE AND THE BEST TIME TO BUY

One of the most important factors in determining risk is to be aware of what phase in the real estate market cycle you are buying in. Unless you are the best psychic on the planet, you will not be able to determine how long a cycle will last, but you can learn to identify which cycle you are in and implement a safer, more informed investment strategy for that cycle. For example, if you want to purchase a property to reposition it, the last thing you want to do is to buy a property that needs expensive cosmetic and constructional changes if the market is in the hyper-supply phase where prices are at their peak, because you would likely be overimproving the property for its potential future value. Even if you find a property with under-market rents in this cycle, you could be in trouble if you pay top dollar for it. If your goal is to improve a property, raise rents, increase the value, and sell at a profit, it makes sense for you to buy during the recovery phase, when prices have hit bottom, and wait until the market is deep into the expansion phase to sell. Here are the four phases of the real estate market:

1. *Recovery*. Preceded by the recession phase, the recovery phase can be identified when unemployment has gone down for two consecutive months, commercial lenders are doing ground-up construction again, and vacancies and declining rental rates have plateaued. The beginning of this phase is the bottom of the market, partly because there has been a year or more of lower sales comparables to bring appraised values down considerably. Prices will gradually be going up now as the economy recovers. This is the very best time to buy, as distressed sellers have faced the reality of where market prices are. Foreclosures have now reached their peak, resulting in many opportunities to buy properties at public auctions and bank owned properties. Seller financing is much more available. Because prices are at their lowest, this is the best time to buy commercial properties that need little work for a good price.

2. *Expansion*. In this phase, the market has recovered: job growth is good, GDP is back to normal, and occupancy and rental rates are going up. There is increasing competition for properties for sale and prices are rising. This is a good time to buy properties that need repositioning with value-add strategies, and financing is more easily attainable again. At the beginning of this phase, prices are set fairly for both buyers and sellers, where neither really have an advantage. This is still a decent time to buy, as sellers are reasonable. At the middle of this phase, it becomes a seller's market; cap rates have been continually coming down, prices are going up, and rental rates and occupancy remain high. New construction starts are shooting up and bare land is being purchased at insane prices for future development. You can tell this is not the best time to buy.

3. *Hyper-supply*. In this phase, there are too many units on the market as a result of the completion of too many construction and rehab projects; the market has too much supply. This causes construction to slow, rental rates to come down, and rental concessions to increase. Surprisingly, a seller's market with high prices can hang on for a long time during this phase. What is truly amazing is how long buyers keep buying at the top of the market. As you already know, this is the worst time to buy.

4. *Recession.* The coronavirus recession was an anomaly caused by a pandemic. But most recessions are the result of out-of-control growth and unrealistically high prices. GDP and rental demand go down, jobs are lost, rent and mortgage defaults increase, and new construction stops. At first, purchases almost stop, as no one knows what properties are worth; financing choices diminish and loan guidelines become stringent, resulting in many buyers no longer being able to qualify for a loan. At first, sellers try to ride it out, hoping to still get good prices. Strange, but it will take about seven months for many to face reality. By then, there will be enough low sales comparables to reduce appraised values. Distressed sellers will no longer be able to hang on, as their NOIs have dropped below their *break-even ratio* (Encyclopedia Topic A, Buying), having pushed many into foreclosure. Their properties will be sold at a big discount. This is a great time to buy. And it is the very best time to buy a property that was purchased during the hyper-supply phase for rehabbing and the owners have crashed and burned, not completing the renovations, the lease-up, or both. Boy, can you snatch a property like that up for a good price.

> **Time and Money Saving Tip**
>
> Would you like to learn how to buy commercial properties that have been foreclosed upon on the steps of the county courthouse? You will want to get some experience with the auction process first by going to many auctions. The best time to buy is when the recession phase of the real estate market turns into the recovery phase. This is when banks have failed at selling many nonperforming notes at a discount and the most foreclosures are in their final stage. You won't know ahead of time what the bank's opening bid will be; the auctioneer will mention this when the auction starts. So look up the deed online at the county recorder of deeds' office, and find out what the original mortgage amount was. Then estimate what the principal balance might have been reduced to. The bank will want to recover that amount plus back taxes, attorney fees, and court costs, and this total will most likely reflect the opening bid price. You will need to know ahead of time what your maximum bid will be. For more on this, go to *auctions–buying at* (Encyclopedia Topic A, Buying).

THE LOWEST-RISK PROPERTY TYPES TO CHOOSE

The type of property you choose to invest in is likely the largest determination of its risk level. Face it, people need a roof over their heads during the best and worst economic times. In fact, during a recession, many lose their homes and are forced into the rental market; this puts apartment buildings at a much lower risk than strip malls, as far as occupancy goes. But then during a recession, Class C-minus multi-family properties in blue-collar neighborhoods are rampant with slow-paying and nonpaying tenants who have lost their jobs, putting the properties at a higher level of risk for poor rent collections than a strip mall, where the tenants have the survival of their business at stake. Surprisingly, Class C-minus apartments are still ranked at a lower risk level than a retail center, because they can bring in new tenants in a matter of weeks, whereas for a retail space it takes an average of seven months to find a tenant, negotiate a lease, and have tenant improvements completed.

I have listed the major commercial property types below in the order of their level of risk during a recession for retaining good occupancy, rent pricing, and collections, with number one being the lowest risk. This is based on my experience lending on and evaluating financials for these property types during all economic cycles and the past three recessions, starting in 2001, as well as on risk assessment analysis for commercial lenders extrapolated from Moody's Analytics.

1. *National credit tenant triple net lease property* **(extremely low risk)**.Tenants of these properties have a credit rating of single A (A) to triple A (AAA) and 15 years or more remaining on the lease. These bulletproof properties are very expensive, with a low rate of return on investment. A property leased to the Home Depot, which has an A+ credit rating on a 25-year lease, has almost zero risk. A building rented to Walmart, which has an even higher credit rating of AA, has an even lower risk. Your chance of getting struck by lightning right now while reading this book is higher than the odds of Walmart missing a lease payment. The downside is that these properties are being sold at a 4% cap, which means that without a mortgage you would be earning 4% annually on your investment.

2. *Class A and B multifamily lifestyle properties* **(very low risk)**. These properties attract more affluent tenants that have good incomes, and, better yet, most have savings and pay their rent during a recession. Some large cities ended up with too many top-of-the-line apartment complexes during the coronavirus recession and had to reduce rents to fill them.

3. *Mobile home parks* **(low risk)**. The majority of the mobile homes are owned by the tenants, not the park. These homeowners have a pride of ownership and keep their homes and yards in tip-top shape. Even during hard financial times, these renters seldom skip their rent; if they do, after a few months the park owner can slap a lien on their home and put a for sale sign on it.

4. *Senior housing* **(low risk)**. 55 and older properties and independent senior living facilities are best in this category. These tenants have retirement income,

which is often more reliable than a job. Assisted care, memory care, and nursing homes are a much higher risk, as they require skilled nursing and very specialized management.

5. *Class C+ multifamily* **(low risk)**. These properties are older apartment complexes in great shape, located in good neighborhoods, with much lower rents than the Class A and B properties. During a recession, they stay full with tenants who pay the rent.

6. *Medical office* **(low risk)**. These properties include physician, medical clinic, outpatient surgery, physical therapy, and lab offices. They represent the safest investment in office properties with the highest rents. As our population ages, medical care is always in demand. Dental offices do not fare as well during recessions, as if dental work can be put off if there is no pain. The downside to medical offices is that when leases run out and are not renewed, the tenant improvements are very specialized and require a complete retrofit for other types of office tenants. Medical office buildings located near hospitals always seem to stay full.

7. *Flex industrial property* **(low risk)**. Made up of smaller spaces with affordable rent, these properties are occupied by business tenants that take pride in taking care of their shops. Each space has manufacturing and/or storage on one side and a sales office on the other. Tenants faithfully pay the rent and these properties tend to stay 100% full. Tenants know that their spaces are in high demand and do not want to risk losing them.

8. *Student housing* **(moderately low risk)**. Student housing overall did well during the Great Recession, as college enrollment went up significantly and student loans were in abundant supply. These properties have a much higher risk if the majority of leases are for the nine-month school year, giving the property low economic occupancy. To remedy this, make sure all tenants sign a year-long lease guaranteed by their parents.

9. *Self-storage facilities* **(moderately low risk)**. Ideally, find a facility that has an occupancy of 85% or more with under-market rents, as vacancies can be slow to fill and you need to remain competitive. This property type runs amazingly low expenses, resulting in one of the lowest occupancy break-even points of all commercial properties. Often all the expenses and the mortgage can be paid at 60% occupancy. Self-storage is in demand during both good and bad economic times. The downside is the risk of a new competitor locating near you; they will undercut your rents, forcing you to lower them.

10. *Class C and C-minus multifamily* **(moderate risk)**. These properties certainly do stay full during recessions, but, as mentioned earlier, rent collection problems resulting from tenants' losing their jobs make them a higher risk. During

a financial crisis, without hands-on management these properties can have a high failure rate.

11. *Mixed-use buildings* (**moderate risk**). These can be Class A and B or C properties with mostly multifamily tenants, but have a substantially higher risk if they average 25% or more office or retail on the first floor. What makes mixed-use properties a moderately high risk is the potential for all the office and retail tenants to move out during a recession, making it difficult for the property to break even. To lower this risk, put in commercial tenants that do well during a recession, such as a utility company office, government office, urgent care, or thrift store.

12. *Retail centers* (**moderately high risk**). Strip malls can be a risky investment and have gotten hit especially hard during the coronavirus recession. But with an experienced manager and the right tenant mix, they can still be a good investment. Buying at the right price and at lower leverage, where the property can run profitably at 70% occupancy, can make this property type recession-proof. Every year it seems that more people are buying more retail items on the Internet, so be sure to mix in businesses like restaurants, hair salons, and other services that will be largely unaffected by the shift to purchasing items online.

13. *Office properties* (**very high risk**). Multitenant office buildings did not fare well during the Great Recession but recovered with time. They really bombed during the coronavirus recession, which has resulted in an oversupply of space as many business owners have discovered that they can save by having more employees work at home.

14. *Hospitality* (**very high risk**). Hotels and motels took a dive during the Great Recession and then amazingly sprang back to peak performance. But it is predicted that it will take a long time for the hospitality industry to rebound after the coronavirus recession. Many of these properties will make great repurposing opportunities, as they can be converted to apartments and student housing.

TEN RISK-LOWERING ACTION STEPS

The third most important question to answer when buying a commercial property has to do with your mental health, or "What can I do to lower my risks when buying so I don't have to lay awake at night worrying about it?" Implementing as many of the following risk-lowering action steps as you can will take a load off your mind.

1. *Choose a property closer to home.* Yes, we have already discussed this earlier in this chapter, but I do want to emphasize again that one of the highest risks is buying far away from home. If a recession hits and your occupancy and rents

drop, you are going to need a hands-on approach, even if you have professional property management. How will you know if the on-site manager is not showing up to rent units on weekends, the lawn is dying, or the parking lot is strewn with garbage? If you can't drive by the property often, you won't know. If income really drops, you can let go of your property manager and handle the leasing and some maintenance and repairs yourself—but you can't do this if you have to get on a plane or drive four hours to get to the property.

2. *Choose a property that retains its tenants.* Multifamily properties that have many tenants who have lived there for three years or longer have a tendency to stay full during tough economic times. These tenants have an attachment to their homes and do not want to lose them. Retail, office, and industrial tenants who have occupied their space for five to 10 years or longer have proven their stability. Most will be stronger, more established businesses that have cash in the bank and lines of credit to make it through a recession.

3. *Choose a property with good historical financials.* You wouldn't want to buy a manufacturing business that had only six months of financials. Buying a commercial investment property that doesn't have a track record amounts to the same thing. A property that has always run strongly in the black is more likely to make it through a recession. You want to collect four years of month-by-month income and expense statements, looking for consistent good NOI. Conversely, fix and flip and unstabilized properties that are totally relying on projections are the highest risks, unless you have experience.

4. *Choose a property where you can negotiate a purchase price based on economic occupancy.* In a seller's market, never pay full price for a property based on a full rent roll when some tenants are paying late or not paying at all. Come on, if only 78% of the tenants are actually paying rent, then the property is worth a lot less. Many sellers and their listing agents are sneaky, and will try and sell the property based on physical occupancy. To accurately determine economic occupancy, you will need to do a *collections verification report* (Encyclopedia Topic B, Due Diligence). What a great repositioning opportunity at the right price!

5. *Choose a property in a large or medium-size market.* Large cities have more industry, job opportunities, and a more diverse economy; these factors will help in surviving a recession. Buying a property in a small town that lacks major industry close by and has few jobs is risky. Buying in a low-income, high-crime neighborhood is even riskier.

6. *Choose a property in which you have walked every unit or space.* Even if you get a property condition report, there is nothing that can equal walking every square foot of the property before you buy it. If you take a contractor with you, all the better. Believe me, you will find things that the property inspector has missed.

The buck stops with you when knowing the condition of the property you are buying and walking the property yourself greatly lowers your risk.

7. *Choose a property with good occupancy and leases*. Buying a property that is already at or above market occupancy and full of high-quality paying tenants on long-term leases is the safest scenario. Buying one that has low occupancy with many lease terms ending soon, or one that cannot cash-flow expenses, is risky.

8. *Judge the cost and time for repositioning a property correctly*. Whether you are making inexpensive operational changes or more costly cosmetic and construction ones, misjudging the cost and time needed to complete the project and fill it with tenants can cause you to lose the property.

9. *Know the market*. This means knowing you are not paying too much for a property based on comparable rents and sales prices in the submarket. If you are planning on repositioning the property, raising rents too high, resulting in low occupancy, or overimproving a property for the neighborhood and its potential value are signs that the buyer did not study the market and the competition. This creates a high-risk investment.

10. *Factor in all the costs correctly*. We are talking about unexpected expenses right before or after closing such as repairs, a more expensive loan than planned on, and, most common, unexpected closing costs like tax and insurance impound escrow accounts and payment of interest in advance on your new loan. Not factoring in these costs will result in your having a lower return on your cash invested and, worse, less post-closing cash for your rainy day fund.

FOUR LEVELS OF RISK BASED ON PROPERTY CONDITION, INCOME, LOCATION, AND OCCUPANCY

1. *Core deals*. These properties have the lowest risk. They are in great condition; are in a good location; have very established, quality tenants; have strong historical incomes; and are fully leased. These properties are the most expensive. You should choose these properties if you want the lowest risk and can afford them.

2. *Core plus deals*. These properties have a higher risk due to the property needing some work, being in a less favorable location, having less-than-stellar historical incomes, having tenants that are of mixed quality, and having lower-than-market occupancy. These are usually Class C properties that are moderately priced. If you find one in a good neighborhood and can give it good management, the risk can be low.

3. *Value-add deals.* These properties have substantial risk just because you are making many untested changes to the property to increase net income and value. These properties need repositioning to achieve their potential. The likelihood for cost overruns and lengthy delays in completing the improvements and reaching market occupancy means these projects have substantial risk. They might not cash flow now, but with some cosmetic work or light rehab, rents can be increased. The only way to lower the risk is experience. If you do not have it, bring in an investor that does.

4. *Opportunistic deals.* These properties have the highest risk, and include those that require major rehabbing or ground-up construction. The greatest risk lies in underestimating the time it will take to build and stabilize (fill to market occupancy) the property. These deals usually have no income for a year or longer, which makes them very risky. Experience is a must. Chapter 11 covers all the steps involved.

CHAPTER 2

Seven Smart Strategies for Adding Value When Buying

This chapter is all about making smart decisions when buying a commercial investment property. First we look at the importance of having your down payment and financing together. Then we examine the benefits of leveraging done responsibly. Defining your property search objectives is covered next, followed by how to do a quick determination of value and how to choose a property that can be recession-proofed. Lastly, we discuss choosing the professional team members who will advise you, and some great tips on making and negotiating offers.

1. HAVE YOUR DOWN PAYMENT, PROFESSIONAL TEAM, AND FINANCING TOGETHER BEFORE YOU GO SHOPPING

Often beginners shop for financing with no experience and before they have a down payment or a team. Worse yet, they make offers first and then shop for their team and financing, after a seller is interested. Both of these methods are totally backwards and may waste your time along with everyone else's. If you do find the right property, do you really want to sabotage your chances for landing it with the listing agent and lender by conveying that you don't have the wherewithal to pull it off? Yes, first impressions really do matter. Here are some great steps to follow before you make your first offer:

1. *Get prequalified for financing at the beginning* by an experienced commercial mortgage broker who is affiliated with many lenders. If you want to just use your bank, make sure that whoever is going to approve the loan reviews the submission package at the beginning. Get deeply involved with the lending process and find out what the qualifications are for the property and the borrower. (Prequalifying yourself for the loan programs you are interested in is gone over

21

in detail in Chapter 11.) You need to know the maximum you can borrow for the property type, based on the property location, your experience, your down payment, and the property financials. You also need to know the closing costs and post-closing liquidity requirement ahead of time. Yes, lenders will not allow you to be broke right after closing—and this way you will know in advance if you need investors to raise additional equity. Lenders hate it when you tell them, "Oh, I know I don't have enough down, but I will raise the money." You will also be finding out what the rate and terms look like, which you will need for filling out the purchase agreement.

2. *Get your team together at the beginning*: this includes your investors, your lender or mortgage broker, your buyer's real estate broker, your property manager, and your real estate attorney. You want to inform your lender and the listing real estate broker about these people. If you do not have the down payment and closing costs needed, lenders will not waste their time with you. Read Chapter 3 on raising investors: it discusses bringing in a high-net-worth investor who could just act as a proxy. Offer to give them a very small percentage of ownership in the property (like 2%) for taking on this role. You can use their personal financial statement to prequalify for loans, and if needed switch them out for another high-net-worth investor down the road. The listing realtor will also likely want to see a strong personal financial statement plus verification of liquidity before signing a purchase contract with you.

3. *Get a letter of preapproval* from a lender or commercial mortgage broker that you can attach to your *letter of intent to purchase*. This will give the listing broker and seller confidence that you will be able to close. Be prepared to also share with them a copy of your bank and/or security accounts to show proof of your down payment. You can have them sign a *confidentiality agreement* that prohibits them from sharing this information with anyone. If you do not have a strong enough personal financial statement or proof of down payment, read Chapter 4 for some great tips on how to get around this step and how to fake it until you make it.

2. USE LEVERAGE RESPONSIBLY

Who wouldn't want to get rich using other people's money? This is the best definition of leveraging. There is simply no better method of growing your net worth over time than buying commercial real estate and financing the majority of the purchase price. I work for many wealthy people. About a quarter of them did it the easy way—they inherited money. The rest used leverage to buy commercial property and get rich. But before we get started on the amazing benefits of leveraging, I'm going to put a damper on the discussion.

There are many get-rich gurus out there who will tell you that they can teach you to buy commercial real estate with 10% down—or better yet, no money down. Most of the programs these people run make money by selling books or coaching programs. At least twice a week our firm gets an inquiry call from someone who does not have any money and thinks that this is okay.

Here's the reality: the best of these mentoring programs work with investors who have a realistic amount of money to put down on a property and are moving from residential to commercial property investment. My friend and colleague Peter Harris is the author of *Commercial Real Estate Investing For Dummies*. He is also a principal at Commercial Real Estate Advisors, a mentoring/coaching firm. He will tell you that trying to buy with little or no money down is a waste of everybody's time. Nevertheless, if you have at least half of the down payment and are tenacious you can pull off getting into commercial real estate investing. He states that putting 20% down and getting the seller to carry the mortgage is the best way to get started if you do not have the experience to qualify for a conventional loan.

The majority of my highly leveraged clients did not make it through the Great Recession, and many in this group are struggling today to hang on to their properties during the coronavirus recession. They were doing what they thought was smart—putting every dime they could muster into buying another property. They would brag, "I have all my money making money for me. I'm not dumb enough to just let it sit there in the bank." Many lost everything. But just about all of my borrowers who hung on to some cash for a rainy day and put 25% or more down made it through. In fact, many were able to pick up bargain properties that investors in the overleveraged group lost.

I met Laurence in 2000 when he applied for a loan to buy his first motel in Bakersfield, California. An elderly couple had turned it over to their kids, who ran it into the ground. It was a mom-and-pop business located on Interstate 5. Laurence had a good business plan to turn it into a flagged hotel using the Travelodge brand. I was able to get him an 80% SBA (Small Business Administration) loan and the sellers carried 10% in second position. It was a roaring success. A little over a year later he repeated this recipe and bought a second motel in Sacramento. By February of 2009 he no cash left, but he did have five motels all purchased with 10–15% down that were hanging on by the skin of their teeth. By 2011, he was working as a car salesman. To keep this from happening to you, keep your down payment to 20–25% or above and keep a minimum of 15% of your net worth in cash.

Now, let's get back to the amazing benefits of leveraging responsibly. Some might think that paying all cash for a smaller property and not having a mortgage is the way to go. But there is really no way this approach can compete with putting 20% down, taking out an 80% mortgage, and buying a larger property that will produce more income from operations and appreciation combined, plus more savings on taxes from higher depreciation. To illustrate this we will compare two income property investors, each of whom has $200,000 to invest in real estate. One buys residential—a duplex for $200,000 cash—and is proud to not have a mortgage payment. The other buys a 12-unit apartment building for $1,000,000 and puts 20% down (also $200,000). The vacancy rate and the expense ratio are the same for both investors. Both properties have net income that goes up 8% per year and appreciation that averages 6% per year.

It seems impressive that in five years the duplex buyer will have earned $174,057 in net cash flow and appreciation on their $200,000 investment, which is an annual *internal rate of return* of 17.4%. But it is much more remarkable that the apartment buyer earned $515,202 in net cash flow (after loan payments) and appreciation. That comes to a 51.5% annual internal rate of return and is $341,145 more than the duplex buyer earned in five years. The duplex owner's equity has grown by $72,097, which is a 36% increase. The apartment owner's equity has grown by $425,370, which is a whopping 213% increase. To top this off, the apartment building produces an annual tax shelter in depreciation of $29,090, compared with $5,818 for the duplex (see Table 2.1).

TABLE 2.1   Buying a Duplex with Cash Versus an Apartment Building with Leverage.

Note: Both have a $200,000 down payment.	**Duplex** $1,200 per unit	**12-unit apartment building** $850 per unit
Annual rent	$28,000	$122,400
Less 5% vacancy	−1,400	−6,120
Adjusted rent	26,600	116,280
Less 32% expenses	−8,512	−37,209
Net operating income	18,088	79,071
Less annual debt service	−0	−51,535
Annual net cash flow	18,088	27,536
Property value in 5 years	272,097	1,360,489
Original price	−200,000	−1,000,000
Capital gain	72,097	360,000
5-year net cash flow	101,960	155,221
Amount earned in 5 years	*174,057*	*515,221*
Equity in 5 years	*272,097*	*625,370**
Annual Depreciation	*5,818*	*29,090*

Assumptions: Net operating income for both properties has been compounded at 8% per year for five years. Appreciation for both properties has been compounded at 6% per year for five years. The 80% mortgage on the apartment property is $800,000 at 5% interest with a 30-year amortization.
*Includes $65,370 in principal reductions on the mortgage after five years.

3. DEFINE YOUR PROPERTY SEARCH OBJECTIVES

Can you imagine how great it would feel to look for a property to buy knowing exactly what you want, what you qualify for, and what the parameters are? Being a proactive investor means you know from the beginning what you are looking for and have experienced team members to help you sort through a large stack of deals to find it. We're talking about not only knowing from the start what the property type will be, but also where you want to buy. What you want to achieve financially from the investment and what size and type of loan you need to get you there. What price range you can afford and your minimum acceptable cap rate. How to estimate the value and what your value-add objectives are. Who your team members will be and what strategies you will employ as a team to win the best deals.

The following sections describe eight objectives you should define at the beginning of your property search.

Property Type

If you are a beginning investor, consider choosing a property type based on the risk level shown in Chapter 1's section The Lowest-Risk Property Types to Choose. Many investors choose multifamily properties because of their lower risk if they have already owned one or more rental homes. This is a natural and good progression. Student housing properties take specialized management. Most other property types do best with experience. *Flex-industrial* properties are low risk and a good type for the newbie. *Self-storage* properties have a moderately low risk if you find one that has 85% or higher occupancy and they are one of the easiest commercial property types to manage (see Encyclopedia Topic A, Buying).

Property Age, Class, and Condition

Are you willing to pay more for a Class A or B property that is under 20 years old, is in excellent condition, and commands the highest rents? These properties weather the best during recessions. You certainly will not be getting calls on weekends that the heating or air conditioning system is broken. Or is a Class C property that is over 25 years old and needs a little work okay? Or are you looking for a fixer-upper?

Responsibility Level and Lifestyle

How will this property fit into your lifestyle? How much time will you have to put into overseeing it? If you want to do absolutely nothing except collect the rent, and you can afford it, you should choose a credit tenant triple net lease property. Apartment buildings, although low risk, require the most management. With poor management they can have a very high risk. Even if you have a decent property manager, you have to keep your eye on them constantly. Residential tenants just seem to demand a lot of attention and need oversight. Light industrial buildings with net leases on them have very few headaches. They have business tenants that take pride in keeping the premises in great condition. It is very unusual for one of these types of tenants to misbehave.

Market/Location

Where will you buy: in your neck of the woods or in another state? Before you can get an estimate on the financing you will qualify for, you will need to know where you will be buying. Most low-priced national lenders such as life companies are very fussy about the size of the market they will lend in; they prefer larger markets. Local community banks prefer lending in areas where they have branches and are usually not fond of out-of-area borrowers they cannot have a deposit relationship with. Are you going to buy in a primary market (population of 1,000,000 or more), a secondary market (population of 500,000–1,000,000), tertiary market (250,000–500,000), or a small market (under 250,000)? Larger markets have more industry and many more jobs and therefore involve a much lower risk than smaller markets. In addition, what kind of neighborhood are you interested in: urban, suburban, middle class, upper class, or blue collar? Are you willing to pay more for a more effluent or high-traffic location?

Lease and Tenant Objectives

If you are interested in buying an office, retail, or industrial property, what quality of leases are you looking for: gross leases—where the landlord pays all of the expenses—or single, double, or triple net leases—where the tenant pays some or all of the taxes, insurance, and maintenance? Also, what is your minimum acceptable average lease term left on the property? Better consult with your lender on this one. Many lenders take commercial tenants off the rent roll if there is less than a year remaining on their leases, and they get heartburn if there are too many month-to-month renters occupying a strip mall or apartment building.

What type of tenants do you want? For retail, office, and industrial properties, national tenants or those that have a well-established business with good credit ratings are best. Even better is if they have more than one location. For a multifamily property, do you have the stomach for mothering your renters and/or property manager? If not, don't choose student housing or a C-minus property in a low economic neighborhood.

Financial Objectives

Is the property going to be a long- or a short-term hold? Are you going to keep this property for retirement? What price range makes sense for your resources? Based on a discussion with a commercial mortgage broker, what type of mortgage can you qualify for and what size loan can you secure? What is your minimum acceptable *cash on cash return* and *internal rate of return* (Encyclopedia Topic A, Buying) on the money you invest? The first looks at how much annual income your cash injection (including renovation costs) will earn annually. The second looks at total earnings over time, including appreciation. Determining your minimum acceptable cap rate and tempering this with the reality of what similar properties are selling for can be sobering.

Financing Objectives

Based on the amount of cash you can raise for a down payment, how much can you borrow? What interest rate and terms do you need to make your financial objectives work? Are you looking for a long-term fixed rate or a short-term mortgage? Do you need to close on a distressed property fast? If so, you will likely need to find a bridge lender. You'll also need to estimate closing costs and allow for a certain amount of post-closing cash. Lenders usually like to see a minimum of either 10% of the loan or 12 months of mortgage payments in the bank after closing. If you do not have great credit or income and are willing to pay top dollar for a property, an owner-carry mortgage may be the way to go. These usually have high interest rates with short terms of two to five years. In that amount of time, you can improve your credit and finances, so you can refinance with a lower-rate conventional loan.

Time and Money Saving Tip

When you find the right property to buy, create a pro forma that has four or more financing scenarios ranging from your favorite to least desirable. The objective here is to know what the worst financing is that you can accept to meet your financial objectives.

Value-Add Objectives

This is the fun one! What value-add opportunities will you be looking for? You may find yourself getting obsessed with creative thoughts about this when you first meet a property. Should you do some remodeling and raise rents through turning over tenants or just increase occupancy over time? Optimize lease potential by attracting better, higher-paying tenants or by adding more rentable square footage? Or is your goal to change zoning and/or density regulations or to repurpose the property for another use entirely? Chapter 7 has some great insights on this subject.

4. FOUR 15-MINUTE METHODS OF DETERMINING PROPERTY VALUE

Now that you know what type of commercial property you are most interested in and your objectives for the property, it's time to go shopping. When sorting through properties that fit your profile, how will you know which ones are a good buy? Many, or even most, will be overpriced. Most sellers know that they need to start out high so that they can come down a bit and end up at the price they really want. You'll need to determine what the property is actually worth. During the beginning of a recession this can be tricky, as comparable sales will likely be overpriced. You can use my *Apartment Quick Analysis Spreadsheet* or *Commercial Property Quick Analysis Spreadsheet* for each property you are seriously interested in to estimate a property's value based on *cap rate* and *GRM* (see Appendix A). You can find a downloadable Excel version of these spreadsheets on my website: https://apartmentloanstore.com.

For the four 15-minute methods of determining value, we are going to use a 16-unit apartment complex that catches your eye. It is priced at $2,200,000. Before you start, you need to find three similar properties that are currently for sale or have sold in the past year. If you are buying during a recession, use properties for sale through LoopNet or your real estate broker that are the same type and a size and quality similar to the targeted property. If you are not buying during a recession you will need to find three properties that have sold in the past year. You need to know the purchase price, cap rate, number of units or square feet, gross rents, and NOI for each property. Here are the four quick methods to determine value:

1. *Price per door or square foot quick valuation method.* This method is really fast. Use the price per door for multifamily properties and price per square foot for all other commercial property types. Calculate the average price per unit or price per square foot for the three comparable properties and the subject property. Let's say that the average price per door is $144,400:

$$16 \text{ units} \times \$144,400 = \$2,310,400 \text{ property value}$$

   Your property is priced on the low side at $2,200,000.
2. *Gross rent multiplier (GRM) quick valuation method.* GRM is the purchase price divided by gross annual rent if the property is 100% occupied. The lower the GRM, the more rent you will be getting for the purchase price.

Start out by calculating the GRM for the property you are interested in:

$2,200,000 purchase price/$258,800 gross annual rent = 8.50% GRM

Next calculate the GRM for each of the three comparable properties and the average GRM for all four properties. Let's say the average GRM is 8.95%:

8.95 GRM × $258,800 annual rent = $2,316,260 property value

This confirms again that the subject property is priced on the low side.

3. *Cap rate quick valuation method.* Capitalization rate, or cap rate, is annual net operating income (NOI) divided by the purchase price.

Here is the cap rate for the subject property:

$166,960 NOI/$2,200,000 purchase price = 7.6% cap rate

Now calculate an average cap rate for the four properties.

Subject Property NOI: $166,960/$2,200,000 purchase price = 7.6% cap rate
Comparable Property 1: NOI $152,800/2,175,000 purchase price = 7.0% cap rate.
Comparable Property 2: NOI $176,950/2,425,000 purchase price = 7.3% cap rate
Comparable Property 3: NOI $140,600/1,995,000 purchase price = 7.0% cap rate

To do this calculation even faster, you just average all the cap rates.

Average of all four properties = 7.20% cap rate which would put the value of the subject property at $2,318,000. $166,960/$2,318,000 = 7.2%. Again, the subject property at $2,200,000 at a 7.6% cap rate is priced below market.

4. *Valuation average method.* This only takes a few minutes. To get the most accurate indication of value for the subject property using a method that you can compute yourself, average the property value yielded from each of three approaches above:

Price per door value = $2,310,400

GRM value = $2,316,260

Cap rate value = $2,318,000

Total = $6,944,660/3 = $2,314,887 average property value.

This property is a great buy!

5. CHOOSE A PROPERTY THAT CAN BE RECESSION-PROOFED

Sorry to start with a disclaimer, but with the exception of buying a commercial property occupied by a credit tenant like Walmart or the federal government that has an insanely high credit rating and 20 years or more remaining on the lease, nothing is truly recession-proof. The Gap, which had a fair credit rating of BB+ in March of 2019, was downgraded toward junk territory with a BB– a year later as a result of stiff competition from online sales and the start of the coronavirus recession. Then they stopped paying rent in April of 2020 after furloughing 80,000 employees and their credit rating tumbled further. The same month, Staples, Mattress Firm, and Subway stopped paying rent. These were all considered good tenants.

Does this mean that commercial property is just too risky to invest in? No. What it means is that just like in all recessions, the coronavirus recession—which was the worst economic tsunami to hit global financial markets since the Great Depression—nearly wiped out hospitality and wounded office and retail properties. Apartments, flex-industrial, self-storage, and mobile home parks seem to always make it through with much less pain.

Many of my clients are just sitting on the edge of their seats waiting for the next recession to hit. They have cash ready to grab good properties at great prices. For their existing properties, they put cash aside to protect them for the next recession, along with other recession-proofing strategies. They did this in the same way someone buying property in a storm surge area in Florida prepares for the inevitability of a hurricane. In a moment I share with you the 10 best recession-proofing strategies.

In most markets, a recession causes commercial real estate values to go down. This is because there is lower demand, and financing becomes more stringent, resulting in fewer buyers being able to qualify. Even though interest rates are usually low during recessions, lenders lend less by lowering their LTVs, raising vacancy, and raising their *underwriting interest rate* (Encyclopedia Topic H, Financing). Appraisers get pressured by lenders to lower valuations by having appraisals reflect lower occupancy, higher credit loss, and rent concessions.

According to Wikipedia, during the 60-year period between 1960 and 2020 there were 10 recessions in the United States, or an average of one every 6 years. If you are buying a commercial property and are planning on a long-term hold it would be smart to pick a strategy that will recession-proof you and your property. What you really want to know is this: If your occupancy takes a dive, how low can it go and still allow you to pay all expenses and your mortgage payment? Can you hang in there until things get better? What resources will you have to enable you to survive?

Which commercial property investors do the best during a recession? During the Great Recession that started in December 2007, my clients who had bought commercial properties with a long-term hold strategy weathered the storm better than those who planned on a short-term hold. The latter group intended to make a bundle in the future and pulled cash out to buy more properties. Although property values went down and occupancies dropped for properties held by many of the long-term hold borrowers, most made it through until occupancy and property values went up again. How did they pull this off? Most had chosen a more recession-friendly property and had enough cash or other sources of income to ride it out. In contrast, some short-term investors who had bought properties to rehab and flip got hurt because once they had completed the renovations the lease-up period was too long because the recession had already started. They just did not have enough capital left to make the mortgage payments, and many in this group lost their properties.

The 10 Best Recession-Proofing Strategies

1. *Have working capital and other sources of income.* Yes, cash is king! There is absolutely nothing that can make you and your commercial property more recession-proof than a nice chunk of cash. Having additional sources of income is a lifesaver too. Working capital is a rainy day fund used to pay unplanned-for repairs, or in the event of a recession to help with expenses and even mortgage payments. Do a quick pro forma on your property to determine what the expenses and mortgage payment will average each month. Then for a multitenant property bring occupancy down to 65% and calculate the monthly shortage you have after paying all expenses and the mortgage. Your working capital fund should be 12 to 18 months of this shortage.

2. *Find a property with a* break-even ratio *that is 75% or lower.* The break-even ratio tells you the minimum occupancy you need to pay all of your expenses and the mortgage on the property. Keeping this at 75% or lower is the next best recession safety strategy after having a stash of cash.

3. *Don't overleverage.* Plan to reduce your personal debts and make sure that all your investment properties are purchased with at least 25% down. It's a lack of positive cash flow that ruins commercial property investors during a recession. One of my clients owned a beautiful historic eight-unit apartment building in San Francisco that was thriving through the Great Recession. But it was the four distressed apartment buildings in Sacramento purchased with 15% down seller financing that took him down. He lost the San Francisco property because he drained it of cash to cover the shortages on the Sacramento properties, which he ended up losing, too.

4. *Refinance with lower payments.* Having lower payments on all the properties you own, including your home, will give you extra positive cash flow during a recession that can be used on investment properties that are not able to make it on their own.

5. *Buy a property at below its value.* There is nothing better that you can do than to buy a property for an even lower price than what it is worth. Let's say that you brilliantly take $125,000 off a $1.5 million purchase price. Well, first of all, think about how long it would take for you to raise rents and lower expenses to earn an additional $125,000 from the property. Most importantly, this windfall will enable you to take out a smaller loan, thus lowering your monthly payments.

6. *Keep your rents below market.* I know, this sounds like leaving a lot of money on the table. But think about it. During a recession, rents get lowered and some tenants move to less expensive properties. If you already have lower-than-market rents, your tenants won't be leaving and you will be attracting renters from more expensive properties. My client who owns a shopping center in Louisville, Kentucky, keeps his rents about 15% under market. I have scolded him for this. But his intention is to keep his property full during both good and bad times and he has. I have a client in Eugene, Oregon, who owns two apartment complexes, a 36 and a 61 unit. He made it through the Great Recession unharmed and is collecting 96% of his rents during the coronavirus recession. He says this is because his rents are lower than his competitors' in his submarket. He always stays full for the same reason. And during bad economic times his tenants don't want to risk losing their homes.

7. *Choose a recession-friendly property type.* Multifamily, medical office, self-storage, and flex industrial properties, as well as mobile home parks and senior housing, have a much better chance of making it through a recession unscathed. In 2008, multifamily occupancy grew as more people lost their homes and moved into apartments. Many of the same people rented self-storage units to hold the stuff that did not fit in the apartment. Mobile home park occupancy stayed strong during the Great Recession. Flex industrial complexes weathered the recession too, with small spaces having reasonable rents occupied by a large variety of businesses.

8. *Don't buy at the top of the market.* This is hard to do if you are buying during a seller's market. As mentioned in Chapter 1, little adds value to a property like not overpaying for it. In an up market you will have to work harder to find decent deals. If there are no good deals, just wait until the market comes down.

9. *Choose a multitenant property with many smaller units.* If you

Time and Money Saving Tip

One of the best ways to make a killing during the recession and recovery phases of the real estate market cycle is to have the cash ready to buy a distressed seller out *fast*. When you submit your letter of intent to the seller or listing agent, include a letter of preapproval from a bridge lender that states they can close in two weeks. If you can pay cash, mention that you will provide verification of funds upon buy a four-unit office or retail building and two tenants fail during a recession, you could be left with 50% occupancy and be underwater.

Also, stay away from retail and office properties where one tenant occupies 20% or more of the total space. The exception to this rule is anchored retail.

request. Bridge loans are expensive but well worth it if you can buy the property for the right price. Buying well below market means you will be recession-proofing the property right out of the gate.

10. *Find a property that has many value-add opportunities.* Buy a property where you can do two or more of these lower-cost value adds: make cosmetic changes and raise rents, increase occupancy, lower general expenses, lower taxes and insurance, optimize lease potential, and attract higher paying tenants. Put together a buyer's pro forma that shows the financial gains from your value adds and that you will obtain a lower break-even ratio in the near future. Boy, does this make your property recession-proof!

6. CHOOSE THE BEST TEAM MEMBERS

Experienced successful commercial property investors have a team of professionals that they usually work with over and over. Consider yourself the president and these people your cabinet. They will advise you and help resolve problems, but the final decision is yours.

Buyer's Real Estate Broker

One of the first members on your team should be your own real estate broker, who will represent you as the buyer. Today, buyers often contact the listing broker when they find a property and just fall into working solely with that broker. Of course the listing broker is thrilled with this—after all, what could be better than not splitting the commission with a buyer's broker? Although uncommon, sometimes the listing broker refuses to split the commission with the buyer's broker. If this happens, buyers have to compensate their own broker. Using the listing broker to represent you is like using the defendant's attorney to represent you if you are the plaintiff in a lawsuit.

My client Jerry was buying a strip mall in Tucson. Four days before the due diligence period was going to run out and his earnest money was going to go hard (nonrefundable), he got the property inspection report in. All the roofs needed major repair or replacement. He got very stressed out working only with the listing agent. He did not have a buyer's broker representing him and it was futile to get the seller's broker to negotiate a lower sales price on his behalf. Talk about a conflict of interest! But he really wanted the property, so he paid the sales contract price and used his own money to do the repairs. Ouch!

Commercial Real Estate Attorney

When purchasing commercial real estate, I cannot stress enough how important it is to get an experienced commercial real estate attorney to represent you. Sure, your family attorney may be able to limp through the process, but this can add a lot of additional time and headache to the closing process. A commercial real estate attorney will have the expertise to review on your behalf the purchase agreement, preliminary title report, easements, encroachments, water rights, zoning ordinances, surveys, loan documents, closing statements, leases, and management contracts. If there are any complications you can refer them to your attorney, who will be a godsend in handling these complicated legalities.

Nancy, one of my best clients, decided to go with a *non-recourse* Freddie Mac loan to purchase a 74-unit apartment building. She insisted on using her family attorney. I knew this was going to be problematic when her lawyer allowed ambiguous language to remain in the due diligence clause in the purchase contract. We requested that her attorney write an attorney opinion letter stating that the limited liability company (LLC) that was going to own the property was set up correctly. This is standard procedure, but he did not know how to do it. The last straw was when her attorney, after reviewing the loan documents, told her to cancel the loan because I had lied to her about it being non-recourse (no personal guarantee required). He had reviewed what is called the *bad-boy carve-outs* (Encyclopedia Topic H, Financing), which converts the loan into a recourse loan if the borrower commits fraud with respect to the property. This is standard language in any *non-recourse loan* (Encyclopedia Topic H, Financing). The lawyer clearly did not understand non-recourse legalese. Because of additional legal mishaps caused by Nancy's attorney, it took an additional three weeks for the loan to close.

Lender or Commercial Mortgage Broker

A banker that knows and believes in you can certainly be a great asset. Keep in mind that a bank only has one lending program with one set of underwriting guidelines. Bank officers are often overworked and may not have the time to evaluate a property that you do not have an accepted offer on.

An experienced commercial mortgage broker will have more than a dozen programs and because they only get paid if they close loans, I assure you they will have the time to review many properties you are interested in for financing. Most will do this with a smile on their face and maybe do a few cartwheels for you. They are amazingly talented at steering you away from properties that are not what they appear to be. They will also be able to accurately prequalify you for the best loan programs. This is the best way to determine ahead of time the maximum amount you are qualified to borrow. They will also be pleased to write a generic letter of preapproval that can be attached to multiple letters of intent. Once you hit pay dirt on a property you can have them write a preapproval letter that applies specifically to that property.

Property Manager

Many of my clients only buy commercial properties where they already have good off-site property managers. Why? Because they can trust them to be the boots on the ground that handle all operations, especially keeping the tenants happy. Your lender will want to review the brochure or website for your property management company. Choosing a solid company will help you get a loan. Chapter 12 has in-depth advice on choosing the right property management company.

Here's another plus: when you find a property, you will want to compile a *buyer's pro forma*. You'll want to make this projection of income and expenses as accurate as possible. A local property manager can give you comparable rents in the market and an estimate of what expenses will run. This doesn't mean you have to commit to using this manager. Potential property managers will be looking to make a connection with you so that they can make a sale. They will be pleased to advise you. You will get some great value-add ideas from them about raising rents and lowering expenses

---

If Only This Buyer Had a Realtor and Lender Watching Her Back

Cindy retired early, at age 54, from her job as a schoolteacher. At retirement she planned to sell her portfolio of five single-family rentals and move into the world of commercial real estate investing. She had read a book that suggested making as many lowball offers as possible through letters of intent. After making 18 offers over two and a half months, she finally hooked the seller of a six-tenant office complex in Phoenix. The asking price was $1.8 million, and Cindy was thrilled to have her $1.65 million offer accepted.

(continued)

(*continued*)

Without having a buyer's real estate broker to represent her, it took over two weeks of negotiating through the listing agent to get a green light from the seller. Getting everything to her lender to start the loan took another few weeks. Three and a half weeks later her bank told her that since she'd quit her job, her retirement did not show enough income on tax returns to qualify for the loan. She wondered why people at the bank hadn't figured this out at the beginning. The good news was that they were going to refund her loan deposit except for the appraisal cost, since she could likely use the appraisal with her next lender. Now she had over seven weeks of her time invested in the deal.

Cindy called a commercial mortgage broker and applied for a new loan that would be rushed through. The seller reluctantly gave her another 30 days to close, but made it clear that there would be no further extensions. Two weeks later the appraisal came in at $1.5 million, $150,000 less than the purchase price. The listing broker told her that not only had her lender used a very conservative appraiser, but that the appraiser was an idiot. The listing broker also said that the report was just plain wrong and that she needed to have the lender order another appraisal. Cindy found out that lenders just don't do that. She asked that the seller lower the price. When the seller refused, she knew that using the seller's broker to represent her had been a mistake. Cindy did not have the extra cash to put down, so she scrapped the deal, along with 10 weeks of her time and $12,000 in loan deposits.

So what could Cindy have done differently?

1. Office properties in Phoenix had a high vacancy rate at the time. She should have done some market research to determine the value of the property. She felt confident that because she was getting it for a much lower price, she was safe in getting a good value.
2. She did not engage a buyer's real estate broker to represent her interests.
3. She did not get involved in the lending process to find out exactly what it would take to qualify. Chapter 11 has everything you will need to know to do this.

7. WINNING THE NUMBERS GAME—MAKING AND NEGOTIATING OFFERS

You really want this property. If you can just get the price down a bit it could pencil out. What's the most you can afford to pay for it based on your value adds, the break-even ratio, and your minimum acceptable *cash on cash return* and *internal rate of return* (Encyclopedia Topic A, Buying)? Putting together a buyer's pro forma will help you determine this.

Buyer's Pro Forma

This is the fun part. It should be enjoyable for you to put together a buyer's pro forma, which is a projection of income and expenses after your value-add strategies have been implemented for the next two to seven years. You will be raising rents and lowering expenses over time. So, for example, you may start out with a break-even ratio of 80%, but your pro forma shows that the ratio will come down to 72% in two years. Now you'll have confidence that your investment is recession-proof and that the property was a good buy. But you also need this pro forma to make sure you are making your minimum cash on cash return and internal rate of return. Go to Appendix A to see a sample of a seven-year budget pro forma. You can find a downloadable Excel version on my website: https://apartmentloanstore.com/.

Determining Your Highest Offer During a Seller's Market

During most of 2019, although most real estate investors were not aware of it, the United States was in the hyper-supply phase of the real estate market cycle. This meant that there was more supply than demand. Remarkably, prices remained high. They reached the point that many commercial properties were overpriced and not profitable for buyers, but—could you believe it—they were snatched up anyway because it was feared that prices would go even higher.

If you are making an offer in a competitive seller's market, how do you know the maximum amount you can safely pay for the property? Here are four methods. I recommend you use all of them on the same deal:

1. *Focus on your rate of return.* Focus on buying at prices that give you the rate of return you want on your cash invested. You will have to look at a lot of overpriced properties to find these.
2. *Focus on your break-even ratio.* As discussed previously, the break-even ratio determines, based on the seller's income and expenses, the occupancy you need to pay all of the property's expenses and the mortgage. If a property's break-even ratio is 80% or lower, it is likely safe to buy it at the seller's asking price. If it is higher than 80%, you'll need to either negotiate a lower price or walk away.
3. *Focus on your down payment and the amount that can be financed.* The purchase price will determine how much needs to be put down and the size loan

the property will qualify for. This is often the best handbrake for paying too much for a property.

4. *Don't buy during the hyper-supply phase.* Go back to Chapter 1 and read the Four Phases of the Commercial Real Estate Market Cycle section and try to determine which phase you are in. If there are too many units of the property type you are interested in already on the market, and rental rates are flat or declining, this is a sign you are in the hyper-supply phase and you should wait to buy.

Determining Your Highest Offer During a Buyer's Market

Who would guess? The beginning of the recovery phase following a recession usually becomes such a solid buyer's market that often it is more competitive than during a seller's market. This is because there are so many more players—more buyers who are motivated to join the game because of so many great deals, and so many more sellers who have hit a brick wall and have to sell. Now the buyers are holding the cards. They don't seem to care if they practically steal a property and make a bundle on the seller's misfortune. So as a buyer in a down market, how do you know if you are getting the best price for a property? Here are three methods; I recommend you use all of them.

1. *Offer 15% less than the purchase price during a recession or recovery phase.* At the beginning of a recession, sellers and their listing agents have a hard time accepting declining values, and prices on properties that have declining rent collections will likely be inflated by an average of 15%. Comparable values will be from a period when properties were stable and worth more. Determine what real

---

Time and Money Saving Tip

If you are buying during the expansion or hyper-supply phases of the real estate market cycle, don't count on your future value adds to make the property a good deal. Whether you can pull this off is an unknown, unless you are highly experienced at this game. Better to work with the seller to be reasonable and come down on the asking price by letting them know that you cannot make your minimum cash on cash return based on what you have to put into the property. Next, estimate the property's value by using the steps outlined in the Four 15-Minute Methods of Determining Property Value section of this chapter. Be sure to read Chapter 6, which is directed at sellers. It discusses in detail how and why commercial property values go up and the methods that listing agents use to determine a property's maximum listing price.

estate cycle phase you are in. Take a look at the Four Phases of the Commercial Real Estate Market and the Best Time to Buy sections in Chapter 1. About seven months into the recession phase, many properties are in foreclosure and appraisers have lowered values. Determine what the property would appraise for based on its current NOI and market cap rate. This is one of the best times to snatch properties for great prices based on what distressed sellers owe the bank. Commercial property will still be priced at more than it will likely appraise for, so you should offer at least 10–15% less than the asking price. At the beginning of the next phase, the recovery phase, prices will be at the bottom. This is the best time to send out many lowball offers.

2. *Determine your offering price based on economic occupancy.* Before making an offer on a property, ask what the physical and economic occupancy is (based on rent collected). If physical occupancy is at 90% and economic occupancy is at 70%, 20% of the tenants are not paying rent or paying on time. Based on current cap rates, base your offer on economic occupancy.

3. *Base your offer on the cost of money.* Determine what you can afford to pay for the property based on the best financing you and the property qualify for. Then base your offer on what you can safely put down and the estimated return on your cash invested after loan payments.

Time and Money Saving Tip

Wouldn't you like to know if a property you are interested in purchasing is in default with their bank or behind on taxes? This is public information. Go to the recorder of deeds' website for the county the subject property is in. Put in the property address and look up the deed. It will have the owner's information, legal description, and a record of all liens filed against the property. If you find that there are many years of back taxes owed or there is a default on the mortgage, there is likely an opportunity to buy the property fast for a good price. Be prepared with a fast-closing bridge loan or cash. If you want to be more aggressive, contact the special services department of the bank that holds the mortgage. See if you can buy the property from the bank for close to what they are owed if they are soon going to take it back. If foreclosure has not progressed that far, ask the bank if they would be interested in selling the mortgage note at a discount or face value. You can then foreclose on the property yourself in the near future and obtain the property at a substantial discount. See *non-performing note purchasing* (Encyclopedia Topic F, Repositioning).

Best Strategy for Making Offers

Expect a competitive market, whether it's up or down. Most buyers use letters of intent to make offers. These are not legally binding and are not meant to replace a purchase agreement, but quickly give the seller all the terms of your offer. If you can have dozens of these letters out on properties that you are interested in at the same time, you can really make some headway with this numbers game.

Negotiating the Sale Contract

Find out as much inside information about the seller as you can. Look at public records to see if there are back taxes owed on the property or if there has been any litigation. This is an indicator that the seller is going through financial stress and likely needs to sell. Maybe the seller is doing a 1031 exchange, has already found a replacement property, and needs to sell quickly. Maybe the owners are divorcing and need to sell. The seller will have done market research and is likely convinced that the property is worth the asking price or even more. If the property is overpriced, put yourself in their shoes and think about how you can motivate them to accept a more reasonable price. Try to set up a meeting with the seller directly and show them with facts and numbers why their price just will not work. Study Chapter 6 on how sellers and their listing brokers determine a property's maximum sales price. This will give you great insight into how sellers manipulate the price up, knowing that buyers are going to offer less and just where to negotiate a lower price.

Your buyer's broker can use a standard 20-page form to fill out the purchase and sale contract. For best results, the first draft of the purchase and sale contract should be written by your commercial real estate attorney, and you and your buyer's broker should review it. Your attorney will know best which side has the bigger stick for each clause of the contract. Also, your attorney stating that something must be stipulated in a particular way is much stronger than the same statement coming

> ### Time and Money Saving Tip
>
> Include multiple price offers in your letter of intent. The seller will be reviewing multiple offers from other people, so why not find out what they are most interested in by making multiple offers yourself? Say, for example, you find a multifamily 8-plex for sale for $595,000. The first offer in your letter of intent should be the highest price offer. For example, you might offer full price, or even more, with 20% down and the seller financing the balance. The second offer listed would be one with a lower price—say, $575,000 with a 70% first mortgage and a 10% owner-carry second mortgage. The third offer would be the lowest price offer—say, $555,000 with a 20% or 25% down payment with the balance being financed elsewhere. You should put all of the main terms of your offer in the letter of intent but leave out contentious ones that might put the seller off. You can bring these up after you get your foot in the door.

from a real estate broker. Ninety days is an optimum amount of time for the closing period for commercial deals, and between 45 and 60 days should be allowed for the due diligence period prior to your earnest money going hard. Sixty days is generally needed for financing, but you will need 90 days if the property inspection reveals unexpected needed repairs that must be bid on and negotiated. Be sure that all time periods start after you have in hand the property financials and all other information that you've requested from the seller. This will motivate the seller to gather those items quickly.

Your attorney will make sure that there are no *contingency clauses* missing in the contract. Contingencies are written to protect buyers from losing their earnest money due to a variety of circumstances. They are actually escape clauses for the buyer in the event of an adverse outcome pertaining to financing, property financials, property physical condition, leases, buyers intended use, environmental concerns, title, survey, water rights, zoning, and more If there is such an adverse outcome, the sale will be canceled and the buyer will receive their earnest money back.

> ### Time and Money Saving Tip
>
> It is standard practice for commercial properties to be sold as is. This puts the onus of discovering the property's financial and physical condition on the buyer. All negatives can be used by the buyer to lower the sale price prior to the financial and inspection contingencies expiring. Although it's not usually done, you can request ahead of time that the seller provide you with a list of any major replacements that are needed: new roof, HVAC system, and the like. That way the seller is admitting at the beginning that the property is being sold with problems. You can also request a list of capital improvements that the seller has made over the last five years. That will tell you about major work that has been done and give you an idea of how well the seller has maintained the property. Most sellers of commercial properties have this documentation.

How to Win the Numbers Game

Yes, this is a numbers game, even more so if it's a seller's market. For example, you might look at 40 properties that are for sale to find 4 that initially meet many of your objectives. You send letters of intent for those. One of those letters gets the listing agent's attention. But you are told that someone else is offering more. So you start all over again. But the good news is that at least you do know what you are looking for and have narrowed your search accordingly. Be sure to ask all of the brokers you talk with to look out for properties that meet your profile. Also, keep a database that lists the high-priority deals for which you've sent a letter of intent resulting in some interest from the listing agent. You should follow up on these every week or two. If you were told previously that there was already an offer on the property, it's possible that it has fallen through.

Jack, a client of mine, makes 20 or more lowball offers a week in North Texas and Southern Oklahoma. He attaches a generic preapproval letter to his letters of intent from me stating that he is qualified to buy the property. He doesn't have a chance to adequately evaluate these properties. His game is to fish in a large pond and play the numbers game. He almost never gets counteroffers, but eventually he will get a bite. And then during the due diligence phase he often finds the property wasn't what he thought it was and offers much less. Since the property was already priced low, this usually kills the deal. Then maybe in four to six months he hits a home run and closes at a great price. Even with all the time and effort involved, he feels it is worth it.

Why not try something more time effective? Give your property profile to several real estate brokers who specialize in the type of property you want and have them do most of the legwork for you. They will also have a network of property owners and might be able to secure an off-market deal for you.

Why not create your own leads? For a $600 annual investment you can subscribe to reonomy.com. It offers one of the largest national databases of commercial property owners in the country. It also can find the actual names of the owners of LLCs and provide contact info for them.

Buying

Actual Versus Potential/Pro Forma Numbers: *Don't get reeled in by the potential numbers*

Would you buy a business based on its potential income? Probably not. So what are sellers and their commercial listing brokers trying to pull when the marketing flyer lists a mix of potential and actual income? As the buyer, it is essential that you do not participate in a seller's shenanigans. When a seller is intent on selling you a property based on possible future income from it, set a precedent from the beginning by saying that you will only be analyzing actual numbers.

Actual Numbers: These are the real current and historical numbers. They are verifiable by the property's current rent roll, trailing 12-month report (T-12), and last full calendar year's month-by-month profit and loss statement on the subject property. Better yet, why not do the same verification of actual numbers that most lenders require? Ask for the last three years of the seller's Schedule Es from their 1040 tax return on the property to see how they reported the property's income on their taxes. Any savvy buyer of a business will request this documentation. You are not asking for their entire tax return, only for the one page that shows the subject property.

Potential/Pro Forma Numbers: These are enhanced numbers showing the property's potential gross income and net operating income (NOI). Often the marketing flyer will show a mix of actual and projected numbers. The intention is to show a higher cap rate, which makes the property appear more profitable. It is a commercial real estate standard that a minimum of 5% is shown for a vacancy rate, and that any credit loss (unpaid rent) is listed as well. But if the property is 100% occupied, this is seldom done. Also, the flyer should show something for management expenses (5% is recommended) even if the current owner is managing it themselves, and something for expenses related to *capital improvements* (see Encyclopedia Topic B, Due Diligence).

Look for discrepancies. If the gross rental income shown for each month is less than what the rent roll is showing, it could mean that some tenants are not paying or are paying late. (See *collection report* in Encyclopedia Topic B, Due Diligence.)

Affordable and Subsidized Housing: *Some great benefits here if you don't mind getting in bed with the government*

Let's not confuse low-income housing with affordable housing. Many low-income apartment complexes in America are Class D. These are cash cows for landlords who will rent to anybody in exchange for hardly ever fixing or maintaining anything.

Affordable Housing: A government-regulated property that has to be kept in good condition. Rents are limited to a percentage of the resident's household income.

Subsidized Housing: A housing subsidy is a government assistance program that helps provide housing for low-income persons. The most common subsidy vehicle is a Section 8 voucher, which is issued by state housing authorities and pays all or a portion of rent. Section 8 vouchers are issued to individuals or families for approved multifamily properties that usually have a mix of subsidized and unsubsidized renters. A Housing Assistance Payments (HAP) contract is a contract for subsidized housing that is issued on an entire building. The US Department of Housing and Urban Development (HUD) administers these contracts. HUD has a contract with the property owner and pays the rent for all of the tenants.

Should You Buy an Apartment Building with Section 8 Subsidized Rents?

Ideally the rule of thumb is to keep the percentage of Section 8 renters at 25%, and no more than 40%, of total residents. These percentages are what Fannie Mae prefers and will give your multifamily property a diversity that is optimum. On the one hand, it is more difficult to sell a property that is mostly Section 8. On the other, there is an advantage in renting to tenants who have Section 8 vouchers because the rents are often slightly higher than markets rents. In addition, you can sleep better at night with the certainty that the rent will be paid. When units are vacated, the housing authority will give you a generous repair allowance to make the unit ready for another resident. You will need to use your own funds for repairs and then get reimbursed, which takes about two months. A major downside is that some of these tenants may be experiencing an economic crisis or have domestic problems that create more property damage. This can create quite bit of havoc for property managers. Keep in mind, though, that many Section 8 tenants are seniors who are usually great tenants.

The Risks of Buying a HAP Contract Apartment Building

In this case HUD is renting the entire building from you and you are getting in bed with the government with a nice spool of red tape. The reporting requirements alone can be daunting. It's best to hire a property management company that has experience with HUD reporting. The risk here is if you or your property manager does not maintain the building properly, HUD can cancel the contract, resulting in 100% vacancy. If you do want to go ahead with the purchase of a HAP contract building, make sure there are three years or more left on the contract. This will give you plenty of time to learn about HUD maintenance and reporting requirements. If HUD doesn't like the way the property is run, it is less likely to cancel the contract and more likely to just not renew it. Keep in mind that multi-family properties with HAP contracts are much more difficult to sell. This is mainly because many lenders will not provide financing to purchase them because of the risk of the property becoming 100% vacant if HUD does not renew the contract.

Auctions, Buying At: *Great prices here, but you have to raise the cash fast*

Did you know that commercial properties can be purchased at auctions for amazingly good prices? Often these are great value-add opportunities. The auctioneer will prepare a due diligence package, which can run from twelve to several hundred pages. Prior to bidding the buyer usually has to show proof of funds or put down a deposit on a credit card or with a cashier's check. A line of credit can work nicely for this. The other option is to get a bridge loan. Many bridge lenders specialize in auctioned properties, are prepared to quickly preapprove a deal, and can close within a few weeks.

Auctions on the Courthouse Steps

Time and Money Saving Tip

So you are buying a property with the intention of improving it, raising rents, and raising the appraised value, followed by a cash-out refinance to take your profit out nine months later. You then intend to invest your windfall by buying another property. Sorry, but commercial banks don't like your getting rich that fast and will require that you own the property for three years before you take cash out based on the current appraised value. This is why so many investors have to sell their repositioned properties to realize a gain.

Most lenders will only refinance 75% of what you paid for the property plus what you put into it over the first two years of ownership. For multifamily properties you can take up to 100% of the cost out with a *Freddie Mac* loan (see Topic H, "Financing) after one year of ownership. For other property types, you can consider *CMBS* (*commercial mortgage-backed security*) loans, a *private fund lender, or a hard money lender,* all of which may enable you to take maximum cash out of a property after a year of ownership.

These auctions are a result of judicial foreclosures or property tax delinquencies, where the court has mandated that the property be sold at public auction. Although there are still some foreclosure auctions where investors gather around the auctioneer on the courthouse steps, most are held in a large room within the courthouse or at a hotel. It is advised that you attend a few auctions beforehand to get the hang of them. Here's how it is done:

1. *Review the due diligence package.* This is provided by the trustee on the properties you are interested in; drive by the property, if possible.
2. *Get your cash or financing together.* In most states and counties you will need to show proof of cash, so have this together beforehand. It's more the exception that you can put 5–10% down and hold the property after your bid has been accepted.
3. *Register with the auctioneer ahead.* In most cases you will need to show proof of funds to verify you are qualified.

4. *Attend the auction.* Be sure to arrive early and obtain an auction bidder card that you will raise each time you are willing to pay the most recent auctioneer's price. Be prepared to bring in a cashier's check for the full amount within one business day.

Other Types of Real Estate Auctions

- **Online Bid Auction:** This is becoming the most popular type of commercial property auction with both buyers and sellers. All bids need to be turned in by a designated date and time, and the highest bidder wins. An advantage is that you can shop for out-of-state properties without having to go to the auction physically. Go to

    https://zetabid.com/commercial-real-estate/
    https://www.tranzon.com/searchseeallcommercial.aspx
    https://www.williamsauction.com/commercial-real-estate-auction

- **Sealed Bid Auction:** Here, bids are sealed and no one—including the auctioneer—knows what they are. The sealed envelopes are opened and the property is sold to the highest bidder.
- **Reserve Auction:** In this type of auction, the seller decides ahead of time the lowest acceptable price for the property. After the bidding is complete the seller does not have to accept the highest bid and can counter it.

Break-Even Ratio: *Knowing this ratio can mean life or death for your finances when choosing a commercial property to buy*

This is likely the most important calculation you can do when buying a commercial property. You will probably get tired of hearing about it, as it is mentioned a dozen times or more in this book. Fortunately, it is quick and easy. The break-even ratio tells you the minimum occupancy the property has to have to pay all the bills and the mortgage. Anything above this is your profit. But more importantly it tells you the minimum occupancy you need to maintain before you have to feed the property cash. If you do not have the time or money to do value-adding, pick a property that has a break-even ratio of 80% or lower. To make the property recession-proof, plan on increasing rents and lowering expenses to a break-even ratio of 75% or less. For a value-add property needing major rehab, the break-even ratio might be 100% at the start, but it may be a worthwhile purchase if based on market rents you are confident that after you do the improvements, re-tenant, and raise rents, the break-even ratio will be 80% or less.

To calculate the break-even ratio for a commercial property, simply add the monthly property expenses to the monthly loan payments and divide the sum by the property's potential gross monthly income at 100% occupancy with current rents.

$$\frac{\text{Monthly expenses} + \text{Monthly loan payments}}{\text{Monthly potential gross income}} = \text{Break-even ratio}$$

Buying

Building Class: *The better the building class, the more expensive the property and the lower the return and risk will be on your investment*

Commercial real estate brokers, lenders, and appraisers have cleverly devised a rating system for the quality of commercial properties. These are Class A, B, C, and D (well, hardly anyone ever mentions Class D, but I assure you these buildings do exist so I'm going to mention them). I wish there were a big sign on each building with its class, as it's often not easy to determine. It's strange, but there is actually no building class rating system, so the classifications are really quite arbitrary. No one seems to agree on exact criteria for determining class; usually the listing real estate broker assigns this based on advertising objectives. The age of the property definitely seems to be a major factor. Class A properties age into Class B and then into Class C, where they will remain indefinitely if they are good looking, well maintained, and located in good safe neighborhoods.. If not, they may be designated Class D. Here are some general rules underlying these classifications:

- **Class A Properties:** These properties are up to 10–15 years old, are in good locations, in excellent condition, and have the best and latest amenities. They command the highest rents and are the most expensive properties in the market. They perform exceptionally well during recessions. Because these properties are so new, repair expenses are much lower.
- **Class B Properties:** These properties were A properties that have become 15–20 years old. They command high rents too, but the rents are lower than those of Class A properties and expenses for repairs are higher. They also do well during a recession.
- **Class C Properties:** These properties are 20 years old plus. They can be in safe, good neighborhoods and are in good condition. They can be in need of minor repairs and/or remodeling. It's strange, but a Class C property can be located in a Class D neighborhood but be considered Class C because it is in good condition and getting decent rents. In contrast, a Class D property in a Class C neighborhood will always be classified as Class D. And boy, are these in great demand among real estate investors—they represent the greatest value-add opportunity for fixers and flippers. These properties perform moderately well during recessions, with the exception of hotels, office, and retail properties.
- **Class D Properties:** These properties are old and worn out. They are in need of major repair or demolition. They are often located in less-desirable neighborhoods with working class tenants who are slow-pays and no-pays. They might appear to be an attractive buy because they have the highest cap rates and are the most profitable. If you get queasy at the thought of being a slumlord you will have to do major rehab on a Class D property. The risk lies in overimproving the property for the neighborhood and appraised value.

I became familiar with Class D apartment buildings when I met Winston early in my lending career. I had come to Cincinnati to refinance his 36-unit property. I could tell right away that it was in a bad neighborhood when I parked my rental car and four teenagers started rocking the suspension. Winston came out, waived his walking stick, and in a very quiet voice told them to move on. He was a very well-dressed older gentleman.

He told some funny stories about his tenants. My favorite was the time a tenant called the police because he hadn't seen the man next door in a long time and thought he had died in his apartment because of a foul smell coming from it. It turned out that his neighbor was a hermit and had not thrown his garbage out in over a month.

This was definitely a Class D property. It just looked bad—cracked walkways, a sagging roofline, and peeling paint. There was the smell of urine in the hallways. But the property cash flowed an insane amount of income. Winston was only spending $2,400 per year on repairs and maintenance ($66 per unit per year) and his rents were high. When I told him he would have to improve the property to get a loan, he told me, "no problem." I asked him how his rent collections were so good in such a high-crime neighborhood. He bragged, "That's because my bodyguard goes with me to make collections and I only accept cash or money orders." I started a loan for Winston but had to cancel it three weeks later. The appraiser called in alarm to say that in one of the units an 84-year-old woman with a walker was negotiating around a hole in the carpet the size of a manhole.

> ### Time and Money Saving Tip
>
> Class A properties are the most expensive and have little or no room to add value. Adding the latest amenities to a Class B property, upgrading its finishes, and adding landscaping and new signage can push it back into being a Class A rating and yield higher rents. Finding a Class C property in a good location with under-market rents that needs just cosmetic work will give you the best return on your investment in a buyer's or seller's market. In a seller's market, watch out for paying too much for a Class C property in a good neighborhood, as they are often priced close to what Class B properties command. Class B properties have much lower incidences of deferred maintenance and run lower repair expenses. In this situation buy the Class C property only if it is in a superior location, is in very good condition, and has plenty of opportunity to raise rents.

Buyer's List of Property Objectives: *When buying a commercial investment property, you need to know where you are going*

Here are eight main objectives to focus on when deciding what, where, why, and how to buy a commercial investment property:

1. **Property Type Objectives:** Determine what type of property you want to buy and why. Do you want a multifamily, senior living, student housing, mobile home park, self-storage, industrial, office, retail, or a healthcare property? Class A, B, C, or D?

2. **Market and Location Objectives:** Do you want to buy property in a *primary*, *secondary*, *or tertiary* (see Encyclopedia Topic H, Financing)? Near public transportation, major shopping, freeways, and the like? Do you need a high-traffic location?

3. **Financial Objectives:** Determine minimum acceptable cash on cash return, cap rate, and internal rate of return. How much can you put down? What is the price range you can afford?

4. **Value-Add Objectives:** Will you raise rents, lower expenses, attract better tenants, do cosmetic work, or do a light or major rehab (see Chapter 7)?

5. **Financing Objectives:** What financing are you ideally looking for: loan-to-value (LTV), fixed interest rate, amortization, or prepayment penalty? What types of loans do you qualify for? (See Chapters 10 and 11)

6. **Objectives for Raising Partners:** Will you be having partners? If so, what qualifications do they need to have or what can they contribute? Do you need a high-net-worth individual, someone with cash to contribute, or someone with experience in a particular area? (See Chapter 4.)

7. **Team Member Objectives:** Who will be your team members? Select your buyer's real estate broker, lender, commercial real estate attorney, experienced partner investors, and property manager.

8. **Exit Strategy Objectives:** Decide whether the property will be a long- or short-term hold, a reposition and hold, or a fix-and-flip. Lay out a plan and a time frame to accomplish it in.

Buyer's Pro Forma: *So where are you going financially with this property?*

If potential equity partners ask you what the *cash on cash return* (*CCR*) (see Encyclopedia Topic A, Buying) will be for the first 5 years, how will you know what to tell them? A buyer's pro forma does exactly that. It is an Excel spreadsheet that lists 2–10 years (based on your hold time) of researched projections on the property for income, expenses, debt service, capital improvements, and net profit. You can compute your expected CCR over time from the projections. Be sure to include these categories on your spreadsheet:

Buyer's Pro Forma, Main Categories

- **Gross Rental Income:** Show the seller's current income and expenses for the first few months. Insert current rents or rent per square foot for vacant spaces. Increase monthly rental income based on your expectations for occupancy and rent growth. Be sure to show how your value-add strategies will be impacting gross rental income and expenses over time. These strategies may decrease gross rental income in the beginning as units are improved and turned over, but increase it later on.

- **Vacancy Rate:** Be sure to allow for vacancies when calculating gross rental income. Use a market vacancy rate, or a minimum of 5% (appraisers and lenders use a minimum 5% vacancy rate).

- **Collection Loss:** Factor in a percentage of the estimated gross rental income that will not be collected due to default.

- **Other Income:** Add in any additional monthly income.
- **Expenses:** For gross leases include line items for taxes (increased to the amount the new owner will pay), insurance, off-site management, utilities (increase your utility costs and most other expenses by 3% per year), repairs and maintenance, trash removal, pest control, cleaning, general and administrative, professional services, and miscellaneous. For office, retail, and industrial net lease properties, you'll want to show the CAM (common area maintenance) expenses that the lessees will be paying as a debit under Expenses and as a credit (because the lessees will be reimbursing you) under Other Income.
- **Replacement Reserves:** Show this item as an expense. This amount shown in this category should cover the cost of major items that will need to be replaced or repaired, such as the roof, the HVAC system, and the surface of the parking lot. Allow $250–400 per unit per year for a multifamily or $1.50–2.50 per square foot per year for office and retail. Ask your lender what amount you should use for this.
- **Debt Service:** Since you have not been approved for a loan yet, it is best to prepare two to three different pro formas, each of which shows a different scenario based on interest rate and amortization.

> ### Time and Money Saving Tip
>
> One of the main purposes of preparing a buyer's pro forma spreadsheet is to impress your lender and investors with it. This is one of the most important tools you have to sell them on your deal. It is not that you are trying to fool them—your pro forma will need be packed with facts, actual numbers, and intelligent assumptions. Knowing how the property will perform over time is very important to lenders. To go along with the buyer's pro forma, write up a narrative detailing your plan for the property and the value-add items you will be implementing. Be sure to show the associated income or expense associated with each month. Show how you will be raising rents and lowering expenses over time. Each income and expense category will need to have a footnote explaining how you determined the amount. Lenders and investors do not like it when they ask how you came up with numbers and you say, "Oh, I'm not absolutely sure, but it seems likely."

Cap/Capitalization Rate (Buyer's Perspective): *If cap rates are going down rapidly, this means prices are skyrocketing and it might not be a good time to buy*

"So, what is the cap rate?" "Oh, this property has a killer cap rate." "I just don't like that cap rate!" These are statements that you often hear from commercial property investors and professionals, who all seem to be obsessed with cap rates. If you know the market, the cap rate will tell you instantly, with just a single number, if the property is a good buy or a bad buy.

What is a cap rate? It stands for capitalization rate. To determine cap rate simply take the property's annual NOI and divide it by the purchase price. For example, if a property has an annual NOI of $80,000 and a purchase price of $1,000,000, it would have an 8% cap rate.

$$Annual\,NOI/Purchase\ price = Cap\ rate$$

The higher the cap rate, the less expensive the property is given its earnings. Real estate brokers, sellers, lenders, and appraisers in the commercial real estate sector often look at a cap rate differently. This could be because they have different incentives, which lead them to form different assumptions about market rents, vacancy rates, and operating expenses. Listing agents and sellers get excited over lower cap rates. They want to get the highest sales price possible and will gather comparables from recent sales of the highest-priced properties with the lowest cap rates. Conservative lenders seem to prefer higher cap rates that lower the property value. Commercial appraisers that work for banks often want to please them and often come in with higher cap rates that conclude a lower valuation. Buyers are usually only interested in the cap rate of the subject property based on current actual rent, income, and expenses for that property. They then want to check market cap rates to determine if the subject property is a good value.

Using the Cap Rate to the Buyer's Advantage

1. *Know your cap rate floor.* Your cap rate floor is the lowest cap rate you can accept in a property you are buying based the money you are investing and your CCR objectives for that investment. When searching for properties to buy, this will help you quickly identify properties that meet your CCR objectives.
2. *Research where cap rates are headed.* This is difficult to do at the beginning of a recession, as the comparable sales are likely from when the market was at its peak. In an up market, have a good commercial real estate broker compare cap rates from like properties that have sold in the past year. This will give you the best indicator of which properties that you are evaluating are a good buy. In a down market, ask the real estate broker to show you a recent history of where cap rates have been and where they think they are going. You need to know if you are buying in a market where cap rates are going down (prices are increasing) or cap rates are going up (prices are going down). If cap rates are going down rapidly in a short time frame and prices are skyrocketing, this is likely not a good time to buy. The last thing you want to do is buy at the top of the market. If cap rates are going up rapidly and prices are falling, you might as well wait until prices hit bottom before you buy. But you will not know that they have hit the bottom for sure until they start going up again.

Cash on Cash Return (CCR): *What percentage is the cash you are investing into buying this likely going to earn?*

What you really want to know when buying income-producing real estate is the percentage your cash investment will be earning annually. Calculating the potential CCR for a property you are buying is the way to do this. If your cash investment is earning 7% or more, this rate of return can be better than that of a bull stock market. To determine CCR, simply divide the annual projected NOI less loan payments by your total cash invested in the property.

$$\frac{\text{Annual NOI less annual loan payments}}{\text{Total cash invested}} = \text{CCR}$$

Four Cash on Cash Return Tips

1. *Loan terms matter.* Finding a loan that starts out with 2–10 years of interest-only payments and combining this with the lowest interest rate you can find will do the most to lower your loan payments and increase your CCR. If you cannot get an interest-only loan, go for the longest amortization you can get.
   To illustrate, let's use a $1,360,000 purchase price at an 8% cap with 25%, or $340,000, down. Net operating income is $108,800. Let's compare your CCR under terms that specify a 20-year amortization, a 30-year amortization, and interest-only payments.

Annual loan payments		CCR
20-year amortization annual payments =	$ 79,194	8.7%
30-year amortization annual payments =	64,418	13.0%
Interest-only annual payments =	50,000	17.3%

2. *Choose properties with quick, low, or no-cost operational value-add strategies.* Obviously, it's best to find properties that have under-market rents and will not take a lot of cash to upgrade.
3. *Property type matters.* Class A and B properties have the lowest cap rates and have few value-add opportunities. Class C properties in decent neighborhoods are the best. Choose a property type that has more than one source of income. Independent senior living produces great CCR with rent on the units plus services like meals, housekeeping, and laundry. Mobile home parks with many park-owned homes receive rent on the pads plus rent on the homes.
4. *Know your floor CCR.* More important than cap rate for many is knowing what their lowest acceptable CCR is. In a low cap rate seller's market it is prudent to choose a property based on value-add strategies and the best financing to achieve the CCR you want.

Commercial Properties' Four Income Streams

Commercial properties have *four* sources of income: rental income, rental increases, appreciation, and depreciation. Here is about what you can expect to earn annually when you put 25% down on a million-dollar apartment complex today:

Buying

Net operating income at a 7.5% cap rate:	$75,000
Less annual mortgage payments	– 46,948
Adjusted net income	28,052
Rental increases	5,400
Appreciation at 6%	6,000
Depreciation $32,727	8,812 (savings on taxes if your tax
Total annual earnings	**48,264** bracket is 25%)

Assumptions: Mortgage payments are based on a rate of 4.75% with a 30-year amortization. Rental increases are estimated at $75 per month for 6 units in a 12-unit property. Property appreciation is estimated to be 6.3%. Depreciation is based on IRS Section 179, which allows the purchase price less land value to be divided by 27.5 over a period of 27.5 years. Land is assumed to be worth $100,000. For all other commercial properties, the value of structures can be depreciated over 39 years. Can you believe it? Just by owning this property—that is, by the way, almost certainly appreciating—you get to deduct *$32,727* in depreciation from your taxes each year. If you are in a 25% tax bracket, you end up with $8,812 more in your pocket instead of the government's pocket. W-2 wage employees and business owners that rent are just not blessed with a tax shelter like this.

Contingency Clauses in the Sales Contract (Buyer's Perspective): *As a buyer, these are your escape clauses for getting out of the purchase contract*

Contingency clauses are written into the sales contract as escape clauses to protect the buyer in the event of an adverse outcome pertaining to financing, title and survey, property financials, property physical condition, leases, environmental concerns, or zoning. If there is an event, the sale is canceled and the buyer receives their earnest money back. The contingencies have time periods whereby the buyer does their due diligence and they are removed after these expire. Once removed, the earnest money will go hard (not be refundable). The main contingency clauses follow (there are more) with suggested time frames:

- **Financing Contingency:** This should be written so that if the buyer cannot obtain the financing they want for any reason, the sale will be canceled and the buyer will receive their earnest money back in full. It takes 30–45 days for a conventional loan to be approved and 21–30 days for a bridge loan to be approved. Allow 45 days.
- **Title and Survey Contingency:** The buyer should have their commercial real estate attorney start reviewing the title report and survey within days of signing the purchase agreement. Is the buyer getting what they think they are? Are there any restrictions such as liens, problems with access, easements, or encroachments? Is there litigation filed against the property and does the seller have the legal right to sell the property? This can take up to 60 days if there are problems clearing the title.

- **Property Inspection Contingency:** The buyer should have all the major systems and components inspected, including structural/engineering, plumbing, electrical, HVAC, roofs, doors and windows, and exterior and interior finishes. It takes an average of two weeks for a property condition report to be completed and up to 30 days after that to get bids on the work needed, so 45 days is recommended.

- **Financial Due Diligence Contingency:** This should be written so that the buyer can cancel the sale if any of the financials the seller submits or fails to submit to the buyer show a financial condition for the property that is more negative than what was portrayed by the seller at the beginning. Items to be reviewed include current and historical rent rolls; three years of income and expense statements; three years of capital improvements; last year's utility bills, leases, and rental agreements; property tax and insurance bills; and tax returns. 30 days should be adequate.

- **Review of Leases and Rental Contracts Contingency:** The buyer is given a reasonable amount of time to review leases and rental contracts. 45 days is good here.

- **Estoppel Letter Review:** For office, retail, and industrial properties only, all tenants need to fill out an estoppel that certifies what their lease term is and that they are not in default of their lease. Estoppels need to go out to tenants right after the purchase agreement is signed. They can sometimes take several months to come in from national tenants, and your lender will not close without them. So allow 60 days, or whenever all the estoppels are in.

- **Zoning and Certificate of Occupancy Contingency:** The zoning contingency addresses whether the property's use is legally permitted under zoning regulations, while the certificate of occupancy contingency pertains to whether all units are legal. 30 days is good.

- **Approval for Zoning Contingency:** If the property is not already zoned for the buyer's intended purposes and requires a zoning change by the planning department or zoning board, this contingency should be added. This can take 90 days or longer.

- **Miscellaneous Contingency Items:** These include environmental concerns, vendor contracts, crime reports, and a list of equipment, fixtures, and supplies that are being sold with the property. 45 days is good.

Time and Money Saving Tip

As a buyer, the very first thing you need to do after signing the purchase and sale contract and before you spend any time on due diligence is to have your real estate attorney review the title and survey. Finding out prior to closing that the seller does not have clear title to sell the property or does not even have the authority to sell it due to pending litigation happens more often than you would think. Also, determine at the beginning if there is an easement or encroachment on the survey that makes the property less usable. I have worked on properties that were landlocked, but the buyer did not know this since there was a road going to the subject property. However, to access the road you had to cross a large gravel area that belonged to a neighboring property, and there was no easement in the title report or survey that allowed access through that property.

Cost per Unit Analysis: *This is the quickest method of determining if the commercial property you want to buy is overpriced*

This is a simple, quick way of determining market value on a property you are interested in buying, but it can only be used for multifamily, senior, and student housing, and for hospitality properties. Start out by finding four to six properties of similar quality and size that have sold in the last year in the same market as the subject property. Then determine the cost per unit for each property. Simply take the purchase price and divide it by the number of units. Then average the cost per unit of all the properties. Next take the average cost and multiply it by the number of units your property has. This should give you a fair determination of value for the subject property. Lastly, compare what your property is being sold for with the cost per unit analysis value.

Deferred Maintenance (Buyer's Perspective): *Be sure to walk through all the units and spaces in a subject property with a contractor to identify blemishes firsthand*

"Deferred maintenance" is a commercial property term. It refers to repairs and capital improvements that have been put off or neglected. If the property you are interested in buying has a lot of deferred maintenance it is usually due to the property underperforming or the seller having financial concerns. It will take a property condition report to accurately identify all of the deferred maintenance items and the cost to remedy them. This report looks at all the major systems and components, including the foundation, structure, roofing, siding, and the electrical, plumbing, and HVAC systems. Most importantly,

Time and Money Saving Tip

Are you paying too much for a multifamily or hotel property that needs minor or major rehab after you add the renovation costs in? Start out by figuring out total project cost. Take the purchase price and add it to the estimated cost for the renovations. Add a 15% contingency factor to the renovation costs for cost overruns (sorry, but because some units will need to be vacated during the renovation and the fact that actual costs usually end up being higher than estimated costs, this is necessary). Then add your loan fees, closing costs, and interest payments during construction. The total should represent total project costs.

Next, find properties of a similar size in the same market that are in good condition and that have sold in the past year and determine the cost per unit for these properties. Then calculate an average cost per unit for these properties. Take that average cost and multiply it by the number of units in your property. This should give you a fair indicator of what your property will be worth after improving it. Is what you will pay for the property plus the cost to reposition it more than the cost of like properties already in good condition? If so, you are taking an unreasonably high risk. Share your figures with the seller and negotiate with them to lower the price. Or, walk away.

Time and Money Saving Tip

If you do not want to risk losing several months of your time plus the deposit on your loan for *third-party reports* (see Encyclopedia Topic H, Financing), read this tip carefully. One it is essential that you walk through all the units and spaces with a contractor and take notes about all the problems you see. I assure you that your contractor will find even more items that need work.

Double Closing: *Use this method if you want to sell the property to someone else at a profit at closing*

If you are good at finding income properties priced below their value, maybe you should consider becoming a commercial property wholesaler and sell these properties immediately using a double closing. Double closings are used by savvy real estate wholesalers who pick up a property for a good price and

of the main reasons fully executed purchases of commercial properties fail to close is because repair items are discovered during the 60 days it takes to close and the buyer insists on trying to lower the sales price each time something is discovered. This really wears the seller down, to the point that the deal is just not worth it for them. Wait until you get the property condition report before you walk through all the units and spaces to get an estimate of repair costs. Then negotiate just once with the seller on all of them at least a week before the due diligence period is up.

then resell the property at a higher price at the closing table. The wholesaler has the purchase contract made out to themselves, an ownership entity they own and always put in, or assignees. They then find a buyer who will pay more for the property and sign a purchase contract with them. To close the transaction they assign the original purchase to the new purchaser. If timed correctly, the wholesaler is paid their profit along with their earnest money at closing, while putting very little or no money into the deal.

Commercial property wholesalers often have lines of credit as a backup plan so that if the resale fails, they can still purchase the property and find another buyer soon after. That way they do not lose their earnest money. Another backup plan is for the wholesaler to find two buyers and have one make a backup offer.

Earnest Money: How Much and Is It Refundable? (Buyer's Perspective): *It is rare that a commercial property purchaser loses their earnest money*

An earnest money deposit of 1% of the purchase price is the average for commercial real estate. However, I have seen it be as low as $25,000 on a $5 million purchase, which is only half of a percent. In very competitive deals I have experienced sellers asking as much as 3%. The rule of thumb here is to demonstrate to the seller that you are sincere; a minimum of 1% is good. If you know you are competing against other offers in a seller's market, 1.5–2.0% could help you win the deal.

As to whether earnest money is refundable: I have worked on hundreds of commercial real estate purchases and it is rare that a buyer cannot back out and get their earnest money refunded. However, once the earnest money goes hard (after contingencies, including the financing contingency, are signed off on), the earnest money is at risk. To counter this risk it is important for the buyer to not sign off on their financing contingency until their loan is approved with no conditions or conditions that can be easily met. Sellers keeping the buyer's earnest money when the sale does not close is the exception in these deals. Why? First, because listing real estate brokers do not want to risk litigation, and second because there are so many contingencies or escape clauses that protect the buyer in the purchase and sales contract. The most popular reason why buyers back out is when the condition of the property is not what they expected, or if they cannot get the financing they wanted.

Effective Gross Income: *You do this calculation to determine the actual gross income*

You are being duped if you buy a commercial property in the same way most people do. Most often they annualize the gross rents listed on the rent roll and subtract last year's expenses to come up with gross annual rental income. They then figure out NOI using that figure.

It makes much more sense to determine the NOI and the value of the property based on effective gross income. This is a more conservative way of forecasting the gross income of a commercial property based on actual numbers. To calculate effective gross income, simply take potential income (at 100% occupancy) and subtract income lost through annual actual vacancy, collection losses, *rent concessions* (see Encyclopedia Topic J, Managing and Leasing), and leasing commissions from the previous 12 months. You will need to get a *trailing 12-month report (T-12)* (see Encyclopedia Topic H, Financing) to determine this accurately. If you cannot obtain the T-12, then subtract a minimum of 5% for vacancy or market vacancy, 3% for credit loss, and actual lost rental income due to rent concessions. If the effective gross income is a lot less than the gross income the seller has reported in the marketing flyer, your job is to politely ask them what they are trying to pull here—and then get the price lowered accordingly.

> **Time and Money Saving Tip**
>
> Now that you know that it is better to use effective gross income to determine the actual property income, you'll want to look at expenses more realistically too. Usually the buyer of a commercial property analyzes the NOI based on the past year's expenses. The problem with this is that expenses always go up. So do what lenders do: we add 3% to expenses when forecasting the first year. You should too. Be sure to look up the current taxes with the county tax assessor's office to make sure they are accurate. Most increase every year. And don't forget to check your lender's insurance requirement, as this could raise your insurance costs higher than what the seller is paying; then get an accurate quote on what the cost will be for you.

Gross Rent Multiplier (GRM): *Is the property you want to buy a good buy? Use this fast method to find out.*

GRM is used as a quick method of determining property value for a rental property. It is based solely on the relationship between gross annual rents and the sales price of the property. The lower the GRM, the more rent you will be getting for the purchase price. Operating expenses are not taken into consideration, so this is a much less accurate method of valuation than an appraisal. The GRM also estimates how many years it will take for the gross annual rents alone to pay off the property without a mortgage.

To calculate GRM, take the purchase price and divide it by gross annual rents at 100% occupancy.

$$\text{Purchase price/Gross rents} = \text{GRM}$$

For example: The purchase price is $1,000,000. The annual gross rents are $120,000. The GRM is 8.33.

How to use GRM. Use GRM to determine if the property you are interested in buying is priced fairly; it will only take 10–15 minutes. Find four properties listed for sale on LoopNet or ask your real estate broker to pull these up for you from the Multiple Listing Service. They have to be in the same market and be similar in type, size, and condition to the one you are interested in buying. Compute the annual GRM on each and then average the results.

As an example, if you find that the average GRM for these properties is 8.75 and the subject property has a 7.75 GRM, you know that yours is priced better than the others and is a good buy. If the property you are interested in has a GRM higher than the average of the comparables' GRMs, you can still buy if you can get it for a price that will allow you to put time and money into repositioning it with higher rent and lower expenses.

What is a good GRM? A GRM of 7 would be great, but you will likely have to choose an older Class C property with more deferred maintenance to get this. A GRM of 8–12 is the average range for GRMs these days. If getting the most net income is the most important thing to you, a GRM of 10 or under will be needed. In or near large cities it is very difficult to find quality commercial properties with a GRM lower than 10. The most expensive properties being sold at very low cap rates can have a GRM of 14–18.

Healthcare Property: *These properties are expensive but are they a safe investment?*

Some healthcare properties have the lowest risk and are some of the most expensive commercial properties to invest in. They consist of medical offices, urgent care centers, outpatient clinics, and surgery centers. In most cases tenants sign a 15- to 20-year lease and build to suit with business loans from their bank. When the landlord pays for tenant improvements the rent skyrockets.

Skilled nursing facilities, assisted living, memory care facilities, and hospitals are a much higher risk because it takes exceptionally good management to run them profitably. If these facilities have too many Medicare and Medicaid patients, they can run in the red.

Industrial Property: *Did you know that a flex warehouse complex is the most sought-after industrial property by buyers?*

Multitenant industrial complexes are right below apartments as one of the safest commercial property investments. This is because the tenants are businesses that take pride in their operations. At the other extreme, single-tenant manufacturing or distribution industrial buildings are much more risky because if the single tenant goes out of business, you'll have a 100% vacancy rate. According to JLL, industrial spaces had a record low vacancy rate of 5.1% nationally in 2017.

Types of Industrial Properties

- **Flex Warehouse:** These spaces average 2,000 to 12,000 square feet, that have an office on one side and a warehouse with a sliding door for deliveries on the other. Flex space ranks as having the highest buyer demand among commercial property types, just below apartments. This makes them difficult to acquire. They are a very low-risk investment.
- **Light Manufacturing Multitenant Building:** These buildings are larger than flex spaces, easily reconfigured, with space for assembling products, storage of inventory, and office functions. They are a low-risk investment.
- **Heavy Industrial Warehouse:** These properties usually house one manufacturing or distribution company and average 60,000 to 500,000 square feet in size. These properties can also house telecom business, such as data hosting centers. These carry moderate risk with a financially strong, creditworthy tenant with a long-term, 15- to 20-year lease (once the lease is up you could have a 100% vacancy rate). Wholesale food distribution warehouse buildings have one of the lowest risks of any commercial property during a recession.
- **Showroom Buildings:** These have one of the highest risks of commercial real estate. This is because they are very large, single-tenant/single-purpose properties. An auto dealership is an example of this type of property: If this tenant goes out of business, what other tenant could use the configuration of this space?

Internal Rate of Return (IRR): This number represents the true value of money invested over time

Are you planning to have investors purchase the commercial property with you? If so, you really want to use the property's projected IRR to sell them on the investment—the IRR will show a much higher rate of return than what the CCR shows. IRR is the value of the money invested over time. This includes not only net annual income over the period of ownership from operations, but also appreciation when the property is sold. In most cases, commercial properties earn much more from appreciation than they do from operations.

Here is an example: Let's say that your group purchases a mixed-use Class C property in a good metropolitan neighborhood for $2.4 million with 25% of the total costs down. The ground floor is vacant and there are 16 apartments on the upper floors that are in good shape. Your plan is to upgrade the apartments with new appliances, fixtures, and floor coverings and then to raise the rents. You plan to attract a national chain restaurant, which will put in its own tenant improvements, to rent the first floor. Then you plan to sell the fully stabilized property in four years for $4.4 million. The example below shows an impressive 49.5% annual IRR: try earning a rate of return like that in the stock market.

To calculate the estimated annual IRR of a commercial property investment, follow these steps:

1. Start out by adding up the total project costs, including financing costs.
2. Calculate the total project net income after expenses and debt service for the time period you plan on owning the property.

3. Calculate your total profit on the investment after selling it by adding the total income and the appreciation over the term of ownership.
4. Divide the total profit by the down payment or cash you originally contributed. This will give you the gross IRR for the total time period.
5. Divide the previous result by the number of years the property is held to get the annual IRR.

A sample calculation follows:

1. Project costs

Purchase price	$2,900,000
Renovation costs	+ $345,000
Financing costs	+ $ 90,000
Total project costs	$3,335,000

Down payment at 25% = $833,750

2. Net income after debt service

Year 1	$65,525
Year 2	+ $160,500
Year 3	+ $170,130
Year 4	+ $180,207
Total net income	$576,362

3. Total profit from income and appreciation

Total four-year income	$576,362
Appreciation	+ $1,065,000 (after sale)
Total profit	$1,641,362

4. Gross IRR

Total profit $ 1,641,362 / Down payment $833,750 = 198%

5. Annual IRR

198% / 4 years = 49.5%

Letter of Intent/Interest (LOI) to Purchase: *Use these to make many different offers on many properties at the same time*

Your LOI is your sales pitch and the first impression that the seller and their real estate broker will have of you. It should get them interested in selling their property to you. Put yourself in the seller's shoes and think about what you can offer that they will find most attractive. You need to also get across that you are qualified to make this purchase. If you are not, then bring on a strong, experienced partner that is and you can say that you are representing this investor. See Chapter 4 for more detail on this.

The LOI does not replace a legal purchase and sale agreement, it precedes it. It is best to make many offers through LOIs to see which ones stick. Being able to mass-produce them quickly is essential. Set up a template so that you can quickly change the pertinent information. Remember that the best deals are highly competitive. The odds are that out of 20 offers, 1 will get a favorable response to your terms. Of those, less than half will make it through the negotiating process and in a seller's market, maybe one in four. To give yourself a competitive edge, attach a preapproval letter from a lender or commercial mortgage broker showing that you are qualified to finance the subject property based on your credit, net worth, and down payment. Offer to show proof of your down payment to the listing broker upon request. That should get their attention, since most offers don't offer that option in the LOI.

What to Include in Your Letter of Intent

1. **Headings:** Insert the date and seller's and/or listing agent's name. Follow these by your name and the name of the buyer broker who is representing you.
2. **Introduction:** List the name and address of the subject property. State briefly why you and your team are qualified to buy this property.
3. **Purchase Price:** Put in the amount of your offer.
4. **Financing:** Show amounts for the down payment and proposed loan. Give yourself the option of either assuming the seller's financing or having the seller carry the mortgage.
5. **Earnest Money:** Put in the proposed amount (1% is average).
6. **Inspection/Due Diligence Period:** A 45-day period is ideal. A 30-day period will be tight. Put in all the contingencies: financing, appraisal, environmental concerns, property condition or inspection report, review of leases, zoning, and title report. For the due diligence period, specify that the period starts once you've received all of the property's financials from the seller.
7. **Purchase and Sale Agreement:** How soon do you intend to sign it after your LOI is accepted? A period of 2–3 business days is good; you want to tie the property down fast.
8. **Escrow Account:** Specify when you will put the earnest money into escrow at a title company. Within 2–4 business days after the purchase contract is fully executed is a reasonable time frame.
9. **Real Estate Broker Fees:** Who will pay these fees? If you have your own buyer's broker, state that you expect the listing broker to split their commission with your broker.
10. **Closing Date:** A period of 75 days is ideal, 60 days is doable, and 45 days is very rushed. Commercial financing takes, on average, 45–60 days.
11. **Closing Conditions:** The conditions that must be met prior to closing.
12. **Closing Costs:** Specify who will pay for title insurance, transfer fees, and the like. Splitting them is recommended.
13. **Prorations:** A proration is a monetary payment that will need to be prorated depending on when the property sells. Rents collected, rental deposits, taxes, and the like all fall under this umbrella. Handle these through your escrow account.
14. **Possession:** State when you will take possession of the property. Usually, this occurs at close of escrow.

Buying

15. **Expiration Date of Your Offer:** Specify the date by which the seller must accept your offer. A time frame of no more than five business days is recommended.

Master-Metered Property: *These properties run the highest operating expenses*

Are your kids terrible about turning lights off when they leave a room? The same goes for tenants who are not paying for utilities. A master-metered commercial property has one utility meter for the entire property or for each building billed to the property owner. This system pertains to electric and natural gas. Master metering was quite popular during the 1960s and 1970s when utilities were cheap, but it makes absolutely no sense today. Operating expenses can run as much as 18% higher than average on master-metered properties. Today, master-metered properties are usually Class C multifamily properties. These systems are prevalent in Class D apartment complexes too. The tenants in these kinds of properties usually have bad credit and cannot get utilities put in their name, so the only way for them to keep the power on is to have their landlords pay the utilities. However, rents are usually high enough to compensate the property owner for this kind of setup.

Time and Money Saving Tip

To increase your odds of getting to the negotiating table on a competitive deal that you really want to land, have your real estate broker call the listing agent. As a third party, they will be able to sell your qualifications and your ability to close the deal best. As a fellow professional, they can find out why the seller is selling. Maybe the seller is doing a 1031 exchange and it's urgent that they sell. Your broker can then tell the listing agent the maximum price you can offer and some of your terms. Your realtor should get a good idea if your offer is wasting the seller's time, is in the ballpark, or how it might need to be adjusted. Then you can submit an LOI that is focused accordingly.

Time and Money Saving Tip

If you find a master-metered property that you are interested in buying, consider putting in a RUBS, or a ratio utility billing system. The utility bills will be prorated and simply passed on to the tenants every month based on the square footage of each unit. The other option—installing meters in each unit—is very costly.

Mixed-Use Property: *Follow these guidelines to invest in one safely*

A mixed-use commercial property has retail or commercial office space on the ground floor and apartments up above. This property type is very popular in urban settings. Mixed-use properties can be an excellent, safe investment under the right circumstances. But under the wrong ones, they pose a much higher risk than multifamily buildings. This is especially the case if more than 25% of the square footage or 25% of the gross income comes from the retail or commercial office space. If fewer than three commercial tenants occupy the ground floor it adds greatly to the risk. It's obvious that the time period it takes to prepare and rent an apartment is a lot shorter than the time needed to ready and rent office and retail space. Also, the demand for apartments is much higher.

To mitigate this risk, having three to four strong commercial tenants on long-term leases of 10 years or more on the ground floor is recommended. If you have only one commercial tenant occupying 20% or more of the building and that tenant moves out, at once you have 20% vacancy rate. This problem is compounded by the fact that it can take between five and nine months to find a commercial tenant, negotiate a lease, and wait for tenant improvements to be completed before the rent starts to be paid. During this time your property could generate a negative net income after debt service and cause your loan to be called.

There is an exception to this rule: if the tenant occupying the entire ground floor is a credit tenant with a high credit rating that has signed a very long-term lease, the risk will be lower. A few years ago I financed a mixed-use property in Los Angeles that had Head Start occupying 34% of the gross building square footage. The US Department of Health and Human Services, which runs Head Start, had signed a 25-year lease. The US government has an excellent credit rating of AA+, so this more than mitigated the risk.

Mobile Home Park: How to rate and finance them

Mobile home parks are often spoken in terms of their quality, which is rated from one to five stars. Real estate brokers quite often market a mobile home park based on its rating. Because there is not a rating agency in the United States that evaluates the quality of mobile home parks, the star rating is really not based on fact. There used to be a Woodall's guide that rated mobile home parks, but this has been out of print for more than 25 years. Since then, mobile home parks have evolved into manufactured home communities with outstanding amenities. Mobile home parks that have 85% or more homes owned by the tenants are a low risk during a recession. At my company, a mortgage banking firm, we categorize mobile home parks into four classes similar to commercial property ratings.

> ### Time and Money Saving Tip
>
> Mobile home parks can be difficult to finance; it's best to find one with owner-carry financing. Banks are not crazy about them because they just don't trust an asset that has almost no brick and mortar to support such high sale prices and homes that can be driven off in the middle of the night. At best, most banks lend at 65% LTV with a 15- or 20-year amortization. Worse yet, mobile homes that are owned by the park only get credit by appraisers for the pad rent when most of the rent is from the home. This results in a much lower appraised value and an even smaller loan. Now if you can move up to a Class A or B property with 90% or more tenant-owned homes, you can get a great loan from Fannie Mae. We are talking about a 10- to 30-year fixed low rate mortgage with a 30-year amortization.

Mobile Home Park Categories

1. **Class A:** These parks are newer manufactured housing communities with low density that look like good residential neighborhoods. They are well located near major shopping. The residents own over 90% of the homes. All of the homes are

Buying

double- and triple-wide and set back from the street. There are curbs and gutters, paved roads, underground utilities, manicured lawns, good road lighting, and usually city water and sewer. These parks have the best amenities, including a community activity building, a gym, a swimming pool, and a playground.

2. **Class B:** These manufactured housing communities are similar to Class A communities but are older and may not be as centrally located. They have at least 90% resident-owned homes.

3. **Class C:** These parks could be centrally located near shopping or be in a rural setting. They have 10–20% park-owned homes and have 50% or more single-wides. They have good street lighting and paved roads. Utilities can be either aboveground or undergound. They can have city water or be on a private system. Resident's homes are well maintained and have yards with decent landscaping that are clutter-free.

4. **Class D:** These parks usually are almost entirely made up of old single-wides. The majority of homes are park owned, which lack the pride of home ownership since the occupants are renting. There are often gravel roads, above-ground utilities, poor-quality landscaping (if any), and clutter in many of the yards. Water and sewer services are supplied by the city or through a private septic system. However, Class D parks throw off the most income of any class and have the highest cap rates of almost any type of commercial real estate. This is because they have two streams of income: rent from the pads and rent from the park-owned homes.

Multifamily Property: The commercial property most in demand by buyers

> ### Time and Money Saving Tip
>
> It may be tempting to purchase a Class D mobile home park that owns all or most of the homes. Yes, they are cash cows, but here's the catch: just like Class D apartment buildings you could be faced with a high incidence of domestic problems, drug problems, and the police calling you in the middle of the night. But most importantly, there are too many slow-paying and no-paying tenants. When tenants own their homes in a mobile home park they almost always pay the rent. If they do not, the park can put a lien on their home and kick them out. So unless this lifestyle is for you, pick a less profitable Class C mobile home park. If you are still determined to purchase a Class D park, be sure to employ an on-site manager who has the personality of an army sergeant.

If you have owned multiple residential rental homes, maybe it's time for you to graduate to a multifamily property. You already have the skills to manage residential tenants. You will save time and money by having all of your units under one roof. With an average national vacancy rate of 5% or less in 2019, multifamily properties and apartment buildings are the most in demand by buyers of any commercial property type, and they do well during recessions. Class A, B, and C properties have just about the lowest risk if the owner lives close by—just under high-credit-rated net lease properties. Because of stiff competition, multifamily property prices are often unrealistically high. In 2019, the United States experienced one of the highest demand for apartments since World War II. This is due to a growing population and the rising price of single-family homes. Those Gen Xers and millennials who prefer renting and living for today versus saving to buy a home further increase demand. Add to the mix our aging population. Many seniors lose their appetite for the continual maintenance that home ownership requires and want to move into smaller, luxurious rentals, often in 55 and older communities.

Multifamily Property Types

- **Garden Style:** This is the most common style of apartment buildings and makes up the majority of Class C complexes. They quite often have a parking lot on one side and a lawn and landscaping on the other. They can be located in urban, suburban, or rural settings. They can range from one to three stories and can be composed of large buildings or townhomes that look like individual homes or condos that are attached.
- **Low-Rise:** An apartment complex that has three to four stories with elevators and that is usually located in urban settings.
- **Mid-rise:** A complex of five to eight stories with elevators that is almost always found in urban settings.
- **High-Rise:** A complex of nine stories or more with elevators that is typically found in high-density urban areas.
- **Micro Apartments:** These are low-rise and mid-rise buildings with high-end amenities that are found in urban settings and often rented by millennials. They command the highest rent per square foot of all multifamily types. Studio and one-bedroom units average 240–500 square feet. The units are designed with space-saving features such as pull-down beds, tables and desks that can be folded up, and small appliances that are hidden. I have developer clients who specialize in building these. They are occupied by millennials and the more serious students love luxurious, comfy, small living units where they can live alone.

Nondisclosure Agreement (NDA): This agreement protects the seller's property financials from being disclosed to their competitors and tenants

Often sellers are not willing to release property financials until the purchase contract is signed. Wouldn't it be great to be able to review the rent roll and income and expense statements early on? And to use them to make an informed decision about buying and financing the property before you put earnest money down? To accomplish this, tell the seller you are willing to sign an NDA, also known as a confidentiality agreement. This is a legally binding agreement that protects sellers of commercial property when they provide property financials and other sensitive documents to a buyer. The potential buyer agrees to not disclose any information regarding the property financials, taxes, the mortgage, past and planned capital improvements, and lease negotiations. Some sellers require that buyers sign an NDA before they release any property information. The last thing the seller wants is for this information to get into the hands of a competitor or tenant. The buyer has to agree to have all other parties that the information is released to—including lenders and property managers—sign an NDA too.

Office Property: *Try to buy an office property that you can recession-proof*

On average a recession hits every six years, and when it does multitenant office properties seem not to fare as well as other types of commercial properties. Office properties got hit especially hard during the coronavirus recession (high-credit-rated government and medical office are an exception to this rule). So it is especially important to make sure that your office property is recession-proofed. To do this, try to get your break-even point to 65% or less. This means you can pay all the property expenses and the mortgage if the occupancy rate drops to 65%. Keeping your mortgage at 65% LTV or lower will also help. Avoid gross leases and go with net leases, where tenants pay some or most of the expenses.

Be sure to screen all new tenants thoroughly. Financially strong tenants will be less likely to declare bankruptcy. National tenants that are creditworthy and tenants with more than one location represent lower risk. Check the credit of the business and the owner. Request three years of tax returns, a current profit and loss statement, and a current balance sheet. Look for tenants that have some cash assets to fall back on, and those that do not have accounts receivable problems

Office Property Types

- **Government Office:** If the government entity has a high credit rating, this is one of the lowest-risk commercial properties you can invest in. Some state, county, and city governments have low credit ratings, so be sure to check on this. In exchange for above-average rents, the property owner usually builds tenant improvements to suit. Leases tend to be 15 years or longer.
- **Medical Office:** This is also a very low-risk property type to invest in. The property can consist of one or multiple medical offices composed of physicians' group practices, outpatient surgery centers, medical labs, urgent care groups, and dental offices. A medical office property is one of the most expensive commercial property types, commanding some of the highest rent per square foot. Leases average 10 years.
- **Office Park:** These low-density office complexes are found in suburban settings and have professional tenants, such as attorneys, accountants, real estate offices, architectural firms, and stock brokerages. Leases average 5–10 years.
- **Executive Suite Office Building:** Rents per square foot for this type of property are also among the highest of any office property. These buildings have a centrally located lobby or waiting room with a receptionist. There can be between 12 and 60 small, 200-square-foot offices, each with a different service-oriented business. If you have a yearning for developing, find an empty office building, get it for a good price, and reconfigure it into executive suites.

Preapproval Letter/Letter of Interest for Financing: *Don't place an offer on a property without this*

Our mortgage-banking firm provides these all the time to help buyers of commercial properties get their offers taken seriously. A preapproval letter, or letter of interest, is a letter from a lender or commercial mortgage broker that prequalifies the buyer for the financing to purchase a commercial property. Including one with your LOI will give you a competitive advantage.

Guidelines for a Preapproval Letter/Letter of Interest

- Have the letter made out to both you and the ownership entity (like an LLC you've created for the property) or to just you personally if you have not named the ownership entity yet.
- Do not use a generic letter that can be used for any property. Make sure the letter specifies the name and address of the property you are making an offer on.
- Make sure that the lender or broker prequalifies both you as a borrower and the specific subject property (this means they have analyzed the property financials) and that the letter specifies an approximate time frame for the loan to close. The property can often be prequalified using the financial information in the marketing flyer.
- If you are working with a bank, the preapproval letter to finance the property will be issued as an LOI. Many banks do not want to take the time to do this until you have a fully executed purchase agreement, which puts the cart before the horse. This is understandable because it does take some time to evaluate you and the property. Ask the bank to help you to get your offer taken seriously. Your second choice is to find a commercial mortgage broker. Unlike bank officers they are 100% on commission and will be pleased to do this for you quickly.
- You will need to turn in your personal financial statement and some financials on the property to get preapproved.

Proof of Funds Letter

Most listing agents know that the number-one reason why purchases fail is because the buyer does not have the down payment and closing costs. So they will want to verify that you have the funds by asking for a copy of your bank and security statements. If you do not want to provide these, you can usually use a proof of funds letter instead. This is a letter from your lender or accountant stating that you have a sufficient amount of money to close the deal.

Purchase and Sale Agreement (PSA) (Buyer's Perspective)

So you've just had your offer accepted. Now it's time to have the purchase and sale contract written up. This is a legally binding agreement between the buyer, the seller, and the real estate brokers. If you are a first-time commercial property buyer, do not even think about getting a template from the Web and doing this yourself. There are so many things that can go wrong prior to closing and this contract needs to protect you from losing your earnest money deposit and litigation. The first step is to have a solid purchase and sale contract drawn up either by a commercial real estate broker who represents you or by your commercial real estate attorney. A standard agreement from your realtor can be under 20 pages; one from an attorney can be 40–60 pages long. If you are having your broker prepare the PSA be sure to have your attorney review it.

In most states commercial properties are sold as is, which means the seller is not providing any warranties as to the condition or use of the property. This puts the burden of discovery for anything that is physically, legally, or financially wrong with the property on the buyer. The most important clauses in the PSA are the contingency clauses, which give the buyer time frames to perform due diligence. This is all the research you will be doing to make sure the deal is feasible. Contingency clauses are escape clauses that allow you to back out of the deal and get your earnest money refunded under specified circumstances.

Main Components of the Purchase and Sale Contract

- Name(s) of the buyer(s) and seller(s)
- Date of possession
- Description of the property and address
- Purchase price
- Earnest money
- Closing date
- Closing cost splits
- Real estate commissions
- "Time is of the essence" clause
- Good title to the property
- Delivery of surveys
- Equipment, inventory, and items included
- Contingency clauses for property inspection, title, survey, financing, financials, zoning/land use, environmental, and leases
- Security deposits and rent prorations
- Lease assignment

Time and Money Saving Tip

As a buyer, it is critical that you take charge of setting the time frames for conducting due diligence and removing contingencies in the purchase and sale contract. Next to buying the property for the right price, allowing enough time for due diligence is crucial. Sellers and their real estate brokers usually prefer shortening these deadlines and closing fast. Try to get a minimum of 75 days for closing (45 days is very difficult) and 60 days to remove all contingencies. Sellers often want to stipulate that the earnest money will go hard (becomes nonrefundable) after the contingency period expires. Forty-five days is often not enough time to get your loan approved and to negotiate with the seller about repairs. Most often you have to put more earnest money down that is not refundable to extend contingency time frames. You definitely do not want to go there if you can avoid it.

Real Estate Owned (REO) Properties for Sale

Although REO stands for real estate owned, it really means bank-owned properties. When banks foreclose on a property they usually clear the title and sell it. You can get the best price if you buy from the bank directly. Larger banks often have bank-owned properties listed on their website. Most of these are residential properties with one to four units.

Finding Bank-Owned Properties for Sale

1. Ask a commercial real estate broker to check the MLS and to give you a list of bank-owned properties for sale.
2. Call the special asset department of commercial banks. That will give you a head start on finding properties that will be foreclosed on soon. See if you can make a deal with the bank early in the process to acquire a property when they complete foreclosure and legally own it. Sometimes the bank will even finance the deal for you.
3. Buy at a public auction. Many banks sell their REOs at public auctions. (See *auctions* in Encyclopedia Topic A, Buying).
4. Use an online listing service, such as LoopNet, Zillow, or Reonomy. All of these services have listings of bank-owned commercial properties for sale.

Rent Concessions (Buyer's Perspective)

A rent concession is a discount in the rent that's used by property owners and property management companies to get tenants when the supply of leased space is larger than the demand. Rent concessions are typically used for new properties to assist with faster absorption. In multifamily properties, a typical rent concession would be to sign a yearlong lease and get the 12th month free. It can also take the form of a physical item, such as a big screen TV. For office and retail properties, it can take the form of a rebate on the rent for the first three months of occupancy.

The problem with rent concessions is that far too often sellers offer rent concessions right before they put the property on the market to fill vacancies fast and make the property more attractive to buyers. They do not always take the time to screen tenants adequately, which can cause problems. Also, when rent concessions are used for every new tenant, lenders will often calculate total annual discounted rent and subtract it from the rent roll, which will lower gross rental income. This in turn will lower NOI, which can result in a smaller loan or the property not qualifying for a loan at all.

A Rent Concession Disaster Avoided

In 2010 I had a borrower that had an accepted offer to purchase a 36-unit apartment building in a low-income neighborhood in Tulsa, Oklahoma. He was excited because the property was 96% occupied and in fairly good condition. From the marketing flyer it appeared that it would more than adequately cash flow the 75% loan he was applying for.

We requested a current rent roll and income and expense statements for the past 12 months and the previous calendar year. It was evident from the gross rents we saw that the property was running at about 76% economic occupancy.

(continued)

Buying

(*continued*)

Worse yet, we obtained rent rolls for the last six months and determined that the property had been at 72% occupancy four months ago.

I was suspicious. How had the seller filled the property so quickly? Had he even bothered to screen the tenants for credit and employment? The answer was no! He had offered very generous rental concessions and had put anyone he found in the building. All they had to do was pay the first month's rent and a $250 deposit and they got the second and third month at half off. Well, many of these tenants had never paid after the first month and several had stopped paying after paying half a month's rent for the third month. But these tenants were still on the rent roll.

Keep in mind that just because someone is on the rent roll does not mean that they are paying rent. My client canceled the sale and avoided buying a property plagued by a rental concession disaster.

Rent Control

Should you purchase an apartment complex that has rent control? Rent control is a government regulation that places a ceiling on rent increases for tenants in multifamily properties. Most people know that New York City and San Francisco have rent control, but it is becoming more mainstream. This is due to multifamily vacancy rates being at a national low, which has been pushing up rents beyond what is affordable for many tenants. Oregon's legislature passed a rent control bill in 2019 that limits rent increases to 7% annually. California is approving similar legislation. Most places in the United States allow rents to be brought up to the market rate when the unit is vacated. Being able to increase rents to as much as the market will bear is the best way to increase the value of any commercial property. Rent control obviously depresses the current and future value of a property. It also discourages new development in rent-controlled areas.

When can a rent-controlled property be a good investment? Apartment buildings in rent-controlled San Francisco have a history of going up in value over time. In fact, they are some of the most expensive commercial properties with the lowest cap rates in the country. There is an upside to rent-controlled properties if you can find one in a high-rent urban location. In that situation, they will still command some of the highest rents around. These are certainly not affordable rental properties. What makes them valuable is that while you are waiting for tenants to move out so you can raise rents to market rate, the high-quality existing tenants never miss a rent payment. Often these properties can be purchased for less than market value because they have rent control. Every year rents can be raised an average of 3–7%. Over time tenants will move out and rents can be raised as high as you want to. With a long-term hold strategy, the property value should soar in 10 years.

Replacement Cost

If you can buy a commercial property that is in good condition for its replacement cost, it is usually a good deal. If you can buy one for less than its replacement cost, it is an outstanding deal. This is usually only possible during a recession or at auction in a foreclosure sale. Replacement cost is what it would cost today to buy the land, get it approved for construction, build the improvements, and tenant the property. Keep in mind that it often takes a developer three years or more and thousands of hours of work to accomplish this. Land costs and building costs are always going up. For the buyer, the rule of thumb is to pay no more, and preferably less, than replacement cost. For the seller it is to get a price that is as close to replacement cost as the market will bear.

However, some commercial properties are worth more than replacement cost. The reality of replacement cost is that in big metropolitan areas such as downtown Los Angeles or San Francisco, it is cheaper to buy an existing commercial property than to build one. Besides, there is just no more available open land to build on. The flip side of this is that in secondary or smaller markets, developers just about always make a profit above what it cost them to buy the land, build, and tenant a property. This profit is often 15% or more than their costs. So most commercial properties today are worth more than replacement cost.

How to calculate replacement cost. You are going to have to take the time to price out the cost of the land, hard costs (the cost of building the structure), soft costs (architectural drawings, surveys, permit fees, etc.), leasing commissions, and tenant improvements. Just ask a few general contractors and a commercial real estate broker what the cost per square foot is to build a similar property today. Then multiply this by the square footage of the building. Ask a commercial realtor what they would expect leasing commissions and tenant improvements to cost for this property. Add this to the building costs. This will give you a pretty good ballpark estimate of replacement cost.

Retail Property

If you are interested in owning a retail property and want absolutely no responsibilities, then pick a single-credit tenant, triple-net-lease property. All you'll need to do is look at your bank account to see that the rent has been deposited and do some light accounting. During a recession, many strip malls dip below 80% occupancy, which puts them in a distressed category. This is a great opportunity to get one for a much better price and wait for better times. Ideally you want to purchase one at a price and with financing where your break-even ratio is 75% or below.

This property type requires a skill set that has a learning curve. Finding the right tenant mix, knowing the right lease terms, and negotiating tenant leases and buildouts is not easy. You need to know your *break-even point* (see Encyclopedia Topic A, Buying) to manage the length of your leases so that you avoid the likelihood of having the lease terms of two to four tenants end about the same time, which could cause you to be in the red after mortgage payments. Here are the main pros and cons of investing in retail:

Buying

Pros

1. *A dependable and reliable income source.* Successful well-screened retail tenants are some of the most reliable tenants when it comes to paying the rent. As businesses, they cannot afford the risk of losing the roof over their head. Retail leases have built-in rent increases each year that you can depend on.
2. *Longer-term leases.* Lease terms for retail spaces average 5–10 years. Once you get a tenant in you won't have to worry about filling the space for a while. Banks love long-term leases.
3. *CAM charges.* Most retail properties are net lease properties, where the tenant pays some or all of the taxes, insurance, and maintenance.
4. *Improvements made by tenants.* Leasehold improvements are often made by the tenants. If you pay for them, you can charge a lot more in rent and get reimbursed with that profit.

Cons

1. *Property values can go down quickly.* During a recession people shop less and put off going to service-related businesses in malls. If you lose many tenants and occupancy falls to a point that the property is no longer running profitably, the value of the property will go down.
2. *Tenants are more difficult to find.* You can rent anyone an apartment, but you'll need just the right tenant for a retail space. Finding that tenant can take three months or longer.
3. *It takes longer to get rent started.* Once you find the right tenant, tenant improvements often need to be made. So if it takes three months to find the tenant and they take three months to build out their space, that is six months without rent.
4. *More vulnerable to area changes.* If a new retail mall is built close by, your tenants could lose business and no longer be able to stay in business. Also, if crime increases in the neighborhood, the property's value could go down and it could be more difficult to sell.

Types of Retail Properties

- **Strip Malls:** These are the most prevalent and popular retail commercial properties. They have a mix of retail stores and restaurants. It's best to mix in some service-related businesses, such as hair and nail salons, dental offices, and tax preparation services, along with some popular national chains, such as dollar stores. Strip malls are low risk when they have a good tenant mix of national chains and mom-and-pops. These usually have a moderate risk.
- **Anchored Shopping Center:** These are most often strip malls with major grocery chain anchor tenants drawing most of the shoppers that trickle out to other stores. These are moderately low-risk investments as long as the anchor tenant has 10 years or more remaining on their lease.

Buying

- **Super Regional Shopping Center:** These are the large malls that have an average of 800,000 square feet or more of retail space and an average of four anchor tenants. Large commercial real estate investment companies mostly own these properties. They have a higher risk because they have to compete the most with online shopping. Vacancies are on the increase.
- **Factory Outlet Mall:** These are filled with national chain retail stores. They usually sell a line different from their retail stores located in super regional shopping centers. Growth is flat in this sector due to competition with online retailers. These represent a moderate risk.
- **Big-Box Retail Mall:** These have anchor tenants like Walmart and have up to 20 retail stores. They are considered a moderate risk.
- **Freestanding Single-Tenant Retailer:** These are almost always triple net properties and most often have national, credit-rated tenants. They have the lowest risk of any retail investment properties with tenants that have credit ratings of AA and above. But the risk is very high for a mom-and-pop retailer.

Return on Investment (ROI) after Value-Adding

What you really need to know when you find a commercial property to buy and add some brilliant value-add strategies is how profitable the investment will be in a certain number of years. The simple ROI calculation below will let you estimate this. Ideally you want to choose a property that allows your cash investment to grow by at least 25% a year after adding value. Most of this will be from appreciation resulting from raising rents. First you need to estimate what the property you are buying will be worth after increasing the rents once your value-add strategies are implemented and the property is leased at market occupancy. Then just do this calculation:

Annual capital gain/Total cash invested = ROI

Here is an example using a 10-unit apartment complex that needs $75,000 in renovation costs:

Purchase price:	$ 950,000	Value in 2 years	$1,200,000
Renovations:	$75,000	Less total project cost	$1,041,500
Closing costs:	**$16,500**	Capital gain or profit	$158,500
Total project cost	$1,041,500		
Mortgage	$712,500		
Cash invested down	$260,375		

Profit $158,500/Cash invested $260,375 = 60.87% ROI in 2 years
Annual ROI = 30.44%

How does ROI differ from CCR? CCR estimates what percentage you will be earning annually on the cash you invested from operations after debt service. ROI estimates the percentage you will be earning annually on the cash you invested based on the appreciated value of the property, less the total amount you put into the property.

Self-Storage Property

Who wouldn't want to get into the self-storage business? It is one of the most recession-proof commercial properties that can often break even at 60% occupancy. During recessions people move into smaller homes or apartments and need to store their stuff. During good economic times they buy more new things and seem to store much of their old stuff. There is no other commercial property that is easier to maintain. To make a self-storage unit ready for a new tenant, all you have to do is sweep it out. Many self-storage properties have outdoor space to store RVs and boats. Some even have trucks that can be rented by the day for tenants moving in and out. Tenants seldom miss rent payments because after they do for two to three months, you can lock them out and sell all their stuff.

These facilities can be built for between $25 and $35 per square foot for metal buildings and between $45 and $65 per square foot for concrete buildings (not including land). This makes self-storage the second least expensive commercial property to build, just after mobile home parks. Self-storage is one of the few commercial properties outside of hotels, senior assisted living, and owner-occupied properties that the SBA (Small Business Administration) considers a business and will fund. An SBA loan can go up to 90% LTV.

Four Classes of Self-Storage Properties

1. **Class A:** These are highly secure facilities constructed with tilt-up concrete or cement block that are 15 years old or less. About a third of the units are climate controlled. There are surveillance cameras everywhere and all the unit doors are secured by sensors. These facilities have paved roads and excellent lighting.
2. **Class B:** These are highly secure facilities with cement-block construction, paved roads, and good lighting. About 20% of the units are climate controlled. These facilities are 15–25 years old.
3. **Class C:** These are secure facilities with good surveillance that have metal buildings in very good condition. Class C properties rarely have climate-controlled units. There are paved roads and good park lighting.
4. **Class D:** These facilities have much lighter security than the higher classes and have older metal buildings that are more worn. There are usually gravel roads and the lighting is of mediocre quality. There are no climate-controlled units.

What it takes to be successful in self-storage. It is getting continually more difficult to get permission from city planning departments to build self-storage facilities. Most cities consider them an eyesore and prefer that they be on the outskirts of town. Although relatively inexpensive to build, they are known to take a long time to fill to 85% occupancy. Self-storage seldom gets to 100% occupancy. This is due to stiff competition.

Buying

So finding an existing facility that has a good history of 85% occupancy or greater is best. On the upside, self-storage has one of the lowest break-even ratios of commercial property types. As mentioned, many can break even at 60% occupancy.

Lowering the Risk When Investing in Self-Storage

- Choose a self-storage facility that is near a population center of 75,000 or more.
- Choose a property that has a traffic count of 25,000 per day or more.
- When buying an existing facility, it is preferable that it be located in a city that is not allowing new construction starts on self-storage. Be sure to check on this with the city's building department.
- When buying an existing facility, make sure it already has good online reviews.
- If building, keep the cost down by building with prefabricated steel. If someone else puts a facility in nearby with much lower rents, you can lower your rates and survive.
- This is not a passive investment. If you don't want to buy yourself a job, it is best to choose a self-storage property that is large enough for you to afford an on-site manager.

Senior Housing

With over 75 million baby boomers in the United States, senior housing is one of the fastest-growing sectors of commercial real estate. With the exception of 55 and older communities that are just apartment rentals, all other types of senior housing are part service business and part multifamily. For this reason, owning a senior housing property is a profession more than a real estate investment opportunity and takes specialized management.

The advantage of investing in nursing homes or in independent living, assisted living, or memory care facilities is that they have two streams of income. They charge not only monthly rent for the living unit, but for each individualized service provided. This can make them highly profitable. On the downside, if over 30% of the residents are on Medicare or Medicaid, which both pay lower rates than private payers, the facility might have difficulty running profitably. Ideally you want 80% or more of the tenants to be on private pay, paying full prices.

Types of Senior Housing

- **55 and Older Communities:** These properties can be composed of a large grouping of single-family homes or large apartment complexes. They can have affordable or market rents.
- **Independent Living Facilities:** In these properties, residents have their own apartments with kitchens. Meals and house cleaning are provided at an extra charge. Entertainment and group activities are usually included with the rent.

- **Assisted Living Facilities:** These facilities are the same as independent living facilities but have licensed skilled nurses and nurse's aides on staff to help residents dress, bathe, and take medications. Residents pay for each service they require.
- **Memory Care Facilities:** These facilities are similar to assisted living but care for residents with Alzheimer's and dementia, supervising them 24-hours a day. Residents live in rooms or small apartments.
- **Nursing Homes:** These are health-care facilities with 24-hour skilled nursing care for seniors who are recovering from illnesses or need specialized medical care.

> ### Time and Money Saving Tip
>
> Would you like to get extra cash back at closing? If your deal is ready to close toward the end of a month, delay the closing until between the second and fourth of the following month. When the escrow officer prorates the rents at closing, you will get 25–28 days' rent. If you were to close on the 27th you would only get 3–4 days of rent at closing. Be sure your purchase contract stipulates that you will be credited with rents showing on the leases and rent roll, not based on what tenants have paid so far. Then the escrow officer will prepare the settlement closing statement this way.

Single-Purpose/Single-Tenant Property

A single-purpose, or single-tenant property, is one that is constructed for one type of business to occupy. An auto dealership is an example. It has a showroom, joined with an auto repair facility. There will be almost no other types of businesses that will be able to lease this type of property. A medical surgery center is another example, but these are a very low risk until the tenant vacates. Most single-purpose/single-tenant properties have the greatest risk level of all commercial properties and are the most difficult to finance. If you lose the tenant, you are not only left with 100% vacancy but also a very small pool of replacement tenants.

Although they usually can be vacant for a long time, vacant single-purpose/single-tenant properties can be repurposed. An example of this is an old Ford dealership on Route 66 in Albuquerque, New Mexico, that was turned into Kelly's Pub Restaurant.

Student Housing

Did you know that most student housing properties are rented by the bed and are cash cows? Renting to students by the bed returns the most rent per square foot of any multifamily property after micro apartments. Some are set up as quads, where four students each have their own bedroom and bathroom but share a kitchen. Others rent by the apartment. As you know, students can be rowdy, messy, and unpredictable. So do not try to manage one yourself unless you live nearby and enjoy mothering. Student housing properties are considered low-risk investments if near a major university or college and are professionally managed by a company that specializes in student housing.

Lowering the Risk of Investing in Student Housing

- Choose a property that is near a student population of 10,000 or greater.
- Always have parents cosign leases.
- Have 12-month leases. Many students want to rent for the nine months of the school year, but this leaves the property only 75% occupied over the year and makes it hard to finance. You can allow students to sublease during the summer to students that have been screened.
- Have an on-site property manager to keep the students in line.
- Increase the deposits tenants pay. When the lease is signed, collect the first month's rent plus two months' rent for a security deposit.
- Have the units furnished. Most students love this and you can get a premium on the rent.
- During the coronavirus recession, college and university students were forced to take their courses online at home. If this becomes a trend for the future, there might be a much lower need for students to live near their schools. This could greatly reduce student housing occupancy, making this property type a high risk.

Buying

PART II

Smart Strategies for Buyer Due Diligence

CHAPTER 3

Outstanding Due Diligence
for Buyers

Getting acquainted with a commercial property after your offer has been accepted goes through the same phases as any potentially long-term relationship. In the courtship phase both sides present the best of themselves to each other. This is followed first by the getting-to-know-you phase, where the real you comes out, and then by the let's-have-a-permanent-relationship phase or the I'm-breaking-up-with-you phase.

"Conducting due diligence," as it's referred to in a commercial purchase and sale contract under the feasibility and inspection clauses, refers to the period of time the buyer has to investigate and inspect all aspects of the property. This is the getting-to-know-you phase, and if done correctly it will allow the buyer to make an informed decision about going forward with the purchase. Due diligence actually starts when you review the numbers in the marketing flyer and compare them to other like properties that have sold or are currently for sale in the market. It then kicks off when you give the seller a *due diligence checklist* (Encyclopedia Topic B, Due Diligence) in the purchase and sale contract and agree on a drop-dead date to complete your research.

As I am writing this chapter, I am thinking that this topic could easily be a book in itself. There could easily be 60 or more individual items that a buyer should inspect, collect, and review for multifamily properties, and a hundred or more for multi-tenant retail, office properties, and net lease properties. These items include the property's current and historical financials, physical condition, title policy, survey, easements, encroachments, UCC filings, environmental concerns, leases, service contracts, taxes, insurance, zoning compliance, and more. For a more complete list, see *due diligence checklist* in Encyclopedia Topic B, Due Diligence.

But don't be intimidated. Try to approach this exercise with some excitement. Think about what it has taken you to find this property and then get your offer accepted. Now that first impressions are out of the way, it's time to find out who this property really is and uncover the facts. Why not have fun being an investigator? Your job is to find out if this property is going to make the money you thought it would. Nobody can represent your interests in this department better than you can. As a bonus you will get to find ways to boost the income that the seller did not see or care to implement.

When the purchase contract states that the property will be transferred "as is," this simply means that the seller is not making a representation as to the condition of the property. This places the burden of conducting due diligence and finding out what's wrong with the property on the buyer. This is standard practice.

This chapter covers 12 due diligence mistakes to avoid, taking a look at whether a property is who you thought it was, calculating how much you need to lower the sales price, and an eight-step pitch to the seller on lowering the sales price. Although this chapter is written for buyers, sellers should certainly find it to be of interest too. The bottom line is that both parties want to close the deal, and seeing the nuts and bolts of their property through the buyer's eyes will only strengthen the seller's ability to negotiate.

TWELVE DUE DILIGENCE MISTAKES THAT BUYERS SHOULD AVOID

1. Taking Shortcuts

It's just human nature to want to see a property you are purchasing as having more current or potential value than it might actually have. After all, you are the one who found this property for sale and had an inkling it was the right one. It just feels good to be positive at the getting-to-know-you phase. I know you will agree that it is much better to dig deeper into uncovering who this property really is, though.

Some buyers are prone to taking shortcuts with due diligence and my job is to shake them out of their downright laziness. Yes, you do need to try and get all the items on the due diligence list done. Many buyers seem to go after the easy ones with relish and lose steam on the difficult ones. And then, what do you know, they run out of time and are forced to make a hasty decision before they have uncovered all the facts.

Sometimes I have to twist my clients' arms to get them to do all the work it takes to evaluate the property based on facts rather than appearances and hearsay. Often they are already overwhelmed at gathering and evaluating over 40 items on the due diligence list, and then I give them even more items as we uncover discrepancies, most often related to the property financials and property condition report.

To safeguard my purchasing clients in determining the property's current and potential future income, I give them my *Commercial Real Estate Purchase Evaluator Spreadsheet* to fill out. You can find an example of this in Appendix A and a downloadable Excel version at my website: https://apartmentloan store.com. After putting in the purchase price, down payment, and the property's income and expenses, this spreadsheet helps determine the property's current NOI and cap rate as well as the projected CCR and IRR over time. You will need to fill out a month-by-month pro forma first to project how the property will do over time. You can use my *Seven-Year Month-by-Month Budget and Summary Spreadsheet*; an example is shown in Appendix A and a downloadable Excel version is on my website. Of course you want to start by crunching the numbers accurately by uncovering the real numbers before they are entered into year 1 of this spreadsheet. Also be sure to do some market research to determine whether rents are at, above, or below market.

To safeguard against unknowns in the property's physical condition, I push my clients toward fully understanding all the major systems evaluated in the property condition report and getting bids on repairs that will stick to the wall.

Time and Money Saving Tip

Far too often commercial investment property buyers paint a rosy picture in their pro formas of future rental increases that are not going to happen. This mostly occurs when investors are buying during the hyper-supply phase of the commercial real estate market cycle that occurs before the recession phase (see the section Four Phases of the Commercial Real Estate Market Cycle in Chapter 1). Sales prices and rents are now at close to or at the top of the market. Watch out for the telltale signs of hyper-supply when there is an abundance of unoccupied units in the market because of new construction. This means rents will be flat or coming down due to oversupply. This can be a recipe for disaster if the buyer is planning on putting more money into the property so they can raise rents, which can lead to overimproving the property for its potential income and value.

About four months after a recession has started, prices will start coming down. This is a better time to buy. An even better time to buy is just after the recovery phase has started, as prices and appraised values are at the lowest. Expect a lot of competition for these value-add opportunities. Now it is safe to project future rental increases over the next five years as the growth phase of the cycle is next, followed by the expansion phase.

2. Not Allowing Enough Time

It is surprising that many sellers and their real estate brokers would like the buyer to get all this reviewing done in 45 days or even less. Could this be because the more time they give the buyer, the more undesirables the buyer may discover? Possibly, but more likely it is because "time kills real estate deals" and they want to close quickly.

Short due diligence time periods often result in the buyer requesting an extension for more time because many items are still pending. Missing tenant estoppel certificates and zoning letters, and waiting for an ALTA survey to be completed, are common causes of delays. Sixty days is a much more reasonable period of time, but if the seller is highly cooperative, 45 days can work. For more complex commercial properties, such as senior assisted living, hospitality, and other commercial properties that are selling real estate with a business, 75 days is what you should insist on.

The harsh reality is that if you have not completed all of the important items on your due diligence list when the clock runs out, you have to either cancel the deal or own the property. At this time your earnest money deposit "goes hard"—meaning it is not refundable if you decide to bail. You can usually buy more time if you put more earnest money down that is nonrefundable. I can assure you that the most distressing experience in buying a commercial property is when a buyer knows they are running out of time on due diligence and has to make a hasty decision.

3. Not Includin a Due Diligence Checklist in the Purchase Contract

As the buyer, writing up the purchase and sale contract is your one chance to get the seller to agree to give you everything you need from them to conduct your due diligence. Always include a complete due diligence checklist as an exhibit at the end of the contract and make sure the seller initials it (see *due diligence checklist* in Encyclopedia Topic B, Due Diligence). The beginning of the purchase contract will include feasibility and inspection clauses that list many due diligence items, but the lists in these clauses will not be anywhere near as complete as your list. Your experienced buyer's commercial real estate broker and commercial real estate attorney can help you make sure the list is complete for the particular commercial property type.

> **Time and Money Saving Tip**
>
> As the buyer, be sure to write into the purchase contract that the due diligence period begins when you have received every item requested from the seller. Also build in an extension clause that should further inspections be deemed necessary, you'll have another two weeks. The idea here is to not have to put more earnest money down for this two-week extension. On very competitive deals that may have a backup offer, this precaution can keep you from losing the deal.

4. Wasting Time on Small, Inconsequential Items

Okay, let's be realistic. It is unlikely that you will have the time to review every item on your due diligence list. Also, turning over one rock commonly leads to uncovering another that needs to be turned over. It is imperative that you prioritize your due diligence list from day one and make sure that you identify the really important items and those that take the longest to complete started first.

Wasting time on smaller, inconsequential items—like trying to get a copy of every utility bill for the past year—might mean that you run out of time to address the most essential tasks. Many items on your legal due diligence list, such as getting signed estoppel certificates from tenants and deciding what to do with restrictive easements, can take the longest to complete and need to be started early. You certainly do not want to leave clearing the title until the end, because it can take two months to clear problems up. Analyzing the property financials and having the property professionally inspected are obviously also very important. But engaging legal counsel to prepare lease summaries (for retail, office, and industrial properties) for you is equally important.

Unless the property is almost new and full of great tenants, it is unlikely that everything you investigate on your due diligence list will be to your liking. You might only have a matter of days prior to your deposit going hard to renegotiate the deal with the seller.

5. Trying to Negotiate the Price Down Too Soon

A property inspection report can be completed in less than two weeks after the purchase contract is signed. Sometimes the buyer has a knee-jerk reaction if a need for expensive repairs is discovered. They want to go after the seller immediately and demand that they pay for the repairs or drop the sales price accordingly.

I cannot emphasize enough that there should only be one negotiation about lowering the sales price with the seller. This should occur about a week before the due diligence period runs out. Have one negotiation about lowering the sales price or getting the seller to pay for repairs that also encompasses the financial negatives you have uncovered during due diligence.

At that time you can let the seller know that everything is going very well with your financing and that you'll be able to close on schedule. The seller in many cases will prefer to lower the sales price for the existing buyer instead of starting the whole process over with a new buyer who will discover the same derogatory items.

Negotiating with the seller piecemeal throughout the due diligence process will make them feel as if you are nickel-and-diming them. This will create a very unstable environment for all parties involved and will likely lead to the deal falling out. The following story illustrates this point.

Negotiate with the Seller on All Derogatories at One Time

One of my loan officers recently had a client who was buying what he thought was a Class C-minus, 142-unit multifamily complex for $7,000,000 in Riverside, California. The buyer was thrilled to be buying this property for around $49,000 per unit, about half of its replacement cost. Better yet, the complex was 96% occupied with affordable rents that would earn the buyer a 13% cash on cash return (CCR) on his investment.

The buyer had walked 12 of the units, which were probably the best ones. These were shown to him by the off-site property manager, who was also the listing agent. The buyer noted that the exterior was in need of some paint and the interiors in need of new appliances, floor coverings, and some cosmetic work. The buyer planned on spending about $4,000 per unit, or $568,000 in total, to gingerbread up the project.

When the property condition report came in a few weeks after the purchase contract was signed, it turned out that the property was really Class D and would take more than $12,000 per unit (or $1.7 million) to bring it up to Class C. There was extensive dry rot, leaky roofs, leaky windows and doors, broken HVAC units, aluminum wiring that would have to be replaced, and termites, plus very worn-out interiors.

The buyer insisted on immediately negotiating with the seller to lower the price by $1,500,000. The seller agreed to lower the price by $750,000. Our firm switched from permanent financing to a rehab bridge loan.

Less than two weeks later the buyer discovered that the property, although 96% occupied, had an economic occupancy of 74%. This meant that 31 tenants were living there and not paying any rent. The buyer again went to the seller and asked for an additional $500,000 reduction in the sales price and they settled on lowering it by $200,000.

Because of the low economic occupancy, we needed to verify rent collections. We requested a cash ledger from the property's operating account for the past two years plus two years of bank statements on the account. Less than a week later and nine days before the due diligence period was up, we discovered that the on-site manager had cooked the books and the tenants in 11 additional units were paying him their rent in cash. This dropped the economic occupancy even further.

> The buyer again went to the seller and demanded another $250,000 reduction in the purchase price. The seller at that point had had enough and told the buyer to shove off. The buyer had had enough too.
>
> The moral of this story is that it is very important for the buyer to walk every unit and to negotiate only once with the seller once due diligence is completed, using all the negatives found as ammunition to lower the price. This seller was not unreasonable and was always willing to negotiate, but the buyer just wore him down.

6. Trying to Do It All Yourself

Conducting thorough due diligence is a daunting job. Use your commercial real estate advisory team and delegate as much as you can to them.

Your Commercial Real Estate Advisory Team

- **Buyer's Real Estate Broker:** Have your buyer's realtor get any items that you need from the seller that are not forthcoming from the listing agent, the seller, or the seller's property manager. You can let one of them get in the seller's face and be the bad cop. Remember, neither realtor will make a dime unless the deal closes, so they will want to assist you with this.
- **Commercial Mortgage Broker or Lender:** These professionals are experts at crunching the numbers and should be used to help you with financial due diligence. They are trained to find discrepancies between rent rolls and operating statements, and will share any concerns about the property appraising at the purchase price. They can also help you get financials that the seller hasn't provided by contacting the seller or seller's property manager for you.
- **Property Manager:** Even if you are planning on managing the property yourself, find a professional property manager to help you. They are experts at reviewing rents and expenses. They will let you know how much they think your rents can be increased and if there are any expenses missing on the seller's income and expense statements. They will also give you suggestions about how to run the property more lean and mean.
- **Commercial Real Estate Attorney:** Have your attorney review the leases, the preliminary title report, legal description, easements and encroachments, survey, and UCC and judgment liens. Their number-one job is to make sure the property has a clear title and can be used for your intended purposes.

7. Relying on the Seller's Numbers

I am not going to come out and say that sellers often lie to buyers. But since marketing flyers put the property's physical and financial condition in its best light, after doing their due diligence buyers might sometimes think they did. Quite often the buyer discovers the property's cap rate is lower than the marketing flyer led them to believe. When this happens the buyer's first thought may be that they are overpaying for the property. In most cases the seller has not intentionally tried to swindle the buyer but was in a rush and left out some expenses.

Another common occurrence is when the seller decides to enhance the net income of the property by transferring repair expenses into the capital improvement category. This lowers expenses and increases net operating income (NOI). Capital improvements are major property replacements that can't be counted as expenses on your taxes. These are improvements to the property that are taxable. Often your lender will request copies of the seller's Schedule Es, which show how the seller reported income and expenses on their personal taxes. Your lender might have heartburn if they find major discrepancies between the tax returns and income and expense statements.

It's also not unusual for the seller to compute the cap rate using gross rent from the rent roll, even though some tenants have not been paying rent because of delinquencies or rent concessions.

And the good news is that it is the buyer's job to uncover this. You need to verify all expenses listed on operating statements and look for expenses that might have been left out. Again, nobody can do a better job at being a sleuth than you. It's your financial future that is at stake.

Was the Marketing Flyer Misleading?

In 2012 I was working on a loan on a strip mall. We had to find out why the gross income showing on the income and expense statements was a lot lower than the gross income on the rent roll.

It turned out that the property had recently been repositioned. Two large, 10,000-square-foot spaces had been made into six smaller stores. It turned out that four of the new tenants were given the first eight months rent free in exchange for putting in the tenant improvements and signing a 10-year lease. These tenants had just completed their stores and had moved in a few months prior to the property being put on the market.

> The buyer was not told about these rent concessions and only found out about them from the estoppel certificates. The listing broker computed the cap rate based on full occupancy minus a 5% vacancy rate and put it on the marketing flyer.
>
> Although the cap rate would have been accurate once the concessions ran out, the buyer thought that the flyer was misleading and was not pleased that they were expected to absorb four to five months' rent from four tenants. The buyer negotiated to have the lost rental income taken off the sales price.

8. Not Verifying Rent Collections

Would you buy a business that was priced based on reported sales even though some customers received but never paid for the product or service? Probably not. If you do not verify rent collections when doing your due diligence, you might be doing just that.

Should you pay full price for a property if there are some undesirable tenants paying the rent late or not paying at all? These kinds of tenant defaults are often not disclosed by the seller. At a minimum, this is something you need to know. Having to re-tenant after you own the property will cost you time and money.

Doing a *collections verification report* (Encyclopedia Topic B, Due Diligence) is a smart move if you find that income and expense statements show less rent collected than reported on the rent roll. This report uses the seller's operating account cash ledger or even bank statements to explain discrepancies between month-by-month rent rolls and corresponding income statements. You then follow this up by requesting an aged receivables report to identify the tenants who are not paying.

9. Ordering Third-Party Reports Yourself If You Will Need Financing

As the buyer it is your responsibility to conduct a physical and mechanical inspection of the property, and to see if there are any environmental concerns. If you are planning on financing the property, do not order these third-party reports yourself. Your lender will need these reports as well, and to eliminate the possibility of any collusion, the lender will not be able to use reports ordered by the buyer. So have your lender order all of the reports, including the property, environmental, seismic, and pest inspections, and any others needed. In most cases the lender's property inspection report will be more thorough. Believe me, you do not want to go through the shock of finding out what is wrong with the property from your property inspector only to have to go through the process a second time with the lender's property inspector, and be faced with paying for two reports to boot.

10. Not Reading Every Lease and Estoppel Certificate

Leases are complex and often difficult to understand. For office, retail, and industrial properties, have your experienced commercial real estate attorney review all the leases and estoppel certificates and prepare a summary for you. Be sure to verify that the square footage and the lease terms are the same as those listed on the rent roll. Look for any landlord obligations that will be passed on to you, such as incomplete tenant improvements that the seller has promised to pay for. Find out if the leases require your tenants to disclose their financial information. Your lender might require this.

11. Failing to Walk Every Unit or Space

This story says it all. My clients Tricia and her husband Rex were both CPAs—smart people who in 2013 purchased a large, 286-unit multifamily property just off the strip in Las Vegas that had been built in 1975. They did not have their own commercial real estate broker and worked with the listing agent. What they loved most about the property was that it was in a great location in great condition with well-manicured lawns. They were told that the property, which was 89% occupied, had been 100% remodeled in 2007 and had been outfitted with all new interiors, including kitchens, bathrooms, windows, doors, and roofs.

We required a property inspection report that was very thorough. The inspector even discovered a broken sewer line and electrical panels that were not to code. Also identified were over 40 health and safety issues, such as cracks in the walkways, rickety railings, broken windows, and dead fire alarms. Still, the report did show the property to be in good condition for its age.

But the inspection did not uncover the hoarder who lived in apartment 17D. She had lived there for 26 years. There were stacks of magazines, boxes, and junk going up to the ceiling, with narrow walkways to navigate through the mess. This should have been reported as a health, safety, and fire hazard. The inspection also did not reveal that 36 of the units had not been remodeled in 2007 and still had the original bathrooms and kitchens, complete with 1970s cabinets and countertops.

Neither the buyers, the listing broker, the property inspector, nor the appraiser walked all the units during the due diligence phase. The inspector should have gone through all 286 units (which would have taken weeks), but chose to take a shortcut. The buyers had nothing in writing that specifically stated which units were remodeled and to what extent. It cost the buyers just over $300,000 to bring those 36 units up to the level of the rest of the complex.

12. Not Responding Firmly to Seller's Pushback

All sellers have been buyers before they became sellers. Many are very helpful and accommodating and go the extra mile to get you everything requested. Some sellers forget what it was like when they had to gather all those due diligence items as a buyer.

Often your lender, your attorney, or an inspector will request additional information. Some of these items might not have been on the due diligence list the seller agreed to, and the seller or their property manager might just tell you that they gave you enough already or ignore the request.

This is where it really comes in handy to have your own commercial real estate broker representing you. Again, these realtors are on commission and only get paid if the deal closes. If you get pushback from the seller, have your realtor be the bad cop. The best approach is to work through the property manager and not try to make their life miserable but to ask them for help in getting the deal closed. If you do not have your own realtor then have your lender or mortgage broker ask the seller for help in getting the remaining items. If you are still not getting results and your money is close to going hard, request an extension based on items not provided by the seller at least a week in advance of the drop-dead date.

> **Time and Money Saving Tip**
>
> Be sure to walk every unit or space and take an experienced general contractor with you. Contractors are trained to see absolutely everything that needs fixing and can give you a ballpark quote on the cost to remedy each. Take notes. This should be done in addition to the property inspection report, which will also include a cost-to-cure estimate. The contractor can give you a bid for all the work that needs to be done, which you will use to negotiate the price down about a week before the inspection due diligence period runs out. Also be sure to put on your due diligence list that you will need access to 100% of the units or spaces.

IS THIS PROPERTY "WHO" YOU THOUGHT IT WAS?

As the buyer, you started out being very excited about this property. Now that due diligence is completed you may know the property even better than the seller. So how do you feel about buying it? If you have a sinking feeling in the pit of your stomach because you have found so much wrong with it, and you know you are done with it, then just be thankful that you did not get married to it. If you discovered some unsavory items, but are viewing this as an opportunity to reduce the sales price and implement some great value-add opportunities, then you will be giving it your best shot at buying the property for a better price.

Fortunately most purchases do not tank because of problems found by the buyer during due diligence. Both sides have to weigh the time and money involved in starting all over again. And remember that the seller was most likely a buyer at some point. They have been in your shoes. They certainly know that it is accepted practice in commercial real estate, or for that matter any business, for the sales price to be validated by the buyer doing due diligence. The seller has likely been expecting you to come up with a list of repairs reported by the inspector. They know that you are going to ask them to pay these costs. Of course, they do not want to pay for them. In most cases the seller will reluctantly cover some costs, but if there are many repairs to be made, they seldom will cover all of them. This seems to be the case in a buyer's market during recessions too.

Obtaining a price reduction because you have found the rental income and/or expenses given to you by the seller inaccurate is more difficult. The seller or their listing agent will likely counter this discovery with comparable property sales that support the agreed-upon purchase price. There are, of course, properties that are well maintained and marketing flyers that are so accurate in reporting the NOI that there is little that the buyer can use to lower the price. But this scenario is more the exception.

Guidelines for Calculating How Much You Need to Lower the Sales Price

Before you negotiate with the seller to lower the price, you will need to know exactly how much you are willing to pay for the property if they hardball you. This exercise will help you to determine the maximum amount you can pay for the property based on the minimum CCR you are willing to accept and the value-add opportunities you can implement.

1. *Make a list of derogatory due diligence items.* Make a list of all the problems you found with the property, both physical and financial. The list should include all necessary repairs and also any loss to the NOI based on inaccuracies given to you by the seller at the beginning. Next assign a cost to each of these and then total them up. Subtract this total cost from the agreed-upon sales price to come up with your lowball price.
2. *Calculate the loss to your expected rate of return.* Now take a look at what you expected the property to earn after the first full year before you did your due diligence. Subtract the total cost of the items from step 1 from the original annual earnings you expected to earn. Then calculate how much this has lowered your expected annual CCR.

3. *Decide on your maximum sales price.* When you go into negotiations with the seller, know ahead of time at what price point you will walk away based on your minimum acceptable first year annual CCR.

4. *If your return on investment is lowered 10% or more, consider letting the property go.* If the seller is not willing to budge on the sales price, consider letting the property go if your expected CCR was lowered by 10% or more. For example, if you were expecting an 8% CCR your first year, and now it has been reduced by 10%, you will now be getting a 7.2% CCR. If this is acceptable, then perhaps you won't want to risk losing the property for this amount. You can still act as if you are going to walk away, but in the end you won't. Finding another property to purchase and going through due diligence all over again might take more time and money and might not produce better results.

Time and Money Saving Tip

I have been blown away by some of my inexperienced clients who have had their projects fail by paying too much for a distressed property during a recession. All of them thought they were getting such a great price. This mistake occurs because it is very difficult to accurately determine the cost of filling vacancies, which includes the cost of your value-adds, the cost of feeding the property during the time it is not breaking even, and the cost of tenant improvements and leasing commissions. Also, during a recession, it is easy to misjudge the time it will take to attract new tenants, get their spaces ready to occupy, and get them moved in and paying rent. This is called absorption, which is very difficult to project during a recession. Plan on absorption taking a lot longer. To remedy all this, be sure to add 15%, including a payment reserve, to the cost of repositioning these properties. Then budget an additional 20% more time for the rent to start coming in on vacant spaces. In this scenario, you really do need to get the property for an even better price than you think.

5. *Value-add strategies might make this property worth more to you.* You have likely come up with some value-add opportunities while doing due diligence. Create a three-year pro forma reflecting the increase in rents and perhaps lowering of expenses. Does this make the property worth buying and at what price? Be sure to weigh in the extra cash you will likely have to put in to implement these improvements. What will the property be worth at current cap rates in three years with the increased NOI? Now determine the most you are willing to pay for the property based on what it will be worth to you once these value-add strategies are implemented.

Coming Up with Your Pitch to Lower the Sales Price after Due Diligence

If you do not find much wrong with the property and decide that you want to lower the sales price after due diligence, the seller will consider this to be acting in bad faith. If you find significant negative changes in the profitability of the property or necessary expensive repairs after conducting due diligence, the seller will expect that you are going to try to renegotiate a lower sales price.

Eight-Step Pitch to the Seller to Lower the Sales Price

1. *Prepare your pitch well.* You want to be well prepared and write out a script for your pitch, or at a minimum have an outline. In most cases this pitch will be made by your buyer's realtor. But I can assure you that because your heart and soul are involved, you are the best one to make it. Your job is to convince the seller that the property is worth less than the agreed-upon price based on the facts uncovered by you and your commercial real estate advisory team. You should provide documentation to support your research whenever you can.

2. *Start out by complimenting the seller.* Keep in mind that the seller has likely been dreading the day when your diligence is completed and you will be asking them for a better deal. Why not start out by disarming them with some compliments? Tell them how professional and helpful their listing agent and property manager have been in getting you all the items needed. Tell them some items that you really love about the property.

3. *Talk facts, not emotion, when making your points.* Make sure your delivery is firm, but polite. Give the seller a list of repairs to remedy and associated costs. Back this up with a copy of your property inspection report. Show them why these numbers do not work, and point out that now that due diligence is complete, the return on your investment doesn't make sense and represents too large of a risk. Back this up by giving them a copy of your projections, showing them why the purchase price does not pencil. It's going to be difficult for the seller to argue with well-presented facts.

4. *Support your pitch using advice from your expert team.* Whenever possible quote advice and supporting data from your property manager, building contractor, buyer's real estate broker, lender, or attorney.

5. *Offer to remove all contingencies.* Offer to remove all contingencies—except that for financing if your loan has not been approved yet—if you can come to an agreement on a lower price.

6. *Practice your script.* Role-play your script with your spouse or a good friend. You want to come off as relaxed and confident in your delivery.

7. *Deliver your pitch to the seller directly.* It's okay if your real estate broker and the listing agent go with you to renegotiate the price with the seller. But your

chances of a favorable outcome are greatly increased if you can present your situation to the seller directly. The best time to get to know the seller directly is at the beginning, when you are first making your offer or right after your offer is accepted. Your relationship with the seller will pay off the most when you need to renegotiate the purchase price after you have completed due diligence. If you can establish a friendship with the seller early on, you can establish the attitude that both of you need to win. The seller needs to get to know you as a reasonable person. When it is time to make your case as to why the sales price needs to be lowered, this will come through for you. After all, you are not making these things up. Your position is backed up by data. The listing broker knows that it is their job to be the bad cop and push back on behalf of the seller. If the seller is not present, you are likely going to hear this from the listing broker, "I talked with the seller and he sees no reason to lower the price and has several backup offers."

8. *Be willing to walk away.* If you cannot negotiate a price reduction that makes the deal work for you, then thank everyone for their time and walk away. If they do not come back to you with a better offer the next day, you can always change your mind and accept their price.

Due Diligence

Buyer$ or Seller$ Market: *Are you buying or selling in an up or down market?*

Recessions happen on average every six years. So up cycles are followed by flat cycles, which are often followed by down cycles. Is there any good reason to buy in a seller's market? Yes! But you need to work a lot harder to find properties that you can add value to without spending too much cash (see Chapter 7). In a seller's market, there is more demand than supply, resulting in a scarcity of decent properties. If you are selling in a seller's market, you are in the best place at the right time. You can get a good price just selling your property as is—even if you have too many vacancies or shorter-term leases. Let's say your property is a fixer-upper. In a seller's market, it will likely go for more than it is worth to someone who wants to renovate it in hope of raising rents.

In a buyer's market, there is more supply than demand. Now the buyer is in the best place at the right time and has a better selection of reasonably priced properties to choose from. But you might want to hold off on buying at the beginning of a recession; prices are likely to fall further. You won't know for sure that they've they hit rock bottom until they start going up again. If you are the seller, you better spruce the property up and get solid leases in place before putting it on the market. You might want to wait until it is a seller's market to sell. Is there any good reason to sell in a buyer's market? Of course! If you have found a larger property that is being sold at a great price, will give you much more income and depreciation, and you can 1031 exchange into it, buy it.

Cap/Capitalization Rate: *Use the commercial appraisers method to calculate it accurately*

The cap rate of the commercial investment property you are interested in buying is one of the most important metrics to investigate when doing your due diligence. Often listing real estate brokers put the property's financials in their best light by mixing in actual with projected numbers. Their goal is to demonstrate that the subject property is worth as much as the most expensive comparable properties with the lowest cap rates that have been sold. But this tactic is misleading. Your job is to figure out exactly what the subject property's cap rate is based on its actual NOI and sales price. The lower the cap rate, the more expensive the property is for its earnings. The higher the cap rate, the better a deal it is for the buyer. Computing an accurate cap rate for the property will give you the best indicator of its value. You can then compare this with other like properties that have sold or are for sale to determine if it is overpriced.

$$\frac{\text{Annual net operating income}}{\text{Purchase price}} = \text{Cap rate}$$

Wouldn't you love to be able to determine a commercial property's cap rate that you are interested in buying accurately, using the same method a commercial appraiser does? This is the best way to determine value. You really can do this yourself.

Commercial Appraiser Method of Calculating Cap Rate

1. Start out by determining the property's effective gross annual income. This includes current rents as showing on the rent roll, plus miscellaneous income, plus CAM (common area maintenance) reimbursements, less 5% or market vacancy (even if there is zero vacancy), less concessions and collection losses.
2. Determine the property's total annual operating expenses based on the actual past 12-month trailing expenses (see list of expenses under *expense checklist* below) and make sure none are missing. Be sure to include something for off-site management—even if the seller is self-managing and you plan to do this too (use 5% if you do not have an estimate). Include something for *capital improvements* (see below) too.
3. Subtract annual expenses from annual effective gross income to come up with the annual net operating income (NOI). Divide the NOI into the purchase price to get the subject property's cap rate.
4. Ask your commercial real estate broker to provide you with the income and expenses of three to four comparable properties that have sold in the past year in the same market and their cap rates. They have data services they subscribe to, like CoStar and REIS, that can provide this.
5. Average the cap rate of the subject property together with the cap rates of the comparable properties. This average will be a much more accurate representation of what the cap rate should be for the subject property. Once you have determined the cap rate, multiply this by the NOI of the property to come up with the property value. For example, if the cap rate is 7% and the property's NOI is $120,000, then the property value based on cap rate is $840,000.

Capital Improvement/Replacement Reserves/Cap-X: *Try to understand what these are so you can put them on your pro forma*

Understanding capital improvement reserves, also called Cap-X or replacement reserves, can be quite confusing. These reserves are for replacement of major items, such as roofing, windows, appliances, carpeting, cabinets, HVAC units, parking lot surfaces, or any item that will last for five years or more. When you own investment real estate, the IRS mandates that you first show these as income on your taxes since they are adding value, after which you can depreciate them. But they kind of seem like repairs, don't they? Most investment property owners think so. Most deduct costs for what should be classified as capital replacements as repairs so that they pay less tax. But when they want to refinance or sell the property—well, what do you know! These same items get taken out of the expense column and put into capital replacements. This lowers expenses and increases the net income, which lowers the subject property's cap rate, which raises its property value.

Can they have it both ways? The answer seems to be yes. Are they cooking the books? Actually not. The IRS is not known for cracking down on this, so it is acceptable. When analyzing property expenses for a property you are buying, be sure to add an expense line for a capital improvement reserve if the seller did not. This is because appraisers and lenders add $150–400 per unit per year to the operating expenses for capital replacements on multifamily, so you should too. Be sure to put Cap-X on your property budget pro forma. Also, if you plan on maintaining the property in good condition, you will be doing capital improvements over the years and should allow for this money. Ask your lender what they recommend you allow for replacement reserves based on the age and condition of the property.

Time and Money Saving Tip

When you request the annual income and expense statements for a property you are buying, be sure to ask the seller to give you a separate list of capital improvements and their related costs they have made over the past five years. This is something a seller will want to brag about if they have replaced major items. If they are hesitant to provide this list, just tell them your lender has asked for it. We almost always do. This will give you an idea of the major improvements the seller has made to the property and what might still need replacing. It is essential that you not only know what the repairs and maintenance will run annually but also plan for capital improvements, which also take cash out of the property.

Collections Verification Report: *Everyone knows occupancy is important, but knowing if a property has rent collection problems is more important*

Would you pay full price for a business whose gross sales were a major part of the value, but which never collected some revenue because some customers refused to pay? Verification of rent collections is verification of sales and is one of the most overlooked due diligence items for buyers of commercial real estate. Unpaid rent should show up as collection loss on the property's books. But often sellers just do not track this. If a property has quality professional management it will show up in an aged receivable report.

Everyone knows occupancy is important. But when buying a property, what's much more important to know is if the property has rent collection problems. Just because someone is on the rent roll doesn't mean they are paying rent. A collections verification analysis looks for discrepancies between month-by-month rent rolls and the corresponding month-by-month gross income from an annual profit and loss statement. Most importantly, it identifies which tenants are paying slowly and which are not paying at all. In other words, you need to know if you are buying a property that has some poor-quality tenants. Having to re-tenant will cost you time and money. In a seller's market, the selling price is seldom discounted for this. You can put this analysis on an Excel spreadsheet like underwriters do or just tally the results on paper.

Six-Step Collections Verification Analysis (This Is How My Underwriters Do It)

1. Request a trailing 12-month report from the seller (the last 12 months of income and expenses shown month-by-month).
2. Compare the gross annual income on the report with the annualized gross rents from a current rent roll. If for the last year the gross income on the annualized rent roll is much higher than the trailing 12-month report, you will need to investigate this discrepancy.
3. Ask the seller why there is more gross income reported on the rent roll. Perhaps there was renovation of several units and tenants were vacated, or something else that explains why rent was not collected. If you are satisfied with the answer and can verify it, then you do not need to proceed further.
4. Ask the seller for 12 months of rent rolls that correspond with the trailing 12-month report. Now compare each month's total gross rents with the 12-month report. You will be able to identify which months have problems with collections. Ask the seller to identify which tenants are paying slowly or not paying at all. You can also get this from an accounts receivable report for this period.
5. If you still cannot verify actual collections, ask for the cash ledger from their accounting software (QuickBooks or the like) for the 12-month period being examined. This will show all cash in and all cash out. You want to focus on the cash in.
6. If the cash ledger brings up more discrepancies you will need to request 4–12 months of bank statements from the property's operating account. This will give you the most accurate numbers on the actual rent collected during this period.

> **Time and Money Savings Tip**
>
> If you discover when doing your due diligence that some tenants are behind or slow in paying rent, here is the best way to get the seller to compensate you for this: Tell the seller that your lender is analyzing the lost rental income and taking it off of gross rental income (we really do this), resulting in a smaller loan. Ask the seller to take six months to a year of this credit loss off the sales price, or give you a credit for that amount at closing. This is not unreasonable, especially when considering the possible cost of re-tenanting and/or eviction.

Commercial Property Purchase or Finance Evaluator: *This spreadsheet tells you a property's current NOI and cap rate plus the projected CCR and IRR over time. Is it a good buy?*

Wouldn't it be great if you had one spreadsheet that could tell you if the property you are purchasing is going to achieve your financial goals? What the actual cap rate and NOI are currently at, plus what your CCR is projected to be your first year and what your IRR will be in seven years when you plan to sell the property? A commercial property purchase evaluation spreadsheet does just that and more (see Appendix A to view samples for apartments and commercial properties). To get the Excel version that I give my clients to fill out, you can go to my website: https://apartmentloanstore.com.

Commercial Property Quick Analysis Calculator: *Use this quick Excel calculator to determine whether the property you are interested in buying is a good buy*

Evaluate many properties quickly for their value based on market cap rates and GRM with this Excel calculator. Just fill in the gross rental income, expenses, purchase price, down payment, and loan details (see Appendix A to view a sample for apartments and commercial properties). To get the editable Excel version for apartments and commercial properties, go to my website: https://apartmentloanstore.com.

Crime Rate Analysis: *Are you serious? Someone was murdered in one of the apartments?*

This one is so important, and so few buyers think about doing it. I am sure they would all like to know that it's not safe for them to be at the property after dark. Crime affects property value, appreciation, and how long your commercial property will take to resell, not to mention the impact on your mental health. Neighborhood crime rates in the United States can range from zero to over 300 incidents per month. Rogers Park, Chicago, the neighborhood I grew up in, is still a safe place today with an average of six crimes per month. Just a little farther to the northeast, East Chicago (which is actually in Indiana) has an average of 86 crimes per month. That's 14 times the crime rate in my old neighborhood.

Determining the crime rate in the neighborhood you are buying in is essential. This can be done free, and in a matter of minutes. Go to https://www.cityprotect.com, and simply find your location on the map. CityProtect compares data from over 1,000 law enforcement agencies. You can pay for a more detailed report at neighborhoodscout .com.

My client Jeff could not figure out at first why a C-minus apartment complex in St. Louis that he had an offer on had been on the market for over 11 months and had occupancy of 74%. Market occupancy was 89%. He found out that there were on average 130 thefts alone per month in the neighborhood and that someone had been murdered in one of the apartment units. Although the price was good, he took a pass.

Due Diligence Checklist: *Be sure you give the seller a copy of this list at the beginning*

Be sure to attach a due diligence checklist as an addendum to the sales contract and have the seller initial it at the bottom. Sorry, but this list has 49 items on it. It's really difficult to gather all of these items in 30 days; 45 days is more like it. Have your commercial real estate attorney review this list to see if anything is missing for your deal.

Financial Due Diligence

____Current rent roll showing when leases begin and end, and for multifamily properties, identifying Section 8 tenants

____Past 24 months of rent rolls if requested by buyer's lender

___Last three years' income and expense statements (month-by-month format)

___Trailing 12-month income and expense statement (month-by-month format)

___Last three years' Schedule Es from seller's taxes on the property

___Last five years' capital improvements and cost (annualized)

___List of rent concessions for the last 12 months

___Aged receivable report

___Accounts payable report

___List of outstanding tenant delinquencies and defaults

___Payroll summary for on-site employees

___Copy of last 12 months' utility bills

___Most recent real estate tax bill

___Accounting of ratio utility billing system (RUBS)

___Management operating budget

___List of any prepayments of rent

___Accounting of all CAM reimbursements collected

___Accounting of all rental deposits

___Account ledger for RUBS

Physical, Mechanical, and Environmental Due Diligence

___Building and site plans

___Survey

___Seismic report

___Engineering report

___Statement of structural alterations made by seller

___Seller's phase 1 or phase 2 environmental report or environmental screening report

___Copy of pest inspection report

___Copy of radon gas report

___Mold abatement report

___Zoning compliance certificate

___Certificate of occupancy

___Parking compliancy verification

Operational Due Diligence

___Copy of all leases with current amendments

___Renewal options signed

___Copies of intent to lease, signed

___Tenant applications and credit reports

___Tenant estoppel certificates

___List of all personal property

___Inventory list of supplies

___Copy of all service contracts, including maintenance, pool, laundry, security, and pest control

___Copy of off-site management contract

___Copy of insurance policy

___List of any pending litigation against the property

___Insurance loss summary for the last three years

Legal Due Diligence (Your commercial real estate attorney will review these with you)

___Preliminary title report

___Property legal description

___Basic or ALTA survey

___Review of easements and encroachments

___Tax, UCC, and judgment liens

___Litigation filed against the property

Environmental Concerns: *Be sure to ask the seller for a copy of their environmental report. If they have a loan, chances are they have one.*

Savvy buyers of commercial real estate ask questions at the beginning about environmental concerns. The last thing they want is to spend their time dealing with the regulatory process involved with a property that may need cleanup. Unless the buyer of commercial real estate has negotiated with the seller ahead of time, the buyer can become totally liable for contamination on the property that occurred prior to the sale. Almost all lenders require an environmental assessment—anything from a simple screening report to a phase 1 report. If contamination is detected it is very unlikely that your lender will proceed with the loan. After all, the liability will be passed on to them if they take the property back in a foreclosure. If your loan is canceled because of this, you will have lost at least a month of your time doing due diligence on the property.

To be proactive, here is the best action to take. Prior to signing a purchase and sale agreement, ask the seller about any known environmental concerns. If they have a loan on the property, they will almost certainly have had to commission some level of environmental report. Ask them for a copy. If the seller discloses that there was contamination that has been mitigated, ask them for a copy of the closure letter from the pertinent federal, state, or local regulatory agency.

Estoppel Certificate or Letter: *Be sure to get these to the tenants the day after signing the purchase contract. They can take a long time to come back.*

Due Diligence

As part of your due diligence when buying an office, retail, or industrial commercial property, it is important for you to review tenant estoppel certificates. Multifamily, hospitality, healthcare, and self-storage properties do not require them. The estoppel's purpose is to have the tenants state the terms of their leases and then certify that the information is true and correct. This is the only way you will know for sure that the leases you were provided have not been changed and are in good standing. Estoppel letters certify the beginning and end dates of the lease, options to renew, rent amount, security deposit amount, the date to which the rent has been paid, and any defaults by the tenant or the property owner. Be sure that your estoppel asks if there are any tenant improvements or repairs promised by the landlord, or if they have any claims against the landlord (see the next topic, Estoppel and Lease Review Checklists). If you are taking out a loan to buy the property, your lender will require tenant estoppels, so be sure to use them. Be sure that you mention in the purchase contract that you will be using your estoppel certificate and include a copy to be attached to the sales contract so that the seller is aware of this. Almost all commercial leases have a provision requiring the tenant to fill out and sign an estoppel letter for the property owner to give to a third party.

Estoppel and Lease Review Checklists: *Be sure to go through this list when comparing estoppels with the leases*

Comparing the estoppel certificates signed by the tenants with the leases is something your commercial real estate attorney will do for you. But I am including a checklist with some of the most important items (not claiming the list is complete) because it is so important for you as the buyer to understand this process and how important it is. After all, each lease represents a part of the income of the property you are buying, and you need to know that what is represented on the rent roll and the leases is what you thought you were buying. Again, only office, retail, and industrial properties require estoppels.

Estoppel Review Checklist

___Compare the lease start and stop dates and rentable square footage with the rent roll to determine that there are no discrepancies.

___Confirm that the description of the lease in the estoppel certificate is the same as what is showing on the lease.

___Check the amount of current rent and security deposit.

___Check as to the exact date the rent is paid through.

___Check to see the date all common area charges, and if a net lease all pass-through charges (taxes, insurance, and maintenance), are paid through.

___Check that there are no tenant defaults.

___Check that there are no landlord defaults.

___Confirm that there is no incomplete construction required by the landlord.

___Confirm that all amendments, addenda, and agreements are represented.

___Check lease extensions and purchase options.

Expense Checklist: *Compare this list of expenses with the expenses the seller has given you for the property to make sure they haven't missed any*

The main purpose of this list is for you to make sure that the seller has not missed reporting any expenses. An example of this is when sellers do not report property taxes and insurance on their income and expense statements because they pay these with their mortgage. Often sellers that do not have professional management lump many expenses together in a general category. An example is the repairs and maintenance category, where they might show one amount for everything instead of breaking out repairs, elevator maintenance, HVAC maintenance, landscaping, decorating, cleaning, and snow removal. If the seller has broad categories, ask them to break these into more detail.

> **Time and Money Saving Tip**
>
> There are two very important steps that buyers often fail to do when tenants fill out and sign estoppel certificates: (1) fail to attach a copy of the lease as an exhibit to the estoppel certificate before the tenant signs it, and (2) fail to have all lease guarantors sign the estoppel certificate. Both of these failures can result in the estoppel being not legally binding.

Commercial Property Expense Checklist

___Real estate taxes

___Water and sewer

___Pool maintenance

___Insurance

___Trash removal

___Elevator maintenance

___Licenses

___Pest control

___Parking lot maintenance

___Ground lease

___Building maintenance

___Security

___Electricity

___Building repairs

___Equipment leasing

___Gas

___Landscape maintenance

___Audit expense

___Resident manager

___Payroll taxes

Due Diligence

___Association fees

___Off-site manager

___Telephone

___Flood insurance

___Advertising

___Leasing commissions

___Wind insurance

___Supplies and cleaning

___Professional fees

___Tenant improvements

___Employee benefits

___Leasehold improvements

___Internet and cable TV

___Snow removal

___Replacement reserves

Expenses, Variable and Fixed: *Go after variable expenses with a vengeance to lower property expenses*

One of the best methods of adding value to a commercial property is to lower variable expenses with a vengeance. They can be managed based on the property's ability to pay them. Some can even be eliminated. During the Great Recession I witnessed many multifamily property owners fire both their on-site and off-site property managers and take on these jobs themselves. This is an example of cutting a large variable expense. Variable expenses include off-site and on-site management, repairs and maintenance, cleaning expenses, and professional fees.

Fixed expenses are not easily changed and stay the same each month for about a year regardless of occupancy. These include property taxes, insurance, common area utilities, and trash removal.

Time and Money Saving Tip

If you have an off-site management company, make sure your management company competitively shops for all maintenance contracts, including landscaping. Sometimes management companies get kickbacks from vendors for choosing them. This cost gets passed on to you and is difficult to catch. The only way to do so is to be a secret shopper and pretend-shop the vendors for a similar-size property. Tell your property manager that you want to get quotes yourself for large expensive repairs. If your management company has a payroll for maintenance and repairs, be sure to continually question the expense and ask them to lower it. Put all variable expenses on a budget and stick to it.

Historical Financials: *It is better to buy a commercial property that has a good, long operating history than one that does not*

Would it not be better to buy a business that has three years or more of a strong operating history as shown on financials and tax returns rather than one that had failed and was resuscitated? As already mentioned, investing in commercial real estate is a business too. Be careful if you're buying a repositioned commercial property that might have been failing a year ago and now is for sale at a top market price. It might have just attained great occupancy, but it won't have any historical financials. Is it really worth as much as a similar property that can show proof of two years or more of success? It could be, if adequate screening was done on the tenants. If the property has been professionally managed there will be a file on each tenant and you should ask to review these. Strong historical financials show that the subject property is one that has good tenants and that people like to live or do business there.

> **Time and Money Saving Tip**
>
> Although commercial property insurance is a fixed expense, it is one of the best items to shop for competitively. Be aware that independent insurance agents are intermediaries and add their fee onto what the insurance company charges. Shopping competitively directly with insurance companies, such as State Farm, Allstate, and American Family Life, can produce much better results. They can use what the independent agent earns to lower the cost. Once you get a price from one, take the quote to another and see if they can lower it. Cutting out the middleman will save you money.

Historical financials show the current year to date plus an additional three years of income and expense statements on the subject property. Be sure to request these in month-by-month format from the seller. This way you can track the history of the income and expenses. By the way, lenders much prefer to make loans on commercial investment properties that have strong historical financials. The ones that do not have these are highly scrutinized.

Buying a Property Without Historical Financials

In 2019 one of my best clients was doing a 1031 exchange and had a 14-unit, $2.4 million apartment complex under contract in a suburb of Seattle as a replacement property. The property was over 40 years old and had just been extensively rehabbed. What he loved about the property was that it did not need anything. Except for the dated design, it was like buying a new building and was priced

(continued)

Due Diligence

(*continued*)

almost as high as one. It showed 100% occupancy on the rent roll. The property only had 6 months of operating history since they had vacated all the units prior to rehabbing it 13 months prior. We asked the seller for the historical financials from when he'd bought the property, since it would have been helpful to see how the property had performed prior to the renovation. He told us that he bought it without any financials.

The six months of operating history that we did have disturbed me. The lease-up went exceptionally fast. They had filled all 14 units in less than three months. The income and expense statements and the month-by-month rent rolls showed that for the last three months they had only collected about 64% of the rent. It turned out that three tenants were late-pays and two were not paying rent at all. One was being evicted. It was obvious that my client was buying a property filled with some terrible renters. It would take over six months of evictions and spotty income to re-tenant the property. My client canceled the sale.

Loss to Lease Ratio: *Wouldn't it be great to know what percentage of a property's rents are under market rate?*

When evaluating a commercial property you are interested in buying or selling, check to see what the loss to lease ratio is, if any. When buying, this number can tell you how much of a value-add raising rents will be in the form of a percentage. When selling, it can tell you the percentage by which your rents are under market. The loss to lease ratio is the difference between what current rents are for a commercial property and what potential rents could be, based on market rents. In other words, how much is the property losing because of the rents being under market?

Let's use an example of a 10-unit apartment building where the units are all the same and rent for $1,000 per month. If market rents for like properties in the market support $1,100 per month, then there is a loss to lease of

Time and Money Saving Tip

This approach can be used to entice the seller into lowering the sales price. A request for historical financials will be on your due diligence list, which should be attached to the purchase contract. Request the corresponding years' schedule of income on the property from the seller's tax returns. Often sellers will refuse to provide these, stating that releasing them constitutes a violation of their financial privacy. Be sure to tell the seller that your lender is requesting these, which they often do. Lenders consider a tax return to be the most verifiable source of a property's income. And, you are not asking the seller for their complete personal tax return, only for the pages that pertain to the subject

$100 per unit. Multiply this by 10 and you get $1,000; multiply $1,000 by 12 and you get an annual loss to lease of $12,000. Assuming that the total gross rental income of the property at 100% occupancy is $120,000 annually, then the loss to lease ratio is 10%. When figuring out the loss to lease ratio for office and retail properties you should use rent per square foot.

Market and Competition Analysis: *This tells you how the subject property compares with its competitors in the market*

If you were to start or buy a business, you would want to know the competition in your market. This is equally important when buying commercial real estate. It's best if you take a more hands-on approach. An experienced real estate broker who specializes in the property type you are purchasing can do a market analysis for you. For larger, more expensive properties you can order a feasibility report. Another alternative is to hire a consultant from Goodkin Consulting or Cushman & Wakefield, or to order a detailed report from a research firm such as CBRE, JLL, or CoStar. Follow the nine steps shown next to complete a modified market analysis yourself.

Nine-Step Market and Competition Analysis

1. *Geographically define your market.* For larger metropolitan communities, look at the competition within 3–5 miles of your location. For smaller markets, look within 10 miles. For very small markets, you might have to use the entire county.

property. In most cases, this is the seller's Schedule E. Compare the income and expenses shown on the tax returns with the corresponding income and expense statements. If the seller is showing an amount of income that is significantly less than that shown on the income and expense statements, which is often the case, you can use this to negotiate a lower sales price. Prior to your financial due diligence period being up, tell the seller that your lender is only able to use the net income showing on the tax returns and that this has resulted in a lower loan amount being approved. This is often the case with commercial banks. Then ask the seller to lower the sales price accordingly. You might end up splitting the difference.

Time and Money Saving Tip

Now that you know how to compute a loss to lease ratio when buying, see if you can find properties that have a loss to lease ratio of 10% or higher. If you can raise the rents by 10%, this will go right into your bottom line. Be sure to estimate the cost of any renovations or tenant improvements you will be spending cash on to charge the higher rents. Make sure that this cost can be recovered within two years. Check with an experienced real estate broker to verify that the subject property does charge under-market rents and to determine what the loss to lease ratio is. Look for opportunities where a property has been poorly managed, rents are clearly under market, and unnecessary rental concessions have been used.

Due Diligence

2. *Determine the vacancy rate in your market.* You can call a local appraiser or talk with several commercial loan officers at banks in the area. They will have looked at many appraisals that have analyzed vacancy rates. Low vacancy rates will support your investment.

3. *Compare rent per square foot.* For office, retail, and industrial properties, this will tell you if there is room to add value by raising rents. It will also tell you how the subject property compares with the competition. Ask your commercial real estate agent to help you find comparable properties.

4. *Compare rent per unit.* For multifamily properties, find at least three comparable properties that are similar to the subject property in terms of age, condition, and number of units. Determine if there is room to raise rents on the subject property. You can look up apartment complexes online or ask your commercial real estate broker to provide you with comparables.

5. *Compare location and amenities with the competition.* How does the subject property look compared to the competition? Does it have superior or inferior amenities? Does it have a workout room, or comfy outdoor areas? How is the landscaping? Is it older or newer? Do your competitors have more or less traffic? Why is this? What would you have to do to the subject property to give it a competitive edge in the market?

6. *Do a sales comparison report.* Ask your commercial realtor to provide you with three comparable properties that have sold in the past year. Determine from this if the subject property is over- or underpriced.

7. *Do a market cap rate analysis.* Ask your commercial real estate agent to get you the income and expenses from three properties similar to the subject property. Average the cap rate that these properties sold at with the subject property's cap rate. This market cap rate analysis will be a stronger indication of what the property is worth.

8. *Do a traffic count.* For retail and office properties, higher traffic locations are more expensive. Spend 20 minutes at your site and at your strongest competitors' sites and literally count cars at different times of the day. You can also subscribe to Esri Demographics, which does traffic counts for more than a thousand locations in the United States.

9. *Check for new construction starts.* Check for new construction starts with the city or the county building or planning department. You need to know if anyone is building a similar type of project near your location.

Millage Property Tax Rate: *Have you checked with the county to see if property taxes are higher than what the seller is reporting?*

Far too often buyers overlook the fact that their property taxes might be higher than what the seller has reported. They mistakenly use the amount on the seller's financials or last property tax bill when calculating expenses for after they buy the property. It's not that sellers are trying to mislead buyers on this. They are just reporting what they paid. But property taxes always seem to go up every year as the millage tax rate is increased. This is the amount per thousand dollars of property value that the property is taxed at based on current tax levies. I can't tell you how many loans I have worked on where I determined the property taxes were much higher than what the seller was reporting. Often the purchase price has had to be lowered.

To determine current property taxes, request a copy of the most recent property tax bill from the seller. Then do a search for millage tax rates on the county assessor's website. This is public information. Look up the current millage property tax rate for the type of property you are buying. Then multiply this by the property value shown on the tax bill. This should give you the most current taxes assessed on the property. Lastly, look up the property by the tax number on the website and see if the property value has been raised. If so, use this value or the current millage value you computed, whichever is higher

If the property you are purchasing is in California, property taxes are reassessed at the purchase price after a property is sold. This is quite a zinger. So be sure to use the current millage rate times the purchase price to determine what your new property taxes will be.

This conversation illustrates the point:

"Are you kidding me?" my client asked. "You're telling me that the property taxes are going up by $19,500 when the county reassesses the property? So I'm buying today based on the seller's property taxes and then once I own it my taxes will zoom up based on the purchase price?"

"Yes," I answered. "In California they do that."

"Well then," he said, "that means I'm buying the property for a 4.7 cap instead of the 6 cap the listing agent said it was. That means I'm getting ripped off and the listing agent lied to me. Why would he put the seller's lower property taxes in the list of expenses and calculate a 6 cap? This is the only property I have identified in my 1031 exchange. What am I going to do?"

Mold Assessment Report: *Don't forget to check for mold*

If the property you are buying is older and in a damp climate, it is a good idea to order a mold assessment report, which will cost $250–400, as part of your due diligence. Commercial appraisers are trained to look for visual signs of mold in commercial properties. If found, it will be necessary to order a limited-scope mold assessment report. The inspector will conduct a visual inspection, collect samples in areas that are affected, and make recommendations for abating the mold. Usually poor ventilation is the culprit. Several types of mold produce mycotoxins, which are harmful when inhaled indoors. California requires owners to disclose the presence of mold in commercial properties to buyers and tenants.

Net Operating Income (NOI): *This simple calculation is the most important one in commercial real estate*

This simple math calculation is the most important number in commercial real estate. It is the foundation for determining everything related to a commercial property's financial condition, including CCR, cap rate, and its value. The NOI is simply the profit the property is earning before debt service. It is rental income minus expenses. But it is actually a bit more than that: gross rental income, less vacancy, less collection loss, less expenses = NOI.

Parking Ratio: *Does the retail or office property you are buying meet the city's parking requirements?*

If you are buying a retail or office property, check with the city to make sure there is adequate parking for each tenant based on their type of business as part of your due diligence. For a multitenant property, you will be adding the number of parking spaces required for each tenant together. Then confirm that the property has at least this number of spaces.

Here is how this can become a problem: Because tenants can change over the years, the current tenant might not have enough parking but has somehow gotten by with it. If the city discovers there is not enough parking after you own it they can make your life quite miserable. They can also require that a tenant move. For example, say a space that was once occupied by a shoe store became a coffee shop at some point. The city may have only required the shoe store to have one parking space for every 400 square feet in the tenant's space. For a food and beverage establishment it might require one space for every 200 square feet, however, which means that it requires twice as many spaces for the coffee shop as for the shoe store. Almost all multifamily properties have off-street parking space requirements. The good news is that the developers would not have gotten their certificate of occupancy (even if the property was rehabbed) if they did not meet the city's parking space requirement. This problem is rare and only occurs when the tenants have changed over to ones that require more parking spaces.

Preliminary Title Report: *This is what you need to check out on the preliminary title report*

Often buyers and sellers of commercial real estate fail to read the preliminary title report thoroughly. You would be surprised at how often a sale has to be delayed or fails to close due to not being able to get clear title on the property. Sellers sometimes do not know that there are mechanic liens, tax liens, or litigation showing on a title. If the preliminary title report is reviewed thoroughly at the beginning, this could have been avoided.

Be sure to have the listing agent pull a preliminary title report the day after the purchase contract is signed. This can take three or four days. You want to get started as early as possible. If there are problems with clearing the title, it can take several months to resolve. This is where it really pays to have a skilled commercial real estate attorney. They are experts at understanding the title report, comparing it with the survey, and watching out for your interests. A preliminary title report has information from the public record that tells the buyer who owns a property, its legal description, liens, easements, and encroachments.

Main Items to Check Out in the Title Report

1. *Who owns it?* Is the seller's name on the purchase and sale agreement the same as it is on the preliminary title report? If not, find out why. It is hard to believe, but it

does happen that someone who does not own the property will try to sell it. (See How I Learned the Hard Way to Read the Title Report box.)

2. *Is the property in foreclosure?* Sometimes the seller does not disclose this, thinking they can sell the property and pay off the lender. If the foreclosure process has advanced to the point that the lender has received a court judgment awarding them the property, then the seller won't be able to get clear title. This will likely mean the purchase contract has to be extended. If this happens, maybe you can get the property for a better price, especially if you can buy it from the bank. Your time is worth money.

3. *Are there unworkable easements and/or encroachments?* I have seen cases where a property really was landlocked, and the only access to it was through an easement that was being contested. I have also seen cases where the property that was being purchased was partially located on someone else's land. This is the definition of an encroachment.

4. *Are there liens that might be difficult to clear?* If there are multiple loans, mechanic liens (liens from work done on the property that was not paid for), and back taxes, is the property being sold for enough to cover them all? Get assurances from the seller that clearing the liens will not be a problem. I had a loan approved on a property that failed to close because of liens on the property for past-due spousal and child support that were much more than the seller expected.

5. *Is the property in litigation?* First, a property cannot be sold or financed when it is tied up in litigation. I lost a loan on a manufacturing plant that was owned by two partners. I knew my client needed the loan to buy his partner out. But he did not tell me that his partner was suing him. I found this out through the title report. Fortunately I did not start the loan. I told my client to come back when the lawsuit was settled.

Due Diligence

How I Learned the Hard Way to Read the Title Report

In my second year doing commercial mortgages I spent over two months working on the refinance of a rock quarry. My client was a large rock-crushing company. The owner was working the equipment on-site and convinced me that he owned the quarry. I think he thought he owned it as well. He had purchased it but the land sales contract was not recorded. He had missed some payments and the company he'd bought it from had a clause in the contract that stated if he fell behind on payments for more than 60 days that it would take the property back. Although I had ordered a preliminary title report within days of starting the loan, I had failed to read it through. If I had, I would have discovered that

(continued)

(continued)

the company refinancing the property was not the company that was listed as owning it on the title report. My borrower did not legally own the property. As you can guess, this deal crashed.

Property Condition Checklist

Why not take charge of the physical condition of the property you are buying or selling from the beginning, by understanding what the property condition report covers? Here is a general list:

___Structural framing

___Pavement and curbs

___Lighting

___Building envelope

___Drainage

___Landscaping

___Roofs

___Fire suppression

___Fencing

___Foundation

___Exterior finish

___Fire and safety

___Plumbing

___Interior finish

___Regulatory compliance

___Electrical

___Boilers

___Common areas

___HVAC

___Signage

___Elevators

___Windows and doors

___ADA accessibility

___Stairways

___Data and phone

Due Diligence

___Mold

___Wood-boring insect damage

Radon Gas Report: *Radon gas is the second-leading cause of lung cancer in the United States. Does your property have it?*

As part of your due diligence, don't forget to test for radon gas. Radon is a radioactive gas that is in rocks and soil and can be under commercial properties in almost every state. With poor ventilation it can build up to dangerous levels. It is the second main cause of lung cancer in the United States after cigarette smoking. A radon gas inspector will place a testing kit in each unit or space and retrieve it in a few days for analysis. If the result is below 4 pCi/L, the property is okay. If higher, they will come back and do a second test. Mitigation usually consists of increasing ventilation. Many lenders require a radon gas report for states that are known to have high levels of radon gas. The western states have the highest incidence.

Rent Comparable Report: *Are the rents at or above market rents? Is there room to raise rents?*

A rent comparable report compares the rent from three to six similar properties with the subject property. The purpose of the report is to determine if the subject property rents are at market, below market, or above market. When buying or selling a commercial property, this report will tell you if there is a value-add opportunity to increase rents.

A commercial real estate broker that wants to represent you will do a rent comparable report for free. If they are not going to represent you, they will charge a small fee. They will not only know some rent comparables themselves, but their companies will likely be members of Costar or REIS, which are market research companies that have current market rents. Property management companies are another excellent source for market rents. Banks and commercial mortgage brokers have access to recent appraisals, which will have this data too.

Seismic Report/Seismic Risk Assessment: *Is the building you are buying at risk of collapsing in an earthquake?*

Is the property you are buying in an earthquake zone? If so, it's important to assess the building's structural risk for earthquake. Ask the seller what has been done to retrofit the building for earthquakes and for a copy of his seismic report. If he financed the property in an earthquake zone he will likely have one. Search online for "FEMA seismic map" to find locations in the United States that are prone to earthquakes. A seismic report estimates the percentage of a building that could be lost in the event of an earthquake by calculating the probable maximum loss. The report evaluates the seismic risk as a percentage of the building's potential loss. A loss of 20% or higher is considered high risk. "Tuck-under parking," where parking is on the bottom level and apartments or shops are above it is considered very high risk. Most buildings that are at risk can be retrofitted seismically.

Stabilized Occupancy: *This is when the property is at market occupancy*

"Is the property stabilized?" or "When will the property be stabilized?" are questions that come up a lot in commercial real estate. A property is considered to have stabilized occupancy when it is leased up to market occupancy. Newly built or rehabbed properties can take six months or more to achieve stabilized occupancy. A brand new apartment building might have only 40% occupancy after the first three months, but be expected to reach stabilized occupancy in another four months when it achieves a market occupancy rate of 95%. Properties that do not have stabilized occupancy have lower NOIs and are worth less than ones with stabilized occupancy. Commercial appraisals for properties being rehabbed or newly constructed will have two values—a lower, as-completed value and a higher stabilized value.

Survey, ALTA: *This survey will show absolutely everything about how the property is laid out*

When buying a commercial property there is no better way to see what you are buying than through an ALTA survey of the property. Not only does it show you accurately where all the property lines, rights of way, and buildings are, but it will also show all walkways, roads, paving, parking, storm drainage, landscaping, and utilities. Just as important, it shows all easements and encroachments, and the zoning and flood-zone classifications. Keep in mind that title reports only provide a legal description of easements, which is usually hard to comprehend. An ALTA survey shows you exactly where it is located.

The seller of the property you are buying might only have a simple boundary survey, which is often acceptable to community banks that can go and see the property easily. Lenders that are out of the area will often require an ALTA survey, which is much more expensive.

Tenant Rollover Risk: *Is the property at risk for many vacancies at the same time?*

When making a decision to buy a commercial property, it is essential to assess the tenant rollover risk. This is the risk associated with leases that are expiring. For office, retail, and industrial properties, the tenant rollover risk is high if many leases are expiring at about the same time soon or at some other time in the future, or also, if they are month to month. A property with a majority of leases with terms of five years or more remaining has a relatively low tenant rollover risk. A property

Time and Money Saving Tip

Be sure to check with your lender right after you have signed the purchase contract if they will require an ALTA survey. If they do require it and the seller only has a regular boundary survey, you will have to order an ALTA survey right away. It can take from two weeks to a month depending on how busy the survey company is. ALTA surveys are expensive and can cost $6,000–10,000 or more depending on the size and complexity of the property. Be sure to go to the same surveyor that did the original survey and ask them for a substantial discount. They should discount their standard cost for an ALTA survey by half since they have already measured the entire property. If the seller cannot find the survey, check with all of the local title companies. Whichever one closed on the property last will have a copy of the survey.

Due Diligence

that has 20% or more of the total square
footage of the leases expiring in one year has a high tenant rollover risk.

Steps to Determine Tenant Rollover Risk

1. For each year, make a list of each lease that is expiring and the amount of square footage that each of these tenants occupies.
2. Sum the amount of square footage for the expiring leases for that year.
3. Divide that total by the property's total rentable square footage. This will give you a percentage of the property's rollover risk for each year.

Your job is to identify time periods in the future that are at an unacceptable risk level for tenant rollover. An example would be a strip mall that has 60,000 rentable square feet with two leases totaling 10,500 square feet expiring in the first year of ownership:

$$\frac{\text{Expiring Leases sq.ft.}}{\text{Total Rentable sq.ft.}} = \text{Rollover risk}$$

$$10,500/60,000 = 17.5 \text{ Rollover risk}$$

Title and Survey Objection Letter:

If there are problems with the title report, your commercial real estate attorney will write this letter

When buying a commercial property, most buyers just assume that everything will be okay with the title commitment and survey. Always assume a problem may exist and have your commercial real estate attorney review these items shortly after signing the purchase contract. If your attorney finds any title defects, such as restrictive easements, encroachments, or any agreements that restrict your use of the property, they will prepare a title objection letter on your behalf. This will be given to the buyer's and seller's real estate brokers, the seller, the title company, and the surveyor. This letter needs to be issued well before your due diligence period is up, as defects can take several weeks to a month or longer to remedy. In most cases the seller will extend the purchase contract to accommodate the estimated time it will take to correct the title defects.

Time and Money Saving Tip

As part of assessing tenant rollover risk, do what most lenders do. They check each tenant's business credit. This is a part of assessing tenant rollover risk that buyers often do not think of doing. Even if the tenant has many years remaining on their lease, if they are on the verge of going out of business they represent a substantial risk for tenant rollover to the property owner. Dun and Bradstreet, Equifax Business, and Experian Business can provide you with tenant business credit reports. Scores range from 1 to 100. A score of 75 or higher is very good. You can check the Standard & Poor's rating for national credit-rated tenants online.

Due Diligence

Trailing 12-Month Report (T-12): Your lender will require this. Ask the seller for it early on.

What you really need to know when buying a commercial investment property is how the property has been performing over the 12 months previous to your signing the purchase contract. A T-12 report does just that. It shows income and expenses month by month, starting with the month preceding the contract and looking back for 12 months. You need this to be in month-by-month format so you can look for monthly discrepancies in rental income and expenses. When purchasing a commercial property, the seller and/or listing agent will most often provide the past calendar year's income and expenses for the property in the marketing flyer. This does not give you an accurate representation of how the property has done recently—especially if you're buying the property early in the current year. Be sure to request a T-12 report from the seller as early as possible and make sure it is included on your due diligence list for property financials. Most lenders require a T-12. To view a sample of a T-12 report go to Appendix A. For an Excel copy that can be filled out, go to my website at: https://apartmentloanstore.com.

Transfer Tax: Check to see if the city or county is going to charge this tax; fortunately, most do not

A transfer tax can be charged by municipalities, counties, or states when real estate is sold to another party. This is really a charge for changing the deed from one owner to another. In a seller's market, most often the buyer pays this tax. The cost can be anywhere from 1 dollar for every 1,000 dollars of value to 2% or more of the purchase price. These states do not allow transfer taxes: Mississippi, Missouri, New Mexico, North Dakota, and Wyoming.

Vacancy Rate: Physical, Economic, and Market

- **Physical Vacancy Rate:** The physical vacancy rate applies to multifamily, mobile home park, or self-storage properties. It is the number of vacant units divided by the total number of units. For office and retail properties, the physical vacancy rate is the square footage that is vacant divided by the total leasable square footage.

Time and Money Saving Tip

Wouldn't you like to take a forensic look behind the scenes of how the commercial property you want to purchase has been managed and performing over the past two years? You might have been told a thing or two by the listing agent or seller, but why not find the truth out for yourself?

Just follow this recipe: Request a T-12 report and also a month-by-month report for the 12 months before the T-12 report starts. Then request the past 24 months of rent rolls for the same time period. If the seller is hesitant to provide this, just tell them your lender needs it. If we are concerned about rent collections, our company does require this. Examine each month's income and expenses carefully.

Here is what to look for:

1. Does the property have a good history of monthly income? Has it been increasing over time or is it up and down? This is

Due Diligence

- **Economic Vacancy Rate:** When you buy a property you should be looking at the economic vacancy rate, not the physical vacancy rate that is showing on the rent roll. The economic vacancy rate is determined by looking at actual gross rental income from rents collected as shown on income and expense statements. For example, you could be told that a property has a 6% vacancy rate, but in looking at rent collected you might find its economic vacancy rate is 9%. Economic vacancy rate is what lenders really look at; they're interested in vacancy based on actual rents collected, not based on rent rolls. To determine the annual economic vacancy rate, take the total annual gross rental income collected from the property as shown on the operating statement for the past 12 months. Now divide that amount by the gross potential income as if the property were 100% occupied during the same time period.
- **Market Vacancy Rate:** The market vacancy rate is the average vacancy rate for the subject property type in a submarket. This is an indicator of supply and demand in this market.

a sign of good or bad management. Most importantly, has the property been operating at well below market occupancy and only showing growth over the past four to six months? Do the rent rolls show more *physical occupancy* than *economic occupancy* (see Encyclopedia Topic A, Buying) when compared to the actual amount of rent taken in? This could mean that you are getting some substandard tenants that were not screened properly and were accepted just to sell the property.

2. Take a look at expenses month by month and line by line. Do the expenses for repairs and maintenance fluctuate? Are there many months for which there is little or no expense for repairs? This should tell you how the property has been maintained. Are there expenses, such as taxes, that are completely missing? Check with the local government to see if the seller is behind on taxes. If so, they might be in financial stress, which is good for you to know.

You can determine market vacancy rate through a quick call to a commercial appraiser or local lender. If the subject property has a 12% vacancy rate and market vacancy is at 7%, then this is an excellent opportunity to reposition the property. Your goal would be to get the property to a market vacancy rate or better.

Wood-Destroying Insect Report: *If you live in a state that has wood-eating insects, you should order this report as a precaution*

As part of your due diligence, you will need to order a wood-boring insect report if your building inspector finds signs of termites and other wood-boring insects, including carpenter ants and wood-destroying beetles. The report will identify the location of the infestation, the extent of the damage, and the cost to remedy it. Alabama, California, Hawaii, Florida, Louisiana, Texas, Mississippi, Georgia, and South Carolina have the highest incidence of wood-boring insects.

PART III

Smart Strategies for Raising Investors

CHAPTER 4

Raising Money and Creating Investor Partnerships

This chapter really gets into the details about how to use other people's money to purchase a commercial property. It covers countermeasures that can offset a lack of money or experience, why using other people's money grows wealth faster, how to get started, why you should use non-recourse funding, what mistakes to avoid with investor partnerships, and the pros and cons of forming a commercial real estate syndication.

BUYING COMMERCIAL REAL ESTATE WITHOUT MONEY OR EXPERIENCE

Let's get this out of the way right now. For those of you who are just starting out in commercial real estate investment, you might prefer that I begin by telling you that it is easy to buy your first commercial property without a down payment or experience. Many real estate gurus who want to sell their seminars and coaching services will sell this to you—or better yet, give you the recipe for how to get investors to come up with all of the down payment. Sorry, but it is not easy to pull this off.

Just think about it. Why would someone want to invest tens of thousands of dollars with you if you have no skin in the game and no record of accomplishment? Would they enthusiastically say to you, "Here—take this $150,000 that has taken years to save and use it to get the on-the-job-training you need so that I can earn an 8% return?" Not likely! After all, there is an abundance of highly experienced deal managers they could work with.

But now I am going to contradict myself. If there is one thing that always gets my attention when the phone rings, it is a drop-dead, mind-blowing property for sale in a good location that has more than one upside. There I go: dropping everything I am working on to start analyzing this shiny new deal. And if you can convince me that you can get control of this property, I'm likely going to lower my standards on my two most important screening questions: "How much cash do you have to put down and do you have the experience?" My attitude will be, "Together, we will find a way to get this closed."

Why? In my line of work, we have to sift through so many mediocre or garbage deals to find the few outstanding ones. That's why we always answer the phone and talk to everyone. The truth is, my staff and I have financed and closed dozens of deals in which the deal's sponsor had almost no money and no experience. They were successful through a mixture of being well prepared and confidence. What they did to mitigate their lack of experience and cash was to implement most of eight countermeasures that I am going to share with you in the following sections.

If you want to get your foot in the door and start wheeling and dealing in this big boy/girl league, and you are willing to do the work, you can likely pull this off too. For those of you that have some cash and experience and plan on raising money from private investors for the first time, many of these items will insure your success.

EIGHT COUNTERMEASURES FOR NOT HAVING ENOUGH MONEY AND EXPERIENCE

1. You Have Found an Outstanding Property

If you are new to commercial property investing, you will need to find the deal first and then find investors. Find a property in a good neighborhood and market with these three qualities:

1. It's priced below market.
2. It can cash flow the new debt service right now.
3. The property has a strong repositioning upside (such as raising below-market rents), has expenses that can be lowered, needs better management, or requires some cosmetic improvements.

If your property embodies just two of these qualities, I will do flip-flops to try to make this deal happen for you. That is because I am confident that private investors are going to want to talk with you.

2. You Can Raise 10% of the Equity in Your Name

I know, this is a hard one for some. But if you can achieve this, it will give you something very important—CLOUT! I can tell you from my work on hundreds of deals that this item is the big one. Achieve this and you can easily increase your odds of putting a deal together by 10.

Even if you have to borrow funds from your parents, siblings, or friends, or refinance your home, it is imperative that you show that you have some skin in the game. Nothing else can give you more credibility as the sponsor and managing partner. Every investor you talk to will ask you how much you are putting in. Do you really want to tell them ZERO?

Before you start talking to investors, put your money in an account in your name. You will need these funds out of the gate for some of the ancillary costs, such as the earnest money, the appraisal and other third-party reports, and the retainer for your commercial real estate attorney and maybe a syndication attorney.

Trust me, you just do not want to have to beg for money for these items. And investors will be put off at the beginning if you ask them to fund these costs. Plus it will give any lender heartburn if they figure out that you are having trouble paying for these soft costs. Applying your own funds to 10% of the down payment will enable you to use *crowdfunding* or to do a *joint venture* with a venture capital firm to raise most of the equity.

3. You Have a High-Net-Worth Individual or Proxy

This individual might actually be a key principal in your deal, putting in much of the equity, or they might just serve as a proxy and use their personal financial statement to prove to the listing agent, seller, and lender that they have the wherewithal to make the deal work. You might very well end up using someone else to replace them before the deal is complete.

Find someone that has commercial property ownership experience—preferably experience with the same type of real estate as the subject property. Ideally this individual will love to teach and can mentor you. Again, finding a high-quality deal will draw such a person to you. Be prepared to offer them 5–10% or more ownership in your venture just for taking on this role and putting up to 10% of the equity into the deal. The ownership percentage should be even higher, of course, if they put even more equity into the deal.

In a competitive seller's market, it is unlikely that the seller or listing broker will make a deal with you without verifying that you have the down payment. And they know you will need experience to get financing. If your high-net-worth individual does not want to give a copy of their bank or security statement, they can get a *qualification letter* from their banker, accountant, or stockbroker verifying that they have the amount needed for the down payment. Lenders and commercial mortgage brokers will also need this to know that you are not wasting their time. It is better if you can show actual proof of funds. Quite often, I have started a loan using one high-net-worth individual's personal financial statement only to substitute another high-net-worth individual's statement prior to final underwriting.

4. You Have Control over the Property

You have a fully executed purchase contract on the property. This is the big one that will get investors and lenders interested in talking to you.

5. You Have the Essential Property Financials

You want to get the current rent roll, a 12-month-old rent roll for comparison, the previous year's month-by-month income and expense statement, and a trailing 12-month report (shows income and expenses month by month for the past 12 months).

6. You Have a Pro Forma Showing Strong Financial Returns from Your Value Adds

This projection will show that after repositioning, the property will have an excess of net operating income (NOI) to support an excellent and ever-increasing *cash on cash return (CCR)* and *internal rate of return (IRR)* after stabilization. The pro forma should show a minimum of five years, or be based on how long you plan to hold the property. You want to support your initial rental increase assumptions with a *rent comparison report* and your lower expenses with a letter from a property management company stating that it can run the property at these expense levels. As a rule of thumb, for multifamily properties you should show your rents increasing 5–8% per year. For other commercial properties, rents should increase 3–6% annually or by actual increases in the leases. Expenses should show a 3% increase each year. You want to fill out a *seven-year month-by-month pro forma*, and then populate the data to a *commercial purchase or finance evaluator spreadsheet*. View examples of both of these forms in Appendix A and find downloadable Excel versions on my website: https://apartmentloanstore.com/.

7. You Have the Best Team

Boy, can this group of professionals make you look good! These seven team members should always be included:

1. One or more high-net-worth partners who can prove availability for the balance of the cash for the down payment (again, you might not use all of them)
2. A partner investor who has experience in owning the same type of property (ideally this will be at least one of your high-net-worth partners)
3. A buyer's real estate broker to represent you
4. A commercial real estate attorney

5. A syndication attorney, if you are forming a *syndication*
6. A commercial mortgage broker or banker
7. A property management company

8. You Have an Outstanding Executive Summary

Your executive summary should be put together professionally, with the main purpose of selling this deal to investors. If you end up forming a *syndication*, a *private placement memorandum* (*PPM*) should be used instead. Lenders also love to see these documents. You want to entice investors with what their earnings from operations and appreciation will be when the property is sold. Estimate what the property will sell for upon exit. You and your investors should earn the most from appreciation, which will be divided up based on the ownership percentage of each partner. Highlight the projected *internal rate of return* (*IRR*) and the *preferred return* they will be earning. You want to impress lenders with the current NOI or the NOI after the property is stabilized. And you want to include both investors' and lenders' bios showing the outstanding experience of your team of professionals and partners.

Be sure to include a description of the property, great exterior and interior photos, aerial photos, demographic information, and a market rent report based on the submarket competition. You'll want to mention the distance to major shopping and freeways. Be sure to highlight a snapshot of what the financing will look like and mention the lenders that are interested. In addition, it is best if you can make this a *non-recourse loan.*

A No-Experience, Almost-No-Money-Down Success Story

Over the years I have worked on financing many deals where one bright entrepreneur was at the right place at the right time with the right property. This individual would then bring in 2–10 private investors to raise the down payment. One of my favorite deals was sponsored by a physical therapist who had no experience and little cash, but who did have the motivation to put the deal together due to his extreme circumstances.

This should have never have happened to Mark. He always planned meticulously and allowed more than enough time for major projects. But in early December of 2010 he found himself staving off a panic attack as the extent of his misfortune hit him. He was supposed to move his practice to a new medical office complex near the hospital in Eugene, Oregon, in March of 2011, but the

(continued)

(continued)

new building was far from being completed. He had been very careful to plan the move using an eight-month cushion ahead of his current office lease expiring. This gave him the four months needed for his tenant improvement buildout plus an additional four months for construction completion delays. The main problem was that he had given up his old space to a new tenant who was planning to move in at the beginning of March, in less than three months. Over a year before, Mark had signed an intent to lease letter with the developer of the new building. The developer was no longer answering calls.

Mark pulled himself together and realized that his established business would not have a home if he did not take action. There was a sign on the new property showing the name of the bank financing the project. Mark contacted the bank only to find out that it had been taken over by a larger bank, which did not know anything about the medical office building. After a few weeks someone from the acquiring bank's headquarters called him and said that the previous bank had taken the property back in distressed condition. The construction was only 78% complete and had stalled. They were planning to sell it at public auction in four months. It turned out that the developer, who was also the general contractor, had gone out of business because of having too many projects going at the same time during the recession. Mark could hardly believe it when he heard his own voice tell the banker that he wanted to buy the property from them.

Mark called me and said that he was going to buy this unfinished property from the bank at a discount. He did not have a clue that he was not qualified. His adrenaline told him otherwise. The construction appraisal valued the property at $2.8 million once completed and occupied. It was estimated that it would take at least $500,000 more to complete it. The tenants were putting in their own tenant improvements. The bank offered to sell it for $2.2 million as is if he took it right away. He told them that price seemed like it could work. I did not care about Mark's lack of experience and cash. Here was a medical office building—one of the lowest–risk commercial property types—that was 68% preleased, in a great location, and priced at a great discount. To top it off, Mark had talked with three physicians who had also signed leases about becoming partners. Two definitely wanted in and the third was thinking about it. The risk lay in completing the construction quickly and possibly losing some of the tenants that had signed on because of the delay.

With the appraisal from the bank in hand, I did some market research and got really excited. It turned out that this property was on a rezoned urban infill parcel and there was almost nothing else that close to the hospital left to develop.

Also the price per square foot for medical space had gone up significantly since the appraisal had been done, which meant that when completed and occupied the property would be worth at least $3.2 million.

Mark and I met with the bank and showed them our pro forma and an estimated cost for completing the construction from a local contractor. We also had a letter from the appraiser estimating the time for *absorption*. The numbers justified a maximum price of $1,800,000. We also showed them my letter of preapproval for financing.

Mark purchased the property for $1,900,000. It would take another $660,000, including a payment reserve, to complete the construction, for a total of $2,560,000. I was able to arrange a $1,920,000, 75%-of-cost bridge loan. Mark put $102,000 into soft costs, which were mostly attorney fees and leasing commissions. That put his cash contribution to the deal at 4%. The remaining equity came in from the two doctors, who put in $269,000 each.

Mark's commercial real estate attorney set up a simple LLC ownership for the property, where the two doctors each owned 40% and Mark owned 20%. They would all run the property jointly, with Mark being the managing partner. We closed the deal in a little over 60 days.

USING OTHER PEOPLE'S MONEY TO GET RICH WHEN BUYING COMMERCIAL PROPERTY

Why use other people's money for the down payment to get started in commercial real estate? To some this might sound lazy, but it is both smart and practical. Because most of the profit from commercial real estate investment comes from appreciation, it makes sense to buy sooner with funds from private investors rather than wait to save the down payment yourself. If you are not blessed with an inheritance or a large chunk of savings and are planning on saving the down payment over time to purchase a larger, more expensive property, one of the major laws of commercial property investment will be working against you. This is the law of forced appreciation, which states that the property you want to buy today and are saving for will be going up in value each year as the current owner raises rents and increases the value. This continually raises the bar for you. This means the down payment you are saving for will be much larger five years from now.

Let's say you are earning $60,000 per year. You decide you are going to give up eating out and vacations so you can save as much as you can in five years for the down payment. How much can you save every year from your salary? If you have a talent for frugal living and do not have a car payment or much credit card debt, maybe $15,000 per year after paying taxes and living expenses. So in five years you could likely save $75,000 for the down payment. This might give you the 25% down on a $300,000 duplex, but it won't get you into commercial real estate. If you rented each unit of the duplex out for $1,250 per month, after 30% expenses and loan payments you might be able to make $7,000 annually. This is not much of a payoff for giving up five years of vacations.

Now let's look at what you could achieve if you said to yourself, "Hey, I don't want to give up the good life and save for five years and end up owning a duplex. I want to own something much bigger now and I'm going to find the investors to make this happen." Who would guess, but bigger is actually much easier in the private investor game. Yes, it is easier to raise larger amounts of money from rich people than smaller amounts from low-net-worth mom-and-pops that are just making ends meet.

Next you find a 16-unit apartment complex priced at $1,250,000. I'm choosing this as an example because this is about the minimum purchase price where you can get an 80% loan that is non-recourse (we'll go into non-recourse loans in a moment) and attract higher-net-worth investors that have the cash. So the down payment at 20% will be $250,000. Let's bump that up to $268,000 to include closing costs. You do the math and figure out that it would take you 18 years to save the down payment plus closing costs if you did this on your own and you were saving $15,000 a year.

So here is what you do. You are going to put in 10% of the equity, which is $26,800. I do not care how you raise this money, but as mentioned earlier, it is important that you are risking some of your own money and not just your reputation. It can be from your savings, a home equity line, or a loan from your Aunt Martha. Next you are going to present a killer executive summary of the deal and land three passive investors that can each bring in $60,300, which represents the remaining 90% of the equity.

Because you found the property and are doing all the work, you will own 25% of the property and each of your partners will own 25%. Will they go for this if you are only putting in 10% of the down payment? After all, this is your deal. Tell them that you are putting in just about all the work over five years and all they have to do is receive their share of the income and have a partnership meeting every three months. Show them how much their investment is projected to grow in five years. The executive summary will need to highlight that the investors will earn a *preferred return* of 8–12%. And that you will not see a dime until they get their preferred return. A return of 10% or more seems to be the best motivator, if the cash flow can afford this.

The balance of the income of the property will be divided according to the operating agreement. When the property is sold in five years at 6% appreciation compounded annually, it will be worth $1,672,782. This is an increase of $422,782, or $105,695 per partner. Each partner will get this amount plus their original cash investment back when the property sells. If we take the net income for five years and combine it with the total appreciation, the memorandum will show a 23.5% annual IRR, which is outstanding. What's even better than that is in five years your 10% cash contribution of $26,800 will have grown to $132,495. This is not a modest increase. It is an increase of 494%.

HOW THE INEXPERIENCED DEAL MANAGER/SPONSOR CAN GET STARTED

The deal manager is called the sponsor. Perhaps you have never owned commercial real estate before, your net worth is not something to brag about, and you are almost broke. But this is your dream. You have been burning the midnight oil searching for good deals on LoopNet and have found a property you cannot stop thinking about. Maybe this chapter is why you bought this book and you can't wait to start pitching this deal to investors.

What you have going for you is enthusiasm, an honest face that can sell winter coats in the Bahamas, and some experience you can extrapolate from. Maybe you fixed and flipped several residential homes. If you don't have real estate experience, maybe there has been another profound success in your life. If this description applies somewhat closely to you, the following sections lay out eight steps you can follow to find investors.

1. Gain the Confidence to Fake It Until You Make It

If you do not have experience raising investors, you will need to learn the jargon and talk the talk with confidence. I fall for it every time. A sponsor wanting financing gets me on the phone and we are turning the gears together on the deal with such synchronicity. They answer every question I ask so intelligently. And then I find out they have very little cash or experience. I've been taken by surprise because they sound exactly like my very experienced wealthy clients—and that's what you need to do. Being overly prepared will be your best ammunition in selling your deal to investors, and lenders. Put yourself in their shoes and think of the questions they will likely ask you ahead of time. Rehearse your answers to these questions.

You will need to know how to crunch the numbers to analyze deals. Study Chapter 3 on due diligence and learn how to determine the strengths and weaknesses of a deal. You do not want to draw a blank when a potential investor asks you what the financing looks like (review Chapter 11 on financing). Talk to a commercial mortgage broker and get several recommendations for the best financing, and what the qualifications are.

Study buying and due diligence in Encyclopedia Topics A and B, respectively. Study as many of the subjects and terms as you can. The *due diligence checklist* will be especially helpful, as it tells you all the items you need to collect from the seller on the property. The idea is to put some of these terms into your language so that you can talk the jargon to investors, real estate brokers, and lenders.

You'll want to be able to discuss why the location is good, your plans for value adding, what the estimated returns on their investment will be, and the exit strategy—or when they will get their money back.

Be sure to brag about your team members—your experienced high-net-worth investor, your buyer's real estate broker, your real estate attorney, your lender or commercial mortgage broker, and your property manager. The experience of your team ensures that this property is going to make it. If someone goes after you for lack of experience, you want to tell them the truth, but emphasize that you have that covered because of your team.

2. Form a Real Estate Investment Company

Would it not be better to send a potential investor to a company website or to give them a business card that has a company name instead of your name? Making a cold call and being able to say "I'm from XYZ Holdings" adds so much more strength to your ability to sell. I know this might seem daunting, but it's actually easy. Simply form a limited liability company (LLC) with a company name you like. You can do this online with the secretary of state corporation division in your state. It's not expensive and you do not need an attorney.

3. Be the High-Net-Worth Investor's Representative

Mentioned earlier in this chapter, you will have an experienced high-net-worth investor to show the strength needed for this deal. You should get the attention of listing real estate brokers and sellers by telling them your company is representing this high-net-worth individual and your job is to find deals for them. Ask them some intelligent questions about the property and be sure to talk the talk with jargon like, "I see that the repairs and maintenance line is only showing as 6% of the gross rental income. Is this number low because some of this expense has been listed under Cap-X (capital improvements)? If so, do you know about how much the Cap-X has been for this period?"

To get the loan terms for your executive summary or PPM, you will also be telling commercial mortgage brokers and lenders that you represent this high-net-worth individual. At a minimum, you will need to know the high-net-worth individual's net worth and commercial real estate experience.

4. Be an Expert at Selling Returns and Risks to Investors

It is best to offer your investors a *preferred return* on their cash investment versus an open return based on what the property earns. With a preferred return they will always get paid their percentage first from any profits after the expenses and mortgage are paid and before you do. This lowers their risk and shows that you have a fiduciary responsibility to take care of their interests. Highlight the estimate of what the property will be sold for upon exit and show them their IRR (combined earnings from annual property net income and appreciation).

Every business investment has risks. Risks can be unexpected downward economic trends, such as higher unemployment, recessions, or the same type of property being built nearby. Stagnant property values due to interest rates rising are another risk. To mitigate these risks, it is always reassuring to demonstrate that the property has a low *break-even ratio*. This means that the property can still pay its expenses and mortgage at lower occupancy levels. Also point out what you are doing to make the investment a lower risk (see the Ten Risk-Lowering Action Steps section in Chapter 1), and *recession proof* (see the Choose a Property That Can Be Recession-Proofed in Chapter 2). Sharing with potential investors that you plan on having some working capital to handle unexpected expenses will especially make them feel more comfortable.

5. Write Up an Executive Summary on a Subject Property

This might not be the property you end up buying. The real purpose of this deal summary is to attract investors and get experience and a level of comfort in doing so. The deal summary should have a good description of the property to highlight your value-add objectives and the exit strategy. You want to mention what their preferred return will be, the annual IRR, the annual NOI for the first two years, and the potential appreciation they will share in after the property is sold. This information should be followed by a financial section, which should be followed with bios of you and your team members.

6. Pitch the Deal to Potential Investors

Be sure to rehearse your presentation in front of your best friends, spouse, or even your kids or your dog. Watch some TED Talks or some YouTube videos that have inspirational speakers who are experts at something. You want your delivery to show that you have confidence in yourself and the deal. Always start your pitch by briefly describing the property, how much you are paying for it, and what it will be worth in so many years after you do your value adds and sell it. Then talk about the preferred return investors will be earning. Yes, you want to draw investors in by telling them about the potential earnings right away.

If you were able to bring in a high-net-worth investor, ask them if they know anyone who might be interested in investing. They will likely know other wealthy people. They could also be on the phone with you to add more credibility when you talk to an interested investor.

Pitch the deal to everyone you know on Facebook. Try joining a Facebook real estate group. Buy a Pro membership on BiggerPockets, which has one of the largest groups of people interested in getting into real estate investing. Make a list of everyone you know. Thirty or more potential investors would be great. You will be surprised to find that those that you think have money to invest might not really have any or be interested, and that someone who appears to have little means could be loaded and interested.

Before you pitch the deal to anyone, write a script. You want to start out by telling them how they can earn a 12% preferred return on their money plus a slice of the pie when the property sells. Again, practice your script enthusiastically. You will find yourself relaxing more in your delivery after your first live presentation. Be sure to get a few back-up investors, as some who initially agree to invest may change their minds.

7. Prequalify Your Investors

Have your investors fill out an *investor qualification form* (Encyclopedia Topic C, Raising Investor Partners). Yes, you are going to prequalify these investors. This exercise has three purposes:

1. It clearly places you in the driver's seat in terms of authority.
2. You will need to know for sure that your investors are who they say they are financially. You will need to collect their personal financial statements and proof of funds down the road.

3. If your investors are going to be passive owners who take no part in running the property, you will need to go the syndicated ownership route and will need to show that they are *accredited* or *sophisticated investors* (Encyclopedia Topic C, Raising Investor Partners).

8. Have Investors Sign a Letter of Intent to Invest

A *letter of intent to invest agreement* (see Encyclopedia Topic C, Raising Investor Partners) is not legally binding and should not be more than two pages. Its main purpose is to summarize the investment and put into writing the investors' financial commitment and when their money needs to be contributed—but even more importantly, to have them make a written commitment, which is much more likely to stick to the wall than a verbal one.

Time and Money Saving Tip

You do not want your deal to crash and burn at closing because one investor does not wire their portion of the equity to the title company at closing. The greatest problem with raising investors is that human beings are not the most reliable forces in the universe. Investors often commit, and because real estate deals take time to close, life happens and they simply change their mind. More often they find a sweeter deal and dump yours.

Be sure to have a stated time in your letter of intent to invest and also in your legally binding agreement or PPM as to when the investor's money has to be put into an escrow account. A good time for this is after the due diligence period in the purchase contract is up and the earnest money goes hard. Once placed in escrow, the investor's contribution will not be refunded if they change their mind unless the deal does not close for any other reason, such as your financing not being approved or other investors not contributing their funds.

Don't Be Taken In by the Right Talk, Charisma, and the Appearance of Wealth

Several years ago one of my best clients referred Ross, a developer, to me for a commercial construction loan. Ross had a solidity about him that impressed me from day one. He had an option to purchase a property with a vacant restaurant in downtown Colorado Springs. His plan was to demolish the existing building and build a five-story, mixed-use building with a large restaurant space on the first floor and 24 apartments on the four upper floors. The total cost would be about $6.5 million.

(continued)

(*continued*)

Ross did not know his exact net worth but said he did not have enough cash or the net worth to do the project on his own. He did own three apartment buildings worth $6 million and he had overseen the ground-up construction of one of them.

What really got my interest was that he had a partner that had a net worth of over $30 million. This partner owned one of the most successful microbreweries in Colorado. I loved their beer. They had recently been purchased by a larger brewery, and according to Ross the investor had tons of cash to invest. I asked him if he had prequalified the financials of his investor and he told me "of course." Ross had the experience and his partner would bring in the financial strength. After viewing the building plans, construction budget, and first five years of projections, I booked a flight out to meet Ross and see the property.

Ross was a well-dressed man in his mid-30s who impressed me with his professional demeanor. The downtown was doing well and there was a lack of rental units in Colorado Springs. I knew I could get this deal done. I had asked Ross for his and his partner's personal financial statements and verification of cash on day one. For one reason or another Ross was not getting them to me. He finally told me that his partner was very secretive and would only show his financials to me. "So you did not actually see his financials?" I asked him. "No, but everyone knows he is as rich as sin." I told Ross that unless I got the personal financials in within a week, I was going to close his file. Ross got me his the next day. He had a net worth of $400,000. He did have ownership in multifamily properties worth $6 million, as he'd said, but he only had 2% ownership in them. This invalidated his experience.

A week later the investor emailed me his statement. He was not worth $30 million, but only about $3 million. I had been duped.

The moral of this story is that even with my 20-plus years of experience, I allowed myself to be taken in by the right talk, charisma, and the appearance of wealth. I don't think that Ross had actually lied to me. He really did have ownership in three apartment buildings. And he really did think his investor was worth $30 million. That was what he had been told.

My purpose in sharing this story with you is that if this can happen to me, a professional that prequalifies people for a living, it can easily happen to you as a deal sponsor. So be sure to ask for proof of financial strength and experience before you waste any time with an investor.

WHAT PERCENTAGE OF OWNERSHIP SHOULD YOU GET FOR PUTTING THE DEAL TOGETHER?

In the example given earlier in this chapter, the sponsor who found the property and put the deal together put in 10% and retained 25% ownership. This is not the norm. But since I have witnessed this happening many times, I am using it as an example to encourage you to go for a larger percentage of ownership. Most experienced investors think the sponsor should only get an amount of ownership equal to the percentage of the down payment they contributed. This is really not fair for the sponsor. They will put in hundreds of hours finding the right property, putting the deal together, obtaining financing, and overseeing operations, followed by refinancing or selling the property down the road.

Most of the profit from commercial investment property comes from appreciation. For this reason alone, as the deal finder and managing partner, you are going to want to make sure to retain as much ownership of the property as possible. I have seen managing partners put none of their own money in and get 10% ownership. And I've seen them put 5% down and receive up to 33% ownership. And I have seen them put 15% down and get 15% ownership. So there are really no rules for this. In most cases, "those who have the gold"—the private investors—think they should rule. But it doesn't have to be that way. I have worked with some sponsors that have the hutzpah to be paid very well for their time. Investors who are new to the game will be pleased to just be earning a generous return on their cash and a percentage of the appreciation when the property is sold. They are much less likely to resent the sponsor getting well compensated for their sweat equity.

Remember that without you—the sponsor—the opportunity would not exist. My recommendation is to bring this subject up to the passive investors with a cocky but respectful attitude. Never ask a private investor what percentage they want, but TELL them

Time and Money Saving Tip

Often new sponsors make the mistake of thinking they do not need to have a quote on financing in their executive summary of the deal and tell investors that they are working on this. What these deal managers are thinking, and rightly so, is that they need to have their investors together before they shop for a loan. Yes, lenders would love that too. But I can assure you that you are going to have difficulty raising strong investors if they do not know what the financing looks like. So even if you have to wing this, you are going to have to present some spectacular-looking financing. This is where your high-net-worth investor or proxy comes in. Use them to get prequalified for the best financing possible. Be sure to include the lender's letter of interest showing the terms of the loan and that they have preapproved your deal in your executive summary.

what they will receive for their investment. The trade-off will be if you give them a preferred return: they'll get paid an agreed-upon percentage of their contribution first and you will only get paid if there is enough profit left over.

Of course, this is negotiable. If you are forming a syndication, you have to have the same rules for all investors in the PPM. You cannot decide to give your sister an extra 10% because you love her more.

Just a note: You cannot charge a fee for raising the down payment. That would make you a broker-dealer, and the SEC will require you to be licensed as such.

WHY NON-RECOURSE FINANCING IS THE KEY TO RAISING INVESTORS

Keep in mind that banks love their recourse loans, which allow them to get personal guarantees from the same group of people that you are going after as private investors: those that have high net worth and plenty of cash. In other words, people who have something to lose should the property fail. Most of your wealthy investors are going to run the other way if they ask you if the loan is non-recourse and you say no, or worse, "I don't know what that is." They see a recourse loan as giving the lender carte blanche to go after their residence, their vacation home, their bank accounts, autos, RVs, and even their child's 529 education account should there be a foreclosure. Only their retirement funds are safe.

A non-recourse loan does not require personal guarantees. What is required is that the property be vested in a single-asset entity, such as an LLC. In the event of a foreclosure, the lender can only go after the LLC and not the individuals. For more on non-recourse lending, see Chapter 10.

The goal is to get just a few high-net-worth investors to put in the equity, as opposed to having to find many smaller contributions from lower-net-worth investors that might not care about recourse. The fewer investors you have, the less difficulty you will have. The wealthy ones are less likely to back out. But be sure to attract a few more investors than you need.

To attract the high-net-worth group, you are going to need to tell them right away that you are arranging for non-recourse financing. And then refer them to the financing section in your executive summary where it explains the terms of the loan. Over 80% of the loans we provide at my firm are non-recourse. They are mostly offered by nonbank lenders and start at around a million dollars. The following sections explain the pitfalls to avoid in investor partnerships.

NINE PITFALLS TO AVOID IN INVESTOR PARTNERSHIPS

1. Not Verifying the Financial Strength and Credit of Your Private Investors

Do you want to risk getting to the closing table and finding out your investor doesn't have the funds they said they had? Or finding out when a lender verifies financials down the road that an investor who told you they have plenty of cash to invest or net worth to help qualify for a loan apparently does not. It will not be fun to find a replacement investor at this stage.

For most types of financing, with the exception of hard money, if the deal manager is not financially strong enough to be a key principal (a borrower that has financial strength and is on the loan), some of the investors will have to be. Do not rely on what they tell you. Require that they fill out an *investor qualification form* and attach their personal financial statement, bank or security statement, and credit report. Of course some will not want to disclose this information to you, even though they are going to trust you to invest their money. Then sign a nondisclosure agreement (NDA) with them, which is a confidentiality agreement. If that doesn't work, have them disclose their financial information to your mortgage broker or lender. The bottom line is that you absolutely have to know they have the big bucks they say they do.

2. Allowing a High-Net-Worth Investor to Highjack Your Deal

This actually happens quite often. The investor you thought was going to mentor you, or even a passive investor that is contributing most of the equity because they are investing, slowly and methodically takes control of your deal. It's obvious that they did not want to go through all the work to find a property this good themselves, but that now they want to control it. They might be the type of person who is an expert on everything. You will find them leading the meetings with your other investors and making the major decisions. You become their lackey. You will recognize the traits of this type of investor early on.

You need to demonstrate your authority from the beginning. When you ask for a private investor's opinion, make it clear when they give it to you that you will be weighing it carefully and making a decision.

3. Making Decisions by Consensus

Be sure to acknowledge the opinions of your private investors. But be warned that if you are going to have an equal vote among all of the investors to make most of the important decisions prior to closing the deal, you might be setting your deal up for an implosion. Not all investors are going to want to take the time to get informed on the complexities of the deal. And you can be sure many will have conflicting opinions. At a minimum, making decisions by consensus just takes too much time. Again, as the managing partner it is important for you to put the deal together and make the important decisions.

4. Not Having Enough Investors

If you have just one or two private investors and one drops out, your deal will likely crash. It is better to raise money from more investors than you will likely need. Some will likely change their minds.

5. Doing a Bait and Switch with Your Investors

The number-one reason that private investors drop out is because they thought they were getting one thing at the beginning and toward the end they are offered less. This often happens when you bring on an investor who is contributing a major amount of the equity, and after you bring other investors in wants a larger share than the project can afford. You then have to get everyone else to accept less. Or perhaps you did not base the offering on *actual numbers*, but potential numbers instead, and now that the real numbers are disclosed the property's earnings have been shown to be lower.

6. Offering to Pay Your Investors More Than the Property Can Afford

This is something you really cannot afford to mess up. Be sure to do your projections carefully. If you are repositioning a property, have your attorney state in the contract with investors that they will only receive payments after the property has stabilized at a certain NOI and debt service coverage ratio for your loan for 90 days.

I have had many clients who have purchased distressed properties that were not cash flowing with the intention of repositioning them. They made the mistake of offering their equity investors monthly interest payments that commenced a certain number of months after closing. If the perfect storm hits, this can be a recipe for a financial disaster. In one case the sponsor had to use an equity line of credit on his home to make interest payments to a retired investor when the investment property leased-up slowly and could not afford them.

7. Having Too Much Time Prior to Closing

Ask anyone in my office what my favorite saying is: it is "Time is not your friend on real estate deals." If you have more than 90 days involved after your offer is accepted you have a much higher chance that the deal will crash and burn. This is because there are so many variables in a commercial real estate transaction that can change or go wrong. With enough time, occupancy can drop to where your financing no longer works, a major tenant could move out, a lien could be put on the property, the sellers could change their minds, or a fire or natural disaster could affect the property. I have twice had the buyer or seller die prior to closing.

8. Not Having the Best Legal Advice

Not having the advice from an experienced commercial real estate attorney at the beginning on how to legally structure your partnership with investors can be a time bomb. This is one of the main reasons why commercial deals take longer to close. For a simple LLC—where you and the investors manage the property jointly—a commercial real estate attorney is all that you need. When forming a syndication and creating a PPM, it is best to use a syndication or securities lawyer that can structure a *multiple-layered ownership*. They will make sure that the complex ownership documents of the general partnership representing the deal manager and the limited partnership, and representing the passive investors, are compliant with the Securities and Exchange Commission (SEC) regulations. These two ownership entities will jointly own the LLC that owns the property directly. Yes, this is complex.

9. Not Having Cash Calls in the Operating Agreement

In 2012, my client Matthew purchased a 56-unit apartment complex in Portland, Oregon for $7.6 million. He planned on putting in $1.4 million in cosmetic and constructional repositioning and then raising rents. The property would be a long-term hold for retirement. He brought in three investors to raise the down payment. The property had four buildings on a slope. In November, a building inspector discovered that the foundation of one of the buildings had shifted due to heavy rains. To issue a certificate of occupancy the city required that all the buildings have their foundations reinforced, which added $360,000 to the project. All of Matthew's investors refused to pitch in and there was nothing he could do about it. If he had put in a "cash call" clause into the operating agreement when the LLC was formed, it would have mandated that all investors put in a pro rata share of unexpected expenses if the property ran out of money. For more on *cash calls*, go to Encyclopedia Topic C, Raising Investor Partners.

FORMING A REAL ESTATE SYNDICATION

If you are planning to have one or more passive investors whose only role is to invest money in your deal and get a return on it, the SEC will mandate that you form a syndication. This involves the sponsor, also called the syndicator, taking sole responsibility for all aspects of the deal—most importantly, the responsibility for combining the equity or down payment money from one or more passive investors in exchange for a preferred return on their cash plus a percentage of ownership. The SEC views this transaction as a security. This is because the investors have to trust the syndicator with their money just as they do when they invest in a publicly traded stock.

SEC Regulation D allows the syndicator to raise unlimited cash from accredited investors who are strong financially and up to 35 nonaccredited investors, called *sophisticated investors*, who do not have the required financial strength but have experience.

Why You Should Form a Syndication

Okay, I understand the draw of being a syndicator and using other people's money: the lure of putting the deal together; of having total control over it; of earning fees for acquiring, managing, and selling the property—and of raising money from investors who don't do a thing except write out a check. Yes, they trust you implicitly. After all, the syndication gives you professional clout.

The main benefit of forming a syndication is that it is easier to raise passive investors who are just looking to invest their money in real estate than it is to find active investors who want to run the property with you and be a key principal on the loan. Plus, as the sponsor in a syndication you get to call all the shots and do not have to make decisions based on consensus, which takes so much less time and preserves your sanity.

Another benefit is that syndications have a PPM, which legally spells out the benefits, risks, and returns on the investment. These documents are often glossy brochures these days. They not only detail the investment but sell it. Right away, the investor will know that their investment is regulated by the government and they will feel protected. They will have comfort in knowing that each class of investor is treated the same.

If you have experience owning a similar type and size commercial property and have the confidence to present yourself as an expert to passive investors, then going the syndicated route will likely have many more pluses than minuses for you.

Why You Should Not Form a Syndication

In my lending career, I have worked on over 50 syndicated deals. I have witnessed many first-time sponsors get pushed over the edge with stress when trying to put together a syndication. This is a very expensive and time-consuming process that requires a securities attorney who will charge you from $450 to over $1,000 per hour. This expense does not pencil for deals under $2,000,000.

Do you really want to take on the fiduciary responsibilities that the SEC will require of you if you are new to commercial property investment? Yes, you can be open to liability if one of your partners decides you bungled the deal and did not explain the risk adequately or did not follow the guidelines in the PPM. If the property underperforms, you alone will carry the risk to your reputation in doing future deals.

Most importantly, if this is your first deal, you will already be overwhelmed with finding the right property, doing the due diligence, finding investors, and applying for financing.

There is such a simple alternative for the newbie. I highly recommend you avoid the syndicated route and form a simple LLC that owns the property, with partners who take an active role in managing the property with you. To avoid regulation by the SEC, your partners have to be involved in the operation of the property and their responsibilities have to be specified in the operating agreement of the LLC. With this method of ownership, you and your partners are bearing the risks and responsibilities together. You can still be the managing partner and take a much more active role. On your next deal, once you have experience and a track record, it can make sense for you to form a syndication.

Creating a Syndication

As mentioned, you will need to hire a securities attorney, also known as a syndication attorney. They will put together a PPM, which will describe the investment in detail and spell out to investors the risks involved and how each investor type will be compensated. Usually a single-property ownership entity LLC will own the property, which will be co-owned by the sponsor's LLC as *general partner* and by the LLCs of the passive investors as *limited partners*.

Raising Investor Partners

Accredited Investor: *If your investors are not going to be passive investors, then you are going to have to get into bed with the SEC*

As the sponsor, or deal manager, if you need to raise money to purchase a commercial property, you might already be thinking of your Uncle Henry, who is loaded, and likely some other folks that have money. Most of these people will have no interest in running a property with you. They just want to make money on their money. It is easier to attract private investors to raise equity if they are passive investors, which means they have no responsibilities whatsoever in running the property. But then things get complicated, as this arrangement will require a *syndication* (see later in this Topic) with a *private placement memorandum* (see later in this Topic), as required by securities law. The Securities and Exchange Commission (SEC) mandates that these passive investors be accredited investors, unless they have a lot of experience investing in commercial properties. To qualify they have to have a net worth of at least $1 million and a minimum annual income of $200,000 if single and $300,000 if their spouse is included. The value of the accredited investor's residence and any mortgage on it are excluded when computing the net worth. The easiest way to have your investors become accredited investors is to have their CPA or banker write an accredited investor qualification letter that verifies that they meet the qualifications.

Cash Calls: *Better to get an agreement from your investors ahead of time that they will put more cash into the deal when needed*

Oh, no! As sponsor, you are seven months into rehabbing a property and it looks like you are going to be about $45,000 short. You hate to ask your investors to contribute, but fortunately you were smart enough to put a provision for cash calls into the operating agreement of the LLC. In the cash calls clause, the investor members agree to put additional funds into the property if needed. The additional funds may be needed for going over budget on renovations, for unforeseen repairs, or for tenant improvements. When additional funds are contributed, it is best to configure them as a loan to the LLC that owns the property. The loan is then paid back to the investors either from income from operations, or more often, when the property is sold at a profit.

Crowdfunding for Raising

Equity: *If you are still short when raising funds to purchase a property, consider a crowdfunding platform*

So you are having difficulty raising enough money for a down payment on your acquisition from investors. Consider filling in the gap with funds raised from a crowdfunding platform. You can raise money from accredited investors that register with the platform. But be careful. If you choose to go this route, it is best not to make up more than 50% of the equity from crowdfunding. This is because crowdfunding investors will expect an ownership stake in the property based on the percentage of equity they contribute, plus a *preferred return* (see later in this Topic) arrangement, where they'll get paid first. Crowdfunding companies use an Internet platform to connect sponsors and investors, and require a sponsor to contribute a minimum of 10% of the equity from their own funds. Crowdfunding investors get a preferred return, paid first on an investment, which averages 10% annually.

Crowdfunding Platforms

CrowdStreet

PeerStreet

RealtyMogul

Sharestates

LendingHome

RealCrowd

Patch of Land

Time and Money Saving Tip

Cash calls can often create discord among partners. Sometimes one partner cannot come up with their share, forcing the other members to come up with more. To avoid having to use cash calls, create a working capital fund instead. At the beginning, have all members contribute some cash to a working capital fund to be used for unforeseen expenses. Keep this money in a separate savings account and not in the property's operating bank account. When used, these funds should be replenished from the earnings of the property. A good rule of thumb for working capital is to start out with 10% of gross rental income and add 5% of operating expenses to this each year. If you are taking out a mortgage that requires *replacement reserves* (see Encyclopedia Topic H, Financing), you will not need much or any working capital because your lender will be collecting funds monthly to be used toward repairs and replacements.

Raising Investor Partners

Equity Multiple: *Wouldn't it be great if you could tell a potential investor that their cash investment will double over a five-year period from earnings?*

Use an equity multiple to tell a potential investor how much their estimated cash contribution will increase over the time the commercial property is owned. Being able to say that your money is going to double is much stronger than saying that it will earn 8%. An equity multiple greater than 1.0 means that the property is earning more than what was invested. An equity multiple less than 1.0 means that the cash invested is showing a loss. An equity multiple of 2.25 means that for every dollar invested an investor will get an estimated return of $2.25, which represents the original dollar invested plus $1.25. The equity multiple is different from the *internal rate of return (IRR)* (see in Encyclopedia Topic A, Buying) and the *cash on cash return (CCR)* (see in Encyclopedia Topic A, Buying) in that it is not in the form of annual percentage of money earned on the cash invested. Instead it tells the investor estimated actual cash they will get back on their investment.

How to calculate the equity multiple: If you are planning on owning the subject property for five years, then estimate the net profit after debt service for each year using a five-year pro forma. Add to this the dollar value of property appreciation when it is sold at a profit in five years. This will be the total profit distributed. Take the total profit distributed to investors and divide this by the total cash equity invested.

$$\frac{\text{Total profit distributed}}{\text{Total cash invested}} = \text{Equity multiple}$$

What is a good equity multiple? 2.0 or more is considered good. But this really depends on how long you plan on keeping the property. For example, if you estimate a 2.0 equity multiple based on rehabbing the property, re-tenanting it, and then selling it for 20% more than you invested in two years (thus doubling the investment), this is really good. However, if you own the property for 10 years and after selling it the equity multiple is projected to be at 2.0, it's not terrible, but certainly not a windfall.

Executive Summary for Raising Investors: *This is your sales pitch to investors*

This report is your sales pitch to potential investors. It is a summary that should mostly highlight the positive aspects of your commercial property investment opportunity but also mention the risks. The report should include the following:

1. **Summary of the Transaction:** With so many people having experienced a huge drop in the value of their stock market portfolios during the coronavirus recession, you want to start out by drawing them in with an estimate of what they will earn on their cash investment. Highlight what they should expect to earn from operations and appreciation when the property is sold. This is the *internal rate of return* (see Encyclopedia Topic A, Buying). Also mention the tax shelter all the partners will share from annual depreciation. Then provide an enticing summary description of the property, why it is in a good location, and then add a strong

simplified narrative of what you plan on doing to the property to add value. Then describe what your *exit strategy* will be. This is one of the most important items, as it tells the investor when they will get their money back plus profit. Talk about what you are buying the property for, how much you will be putting into it, and what you will sell it for after your holding period. A four or five year period is a good amount of time to add substantial appreciation to the property and realize the financial returns of your value-add improvements. If you are offering a *preferred return*, mention what that will be. Highlight what they should expect to earn from operations and from appreciation combined when the property sells. If there are any problems with the property—management is a likely one—you are going to talk about how you are going to solve them.

2. **Financial Summary:** The next section is going to be a financial synopsis. Include a current roll and show a pro forma rent roll showing where rents will be when you have repositioned the property. Show the previous year's actual income and expense statement and your five-year pro forma statement showing the property improving over time. You are going to conclude with a summary of the financial strengths of the investment.

3. **Risks:** Mention what the perceived risks of the investment are and how they can be mitigated. If you are buying during a recession talk about what you will do to make the property *recession proof* (see Encyclopedia Topic A, Buying) for the future. Another risk is slower than anticipated lease-up. Talk about how you will be working with the property manager to offer *rental* concessions to remedy this.

4. **Demographic and Market Information:** Ask your buyer's real estate broker to pull up a CoStar or REIS report showing demographic and market information on the property location.

5. **Team Bios:** If you do not have much experience, put your bio last. Include bios for your buyer's real estate broker, your commercial real estate or securities attorney, your property management company, and your CPA.

Exit Strategy: *Your investors need to know how long you plan to hold the property based on financial objectives*

The exit strategy is simply your short- or long-term plan for holding the property prior to selling it. It is essential when attracting investors to be able to show them how this strategy maximizes the return on their investment. Your exit strategy will dictate what type of investor you need to attract. Some investors are looking for a long-term hold of 10 years or more for income. Others want a short-term hold—to get their money back within 3 years after reaping the benefits from the value adds implemented. For the long-term investor it could make sense to sell the property when a mortgage matures in 10 years and prepayment penalties expire. Also at this time the property might need many more repairs. Why not pass these on to the next buyer as a value-add opportunity?

Be sure to have a plan B for disposing of the property should the economy change or if there are major occupancy or tenant changes.

Expenses Incurred by the Sponsor: *It is so much better if you don't have to ask your investors to come up with these expenses*

What kind of image will you have as the manager of your deal if you have to nickel-and-dime your investors at the beginning? Investors, lenders, and even joint venture partners are going to be put off if the *sponsor* (later in this Topic) appears to be broke and wants to use 100% other people's money to get the deal started. They expect you to contribute a minimum of 10% of the down payment. Just out of the gate, as sponsor you really need to have the money for the earnest money deposit, third-party due diligence reports (such as the market study), the property condition report, and even the deposit required to start a loan. Don't worry, you can get credited on these funds toward your share of the down payment. Your investors are not going to want to contribute their funds until due diligence is completed and contingencies are met and financing is approved. If the deal does not close, you will most likely get the earnest money back, but everything else will be lost.

Joint Venture Institutional Capital Partner: *Watch out for these guys, as they can be greedy*

If you have a solid development or repositioning project in a great location and are having difficulty raising investors or just don't want to bother doing it, your last resort may be to bring on a joint venture institutional partner. Their minimum deal size usually starts at $10,000,000–20,000,000. Be careful, as they are experts at having the contract and the profits heavily weighted in their favor. They will require you to have a minimum of 10% of the equity (that is, 10% of the down payment). If you are contributing less than 20%, they will most likely insist on being the managing partner; that is, being in charge on the deal. On the positive side, it won't be a problem if you are not financially strong enough to qualify for financing. And you can count on them being well connected with top lenders, relieving you of the time involved with this piece.

If the joint venture capital partner is putting in 70–90% of the down payment, they will view themselves as owning 70–90% of the project. The largest venture capital firms have a lot of their own money to invest. But most operate from funds they have raised from banks, insurance companies, pension funds, and institutional investors. These funds have rigid rate of return requirements and expectations to get the funds back in a set amount of time. This results in a preference for shorter holding periods of three years or less. They also want preferred returns on their cash invested to be 10% or more. They will not likely want you to see a dime of the profits until they get all of their equity back plus their preferred return. How much are they open to negotiation? If your deal is in their wheelhouse and they love the location, you can fight with them for a better deal and likely get it. Be sure you earn a hefty portion of the *sponsor promote* (see later in this Topic)—at least 25% or more. If this is a development project and you are going to be the lead developer, try for three quarters of the development fee and do not accept less than half.

Investor Qualification Form: *Don't be shy about prequalifying your investors*

Yes, having your investors fill out this form is a must. It will be quite uncomfortable when the time comes for your investor to contribute their funds if they say to you, "Well, I thought I had the money." This form will give you most of the information needed to know your investor's net worth, liquidity, credit scores, and commercial real estate ownership experience. And don't be shy about asking them to attach their personal financial statements, schedules of real estate owned, and a copy of their bank or securities statements showing proof of funds being contributed. This info has a dual purpose: (1) to verify that your investor has the financial wherewithal to invest, and (2) to document your investor's financial strength when you apply for financing. You will also be asking the investor if they are willing to be a key principal on the loan. As long as the loan is *non-recourse* (see Encyclopedia Topic H, Financing) and they do not have to personally guarantee it, they might be willing.

If your investors are hesitant to provide this personal financial information, then tell them you are willing to sign a confidentiality agreement. If that does not do it, then they will likely supply their financials to a commercial mortgage broker, who can screen the investors for you. The bottom line here is that you cannot afford to just take someone's word that they have the money. They could be planning to borrow it from a family member who does not come up with it.

> **Time and Money Saving Tip**
>
> It is always best to be very well prepared when approaching JV capital firms that specialize in your type of commercial property. Your first step is to get them to drool over the deal. To get an upper hand you will need to contribute 25% or more of the equity. Don't give them a chance to tell you what the terms are, as if they are written in stone. It's better for you to start by telling them what terms you are offering them. Remember that they need deals like yours or they would not be talking to you. Most importantly, the majority of the profit on this deal will come from selling the property after the property is built and occupied or when your value-add strategies are put into place. So you want to make sure you get the largest share of the property as you can.

Letter of Intent to Invest: *Having your investors put in writing the amount they are verbally committing to invest will make it much more likely they will follow through*

A letter of intent to invest is a non-legally-binding agreement used by a sponsor when raising investors to purchase a commercial property. The letter has a dual purpose: (1) to have investors put their verbal commitment to invest in writing, and (2) to have the sponsor put in writing the expected returns the investor will earn.

Contents of a Letter of Intent to Invest

Investor's name

Amount to be invested

Sponsor's fee

Sponsor's name

Expected holding period

Investor's expected returns

Property address

Amount to be financed

Investor's percentage of ownership

Purchase price

Time period for purchase

Sponsor's percentage of ownership

Pari Passu (in Commercial Real Estate Partnerships): *This is a mouthful, but if you are doing a syndicated transaction, you need to know what pari passu means*

"Pari passu" means an equal distribution to all partner classes, or when the project manager or sponsor earns exactly the same amount as coinvestors under the same distribution structure. This term is used frequently in syndicated commercial real estate partnerships when deciding how profits will be divided among different classes of partners. For example, in a syndicated partnership the Class A investors may get a preferred return of 8% on their investment before Class B investors receive a dime. After that, any excess profits may be distributed pari passu, or equally, to both classes based on the pro rata share of the property that each investor owns.

Time and Money Saving Tip

If you are the sponsor, just remember that you hold the reins. If you can start out by structuring all earnings in a pari passu distribution, the profits will be distributed to you in the same way and at the same time as your private investors. If you have enthusiastic, inexperienced investors, try staying away from the preferred returns that experienced and institutional investors and joint venture capitalists demand. When you give them a preferred return, they get paid first. If there is any profit left over, you as the sponsor get paid. On projects that require substantial repositioning, such as rehabbing the property, it is possible that if your investors get a preferred return, you will not see a dime of earnings until the property sells many years later.

Peer-to-Peer Funding for Gap Equity Raising: *Just a little bit short on the down payment? This can fill the gap fast*

As the sponsor, if you are short on funds for the earnest money deposit or other project costs, you can bring in a little cash using peer-to-peer funding. These loans are unsecured and go up to $50,000. These online lending sources are called peer to peer because the lenders get their funds from a multitude of investors that invest small amounts. On the downside, expect a loan fee of one to six points. Interest rates are high and based on your credit score. These funds can also be used in the case of an emergency if you are short of funds at the closing table.

Peer-to-Peer Lenders

Prosper

Peerform

LendingClub

StreetShares

Upstart

Preferred Equity: *This is like a second mortgage if you need higher leverage*

As a commercial real estate project sponsor you may find it difficult to obtain the loan amount you need. You might need 80% financing and are only able to qualify for 70%. A preferred equity investor can add their funds to your down payment to fill the gap. This is not a loan. The preferred equity investor will be an owner of the LLC or limited partnership (LP) that owns the property. They will hold a higher position in the capital stack and get paid first from profits, before the sponsor, who has common equity, gets paid. The capital stack has senior debt at the top followed by preferred equity, followed by common equity. Preferred equity investors expect high returns for the risk they are taking—typically 12–16%.

With the exception of bridge lenders, most first-position lenders will not allow secondary financing and will only allow a soft preferred equity structure (see below). A plus is that senior debt loan documents will not allow the preferred equity investor to file a lawsuit against you to recover their investment should the property fail. In fact, the preferred equity investor's only recourse is to have you removed as the managing partner and put themselves or someone else in your place.

Soft Preferred Equity Structure: This is much more acceptable to your first-position mortgage lender because the preferred equity investor will be limited by the following: (1) They cannot require interest payments if the debt service coverage ratio is too low, (2) They cannot raise the interest rate if there is a default, and (3) They cannot have a set maturity date for the repayment of the investment.

Hard Preferred Equity Structure: It is unlikely that you can get your first-position mortgage lender to allow this structure, unless they are a hard money lender. They will view it as a second-position mortgage. This arrangement is structured very much like a loan, with interest-only payments paid monthly by the sponsor, even if the property cannot afford it. There will be a maturity date by which the original investment is to be repaid, and the interest rate is sure to go up in case of default. A hard preferred equity structure is viewed by the first-position mortgage lender very much like a loan. The lender will require that the property have sufficient net operating income to hit the minimum debt service coverage ratio after paying the mortgage and the preferred equity payments.

Preferred Return: *Offering to pay your investors a preferred return should grab their attention*

Offering investors a preferred return is one of the best ways you as a sponsor can attract them, especially if you are planning on contributing less than 20% of the equity and the investors will be putting in 80% or more. A preferred return means that they will get paid first from the operations of the property, cash-out refinancing, or sale of the property. They will be paid before the sponsor, who is a subordinate investor, gets paid anything. This shows the investor that you have a lot of confidence in the project's success. The downside is that it puts you at risk of not realizing any income for your hard work until after your partners have been paid their preferred return. This could be years.

If you are only going to contribute 10–20% of the equity but want to own 25% or more of the project, offering a preferred return to your investors who are contributing most of the down payment can be a good trade-off for your larger share. But be cautious about what you offer. During times that the stock market performs well you will need to offer your investors a preferred return of 8% or more to really get their interest. A 10% preferred return seems to attract a huge amount more interest. If the stock market has been tanking, 6% can be acceptable. But be sure to do your pro forma carefully to make sure the property can afford this. Also, pay your investors monthly or quarterly so you do not get behind. Remember that any time the property cannot afford to pay this preferred return, the interest will compound, meaning that you will be getting into increasing debt to your investors.

A Preferred Return Disaster Story

In 2011 my client Nate was fortunate to find a value-add redevelopment opportunity right in his back yard in Madison, Wisconsin, where he had gone to school. He knew the University of Wisconsin was experiencing a shortage of student housing. There was a 108-room hotel 1.6 miles from campus for sale for $11.6 million. The rooms were all suites and Nate's idea was to change them into efficiency apartments for students. He needed to put in about $810,000 to upgrade all the units. With closing costs, the total project cost would be $12,658,000.

Nate brought in his wife's parents and four other investors to raise the down payment. We did an 80% of cost bridge loan. All the investors were promised a 14% preferred return on their money from the day they contributed it. We closed in October. Nate was planning on completing the project in June of the following year, which allowed plenty of time to lease it before students arrived in September. Unfortunately, due to bad weather the project was delayed for several

(continued)

Raising Investor Partners

(*continued*)

months, and then it took much longer than expected to complete. Also, Nate had hired a mom-and-pop management company that did not prelease the units early enough. The result was that when the certificate of occupancy was issued in September, the property was only 44% leased. By that time most students had already found a place to live. Nate had missed the school year and would have to wait a full year before the property would hit market occupancy and be financially stable. The greatest problem for Nate was the 14% preferred return provision, which had to be paid to his investors before he got paid. The interest on it compounded for 23 months before the property generated a profit from operations to start paying it down. Nate put thousands of hours into the project without seeing a dime of earnings until the property was sold five years later.

Private Investors: *There are many people with capital sitting in the bank or stockmarket who would love to diversify into your commercial property investment*

Private investors are individual investors, not joint venture capitalists, crowd-funding platforms, or hard money lenders. Private investors invest money into your deal from their savings, their home equity, or their retirement accounts. The best ones are actually the inexperienced ones who are investing in commercial real estate for the first time. This is because you can offer them a simple return (not a preferred return) on their money that will be attractive. They are not as greedy about ownership share as experienced investors are. With private investors, you can take a larger percentage of ownership than the percentage of the down payment you contributed. The experienced investors will want a higher preferred return and a percentage of ownership of the property equal to the percentage of equity they contributed or more. They will try to keep your percentage of ownership down to the percentage of equity you contributed.

Time and Money Saving Tip

Finding private investors to contribute equity to your deal can be daunting. This approach has worked very well for many of my deal sponsor clients: Offer your friends and all the real estate professionals you know a commission of 5% of the money raised for your deal from investors they find. Talk to all of the real estate brokers, mortgage brokers, and property managers you can. By receiving 5%, these professionals can afford to split the commission with others if needed. Be sure to draw up a contract that states that the commission will be earned only after the money has been raised, put into an escrow account, and the deal has closed. You will need to check with the state the real estate brokers are licensed in to confirm that it is legal for them to earn commissions from raising investors.

Private Placement Memorandum (PPM): *This tells your passive investors everything they need to know about the deal, how they will get paid, and the risks involved*

If you are raising passive investors you will need to do a syndicated transaction, which will require a private placement memorandum (PPM). What I love about PPMs is that they tell you everything you need to know about how a deal is structured; you need not have an executive summary for the deal. These days PPMs are brochures that are designed to sell your deal to investors, with every detail they need to know about the property. PPMs also protect you by ensuring that you are complying with Securities and Exchange Commission (SEC) rules. Most importantly, a PPM describes the financial objectives of the deal and how each class of partner will be paid, along with the benefits of investing in the property, all the terms of the deal, and the risks associated with the investment.

Distributions of income have to be made using the same formula for each individual in a particular investor class. As the deal sponsor, you cannot favor one investor over another through preferential returns. Although it is possible for you to use a template and put together your own PPM, it is a very technical document and using a syndication attorney is highly advised. This will greatly decrease the possibility of not following SEC rules and limit your liability should one of your investors decide to file a lawsuit against you in the future.

What Is in a Private Placement Memorandum?

Offering summary

Risk factors

Subscription agreement

Team member bios

Property description

Local market data

Sources and uses of funds

Financing proposal

Operating agreement

The offering

Cash flow projections

Conflicts of interest

Eligible investor criteria

Appraisal or market study (optional)

Real Estate Investment Company and Branding: *Be sure to offer your deals from your own real estate investment company*

When attracting investors and talking to listing brokers about your deal, wouldn't it be better to say, "This is Susie Stanford from Stanford Investments" instead of

"This is Susie Stanford"? My clients who have formed real estate investment companies have been much more successful. This is simply a company that either owns real estate, raises equity from investors to own real estate, or both. It is easy to set up, inexpensive, and you do not need an attorney; you can just set up an LLC with your state. Starting out, there are no regulatory requirements. You can talk to investors as much as you like about specific properties. However, if they make a decision to invest as passive investors (investors who are not involved in running the property), you will need to follow SEC rules. If your investors share management duties with you, there are no SEC regulations.

Owning an impressive-sounding company will give you much more clout. Be sure to brand your company. Branding starts out by thinking about how your company is unique and better than the competition. Then create a great logo and add a mission statement that describes your uniqueness. This can be used on your business cards, website, and advertising. Next, put together a company website that has a synopsis of the properties you have owned or worked on. Most importantly, show the properties you are offering investment opportunities on, along with summaries about them. Be sure to have bios on yourself and your professional team members on the site too. If you include educational articles, forms, and worksheets for evaluating properties you can send people to your website to retrieve them.

Securities Attorney: *Don't leave home without one if you are forming a syndication*

As the sponsor, if you are planning to raise passive investors and form a syndication, you will need to engage a securities attorney, also known as a syndication attorney, to draft the documents. These documents will include the *private placement memorandum* (see earlier in this Topic) required for a syndicated partnership. The SEC regulates these partnerships. Sure, you can find templates online or see if your real estate attorney can pull off drawing up a PPM. But each deal is unique and has different moving parts. How will you know for sure that you are covering all of the disclosures required to be compliant with SEC regulations? A securities attorney will make sure that you, the sponsor, who is now called the "syndicator," and your investors are protected legally.

Securities attorneys are some of the most expensive, with partners charging between $750 and $1,100 per hour and associates charging $450 to $650 per hour. Securities attorneys do not handle anything related to title work or closing the transaction. You have to hire a local commercial real estate attorney for that.

Self-Directed IRA Investment in Commercial Property: *By investing your IRA in commercial real estate, it will have two sources of income*

Did you know that you or your investors can convert an IRA into a self-directed IRA to invest in commercial real estate? Your IRA will own the real estate in an IRA LLC, instead of you personally. It doesn't get much better than this—your retirement will not only be earning money from the profit from operating the property, but from appreciation as well. If you do not have enough in your IRA to purchase a property outright, you will have to get a *non-recourse loan* (see Encyclopedia Topic A, Financing) for the balance. Non-recourse loans are a must because they do not require a personal guarantee. This means the lender cannot go after you personally. This is what makes it possible for you to invest your IRA in real estate if you have a loan. These loans only go up to a maximum of 55% loan to value. Just as with a regular IRA, you will not be able to take any income from the property without being penalized until you reach retirement age. If you use a Roth IRA, it will have been funded with money that you were already taxed on—so you can take a distribution from the property at any time.

Sophisticated Investor: *If you are forming a syndication, consider asking your accountant or real estate broker to invest with you as a sophisticated investor*

If you are forming a syndication with passive investors and cannot find enough high-net-worth individuals to become accredited investors as required by the SEC, consider asking your CPA, mortgage broker, real estate broker, or attorney to invest. They can likely qualify as sophisticated investors. Most passive investors are *accredited investors* (see earlier in this Topic) who have enough net worth and cash to qualify. For those that do not, the only other option is to be a sophisticated investor. To qualify, you have to have extensive knowledge and experience in finance and business that qualifies you to understand the financial risks of investing in commercial real estate.

Sponsor of a Commercial Real Estate Investment: *This is your deal, so own it*

I don't know any other way to say this, but most sponsors of commercial property deals, if they are not exceptional multitaskers, are going to be in over their head. The sponsor is responsible for finding the property, negotiating the offer, doing all the due diligence, negotiating with the seller about repairs, attracting investors, applying for financing, overseeing the management of the property, and financial reporting to partners and lenders. And let's not forget disbursing profits to partners and requesting money from them for expensive repairs. Eventually it is their job to refinance the property or sell it. In most cases, the sponsor is the managing partner and signs the purchase agreement, loan documents, leases, and contracts. Whew, that's a lot!

Two Important Tips for Sponsors
1. *Take ownership of the deal.* I know I already mentioned this in Chapter 4, but it is so common, I'm going to hit you over the head with it again. Don't let a high-net-worth investor with more experience than you hijack your deal. We are talking about them calling the shots. This especially happens when that investor is needed as a major key principal on the loan. You don't want two artists painting the picture—they would not have this great opportunity to invest if it were not for you! Let them contribute their knowledge, but they do not get to run the show too.
2. *Get paid what you are worth.* Let's face it—as the sponsor, going for a larger ownership stake in the property is the most valuable negotiation you can have with your investors. Most of the profit on the investment will be made from appreciation when the property is sold. Experienced investors will always expect the sponsor to own a pro rata share of the property equal to what they contributed toward the down payment. But the ownership stake is more negotiable than you would think. First-time investors are much more open to the sponsor owning more than a pro

rata share. What about all the time you put into finding the property, negotiating the purchase, and saving the deal from crashing? And then the thousands of hours of work it will take for you to oversee the property over many years. This is your deal! Isn't that worth something? So what if you are only investing 10% of the down payment and they expect you to own 10% of the property. Tell them, "I don't think so." Declare the percentage of ownership you want for yourself at the beginning. Even if you're only putting in 10% of the down payment, just tell your investors you will be retaining 20% ownership; if you've put in less than 10%, then 15%. And don't be shy about charging for your services. Here are five additional ways that sponsors can get paid:

Five Additional Sources of Income for Sponsors

1. **Acquisition Fee:** As the sponsor it is acceptable to charge 0.5–1.0% of the gross rental income for finding the property, finding investors, and putting the deal together. I have seen sponsors charging up to 2.0%.
2. **Asset Management Fee:** This is for overseeing the operations of the property over time and implementing the value-add strategies. This fee is usually 1.0–2.0% of gross monthly rental income. This fee is not usually charged if the sponsor is earning a fee for managing the property.
3. **Management Fee:** If there is not going to be a property management company and the sponsor takes on this job, the typical fee is 3.0–4.0% of gross monthly rental income.
4. **Sponsor Promote:** If the property ends up earning more than projections, the sponsor typically gets 25% of the overage after preferred returns are paid (more on this in the next topic).
5. **Refinancing or Disposition Fee:** For refinancing or selling the property, the sponsor usually charges 1.0% of the loan amount or the purchase price.

Sponsor Promote: *If earnings exceed expectations, the sponsor should get rewarded*

As the sponsor of a commercial real estate deal, you have to love the "sponsor promote" concept. Although this is a reward, you'll have to wait for it. This device entitles the sponsor to a higher portion of the profits once the income of the property exceeds certain thresholds in two circumstances: (1) when sponsors are sharing a pro rata share of the profits pari passu with their investors, and (2) when a *preferred return* (see earlier in this Topic) is given to the

Time and Money Saving Tip

As the sponsor, think about preserving your cash flow. When raising equity, it is a better deal for you if you offer your investors simple instead of compounded interest. Inexperienced investors will often be okay with this. And do not pay anything out until the property income exceeds its break-even ratio (after all monthly expenses and the mortgage payment are made) for 90 days and the property can afford it. Put into your contract with investors that they will receive payments once you investors and the sponsor is not realizing any income from the property until the preferred return is paid (after that it is typical for the sponsors to earn a much larger share of the excess income, called a *waterfall*, as a sponsor promote).

reach a certain break-even ratio and the debt service coverage ratio on your loan gets to a certain level and is sustained for 90 days. If you are doing a fast fix-and-flip, you'll want to defer paying your investors anything until you sell the property.

For example: As the sponsor, you have successfully repositioned a property. After the property has been re-tenanted and the net income has exceeded financial goals, you receive an additional 25% of the excess profit. Yes, you can negotiate more. The remainder is then divided in pro rata shares according to the percentage of ownership.

As the sponsor, be sure to always negotiate a sponsor promote that gets paid quarterly. Be wary of crowdfunding platforms, venture capitalists, and sophisticated investors (highly experienced investors) that hold back on the sponsor being paid the sponsor promote until their preferred return and all of their cash contributions are repaid.

Syndication: *If you are raising passive investors for your deal, you will have to form a syndication.*

A real estate syndication is a group of passive investors who jointly contribute the equity to purchase a property with a sponsor who is putting together the deal. Because the investors are just investing their cash, have no role in overseeing the property, and are trusting that the sponsor makes good decisions, the SEC views this as a security investment, similar to investing in the stock market. A *private placement memorandum* that describes the terms and the risks of the investment is required.

In a real estate syndication, the one who finds the property and manages the acquisition is called the syndicator (also known as the sponsor). The syndicator is responsible for every aspect of putting the deal together, including financing, overseeing operations, and selling the property. As a passive investor you want to make sure the sponsor has some equity in the deal—a minimum of 10% will give them skin in the game. The sponsor will be putting in hundreds, if not thousands, of hours of their time in sweat equity.

A real estate syndication is usually set up with the passive investors owning their share of the property in a limited partnership LLC. The sponsor usually owns their share in a general partnership LLC. Both of these entities jointly own the subject property, which is owned in a single-asset LLC. The sponsor is responsible for disbursing funds first to the limited partners, who are Class A members and who usually get a *preferred return* (see earlier in this Topic). The sponsor is a Class B member and does not typically get paid until Class A members are paid.

Tax Shelter for Investors: *Your investors will be getting a large break on their taxes*

As the sponsor, be sure to sell your investors on the phenomenal tax shelter they will be getting. We are talking about depreciation. A $1,000,000 multifamily property will be depreciated over 27.5 years. This means the partners can each deduct their pro rata share of $32,727 annually (this assumes that the land is worth $100,000, which cannot be depreciated). All other commercial properties are depreciated over 39 years.

Waterfall: *As sponsor you can get a waterfall of excess profits over and over*

This is where being a deal sponsor really gets rewarding. A commercial real estate waterfall is a mechanism that distributes extra profits to the sponsor through a device called the *promote* (see "sponsor promote," earlier in this Topic) that flows repeatedly as financial goals are met or exceeded over time. This mechanism is called a waterfall because each time a net income projection is achieved the sponsor is paid a promote, and then if it overflows again, the sponsor is paid another promote. It is usually structured so that the investors receive a smaller portion of each promote. Waterfalls can have many tiers of hurdles to achieve before they flow, based on *cash on cash return* and *internal rate of return* (see Encyclopedia Topic A, Buying) expectations.

Here is an example: The sponsor prepares a pro forma showing a projection of net profits for each year-end on a five-year hold. That profit, once met for the year, is distributed according to the operating agreement. Once the hurdle of distributing the projected profits is met, the amount of profits above that is the waterfall, of which 25–50% goes to the sponsor and 50–75% goes to the investors. How the waterfall is shared is, of course, negotiable. If the sponsor fails to make the hurdle, then the loss is usually carried over to the next year's hurdle, which may or may not create a waterfall.

Property Ownership Entity

C Corporation: *This type of commercial property ownership is subject to double taxation*

Very large commercial real estate holding companies often prefer to own commercial property in C corporations because profits are taxed at much lower rates. This makes sense if the company's main goal is to buy more property with the profits. Another advantage applies to owners who own 10 or more properties in the corporation. When they are applying for a loan personally, they do not have to submit balance sheets, profit and loss statements, and K-1s for each property. This is because they receive all property income from the corporation as an employee, and that income is summarized on one W-2 wage statement. Another benefit for large real estate companies is that there is no limit to the number of shareholder investors (S corporations are limited to 100). A further benefit is that the personal liability of shareholders is limited to their percentage of investment in a property.

Owning commercial investment properties in a C corp makes absolutely no sense for a smaller investor who owns less than 10 properties. The main downside to C corporations—double taxation—will hit them hard. Corporate earnings are taxed first and then when earnings are distributed to individual owners, are taxed again on their personal returns. Another negative is that corporate losses cannot be passed on to personal returns. They can only be passed on to the corporation the following year. To avoid double taxation, make sure all corporate profits are paid out as salaries to owners and show the corporation as not making a profit.

Delaware LLC: *Why do so many commercial property owners choose to vest their property in a Delaware LLC?*

There are many perks to owning your commercial property in a Delaware LLC. You do not need to live in Delaware and the property does not need to be located there, and an LLC can be set up quickly online for a nominal cost, without an attorney. Why is this so popular? Because doing so provides more benefits than forming an LLC in any other state. Here are the top benefits:

1. **Remaining Anonymous:** Many states require you to disclose the names and addresses of all members of the LLC. That information becomes public record and each partner can be solicited. Worse yet, anyone can identify the extent of your real estate wealth. In Delaware, members' contact information is not required to be

listed on the certificate of registration. Only the IRS will know the identity of the members.

2. **Better Safeguard of Your Personal Liability:** Although all LLCs provide some personal asset protection from creditors or lawsuits, the Delaware LLC Act provides more protection than any other state by strongly protecting the LLC against its members' creditors.

3. **Strong Enforcement of the Operating Agreement:** Let's say that your operating agreement states that certain members have to perform specific duties and that all members have to contribute cash if certain events occur. With a Delaware LLC, this becomes legally enforceable.

4. **A Delaware LLC Can Operate in Any State:** Your property can be located in any state and you only pay state tax and file in the state in which the property is located.

5. **Protection from Lawsuits by Minority Investors:** As long as the manager is not self-dealing (making decisions that only benefit the manager), they are protected from lawsuits from minority investors. This gives the managing partner the ability to take risks that they deem to be safe.

6. **A Separate Court for Dispute Resolution:** Delaware has a separate court, called the Court of Chancery, to efficiently resolve disputes involving the LLC. Cases are resolved quickly. There are no jury trials and judges are highly experienced in real estate and business cases.

Delaware Statutory Trust (DST): This can be a godsend for 1031 exchange investors who are running out of time to find the right replacement property

If you are a deal sponsor: If you are trying to raise investors to purchase a large high-quality commercial property, owning the property in a Delaware Statutory Trust may be the way to go. Some benefits are that you can use 100 or more investors and that the property does not need to be located in Delaware and the names and contact information of the sponsor and all investors is kept secret. The top advantage is being able to attract *1031 exchange* investors who have just sold or are about to sell a property. They can invest the deferred proceeds tax free into owning a pro rata portion of your property as a replacement property. The IRS has given their blessing for DSTs to do just this. Usually investors have to put in a minimum of $100,000, but this is not set in stone. Investors will not own their share as a partner but as an individual owner within the trust. As the sponsor, you become the master tenant and call all the shots. The investors are passive. Another benefit to attracting 1031 exchange investors is that if they are required by the IRS to replace debt, they can meet this requirement as long as the property they are investing in has debt. A plus for these investors is that they do not have to qualify for financing. As the sponsor, you can recoup expenses for the formation of the DST and marketing as well as charge fees for administrating the DST.

For the 1031 Exchange Investor: If you have not been able to identify the right property for your 1031 exchange funds and are running out of time, choosing a high-quality property being offered in a DST could be a blessing and save you a big capital gains tax bill. Also if you have leftover 1031 exchange funds that are taxable after finding a replacement property, consider using them to invest in a DST.

As a Passive Investor: If you do not have 1031 exchange funds to invest, you could also benefit by owning a small piece of a lower-risk large Class A or B institutional-quality commercial property that is being offered in a DST. Annual returns average 5–7%. You will share in the income from operations and appreciation, and also have a share of the depreciation as a tax shelter. Once the property is sold, your annual *internal rate of return* could be 10% or more, as it includes appreciation.

As an investor in a DST, watch out for sponsors who are offering a share of the property to you by raising the acquisition price higher than the amount they are paying for the property. This is done legally, but is not disclosed. Be sure to ask sponsors for a copy of the original purchase and sales contract. If they will not provide this, they have almost certainly marked up the original price.

General Partnership (GP): *Smart sponsors have their general partnerships owned by a corporation*

When passive investors own their share of the property in a limited partnership, the sponsor will own their share of the property with other managing partners in a general partnership agreement. Because there is unlimited liability for general partners, these days, most sponsors have them owned by a corporation, which protects them from being personally liable.

A general partnership can have two or more partner/managers, each of whom can make decisions on behalf of the partnership. General partners are usually the managing partner and sign purchase contracts and closing documents, and take on the role of being key principals on loans (applying for financing and signing the loan documents).

> **Time and Money Saving Tip**
>
> As sponsor, if you own your share of the property in a GP or LLC with other managing partners who each have the right to make major decisions, be sure to own 51% or more of the ownership entity. That way if you cannot come to a consensus decision on major issues, you'll have final say. Fifty-fifty ownership can create deadlocks and stalemates.

Individual Ownership/Sole Proprietorship: *This is fast and easy, but leaves the property owner personally liable*

It is rare these days that investors choose to own commercial property in individual ownership in a sole proprietorship due to having no asset protection. However, there is no faster or easier way to own a property. Income or loss is reported directly on Schedule E of your 1040 federal tax return. But unlike an LLC, LP, or corporation, there is no protection from personal liability in a sole proprietorship. Sole ownership works best for investment property owners that do not have partners and so can call all the shots. A benefit is that in community property states, they can leave the property to anyone they wish in their will.

Joint Venture Agreement: *As sponsor, you can often negotiate a better deal with a joint venture partner*

If you are the sponsor bringing in just one partner and you are contributing little or nothing toward the down payment, you will likely get a better deal by doing a joint venture agreement with them. The main advantage is that there is a lot less red tape, and it is common for you to end up with a larger share of the pie than in standard partnerships, where it's expected that each partner's ownership percentage is based on the same percentage of equity they contributed.

In a JV, there is an operating member who is the *sponsor* (see Encyclopedia Topic C, Raising Investor Partners) that created the deal, and a capital member who is contributing money, a building, or undeveloped land toward the down payment. The capital member usually wants very little responsibility or involvement in the deal. Both parties sign a JV agreement, which states how much equity will be contributed by each, what percentage of ownership each will have, how profits will be distributed, how the property will be managed, what duties each member will have, and what the exit plan is. Each JV partner is liable based on the share of capital they contributed. For asset protection the property is usually owned directly by a single-asset LLC or by a limited partnership (LP).

I have made loans to joint ventures where one party contributed a rundown apartment complex as equity and the other used their expertise and time to rehab and reposition it. Another example is where someone owned a valuable infill lot in Portland but did not have the money or experience to develop it. They did a joint venture with an experienced developer. The down payment for our loan was based solely on the land's value.

Limited Liability Company (LLC): *You are fully protected against liability with this*

The best, easiest, and least expensive way to own a commercial investment property by yourself or with your partners is to form an LLC. An LLC is the most popular commercial property ownership structure in the United States, so I am including the most detail on it. When many partners are involved, it is strongly advised to have a commercial real estate attorney create the LLC document so that all members are protected. An outstanding benefit of an LLC is that individual owners are protected from liability for the property's debts or lawsuits filed against the property. This type of ownership entity is considered a hybrid because it combines the best traits of an S corporation, a partnership, and a sole proprietorship. An LLC can have one owner or many partners. Another advantage of forming an LLC is that income passes through directly to each member's personal taxes, just like a sole proprietorship. Each partner is given a K-1 at tax time, which shows their pro rata share of the property's annual net income

An LLC's operating agreement, or articles of organization, legally identifies the sponsor as the managing partner and the duties of the other members of the LLC, along with their percentage of ownership. It also defines the financial agreement among partners. It is imperative to have an operating agreement that will prevent any misunderstandings among members as to duties and financial agreements. Also, in the event of any litigation between partners, the court will use the operating agreement to uphold the intent of the members.

Essential Items of the LLC Operating Agreement/Articles of Organization

1. **Organizational Structure:** States when the LLC was formed, its term, purpose, who the members are, what the members' duties are, and what percentage of ownership they have.
2. **Management and Decision Making:** States whether the LLC will be managed by one member or by all members, and what each member's duties are. Also states whether decisions will be made by the manager or by consensus of all of the members. Votes can be assigned equally or according to percentage of ownership.
3. **Contributions of Capital:** States how much each member has contributed at the beginning. Also states what the process will be if *cash calls* (see in Encyclopedia Topic C, Raising Investor Partners) for additional contributions in the future are needed.
4. **Distributions of Earnings:** States how the profits will be distributed among members of the LLC. Also states whether they will be distributed monthly or quarterly, and what happens if there are losses. Also should address how profits will be distributed if the property is refinanced or sold.
5. **Changes to Membership:** States what happens to a member's ownership share if they sell their interest, die, get divorced, or become mentally or physically disabled or financially insolvent due to bankruptcy.

Time and Money Saving Tip

If you are bringing in partners who do not want to do much but other than invest their money, but you do not want to go through the expense and red tape of forming a *syndication* (see Encyclopedia Topic C, Raising Investor Partners), which will be regulated by the Securities and Exchange Commission (SEC), here is what you need to do. Form a multipartner LLC. In the operating agreement of the LLC, be sure to identify your partners as co-managers and assign them duties that correspond to their talents. They will have to agree to be involved at a small scale. Make sure you are the managing partner and have final say.

Time and Money Saving Tip

A divorce between partners of a commercial investment property can be worse than a couple divorcing. Be sure in the operating agreement of your partnership ownership entity to specify exactly how and under what terms a partner can exit and sell their share prior to the partnership maturing. Agreeing on how much the exiting partner will receive for their share seems to be the main hot button, so be sure to put the method for calculating this and determining the property value in the operating agreement too. To determine value, be sure to have a third party that does not have a vested interest in the property choose the appraiser.

Property Ownership Entity

6. **Dissolution of the LLC:** States how and when the LLC can be dissolved when the property is sold.
7. **Right of First Purchase:** States how members can buy each other out, and how the property will be valued.
8. **Financial Reporting to Members:** States when this will be done—usually annually.
9. **Involuntary Withdrawal of a Member:** States that a member can be removed in the case of death or becoming physically or mentally disabled.

Limited Partnership (LP): *If you are a passive investor, this is how you will own your share of the property*

A limited partnership has one or more general partners and one or more limited partners. When the sponsor and managing partners own their share of a commercial investment property in a GP, the passive partners, whose only role is to invest money, will own their share as a limited partner. The most attractive benefit of being a limited partner is being free from liability. This does not mean that they cannot lose their original investment should the property fail. It is common for LP agreements to have cash calls where the partners have to provide additional capital under defined circumstances, such as if the property is in need of major repairs. Limited partners are given a rate of return or a preferred rate of return on their investment during the term agreed upon in the LP. Usually the property has to be sold by the general partner when the term expires to return the original investment to the limited partners. At this time, appreciation from the sale of the property is distributed to the limited partners. Income to limited partners is passed through to their individual taxes through K-1s issued by the sponsor or their accountant.

Multiple or Layered Ownership Structure: *Most commercial real estate investment properties that have partnerships owned in layered ownership structures*

In more complex commercial real estate ownership structures, the property can have two or more layers of ownership entities. For example, a shopping mall could be owned directly by an LLC, which is owned jointly by a GP and an LP, as shown below.

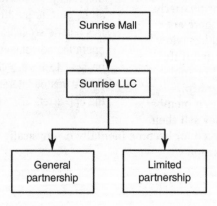

S Corporation: *The corporation is not taxed separately. Income is passed directly to the owners' taxes*

If you own your commercial property in an S corporation you will not be subject to double taxation. S Corps are not taxed at the corporate level. Income or loss is passed on to the owners' personal taxes. Owners are also protected from personal liability, and earnings are not subject to self-employment taxes if they are taken as owner capital draws instead of W-2 wages. An S corporation is a much more complicated ownership structure for owning commercial real estate. S Corps have shareholders and stockholder meetings for which you're required to take minutes. Owning the property in an LLC is much simpler and gives you the same protection against personal liability.

Often developers that specialize in ground-up construction and plan on selling the property upon completion prefer owning the property in an S corporation. This is also the case for someone whose business is fixing and flipping commercial properties. In both of these cases the income is subject to a self-employment tax, which can be eliminated with an S corporation. Rental income is not subject to a self-employment tax.

Time and Money Saving Tip

If you have owned a parcel of land personally for a long time and you have gotten it rezoned to where you can now subdivide it and sell lots, the property can go up three times or more in value. The IRS will consider you to be a real estate dealer when you sell the parcels. All income from appreciation will be taxed as ordinary income and subject to the highest income tax rates. State taxes will apply too. Here is a way to pay the lower capital gains tax rate on the appreciation portion of your profit.

Form an S corporation and sell the land to it with a small amount down and payments that are due annually. Payments will be made from income from selling the lots. You will need to have owned the land privately for at least a year prior to selling it to the S Corp. A good portion of your profit will come from the appreciation, which will be taxed at the lower capital gains rate. The balance of your profit from selling the lots will be from you being a real estate dealer and will be taxed as ordinary income. But the blended tax rate will be a lot lower.

Single Asset Ownership Entity: *Be sure that your commercial investment property is owned in a single-asset ownership entity*

Smart owners of commercial properties practice asset protection. They know to own each of their investment properties in a separate, single-asset ownership entity. This means that that entity owns nothing but the subject property. Smart owners know to never own a property in their name personally, with the exception of their personal residence. This protects them in the event of a lawsuit. If a tenant breaks their hip by tripping on a crack on a walkway at your apartment complex that is owned by a single-asset LLC, they cannot go after you personally or any of your other properties. They can only go after the subject property.

Tenants in Common (TIC): *If you have many partners and own your share in a TIC, you can easily sell your share*

If you plan on owning commercial property with partners and you want the easiest way to sell your share or pass it on to your heirs, consider owning your share of the property in a tenants-in-common structure. What is unique about a TIC is that each partner can sell their interest without the consent of the other partners. In a TIC, the IRS limits the number of partners to 35. Each one owns a percentage of the property and are entitled to the same percentage of the profits. The partners become cotenants in their ownership. A TIC agreement is drawn up to represent the partners. If a tenant wants to sell their percentage of the property in the future, their partners have the first right to buy it.

On the negative side, if there is a need for a cash injection to pay for expensive repairs it is up to each tenant to decide if they want to participate. If they choose not to, the partners that did contribute will be reimbursed upon a refinance or sale of the property from the shares of the partners who did not participate. Another negative is that all tenants are personally liable for the property and for the loan based on their percentage of ownership. Be sure that your TIC partners have good credit and are financially strong enough to be key principals on the loan. Recourse lenders will require all of the partners to sign the loan documents and the personal guarantees. In the case of a default, if one partner is not on the loan, the lender would not be able to foreclose on their share. Many recourse lenders often do not favor TICs. This is because if there is a default, the lender has to go after each partner individually according to their percentage of ownership.

> **Time and Money Saving Tip**
>
> If you are interested in owning a commercial property as tenants in common with your partners, make sure the property is owned directly in an LLC. This will protect the owners from personally being liable for the property. The LLC can then be owned by a TIC structure. Combine this layered ownership structure with non-recourse financing and the LLC, not the individual partners, will be liable for the loan in the case of default.

PART IV

Smart Strategies for Sellers

CHAPTER 5

Hold, Cash-Out Refinance, Sale, or 1031 Exchange?

Max is a retired orthopedic physician client from Bellevue, Washington, who holds his investment properties forever. He never does a cash-out refinance and he never sells to use his equity to buy a larger property that will produce more income. He only buys another commercial property when he has saved the down payment.

I started lending to him 18 years ago when he was in his early 50s. His net worth at that time was a robust $4.5 million. Today his trust owns three apartment buildings; a large, 16-unit suburban office park; and half of the surgery center building where he used to practice medicine. Nineteen years later his net worth has grown by a whopping 270% to $16.6 million. He has been religiously paying his mortgages down, which now total $2.3 million. He plans to leave his real estate empire to his kids mortgage free.

At times, when his mortgages matured, I would try showing him the benefits of cash-out refinancing or selling to buy more property. "No, I'm not interested in that," he would reply. As far as selling, he would say, "That is such a waste of time—all I'd be doing is trading what I know, which is well maintained, for something that who knows what condition it is in or who the tenants are."

To his credit, he had made it through the Great Recession—and will likely make it through the coronavirus recession with just a few scratches. As a conservative investor, he is about as bulletproof as you can get. Max is the extreme definition of a conservative, long-term hold commercial property investor.

My client Conrad has built his net worth through commercial real estate in a different way. He has taken calculated risks energetically yet conservatively in the Bay Area in California. He started with a lot less than Max, but has increased his wealth in roughly the same amount of time by using the funds from cash-out refinancing and selling to buy larger properties that are more financially rewarding. He would say that paying down debt is reverse leveraging and just leaves a ton of money on the table.

When I met Conrad in 2002 at the age of 28, he had a net worth of about $230,000. I lent him the money to buy his first investment property—a fixer-upper 6-plex in Oakland, California—for $380,000. Two years later, after some light remodeling and substantial rent increases, the property appraised for $560,000. He did a cash-out refinance and bought a 12-unit apartment building. In 2006 he sold an 8-plex for $750,000 and used a 1031 exchange to buy a 36-unit.

Conrad weathered the Great Recession because he was not able to leverage above 70% LTV (property values were high) and invested only in multifamily in the Bay Area. Apartments did not drop in value there, and he has great talent for repositioning. Currently he has 94% of his tenants paying the rent during the coronavirus recession because many of them are middle class and have savings. Conrad has repeated the cycle of selling and cash-out refinancing nine more times and today, 18 years after I financed his first commercial property, he is worth $30.8 million. That's an increase of 747%, which blows Max's gain of 270% away.

Conrad's strategy is to do cash-out refinances conservatively over time on properties that are showing growth while divesting himself of properties that have reached their potential, and in both cases leveraging cash intelligently so as to buy more property.

In both of these examples, my clients thrived because they purchased properties in solid economic markets where commercial properties were not hurt much by the Great Recession. It is clear that Max's investment strategy is just about as safe as one could get. If his economic occupancy were to drop below 50% on all of his properties he could still pay all the properties' expenses and mortgages and still run profitably. Conrad, although much more of a risk taker, has made calculated decisions, always with the awareness that another recession could be around the corner. He needs to keep his economic occupancy at closer to 75% to break even. His strategy has been to cash-out refinance only when he finds a dynamite property to buy. He sells when he feels his original property has reached its peak, and then always finds replacement properties at good prices with value-add potential. He would tell you that he follows four basic rules:

1. Don't take cash out of a property to buy another unless the original property can afford it. This means the property with the new larger mortgage is recession-proof, having a *break-even point* of 75% or less and a *DSCR* of 1.30 or higher on the new mortgage.

2. Don't take cash out of a property to buy another unless the property you plan to buy has at least two value-add upsides. These could be getting the property for a great price in a down market, raising rents after cosmetic changes, re-tenanting, or more cash flow after lowering expenses. Also, more depreciation is always an upside

3. Don't take cash out of a property to buy another unless you have a strong exit strategy, such as selling and making a 15–20% profit, which you can leverage into another property

4. When doing a 1031 exchange, it's okay to sell during a flat or down market if you can leverage your equity into a replacement property that gives you much more net income and depreciation than the original property did.

Max likely sleeps a bit better than Conrad. But it is impressive how much more Conrad was able to increase his net worth over about the same amount of time than Max by cash-out refinancing and selling. This chapter goes into detail about the benefits of cash-out refinancing, how to determine whether it's a good time to sell, the benefits of doing a 1031 exchange, and when and how to use a reverse 1031 exchange.

CASH-OUT REFINANCING TO PURCHASE MORE INVESTMENT PROPERTY

Who could argue that it is smart to use the equity that is locked in your commercial property to buy more property through a cash-out refinance? If you have 40% or more equity in your commercial property, you could be a candidate to cash-out refinance and buy another property. The catch is that your existing property has to be able to cash flow the larger loan. You can do this over and over and it will never be a taxable event. But as mentioned earlier, you need to be careful to not over-leverage the original property by putting a mortgage on it that raises the break-even ratio to above 75%, a level that will make it less recession-proof.

Keep in mind that most banks do not like doing cash-out refinances. They would much prefer that you keep more equity in your properties. They just do not trust what you might be doing with all that cash out. It's almost like they think you are going to Las Vegas with it. Yes, you've told them that you are buying this great investment property with an amazing upside. But that just creates uncertainty and banks hate uncertainties. They do not know that you will not run the property into the ground. What stresses them out even more is that you are putting a financial burden on the existing property by increasing the mortgage. Don't worry—Fannie

Mae, Freddie Mac, commercial mortgage-backed security (CMBS) loans, and private lenders are okay about cash-out refinances for any reason if the DSCR is 1.30 or above

When Is Cash-Out Refinancing the Best Option?

1. *The income, appreciation, and depreciation from two properties are better than those from one replacement property.* The benefit of cash-out refinancing versus selling is that you get to have your cake and eat it too by keeping the original property. Now you have two properties earning income and appreciating, and you're saving money on taxes from depreciation. It is unlikely that you can sell the original property and find a replacement property that will give you more appreciation than owning two properties. But you might not have more annual net income after debt service if the cash-out refinance lowers your profit too much on the original property. Be sure to do an analysis on this.

2. *You'll have more tax savings from the depreciation of two properties.* Unless you are close to depreciating the original property out, keeping the depreciation on the original property plus the depreciation on the new property with a low down payment from a cash-out refinance will create much larger income tax savings.

3. *You don't want to even think about tax consequences.* Over the many years that your property goes up in value you can continually refinance and pull cash out to buy more property and still keep the appreciation and depreciation benefits that the original property provides. Whenever you sell a property, you can be faced with paying capital gains taxes on the profit. Sure, you can do a 1031 exchange and can put the tax bill off almost indefinitely, but about 10% of these exchanges fail. This is often because the investor has targeted the wrong property or is not able to close on time.

4. *Economic times are bad.* If you sell your commercial property in a bad economy for a 9% cap rate you are likely leaving money on the table. In two or three years cap rates might be at 7% and the property will be worth a lot more. In this situation, your income and net worth will likely grow more by buying a second property at a bargain from the proceeds of a cash-out refinance.

Time and Money Saving Tip

When cash-out refinancing to buy another investment property, find a loan that has the lowest rate plus two years or more of interest-only payments. The interest-only payments will lower your debt service substantially and thus lower the property's break-even ratio. Your goal is to increase rents enough so that after the interest-only period is up the property is again recession proof.

Four Crucial Mistakes to Avoid When Buying Another Property Through a Cash-Out Refinance

1. *You don't build a safety margin into your loans.* Make sure your cash-out refinance loan and the loan on the new property is at a 1.30 debt service coverage ratio (DSCR) or higher. This means that for every dollar of loan payment you make after paying all the expenses on the property, you have an extra 30 cents left over for profit.

$$\text{DSCR} = \frac{\text{Annual net operating income}}{\text{Annual loan payments}}$$

   This will give you a safety net should there be a recession or a major tenant rollover event.

2. *You don't have a long-term fixed rate.* Unless you are fixing and flipping with a short-term loan, be sure to lock in a low interest rate for five years or longer on both loans. This will be your insurance policy. You want enough time to raise rents and lower expenses before your interest rate goes up due to a rate adjustment or loan maturity.

3. *Your break-even ratio is 75% or lower.* The break-even ratio is the minimum occupancy the property has to have to pay all expenses and the mortgage on the property. It's best to keep this at 75% or lower on both properties. This will give you a safety margin, and help recession-proof your investments.

4. *Rents are now lower than market in each location.* Make sure there is a strong upside on both properties: rents can be raised further, expenses can be lowered, or the property is in a superior location.

IS THIS A GOOD TIME TO SELL YOUR COMMERCIAL PROPERTY?

So a real estate broker has shown you comparable sales, has reviewed your property's financials, and has told you that he can get you a killer price right now. You are convinced this is the best time to sell. But think about it: another investor, who has likely reviewed comparable sales plus your property's financials, has come to the conclusion that this is the best time to buy your property. How can you both be right?

This is evidence that determining the best time to sell is just as much an intuitive process as an analytical one. The rule of thumb is to sell when values are at their peak. But how can you possibly know that they are not going to go higher?

Conversely, it makes sense to hold until better times when values are low. When cap rates hit historical lows and the market value is just too good to resist selling, you might wonder why someone would pay so much for your property. You certainly would not pay that much. Often buyers see value-add opportunities that you have likely not thought about. Also, there can be a herd mentality in buyers when the same real estate professionals that convinced you that this is the best time to sell have convinced them that this is the best time to buy—that commercial property values are going to keep skyrocketing.

An interesting fact is that when interest rates rise significantly, cap rates rise and property values become stagnant or fall. This is primarily due to buyers not qualifying to borrow as much due to higher interest rates. They either have to put more down or get the property for a better price. With multitudes opting to get a better price, the market is affected with a downward trend.

The flip side of this is most sellers become buyers. If you are selling when prices are hitting historical highs, can you find a replacement property that is better than what you are selling? More likely, you will just be trading like for like. Here's what you can do to prevent this: Determine again who you are as a buyer. What are your main objectives? Are you looking to increase your income over time? Lowering your taxes by finding a property that has more depreciation? Are you looking for a lifestyle change, so you need to find a replacement property that is in better condition and requires less management? Do you want to buy a net lease property where you have no headaches whatsoever? Does it excite you to find a property to improve? Do you want to take on a rehab project or perhaps just find a retail property where you can add value by changing tenants? Or do you just want to find a property out of state, where commercial properties are less expensive and produce more income?

Best Reasons to Sell

1. *You are offered a great price.* Maybe you were not planning to sell but were offered an above-market price. If you own a large Class A or B property, institutional investors, or REITs (real estate investment trusts), which are looking for properties in good markets with strong historical incomes, will often pay more. They are much less concerned with return on investment than with investing money that's just sitting there. Investors that have accumulated a lot of appreciation on a property over time and want to do a 1031 exchange to purchase your property can also afford to pay more for your property. Of course, if you are offered a great price, you can do a 1031 exchange on a larger property yourself without paying any immediate capital gains taxes, receiving the benefit of more income and depreciation.

2. *Cap rates are at a record low.* If the economy is strong and cap rates are at a record low, creating the most favorable seller's market in a long time, it may be time to sell. It also may be time to sell if there is high demand for your property type in the market. Remember that the economy always goes in cycles of times that are good, mediocre, and bad.

3. *Major tenants have renewed long-term leases.* This not only increases the value of your property, but also makes it much more advantageous for the buyer to pay more for the property. Not only will they have a more secure long-term income, but it will make it easier to get a loan. This is because there is low tenant rollover risk.

4. *Your value adds are complete.* It may be time to sell if there is just nothing more you can do to improve the property or the net income in the immediate future.

5. *There is a value-add opportunity for the buyer.* If you have just not had the time, money, or energy to make your property all that it can be, this can make the property very attractive to a buyer. Most buyers are the most excited when they can use their ingenuity to add value to a property they are buying. Yes, sometimes you can get more for a property than it is worth by selling what has immense value but does not cost you anything—the opportunity to add value.

6. *The property is stressing you out.* If a property never stops demanding attention, you might need to sell it and buy something that has close to zero headaches, such as a triple-net-lease property.

7. *You've found a dynamite replacement property.* You might want to sell if you find a replacement property that represents an opportunity you just cannot pass up with an upside that your current property just does not have.

8. *You need more depreciation.* If you need to reduce your income tax bill, you may want to sell and purchase a larger property—the larger the property or purchase price, the larger the depreciation. Or perhaps you have owned the property for a long time and are soon going to have depreciated it out.

Hold or Sell Analysis

Doing an analysis to determine if you should keep or sell your existing commercial property can be even more rigorous than analyzing a property you are interested in buying. It is likely far more enticing to delve into finding a replacement property. To start, you will need to create one 3- to 10-year pro forma for your existing property and one for the replacement property to analyze the potential income of each. Your goal is to determine which has the best *internal rate of return* (*IRR*). The IRR estimates what a property will be earning over time in net income and appreciation combined.

To do a buy or sell analysis, you will need to have the current rent roll and trailing 12-month income and expense report for each property. Whichever property has the highest annual IRR is the best one to choose. Follow these three steps:

1. *Determine your investment base.* Figure out the amount of equity you have in your existing property today. Take what you think you can sell it for and subtract your mortgage. This number is your investment base. It is also the maximum amount you will be investing in the property you want to purchase. Don't forget to add in estimated closing costs to this calculation.
2. *Decide on a holding period.* Decide how long you will hold the properties. Be sure to use the same holding time period for both properties.
3. *Calculate your IRR.* You will need to do this for both properties. You are going to fill out a pro forma for the holding time period showing income and expenses. Be sure to show rental income going up over time based on expected rental increases and value-add objectives. Raise expenses 3% annually for inflation. If you are going to lower some expenses, show that too. Lastly, you need to estimate a date when you will sell each property and what will it will be worth at that time. Let's say you are doing a five-year pro forma and estimate that both properties will appreciate at 6% per year. To figure out which has the highest IRR you will need to compute five years of net earnings after debt service and add to this the amount of appreciation for each property. This will give you an estimated IRR on both. The higher number wins.

YOU'VE GOT TO LOVE THE 1031 TAX-DEFERRED EXCHANGE

Only in America can you sell your property at a profit and postpone paying the capital gains tax almost indefinitely. Under IRS Code 1031 you can legally do just that. I have seen more of my commercial property clients increase their wealth through repeatedly doing 1031 exchanges than through any other method. What they do is take 100% of their equity, which has grown over time, and buy a larger property with a much higher net operating income (NOI) and opportunity for depreciation. If valued higher, the replacement property will also likely experience greater appreciation when it sells than the original property. So this is a triple whammy. Your wealth is really soaring upwards—propelled by increased net property income, increased appreciation, and more money to invest because of more depreciation, thus lowering your taxes.

There is somewhat of a misunderstanding that doing a 1031 exchange will let you completely avoid paying capital gains tax. It is only supposed to be a method of deferring taxes. Fortunately, there is a catch in the investor's favor. You can do it over and over indefinitely and maybe get away without paying much or any capital gains tax. Eventually the taxes will be due, when you sell a replacement property and do not buy another replacement property with a 1031 exchange. But here's the loophole: upon your death, through what the IRS calls the step-up in basis rule, your heirs will receive a new value basis based on the market value of the property at that time. Your heirs will need to order an appraisal and tell the appraiser that they need it for an estate valuation. In most cases the appraiser will come in with a lower value for the property. It is possible to diminish all the deferred capital gains tax or even have them disappear altogether. A good tax attorney can help greatly with the process.

How a 1031 Exchange Works

1. *You can exchange into any real estate of a like kind.* "Like kind" means that both properties have to be used for investment purposes or in a business. You can take

Time and Money Saving Tip

When you do a 1031 exchange, 100% of the equity from your relinquished property has to go into buying the replacement property.

Let's say that you would like to do a 1031 exchange to avoid paying capital gains taxes at present, but you would also like to take some cash out for another purpose. The IRS will not allow this.

But here is a way to do it. Fortunately, the IRS does not prohibit you from doing a cash-out refinance on the replacement property soon after you buy it with 1031 exchange funds. They also do not stipulate how long you have to wait to do so. You can do this and get as much of your cash out tax free as you want and use it for whatever purpose you want.

Purchase the new replacement property with the proceeds from your 1031 exchange and a temporary loan if you do not have all of the cash you need. Make sure that the loan has no prepayment penalty, or has one with a very short exclusion period. Credit unions make low interest rate commercial loans without prepayment penalties. A more expensive bridge loan can accomplish the same thing. Then soon after closing on the replacement property, do a cash-out refinance perm loan on the replacement property and pay off your temporary loan. This is a legal way to take cash out for another purpose from 1031 exchange funds.

a single-tenant warehouse building that is occupied by your business and exchange it for an apartment building, but you cannot exchange it for a primary residence that you plan to live in. As long as it is real property you can exchange into real property anywhere in the United States. I did try financing a marina once and that did not work. My borrower was selling two office buildings and because the marina was over water and not on land he could not do a 1031 exchange. The IRS would not allow that anymore than it would allow you to sell an industrial building and exchange it into a yacht or an RV.

2. *You have to own the replacement property in the same name as the original property.* So if the property that you were relinquishing was vested in the name Golden State LLC, you have to vest the replacement property in the name Golden State LLC.

3. *You have a set time frame to do the 1031 exchange.* From the date that you sell your relinquished property, you have 45 days to identify up to three replacement properties and up to 180 days to close on the replacement property. The 45-day identification period is difficult in a seller's market. The 180-day period is not usually a problem. The IRS does not make any exceptions to these time frames. If you fail to meet them, the consequence is brutal: you have to pay the capital gains tax. On the positive side, the IRS does not mandate a minimum time that you have to hold the replacement property.

4. *You have to use an exchange agent.* You cannot have the funds from the sale of your relinquished property go to you personally. They have to be deposited with a certified tax-deferred exchange agent, also called an accommodator. Almost all title companies have a 1031 exchange department. The accommodators are intermediaries who know just about everything about doing a 1031 exchange and will guide you through the process. As a backup you should have your commercial real estate attorney oversee the process. You can find a 1031 exchange checklist for the entire process in Encyclopedia Topic E, Selling.

Why 1031 Exchanges Fail

Tim Marshall is a leading expert on the 1031 exchange process. He is the owner of TM 1031 exchange. Located in Pacific Palisades, California, his company specializes in matching 1031 exchange investors with suitable quality properties nationally. Tim states that 1031 exchanges fail to close for three main reasons:

1. Property owners did not know ahead of time the specific type of property they wanted to exchange into.

2. Especially during a seller's market, the 45-day identification period is just not long enough, and many investors did not get started looking for replacement properties early enough. Sellers should do this well ahead of selling their relinquished property.

3. First-time 1031 investors just fail to study and understand the 1031 exchange process.

I would add another one: when they need financing, investors fail to get deeply involved with the loan process at the beginning and find out too late that they do not qualify for the financing they have applied for. If this does occur, there is often not enough time to apply for and close on another loan.

A 1031 Exchange Disaster Story

My clients Louise and Fred were so excited when they phoned me to say that they had sold their Los Angeles commercial bathroom installation business and its warehouse building to an employee. The real estate alone was sold for $1.45 million. They planned on doing a 1031 exchange and buying an apartment building in Southern California.

During the last month of the closing period they shopped relentlessly and found three possible replacement properties for sale. They planned to identify all three for their exchange. Upon a preliminary review of income and expense statements, only one of these gave them their minimum return of 8% on their investment. They identified that property for their exchange but did not make an offer on it.

Then, 35 days after their property had sold and with only 10 days left in their identification period, they found the perfect replacement property—a recently remodeled 14-unit, 32-bed student-housing property near USC. At 93% occupancy and with a $2.8 million purchase price and an 8% cap rate, this was a cash cow. Their cash on cash return would be an impressive 14%. They quickly identified the property for their exchange, offered full price, and got it under contract.

There was one catch, which really disturbed me. They would have to close in 45 days. The seller had to pay investors back during that time frame and would not budge on it. In the lending world, we like to have a minimum of 75 days to build in a safety net. When a 1031 exchange is involved, 90 days is even better. I recommended that the borrowers go with the other property they had identified. Although it had a much lower return on their investment, the seller would give them 90 days to close if needed. They insisted on buying the student-housing property.

I had already preapproved Louise and Fred for financing and had started analyzing the student housing property financials. I was immediately concerned that the property only had nine months of operating history, with only the last

(continued)

(continued)

four months showing good occupancy. The seller had bought the property without financials 14 months earlier and had emptied it for renovations, so this did make sense. With student housing especially, though, we like to see more historical numbers. This is because the annual economic occupancy is often lower than the physical occupancy showing on the current rent roll.

I felt encouraged when the listing agent told us that all the students were on annual leases guaranteed by their parents. I requested copies of the leases early on, but after three weeks they were not forthcoming. So I requested month-by-month rent rolls going back nine months from when the tenants first started occupying the property. I wanted to see how the property had been filled with tenants. I found that the rent rolls showed a lot more income than the income and expense statements did for that nine-month period. What had happened to that money? So I requested bank statements from the operating account to verify collections. The seller refused to produce these, saying that it was a ridiculous request that they had never heard of a lender making before. I finally told the listing broker that we would have to cancel the financing if they did not produce the leases and the bank statements.

When we got the leases in, I could see why the seller did not want to show them. All of the students had been given heavy rent concessions. To move in, they only had to pay a $400 deposit and the first month's rent. The second month's rent was free. This explained how they had filled the place so quickly and why the income and expense statements showed so little gross rental income.

When I asked the listing agent about this he told me that the seller had started renting the property out in April, which was just too early for students to commit for the next school year, so they needed incentives. But I still wanted to make sure that the tenants listed on the rent roll were paying rent. I threatened again to cancel the loan if we did not get the bank statements. We got them and found that rent collections were poor. Out of 26 students, 7 had never paid another month's rent and were being evicted. This meant that the seller had filled the property with practically anyone he could find so he could sell it fast.

This was not the property my clients thought they were buying. They offered a lower price, which the seller refused to accept. Fred and Louise canceled the sale. The only other property they had identified in their exchange had been sold to someone else. They would now be hit with the substantial tax bill they were trying to avoid in the first place. After 16 years of owning their industrial property, it had gone up a great deal in value when they sold it. They now had to pay capital gains tax on the profit and pay *depreciation recapture tax* on the amount they had sold it for above the depreciated value.

PUTTING THE CART BEFORE THE HORSE: THE 1031 REVERSE EXCHANGE

As mentioned, in a seller's market—or, for that matter, any market—45 days is often just not enough time to identify one good replacement property (let alone three) under the guidelines for a 1031 exchange. What if you could put the cart before the horse and find your replacement property first? You can even do this leisurely if you like. This only gets better—you can wait to put the relinquished property on the market until after your offer has been accepted on the replacement property. You just need to close on the sale of the relinquished property within 180 days after closing on the replacement property. Sound good? Well, can anything this good really be this good?

If only it were that easy, but I'm afraid it is not. What it is, is complicated. But with professionals guiding you through the process, it is likely worth the pain. After all, if the government is going to create such a big loophole they are not going to make it simple.

Here's the catch: before you have sold the property you are relinquishing, you need to find the property you want to exchange into. Well, how are you going to pay for it? You have not sold your property yet. It is unlikely the seller will wait until you find a buyer. So either you have to have the cash sitting there to buy the replacement property or you'll have to take out a loan. Most people choose the second option. The loan will need to cover your down

Time and Money Saving Tip

A common reason that 1031 exchanges fail is because during the due diligence process the buyer finds out just prior to their earnest money going hard that the replacement property has less net operating income than represented, or costly repairs that were not identified by the seller or anticipated by either party.

To protect yourself, follow these two steps:

1. Be sure to specify in the sales contract that the financial due diligence contingency period will not start until you have received all of the property financials. Get a commitment from the seller to supply these within five business days of signing the purchase contract so as to accommodate your 1031 exchange deadlines. If the property is earning less than you anticipated, you can get out early.

2. Most sellers know the physical condition of the property they are selling. Even though the responsibility is on the buyer for finding out anything wrong with the property, ask the seller for help by giving you a list of capital improvements they have made in the last five years and any large items still needing repair or upgrading. Be sure to negotiate who will be paying for these costly items at the beginning of the sales process and spell it out in the sales contract. Keep in mind that it is not standard practice for sellers

payment on the replacement property. Well, the loan cannot be made to you; it has to be made to a third party special-purpose entity, and they have to provide you with a master lease to run it. Yes, as mentioned, the process is complicated and many choose to not start the process because of this. I have simplified and reduced it down to seven steps. Having an experienced commercial real estate attorney oversee and advise you on the process is advised.

Seven-Step 1031 Reverse Exchange Process

1. When filling out the purchase contract for the replacement property, you will need to have it assigned to a third party entity called a "special-purpose entity." A reverse exchange accommodator (you can find them at title companies) will open an LLC that is under their control for this purpose. You are not allowed to own the replacement property directly or through an ownership entity under your control.

2. You will then enter into an agreement with the accommodator to have the special-purpose entity take title to the replacement property at closing.

3. If you cannot fund the purchase of the replacement property yourself, you will have to apply for a temporary cash-out refinance bridge loan against the relinquished property to come up with the down payment to buy the replacement property. Bridge lenders can take additional collateral from other properties you own if needed, and most will be pleased to make a loan to facilitate the reverse 1031 exchange process for you. You ideally want to pull out your equity in the relinquished property, which should be about the same as you would be using if doing a regular 1031 exchange to buy a replacement property. The loan will actually be made to the special-purpose entity, but you will have to qualify for and guarantee the loan if it is recourse. The loan will need to have no prepayment penalties because you will be soon selling the relinquished property.

4. The accommodator prepares a purchase agreement to have the special-purpose entity sell the replacement property to you at closing and a master lease that allows you to control and manage the property prior to that closing.

---

to do this, but you are going to ask them to disclose needed major, expensive repairs at the beginning. Then expedite the property condition report.

If you do not take these two steps, you could find yourself boxed into a corner. The seller will know that you are doing a 1031 exchange and have to close on their property—so should you find that the property has lower income than represented or more repairs than anticipated, you'll have a very weak position to bargain from when you get close to your due diligence periods expiring. When this occurs, in most cases the buyer has to eat these unsavory items because it is less of a hardship to do so than not closing and paying the capital gains taxes.

5. In most cases, you are going to use the bridge loan proceeds that were taken out on the relinquished property as the down payment on the replacement property, so you will need to apply for a permanent loan on the replacement property. Then, 45–60 days later, closing takes place on the replacement property, which is now owned by the special-purpose entity.

6. You have a buyer for the relinquished property and you go through a typical 1031 exchange process with an intermediary accommodator. You sign a contract authorizing the intermediary to use the funds in your exchange account to purchase the replacement property from the special-purpose entity. You have 180 days to close from the date of the closing of the replacement property.

7. You close on the sale of the relinquished property with the funds going to pay off the bridge loan and the balance going to the accommodator, who will set up a closing where the replacement property will be transferred from the special-purpose LLC to you. Any excess funds that go to you that are subject to capital gains should be used to pay down the loan on the replacement property.

Whew! As I said, it's complicated.

CHAPTER 6

Adding Value in the Selling Process

This chapter is all about getting the best price and adding value when selling your commercial property. Discussed are why and how commercial properties increase and decrease in value, a power real estate broker's method of determining the highest sales price, 12 mistakes to avoid when selling, doing value-adding before selling, whether you should do a for sale by owner, whether you should owner-carry, and doing a master lease purchase.

DETERMINING THE MAXIMUM SALES PRICE

Let's start out by looking at six reasons why commercial property values go up.

First, there is an expectation that they will increase. From the moment an investor decides to buy a property, whether they intend a short- or long-term hold, they have likely been burning with desire for the property to skyrocket in value. You cannot underestimate the power of intention. Unfortunately, whether the property's value goes up or not has more to do with your ability to raise rents over time than pure intention.

The second reason is the innate drive of the investor to raise rents. However, the ability to raise rents is dependent on what the market can bear. Raising rents raises NOI, which raises appraised value.

Third, commercial real estate brokers add fuel to this fire. They know that if they want to get a listing that they have to drive the price up as high as possible. The best of them know they'll have to temper an attractive price with sales comparables in the market and cap rates. But if the property is an office or retail property, the limitations in the leases on raising rents and the quality of your tenants can put this fire out fast.

Fourth, the law of supply and demand affects property values. The more demand there is for a commercial property type during the expansion phase of the real estate market cycle and the scarcer new listings become, the higher the price will be. In many metros there are few, if any, new commercial lots left to build on. This intensifies the scarcity factor.

Fifth, interest rates are a factor. When rates are low, the net operating income (NOI) of the property will support a larger loan amount for the buyer and a higher sales price for the seller. Of course, the opposite is true if rates are high.

Sixth, today's replacement cost of building a property similar to an existing property is a factor. In an environment in which commercial land and construction costs are going up, existing properties will be worth more.

Now let's look at six reasons why commercial property values go down.

First, a recession occurs as a result of high unemployment and the purchasing of fewer goods and services, resulting in lower demand for rental units, which results in lower rents and occupancy. This lowers NOI, which raises cap rates which lowers property value.

Second, the recession has an immediate affect on financing as underwriting guidelines become stringent, resulting in fewer buyers that qualify. Often lenders lower loan to value and raise DSCR. This creates smaller loans, which results in larger down payment requirements, which creates a smaller pool of eligible buyers. This creates more supply than qualified buyers, forcing prices down.

Third, there are too many construction starts and units for rent during the hyper-supply phase of the real estate market cycle. This is when there are more units available for rent than the market can absorb. This lowers rents and encourages rental concessions, both of which lower net operating income which lowers property values.

Fourth is a decrease in economic occupancy during a recession. The property might have good physical occupancy but many multifamily tenants have lost their jobs and office and retail tenants have lost customers, resulting in poor rent collections. This mostly hits Class C properties during a recession.

Fifth, appraisers are pressured to lower valuations during a recession. Lenders no longer trust values from comparable properties that sold before the recession. They know values are coming down and this terrifies them. As the recession progresses, distressed commercial property owners need to sell fast and lower their prices to avoid foreclosure. Appraisers are pushed toward using recent higher-cap-rate comparables that lower property values.

Time and Money Saving Tip

The best time to sell a commercial property is when it has reached its potential, which is evident when rent increases and NOI along with ROI have been stagnant for several years. For office, retail, and industrial properties, if selling can be timed just after major tenants have renewed long-term leases, all the better.

Now, if you want the perfect recipe for increasing wealth, you want to put your prop-

Sixth, whenever interest rates sky-rocket, commercial real estate prices come down accordingly, as the NOI of the property now supports a smaller loan amount. This brings prices down, as there is a smaller pool of investors that can put a larger amount down to support the higher prices.

Surprisingly, most sellers of investment commercial property do not dwell much on the likelihood of their property value's coming down someday. The moment they take title, most know that when they sell they are going to make a killing. If they do get caught in a recession, and cannot get their price, as long as they have the cash to ride it out most will wait until the real estate market goes up again to sell. From a nuts-and-bolts standpoint, commercial properties should go up in value because they have been physically improved, repositioned, or repurposed, resulting in higher rents over time. But if the real estate market takes a nosedive, lower rents, collection losses, and poor occupancy can bring those values down again. The good news is that history has shown that the bust periods are temporary.

erty on the market during the expansion phase of the real estate market cycle. The expansion phase follows the recovery phase after a recession. You can identify the beginning of the expansion phase when job growth and GDP have increased steadily for four months, new housing starts are on the rise, and there is evidence of new commercial construction again. At this time rents will be going up and vacancies and rent concessions will be coming down.

Now it's a seller's market again and there will be an ever-increasing competition for the best turnkey Class A and B properties and the worst Class C and D properties that have value-add potential. Lenders have lowered their requirements and there is an abundance of buyers that qualify for larger loans on all commercial property types, driving up prices. In the expansion phase, buyers will often pay more than a property is worth because of their expectation that prices will still be going up and their intention to raise rents over time. Now after selling for a great price, you can leverage your equity through a 1031 tax-deferred exchange into buying a larger property with much higher net income and depreciation.

Going back to the 1865 recession, real estate prices have always recovered and gone up over time.

How do rents affect appraised values? If your property's rents have gone up, an appraiser will choose sold properties with a correspondingly higher rent per square foot as comparables. This will raise your property's value. Conversely, if the property has become more derelict over time and rents have been stagnant and expenses have risen, then the property will be compared with lower-quality properties, which will lower the valuation. It's strange, but in an up market, the momentum from property values going up and the scarcity of properties for sale will likely pull these fixer-upper properties up too.

POWER BROKERS ARE HIGHLY SKILLED AT PUSHING UP THE SALES PRICE

One of the greatest factors in raising commercial property values is something I call "the power broker force." Top-producing commercial realtors consider it sport to raise property values in their communities. I have seen them do this in many of the markets I lend in nationally, and they do it with relish. They use their arsenal of tested recipes to push prices up and cap rates down.

Nancy Lemas is a power broker in Boise, Idaho. She reminded me recently about all the fun we had together closing $44 million in commercial properties in 2016. She was the listing broker on each deal. I'm not sure I would quite call it fun. For me it was very much like skydiving—exhilaration at the beginning followed by worrying about whether the chute would open.

My job was to create loans for four of her properties that carried record-breaking prices, and although it had been an up seller's market for close to seven years, I was worried that there were just not enough comparables that had sold at comparably low cap rates for them to appraise at their purchase price. We did close on all four purchases, which resulted in sales comparables that lowered cap rates and increased property values on future sales in this market.

I have personally witnessed Nancy push the envelope by increasing commercial property values above what they are logically worth. She does this with her intellect and her bold personality. She has the most thorough, and I think the most accurate, method of determining maximum sales price that I've seen. Here it is:

The Nancy Lemas Seven-Step Method for Determining Maximum Sales Price

1. *Do a market analysis to determine the initial value.* Nancy starts by collecting the current rent roll and the past 12 months' income and expense statements on the subject property. She will then do an analysis of the best market comparables with the highest rents to determine the lowest market cap rate for the property type. She will then apply that cap rate to the subject property's NOI to come up with an initial value.

2. *Compute the value using potential rents.* If the market rents are higher than the subject property's rents, she will do a second analysis on the subject property that reflects potential rents. This will increase the NOI, lower the cap rate, and raise the property value higher than the result from step 1.

3. *Compute the value for out-of-state buyers.* Nancy does extensive marketing to out-of-state buyers who are looking for lower-priced properties with higher cap rates in less expensive states. Often these buyers are doing a 1031 exchange because their equity in an existing property has grown substantially over time.

These buyers will pay the most for a property in a middle market like Boise, Idaho. She comes up with a higher sales price for this group.

4. *Adjust value for an up or down economic cycle.* Nancy not only looks at the inventory of current sales of the same property type but also looks up all new and planned construction starts nearby to determine the demand now and the near future. If it's an up market and demand is high, she will push the price up accordingly. If it's a down market and demand is low, she will keep the price down.

5. *Compute an average sales price from steps 1–4.* The sales prices calculated for initial value, potential value, out-of-state buyer value, and economic cycle value are averaged to come up with an average sales price.

6. *Know about the best financing available.* Nancy will check on the lowest rate financing available with the highest loan to value and figure out what the annual loan payments will be for the buyer if they put down 25–30%. She then computes the buyer's return on their investment with these loan payments. If the return is too low, she will adjust the sales price down accordingly.

7. *Adjust the sales price to fit the buyer's expectations.* Nancy puts herself in the buyer's shoes and thinks about what they would be willing to pay for the property and why. Buyers think in terms of earning a minimum of 5–6% minimum *cash on cash return (CCR)* on their down payment during their first year of ownership. If the CCR is less than this she will adjust the maximum sales price down accordingly. In an up market, Nancy will then add at least 10% to this price as a cushion to come up with the final listing sales price. She will then advise the seller to be prepared to come down 10% if needed.

In conclusion, your commercial property is worth what a buyer is willing to pay for it. Many properties are priced too high simply because the seller is not able to connect the dots on what the buyer's expectations will be or what outside drivers are (e.g., recession, market absorption rates, and sales comparables). These properties tend to stay on the market for a long time and experience many price reductions. Buyers can easily check to see how long a property has been for sale, and if it has been over six months, they are going to expect a discount. There are exceptions to this. For deals of $10 million and above and for newer properties that are in excellent condition, institutional investors and real estate investment trusts are often willing to pay more than the property is worth because they have a lot of cash just sitting. They are willing to accept lower returns on their investment, but the properties have to be turnkey with very low risk, a strong operating history, great tenants, excellent collections, and an outstanding location.

TWELVE MISTAKES TO AVOID WHEN SELLING YOUR COMMERCIAL PROPERTY

1. *Pricing the property too high.* Yes, I know. The buyer is going to make a lower offer, so you should price the property high so you can come down a bit. Although there is substance to this logic, just be aware that if you price it too high you will likely be reducing the number of potential buyers. Buyers can do a lot of research on the Internet. Information on property values is abundantly available these days. If they find comparables that are priced lower, they will pass on your property. Do the math. If they put 25% down on your property and finance 75% at today's interest rates, what will their CCR be at your sales price? If it is 6% or more, you are likely good to go.

2. *Not knowing your prepayment penalty on your current loan.* My client Arty was buying an apartment building in North Carolina. He was at the title company signing closing documents when the escrow agent told him that the seller had just canceled the sale. The seller had just seen the payoff on their loan, and they were shocked to find out that they had a prepayment penalty of over $400,000. Ouch! This created a legal quagmire that I am not going to take the time to go into. When I speak to commercial real estate brokers, I will often ask for a show of hands if they ever got burned because their seller did not know they had a prepayment penalty on their existing loan. Many hands will go up, followed by many war stories. Prior to listing your property for sale, double check your mortgage note to verify that you do not have a prepayment penalty looming in the background that can bite you.

3. *Not having all property financials prepared.* It's just going to slow everything down if you do not have all the property financials and *estoppels* together before you list your property for sale. For starters, your real estate broker will need them to determine the sales price and prepare the marketing flyer. The due diligence period will most likely not start until the borrower has collected these. And the buyer cannot apply for a loan without them. To start with, prepare the last three years of income and expense statements and a current rent roll. The lender will likely ask for a *trailing 12-month* report (month-by-month profit and loss for the last 12 months). Be sure to start collecting estoppels on day one, as I have had this take months for national tenants. Only commercial properties that have business tenants need estoppels.

4. *Showing less income on tax returns than the property financials show.* Okay, it is understandable that, like many commercial property owners, you want to pay less tax. You may have written off many capital improvements, which are not deductible, as repairs, which are a deductible expense. Now that you are selling the property, why not have your cake and eat it too? So you reverse the process

by taking the capital improvements that were written off as repairs and put them back into capital improvements.

Although this practice is not illegal (the IRS does not go after property investors that do this) it can be thought of as misleading to the borrower and their lender. Lenders and astute buyers quite often request Schedule Es from the seller's tax returns to verify income and expenses. If there is a discrepancy between the income and expense statements and your tax returns, don't be surprised if the buyer asks you to lower the sales price.

The remedy for this is to point a finger at it. Just tell the buyer and the lender that this is what you have done. Most lenders don't care since the IRS doesn't care. And since you were honest about it, the buyer can't really ask you to lower the sales price. Be sure to give the buyer a separate list of capital improvements and their costs for three years.

5. *Not disclosing tenant defaults.* Let's face it: if you have some tenants that are in default on their leases, how will your buyer know? It's not that you plan to lie to them, but if they don't ask, would it hurt if you just did not bring it up? Should you tell them?

    YES, you should tell them! And yes, the buyer will find out. Your real estate broker and the buyer will assume that everyone on the rent roll is in good standing unless you tell them otherwise.

    If you have late-paying or no-paying tenants and do not disclose this, I assure you that at a minimum, the buyer's lender will find out. And they will think you misled them and that your financials might be fraudulent. Underwriters are trained to look for discrepancies between rent rolls and income statements for rent collection problems. If they don't find out from these documents, they will find out for sure at least for the commercial properties where lenders require tenants to sign an estoppel certificate. These certify the lease terms, that there are no defaults, and when the rent was last paid. The tenant is committing a federal crime if they lie on a lender's estoppel certificate.

6. *Not disclosing rent concessions.* Rent concessions are used to fill vacancies quickly. They are a discount in the rent for a period of time in exchange for signing a lease quickly. Quite often rent concessions are not disclosed to buyers. They will certainly be discovered by the buyer's lender because the rent roll will show more gross rent than the income statements. It's best to disclose this at the beginning and ideally be able to explain that the concessions are not ongoing. Again, you do not want the buyer to use these to lower the sales price.

7. *Having short remaining lease terms or month-to-month tenancies.* If you have very-short-term leases, you could leave this as a value-add opportunity for your buyer. But the problem here lies in the fact that many lenders feel insecure

with month-to-month tenancy for multifamily properties or with most other commercial property leases that have fewer than two years remaining. They are concerned that many tenants might move out at the same time, making it difficult for the buyer to make the loan payments. So this can present a problem for your buyer. Furthermore, with the exception of multifamily properties, the lender will not fix the rate of the loan for much longer than the average of all of the lease terms. So if your buyer wants a five-year fixed rate mortgage or longer and the remaining lease terms average fewer than three years, the rate will likely be fixed for only three years.

8. *Disclosing some or all known repairs to the buyer.* Telling the buyer about everything that is wrong with the property prior to signing the purchase contract might seem noble and honest, but this is not how it is done. Most experienced real estate brokers will suggest not disclosing the physical needs of the property during the offer negotiations, as this will just slow down getting the property under contract. The buyer will want to bargain with you on the sales price at the beginning and then again after they get their property inspection report. It is smart business to just handle this once, based on the property condition report. It is accepted practice to place the onus on the buyer to do a thorough property inspection, thus determining the physical condition of the property.

I've worked on hundreds of real estate deals and I have never seen a property inspector find that nothing needs repair—even on newer properties. They do need to earn their fee. For the majority of purchases I have worked on, the buyer will request a reduction in the sales price for a variety of reasons just prior to the due diligence period being up. From the seller's perspective, it makes sense to negotiate repairs along with other price-reduction requests at the same time. Major repairs, such as the need to replace the roof, should be disclosed to the buyer at the beginning.

9. *Not sprucing up the property.* Just as when you sell a car, give the property you are selling some shine. Maybe a new coat of exterior paint. Some new landscaping can do wonders to revitalize the property. And don't forget the parking lot. Having it resurfaced and restriped can make the property look 10 years younger.

10. *Not time-managing the deal.* I have a saying that my staff at the office probably gets a bit tired of but that they agree with: "Time is not your friend on commercial real estate deals." My colleague, Albuquerque real estate broker Rob Powell, says this better: "Time kills deals." Both buyer and seller are finicky. The longer the deal takes, the more "what ifs" are asked. The fact is that the longer it takes, the less likely it is that the deal will close. At my firm we have noticed that for every week the closing is delayed beyond the date specified in the purchase contract, the chance the deal will never close increases by 10%.

As the seller, if you do not provide the property financials quickly, the due diligence period will take longer. If the buyer is not preapproved for financing correctly at the beginning, they will likely not get their loan approved. They will then have to start the loan process all over again with another lender. This will add an additional 45–60 days to the closing or even kill the deal. Check in with your real estate broker often and make sure they are time-managing these 10 critical dates:

Ten Critical Time Management Dates

1. **Due diligence start date:** The due diligence period usually starts when the buyer has been provided with all of the property's financials, leases, and a copy of the survey.
2. **Loan confirmation date:** The date the buyer starts their loan.
3. **Estoppel receipt and due dates:** The date on which tenants receive their estoppel and the date they must turn in the estoppel. Not being able to obtain a signed estoppel from a tenant has killed many deals in our firm over the years.
4. **Appraisal deadline**.
5. **Environmental report deadline**.
6. **Property inspection completion date**.
7. **Financing contingency date**.
8. **All due diligence and financing contingencies are met date:** The earnest money goes hard.
9. **Final date to negotiate changes in the sales price**.
10. **Closing date**.

Also be aware that delays caused by legal counsel for the buyers, lenders, or sellers are one of the top reasons closings are pushed past the drop-dead date. Property insurance that doesn't meet the buyer's lender requirements is another. These items need to be time-managed too.

11. *Not mandating on the lease that the tenant has to provide financials*. Often for office, retail, and industrial properties, your buyer's lender will need to approve the quality of the tenants' financials. Failing to have this provision in your leases can create a problem for you or your buyer in obtaining financing. Most national tenants are used to providing this information but often procrastinate. Most other tenants just do not want to comply with this provision, even if it is in their lease. This can kill your buyer's loan.
12. *Choosing the wrong real estate broker*. Very few commercial properties are so fabulous and priced so affordably that they just sell themselves. Having the very best real estate broker will make this very technical process much less

technical for you. Most of all, their experience will keep the deal from crashing and burning.

If you do not already have a broker that you have worked with before, how do you choose one? Unfortunately, usually the real estate broker who says they can get the highest price is going to win your business. If they don't show you the market analysis that proves that price is attainable, be wary.

What is much more important is finding a broker who is actually working diligently to sell properties and not just to land deals. These brokers will be experts in their field and will likely already know someone who is interested in buying your property. They will also know many of the other major commercial realtors in the area and be willing to share their fee with them. They will have many methods of marketing, including various online platforms. They will have a long referral list of satisfied customers who you can talk to. Their marketing flyers and online property brochures will be outstanding and based on facts. They will screen every buyer carefully for verification of down payment, experience, and financing. These realtors have enough experience to know if the buyer's financing has holes in it, and they get involved in plugging those holes. And they likely know where the best sources of financing for your property are and are bold enough to get involved with the buyer on this. They will answer the phone most times you call and make you feel like you are their only customer. Most of all they will tell you what they really think and not just what you want to hear.

Lastly, do not use a residential real estate broker who does not have commercial real estate experience. This is like going to a veterinarian to have your gallbladder removed. They could probably wing it, but you're not going to do that. Commercial really is a different animal than residential real estate. A commercial property is income based and has a different due diligence list.

VALUE-ADDING BEFORE SELLING

Most buyers are trying to find a commercial property with an upside. So as the seller, why not create this upside and increase the property value for yourself? If your property is currently worth a million dollars at an 8% cap rate and has an annual NOI of $80,000, increasing the bottom line by 15% can increase the value of the property by $150,000. The best way to achieve this is to tackle it from both ends by increasing rents and decreasing expenses.

Major value-adding is called repositioning. Go to Chapter 7 for a lot more on this subject. Repositioning value-adds can be divided into three categories:

1. Operational, which cost little or nothing and consist mostly of increasing rents and decreasing expenses.
2. Cosmetic, which are moderately expensive and include improvements such as a new coat of paint or new floor coverings.
3. Construction, which are expensive and include improvements such as adding more square footage or doing a major rehab.

Try to stick with low-cost and low-risk operational value-adds. If cosmetic work is needed, try to confine it to light cosmetic work: paint the ugly cabinets instead of replacing them.

Compare your rents with your competitors to determine if they can be raised.

Have an experienced property manager review your expenses for where there can be decreases. Often decreasing expenses can be as simple as shopping for cheaper insurance or lowering your property tax bill. Going through all your expenses and trimming a percent here and there can really add up.

Any leases coming due? For office, retail, and industrial properties negotiate longer-term leases before you put the property on the market. This represents a minimal expense and can make your property worth more simply because it lowers the buyer's risk, which means they can qualify for much better financing. For multifamily properties, raise rents to the max whenever you can. It is unlikely that a tenant will move out for a $50 increase given the cost of moving.

Ultimately you are going to have to carefully weigh the cost and time involved with value-adding to determine if it is going to be cost effective. And if you are doing some rehab, be sure to include your loss of income due to the lost rents when you have to vacate spaces while improving them.

With the exception of multifamily and hospitality properties, costly cosmetic changes that just make the property look better do not necessarily raise rents and increase the property value. Take a look at your competition. If they are getting higher rents than you because they have better interior finishes, floor coverings, and fixtures, then maybe you should follow suit. But it could be they are doing better just because they have a better location. For an apartment property in a low-income neighborhood, there is a limit to what your tenants can afford to

Time and Money Saving Tip

It might be hard to believe, but often sellers come out ahead on profit by selling potential value-add opportunities with the property. Many buyers are only looking for properties that have a great upside, and this is something you can make money on.

Having many value-add items that are left for the buyer to drool over can entice them to pay more than the property is worth right now. You are appealing to the fixer-upper crazed investor. They just love being able to use their ingenuity to improve the property to make a killing in the future.

pay. So be careful to not overimprove the property. If you have an apartment or office building built between the 1960s and the 1980s, it will always be a Class C property that won't command the higher rents of a Class B property, no matter how much you improve it. Keep in mind that appraisers will always constrain the value by comparing it to other Class C properties.

Selling the upside for a premium happens more often when there is a shortage of similar properties in an up seller's market. But I have seen fixer-uppers go for more than they should have in down markets. Have your real estate broker highlight these value adds in the marketing flyer. Best of all, you will be getting paid to leave all the work of improving the property to the buyer. In the story below, the buyer came out quite well doing just this.

Selling Value-Adds at a Premium

In 2016 I financed a 1944 C minus multifamily property in Portland, Oregon. It was composed of 16 units and had a brick exterior, peeling paint trim, and a very brown lawn. It also featured worn-out interiors with 1980s appliances and teal green linoleum floors. I remember asking the listing agent to get the lawn watered, hoping it would turn green by the time my appraiser came out.

This property was in a great hipster neighborhood, and sold after being on the market for five days. My client bought it for $2,445,000 at a 5.5% cap rate and acted like he was stealing it. I told the buyer that the property was grossly overpriced—that five-year-old Class A apartment buildings down the street were being valued at the same cap rate. He told me he had made one of the smartest moves in his life and snatched it by offering $140,000 more than the listing price.

Apparently there was a bidding war. The 84-year-old seller had hardly raised rents or done any maintenance in the 16 years he owned it. I practically yelled at my client, "This property is a wreck—the sales price was already $260,000 more than what it was worth, and you had to offer $140,000 more? Are you nuts? And on top of all that are you really going to put another $18,000 per unit into it and hundreds of hours of work to fix it up?"

The property ended up appraising for much less than the sales price, which I knew it would. To add insult to injury, there was only enough NOI to support a 56% loan. I had to do a cash-out refinance on another of the buyer's properties to increase his down payment. The buyer planned to use his own funds to modernize the interiors.

Fortunately for the buyer, this was an up market and the neighborhood was highly sought after. Fourteen months later the property was not only a classic beauty but the buyer had raised the rents from an average of $740 to $1,070. That was an increase of 46%. The property at that point was 100% occupied and worth $3.1 million, and he was over $300,000 ahead. I told him I was wrong about him putting too much money into the project and reminded him to keep the lawn watered.

WHY YOU SHOULD DO A FOR SALE BY OWNER

- *You'll save the real estate commission.* With an average commercial real estate commission of 6% on deals of $5 million and under, this should be a no-brainer. You should get paid well for your time when selling the property yourself. On a $2 million sales price, you'll have $120,000 more in your pocket. Why pay a middleman?
- *You know your property better than anyone.* You and you commercial property have grown up together. How often is the listing broker going to ask you to answer questions the buyer has about the property? Why not have them go straight to the horse's mouth themselves?
- *You can sell the property yourself online.* There are many online platforms that feature commercial properties for sale by owner. Unfortunately the largest commercial-property platform, LoopNet, does not allow by-owner listings, but they do allow commercial properties for sale by owner if they are also owner-carry. Here are some online platforms that allow for sale by owner listings:
  - BuildingsByOwner.com
  - FindMyRoof.com

  You can also advertise to commercial real estate groups on Facebook or list the property for sale on Craigslist.

WHY YOU SHOULDN'T DO A FOR SALE BY OWNER

No matter how great your property is or how organized you are, selling a commercial property is a very complex and technical endeavor. If you have sold a home yourself successfully, you might be tempted to do it with commercial real estate. Even if you are selling a simple single-office property zoned commercial, it might appear to be as easy as selling a residence, but it is not as easy. The difference is that with commercial property, you are selling an income stream with the brick-and-mortar attached. Unless you have done it many times before, selling your commercial property yourself, in my opinion, is like an elementary school teacher trying to teach a graduate level university business course.

BENEFITS OF WORKING WITH AN EXPERIENCED COMMERCIAL REAL ESTATE BROKER

An experienced commercial real estate broker can help a seller through:

- *Analyzing the sales price correctly.* Commercial real estate brokers are experts at determining the market value of your property and the maximum sales price, as I illustrated with the Nancy Lemas system above. They have access to services such as CoStar and REIS that can supply them with the latest comparable commercial property rent and sales data. You can subscribe to these too, but it is expensive. They also can get rental comps directly from property managers they network with.
- *Verifying the buyer's financial strength and experience.* Commercial realtors are not shy about doing this. They will ask for copies of the buyer's bank and/or security statements to verify that they have the down payment plus closing costs. Are you comfortable doing this?
- *Negotiating and writing up the offer to the seller's advantage.* An experienced commercial real estate broker will know how to write the purchase contract correctly. This is huge, especially when negotiating the contingencies for financing and due diligence contingencies for property financials, property inspection, review of leases, and more.
- *Marketing.* Commercial real estate brokers know a lot of people that invest in the type of property you are selling and can pitch your property to them. Through multiple listings or just through relationships with their colleagues, you will have enlisted many commercial real estate agents to sell your property, especially if your listing broker is willing to split their commissions, which most are willing to do. Your property will be advertised nationally on LoopNet, the largest online platform for selling commercial real estate. If your property is in a state with higher cap rates, low-cap-rate buyers from states like California will be interested. As mentioned, LoopNet does not allow for sale by owner listings unless they are also owner-carry deals.
- *Time-managing the deal.* Commercial realtors are experts at time-managing a deal's critical dates that were mentioned earlier. They are also experts at making

sure ahead of time that there is a clear title and that the buyer and their lender get the property's financials on time.

- *Negotiating a sales-price reduction prior to the earnest money going hard.* Almost all buyers are going to request a lowering of the sales price because of property condition or discrepancies in property financials. What if the property does not appraise at the purchase price for your buyer? Are you confident you can negotiate with the buyer yourself and keep the sales price up there? Experienced brokers do this all the time. As a third party they can just say, "My seller is not going to accept that. Here is what I can get them to accept."
- *Solving problems and closing issues.* There can be problems with clearing the title and issuing title insurance, surveys, commercial endorsements, easements, and disagreements between the buyers' and sellers' legal counsel. Commercial realtors are not only experienced at solving these problems, most love the challenge.

SHOULD YOU OWNER-CARRY?

In commercial real estate, owner-carry mortgages are sometimes a marriage between a buyer who doesn't have much money or experience and a seller who owns a distressed property. Yes, this can get worse if the buyer has weak or bad credit and cannot qualify for a loan elsewhere. Now, does that sound like a match for a good long-term relationship? As the seller, do you really want to be legally tied to someone who needs something from you—like a handout? Maybe that seems harsh, but I'm calling it the way I see it.

The flip side is that if you are willing to prequalify the buyer as a bank does, this can be a good marriage. Also, you are almost certainly going to get a higher sales price.

As the seller, you usually need something too. The property is often underperforming, having too many vacancies or some tenants not paying rent. It might even be 100% vacant. Sometimes it is just in a very isolated small town, which makes it difficult for a buyer to get conventional financing. The property often will have a long list of neglected repairs due to lack of money, poor management, or both. These properties often do need new blood. At a minimum they need new management. Most often they need to be repositioned. In most cases the owners just do not have the energy or funds to tackle this.

Don't get me wrong, there are some good, decent people out there that need an owner-carry, and have the experience, drive, and commitment to make this a success for both parties. Some of them just do not have the net worth or experience required by a conventional lender. If their credit score is 640 and above and they can put at least 20% down, this might be a good fit. Be sure to verify that the buyer will not be broke after closing (that they will have some post-closing cash). The most important thing to owner-carry borrowers is a smaller down payment than required by the bank and monthly payments that the property can afford. Interest rate and loan maturity doesn't seem to be a major issue for them.

ALTERNATIVE TO OWNER-CARRY: THE MASTER LEASE PURCHASE

If your property is distressed, or just having difficulty selling right now and you just need to get away from running it, consider selling it using a master lease purchase. A master lease is most often used when a seller/lessor wants to lock in a higher price today than the property is worth based on its occupancy, net income, and/or condition. In most cases, the seller does not have the financial means or motivation to improve the property. In exchange, the buyer—who likely does not have the down payment for traditional financing—has an abundance of motivation and energy to improve the property. There is no loan involved, so both parties need not worry about that.

The buyer/lessee can take from two to four years to reposition the property— remodel it, re-tenant it, lower expenses, and raise rents. The lessee makes monthly payments to the lessor. At some specified future date, the lessee has the right to purchase the property for the amount agreed upon when the master lease was signed. When the lease is up the property will usually qualify for quality permanent financing, and the buyer will have raised the down payment from the property value increasing. The buyer/lessor gets the benefit of appreciation. The seller/lessor has the benefit of getting more for the property than it was worth today and the disadvantage of having sold the property for less than it will be worth when the lease expires.

It is standard for the lessee to put as little as 10–15% down when signing the master lease. These funds are credited toward the purchase price for the buyer as long as the future sale goes through. The buyer/lessee loses these funds if they choose not to buy the property. One great benefit of a master lease for the seller/lessor is that you keep legal title to the property. If the buyer/lessee defaults on the lease, it is easy and fairly quick to take the property back since you still own it. The lessee has equitable title, not legal title, which allows the lessee complete authority to run the property and benefit from the property's income, appreciation, and depreciation.

Example of How a Master Lease Is Used

In 2005 my client Mark came across a large, 140,000-square-foot empty manufacturing plant located just off a busy freeway interchange in Iowa. The property had been for sale for close to two years. At $1,200,000, the property was practically being given away. The owner had died and his wife did not have much interest in re-tenanting the property. Mark had a brilliant idea. He called major national clothing chains and got interest from four to locate stores at this location. He still needed another 12. His idea was to repurpose the property into a factory outlet mall. He offered the widow full price with 10% down on a three-year master lease. The widow was pleased to be getting monthly payments and to be done with paying the taxes, insurance, utilities, and security on the property.

Mark did a cash-out refinance of $950,000 from an apartment property he owned to pay for the buildout and 18 months of master lease payments. This consisted of building new walls to separate the 16 spaces; new plumbing, electrical, and HVAC; plus resurfacing and increasing the size of the parking lot. The tenants would be getting a break on their rent to put in their own tenant improvements.

After 16 months Mark had managed to get nine more leases signed. This took much more time than anticipated. He had no idea it would take so long to negotiate leases with national chain stores. He really started worrying when it took seven to eight months for the tenants to build to suit and move in. They did not start paying rent until they opened for business. This was about double the amount of time he had planned on.

Mark had to use an equity line of credit to keep things going. But this is where having the property positioned at such a good price saved the day. Twenty-eight months after Mark signed the master lease, the property was 82% occupied and running profitably. Although not on the market, an investor offered him $3,400,000 for the property. He countered for $3,800,000 and sold the property, paid the master lease off, and made a profit of over $1,400,000.

Selling

1031 Exchange Checklist: *This is a gift from the government that only a select few are lucky enough to take advantage of*

I have seen many of my clients get amazingly wealthy in less than 10 years by doing 1031 exchanges. Section 1031 of the US Internal Revenue Service tax code is one of the greatest gifts around to property investors. It's almost as if someone at the US Treasury Department woke up one day and said, "What is the best way to make personal wealth grow? Let's have people invest in a property. As that property grows in value over time, let's allow them to sell it at a profit. And let them invest that profit tax deferred into a property of greater value. Then let's allow them to repeat the process over and over."

A 1031 tax-deferred exchange enables owners of real estate to sell a property and use the equity from the sale to purchase a replacement property while deferring federal and state capital gains tax on the original property to a later time. Here is a checklist to use if you are thinking of doing a 1031 exchange:

Checklist for a 1031 Exchange

_____*Choose your advisors.* Choose the best buyer's real estate broker, lender or mortgage broker, and tax attorney to advise you on your exchange.

_____*Choose a qualified intermediary.* Also called an accommodator, a qualified intermediary handles the paperwork, sets up escrow, and holds the funds from the sale of your relinquished property.

_____*Determine whether your property qualifies.* The relinquished and replacement properties must be of a like kind, meaning that both have to be used for investment purposes or used in a business. You can take an apartment building and exchange it for an office building, but you cannot sell the office building and buy a primary residence with the proceeds.

_____*Decide on the type of replacement property.* What commercial property type, location, and price range are you looking for? What other characteristics are you looking for? Start looking for your replacement property right away.

____*Choose a replacement property based on the parameters of the relinquished property.* You must buy a property for as much as or more than you sold the relinquished property for. Also you must obtain at least as much financing for the replacement property as you had remaining on the loan for the relinquished property. Lastly, you must use all the cash you received from the relinquished property to buy the replacement property.

____*Fill out the sale contract correctly.* When selling your relinquished property, make sure the sale contract is written so that you can assign the contract to the qualified intermediary who will be purchasing the property on your behalf.

____*Start the identification and closing period clock.* The 45-day identification period and 180-day closing period for your replacement property starts on the day the sale of your relinquished property closes.

____*Identify the replacement property.* You can identify up to three replacement properties within the 45 days allowed.

____*Sign the purchase contract for the replacement property.* Be sure to put the buyer's name or assignees as the purchaser. The property needs to be assigned to the qualified intermediary as buyer.

____*Fill out the exchange paperwork.* Your qualified intermediary will do this for you.

____*Close on the replacement property.* Your qualified intermediary will handle the escrow to close on the purchase of the replacement property.

As-Is Clause: *This clause in the purchase and sale contract protects the seller*

By putting an as-is clause in the purchase and sale agreement (PSA), the seller is establishing that the onus of determining the physical and financial condition of the commercial property being sold is on the buyer. Often sellers have had the property professionally managed and they might not be totally informed on every aspect of the property's physical and financial condition. So it's up to the buyer when they do their due diligence to determine the condition of the property. The as-is clause protects the seller and states that they are not making representations and warranties of any kind, that the buyer is purchasing the property subject to any information they find while doing their due diligence, and that any due diligence items provided by the seller may or may not be accurate.

When a buyer does their due diligence thoroughly, they will likely find things out about the physical and financial condition of the property that the seller may not even been aware of. This is especially the case when sellers have had the property professionally managed. If the buyer's real estate agent or attorney prepares the first draft of the purchase and sale contract, it may state that the seller is making many representations and warranties. It is an acceptable and recommended practice for the seller to tell the buyer about major replacements that are needed such as roof replacements. It should then be mentioned in the purchase contract that the buyer is buying the property as is including these major replacements.

Broker Cooperation Agreement: *Get 10 times more exposure for the property being sold when you get your real estate broker to agree to network with other realtors*

As the seller, be sure to choose a listing broker who is willing to share their fee by signing a broker cooperation agreement with the buyer's real estate broker. Most brokers will do this but some will not. They will insist that the buyer's real estate broker collect their fee from the buyer. Well, not many buyers are expecting or willing to do this. You will be greatly limiting your exposure to buyers if your listing agent is not willing to share their fee. If your real estate agent networks with other realtors, your property can get 10 times more exposure. Listing brokers most often split their commission equally with the buyer's broker, but some pay a flat fee of 1–2%.

Cap/Capitalization Rate (Seller's Perspective): *Be sure to put an accurate cap rate that is based on actual numbers in the marketing flyer*

The cap rate shown in your marketing flyer is one of the most important factors motivating a buyer to be interested in purchasing your commercial property. Remember when you were a buyer searching for the right property to buy—looking on LoopNet or through multiple listings? You likely looked at the sales price first, then the cap rate, and if those two looked attractive, you went through the property photos. If you liked a property, you then looked for verification of its value from cap rates shown for other, like properties for sale.

If your property has a lower cap rate than most of the others, the buyer will think it is priced too high and likely pass on it. Listing brokers know this and sometimes put pressure on sellers to mix actual and potential numbers to come up with a cap rate in the marketing flyer that is higher and will get the buyer's attention. In this case, though, say a buyer makes an offer on your property based on the higher cap rate. When they do their due diligence, they'll find out the cap rate is lower than what they were told it was. The buyer will now feel at best that the deal was misrepresented and at worst that they were lied to.

> **Time and Money Saving Tip**
>
> If your property is being marketed with a lower cap rate and a higher sales price than competing similar properties for sale, be sure to highlight why it is worth more in the marketing flyer. The reasons might include your superior location, the age of the property, strong anchor or national tenants, long terms remaining on leases, three years or more of strong historical occupancy, and major improvements you have made to the property.

The cap rate that your property is marketed at will be heavily scrutinized by the buyer, the buyer's real estate broker, the buyer's lender, and the appraiser. If this group is convinced that you inflated the cap rate, they will not only have the data to prove it but the professional knowledge to use as ammunition in lowering the sales price.

Commercial Real Estate Buyer Types: *Think about what type of buyer will be most interested in your property and then put yourself in their shoes*

Have you thought about how important it is to know what type of investor will likely be buying your property? Will it be a fix-and-flipper or a buyer who will hold the property for the short or long term? What is it about your property that will motivate them to make an offer? Prior to putting your commercial property on the market, talk to several real estate brokers to get their opinion on this. Then decide on the most likely profile of the buyer. From this you can determine the highest sales price on the current market comps for your property type. Then put yourself into the buyer's shoes and ask, "If I were buying my property with this goal in mind, would I pay that much for it?

Types of Investors

- **Developers:** They might be looking to demolish existing structures and do ground-up construction, or they might use the property's good bones and change it into something with a different purpose.
- **Repositioners:** Under-market rents will get their attention. They will likely have a list of value adds they can do to increase the rental income, lower expenses, and increase the value of the property. This can range from cosmetic changes to major rehab. Many repositioners will plan to sell the property in a few years at a profit. Others are intent on a long-term hold.
- **Buy Low, Sell High Wholesalers:** These investors only buy properties they can practically steal. Their only intent is to buy wholesale and resell at a hefty profit. They are not planning to put much, if any, money into improvements. Sometimes they have a buyer lined up even before they close on the property.
- **Long-Term Hold Investors:** These investors are looking for a long-term income stream, often for retirement. They are willing to pay top dollar today, knowing that over time rents will increase. They are looking for properties that are in very good condition with great tenants and leases.
- **Institutional Investors:** These are REITs (real estate investment trusts), pension funds, and commercial property investment companies that have a ton of money to be invested. They will pay top dollar, even more than a property is worth, for a Class A or B property that is in a great location.

I have a client in Portland, Oregon, who had a $28,000,000 office building that I did a construction and permanent loan on in 2013. His plan was to hold onto it for retirement and then pass it on to his kids. But soon after it was stabilized with great long-term lease tenants, a REIT offered him $34,000,000 for it. The offer was too good to refuse.

Commissions, Commercial Real Estate Brokers: *What is the going rate for a real estate broker's commission?*

Commercial real estate brokers are salespeople, so of course their commissions are negotiable. But keep in mind that the buyer's real estate broker will be splitting the commission with your broker. If you negotiate a commission that's too low, both realtors might show other comparable properties before they show yours. You will likely get more realtors working hard to sell your property if there is enough commission to share.

Average Commercial Real Estate Commissions

For a property priced at $5,000,000 and below, commissions average 6%.

For a property priced $5,000,000 to $25,000,000, commissions average 4%.

For a property priced at $25,000,000 and above, commissions average 1.25–1.50%. The entire amount is retained by the listing broker; the buyer's real estate broker has to be compensated by the buyer.

Confidentiality/Nondisclosure Agreement **(NDA), Sellers:** *Be sure to protect yourself with this before disclosing confidential financial and operational information to buyers*

> ### Time and Money Saving Tip
>
> Be bold and ask your listing agent for a rebate of between 1/4 and 1/3 of the gross commission if they sell the property themselves without a buyer's agent. No, it won't hurt to ask. Say, "I am willing to list the property with you if you are willing to give me a rebate if you sell the property without a buyer's agent being involved." Rebates to sellers from real estate commissions are illegal in some states, and the realtor will tell you right away if it is. The best way to get around this is to write the contract up so that the commission is lowered to a certain amount if there is not a buyer's agent involved. This is legal in all states.

As the seller of a commercial property, you will be providing the buyer with confidential financial and operational information that could be used against you by one of your competitors or tenants. To avoid this, be sure to have the buyer sign an NDA. This enables you to disclose sensitive information about the property's finances, leases, property management, service contracts, and more to the buyer. When signing this agreement, the buyer is obligated to keep all information confidential. Anyone that the buyer provides the documents to, including lenders, must also sign the agreement.

Contingency Clauses in Sales Contract (Seller's Perspective): *Make sure you give the buyer enough time, but not too much time, on these*

Can you imagine selling an automobile and having the sale contingent on seven or more contingencies? Contingency clauses in the purchase and sale contract are escape clauses designed to protect the buyer. Yes, this does seem to put the buyer at an unfair advantage. But then, you have to remember that the buyer is buying the property as is, so maybe this is fair. The burden of finding out what's wrong with the property falls on the buyer. They have the right to know what they are buying. But using the faults they find to lower the sales price can be sport for some buyers. Unless the property is practically new and the financials are in stellar condition, you can bet they will do exactly that. Although there can be dozens of contingencies, here are the most popular:

Contingencies in the Purchase and Sale Contract

- **Financing Contingency:** As the seller, you or your real estate broker should make sure that perspective buyers are qualified for financing the purchase of your property. If they are not you will not likely know until a few weeks before closing, when they ask you to extend the financing contingency (see Chapter 11 on getting preapproved commercial loans). Beware of buyers who get their foot in the door by faking it until they make it. Before the purchase contract is signed, be sure to screen buyers for these items: all key principals' personal financial statements, proof of liquidity, and a current credit report. This might sound like a lot to expect from a buyer, but the best commercial real estate brokers do ask for these items. Lenders these days expect the buyer to have previous ownership experience with the same type of commercial property, so screen the buyer for this too.

Don't be shy about asking for advice from a commercial mortgage broker or from your banker about what it will take for a buyer to qualify for a loan on your property. Make sure the buyer has a letter of interest from a direct lender or a letter of preapproval from a commercial mortgage broker.

It will take between 30 and 45 days after you provide the buyer with all the financial due diligence items for their loan to be approved. So **45 days** is a good time period for a financial contingency.

- **Property Inspection Contingency:** A property inspection report should be completed within two to three weeks. All the major systems will likely be inspected, including the structure, roofs, windows and doors, engineering, plumbing system, sewer, and electrical and HVAC systems. If a major repair or replacement is uncovered, it may take additional time to get an accurate bid. A period of **30–45 days** should be enough time for the inspection contingency.

- **Financial Due Diligence Contingency:** To speed the financial due diligence process up, **make sure** that you or your property manager have all of these items ready for the buyer's review prior to receiving offers: current rent roll showing lease beginning and ending dates plus square footage, trailing 12-month income and expense statement, income and expense statements for the last three calendar years, most recent year's utility bills, and property tax and insurance bills.

- **Lease and Rental Contract Review Contingency:** Be sure to provide the buyer with copies of all rental contracts and leases with any addendums along with an accounting of all deposits. An adequate time frame is **30 days**.

- **Estoppel Certificate Contingency:** Estoppel certificates are only needed for office, retail, and industrial properties. Estoppels have tenants certify what their lease terms are, any amendments, and that their leases are in good standing. Allow **45 days**, as some tenants, especially national ones, can take even longer than this to get them in.

- **Title Contingency:** Have your listing agent pull a preliminary title report. Check to make sure that the property owner listed on the title is the same as the one on the purchase contract as the vesting might have changed and not been recorded. Make sure there are no liens. If the buyer discovers you have tax liens they will think you are in a weak position and need cash, and they will likely use this against you to lower the price. If there are any problems with easements or encroachments be ready to explain these and work out a solution. Allowing a period of **45 days** is good, just in case there are any problems with clearing the title.

- **Survey Contingency:** Be sure to provide the buyer with a copy of the property survey. If the buyer needs the survey upgraded to an ALTA survey, make sure that they agree to pay for it, as it can cost $10,000 or more. A period of **30–45 days** should be sufficient.
- **Verification of Zoning Certificate and Certificate of Occupancy Contingency:** If you do not have copies of these, encourage the buyer to obtain them from the city or county government early on, as they can take time to obtain. A period of **30 days** is adequate for these.
- **Environmental Contingency:** Provide the buyer with any environmental reports you have for the property, including screening reports and phase 1 or phase 2 reports. The buyer will likely have to obtain a new environmental report for their loan. A **45-day** period is usually adequate for this contingency, but you will need to extend it if a phase 2 report is needed.
- **Operations Contingency:** Provide the buyer with copies of your management contract; vendor contracts; your insurance policy; and a list of the equipment, furnishings, fixtures, and supplies being sold with the property. A period of **30 days** is adequate.
- **Other Sale Contingency:** This contingency gives the buyer enough time to sell **another** property so he can buy yours. In a seller's market you will not likely want to include this one.

Depreciation Recapture: This is how
the government gets its due

While you owned your commercial property you were given this great gift from the government called depreciation. This has lowered your taxes for each year you've owned the property. But did you know that upon the sale of the property the government is going to take this gift back? Sellers know that they will be facing capital gains taxes if they sell a property and do not do a 1031 exchange. But often they don't know they'll also owe depreciation recapture taxes. "Depreciation recapture" refers to the taxable event that occurs when you sell an income property and are taxed on the total amount of depreciation you wrote off during the period you owned it. Only buildings can be depreciated, so there is no depreciation recapture tax on the sale of undeveloped commercial land.

Time and Money Saving Tip

If the buyer requests an extension on the due diligence period or for any other contingency for a reason that is not due to a delay caused by the seller, be sure to agree to this only if the buyer puts down additional earnest money. A minimum of $10,000, or a quarter of 1%, is recommended. You want to demonstrate to the buyer early on that you are not a pushover who is willing to give them something for nothing in return. They are tying up your property for a longer duration, which is a risk to you. Also, requiring an additional deposit will make the buyer take completing their due diligence more seriously.

Selling

To determine the amount that will be subject to a capital gains tax upon the sale of your commercial property, take the price you are selling the property for and subtract from that the original price you paid for it. This will give you your gross profit on the property. Now subtract from that amount the total cost of all the capital improvements you made to the property over the years you owned it. The balance is your adjusted net profit, which is the amount that is subject to a capital gains tax of 15% or 20%, depending on your income. Now add up all the depreciation you took since you owned the property. The depreciation recapture rate amount will be 25% of this total. Ouch! To avoid this you will need to buy a replacement property and do a 1031 exchange.

Letter of Intent/Interest (LOI) (Seller's Perspective): *How some buyers are experts at misleading sellers with LOIs*

A letter of intent to purchase can be a useful tool for both buyer and seller, as it quickly identifies the buyer's offering price, earnest money, contingencies, and closing date. But far too often the buyer's purpose is to get their foot in the door and tie up the deal. When speaking at commercial real estate seminars about financing, I have sat through many great presentations by commercial property investment gurus. They usually teach buyers to send out dozens of one-page letters of intent offering full price and great terms. The idea here is that one will stick to the wall. Some of these buyers are not acting in good faith. They really intend to get control of the property so they can buy time while they raise the down payment. Worse yet, they are taught to dump the property if they cannot find enough wrong with it to get a much better price.

If you receive an attractive LOI it is important to let the prospective buyer know that you will be screening their experience, financial strength, and proof of down payment extensively. Be wary of any buyer that is short on funds but tells you that they have a high-net-worth investor coming on board. Tell them you need to talk to that person.

Time and Money Saving Tip

With the exception of 1031 exchange buyers, be wary of buyers who want to put "and/or assigns" by the name of the buyer in the purchase and sale contract. In my many years of experience I have encountered some buyers who are actually wholesalers whose intention is to assign the property to someone else and sell it at a profit. Quite often these buyers dupe us too. They will obtain a letter of interest from us so that they can show the seller that they have applied for a loan. They often even sign our letter of interest to start the loan, but they fail to wire the loan deposit that goes along with it to start the loan.

This problem arises when you have decided to sell the property to a buyer you feel comfortable with and have likely checked their financial strength. You never intended for them to be able to sell their interest in the property to someone else, who may not be qualified. The remedy for this is to put into an addendum of the sale contract that "assigns" can only mean assigning the rights to an ownership entity like an LLC that has not been determined yet, and that it does not mean assigning it to another party. Be sure to state that the individual buyer you are working with has to be a partner in this LLC.

Listing Agreements/Contracts: *As the seller, you are holding the cards. You decide what type of listing agreement to have with a broker*

Top-producing real estate agents will tell you they are only willing to sell your commercial property if you sign an exclusive right-to-sell contract with them. Often they will refuse to discuss any other type of listing. Is this in your best interest and should you be bullied into it? Look at the types of real estate listing contracts below and decide which one fits your needs and those of your property best. As the seller, you are holding the cards. Most real estate agents would rather list the property with the type of contract you prefer than not at all.

> **Exclusive Right-to-Sell Contract:** This gives the listing agent an exclusive right to sell the property and get paid a commission regardless of who finds the buyer. This type of contract mandates that the buyer or their buyer's agent must go through the listing agent.

> **Exclusive Agency Contract:** This gives the seller the right to sell the property directly themselves without paying a real estate commission and list the property with one real estate company. The listing agent is only paid a fee if the buyer comes directly to them (and not the seller) or through any other real estate firm or real estate agent.

> **Open Listing Contract:** This gives the seller the best of all worlds. They can sell the property themselves and not pay a real estate commission, or they can list the property with as many real estate agents as they want. Whichever agent brings them the buyer gets the commission.

> **One-Time Showing Contract:** If the seller wants to sell the property themselves without an agent, but is willing to consider offers brought to them by any real estate broker, this type of agreement is used. A real estate agent will call the seller, who has the property listed as for sale by owner, and tell them that they have a buyer who is interested. They will then get the seller to first sign a one-time showing contract.

> **Time and Money Saving Tip**
>
> If you have had interested buyers approach you directly who have not yet made an offer and you are getting ready to list the property with a real estate agent, consider putting a listing exclusion into the listing agreement. This excludes potential buyers who approached you prior to signing the contract from being covered by that contract. In other words, if one of these people ends up buying the property, the listing agent will not get a commission. The listing agent will, of course, insist that this is not the way to do business and might walk away—but then maybe come back, since it could be better to get the listing under your terms than not at all.

Loan Assumption: *What about the buyer assuming your mortgage?*

If you need to sell your commercial property and your loan has a high prepayment penalty, it might be a great benefit to have the buyer assume your existing mortgage.

Selling

Check your mortgage note and see if your loan is assumable. When selling your commercial property, having a great, low-interest rate loan that is assumable may be of great value to a buyer if rates have gone up. Most often sellers think about having their loan assumed when there are three years or more remaining on a declining prepayment penalty. But sometimes they will not be able to sell the property at all unless the buyer assumes their loan. This will be the case if they have a *yield maintenance* or *defeasance prepayment penalty* (see Encyclopedia Topic H, Financing) and rates have gone down a lot since they took out the loan. In this case the prepayment penalty will be humongous. But here's the problem: if rates have gone down, the buyer will do much better to take out a new, lower-rate mortgage than to assume your higher-rate one. So to persuade them to assume your mortgage you will need to have an irresistible property or to give them some incentives.

Community bank loans are almost never assumable, but loans from regional banks and capital divisions of major banks usually are. All securitized loans, including those from Fannie Mae, Freddie Mac, and HUD, as well as commercial mortgage-backed security and life company loans, are assumable. To assume your loan, the buyer will need to qualify under similar guidelines that you applied under. They will also need to pay an assumption fee, which is usually 1%, plus the cost of whatever third-party reports are needed (for sure a new appraisal and often a property condition report).

Negotiating Repairs with the Buyer: *How much the seller pays for repairs is based on supply and demand in the market and two other factors*

Remember that you are not making any representation in the purchase contract as to the condition of the property. If the buyer has a property inspection done that shows major expensive repairs, they will almost certainly ask you to pay either half or the total cost. How much each party pays is based on three factors:

1. Supply and demand for your property type
2. Whether the buyer can recover the repair expense over time by raising rents
3. Whether the buyer can finance the renovations with their loan

Last year one of our clients lost an $8,200,000 apartment complex he was in the process of buying in Sacramento. This property was exactly what he was looking for. The property inspection report found over $700,000 in needed replacements or repairs. The buyer first tried to get the seller to pay for all of this, and then tried to get the seller to split the cost with him. It was a seller's market. The seller knew this and also knew there were no fixer-uppers left in the neighborhood. He was selling it as a repositioning opportunity. So he refused to budge on the sales price, period. Because our client was going for maximum leverage with an 80% loan, there was no room for us to finance the repairs with the mortgage. So the buyer backed out.

So if supply is low and the property is in a dynamite location, the seller can likely hold firm on not paying much or anything toward repairs. The buyer may be thinking that if they don't buy now, prices are going to continue to go up and they'll end up paying full price anyway. Also if they can refinance the repairs with their loan, they can

Selling

recover the renovation money and more over time. On the other hand, if it is a down market and there is a high inventory of similar properties for sale, you as the seller should consider offering some reduction in price. If you put the property back on the market, the next buyer will likely come up with the same list of repairs and you will be back to square one.

Online and Multiple Listing System (MLS) Marketing: *Yes, you do want to choose a listing agent who will market your property on MLS and websites like LoopNet*

With all the online commercial property listing websites these days, such as Loop-Net, is it necessary to choose a listing agent who will list the property on MLS? Well, this is one way you will know whether they are willing share their commission with another agent. Only other real estate agents can view MLS listings. Today, MLS is still a very viable and proven way for realtors to network and find buyers for each other's listings. Why not have as much exposure as possible? The argument against this is that the majority of real estate agents on MLS are residential agents. This is true because there are a lot more residential than commercial agents. But, although few residential realtors understand commercial real estate, they likely know people who invest in both residential and commercial properties. Most importantly, commercial buyers certainly don't seem to care if a realtor is residentially oriented.

Today more buyers find their commercial properties online than any other way. This is a bonus for listing real estate agents and for sellers. For listing brokers, the bonus is that buyers call them directly and are seldom represented by a buyer's agent—so they won't have to share their commission. For sellers, the bonus is that when a buyer works directly with the listing realtor who represents the seller, there is really little representation for the buyer. This can give the seller an advantage in negotiations. LoopNet is the number-one online marketplace for selling commercial real estate. There is also CoStar Group (which owns LoopNet), RealNex, CityFleet, Rofo, Craigslist, and more.

Owner's Title Insurance Policy: *It is really worth it for the seller to purchase this*

Although not mandatory, it is highly recommended that you purchase an owner's extended title insurance policy. This protects the owner against any claims brought against them for defects in the title and pays for all legal fees.

> **Basic Policy:** Guarantees clear title and covers the owner for any title defects during and before they purchased the property, including liens from mortgages thought to be satisfied, fraud, and recording errors.
>
> **Extended Owner's Coverage Policy:** Covers everything in the basic policy plus protects the owner from errors in legal descriptions, surveys, encroachments, easements, zoning, mechanic liens, and tax liens.

Private Sale: *Do this if you do not want your tenants to know you are selling the property*

If you do not want your tenants to know your commercial property is for sale, it is best to sell it through a private sale. A seller needs a private sale when they are negotiating longer-term leases with tenants to increase the value of the property prior to a sale. If tenants know you are selling the property, they will be in a position to negotiate much better lease rates and terms. When a private sale is conducted, there are no signs on the property and the listing does not appear on the Internet or MLS. What makes this approach work is using a top-producing commercial real estate broker who specializes in your property type. They will likely know many investors that will be interested in your property. They can also make the listing available to a few select real estate agents in their company who will keep it confidential.

Property Condition Inspection Report: *Wouldn't it be great to know before you put the property on the market what it needs in repairs?*

Sure, your buyer will be ordering a property inspection as part of their due diligence. Wouldn't it be great to known prior to putting your property on the market the approximate amount the buyer will ask you to take off the price due to the defects they found with their inspection? If you do not want to go through the expense of a property inspection report, consider walking the property inside and out with an experienced licensed contractor and taking notes on all needed repairs. Then get a ballpark quote for them. A definitive knowledge of the work your property needs and its cost will give you a competitive edge. Once the buyer completes the property inspection due diligence, they will want to negotiate lowering the sales price with you to pay for the repairs. Doesn't it make sense for you to determine what you are willing to pay for well ahead of time?

Property Condition Report: Major Items

Major Systems

Electrical

HVAC

Cable and phone

Boilers

Plumbing

Fire suppression

Elevators

Building Evaluation

Foundation

Façade

Roof

Railings and balconies

Building envelope

Exterior finishes

Doors and windows

Time and Money Saving Tip

Be careful about being nickel-and-dimed by the buyer who seeks multiple reductions in the sales price based on inspections of the property. The buyer will often order their own property inspection report within days of signing the purchase contract. Two to three weeks later they will come up with a list of items in need of replacement or repairs and the estimated cost to address them and request that you lower the sales price to cover these. Here's the problem: if they are getting financing, their lender will not be able to use a report ordered by the buyer and will order another one—likely more in depth. More items are likely to be found and the buyer will request another reduction in the sales price. When you are approached the first time, ask

Selling

Outdoor Improvements

Pavement

Lighting

Swimming pool

Drainage

Signage

Fencing

Interior Elements

Appliances

Floor coverings

Fixtures

Finishes

Health and Safety

ADA compliance

Fire extinguishers

Smoke alarms

Mold

the buyer if their lender has ordered a report as well. If the answer is yes, than tell the buyer you will only be negotiating with them one time on property condition.

Time and Money Saving Tip

Consider putting into the purchase and sale contract that should the property not close for any reason other than the seller being in default, that the buyer will provide you with a copy of any third-party reports at no cost to you. After all, the buyer will have no further use for them and they may be of value to you. Included will be a survey, property condition report, environmental report, and seismic report. If any of these reports were ordered by the lender, they will belong to the lender and you will have to get their permission to get copies.

Realized Gain: How to calculate what your capital gains taxes will be when you sell the property

If you are not going to do a 1031 exchange after selling your commercial property, wouldn't you like to know what your capital gains tax will be? You will be taxed on your realized gain. To compute your realized gain you have to first compute your cost basis. Start with the purchase price and add to it any other closing costs that are on your settlement statement that are not related to your loan, taxes, or insurance (look up IRS Publication 551). Next add to this amount any capital improvements you have made since owning the property (these are not repairs and maintenance, which show as expenses). This will give you your adjusted cost basis. Next subtract this amount from the sales price. This will give you the amount that is subject to capital gains tax.

Don't forget to allow for *depreciation recapture tax* (see Encyclopedia Topic E, Selling) on top of capital gains taxes.

Time Is of the Essence Clause: Take this a step further by enforcing time frames for contingencies

Most boilerplate purchase and sale agreements have a brief "time is of the essence" clause or statement, but it can be very vague. This needs to be strengthened, stating that each contingency period time frame is to be enforced. Write in an addendum as to under what circumstances the seller is willing to extend more time for contingencies and due diligence, and what those time periods will be.

For example, the financing contingency clause might state: "This offer is subject to the buyer obtaining satisfactory financing within 45 days. The financing contingency period may be extended for up to 14 days if required by the lender, with the buyer giving notification to the seller prior to the expiration of the financing contingency period. Or it can be extended for an additional 30 days with a $10,000 nonrefundable deposit should the purchase be canceled as a result of the buyer not closing on time."

Selling

PART V

Smart Strategies for Repositioning

CHAPTER 7

Unlocking Hidden Wealth with Repositioning

"**H**ow did you even think of doing that?" I remember asking Ann Clouse. "I saw the whole finished project in my head just as you see it today," she answered.

In 1992, Ann had found an abandoned poultry warehouse on the bank of a roaring creek in the tourist town of Ashland, Oregon. Her idea was to change it to a boutique hotel with a restaurant. But that's not all. All the living quarters would be small apartments with different themes. One would be designed like a traditional Japanese ryokan; another had an antique French scheme that would have been recognizable to Marie Antoinette. There were seven large suites, each decked out with its own theme. The hotel was a huge success.

Ann was a retired set designer from Hollywood. I am sure she did not know she was repositioning, let alone repurposing commercial real estate.

Repositioning refers to making management or physical changes to a property to improve its earnings and value in the marketplace. Repositioning can be as simple as raising rents and lowering expenses or as complicated as rebranding the property with a new name and look or doing major rehab. I have been amazed at what my clients have come up with to bring a humdrum property up to its unrealized potential. The best of them had a knack for unlocking the hidden treasures that others missed to increase the property's value without spending too much money to pull it off. Repositioning is where the real estate investor gets the same creative entrepreneurial opportunity as a developer, with much less risk, time, and headache.

The art of repositioning lies in finding a property that is underperforming and/or mismanaged, buying it for the right price, and then choosing the right value-adds to create the best bang for the buck.

Performing value-adding to enhance the physical and/or financial condition of a commercial property, thereby increasing the value, is what repositioning is all about. This chapter starts out by telling the stories of two investors who repositioned properties through diametrically different approaches, then goes into the three types of repositioning, tips for choosing the best property to reposition, a nine-step repositioning business plan, and concludes with repositioning pitfalls to avoid.

Over the years, I have had clients who just did not have the right temperament for repositioning. They could not be bothered to study the restrictions of the market and made decisions based on their feelings rather than on the data. Often they went on to spend too much money on the property based on what they felt it needed, not based on what they or the property could afford. If I was working on their financing you can bet they had a good business plan—but this did not mean they followed it. It was sad to see some of these projects break even at best and at worst fail completely. More often, I worked with repositioners who studied the market, stayed with their plan, made small changes en route, and then reaped the reward of a good return on their investment. The following two examples illustrate these two different outcomes.

REPOSITIONING A 246-UNIT MULTIFAMILY PROPERTY IN OKLAHOMA CITY

"You aren't going to believe this," my client Dr. Bob said to me. "I just tied up a 246-unit apartment complex in Oklahoma City that is being sold for $21,600 per unit. I put in a letter of intent for full price to snatch it. I'll pay a lot less, of course, after I do my due diligence."

I interrupted with "What is the occupancy?"

"Oh," he said, "it's only 68%, but that's because 45 units are not rent-ready and still need to be remodeled. Hey, don't give me a hard time on this one, Terry! You know I hit a home run the last two times in LA. I can buy four times more units for the same price here. You just watch. I'm going to make a million dollars in two years."

I asked him, "Are you willing to move there to oversee this rehab project?"

He snapped back, "Yeah, right, like I'm going to shut down my practice in San Diego and move to the boonies? Don't worry; I'll have boots on the ground."

This was October of 2009, just as the country was starting to pull out from under the weight of the Great Recession. At first glance, this did look like a good repositioning opportunity. The property, built in 1974, was in decent condition and could break even at its current net operating income.

Apparently, a group of out-of-state investors had bought the property as a bank-owned property (REO) in 2007 for $12,500 per unit and remodeled about 80% of the units before running out of money. Worse, their private loan had less than a month left before maturing. It was all blamed on a terrible property manager who was also the rehab project manager. To top this off, the partners spent most of the 17 months they owned the property in combat with each other. Wow, I thought—unfinished project, partners who need a divorce, plus a loan that is due! Hey, this could be a winner at the right price!

But I still tried to talk Dr. Bob out of it. I had seen too many train wrecks from out-of-state buyers thinking they could reposition a property and supervise the rehab over the phone. Projects being repositioned have so many moving parts creating havoc that the owner really does need to be there just to get in someone's face when they do a substandard job or don't keep a commitment.

My doctor buddy was not worried at all about living out of state. He had successfully repositioned two much smaller apartment buildings in West Los Angeles, increasing their net income and value substantially. I told him to get a budget for renovating the 45 units, and just stick to it. This wasn't his Los Angeles apartments where there were BMWs in the parking lot. This was a blue-collar neighborhood where rents were flat, the median income for a family of four was $34,000, and you could buy a home for $47,000.

My client got the price down to $18,000 per unit. This was still more than it was worth based on the property's current occupancy, net operating income, and unfinished units. We closed with a bridge loan that was 65% of cost and 70% of completed stabilized value in 28 days. Dr. Bob paid $4,428,000 for the property and, as planned, put $306,000 into finishing the interiors on the 45 units in the first eight months.

This would have been a perfect place to stop since his exit strategy was to increase rents and sell the property in two years. But he did not seem to have an off switch for spending. The HVAC units were old, inefficient, and breaking down, so he put $268,000 into replacing them with energy-efficient units. Now all the leaky doors and windows were staring him in the face—so he replaced those, too. He was told that the roofs only had about four years of useful life left, so yes, as you guessed it, he just had to replace those too. Then the unsightly fencing and landscaping became an eyesore and had to be brought up to the standards of the rest of the property. These items added an additional not-planned-for $644,000 to the project. And I almost forgot the $66,000 to put tenants up in hotels while their units were being worked on.

Here is how the project turned out. Dr. Bob was not happy that he had to wait three years to sell the property. During the first year, he raised rents too aggressively and lost many tenants. In his pro forma, rents were going to be raised 8% during the first year to bring them up to market rents. This would raise a $425 one-bedroom unit to $459. Dr. Bob put them up to $500, which was an increase of 18%. He did not think tenants would move out for $75 per month, but many did.

Although he had made the complex a much more attractive and better place to live, Dr. Bob broke the first two rules of repositioning: (1) paying too much for the property based on the cost to improve it, and (2) making costly improvements that will not increase the net operating income and value.

Dr. Bob sold the property for $5,850,000 after putting $5,444,000 into it. This gave him a profit on appreciation of $406,000 in three years, not the million dollars he was expecting in two years.

REPOSITIONING A 38-UNIT MULTIFAMILY PROPERTY IN GARLAND, TEXAS

"Hey, Terry, I think I have found it," Nina told me. "I talked with the owner, and this property just needs a little TLC and a big stick." Nina was a retired schoolteacher—"a loving, but mean teacher," as she described herself. She was showing me photos of a 38-unit apartment complex in Garland, Texas, a suburb of Dallas.

Nina had successfully fixed and flipped nine residential duplexes and 4-plexes and decided to move up to repositioning a multifamily property. This one was a for sale by owner (FSBO) property.

Nina went on to say, "The owner is over her head managing the property. She inherited it from her dad, and she has a wild bunch of hooligans living there." There were problems with junk in the yards and patios, rent collections, and units not made ready to rent. "Can you believe it?" Nina went on to say. "The owner is renting to a lot of her friends, her adult kids, and other relatives –well, not really renting. Many are not paying rent. She says she cannot evict her Aunt Ricki, who has not paid rent in five months." Aunt Ricki was 76, had emphysema, and was on oxygen.

This was July of 2013. Nina was looking at purchasing an 8-plex and saw this larger neglected property next door. She tracked the owner down and asked her if she would be interested in selling. "Sure," the owner replied. "If you want to pay me $1,500,000, it's yours." This was about what it would be worth if it were in good condition with good paying tenants. Nina asked her for the property financials and the seller told her she did not have any because she was terrible at math. Nina told her she would get back to her in a few days.

We pulled a preliminary title report on the property and found that the seller did not have a mortgage but owed four years of back taxes. Nina was able to get copies of the last two months' utility bills after finding out the property was *master metered* for electricity. This meant that the owner was paying for the tenants, heating, air-conditioning, and lights.

We put together a pro forma based on market rents, expenses, and those utility bills. It helped that we had just closed a loan on a property in nearby Fort Worth that was of a similar size and condition that was also master metered. Having the appraisal meant that we could accurately project the income and expenses. Nina made a list of value-add strategies she would do.

The property appeared to be in fair condition. After four years of neglect, it mostly needed, as Nina put it, a good coat of paint and a good scrubbing. I asked Nina how much cash she could put into sprucing up the property. She only had about $70,000. This meant that she would have to focus almost exclusively on operational repositioning, which would cost very little.

It was clear that for the right price this was an outstanding repositioning opportunity—but only if Nina could get the property for a maximum of $1,250,000. Nina sat down with the buyer and told her, "Look, you're about to lose this property to the county for those back taxes. I can pay you $1,100,000 in cash. We can close in two weeks." They settled on $1,200,000 and an agreement that Aunt Ricki could live there rent-free for an additional six months.

Nina acquired the property with a two-year term bridge loan, putting 25% down. I built an eight-month payment reserve into the loan, which would give her time without payments to get the property in shape.

Here is how it turned out. All the tenants were on month-to-month rental contracts or no contracts. It took seven months for Nina to evict all the no-pays and slow-paying ones (she had projected four months for this). She rebranded the property with a new name, logo, sign, and website. She ran credit, background, and employment checks on all new tenants. She instituted a Ratio Utility Billing System (RUBS), where the master-metered electricity was prorated monthly and billed back to the tenants. This lowered her expenses by $56,000 per year. She lowered the insurance bill by $2,200 annually by shopping competitively. She made ready all of the apartments and achieved 95% occupancy in eight months, raising rents by 7%. None of these items cost money, just time. It cost her $7,200 to implement a water conservation program, putting in water-saving showerheads and toilets. The benefit was lowering the water bill by $18,000 per year. She spent $19,000 to clean up the property and give it a fresh coat of paint. Another $55,000 was spent on painting the interiors and replacing some floor coverings and appliances.

Twenty-two months after she purchased it, we had Nina's apartment complex appraised for permanent financing. She had decided to hold on to it and have it professionally managed. Because the net operating income was increased, the value shot up to $1,685,000. Nina's cost to purchase the property plus improvements was $1,281,800. Her repositioning had earned her $403,200 in equity in less than two years, and doubled her cash investment.

MANAGE YOUR REPOSITION PROJECT ACCORDING TO A PLAN

These two stories illustrate two different approaches to repositioning with drastically different results. One was managed according to a plan and the other had a plan that was not managed. Both Nina and Dr. Bob bought Class C multifamily properties in neighborhoods where rents were flat. Both properties were in fair to good condition. Both paid slightly more than the properties were worth based on economic occupancy and net operating income.

So how could the *rate of returns* (*ROI*) be so vastly different between the two? Nina earned about the same amount of money in appreciation in less than two years as Dr. Bob did in three years, investing a fifth of what he did. Dr. Bob had more money to invest and bought a much larger property than Nina did. His down payment plus improvements came to $2,406,100. Her down payment plus improvements came to $401,512. His annual *internal rate of return* (*IRR*) (see Encyclopedia Topic A, Buying), including net income plus appreciation, came to 11%. She hit a whopping 52%.

Nina made mostly low-cost operational changes. She just did not have the cash to do it any other way. Dr. Bob used mostly costly constructional upgrades and medium-cost cosmetic ones. This approach had worked well for him in affluent Los Angeles neighborhoods, but not in a low-income neighborhood in Oklahoma City. In short, he overimproved the property for its potential return and value.

THREE TYPES OF REPOSITIONING

1. **Operational Repositioning:** These changes cost little and have to do with improving operations. Just as in any business, improving management is always a good place to start. Begin with comparing the subject property's rents with those of competitors and make a plan to increase them to market rents if they are lower.

   Fill all vacancies, even though it will take a lot longer to screen the tenants carefully. If you put anyone in who has a pulse, you are just solving one problem today to create another in the near future.

   Go over each expense line by line and analyze where they can be lowered. A good property manager or commercial mortgage broker can help you analyze expenses and identify the ones that are too high. If the property manager is contracting out service for repairs, maintenance, and landscaping, make sure these services are competitively shopped. Go to the *Operational Repositioning Checklist* in Encyclopedia Topic F, Repositioning.

2. **Cosmetic Repositioning:** These changes are of moderate cost and change the property's appeal to tenants. They include: restriping the parking lot, light landscaping, interior and exterior paint, new floor coverings, appliances, and furnishings. To see a complete list, go to the *Cosmetic Repositioning Checklist* in Encyclopedia Topic F, Repositioning.

3. **Constructional Repositioning:** These changes are expensive and have a construction component. Sometimes they involve increasing square footage and major rehab or new construction. They include adding amenities like a swimming pool and fitness center—replacing roofs, windows, doors, and major systems like plumbing, electrical, and HVAC. To see a complete list, go to the *Constructional Repositioning Checklist* in Encyclopedia Topic F, Repositioning.

TIPS FOR CHOOSING THE BEST PROPERTY FOR REPOSITIONING

1. **Choose a Property That Needs Mostly Operational and Cosmetic Upgrades:** These changes are most likely to create the largest return on the money you invest in improvements, due to the lower cost to implement, shorter time period to complete, and not having to vacate good paying tenants. Major constructional changes should only be done if you can get the property for the right price, have working capital to cover cost overruns, and the appraisal supports an absorption time frame that shows that the property can be completed and leased before the money runs out.

2. **Choose a Property That Is Poorly Managed and Underperforming But Not Overpriced:** The best opportunities for repositioning are properties that are poorly managed. Often these properties have an owner who is burned out, going through emotional distress, undercapitalized, or all three. These properties are in need of operational changes—raising rents, lowering expenses, and filling vacancies. They also will likely be in need of cosmetic and constructional improvements that can be done over time. In an "up" seller's market, these properties are usually overpriced. If this is the case, you will need to convince the seller that the price needs to be lowered because of the time and money it will take for you improve it. In a down market, economic occupancy will likely be low, putting financial stress on the seller. You want to offer a very low price and offer to take this property off his hands by closing in 30 days or less with a bridge loan.

3. **Choose a Class C Property That Is Below the Quality of the Market:** Almost all of the similar-type properties are in much better condition with better-quality tenants paying higher rents. An example is to find a Class C apartment property in an upscale market that is surrounded by Class A and B properties. You can remodel the units, improve the landscaping, and add a playground and some outdoor sitting areas. You will likely only bring the property up to a C+, which will not command the rents of a Class B property. But you will be able to greatly increase rents and property value.

4. **Choose a Property with Additional Square Footage That Can Be Developed:** This can be an industrial, office, or retail complex that has additional land, common areas, or open not-rentable space that can be developed into useable square footage that can be occupied by new tenants. For multifamily properties, choose a property that has an additional lot that can be purchased for a fair price to build more units.

Time and Money Savings Tip

If your intention is to fix and flip, don't make the mistake of focusing on what you think the appraiser's first impressions of the property will be. Commercial appraisers just aren't wired that way. And don't think that adding amenities like a swimming pool or fitness center will necessarily increase the appraised value. What it comes down to is that the income approach is king in a commercial appraisal, which is based on net operating income, not the physical condition of the property or its amenities.

The appraiser starts out by computing the capitalization (cap) rate on the subject property based on its net operating income. Most appraisers do not want to kill a sale, so they will do whatever they can to then find comparable properties that support the cap rate that the subject property is showing. In the sales-comparable approach, the appraiser will try to find comparables that are close in supporting the value in the income approach. They will then deduct the cost of major deferred maintenance items from the value. Overall, this will not lower the appraised value much if you have greatly increased the net operating income.

5. **Choose a Property Where You Can Keep Most of the Current Tenants in Place:** It will increase your risk substantially by adding a lot more cost to your project if you have to move out, relocate, or compensate good tenants to do cosmetic and constructional changes in their spaces. Having to give existing tenants free rent or pay for the loss of their income during construction is very expensive. Being able to retain at least 75% of existing rental income while you are doing your value-adds will help you get better-quality financing. Finding a

property where you can make changes with minimal disturbances to existing tenants is a plus.

6. **Choose a Property That Can Be Repositioned within an Effective Time Frame:** The longer you take to make repositioning changes and start collecting those higher rents, the higher the risk that the project will fail. Time is the hidden expense that many repositioners are not aware of until it takes them much longer to complete a project than expected. They then get to experience paying more interest on their loan and having to pay expenses on the property without adequate income. Also, if you take too much time in an "up" market, the market could take a downturn, lowering the demand for your property.

THE BIGGEST BANG FOR THE BUCK

Repositioning successfully is about achieving your ideal rate of return (ROI) on the cash you invest. This is a balancing act between the price you pay for the property, the target net operating income you are seeking, and the amount of money and time it will take for you to get there.

Nine-Step Repositioning Business Plan

A repositioning business plan is your blueprint to: (1) design your repositioning project so it is lower-risk and profitable; (2) to establish time frames for all value-adds to keep the project running at maximum efficiency and profitability; and (3) to define the maximum purchase price based on the amount of money you plan on for improvements.

At the heart of the business plan is knowing the competition, understanding the demographics, and market conditions, and coming up with the right list of value-adds. Creating a pro forma that is supported by market data and shows that your target rate of return is attainable is the meat of the business plan. You will be able to use this business plan to raise capital from private investors and lenders.

1. **Research the Competition:** This is a fun one. You are going to be doing your own mini market feasibility study. Once you find a property that is a good candidate for repositioning, find at least three to four similar properties in the same market. Go inspect these yourself and take copious notes as to property condition, quality of the tenants, quality of the patrons, quality of cars parked, and traffic count. Make a list of all the items that make these properties better or worse than the subject property. What can you do to give your property a competitive edge? If the competition is doing better, why? Is it

tenant mix, location, condition of the property, amenities, or a combination of all these?

2. **Conduct Market Research on Rents and Determine the Property Value:** Your job here is to determine the value of the subject property as is. Have your real estate broker, bank, or commercial mortgage broker supply you with at least three comparable sales of a similar property type and similar size in the same market. This will give you comparable rents and the market cap rate. For multifamily and hospitality properties, comparable rent will be price per unit. For office, retail, and industrial properties, use rent per square foot. It would be a plus, of course, if you can physically inspect these properties to determine if they are better, worse, or about the same condition as the subject property. Next determine the cap rate of the subject property.

$$\frac{\text{Net operating income}}{\text{Sales price}} = \text{Cap rate}$$

Based on cap rate, break-even ratio, and property condition, is the subject property priced fairly, or overpriced? Is there room for you to spend money on the property and how will this increase its value?

Time and Money Saving Tip

If the market is transitioning from up to down, or in the event of a recession, it is even more imperative to check the economic occupancy (based on rents collected) of the property you are buying and repositioning, as well as to add up and annualize rent concessions, which if present will most likely be ongoing. Credit loss from unpaid rents increases during a recession due to the ripple effect of fewer goods and services being purchased. The easiest way for sellers to raise occupancy at these times is to offer generous rental concessions. The purchase price will need to be adjusted down if rent collections are down and/or there are extensive rental concessions. In an up seller's market you might end up paying more for a property that has great potential for bringing in more income. But in a down buyer's market, you should always pay less.

In a down market, rental concessions should be annualized and subtracted from gross annual rent, as they are not likely to go away until the market swings the other way. Make it clear to the seller that the price you pay for the property has to be based on actual annual gross rents collected. Most of all, you want to make sure that the total project NOI does not raise your break-even ratio above 75% on your first year of operations' pro forma after all your value-adds have been implemented and the property has been leased up.

3. **Conduct Demographic Research:** Your experienced buyer's real estate agent can pull up market data for you on key economic and demographic indicators for your project from market data services like Costar and REIS. For larger projects of $5,000,000 and up or if you are making expensive constructional changes, consider having a market/feasibility study done. This gives you all your major competitors and construction starts, and will tell you accurately what market rents and tenant profiles are, along with supply and demand, within a three- to five-mile radius of the subject property, as well as estimates for rent growth and time for stabilization. The last thing you want to do is to reposition a property for a specific type of tenant who is not going to like the location.

4. **Create a Pro Forma and Determine Future Value:** Create a three- to five-year pro forma, or use the time period you plan to hold the property. Show existing rents to begin with and then show rents decreasing during months you are repositioning if you will need to move tenants out. Then show rents increasing and any expenses decreasing as you forecast this over time. Be sure to put in some *rental concessions* if you are in a market that is using them. Where is the net operating income forecasted to be in two and three years? What will the property be worth (use current cap rates) at these future times? What is your ROI expected to be at exit (see step 6)?

5. **Make a List of Operational, Cosmetic, and Constructional Changes and Costs:** At a minimum, get a ballpark quote from a general contractor or property manager on what the cost will be to do the items on your value-add

Time and Money Saving Tip

Market vacancy tends to increase steadily over time during a recession until it peaks and the recovery phase of the real estate market cycle begins. Of course, there is no way of knowing when it's going to get better. If you are buying a commercial property with the intention of repositioning it during a recession, be conservative and put in at least two tiers for vacancy in your operating pro forma for the first two years after your value-adds have been implemented. For example, if the current vacancy is at 7%, do a pro forma reflecting 15% for the first year after your value-adds are completed. Then do a second pro forma at 10% vacancy for your second year assuming occupancy will be improving. You can show a third year at 7% if you like. If the NOI does not support the deal at 15% vacancy after raising rents and lowering expenses, consider offering a lower purchase price, or walk away. For your pro forma you can find an example of the Seven-Year Month-by-Month Budget and Summary Spreadsheet in Appendix A, and a downloadable Excel version on my website: https://apartmentloanstore.com/.

list. If doing everything on your list means you will not hit your target ROI (see the next step), then prioritize the list and remove some items to put you back on budget.

6. **Project Your Rate of Investment (ROI):** If you purchase the property for a specific price and you spend the amount of money on value-adds forecasted in step 4, what will your ROI be when the project appreciates on a hypothetical date in the future? There are two types of ROI when repositioning shown next. Decide your target ROI for both.

ROI Based on Purchase Price plus Cost of Value-Adds

This metric calculates the ROI percentage, based on the total project costs (purchase price plus value-add improvements), as it relates to the future appreciated value. Ideally, you want this ROI to be at least 15%; 20% would be superb. Here is an example:

$$\frac{\text{Appreciated value} - \text{Project cost}}{\text{Total cost}} = \text{ROI}$$

Let's say you buy an office complex for $4,500,000 and put $650,000 into cosmetic and constructional upgrades, bringing your total cost to $5,150,000. In three years, based on market cap rates and the property's net operating income, the property is worth $6,000,000. Your ROI is 16.5% on appreciation alone.

Appreciated value	$6,000,000	$850,000
Less total cost	−5,150,000	5,150,000 = 16.5% ROI
Balance	$850,000	
Annual rate of investment = 5.5%		

ROI Based on Down Payment plus Cost of Value-Adds

This is the metric that most commercial property investors prefer to use. It calculates the ROI on your down payment plus cash invested in improvements, as this relates to a percentage of the appraised value. Ideally you want this ROI to be at least 40%; 65% or more would be great. Let's say you are putting 25% down on the earlier scenario, which would be $1,125,000. This plus the $650,000 in improvements comes to $1,775,000. Here is your ROI in 3 years:

Appreciated value	$6,000,000	
Less down payment plus improvements	−1,775,000	
Balance	4,225,000	4,225,000
		6,000,000 = 70% ROI
Annual rate of investment = 23%		

7. **Determine the Maximum Purchase Price and Cash Injection for Repositioning:** Based on your pro forma, the projected ROI, and *internal rate of return (IRR)* after doing your value adds, determine your maximum sales price.

8. **Put It All in a Time Frame:** Yes, I know, I'm bugging you about this again. But time is not your friend on real estate deals, especially when repositioning. Make a list of all the steps for each repositioning item and assign a completion date for each. Get anyone who is responsible for working on each item to sign an agreement to complete it by a specific date. For cosmetic and constructional work, consider giving workers and contractors a bonus if they finish early and a penalty if they finish late.

9. **Choose the Best Experts for Your Team**

   ▪ **Buyer's Real Estate Broker:** A buyer's broker will help you with market research, seeing leasing value-add opportunities such as improving tenant mix, and negotiating the best sales price possible.

   ▪ **Property Manager:** An experienced offsite property manager who specializes in your commercial property type can help with evaluating the quality of the property and give you their professional opinion on the maximum rents you can attain after your value-adds. They will also give you an opinion of what can be done to lower operating expenses. They can help you with your pro forma and create an operating budget for you, as well as give you advice on the best tenant mix.

   ▪ **Commercial Mortgage Broker or Lender:** An experienced commercial mortgage broker will likely have more time than a bank to give you expert market advice on property value, rents, and expenses. Most importantly, they can give you a proposal for financing that will tell you if you can achieve the loan you are looking for.

   ▪ **Designer and/or Architect:** If you are doing very simple light constructional changes such as changing non-load-bearing walls, a low-cost designer can make a drawing for you at a fraction of the cost of an architect. The advantage during this stage is that you can try many designs out at a nominal cost. Architects are trained in design and engineering plus project management. They are a must for more complex projects that need major constructional changes. For these projects to get a firm bid from a contractor, an architectural drawing will be needed. To save money you can start out working with a designer to try out different ideas. Then take your concept to an architect, who can create floor plans and elevation drawings that you will need for government approvals, your lender, and your contractor. When choosing an architect, find one who specializes in your commercial property type. You might have to talk to a few to find one you can collaborate well with. Between the two of you, you can really make this project sing!

■ **Contractor:** Choosing the right contractor for constructional changes and major rehab can make or break you. You want one who can get the job done the way you want, on budget and on time. They should be able to provide you with a ballpark quote to begin with and then a line-by-line construction contract. Ask for a list of projects they have completed, and references on them. After the purchase contract is fully executed, ask several contractors to give you a ballpark quote. This is likely to be accurate within 15% and will give you some idea of the cost to plan for.

Fourteen Repositioning Pitfalls to Avoid

This list comes from mistakes I have observed my clients making while repositioning:

1. **Paying Too Much for the Property:** This is the number-one mistake when doing expensive cosmetic and constructional changes. About 15% of my experienced rehab clients find at the end that, after cost and time overruns, they paid too much for the property. This can soar to over 50% for inexperienced rehabbers. You are not going to have an accurate estimate of what it is going to cost you for value-adds until you get written bids for them. Also if the lease-up takes longer than expected and you have loan payments to make, and your payment reserve has run out, this will cost you money. So assume the project is going to cost more than your initial budget. Even though it might mean you have to make 40 offers to get one to stick, finding an underperforming property at a great price will lower your risk and ensure your success more than anything else.

Time and Money Savings Tip

Cosmetic and constructional repositioning projects more often than not go over budget. In fact they go over budget to a much greater extent than ground-up construction projects do. This is because when repairing one item another is often found that needs replacing. Be sure to budget an additional 15% of your renovation budget as a contingency fund for unexpected expenses. Also increase your payment reserve (which covers loan payments until the property can make them) by an extra 20% to allow for the property taking longer than projected to break even and be able to make the payments on its own. For example, if you are planning on an eight-month payment reserve, increase it to 10 months.

2. **Making Changes That Will Not Increase Net Operating Income (NOI):** Increasing the bottom line is why you are repositioning in the first place. To increase the value of the property you need to increase the NOI. If you intend

to fix and flip, any change to the property that does not increase NOI should be eliminated.

3. **Overspending for the Potential Return:** Choose costly cosmetic and constructional value-adds carefully. It is often a delicate balancing act to choose the improvements that will give you the best chance of making your expected return on investment. If you overspend on improvements for the property's potential return, you might find yourself making a much smaller profit than intended, or, worse yet, being in the red.

4. **Misjudging the Absorption Rate:** The absorption rate is the time frame planned for the property to reach market occupancy, called stabilization. Few anticipate this hidden risk. I have had repositioners lose their property because of this alone. The greatest danger lies in not reaching the occupancy needed to break even before the money runs out.

5. **Choosing a Property with Little or No Cash Flow:** This greatly increases the risk. Being able to do cosmetic and constructional value-adds where you can work on one or a few units or spaces at a time while retaining most of the property's rental income is a plus. Designing your repositioning project so the property can pay its own expenses and some of its loan payment while underway is a huge plus.

6. **Not Knowing Your Maximum Purchase Price:** Guesstimating the maximum sales price you can afford when value-adding is dangerous. So be sure to do all your homework on market research and the cost of your changes to the property to determine the maximum sales price. In a seller's market, you might need to offer more than your maximum purchase price to be able to snatch a property. But if you are good at negotiating you can then bring the price down to your maximum purchase price prior to your due diligence period being up.

7. **Thinking You Can Change the Class of a Property:** If the subject property is a Class C in a submarket that has many Class A and B properties that are booming, be aware that it is not practical or easy to upgrade the property to a Class B. Class A and B multifamily properties have palatial exteriors, high ceilings, roomy interiors, and luxury amenities. Taking an older Class C property and thinking you can bring it up to a Class B by putting in granite countertops and stainless steel appliances is not going to do it. It's still going to have the look and feel of a Class C property. This is the case for office and retail properties, too.

8. **Living Out of State:** Acquiring a property that needs repositioning out of state greatly increases the risk of failure. The exception to this is if you already have experience owning commercial property in that market. Buying in your own backyard means that you likely know and understand the local economy and can more accurately identify undervalued and underperforming assets. Also, you will have better access to the best professionals—the right real estate broker,

property manager, lender, and contractor. It is imperative that you are on-site most days to oversee the implementation of value-adds and the lease-up of the property.

9. **Selling Too Early:** Be sure to not put the property on the market before you have completed the renovations and filled it with quality tenants. Ideally wait a minimum of three months, when new tenants have a positive record of paying the rent. If you sell after repositioning too early, before you have reached market occupancy, the buyer is going to want to discount the sales price. Also, filling the property quickly with tenants who have not been properly screened, and giving them rent concessions as an incentive to move in, will likely come back to bite you. This is because some of these tenants will be slow-paying or no-paying. Your buyer or their lender will discover this and either cancel the sale or insist on a much lower sales price.

10. **Putting in the Wrong Tenant Mix for Shopping Centers:** Taking the time to create the right tenant mix when repositioning a shopping center is essential. It pays to hire a skilled retail-leasing agent to advise you and help you find the right tenants. If you do not have a grocery-anchored shopping center, try to attract some national tenants that will be your anchors, like a Starbucks or dollar store. Then mix in clusters of shops that complement each other. Having a popular restaurant chain and some service business is a plus too. Someone grabbing a bite to eat or going to visit a chiropractor at your location will likely do some shopping afterwards.

11. **Being Undercapitalized and Not Having Working Capital:** As mentioned earlier, if you are doing mostly cosmetic and constructional changes, it is more likely than not that your repositioning project will cost more and take longer than planned. It is very common when doing cosmetic changes to find constructional changes that were not planned for. An example is thinking that you are just going to replace roof shingles, but when they are removed, you find that the subroofing needs to be replaced.

    Banks and the best bridge lenders that make rehab loans will approve the loan only if the borrower has sufficient backup capital. The worst bridge lenders hope that you will run out of funds when you have 90% of the project completed. They can then foreclose and reap huge benefits without having put in much effort. Having working capital or a rainy day fund of at least 15% of the project's cost (the purchase price plus renovation costs) is imperative to cover the unknowns, including an unforeseen change in the economy.

12. **Choosing a Flaky Contractor:** Flaky contractors continually run behind schedule and blame others for their mistakes. Even worse, they find some reason to increase the construction contract. Sometimes they underbid to land the contract, knowing they will make it up on change orders. Be sure

to only hire licensed, bonded contractors who have good references. Get a list of projects they have completed to make sure they have the experience to complete yours. If your lender is a bank and has not worked with the contractor before, they will check their business and personal credit. In your construction contract, have a clause put in that all change orders and their cost have to be approved by you. Without this, a flaky contractor will just bill you for changes at an exorbitant cost.

13. **Choosing Poor Real Estate Agents or Property Managers for the Lease-Up:** Putting the lease-up of your repositioned property into the hands of an over-worked, underpaid professional will cost you a ton of money. The longer it takes to fill those units, the longer it takes for the property to run profitably. The property management business, especially for multifamily properties, is one of the least cost-effective businesses on the planet. It is so labor intensive that many management company employees only have time to give proper service to the squeaky wheels. Of course, there are management companies that do an excellent job. One of my clients who had rehabbed an apartment complex found out that their property manager was taking weekends off and not showing the units. Weekends are when most renters are off work and are looking for rentals.

For office, retail, and industrial properties, real estate agents handle leasing. Property managers who are managed by property owners do a much more effective job. Give them your expectations in writing and get them to give you a report weekly. Brainstorm with them on ways to find good tenants. Don't

---

Time and Money Savings Tip

Be extra-cautious about buying a property for repositioning in an extended up seller's market. In this situation there is such a shortage of properties on the market that the properties in need of value-adding go for almost as much as properties that do not need much work. The United States had three long boom periods since 1991. In that year, the real estate market kept going up for 10 years. Then there was a six-year boom period, followed by another 10-year one after the Great Recession in July 2009. In all three instances it had been long enough since there had been a recession that sellers and buyers seemed to forget all about them. When buyers purchased real estate at the end of these periods, they were buying at unprecedented high prices that could only fall quickly during the recessions that followed.

The very best scenario is to pick up a property where the seller made costly cosmetic and constructional upgrades during a boom time and then got caught midstream when a recession hit. Running out of money before they could get the property stabilized, they are forced to sell below their cost.

allow them to offer *rent concessions* without your approval. Communicate with them at least once per week. Don't be afraid to be the squeaky wheel.

14. **Not Getting at Least Three Bids When Doing Major Rehab:** This is something you want to do right after the purchase contract is signed. Be sure to have it put in the sales contract that contractors can inspect the property. I have seen bids vary by 20% or more for the same work. Schedule the contractors to inspect the property on separate dates and make sure they all know you are having three contractors bid on the project.

Repositioning

Absorption: *The second reason repositioning projects fail is the misjudging of absorption*

What if it takes you 50% longer than you planned to fill your repositioned property with tenants? How much longer would it take to reach your *break-even point* (see Encyclopedia Topic A, Buying), where you are paying all the expenses and the mortgage? At some point, you are not going to be able to sleep at night knowing that you are going to run out of money. Absorption is the amount of time it takes to fill vacant units in a market based on the number of units available. Absorption can be your friend in an up market or your enemy in a down market. Unfortunately, it is based on the whims of supply and demand for that property type. The number-one reason repositioning projects fail is the owner overspending for the potential return on the investment. The second reason is misjudging the absorption rate.

Absorption rates for a commercial property type are positive, negative, or flat. Multifamily property absorption rates are measured by the number of units vacant on the market divided by the total supply of units during a specific time period. The rate for office, retail, and industrial space is based on the amount of square footage vacant in the market divided by the total square footage of the total supply in the market of that property type during an allotted amount of time. Give a commercial property appraiser a call and ask them about absorption rates for your property type in the market. You can also call your commercial banker, who will have many recent appraisals and can look this up for you. Your repositioning pro forma is going to need market absorption rates to be accurate.

The worst scenario for absorption is when midway through leasing a repositioned property a recession hits, greatly slowing down absorption. I can tell you that my clients who had four to six months of working capital to cover all expenses and mortgage payments for their property made it through this hurdle.

Positive Absorption: There is more leased than vacant space in the submarket.

Negative Absorption: There is more vacant than leased space in the submarket.

Adaptive Reuse (Repurposing): *Taking an old building, using it for a different purpose, and making it beautiful*

Did you know that old historical buildings—even warehouses that have been repurposed as office buildings—often get the same, if not higher, rents than Class A properties in the same neighborhood? This is because they usually have so much more character. They provide an aesthetic and artistic experience that top-of-the-line new properties cannot compete with. Often these repurposed old properties have amenities such as indoor and outdoor common areas, grand lobbies, conference rooms, gyms, and cafés.

Adaptive reuse is when you take an existing building and repurpose it for another use. In many mid-size or smaller towns you will find what was once an old abandoned train station with a lot of historical character turned into a classy restaurant. Repurposing an old obsolete property can be close in cost to new ground-up construction, but is usually less. It really helps if you can obtain the building for as close to the value of the land as possible to make the project economically feasible. Be sure to allow extra time if the property has to be rezoned or a local variance has to be obtained.

Appreciation, Forced: *I know we are told not to force things, but forcing your rents up will raise the property value*

Appreciation of a commercial property is an elusive concept. Sure, you can buy a property and hang on to it long enough, like 7 to 10 years, and it will likely go up in value. But if you want control over this and want your property value to go up fast, the best way to accomplish this is to use forced appreciation—and the best way to do this quickly is through repositioning. Forced appreciation is the method of increasing rents and lowering expenses in a short amount of time, thus dramatically increasing the net operating income and property value. This involves making just the right upgrades

> ### Time and Money Saving Tip
>
> If you find an old building that has become functionally obsolete or, better yet, abandoned, check for local city or state grants or very-low-cost loans that encourage economic investment and revitalization of old buildings. State and federal historical preservation programs can be very useful in raising money. Municipalities often offer gap financing—very-low-cost second-position loans—for renovating old or abandoned buildings. Also, check to see if the building will qualify for a 20% tax credit from the Secretary of the Interior for certified historic structures.

to the property and then raising rents as quickly but intelligently as possible. Buying a property for less than it is worth is difficult during an up market. But finding a property that has under-market rents that can be repositioned is always doable. This is because procrastination in raising rents is so common. Many landlords just don't want to confront longtime existing tenants with rental increases. It's interesting, but when these properties sell, the new owner doesn't seem to have a problem with this.

I have clients who have become wealthy by specializing in forced appreciation by implementing lower-cost *operational and cosmetic repositioning* (see the Cosmetic Repositioning Checklist and Operational Repositioning Checklist later in this Topic) upgrades. The best properties to buy for repositioning are those that have been poorly managed and owned by worn-out owners. These properties are notorious for having under-market rents and over-market expenses. Finding properties that have higher-than-market vacancies, rent collection problems, and the overuse of rental concessions are great for creating forced appreciation through repositioning.

Ballpark Quotes: *These just about always underpriced quotes could put you into a pickle financially*

I have to be blunt about using ballpark quotes or estimates when buying a commercial property that needs constructional repositioning. Sure, this can work for light cosmetic changes such as painting and new floor coverings as long as you have the measurements. But when making your decision to buy a property that needs expensive constructional changes, don't even think about basing it on ballpark quotes. Many of my clients have started out their projects this way. The problem is that all, and I'm not exaggerating, *all* of them ended up paying more for the work. We are talking about 20% to even 50% more. This is because a contractor has to have a detailed list of all the work needed, and actual measurements to quote each item accurately. The only way to know what the project is going to cost is with a construction bid or contract. You can get away without architectural drawings, but a design drawing is a must to get a construction bid for a rehab project. Sure, go ahead and tie a property up based on a ballpark estimate for the constructional work. But until you get a property condition report and an actual bid from a contractor, you will not know if the project is economically feasible.

Building Codes and Permits:

Be prepared to bring old properties up to current building code standards when doing major rehab

Be aware that making constructional repositioning changes to a commercial property will most likely trigger the need for building permits, inspections, and, if the configuration of the space has changed, a new occupancy permit. Where it really gets expensive is when changing major systems like the structure itself and having to bring the entire building into compliance with current building codes, including fire and safety. Usually, if you do not build on to the structure, construct or remove walls, or add new plumbing or electrical work, a building permit will not be required. I had a client who put in a new HVAC system in an office building. The cost

---

Time and Money Saving Tip

Contractors will sometimes bid constructional rehab projects low, knowing you will likely need change orders that they can make a killing on later. In fact, when inspecting the property, they might see items that they think you might have missed and plan to point these out to you later. Their hope is that they can trap you with change orders where they can charge you whatever they want and increase their profit. Anything that is not in the contract is fair game for a change order. Be sure to have an inspector other than the contractor go through the property and your design drawings carefully, looking for additional items that were not in the construction contract that might come up later. Then get a separate bid on them from your contractor. You can decide later whether you want to take action on those.

of bringing the ductwork up to current fresh air flow standards added a third more to the cost.

Competition Analysis: *Is your property more tired and worn out than your competitors'?*

To raise rents and bring your repositioned property to its optimum, do a competition analysis. Take a look at your subject property's condition and amenities to compare it to the most successful commercial properties of the same type in the market. By comparing three to five of your top competitors, you can determine what needs to be done to the subject property. To stay competitive, commercial properties usually need to be renovated every 10 years. Here are some items to analyze:

1. How old is your property and when was it last upgraded? Have your competitors improved their properties more recently?
2. How does the overall condition of your property compare to the competition? Is it out of date, grossly worn out, somewhat exhausted in spots, or just a little tired? Take a look at the entrance, lobby, common areas, interior and exterior finishes, parking lot, walkways, and landscaping.
3. Does the best of the competition have special amenities that your property lacks like enticing parklike outdoor common areas, comfy furniture, a workout room, or a café?
4. What are people saying about your property and the competition on social media?
5. How does the traffic count of your property compare with the best of your competitors?

To answer these questions, get the assistance of an experienced commercial property-leasing broker who specializes in your property type. They can tell you which of your competitors have recently repositioned their properties, exactly what they did, and how much rent they were able to get. They might even arrange giving you a tour of one of these properties. Get their opinion on how much you can raise rents if you upgrade the property to the level to your top competitors. Then determine the cost and whether the improved net operating income will justify the expense and achieves your rate of return goals.

Constructional Repositioning Checklist: *Check off your ideal constructional improvements*

Constructional repositioning usually involves light or major rehab and replacement of one or more major systems. Often building permits are required and sometimes rezoning and a new certificate of occupancy may be required. Constructional changes can include adding more rentable square footage, creating appealing outdoor common areas, or adding a fitness center, playground, dog park, café, covered parking, or storage units.

___ Electrical system   ___ New fencing   ___ New landscaping
___ Plumbing system   ___ New framing and trusses   ___ Swimming pool
___ HVAC system   ___ New windows and doors   ___ New outdoor area
___ Roofs   ___ New gutters/downspouts   ___ Fitness room
___ Sewage and septic   ___ Handicap access   ___ Playground
___ Foundation work   ___ New tubs and showers   ___ New lobby
___ New siding   ___ Tiling work   ___ New rec building
___ Stonework   ___ Drywall installation   ___ New security features
___ New decking   ___ Parking lot resurfacing   ___ New square footage
___ New walkways   ___ New subflooring   ___ Storage units
___ New insulation   ___ Carports

Cosmetic Repositioning Checklist:

These items can really give your property a whole new look and raise your rents, without breaking the bank

Cosmetic repositioning upgrades are moderate in cost. They can dramatically change the look and feel of a commercial property attracting a much higher-grade tenant willing to pay higher rents. They do not require building permits.

Time and Money Saving Tip

When making constructional upgrades there are often inconveniences to existing tenants such as excessive noise, dust, and inadequate access to their rental spaces. The last thing you want is for them to be unhappy and threaten to move. Just letting your tenants know you care about them can make a huge difference. The bottom line is that it is essential for you to communicate frequently with your tenants as to the overall scope of the work, what work will affect them, and the daily work start and stop times. You or your property manager should contact each tenant by email weekly and ask how the construction work is affecting them. When complaints arise, meet with the contractor to work out a remedy. Then contact the tenant and let them know you are on it!

___ Restriping the parking lot   ___ New bathroom vanities
___ Repairing cracked walkways   ___ Painting kitchen cabinets
___ Manicuring the landscaping   ___ New kitchen cabinets
___ New interior and exterior paint   ___ Repair fencing

Repositioning

___ New fixtures   ___ Replace fencing

___ New floor coverings   ___ New furnishings in common areas

___ New appliances   ___ New signage

___ New kitchen countertops   ___ Refurbish the rental office

___ New window coverings   ___ Install gas barbeques

___ New lighting fixtures   ___ New appliances

___ New bathroom fixtures   ___ New baseboards, moldings, and trim

Design Drawings Versus Architectural Drawings: *For constructional repositioning you might be able to use a designer instead of an architect and save a bundle*

When making constructional repositioning changes to a commercial property, you will need drawings to get a construction bid and contract. For many projects, design drawings done by a drafter will be adequate. For major constructional changes requiring engineering, a licensed architect will be required. Drafters charge between $50 and $80 per hour, whereas commercial architects charge 6% to 10% of total project costs or an average of $150 per hour.

> ### Time and Money Saving Tip
>
> Many of my clients have overly improved commercial properties based on their personal taste and feelings. It's almost if they thought they were going to live or work there. Be sure to choose cosmetic and construction upgrades based on what the property needs and can afford. Sure, improving the property just the way you want it might give you the good feeling of pride of ownership. But if you fail to achieve the rate of return on your investment that you wanted, you are being counterproductive. So make sure the property can support the improvements that are on your wish list. If not, maybe take a detour from some of your tastes.

Distressed Property: *Be wary of buying a distressed property in a bad neighborhood*

A commercial property is considered distressed if it has 80% occupancy or less in a market that has 90% occupancy or more for that property type. Distressed properties are often an eyesore as well. If the condition is due to poor management, this can be a great opportunity for repositioning. Usually these properties just need inexpensive operational and cosmetic changes. A new property manager who rules with an iron fist and is more aggressive at leasing might be just what is needed. A distressed property that is in an undesirable location or low-rent area may not be a good candidate for repositioning. Maybe the property is better off left as a Class D with the rents kept low. You don't want to overimprove the property and not be able to raise rents because the average wage earner in the neighborhood cannot afford it.

Economic Obsolescence: *Be careful that the property you are thinking about repositioning is not going to be economically obsolete*

Economic obsolescence is a drop in property value caused by factors outside of the property itself. Probably the best example was the glut of office space on the market after the COVID-19 economic crisis and recession. So many workers got used to working in home offices and their bosses learned to love saving money on rent. Another major factor is too many same-type commercial properties being built and coming on-line at the same time. These new properties have much better amenities and although they have higher rents, they pull tenants away from older worn-out properties. The opposite circumstance can also cause economic obsolescence. This actually happened in the three most expensive neighborhoods in Portland, Oregon, in 2016, when too many new high-end luxury multifamily units entered the market at the same time. Occupancy, rents, and property values took a plunge for three years. Another cause is a change in the economy where major industries nearby have laid off workers.

In an up seller's market, be wary of properties that appear to be a good deal and are priced lower than other like properties are. These commercial properties might be experiencing economic obsolescence resulting from a rise in crime in the neighborhood. This can lower a commercial property's ability to attract better-quality higher-rent-paying tenants. During a recession, be careful to check the number of units or spaces available for rent in the market of the subject property's type. If there are too many, you have a renter's market where rents are freefalling. Worse yet, market vacancy might be so high that the property you are interested in purchasing might have become or will soon become economically obsolete.

Energy Management System (EMS): *These systems are amazing in how they lower your energy bill by themselves*

When repositioning, one of the best ways to cut down on utility expenses on your commercial property is to install an energy management system, which monitors the consumption of energy, lowers it, and curbs waste. It is a computerized system with sensors that collect data so that you can make informed decisions. The system will analyze energy consumption and make recommendations to reduce energy use. It will also monitor your HVAC and lighting. Some of these systems can tell you how much you are spending on energy consumption in real time.

If you have an older building with no energy controls or monitoring, consider installing smart building control sensors. Electricity consumption can be lowered by as much as 25%. Heating, cooling, and lighting are turned off when rooms are not occupied. HVAC systems are monitored to run economically. Check to see if there are energy grants in your area to help pay for the cost of the system.

Functional Obsolescence: *See if you can find a property that has become functionally obsolete. They can be great candidates for repurposing*

In 2011, a client of mine needed to refinance a 60,000-square-foot single-tenant warehouse on the outskirts of Colorado Springs. A food distributor had occupied it for over 30 years. The loan I had done on the property 10 years prior was maturing in three months. Because the tenant had just over a year left on their lease, I could not do another permanent loan without the tenant signing a longer lease. They kept stalling and would not renew their lease early. I had to place an emergency two-year bridge loan on the property. Due to stiff new competition, the distributor went out of business in less than a year. Now the building was 100% vacant. My client could not find another tenant. The problem was that the facility had become functionally obsolete because the ceilings were only 18 feet high. Times had changed and distribution facilities wanted ceilings to be 30 feet high so they could use the latest computerized racking systems that are designed to save space. My client ended up losing the property.

Functional obsolescence occurs in a commercial property because of design features that are out of date. These can be excellent opportunities for repurposing if they are located in the right place for the right price. However, these properties have often been vacant for a long time and redeveloping them may not be cost-effective.

Master Lease Agreement

If you are lacking the down payment or credit to buy a property that has been neglected and needs repositioning, consider acquiring it with a master lease agreement. This is a lease with an option to purchase a commercial property. Sellers are the most open to doing this when a property has been on the market for a long time and they need to sell due to financial hardship or low motivation to maintain the property. A master lease option can be a great tool during a recession when conventional financing is more difficult for buyers to obtain. Here's how it works:

> **Time and Money Saving Tip**
>
> The beginning of the recovery phase following a recession phase of the real estate market cycle is the best time to pick up commercial repositioning opportunities for rock-bottom prices. This phase is not easy to identify, because so many aspects of the recession are still lingering. Rents and occupancy rates are flat now and no longer declining. Unemployment and GDP are flat or declining just slightly. This is the very best time to pick up foreclosed properties at public auction, and many financially distressed owners have reach their peak of discomfort and have to sell.

- You approach a seller to take over all the financial and operational responsibilities of running the property by putting it on a master lease. You tell them that you can only put 10–15% down on an agreed-upon purchase price because you will need to put money into improving the property. In exchange, you will be getting an option to purchase the property at a set price in three to five years. You will receive equitable title and the seller will retain legal title.
- You receive all the income from the property and pay monthly payments to the seller until you purchase the property or the master lease agreement expires.
- You are responsible for managing the property and paying all the expenses for the property, including taxes and insurance.
- You have control over doing operational, cosmetic, or constructional repositioning upgrades at your expense.
- You also receive the tax benefits of the property.

- You can purchase the property at any time during the agreement and receive legal title. If your repositioning project fails, you have to continue making payments to the seller, but you can give the property back when the master lease agreement expires.

Nonperforming Mortgage Note Purchasing: *You can get up to 30% free equity in a property buying a nonperforming loan*

Another way to acquire commercial properties that need repositioning is to buy nonperforming commercial mortgage notes from banks with the intention of foreclosing. This might sound like a mean and predatory way to build your commercial real estate empire, but if you have the appetite for it, it can be highly profitable. These notes can often be purchased for 90% of their face value, so you could be earning 10% equity out of the gate. For more in-demand properties, you have to pay 100% of the note value. Then, once you foreclose, you acquire the property owner's equity, which is often 20% or more. These properties have often been mismanaged and are ripe with repositioning opportunities.

The best time to pick up a nonperforming note is seven months to a year after the start of a major recession. Bank regulators will pressure banks to get new valuations on the commercial properties they have on their books. If they have gone down in value, and they usually do, the bank will call the loan due and payable (yes, they can do that even if the borrower is current) and give the borrower on average three months to refinance elsewhere. If the borrower is not able to pull this off, the bank will likely prefer to sell the note than to further distress themselves and the customer.

Once a borrower has missed three payments, the mortgage is considered nonperforming. The bank will then refer the loan to their special asset department. It's strange to call these bad loans special assets; I am told that the intention here is to fool shareholders. "Special assets" listed as an asset on a bank's balance sheet sounds like something special, doesn't it? Banks sell these notes when they need to increase liquidity to meet regulatory requirements.

To purchase these notes you have to have either cash or a line of credit. You can also use a hard-money lender, who will take a collateral assignment of the note. If there is 35% or more equity in the property, you can sometimes borrow with very little down. It's best to get the loan for a minimum of two years to give you more than enough time to foreclose on the property, and it's best not to buy a mortgage note in a small town where it can be difficult to keep the property occupied. Stick with communities of 75,000 or more, which will also make it easier in case you need to sell the note. Call a commercial loan officer at any bank and ask to speak to their special asset manager to find out if they have any commercial mortgage notes for sale. You can also subscribe to distressedpro.com, which can refer nonperforming notes to you, along with the name of the decision maker at the bank or credit union holding the note.

Operating Budget Pro Forma: *This is your blueprint for how you expect the property to do once it reaches stabilized occupancy*

Creating an operating budget for the property you are repositioning for once it reaches *stabilized occupancy* (see Encyclopedia Topic B, Due Diligence), is critical for maintaining goals for rental income and expenses after repositioning is completed. This is so important because a budget creates the expectation for hitting and maintaining a net operating income that will increase the property value. Start out by preparing a pro forma of rents for each unit or space. Then project rental income and expenses month by month for the first two years after the property is stabilized. Prior to doing the operating budget pro forma, you will need this to create your *repositioning pro forma* (see later in this Topic), which shows how the property will perform during repositioning.

A property manager who has experience in your commercial property type can help you determine market income and expenses for the budget. They will research existing leases, vacant spaces, lease rollover, and rental concessions to come up with a realistic budget for rental income. Then analyze historical expenses, vendor contracts, and planned capital improvements for the budget. Your permanent loan lender will require you to submit an operating budget with your loan package. You can find an example of a seven-year budget pro forma (the Seven-Year Month-to-Month Budget and Summary Spreadsheet) in Appendix A and a downloadable Excel version on my website: https://apartmentloanstore.com.

Operational Repositioning Checklist: *These can greatly increase property income and value without costing much at all*

Operational repositioning changes give you the biggest bang for the buck since most cost only your time. Go through this list and choose as many as you can to implement. Most either do not cost anything or cost $250 per unit or less.

___ Raise rents and lower expenses	___ Implement a water conservation program
___ Make units or spaces rent-ready	___ Lower property taxes
___ Fill vacancies	___ Add vending machines
___ Clean and remove junk	___ Rent parking spaces
___ Replace poor-quality tenants	___ Install security cameras and security signs
___ Renegotiate longer-term leases	___ Charge a pet fee
___ Change signage	___ Lower insurance cost
___ Rebrand the property	___ Competitively shop vendor contracts
___ Design a new website	___ Instigate a ratio utility billing system
___ Change the tenant mix	___ Create a new Facebook page
___ Change management companies	

Raising Rents: *Higher rents mean a higher net operating income, which means a higher property value*

You have to raise rents when repositioning to increase property value. It is a false assumption that just making a commercial property look good will create a higher appraised value. This is because the income approach in a commercial appraisal is king and will overtake any first impressions the appraiser might have about how great the property looks. The capitalization (cap) rate originates from this approach in the appraisal. Read on about why this has the most influence on appraised value.

How Does Raising Rents Raise Commercial Property Values?

Commercial real estate brokers price a property based on market cap rates. Higher rents will raise net operating income, resulting in a lower cap rate, resulting in a higher sales price. If you want to refinance and pull cash out in the future, you will need the property value to go up. Here is why raising rents will make this happen: (1) The appraiser will do a quick cap-rate analysis on the subject property first, as a marker. The net operating income being higher because you have raised rents will result in a lower cap rate and higher value. (2) To determine the cap rate that goes into the appraisal, the appraiser will average the net operating income of your property with four to six other similar properties in your market that have sold in the past year. If your rents are higher, the appraiser will be more inclined to choose properties for comparison that have similar higher rents. These properties will have higher values and pull the value of your property up in the appraisal.

Ratio Utility Billing System (RUBS): *This system bills tenants for any utilities paid by the property owner*

If you are repositioning an older multifamily property that is *master-metered* (the landlord pays some or all utilities) (see Encyclopedia Topic A, Buying), putting in a RUBS will lower your expenses more than any other item. On master-metered properties, the units are lacking submeters for electric, gas, or both. The cost of installing these is often prohibitive based on the investment's potential return. A RUBS costs just about nothing. What you are going to do is bill the cost of gas, electricity, water, sewer, and trash back to the tenants. The total monthly expense for these bills will be prorated for each tenant based on the percentage of square footage the tenant occupies out of the total rentable square footage of the property. To start the program, you have to wait until two months prior to each tenant's lease expiring to give them *notice that on their new lease they will be paying a reimbursement to the landlord for utilities.*

Rebranding: *Be sure to rebrand the property you are repositioning to give it a new image*

When repositioning a commercial property, it is usually essential to rebrand it to let the public know that it has a new look, new management, and new reputation. This is especially the case when a property has been poorly managed or has a tired, worn-out feel to it. Branding happens to commercial real estate whether the owner is aware of it or not. The property has an image associated with its name, and people either like it, dislike it, or are indifferent to it. If you are spending the time and money to reposition a property that has an injured or bland reputation and now has had a facelift and is attracting better-quality tenants, then rebranding it with a new name, logo, and website can really help boost its new image.

Rebranding To-Do List

1. Choose a name for the property that defines the image you want to portray. Using the name of the city in the property's name will help with Internet searches.
2. Check with your state's Secretary of State to see if the name you want to use is available. Subscribe to knowem.com, which can help you check all social media, including Facebook, LinkedIn, Twitter, and many more.
3. Create a budget for rebranding. Having logos and websites professionally designed can be expensive.
4. Have a logo and business cards designed.
5. Have a professional website designed that sells the image of your property and is user friendly. Having a virtual tour feature of common areas and unit types or spaces is a plus. For multifamily properties, have floor plans and rents showing for each unit type. Make sure you have your Google reviews highlighted at the top. If you get less than four stars you can take the reviews off the website. Create a new Facebook page, and make sure you get lots of likes. Create a blog feature with articles about the property and have tenants respond.
6. Put your rebranding plan on a timeline. Be sure to start early, as finishing it will likely take longer than you think.
7. Decide on a launch date and publicly announce your rebranding to the local media and chamber of commerce.
8. Notify the postal service, Federal Express, and UPS, as well as your bank accounts, city, state and federal governments, and insurance companies, of your property's name change. Notify all vendors as well.

Rehab Construction Contract: *Make sure you get a lump-sum contract with one price for all work being done*

Be sure that your rehab construction contract is a lump-sum contract in which the contractor agrees to a set price for all work performed. Stay away from cost-plus contracts that charge you for labor, materials, and all ancillary fees. Do not accept a lump-sum contract with a general list of items to be completed. The contract should contain a line-by-line list with the costs for each relevant job. This way you can evaluate the cost for each item. The quality of materials for each installation needs to be clearly stated. Be sure that the contract includes these essential items:

1. The name of owner, the general contractor and license number, and the property address.
2. An Exhibit A that has a list of all the work to be done, line by line with associated costs and a description of all materials.
3. The contract price and how payments will be made. It's best to make payments when the work has been completed and inspected. Your lender will require this.
4. Start and completion dates.
5. Materials and labor—the contractor will be paying these.
6. Licenses and permits.

Repositioning

7. Change orders.
8. Warranties.
9. A time is of the essence clause.
10. A certification of completion.

Repositioning Pro Forma: *This will esti-mate what your income and expenses will be while repositioning*

A repositioning pro forma is your financial blueprint for the property's cash flow month by month during the time you are repositioning it. It shows you month by month the projected income going down as tenants are vacated, and up as you add new tenants. It also projects expenses along the way. Most importantly, as more rental spaces are occupied with higher-paying tenants, it will predict when the property will break even, paying all expenses and loan payments on its own. It will also tell you if, when, and how much you need to feed cash into the property.

Time and Money Saving Tip
For rehab projects, be sure to put a liqui-dated damages clause, which specifies an amount of money that must be paid for failing to complete work on time, into your construction contract, since it will cost you money for each day that the construction is delayed. Delays due to situations beyond the contractor's control, such as weather, and changes made by the owner should be exempt. Set an amount per day for each day the construction is delayed. If you like, you can give the contractor a bonus for each day the construction is completed early.

Start with creating a projected rent roll, which shows where rents for each unit or space are estimated to be after the repositioning is completed. On an Excel spreadsheet, follow these simple instructions: Show the projected income and expenses month by month over the time period you project the repositioning project to take or one year, whichever is longer. Show rental income increasing over time as units or spaces are completed and rented. Show monthly expenses line by line and mortgage payments as well. Create a footnote for each expense to explain how you determined it. Your lender will want to know this. Go to Appendix A to find a sample of a repositioning pro forma. You can find an Excel version on my website: https://apartmentloanstore.com/.

Re-Tenanting Plan for Retail Repositioning: *This is your chance to decide ahead what type of tenants to attract to enhance your net operating income and property value*

If you are repositioning a strip mall, office, or industrial property, and have empty spaces now or leases expiring in the next two years, this is your opportu-nity to increase the income and value of the property by making a re-tenanting

Time and Money Saving Tip
It is essential that you know what the new features you are adding are worth in increased rent. For multifamily properties, did you know that providing washer and dryer outlets is worth around $35 per month? Providing washers and dryers in the units is worth $50

plan. The payoff will be to attract better-quality tenants who will pay more rent as well as increase traffic. If this is in a landlord's market due to a shortage of same-type rental space, this could be the perfect time to change a property from having *gross leases* to having *net leases* (see Encyclopedia Topic J, Managing and Leasing). If it is a renter's market during a recession or in the recovery phase of the real estate market cycle, you might have to hunker down and lower rents and offer rental concessions.

Start out by making a plan for any operational, cosmetic, or constructional repositioning improvements you need to make. Get advice from a retail leasing agent on tenant mix. If this is a strip mall, attracting popular national chains can act like having many anchor tenants and draw more shoppers. Popular restaurant chains can also be a larger

to $75 per month. Covered parking spaces can be worth $50. Building storage units can be worth from $45 to $75. Modernizing interiors with new crown molding, floor coverings, appliances, countertops, and fixtures can add $100–$150 per month. Of course, the demographics of the market have to support the maximum rent.

Time and Money Saving Tip

You might be surprised, but most low-income multifamily tenants cannot live without high-speed Internet and premium cable TV with Showtime and HBO. Where this might cost you $30–40 per unit per month to buy in bulk, you can offer it to your tenants as an option for $75 per month, and most will pay it. This will be a savings for them and more profit for you.

draw. Spread out service-related businesses like dental offices and nail or hair salons. If this is an office or industrial property, try attracting some national tenants or ones that already have more than one location. They are most likely to be successful over time. Contact a local real estate leasing agent that has a talent for attracting national tenants, as well as local mom-and-pop businesses that already have several locations.

Retail Re-Tenanting Plan

1. Model your re-tenanting plan after successful similar properties in your market. Take notes as to their anchor tenant, national tenants, and overall tenant mix.
2. Work with a highly experienced retail real estate leasing agent to advise you on the types of tenants to attract, what current lease per square foot rates are, and what to expect for tenant improvements. Is it better for you to pay for these and pass the cost on to the tenant in higher rent, or have the tenant pay them?
3. Attract as many tenants as you can that will weather a recession. National chains like the Dollar Store, Michaels, and fabric stores and hair salons do well during recessions.
4. Project your ideal tenant profile and tenant mix. From this, project your gross income increasing over time. Then create a three-year pro forma showing the improved income and estimated expenses.

5. Make a list of any operational, cosmetic, or constructional changes that will need to be done to make the property appealing to your new higher-rent-paying tenants. Get an estimate on the cost.
6. Make sure you have the financing lined up to cover repositioning expenses, tenant improvements, and leasing commissions.
7. Have your leasing agent market the available spaces. If you insist on doing this yourself, you can list the spaces for lease on LoopNet, Costar, and Craigslist.

Revitalization Zones/Urban Revitalization: *Buy a rundown building in a revitalization zone for great tax incentives and a low-rate second-position loan from the city*

If you would like to repurpose or redevelop a commercial property and be rewarded with tax incentives, low-interest-rate loans, and a reduction in permit fees, finding an old property in a revitalization zone may be your ticket to success. Previously known as urban renewal, urban revitalization improves cities by redeveloping vacant rundown buildings. This increases commerce to the area, property values, and property tax revenues. Most cities offer gap financing in revitalization zones, which means that they will go into second position behind your first mortgage, resulting in a much higher leveraged deal. If you are renovating a historic building, check and see if the property qualifies for federal historic tax credits.

Tenant Profile: *What kind of tenants do you need to attract to reach your repositioning financial goals?*

Far too often, commercial properties get filled with tenants randomly, without a plan. What type of tenants do you want to attract? What repositioning tactics do you need to apply to draw the best-quality tenants to your property? Look at the most successful competitors for your property type in your market. What is their tenant profile like? For multifamily properties, do your competitors have better-quality autos in the parking lot? Are their properties about the same age but have a better feel to them than yours? Are the decks and patios kept more clean and free of junk than yours? Do you need new siding and landscaping?

Make a list of repositioning items you would need to do to bring your property to the level of you best competitors in your property class. Can you afford to make these upgrades? Are they likely to attract higher-rent-paying, more affluent tenants? For office, retail, and industrial properties, what is the tenant mix and tenant quality like for the best of your competitors? Do they have more national chains? What does the exterior of the property look like compared to yours? Do you need to resurface the parking lot? Make a list of the changes to the property needed to attract your ideal better-quality, higher-rent-paying tenants. Consult with a commercial real estate broker and/or property manager to create your ideal tenant profile and tenant mix, along with a budget and timeline for achieving this.

Variance Analysis: *This is an accounting system to track if you are doing better or worse than your repositioning pro forma has forecasted each month*

A variance analysis is an accounting action that examines the difference between your planned income and expenses on your repositioning pro forma and what actually occurs. Your job is to scrutinize each rental payment and expense. If there is a variance from what you planned on, what caused it? If the variance has created a negative outcome, what needs to be done to improve it? For example, on month 7 of your pro forma you are expecting the property to be 75% leased and you need to rent three more units to achieve this. Why is the lease-up going slower than anticipated? What can you do to remedy this? You also notice that landscaping maintenance has been trending upward by 18% during months 4–7 above your budget for this expense. Why?

> **Time and Money Saving Tip**
>
> To create the most value when repositioning, being able to retain good existing tenants along with attracting high-quality, higher-rent-paying tenants is the best recipe. Often too much attention is placed on attracting new tenants, and the value of retaining existing tenants who might not be able to afford the new rent is ignored. Keep in mind that it can take 7 to 10 months to fill an office or retail space and 4 to 6 months for industrial space after improvements. Sure, your goal is to get more rent, but be careful to keep the property as full as possible en route. In other words, it is better to plan on increasing rents over a longer duration of time and fill spaces or units when it makes sense to do so. The last thing you want is to run the property for six months or longer at below 85% occupancy.

To create a variance analysis, make a copy of your repositioning pro forma. Add two more columns by each month's income and expense line items, one for pluses and one for minuses. Then tally the pluses and minuses at the bottom.

Water Management/Conservation Program: *This will save money and help you attract green-minded tenants*

Lowering water consumption on your commercial property will obviously save money but, more importantly, is a mandate of the green movement to lower water shortages. Surprisingly, the EPA has listed office buildings as the largest consumer of water, accounting for 25% of total water usage, followed by multifamily and hotel properties, restaurants, and hospitals. Apartment buildings can advertise the EPA water score to measure the building's water use and show green-minded tenants that this is a great place to live. Landscape watering is responsible for the majority of commercial property water use. A basic water management program is not expensive and involves monitoring water usage carefully, looking for leaking water lines, and installing water-restricting toilets, urinals, faucets, and showerheads. Recovering gray water and using it to water lawns and plants can save the most for office buildings, but is a more substantial investment. Reviewing several years of water bills will show you seasonal changes in consumption. If water consumption has suddenly skyrocketed, it could mean a leak in a water line.

PART VI

Smart Strategies
for Developing

CHAPTER 8

Why Developers Are at the Top of the Food Chain

This chapter dives deep into what it takes to be a commercial real estate developer: what they are made of, how much they earn, their best traits, how they spend a typical day, becoming a developer without experience, and 14 mistakes to avoid when developing commercial property.

WHAT ARE DEVELOPERS MADE OF?

One of the only jobs I know of that is of the same magnitude of ambition, financial risk, and time involved as a Hollywood writer/director is a commercial real estate developer. Both ventures start with an inspiration followed by putting the vision down on paper. Then market research is done to determine whether the project is viable, followed by an estimate of cost and time. Then the transaction has to pass muster with high-ranking authority figures. Oh, and let's not forget the pitch to bring on investors and get financing.

Both ventures take an average of 20,000 hours. This means working every day for over three years except major holidays and your birthday. Both require a large team of professionals and grunt workers to pull it off. Both cost an exorbitant amount of money representing a daunting risk. Both are likely to go over budget. If successful, both can produce a large amount of profit, residual income, accolades, and, best of all, endorsements for future projects. In the event of failure, the brains behind both enterprises will likely end up broke and be considered has-beens.

Commercial developers are at the very top of the real estate food chain. They take the largest risk and have the potential largest rewards. They conceive of the project, find the land, put together a team of experts, negotiate with city planners, bring in roads and utilities, find investors, apply for financing, and then go on to manage the construction and lease-up. The job requires an in-depth understanding of urban master planning, building codes, architectural design, structural and civil engineering, geotechnical soils, environmental engineering, and so much more.

It does not really make sense, but there is no college degree or license required to become a commercial real estate developer. In fact, there are only nine universities in America that offer a major in real estate development. What is strange about this is that developers hire or collaborate with architects, landscape architects, engineers, surveyors, land use planners, urban planners, soil consultants, transportation consultants, and environmental consultants who are all required to have a professional degree or certification.

Developer Roy Carver

In 1974, Roy Carver graduated from USC with a degree in business and finance. During his last two years of school, he got a job with a large southern California homebuilder. For $14 per hour, he was tasked with determining the best locations to build homes based on market and demographic data.

One of his recommendations was Encinitas, California, located on the Pacific Coast 25 miles north of San Diego. It was a sleepy little town back then and today has some of the most expensive oceanview real estate in the state.

Roy discovered a love for real estate, and a few weeks after graduation bought an acre of land in Bakersfield, California, to build a 20,000-square-foot industrial building. His total cost for the project was $160,000. Within a month of starting construction, the building was leased. Upon completion in three months, Roy sold the building for $280,000. He made a cool $120,000 profit, which was a fortune at that time, especially for a 23-year-old. The day after closing, he optioned the adjoining land to repeat the process. He was hooked on commercial real estate development.

Over the next 45 years, Roy went on to develop more than two million square feet of commercial real estate costing over $250 million. These projects were shopping centers and industrial, office, and apartment buildings.

I met Roy in 2010 when he came to me for financing a 178-unit luxury micro apartment building on a piece of land he owned near the University of Oregon in Eugene. My first reaction was that it would be difficult to finance, since all the units were 500 square feet or less and the rents were much higher per square foot than any other multifamily properties in the area. Making this even more difficult was that there were no comparable apartment buildings in the market that were made up of all one-bedrooms and studios. Lenders just do not want to be the first of something.

But I was impressed by Roy's level of experience and his enthusiasm. He drove me around the neighborhood, showing me that all the competition was made up solely of two- and three-bedroom units. Roy had discovered something no one else had: a severe lack of single-occupancy units in the three miles surrounding the university. His concept was that many more serious students would prefer living alone and would pay a premium in rent for a high-end comfy small space that they did not have to share.

We ordered a market study and it showed that Roy was right. Only 15% of the multifamily units in the market were one-bedroom and studios. The project was approved for a HUD construction loan. With Roy's skill with managing the construction schedule, and offering the contractor a bonus for every week they finished early, the project was completed two months early and came in just under budget. Prior to completing construction, it was 60% preleased and 95% leased soon after completion. Roy and I went on to work on two more large apartment complexes in Eugene—all three totaling more than $80 million.

Roy is my favorite developer client. In my opinion, he has the perfect temperament for developing. He is unfailingly polite, yet firm when dealing with incompetent professionals. He is so upbeat and positive that when he has the worst of days, you would think he had just spent the day at an all-inclusive resort. He is the best number cruncher I know—even better than I am, and I thought I was good. He does up to 10 different pro formas, covering the best and worst scenarios for rent, expenses, and mortgage payments, and then picks something in the middle. He overprepares for everything.

When he has his concept meetings with city planners, he makes sure his architect, contractor, civil and structural engineers, and traffic engineers are there. He says the process has gotten much more complex and time-consuming over the years. Back when he started, single entrepreneurs could handle the entire process themselves. These days there are so many compliance issues and codes that only large development companies and real estate investment trusts (REITs) with large staffs can wade through the quagmire of regulations efficiently.

HOW MUCH DO COMMERCIAL DEVELOPERS MAKE?

Although it will likely take years before a commercial developer sees a dime of earnings, they do not seem to mind waiting. They know it is going to be a large paycheck. To make this statement stronger, let me just say that there is nothing in the real estate business that pays better than commercial real estate development does. This is because it costs a lot less to build a property than what it will sell for after it is completed and fully leased. Depending on whether it is an up or down market when the property is completed and stabilized, the earnings on appreciation can range from 18% to 25%. Profits can hit 50% or more for building homes in subdivisions and condominium developments.

I have a client in Seattle who I started working with in the late 1990s. His first project was building a light industrial complex, which was cheap to build at $560,000. He used mostly other people's money to get started and today he is worth over $90 million. Another client built a 158-unit luxury multifamily complex in Portland, Oregon, in 2011 for $18,400,000 and upon completion it was worth $22,500,000 at a 6.5 cap rate. This was a profit of $4,100,000 in just over three years. He then held the property for six years and sold it for $27,800,000 to a real estate investment trust (REIT) in a 5.0 cap rate market. This put a profit of $9,200,000 in his pocket.

HOW DO COMMERCIAL BUILDING DEVELOPERS EARN MONEY?

For finding the land, and building on it, commercial developers can make money in seven different ways:

1. Appreciation, which is where the largest amount of profit is realized when the stabilized property is sold.
2. A development fee, which averages from 3% to 5% of total project costs (I've seen as high as 8%), can usually be financed with the loan. Banks do not like to see this fee go over 4%.
3. Income from operations—a developer should earn a percentage of the property's net income after debt service equal to their percentage of ownership, but there is no hard and fast rule on how this percentage is determined. I have seen some invest 15% of the equity and own 25% of the project. Often, investors are paid a *preferred return* first, before the developer earns anything.
4. An asset management fee for overseeing the operations and finances of the property during construction and working with property managers during lease-up as well as providing the partners with quarterly financial reports, K-1s at tax time, and distributing profits. This averages 1% of the construction costs. If the developer is charging more than a 4% development fee, the asset management fee is often waived.
5. A property management fee for offsite managing and leasing the property if the owners do not hire professional management. This averages 4% of gross rents.
6. A disposition fee for selling the property. This can average 1% to 2% of the sales price.
7. A *sponsor promote* or *waterfall*, which is a percentage of any excess profits over what was projected in the pro forma.

HOW DO COMMERCIAL LAND DEVELOPERS MAKE MONEY?

Some land developers specialize in buying raw land and hold on to it over time. Many buy land with the intention of obtaining approvals for zoning changes or other entitlements for future development. This can include having the land rezoned, obtaining a variance, grading it, bringing in utilities and roads, and then selling lots that are ready to build on. Many raw land developers intend to build on the land themselves.

Buying raw land that is zoned agricultural or is located outside of the urban growth boundary and having it annexed to the city and rezoned to residential for a subdivision or multifamily development can increase the value three times or more. Taking residential land and having it rezoned commercial can more than double the value. Taking a raw land parcel and having it rezoned and fully entitled (see *entitlement process* in Encyclopedia Topic G, Development) so that it is shovel-ready for commercial construction can triple or quadruple the value.

TRAITS OF THE BEST COMMERCIAL REAL ESTATE DEVELOPERS

Commercial real estate developers are my favorite people to work with. The best of them are big people on the inside who have the uncanny ability to laugh at their mistakes and the mistakes of others and move beyond them. They have great people skills and can spread excitement and enthusiasm for their project on to their team and other professionals in a way that becomes contagious. They have an unwavering focus to see their project through to completion. They are a group of fiercely creative and innovative hard-working entrepreneurs who spend less time complaining and more time finding solutions. Some of the experienced ones are so brilliant and guide their projects with such precision that I rank them up there with neurosurgeons and nuclear engineers.

Many of the newbies bypass studying what is a very technical process and just learn as they go. They are so intensely motivated by their vision that they just fly by the seat of their pants, bumping into all kinds of unforeseen obstacles en route. Often they make one mistake for every two right decisions, which can tack on an extra year or more to their project's timeline. When this happens, some think about throwing in the towel, but seldom do. They have invested just too much of their own and other people's time and money to be able to live with themselves if they did.

Ten Top Traits of Successful Commercial Real Estate Developers

1. **Having a Love of the Deal:** Starting out with being able to spot potential in a raw piece of land that can be rezoned or an urban infill lot that is just clambering to be made into a mixed use building; lying awake at night thinking

about securing the property with an option to buy or going into a joint venture with the seller; thinking about the right people to bring onboard to make it all happen—having a love of the deal is what makes this job fun.

2. **Having Good People Skills:** I have worked with some developers who have specialized in throwing tantrums when they did not get their way. One resorted to yelling and threatening to sue the Denver City Council members when they rejected his appeal. The best developers know that they need to stay firm with their goal, but keep their cool when they are confronted with opinionated city planners and team members who are more subjective than objective. Many have learned to thank them for their contrary opinion and then go on to ask for their help in solving the problem. Having good diplomacy skills—being able to schmooze with sellers, city planners, investors, lenders, and contractors is a must. Being able to inspire your team of professionals through encouragement, rather than an iron fist, is paramount.

3. **Having Good Leadership Skills:** I have worked with developers who had good people skills but not good leadership skills. Often they were just too nice. They try and get someone else to be the bad cop when everyone knows it is really coming from them. The best developers know that the buck stops with them and take accountability. They understand the magnitude of the project from the design phase to lease-up. They know it is better to pay a bit more for the best professionals than to hire the cheapest ones. They take responsibility to make sure all their team members keep the highest-quality standards and deliver on time frames. The worst developers have no interest in leadership and just want everyone to be happy. This results in the project running itself, and most participants—including the developer—being unhappy.

4. **Having Great Problem-Solving Skills:** Yes, this is the big one. It might seem like you never have a day off from trying to figure out a solution to something. Here are some of the problems that my developer clients have faced:

- The owner of the property next door agreed to sell an easement for an access road since the subject property is land-locked, but now the neighbor does not want all the traffic coming past them and wants the road to come from the other side, which makes the layout of the design impractical.

- The city planners don't like the hardy plank exterior finish and want stucco instead, which adds too much to the cost and blows the budget up. This results in the architect and contractor having to do value engineering to cut the project cost down in other areas.

- The city wants the developer to donate part of the land as a park in exchange for approving utility entitlements. This axes the plan to sell that parcel off to a developer wanting to build a small strip mall there.

- The architect left off many important details in the specs that go with the drawings, resulting in costly change orders.

In order to both prevent and solve problems like these, a talented developer will know that they cannot do it alone. They know when to bring in their team of professionals to assist them. They also have a gift of focusing more on finding a solution than on the inconvenience that the problem is presenting. Most of all, they expect things to go wrong. And when they do, they have the discipline to not overreact emotionally.

5. **Having Perseverance, Patience, and the Ability to Adapt:** You have heard the expression that building always takes more time and money than expected. Well, commercial real estate development specializes in this. I have had development clients who expected the planning department to approve their plans within four months of the initial plan review meeting, then had to wait five months for their first design review meeting after the plans were completed, and then wait an additional three months for the department to review the changes they had requested. During these unplanned-for eight months, the cost of materials and labor went up, resulting in a project that no longer penciled. So they had to work with their architect and contractor to lower building costs. After pulling permits, multifamily developers are always looking over their shoulder for competing apartment building starts that will force them to compete for tenants at the same time. To adapt, the developer has to start marketing early, prelease prior to getting occupancy permits, and offer lower rents and rental concessions if needed. Having perseverance and patience and the ability to adjust to another plan is a must.

6. **Being Able to Make Decisions Quickly:** Sitting on the fence, putting off major and minor decisions, is not something a developer has the luxury of doing. Knowing that even small delays cost money, the ability to make informed decisions quickly is essential. Sometimes developers have so many changes thrown at them at the same time that they become paralyzed and want to take a nap. The solution is to bring in your team members to provide you with the advice needed to make a decision.

7. **Being Able to Multitask and Prioritize:** In one day, a developer might have to work with the architect to reduce the square footage of the property to save money, work with a landscape architect to design the landscaping, provide a list of financial items to their lender, call on several potential investors, and talk to potential tenants about leasing. Being able to know what your most important tasks are each day, prioritizing them, and then being able to multitask to accomplish them is an important skillset.

8. **Being Willing to Bring On Experts When Necessary:** Acknowledging that you need help to move the process faster by bringing on a mentor with extensive development experience or a talented land use attorney to negotiate with the city when obstacles arise is critical.

9. **Being Good at Raising Capital:** Having a talent for raising money from private investors and lenders is a top quality for any developer. The best give effortless, professional presentations in which the selling points are presented as facts that take flight and inspire participation. Questions are prepared-for in advance with well-rehearsed answers. I have developer clients that always use a *syndication* with a *private placement memorandum* (see Encyclopedia Topic C, Raising Investor Partners) to raise equity for their deals from strangers. They have become good at this skillset. Other developers have a knack for raising down payment funds from a few of their friends and business associates, and often use the same investors over and over. Experienced developers know what kind of loan their project will qualify for and know the best sources of financing to achieve this. They know how to get lenders drooling over their deals too.

10. **Being Good at Managing Time and Money:** As a commercial real estate developer, you are responsible for calculating conservatively the expected *internal rate of return* (*IIR*) on investment for yourself and your investors, and then delivering something close to what you have promised. This is a very high level of responsibility that takes excellent time- and money-management skills.

    Prior to having your construction contract signed, the costs of materials and labor could be going up weekly, along with interest rates. After you start building, the longer you take for getting your

---

Time and Money Saving Tip

To speed up your building plan review, hire a third-party plan reviewer. They will make sure that the plans are compliant with state and local building codes before you submit them to the city. In fact, they will forward the preapproved plans to the city for you, giving the plan reviewer confidence that the plans meet current requirements. This can eliminate three to six months of costly waiting times to have your architect revise the plans and specs several times and then having to wait each time for another opening in the planning department schedule. Fees for a commercial plan review start at about $2,500, and are without question the best money invested for many of my developer clients.

Time and Money Saving Tip

Overseeing the construction budget and time frame for building will take continual adjustments. When one item goes up due to a major change order, you can try reducing the cost of another item; otherwise, you will have to put in additional funds. If one subcontractor gets delayed due to weather, you can see if you can speed up the project in another area. Check out Monday.com. It is a task- and time-management system with a dashboard that allows developers to see all the aspects of the work being done, along with the deadlines for each. On larger projects you can hire a construction due diligence and monitoring company, such as Currie and Brown.

certificates of occupancy, the more interest it will cost you on your loan and the more time you will spend burning through money without having any money coming in.

Using a *predevelopment checklist* for all tasks and assigning a time frame to them will help you keep them on target, which will save money. Managing the cost of the project is a continual battle as you, your contractor, and building inspectors come up with the unex-

Time and Money Saving Tip

Be sure to build in a 5% contingency for cost overruns into your construction costs. Your lender will almost certainly require this. Also, putting aside 4% of total hard costs as working capital will allow you to sleep better at night when going over budget or taking longer to lease-up the project. This should make your development financially bulletproof.

pected need for change orders that can dramatically drive the cost up. Always remember that the general contractor can charge you whatever they want for changes outside of the construction contract.

WHAT IS THE TYPICAL DAY LIKE FOR A COMMERCIAL DEVELOPER?

The early stages of the development process can be much more fun and easygoing. In a typical day you might start your morning working with your architect and builder to creatively cut down the cost of the project, then squeeze in a meeting with your property manager to review projected income and expenses, and then have several calls with possible investors. In the afternoon you may have a meeting onsite with the surveyor to measure out where the setbacks are that the city is requiring so you can then stake out the footprint of the building to see where it will be placed. After that you have a call with your lender so you can estimate the size of the loan and finish your pro forma.

As you get deeper into the project, many of your days will be bumpy and have some emergencies. A developer client of mine woke up one morning feeling like he was a 911 dispatcher. He was building a $24,000,000 mid-high-rise student housing building near Portland State University. Late in the afternoon before, he had his first plan review meeting, which did not go well. The planning department wanted him to make the building a floor shorter to protect the solar rights of his neighbors. They also did not like the extended size of the balconies. The worst item was that they wanted him to add a floor of subterranean parking, which did not make sense since this was a high-density urban infill lot with public transportation close by. Also, just about everything the residents would need was within easy walking or biking distance. None of these items had come up in the preapplication meeting.

The next morning my client was in a state of anger and panic, firing off calls to his entire team. His contractor told him the additional parking would add close to a million dollars on to the project and advised going back to the city and suggesting stack parking. His attorney thought hiring a powerful land use–planning attorney to appeal the parking issue with the city council was the best move. Ultimately, the planning department killed the deal by adding so much more to the cost and then eliminating a whole floor of income that the developer's and his investors' rate of return was lowered to a point that the deal no longer made sense.

CAN YOU BECOME A DEVELOPER WITHOUT EXPERIENCE?

You do not likely want this job if you are doing it just for the money. In my opinion, you have to have a love of building something plus the ability to handle an immense amount of detail—and it wouldn't hurt to excel at multitasking and motivating a team of people. This is not something you will be doing alone. The results you create

Time and Money Saving Tip

The mistake that most new developers make is not being prepared for a recession during the predevelopment stage in an up market. This is where developer trait number 5 really comes in: having perseverance, patience, and the ability to adapt. Should a recession hit prior to getting your construction loan funded, your lender might lower the loan to cost or even deny the loan. In this situation, I have even seen construction lenders cancel loans after a commitment letter was issued just by using one of the weasel clauses such as "a change of the financial condition of the property or borrower." Believe me, they will come up with something. Much worse, one of my client's banks completed construction funding for 70% of phase one of a large multifamily development, and then backed out when the Great Recession was well underway. They had committed to financing phase two as well. This didn't make sense, since the units were in 4-plexes with their own certificate of occupancy and each completed one leased. The developer was quick to adapt and engaged me to place a private loan to complete phase one and phase two.

Probably the worst time for a recession to hit is when you have just started lease-up, you are still on your construction loan, and a renter's market develops during the hyper-supply or recession phase of the real estate market cycle. With reduced rents you might have difficulty qualifying for a permanent loan. The best way to protect your development if a recession hits while the project is in the construction or lease-up phase is to (1) be prepared with plenty of will only be as good as your ability to learn and adapt quickly and the quality of your team members.

If you have zero experience, I highly recommend that you work for a development company or a REIT for two or three years and learn the trade. Otherwise, bring on an experienced developer as a partner to mentor you.

working capital to feed the property until the market starts recovering; (2) negotiate with your lender to lower the interest rate and extend your loan term to give you time to recover. After all, there is nothing worth less to a construction lender than an incomplete, unstabilized construction project that has no income.

Developer Landon Crowell

Landon Crowell owned a small commercial building in Southeast Portland, Oregon, where he operated his hair salon. In 2014, a friend approached him about buying this property and two adjacent lots from a neighbor to build an apartment complex. Landon agreed to sell. The city ended up rejecting the project for being too large for the neighborhood. When this happened, Landon had a lightbulb go off in his head. He thought, "Why don't I build a smaller multifamily building just on my property?"

Although my firm seldom works with developers who are inexperienced, meeting Landon was a breath of fresh air. Landon talked the talk and walked the walk of a developer and was bringing in an experienced general contractor with development experience as a partner who could mentor him.

I was blown away that Landon had conceived of and designed a 16-unit, six-story, net positive apartment building himself. Net positive meant that the building made its own electricity and used less than it produced, and could sell the excess to the city. This would be the first of its kind in Portland. The building would also be green—LEED Gold Certified and provide electric-powered cars to tenants. On top of that, Landon had arranged for $750,000 in energy and urban renewal grants. The total project costs came to $7,100,000. We preapproved Landon for a $5,400,000 HUD construction loan.

In February of 2016, Landon had his preapplication meeting with the city planning department. It was then that he first got the drift that his architect had not conformed the plans to building codes. In fact, it was quite evident that the project was over the architect's head. Although he had the plans revised in 30 days, the city put him off for seven months for a plan review meeting. They were clearly irritated by the architect's lack of knowledge at the October meeting.

(continued)

(*continued*)

Although the quality of the plans had improved, they still did not meet all the codes. The city would consider the project if some changes were made. The balconies would have to be removed, the building height would have to be lowered, and they hated the paint color. Landon had two more design review meetings in November and December. Each time the city wanted more changes and were irritated that the architect had still not completed the plans correctly. I might point out that the architect missed most of the meetings with the city. In March of 2017, the design review commission decided that the building did not blend in well with the neighborhood and rejected the project.

Landon, being Landon, was not going to give up and appealed the decision with the city council in April, which rejected it after four neighbors showed up and complained that the building would be an eyesore for them. Landon pointed out that beauty is in the eye of the beholder, and threatened to appeal it again to the Land Use Board. In August of 2017 the city council green-lighted the project.

Unfortunately, by then 19 months had gone by and Landon had lost his energy grants. Compounding this was rising building material and labor costs that had increased the project by over $1,400,000. On top of this, interest rates had gone up. The project no longer penciled and we could no longer finance it.

But wait. As you can probably guess, this saga is not over yet. Landon spent another two years trying to raise money from investors to replace the grants he had lost, and once that was accomplished, he had a hard-money loan ready to cover the balance. As his contractor started lining up subcontractors in early January of 2020, Prosper Portland, his urban development lender for the city of Portland who had backed the deal from the beginning, lost their appetite for it. This should have been fatal. Again, as you already know, Landon was not going to let it die and miraculously brought it back to life when he found himself pitching the deal to a wealthy investor. This guy loved it, and was able to easily place a low-interest-rate construction loan at his bank.

Sorry, I wish I could give you a happy ending, but as I write this, Landon has just put the permit-ready land on the market. In mid-March 2020, the bank suddenly decided to no longer do ground-up construction because of the COVID-19 economic crisis and canceled the loan. Landon finally gave up. Choosing the wrong architect, not having hired a third-party reviewer to bring the plans to code at the beginning, not knowing that the city planners quite often put inexperienced developers at the back of the stack, and dealing with the adage "time kills deals" were tough lessons for Landon. To his credit, he says he would like to develop another property someday, since he knows the ropes.

FOURTEEN MISTAKES TO AVOID WHEN DEVELOPING COMMERCIAL PROPERTY

1. **Buying the Land Before It Is Rezoned and Entitled:** Purchasing the land right away with the hope that you can get it rezoned and approved for all *entitlements* represents one of the highest risks in commercial real estate. Just about all my experienced developers tie the land up in the purchase and sales contract for at least four to six months with options to extend the contract to give them time to get a green light with city planners. Sure, it is going to cost them some money if they do not get the project approved with the city, but this will be much less of a loss than owning a piece of land they cannot develop. In an up seller's market, they have to pay full price for the land and put up more earnest money that will go hard every time they need to extend. In a down market, most sellers will allow the developer to extend without putting more money in.

> **Time and Money Saving Tip**
>
> If you do not have all the down payment together and need to bring on investors for your development project, see if the landowner who is selling the land would like to venture with you and become a partner. You will be signing a *joint venture agreement* (see Encyclopedia Topic D, Ownership Entity) with them. If they have owned the land for a substantial amount of time (over three years), it might have enough value to cover much of the down payment. If your plan is to hold the property for a long time, they will end up with good income for many years and still have their equity growing in the completed project. If you are planning to sell right away after the property is completed and leased, you can cut the landowner in on the appreciation and they will greatly increase their investment.

2. **Overestimating the Rate of Return When Crunching the Numbers:** This seems to happen often, even with more experienced developers, because it is so easy in the beginning to overestimate the profitability of the project. You can count on this happening if you start the project out in an up market and by the time you are ready to lease it, it's a down market with lower rents. It's much better to be conservative. Follow my developer client Roy Carver's method of creating 6 to 10 pro formas reflecting the best and worst of rental income, expenses, and loan payments, and pick one in the middle. Going over budget on construction costs happens most of the time. Be sure to add at least 5% to your initial estimate of construction costs.

3. **Overbuilding for the Market and What the Project Can Afford:** It is easy at the beginning to design a development project that will cost more time and money than what the project can afford based on market rents. You need to start

by doing market research to determine what rents and expenses will realistically be. If it is an up market, lower the rents by 5–10% as a hedge against a possible recession. See if it still pencils. Work backwards from there to determine how much you can pay for the total project, then scale the project based on that number and what you need the *internal rate of return* to be.

4. **Not Having the Cash for Predevelopment Costs:** Predevelopment is the first stage of development and includes everything that has to be done prior to construction, including: acquiring the land, all due diligence, surveys, building plans and specs, applying with the city, obtaining entitlements, pulling permits, and applying for construction financing.

Being underfunded for this expense or not allowing extra funds for time delays during this phase can create financial havoc. Having to go to your investors and ask for predevelopment money to cover earnest money, attorney and architectural fees, and the city application fee can be a problem and an embarrassment. It's just the wrong thing to do.

Most investors do not want to contribute money until all the predevelopment work is completed and the project is shovel-ready with construction financing in place. Keep in mind that lenders do not like to see that the developer is short on covering predevelopment expenses when they apply for a construction loan. One good thing—keep a list of all your predevelopment expenses and receipts; you can apply those expenses as soft costs toward your down payment requirement.

5. **Not Having the Construction Costs Value Engineered from the Beginning:** Be sure to be involved from day one with having the project designed cost effectively. Architects can be brilliant at *value engineering* (designing the project the most cost-effective way). Ask your architect to design the buildings with your budget in mind. This starts out as a cost per square foot. Get involved in the cost of every aspect of the construction, from building height to exterior finishes. Ask your architect's opinion on which way to go to design each item so that it has the best utility and aesthetics for the cost. Then have a meeting with your architect and your contractor and have the three of you brainstorm the most cost-effective way to build the project.

6. **Overpromising and Underdelivering to Investors:** I have seen more investors drop out because the project costs increased and the estimated rate of return decreased than for any other reason. When bringing on investors early on during predevelopment, it is important to give them a range of the time expected and project costs, as well as expected earnings on their investment. Then be sure to raise more capital than you think you will need; you can always take less. Be aware that until you get a commitment letter for financing, you will not know for sure the size of your loan. If project costs increase

significantly at the 11th hour and you have to go back to your investors and request more cash, they often perceive this as a bait-and-switch tactic and will drop out.

7. **Not Getting Prequalified Accurately for Financing:** Until your construction appraisal is done, and you get a commitment letter for construction financing, you will not know for sure the size and terms of your loan. Unfortunately, more often than not, the letter of interest will have better terms than the commitment letter. Finding out just before you are going to pull permits that your loan has been approved at a 70% instead of an 80% loan-to-cost ratio will be a shock that will not be easy to recover from. At the beginning, be sure that your lender has everything they need to accurately give you a quote (see *commercial construction loan submission checkist* in Encyclopedia Topic H, Financing). Be sure that whomever is going to approve your loan reviews and preapproves the entire package early on for the financing you are quoted.

8. **Choosing the Wrong Professional Team Members, or Leaving Some Out:** Choosing the wrong architect seems to be the number-one wrong decision that many of my developer clients make. This often results in it taking three to four times longer to get the project approved by the city. Most developers find it cost prohibitive to change architects midstream. Architects have different specialties and levels of skill. Most of all, they need to be familiar with and understand all the complex building codes and be willing to attend plan review meetings. They need to have a good working relationship with structural and civil engineers. Hiring a good land use attorney is a must for many projects. Going with the cheapest professionals is most often the wrong decision; better to choose the ones that have the most experience and good references working on your property type. Taking shortcuts by not hiring all the professionals needed for the project to save money will just cost you more time and money in the end. See The 15 Professionals Commercial Developers Team Up With in Chapter 9.

9. **Not Planning for Delays (Planning Department, Entitlement Approval, and Construction):** It can take three to six months to get the land rezoned. It can take four months to over a year to get your building plans approved. Delays most often occur because of city workers being overworked and understaffed, and because of poor-quality preliminary drawings. If it takes a lot longer for you to get your development project approved by the city than you anticipated, this could mean a large increase in building cost. It could also mean losing one or more of your investors. Submitting preliminary plans at the first plan review meeting that have many errors and do not meet all the building codes will likely cause the city planning staff to put your project on a back burner. When you are able to start construction and what the weather will be like at that time can cause a delay that was not planned for.

10. **Spending Money on Full Plans and Specs Too Soon:** The cost of full architectural plans and specs can cost from $75,000 for a small commercial property to over $1 million for a large property. Some of my less experienced developers have spent the money to have full plans done too early, before the project is approved by the planning department, with the intention of breaking ground faster. If the project is not approved, this money has been flushed down the toilet. My experienced developers only spend the bare minimum on drawings at the beginning. They have just enough done to get preapproval from the city, knowing that entitlements will be approved. They bargain with their architect and will spend at most $5,000 or 5–10% of the architectural budget just for a preliminary site plan, floor plan, and elevation drawings. This is all you need for submission and entitlement preapprovals. Not all architects will work with developers to keep the initial cost for plans down, so be sure to ask them for help on this. They will earn big bucks if they get to do the full plans and specs.

11. **Being Unprepared and Undersupported at City Planning Meetings:** You want your expert team to be able to answer questions that the city planning staff will have. Be sure to have all your development team experts at the meetings: your architect, structural and civil engineers, mechanical engineers, transportation consultant, landscape architect, geotechnical soils consultant, and land use attorney. Think about all the time that will be saved by having your experts work out solutions with the city directly at the meetings, as opposed to having to query them afterwards and then have to wait for another meeting with the city to resolve issues.

12. **Underestimating the Power of Your Angry Neighbors:** Your development project may affect the neighbors in a positive or negative way. The proposed buildings might be viewed as an eyesore and there might be concerns about traffic and street parking. In almost all cases, the surrounding community will be notified of the proposed project plans. The city council will hold a public hearing where citizens can express their views. Unfortunately, there are often more angry opposing views than calm supportive positive ones. It really makes sense to get the opinions of your neighbors ahead of the public hearing so you can counter subjective negative views with objective comments. Be sure to bring with you some supporters of your project that have loud but polite voices to city council meetings.

13. **Not Having a Large Enough Contingency and Working Capital Fund:** Commercial development projects usually go over budget. Although almost all developers have a contingency (extra money in the budget for cost overruns), as this is required by lenders, it is sometimes not adequate. Five percent is average for a contingency; consider upping this to 8%. Also plan to have 3–4% of the hard costs in working capital to make your loan payments if the property takes longer to lease.

14. **Not Being Continually Hands-On:** The best developers work with intense focus, supervising their team to make it through all the predevelopment tasks and approvals. They might take a break once they get approval to pull permits. But once construction starts, they know they have to oversee the construction and avoid costly delays. Other developers have inconsistent focus and mostly allow their professional team members to take the reins during preconstruction—and then blame them for problems and delays that arise. They then go on to allow the construction to go on autopilot. As the developer, this is your project. Take a hands-on approach to supervise it from beginning to end.

CHAPTER 9

50 Steps of Developing and That Isn't All of Them

Are there really 50 steps in developing commercial real estate? To give you a clue, if you were to look over the City of Phoenix's applications for commercial building permits, you will find over 140 items to provide. The 50 steps are just some of the main To-Dos. I have outlined these later in this chapter. The truth is that there are many, many more. I just did not want to scare anyone away with a really big number.

Let's look at just one of the 50 steps: the construction budget. The budget for a recent $32 million mid-high-rise building our firm financed included 1,159 items to build, install, complete, or purchase. Smaller buildings might have as few as 400 items. Okay, so the developer is not going to have to do the work on all those items, but they are responsible for choosing their quality and overseeing their installation. At a minimum, I think you will agree, they do need to know what each item is and how it is used.

If we start with site selection and tying up the land, then add the feasibility research, due diligence items, and requirements for building permits, entitlements, building plan review, and include financing, you can easily have a list of over 200 items to gather, investigate, take care of, design, or oversee. And on top of that, the developer still has many tasks to do with making distributions to investors, leasing, overseeing operations, refinancing, or selling the completed property.

If this seems impossible from where you are sitting now, please do not get discouraged. Only the most experienced hands-on developers who have also been contractors know what every item is or how it is applied. The good news is that you do not need to know everything, and you are certainly not going to do everything. This is because you are going to team up with many professionals.

This chapter really dives deep into the nuts and bolts of the commercial development process. My goal is to give the reader a very thorough representation of all the work and time involved. Covered are the 15 professionals that developers team up with. Then the chapter goes through chronologically the five stages of development, with all the main steps and time frame involved for each.

Developer Chris Marsh

Chris Marsh just doesn't think small. He is my most prolific developer client. Where most developers are overwhelmed with their one deal, Chris currently has four development projects, costing over $250,000,000, in different stages, going on at the same time. These range from a 40,000-square-foot wet-lab office building in Portland, Oregon, to a 210-unit multifamily high-rise on the Vancouver, Washington, waterfront. Oh, and I should add that Chris also runs two multimillion-dollar medical and data technology companies. And let's not forget that somehow he finds the time to sit on the board of six large corporations.

Chris Marsh has created and sold 14 successful companies and has overseen 45 merger and acquisition deals. As an angel investor, he has invested millions of dollars in getting new companies off the ground. With 28 years of commercial development and building experience, he decided four years ago to invest his money in building new commercial buildings for himself instead of investing in other people's ventures.

So how does Chris handle so many development projects at the same time? To pull this off, he created Summit Development Group, a development company employing 12 of the most talented professionals he could find. He recruited his project engineer from the City of Portland. His crewmembers are so devoted that they seem to thrive on putting in extra hours on evenings and weekends. You would think they owned the company. Well, in a way they do. Chris sets aside 30% of all the profits from every deal for his staff—talk about an incentive!

Chris knows how to create synchronicity throughout the complicated commercial development process. One of his sayings is "If you push too hard, you will break things." One of the things I have learned from him is that a developer just can't do it all themselves and that bigger is actually much easier than smaller.

As a one-project-at-a-time developer, you can create some of the same benefits as Chris does with a large development company. To do this you can be the project manager, then bring on a contractor who has development experience and other professionals as active limited partners in your projects. Have each one be in charge of a specific area of the process. Of course rewarding them with a generous piece of the action is a must. Then you can use the same team of professionals over and over on future projects. Although you will be getting a smaller piece of the pie, you can sleep better at night, just as Chris does.

THE 15 PROFESSIONALS COMMERCIAL DEVELOPERS TEAM UP WITH

1. **Commercial Real Estate Attorney:** Many of my developer clients tell me that this is the most important team member. A commercial real estate attorney will advise you on the preliminary title report, write up the purchase contract so it is in your favor, help you form an LLC to own the property directly, form another LLC to own your share with other general partners with limited liability, and form limited partnerships to provide a safe haven for your investors. They can also advise you on issues with the city, write up your leases, advise you on disposition, and so much more.

2. **Land Use Attorney:** They can advise you on zoning, other entitlements, construction permits, easements, and all land use ordinances. They can really make a difference in your plan review meetings with city planners. Where the planning staff is often subjective, a land use attorney who knows as much if not more than they do can help make the process much more objective.

3. **Lender or Commercial Loan Broker:** It is important that you start talking with a lender or commercial loan broker early on. You need to know what type of financing you and your partners, plus the property, will qualify for. It can cost you two months or more if you apply for the wrong loan that is not going to get the job done. For your pro forma, you need to know what the interest rates and terms will likely be. For your total construction costs, you need to know what the down payment, loan expenses, interest expense, during construction, and closing costs are likely to run.

4. **Architects:** As mentioned, choosing an architect that gives you the best price, but does not have the training and experience to produce the plans and specs to code for your development, is one of the main reasons commercial development projects are delayed or fail. If your preliminary plans are not to code at your first plan review meeting, your application will likely be put at the bottom of the stack. Your architect will usually give you a package deal that includes the civil, structural, mechanic, electrical, and plumbing engineers, as well as a landscape architect. Best to let your architect choose these professionals based on their great relationship on past jobs. Make sure you choose an architect who specializes in your property type and is willing to go to all the planning meetings.

5. **Structural Engineer:** They work with the architect to make sure that the foundations and building structures can support the weight of the building. They work with soil consultants to make sure the building will not sink. They create structural drawings for city planners and the contractor to follow.

A good structural engineer can create cost-saving designs that exceed building codes.

6. **Civil Engineer:** They design the infrastructure to code for land development, including streets, walkways, parking lots, systems for storm drainage, water, sewer, electricity, gas, cable, and telephone. They employ surveyors who prepare a site map showing boundaries, rights of way, and easements.

7. **Mechanical, Plumbing, and Electrical Engineers:** They design the HVAC, plumbing, and electrical systems, making sure that all are located correctly and meet codes.

8. **Landscape Architects:** They creatively design the location of plants and trees to meet city codes. They also design the location of walkways, outdoor common areas, outdoor lighting, water features, and retaining walls.

9. **Traffic and Transportation Consultants:** They measure the impact the new commercial property will have on existing roads and intersections and the people who live and work nearby. If there are conflicts, they are experts on finding solutions. They also know the best location for traffic lights. The developer has to hire this professional.

10. **Land Planners:** They usually work on larger projects, especially where there is a master planned community. Designing a topographical map, they show the unique features and constraints of the land, including steep inclines and the location of floodplains. They help create a site plan based on the characteristics of the land.

11. **Geotechnical Soil Consultants:** You want to hire them right after signing the purchase contract. They determine if the characteristics of the ground can support the proposed buildings and calculate the size and depth of foundations. They are also experts in specifications for making a structure earthquake-proof based on the ground characteristics and seismic data.

12. **Noise Consultants**: They measure the effect that surrounding noise will have on the proposed building and make recommendations for mitigation. For example, if a building is close to a major freeway, they might recommend thicker walls and glass for the side of the building facing the freeway. Sometimes a soundwall will need to be constructed.

13. **Environmental Consultants:** They conduct field and desk research to determine if a site and surrounding sites are contaminated or if the development will impact the Endangered Species Act or the Clean Water Act. For contamination, there are two levels of reports: (1) a phase 1 report, which is based on desk research, and (2) a phase 2 report, which includes extensive soil and water testing. To meet federal, state, county, and city regulations and to get financing, a developer needs to know whether the property is contaminated.

14. **General Contractors:** They are responsible for every aspect of building the project. They hire all the subcontractors for plumbing, electrical, HVAC, framing, drywall, and many more. Be sure to get references on the contractor and get a list of projects they have completed. Make sure they have the experience for the type of construction your building will require. The contractor with the lowest bid might not be the best choice.

15. **Property Managers:** They specialize in leasing and managing specific types of commercial properties. They help create a budget for income and expenses. You want to team up with them well ahead of completing construction to come up with a plan for leasing the property. It is important that the developer team up with a good property management company that specializes in the property type and size. (See Chapter 12 on property management and leasing for more details.)

Developer Eric Myers

Eric Meyers is my most humble and one of the highest-skilled developer clients. He has the advantage of having extensive contracting as well as developing experience. He says, "Being a commercial developer is anything but glamorous. You are the lowest person on the totem pole. To be more exact, you are the butler, to make sure everyone else has what they need to do their job."

Eric says that many developers try to flex their brilliance and authority muscles with city planning staff. Eric uses the opposite approach. He knows that they have the power and, as overworked and underpaid city employees, they can make or break your deal. He always treats them respectfully and asks for their help in solving complex problems.

Eric got his license with the Oregon Contractors Board at the age of 14, and at the age of 21 developed and built his first speculative property. He has since delivered over $350,000,000 in complex construction projects across a broad range of commercial property types. These have ranged from an urban infill mixed-use building to the repurposing of a 40,000-square-foot warehouse into a Class A office building.

Along with doing his own deals, Eric has worked as a project manager for two large development companies. Where Eric really excels is in his ability to coach and motivate other people. Although he has to oversee their work, he does not

(continued)

(*continued*)

come across as being any better than they are. After all, he has done most of their jobs and they respect him for this.

Our firm recently financed the construction of a 104-unit, $19,700,000 multi-family complex in Gresham, Oregon, for Eric. I was impressed by his level of skill and consistently good mood. What really amazed me was his tying up the land for a ridiculously low price of $1,200,000. This was one of the last infill lots in Gresham. Since it was in a flood plain, no one wanted to do the work involved to get it to comply with FEMA. Eric brought in a hydrologist who updated the flood plain map that confirmed that the buildings would be out of a flood zone. Although it took seven months, he successfully negotiated with FEMA to green-light the project. The result was overdoubling the land value.

THE COMMERCIAL DEVELOPMENT PROCESS—FIVE STAGES

Okay, so now we come to the meat of these two chapters on commercial development. If you do not have much interest in developing commercial real estate someday, I recommend you just glance through this section. But if this subject does raise your blood pressure like it does mine, with a spark of excitement, do take the time to go through this section slowly.

Commercial development is one of my top specialties. I have included just about all the major and minor steps involved to give you a glance of the entire process. They are listed in the order in which it is best to do them, based on my experience. My intention is to provide you with enough details to know if commercial development is right for you. I have included rough time periods for the major steps of the process. The better the quality of your team of experts, the less time it is likely to take.

Stage One: Predevelopment

Although predevelopment is shown to take close to a year, I have seen this happen in as little as six months for smaller, simpler projects that the city feels are greatly needed.

Creating the Vision and Site Selection

Many of my developer clients tell me that the vision of the project is the best part of their job. They lay awake at night thinking about just the right project for just the right piece of land. Then one day they come across a land parcel that is even better than what they had envisioned and the buildings start sprouting up in their mind. They just know that's it! The only time they feel equally inspired is when they get their certificate of occupancy and walk through the finished project.

As I am writing this, my client developer, Roy Carver, has recently completed the construction of 35 Club, a 110-unit, six-story, luxury apartment complex in Eugene, Oregon. It has stunning Willamette River views and is a few blocks away from Whole Foods and major freeways. It will command the highest rents in town. This property is branded with the motto "Where Luxury Meets Location."

I asked Roy how he came up with the vision for this beautiful mid-high-rise building. He said that he was pretty burned out after completing his last project, a 139-unit micro-apartment complex a block from the University of Oregon. But about five months later he started having a vision of doing another project. This one would be the premier apartment building in town and have the best amenities and great views. It would not be attracting mostly students this time, but millennials, generation Xers, and affluent seniors. It would be located close to major freeways and shopping. He got in his car and drove to an area of town that met this description. He saw a large piece of land with a little house on it that was occupied by a CPA. He checked on the zoning of the property and found that it was beyond perfect. It was zoned C2 Commercial. This meant it had unlimited density. The land also had zero setbacks, which meant he could place the building from property line to property line. That afternoon, he cold-called the accountant, who showed an interest in selling. He was able to pull up a tax map of the property from the city website showing all the dimensions. Later that evening at his kitchen table, he started laying out the building. Two weeks later, he tied up the land with a purchase contract.

Initial Feasibility Research

Now that you know what you want to build and have found the land you are interested in buying, it is time to check out whether this parcel will work for your vision. This step can actually be quite easy and take less than a week.

Pull up a tax map of the parcel online and check the zoning and dimensions. Do an initial layout of the buildings. Do you have room to build what you have in mind? Call a few contractors and get an idea of what it will cost per square foot to build and come up with a rough cost. Check out rent comparables and talk to a property manager about what expenses should run. Do a back-of-the-envelope pro forma to determine if the projected net operating income is large enough to support the project.

If you are building apartments, how many units can you build? What will the cost be per unit for the land? If it's below $15,000 per unit, this should be a plus—it should be below $20,000 per unit for more expensive urban locations. If you are building industrial, office, or retail, what is the cost per square foot for the land? What are comparable land parcels selling for per square foot? Is this a better location or inferior?

Go to the city and ask for a zoning and development handbook. Check out the availability of utilities, building setbacks, parking requirements, parking setbacks, landscaping requirements, lighting requirements, and offsite public requirements for this parcel. Does it pencil for what you want to accomplish? Take some time to research the competition and demographics. Ask the city what the traffic count is for the site.

If all this initial research is positive, it's time to have your first meeting with an architect. Often they will give you a lot of free advice when you are in this initial concept phase. This is all done before you make an offer.

Letter of Intent to Purchase Land

Most developers use a one- or two-page *letter of intent* to make an offer to purchase the land. It is best to keep this simple and offer the most favorable terms that will likely be acceptable to the seller. You can put a lot more detail into making a deal that works for you into the purchase contract.

Purchase and Sales Agreement (PSA) for Land Purchase

This is where your commercial real estate attorney begins their work. They know exactly how to write this up in your favor. Hopefully, the seller will be pleased to not fork out the money to have their attorney do this. A purchase and sales agreement for purchasing land to build a commercial development has many contingencies, including those for zoning, availability of utilities, road access, geotechnical soil testing, environmental testing, approval from the planning department, approval for the entitlements, financing, and so much more. Your attorney will be sure to protect you on all of these.

Time and Money Saving Tip

You really do not want to close on the land until all your entitlements are approved, which can easily take up to a year to accomplish. Strategize ahead when negotiating the purchase contract to outmaneuver the land seller. If just one entitlement is not approved, you will not be able to build. Most land sellers are thinking of getting their money in six months or less. You ideally want to get close to a year. In a down market this is possible. In an up market, try and get at least six months with extension provisions in the sales contract. After each time period, your earnest money will be refunded or goes hard.

First Month after Purchase and Sales Contract Is Signed

Due Diligence

- **Reviewing the Preliminary Title Report:** Having your commercial real estate attorney review the title report is the first thing you do. When you open up title and escrow with the title company, they will pull this up for you. The last thing you want to do is to spend six months or longer with city approvals and then find out the title to the land has problems that cannot be resolved.

- **Feasibility Study:** You should order this day one. A feasibility study gives you market rents and expenses, plus shows all the competition. Most of all, it will give you a factual opinion on how doable your project is. If the study supports your project, it will be much easier to obtain investors and financing. The study will take six to eight weeks. These reports are expensive and can run from $6,500 to $20,000 or more depending on the scope of the work. For small projects, you can have a commercial real estate broker put together a report showing market data that either supports or does not support your deal.

- **Geotechnical Soil Report:** You need to know right away if the soil cannot support the building. So order this day one as well. It will take four to six weeks to get this report.

- **Architect:** Engaging a good architect who specializes in your property type to prepare a preliminary site plan, floor plan, and rough elevation drawing should be done during the first week after signing the purchase contract. You will need these drawings to get a ballpark quote from a contractor and for your first city plan review meeting. It will take at least 30 days to get a contract together

If the process with the city is going well, get the seller excited about eventually closing by telling them this. You will likely have to buy more time by putting down more earnest money, though. Extend the purchase contract in three- to four-month increments. This is the most land sellers can usually tolerate, and it won't make sense for them to start over with another buyer. Even though you could lose some earnest money if the project doesn't get approved, it is much less expensive than purchasing a land parcel that you cannot build on.

Time and Money Saving Tip

Ask the architect if they would prepare a rough, preliminary site plan within the first week or two of your first meeting with them for initial discussions with the city. You want this to be at no cost to you and without having to sign a contract with them.

If the city reacts favorably, then prior to having the contract signed, offer the architect from $3,000 to $5,000 to prepare a preliminary site plan, floor plan, and rough elevation drawings for the city plan review meetings.

with the architect and 30–45 days to get these initial drawings done.

- **Contractor:** Once you have the initial three drawings from your architect, meet with a contractor to get a detailed estimate on construction costs.
- **Estimate Total Project Costs:** Once you have a more solid estimated construction budget, you can put together an estimate of total project cost. You will need this to communicate with lenders on the financing available. Be sure to include the equity in the land, plus *hard costs* and *soft costs* (see Encyclopedia Topic G, Development).
- **Prepare Researched Pro Forma:** This should show projected rents, expenses, and loan payments monthly for a minimum of three years, starting with the first month of lease-up. It's best if you can wait until your feasibility study comes in to get the most accurate market rents. But you can also get this from interviewing property managers and commercial real estate brokers or going online and looking up apartments in the area if you are building a multifamily building. A property management company that specializes in your property type can give you a good idea of market expenses. You will need this pro forma to sell the project to investors and get a quote on financing.

You do not want to sign a contract with the architect yet. You are also going to have the hutzpah to ask them to go to the plan review meetings with you.

It might seem like you are asking a lot, but many of my experienced developers follow this process with their architects, who want to win their business. The architect understands that you want to keep costs down to a minimum until you know the project is approved. Full plans and specs are the most expensive item on your soft cost list, so you want to have all the entitlements approved before you engage the architect and give them a substantial payment.

Time and Money Saving Tip

There is nothing that will cut down construction costs better than having an architect and general contractor team up to do *value engineering* (see Encyclopedia Topic G, Development) at the beginning. To do this, pick one of the best contractors who specializes in your property type and tell them that you want them to be on your team and that you want to do a *cost-plus contract* (see Encyclopedia Topic G, Development) with a guaranteed maximum.

As long as the maximum is within your budget, you will be safe in doing this and likely save more money by having the project value engineered than take it out to bid to many contractors. Not only will the architect and contractor brainstorm the best, most cost-effective design, but both will also likely

45–60 Days After Signing the Purchase Contract

- **Financing Estimate:** After your feasibility study is in, it's time to get several lenders excited about funding your deal. It's too early to apply for a construction loan because the information on the application cannot be more than 90 days old and it will take longer than that for it to be available. But now that you have a more accurate estimate of project cost and a pro forma on income and expenses, it's time to have your lender decide how much they will lend you. Construction financing is based on a percentage of total project cost and ranges from a low of 65% to 85% of cost. You need to know what it will take for you, other key principals, plus your project to qualify. Most of all you need to know how much of a down payment you have to come up with. You might find that you need to bring in an investor who is stronger financially to be a key principal on the loan.

be willing to come to the city plan review meetings to show off their synchronicity, give your project more clout, and make the meetings more efficient.

Time and Money Saving Tip

If you are building a multifamily, senior housing, or mixed-use project during a recession you will find that most banks will only lend up to 65% of cost or not be doing commercial construction loans at all. If your project is $5,000,000 or more, consider applying for a HUD/FHA construction rollover to perm loan, which during the Great Recession still went to 83% of cost. They are at 85% of cost as I write this. HUD's mandate is to supply more quality housing in America during all economic times. These loans are easier to qualify for and do not require tax returns, but they do require an experienced team. On the downside, it will take nine months or longer to close. You might have this much time if you start the HUD loan process early.

- **Order a Traffic Study:** For urban developments, a traffic study is often needed to access the impact traffic to and from the site will have on public streets and surrounding neighborhoods. Not all developments need a traffic study. Go to the city planning department and introduce yourself. See if you can speak with the senior planner. Show them your preliminary site plan and ask their opinion of how much of an impact on traffic your development will have. Then determine whether you need a traffic study.

Two Months After Signing Purchase Contract

Planning Department Application

Many developers want to have their geotechnical soils report in to know the building can be built on the site before applying with the planning department. If you want to rush the process, you can apply with the city right away by filling out an application and paying a fee. Planning department approvals are required before you can submit an application for building permits.

Preparing Entitlement Documents

Entitlements are legal agreements from government and regulatory agencies that give you permission for zoning variances, utilities, road approvals, greenway approvals, landscaping approvals, use permits, and more. You want to start filling out these documents as early as possible, as they can take anywhere from 3 to 12 months to get all the entitlements approved. Your professional team of consultants will be a great help with these.

75 Days After Purchase Contract Is Signed

Preapplication Site Plan Review Meeting with the Planning Department

Once the application is accepted by the city, a kickoff meeting is scheduled with a city planner and the developer to discuss the project and go over critical issues. The developer should at a minimum bring their architect to this meeting. If the project has many challenges and other building department employees are attending, it would be wise for the developer to also bring their civil engineer, land use attorney or planner, and traffic consultant to this meeting. An initial rough site plan should be brought to this meeting.

Three Months After Purchase Contract Is Signed

Plan Review Meeting

You will need to bring to this meeting the site plan, floor plan, and elevation drawings. See if you can get as many of the building departments to attend the meeting and have your full team of professionals there—architect, civil engineer, structural engineer, land use planner, and traffic consultant. If the city wants changes made, you will have to make them and schedule another plan review meeting. If minor changes are needed, the next plan review meeting could be scheduled in about 30 days. If there are major changes it will likely be much longer.

Four to Five Months After Purchase Contract Is Signed

Public Hearing

Most commercial construction projects will require a public hearing to hear the opinions on the development from neighbors and any residents who may be affected. Usually these concerned citizens come with negative feedback. Be sure to invite people you know who support your project to attend to give positive feedback. Having your land use attorney do an objective presentation should help give you a more favorable outcome.

Planning Department or City Council Approval

For many municipalities, the planning department can green-light the project. For some cities, the city council must give final approval at a public hearing. If the planning department rejects the project, the applicant usually can appeal the decision to the city council. If they turn it down, many states have a Land Use Board of Appeals where you can appeal the decision.

Six to Eight Months After Purchase Contract Is Signed

Entitlement Approval

It is wise to have all your entitlements approved before you close on the land, have full plans and specs designed, and finalize the construction contract.

Investor Money Goes into Escrow Account

Now that all the entitlements are approved, this is the perfect time to have all investors deposit their funds toward the down payment into an escrow account. This way they will be fully committed and you can show proof of the down payment to your lender. An investor will only be able to get their money back if the project does not move forward because of financing or some other unforeseen reason.

Time and Money Saving Tip

Often private investors will be reluctant to put their money into escrow, committing their funds until financing is approved or building permits are issued and the project is shovel-ready. You simply cannot take the risk of their changing their minds at that late a date. Make it clear to them at the beginning that they will be required to put their money into escrow once all entitlements

Close Escrow on the Land

Now that the project has been approved by the city with all the entitlements approved, it is safe to close on the land. You will need to have the funds allocated for this ahead of time, as construction lenders really dislike lending on the land as part of the construction loan. It's always best for you to already own the land when you apply for the construction loan so the lender knows that the title is clear.

Have Full Plans and Specs Designed

This is the most expensive of all the soft costs. You have waited until all entitlements are approved to get these started. Contractors and subcontractors will need these to come up with a construction budget so they can bid on the job. Later you will need these to pull building permits.

are approved. Tell them that your lender will require that the down payment is committed. Should construction fail to start for any reason they will get a full refund unless some of their funds have gone to purchase the land.

Time and Money Saving Tip

Once the land is entitled it is worth a lot more. If you are short on funds to close on the land, this is a safe time to use some of your investors' money. If that won't work, you can use a short-term private land lender. They lend an average of 50% of the land value and love fully entitled land. The money will be expensive, but they can close in as little as two weeks.

Apply for Construction Financing

You will have already had the project preapproved for financing. Unfortunately, so much time has gone by that the entire file has to be updated. Your construction loan will be a percentage of cost of the final construction budget plus the land and all soft costs.

Eight to Nine Months After Purchase Contract Is Signed

Construction Bidding and Signing a Construction Contract

You will need to have your plans and *specifications* (*specs*) (see Encyclopedia Topic G, Development) 90% completed to get firm construction bids. Allow at least 30 days. Either take the project out to bid to four to five contractors or enter into a cost-plus contract with a guaranteed maximum. You will need a line-by-line construction contract for financing; this will take at least 30 days.

Create a Final Project Budget

Now that you have your final construction budget and contract, you can create the final project budget. This will include the value of the land plus soft costs and the hard costs to construct the building and infrastructure. Soft costs include architectural fees, all other professional fees, construction loan costs, and all ancillary expenses outside the construction contract.

10 Months After Purchase Contract Is Signed

Construction Loan Approval

This is a monumental step to have achieved and now it's time to pull building permits. These are expensive and they expire, so you do need to have your construction loan approved first.

Pulling Building Permits

Now that the plans and specs have been reviewed and found to be in compliance, and all entitlements have been approved, and your construction loan has been approved, building permits are issued once you pay a hefty fee. These allow the construction to begin and the work to be inspected.

Step Two: Construction

11 to 12 Months After Purchase Contract Is Signed

Preconstruction Meeting

The developer, acting as project manager, will have a meeting with the general contractor, all the subcontractors, and the architect to discuss how they will be working and solving problems together, as well as establishing time frames for the various stages of construction.

Survey Staking

The property lines will be staked out first, then the site will be rough-graded. Then the utilities are staked, followed by the outer and inner walls of the buildings. The walkways and parking lot will be staked out after the building is completed.

Grading, Site Work, and Conduit Installation

The property is excavated and sculpted with earth-moving equipment to conform to the site plan. Then PVC pipes are run for electrical, gas, water, and sewage.

Pour the Building Foundation

After careful soil testing the soil is compacted, then footings for the foundation are excavated and a concrete base with rebar is poured that can bear the load of the building.

The Building Is Built

Framing the exterior and interior is done, the building envelope is completed, and roofing is completed. Now that it is dry inside, plumbing, electrical, HVAC, and ductwork are installed. Sheetrock, interior finishes, and lighting are next.

Paving Parking Lot, Roads, and Walkways

Now that all the heavy equipment has been moved offsite, the parking lot, roads, and walkways are paved.

Landscaping

Trees, shrubs, and lawns are put in according to the landscaping plan.

Offsite Work

This includes work done outside of the property, including sidewalks and access roads. These can be done any time during construction.

First Punch List

Once all the major systems have been inspected and approved, a preliminary punch list is used to identify any work that still needs to be done.

Temporary Occupancy Permit Is Issued

Once you obtain the first punch list, a temporary occupancy permit is issued, usually for 30 days. This allows the property to be occupied.

Closing Out Construction Punch List

Once all the items have been completed on the first punch list, a closing out punch list will be created, showing any items that are still substandard.

Architect's Punch List

An inspector hired by the developer or architect will go through and make sure all the finishes and installation of fixtures are perfect and that there are no flaws or blemishes in the craftsmanship. These items can range from walls that are not painted properly to cabinets that are missing knobs.

Certificate of Occupancy Is Issued

Once all the remaining items that needed work on the punch list are completed and a final inspection is made, the municipality will issue a certificate of occupancy. Now the property can be legally occupied.

Step Three: Lease-Up

Coordinating Leasing Marketing with Off-Site and On-Site Management Personnel

It's the developer's job to give instructions and to oversee property management. Many office, retail, and industrial spaces are often preleased prior to construction. Multifamily units are often preleased up to four months before the building is completed.

Tenant Improvement (TI) Construction

On office, retail, and industrial properties, if the property owner is doing the lease-hold improvements, they can be completed during the construction process to the tenant's specifications. A construction permit will need to be pulled for each space. If the tenant is doing TIs, they need to get their own building permit and these are started once the shell of the building is up.

Setting Goals with Property Management for Stabilization

Setting time frames for achieving occupancy goals with property management is one of the developer's most important responsibilities. The longer it takes to fill the property to market occupancy, the more money it will cost you. A website for the development will have been completed during early construction. Approving a marketing campaign, a time frame for lease-up, starting rents, and approving rental concessions with your property manager are essential.

Step Four: Overseeing Operations

Creating an Operating Budget for Income and Expenses

This is done with your property management company. You want to set realistic goals for each line item. These goals should be based on criteria that can be substantiated.

Evaluating Income and Expenses

Often during a landlord's up market, rents can be raised if the property is leased quickly. In a down market or recession, rents often have to be lowered and rental concessions have to be carefully implemented. Managing rental income and expenses with your property manager is one of the developer's most important tasks.

Quarterly Reporting and Distributing Income to Investors

This is something you can have your accountant or property manager do, but this is the developer's responsibility. You will need to fully understand the numbers, as your investors will have questions that you do not want to have to answer with "I don't know, but I will find out for you."

Step Five: Refinancing or Selling

Applying for Permanent Financing to Take Out the Construction Loan

Yes, the developer is responsible for this, too. Often a permanent loan will be in the works just prior to the property being stabilized. If the lease-up is going to take long, you might have to

---

Time and Money Saving Tip

As the developer you have been working on your project almost every day for likely two years or more. Now that you have obtained your occupancy permit and are ready to get paid back for your hard work, a major recession hits. The property is leasing up at a snail's pace. Your property manager wants to lower rents by 20% and offer a generous concession: tenants who sign a year's lease get their deposit cut in half and their second month rent-free.

Be wary of property managers who lean toward excessive cuts in rent and overly generous rental concessions. Many are pulled to do this because it makes their job leasing the property so much easier. Be sure to do a complete analysis of all your competitors' rents and base where you set your initial rents on this. Don't forget that if all your rents are too low, you might not have enough net operating income to qualify for permanent financing. If you have to offer rental concessions, it is better to get a larger deposit, as this ensures better-quality tenants. Also offer a free month's rent between months 6 and 12 of a one-year lease as long as the tenant has always paid the rent on time. This rewards the tenant for being a good tenant and lowers the risk that they are looking to scam you by paying a very small deposit, the first month's rent, and then not paying any more rent.

ask your lender for an extension on your construction loan, or apply for a *mini-perm loan* (see Encyclopedia Topic H, Financing) to take the construction loan out.

Putting the Property on the Market

If your plan is to sell the property after it is fully occupied, or years later after a long-term hold, it is the developer's job to list the property and make decisions with the listing broker.

Refinancing the Permanent Loan

Years later, if you plan on holding the property after the permanent loan has matured, it is the developer's job to refinance it.

Development

Absorption Schedule: *Be sure to figure this out to estimate when the property will break even*

For a developer to determine accurately what their total project cost will be, they need to know the absorption schedule. An absorption schedule is an estimate of the timeline for a newly developed property to reach *stabilized occupancy* (see Encyclopedia Topic B, Due Diligence) once the *certificate of occupancy* (see Encyclopedia Topic G, Development) is obtained. For example: The absorption schedule indicates that the property will be 60% leased within four months of completion. Feasibility studies and commercial construction appraisals have an estimated absorption schedule, which is one of the most important metrics for developers and their lenders and investors. The developer needs to know how long it will take for the property to be able to break even once the construction is completed; they may need to inject extra money into the project until then. For the lender to estimate construction interest and the loan term, they need to know the time it will take to construct the property and the absorption schedule. The developer will need to know the

Time and Money Saving Tip

Of all the commercial construction projects I have worked on, very few reached stabilization that matched the absorption schedule forecasted in the feasibility study or construction appraisal. This is because during the average 18 months or longer it takes for construction and leasing, there are so many variables, including the weather, the reliability of the contractor and subcontractors, the thoroughness of plans and specs, change orders, the quality of property management, the amount of preleasing, the time of year the construction is completed, the number of new rental units or spaces coming on line, of course the real estate market changing from up to down or vice versa, and so much more. Therefore it is really important to negotiate a larger interest payment reserve and longer term on your construction loan than your lender has determined from the absorption schedule. If your lender wants to give you a loan term of 18 months or less, fight hard to get 24 months. If they have budgeted 10 months of interest payments, request 12–14 months. This often means negotiating a larger construction loan. Also, having 4% of absorption schedule to know when their investors can start getting draws on their cash invested.

Bid and Award Process: *When getting bids, make sure you are only choosing the best contractors*

It makes sense to use competition to get the best price for your construction project, and the best way to do this is to get four or more of the best general contractors to bid the job. Unlike construction estimates, a bid is considered to be a firm price. If anything is left out, or you change materials, you are inviting costly change orders down the road. To request bids, you will need to have plans and specs completed by your architect. The contractor with the lowest price is usually awarded the job. This process averages four weeks because the general contractor has to get bids from all the subcontractors. The good news is that there is always a deadline in which all the bids have to come in. These days, contractors can use bidding software that will better ensure that their bids are accurate and profitable. Today construction bids can be submitted online.

Bike Score: *Choosing an urban location to develop that has a good bike score will make it far more rentable*

Many people these days are looking for a place to live or work that is bikeable. If you are building in a urban area, why not choose a land parcel that has a good bike score? This may make the property more valuable and desirable for many tenants. Be sure to post the bike score on your property website and promotions. Bike score, based on data collected by the research company Walk Score, measures how good a location is based on the time it takes to run errands and get to major shopping and schools from the property. A bike score of 90–100 is rated "Biker's Paradise" and means that most errands can be accomplished on a bike; a score of 70–89 is rated "Very Bikeable" and means that most errands can be accomplished on a bike; and a score of 50–69 is rated "Bikeable," which means that some errands can be run on a bike.

the hard costs in working capital put aside for the construction and absorption taking longer can mean life or death for your project.

Time and Money Saving Tip

If you receive a construction bid that is far below all the others, take the time to thoroughly investigate the integrity of the contractor; you seldom get something for nothing in ground-up construction. The contractor might be in the habit of taking on more projects than they have the capacity for, which can cause a major delay on your project. Worse yet, if they are running the job on a very small profit margin they might end up cutting corners to turn a profit. The most common way contractors make up for losses is by charging exorbitant prices for change orders. They really can charge you whatever they want.

Before you sign a construction contract, be sure to get a list of all the projects the contractor has completed in the past 10 years along with their references. Be wary if the contractor has changed the name of their company. Take the time to do a background check and credit check on the contractor personally and on their company.

Brownfield: *Finding a brownfield urban infill lot to build on could be a gold mine*

You might have never thought of looking for a brownfield property to build on. Doesn't sound very appealing, does it? But buying one for the right price and location can be a great investment. A brownfield lot is a parcel of land that was used previously for an industrial purpose that resulted in the land's being contaminated. It could also be created by a gasoline spill that contaminated many lots in town, rendering them vacant. It is estimated that there are over 450,000 brownfield sites in the United States. Often the land can be cleaned up and developed cost effectively. Ideally, look for a brownfield urban infill parcel that can be purchased for a great price. Then apply to clean up the property through the Environmental Protection Agency's (EPA) Brownfield and Land Revitalization Program. You will need to get the land at an exceptional price because it can take a year or longer to get the land cleaned up and approved by the EPA.

Buildout: *The tenant in a new strip mall will be provided with a cement slab and perimeter walls showing the studs. Will you do the buildout or have the tenants do it?*

When building an office or retail building, you will need to know if you are going to provide the tenant buildout or have the tenants construct and pay for it themselves. First-generation spaces with no buildout just have a concrete floor and the studs are visible in the perimeter walls. The buildout consists of all the interior components of each space: interior walls, dropped ceilings, lighting, electrical, plumbing, HVAC, bathrooms, carpet, fixtures, and interior finishes. It can be much more profitable for the developer to do the buildouts, finance the expense, and pass the cost along in the form of much higher rents to the tenant. Keep in mind that you will need to pull a separate building permit for each space, which is expensive; if the tenant does their own buildout they will pay for the building permit for that space. If you are preleasing prior to construction, you can ask the tenants their preference. Would they prefer to do their own buildout, or would they rather have you build their space to suit them?

Build-to-Core Strategy: *You could save 20% or more by building a new property in on an expensive urban infill lot*

If you have been looking for a Class A or B commercial property to purchase and prices are just too high, consider a build-to-core strategy. Core real estate is the lowest-risk commercial property to invest in. These properties are either Class A or Class B, in great locations, and have a good history of stable, predictable cash flows. A build-to-core strategy involves building a new Class A building in a low-cap submarket when the price to buy an existing property becomes too high. To accomplish

Time and Money Saving Tip

If you are new to commercial development and have some land you want to build on, consider getting a mentor. Steering a project through city planning the entitlement process is a daunting endeavor. Find a property that has been built in the past five years that is similar to what you want to do. Google the name and address of the property and see if you can find out who the development company was. Then contact the developer and see if you can meet for coffee—developers love talking shop. You can offer to pay them as a consultant or cut this, you have to either find an infill lot and do ground-up construction or repurpose an older building in a great location. Building to core can save 20% or more of the price of buying an existing | them in for a small percentage of ownership on your project to help you get it off the ground.

Class A or B property in an up market. Property values also increase if rents go up significantly by the time the new property reaches *stabilized occupancy* (see Encyclopedia Topic B, Due Diligence).

Car Stack Parking: *If you are short on space for parking, consider installing this*

If you ever walk by a commercial property with car stack parking, you will stop dead in your tracks and look in awe at cars parked one on top of another. If your construction development is on a small urban lot and there is not enough space to build the building and meet city off-street parking requirements, car stack parking could be a solution. This is a lift system that allows you to stack more than one car in a parking space. Although some independent car stack parking systems are automated and can be operated by the public, dependent systems where an attendant raises, lowers, and moves the cars are more common. Dependent lifts can stack cars from two to six high.

Certificate of Occupancy (C of O): *This is what you have been waiting for all those months of construction. Now the property can be legally occupied.*

Once final inspections have taken place on all building systems and all items on the *punch list* (see Encyclopedia Topic G, Development) have been remedied, it is time for a city building inspector to sign off on the completed building and give you a certificate of occupancy, which certifies that the building has met all codes and can be occupied. The C of O will stipulate what use the property is approved for, such as multifamily, mixed-use, retail, or industrial. With a multifamily property, the number of legal units will be specified. The fee for a certificate of occupancy is based on square footage.

Conceptual Design: *This is a 3-D drawing of how the building will look when completed*

Be sure to have your architect produce a great conceptual design drawing that can be used to get investors and lenders excited about your project. Today these are 3-D drawings that depict exactly how the building will look, function, and fit into the surrounding area. They even show landscaping and people milling about. Some of the best even depict great views from the landscape surrounding the building. I have witnessed potential investors who did not seem to have much of an interest in a property fall in love with it because of a great conceptual design drawing. To produce these drawings, an architect has to take into consideration not only the developer's concept for the building, but also how the lot and setbacks are situated and building, parking, and landscaping codes.

Construction Contract Pitfalls to Avoid: *Watch out for these when signing a construction contract*

Most construction contracts start out as templates on the general contractor's computer. This puts the contract in favor of the contractor. As the *developer* (see later in this

Topic), it is important to have your commercial real estate attorney rewrite some clauses to even out the playing field. Also, have your lender review the contract to make sure the construction draw provisions are acceptable to them. Here are some of the most common pitfalls to avoid:

1. **Change orders clause:** Change orders are to be expected due to, for example, errors in drawings, mistakes made by soil consultants, or design changes. Be sure the contract clearly states how change orders are to be submitted and a time frame for the contractor to respond and remedy any problems. Most importantly, change orders can arise from the contractor not being able to obtain agreed-upon materials. In this case, be sure the contract clearly states that the contractor must bear the cost of more expensive replacements, rushing the materials, or lowering the construction costs for inferior or less desirable replacements.

2. **Certification of work completed and payment clause:** Often a boilerplate contract will leave it up to the contractor to certify that a certain amount of work has been completed and that payment for such work is due. Make sure that the construction contract allows you, your lender, your architect, or a third-party construction monitoring service to verify that work has been completed before payment is made. Also, be sure the contract has a clause that allows for any disputes over completion to be resolved easily and gives you 30 days to resolve the dispute without a work stoppage.

3. **Construction delays clause:** This clause protects the contractor with extra compensation should there be an event beyond their control that causes a delay in construction. These can include "acts of God" such as severe weather, natural disasters, or even national shortages in building materials. Be sure to put into the contract only the events that you feel are worthy of costly delays and additional compensation to the contractor; also include a maximum amount based on a percentage that affected construction costs can be increased.

4. **Completing the construction on time clause:** With the exception of delays that are out of the contractor's control that are listed in number 3, put in a penalty for each day that the construction is completed late. You can also provide an incentive to the contractor by rewarding them with a bonus for each day the construction gets completed early.

5. **Monetary assurances clause:** In this clause, also called the "securing the parties' performance clause," you will be required to certify that you have raised the capital needed to complete the construction in the event that there is a mistake in the drawings and work you did not plan on is needed or the contractor does additional work that you did not approve and your financing will not cover the deficiency. In this event, if the contractor goes over budget, and you request more time to raise more money, the contractor may file a mechanics lien without giving you enough time to remedy the situation, which will bring all work to a halt and can cause costly delays as well as legal expenses. Be sure to have your attorney write into this clause that the contractor must get your written permission to perform any additional work outside of the contract, and give you a minimum of 30 to 45 days to raise more capital before filing a mechanics lien, should you go over the construction budget.

Construction Monitoring: *Having a specialist do this for you will pay for itself by making the construction project more productive*

Do you have the time and ingenuity to monitor each aspect of your construction project for not only quality but also compliance, accounting, and time frame? As the developer for larger commercial construction projects, consider hiring a third-party construction monitoring service like Currie and Brown or Guidepost Solutions to give you more project control. They will give you continual reports on construction progress, costs, and notify you immediately if it is falling behind schedule. They will also check to make sure your contractor is not substituting unapproved materials, committing fraud, and give you a heads-up if the project is going over budget. They are experts on catching early on if the construction is not conforming to the approved plans, specs, and building codes.

Lender Construction Monitoring

Lenders perform a different form of construction monitoring. The same term refers to their verification that a certain amount of work has been completed before releasing funds for that work to the general contractor. Local banks usually do construction monitoring themselves, whereas out-of-state lenders usually hire a firm to do this for them.

Cost per Square Foot: *Did you know that cost per square foot estimates can be as much as 20% off actual cost?*

So you have found the perfect land parcel and you want to build a commercial building on it. You know how much the land is going to cost, but you are dying to know what the construction cost will be. So the first thing you do is contact an architect, contractor, bank, or even a real estate broker and ask what the going cost per square foot is these days to build. The answer will always be given to you in a range of costs, such as for multifamily, from $150 to $185 per square foot. If you ask another expert, you will get a different answer. Cost per square foot estimates for construction costs can easily be 20% off actual costs when compared to accepted construction bids, because with actual bids the contractor has the complete plans and specs and the quality of materials has been specified. These plans are based on the data from geotechnical soil, civil, and structural engineers. The bottom line is that cost per square foot can be used to give you a ballpark or very rough, speculative estimate of cost, but don't expect it to be accurate.

> **Time and Money Saving Tip**
>
> If you are doing a construction loan with a lender that is out of state and they are using a third-party firm to do the construction monitoring, make sure that your lender is behind creating a construction draw process that is efficient. Find out ahead of time what the average turnaround time is for getting work inspected, since the lender will not pay construction draws until this has been done. Subcontractors expect to be paid soon after they have completed a section of work. Often these construction-monitoring firms are out of state and will schedule inspections on your project based on what is convenient for them, not based on what is best for your construction crew. Slow-paid subcontractors often threaten to jump ship to work elsewhere, where they will get paid on time.

Development

There is one exception to this and that is when your architect and contractor are working together with design drawings to do *value engineering* (see Encyclopedia Topic G, Development).

Cost per square foot varies greatly based on demand, property location, building height, quality of materials, number of stories, terrain, impact fees, building permit fees, and so much more. I have had a similar size three-story garden-style apartment complex be quoted at $1.65 per square foot in Bakersfield, California, and $3.00 per square foot in Korea Town, Los Angeles. Commercial construction always costs a lot more in large cities, largely due to the cost of getting everything to the site, and often having to build a parking structure or subterranean parking.

Cost-Plus Construction Contract: *This can work if the contractor agrees to a guaranteed maximum price*

In a cost-plus construction contract, the contractor gets paid for all expenses plus a contractor fee based on a percentage of the total. Expenses include direct costs such as materials and labor as well as indirect costs for overhead, which cover rent, insurance, office expenses, and mileage. General contractors usually charge from 10% to 15% of total costs for their profit.

When to Use a Cost-Plus Construction Contract

Using a cost-plus contract is only advisable if you can get one with a guaranteed maximum price. If the maximum amount is within your budget, then there are definite advantages in going this way. If you are on a tight predevelopment schedule and want to avoid the timely bidding process, this can easily trim six weeks or more from the predevelopment time frame, as well as cutting out the time it takes to check out the credentials of many contractors. Being able to choose one contractor who you know does outstanding work and specializes in your property type can save time.

Density: *Look at the price of the land based on its zoning for density*

When choosing a land parcel to develop, don't look only at the price of the land; look at the price based on

Time and Money Saving Tip

Choose the best architect and the best general contractor you can find. Offer to pay the contractor on a cost-plus contract with a guaranteed maximum (make sure the guaranteed maximum amount is within your budget). The purpose of this is twofold. First, this is the most effective way to save money on total project costs by having your architect and contractor team up from day one to do *value engineering* (see Encyclopedia Topic G, Development) on the design. This can trim an average of 12–15% off the *hard costs* (see Encyclopedia Topic G, Development). Second, because these two experts designed your building together, their total comprehension of the project and their attendance at city planning meetings will help the approval process go much faster.

Development

density. Zoning determines density, which refers to the number of units or buildable square footage allowed per acre. Paying more for raw land that is zoned for high density will often produce a greater return than paying less for the same size parcel that is zoned for low density. I have a client who paid $1,850,000 for a land parcel in Denver that seemed very expensive for 1.4 acres, but its zoning for unlimited density for multifamily made it cheap. My client was able to build 147 units on it, which came to $13,504 per unit for the land. For multifamily properties, density can go from unlimited down to 12 units per acre. Density for office, retail, and industrial buildings is based on the floor area ratio, which is the ratio between a building's floor area and the size of the land.

Development Fee: As the developer, be sure to get paid a fee for your expertise and time

The developer is expected to charge a fee for the services they provide. With some lenders, this fee can be financed as a *soft cost* (see Encyclopedia Topic G, Development). Most often, they will not let this fee be paid to the developer until the project is completed. The developer's responsibilities start with *predevelopment* (see Encyclopedia Topic G, Development), which can take six months to a year or more, then go on with construction, taking a year or more, then lease-up, six months or more. The

> ### Time and Money Saving Tip
>
> If you find a parcel of land that is offered for a great price because it is zoned for low density for multifamily, consider applying for a density bonus. You will have to commit to building affordable housing, where a certain number of units have affordable rents. For some municipalities this can be as low as 15% of total units. In exchange, you can greatly increase the density, which should make the property more profitable, even with the lower-rent units, than building without the density bonus. Another bonus is that the price of the land per unit will be low.

> ### Time and Money Saving Tip
>
> Be careful when co-developing a project with a joint venture capital firm that is contributing most of the equity. They often want to be the lead developer and will demand 75% of the development fee. This is your project, and you should control it. That 75% of the development fee should go to you, regardless of the percentage of cash you have contributed. By earning a larger percentage of the development fee you are declaring that you are the lead developer and getting paid accordingly.

development fee ensures that the developer is paid for their time. Development fees are usually charged on a sliding scale: 4–5% for projects of $5 million to $20 million, 4% for projects of $20 million to $30 million, 3.5% for projects of $30 million to $40 million, and 3% for projects of $40 million and above. This fee is, of course, negotiable. I have seen them go as high as 10%. Banks do not like to see development fees over 4%, whereas private lenders seem to be okay with higher fees, up to 6%.

Developer's Responsibilities: *Do a developer's responsibilities ever end?*

Most people have the impression that a developer will mostly be overseeing the ground-up construction. But there is so much more than that. The developer is responsible for conceiving of the development, finding the land, doing all the predevelopment work, such as: hiring project consultants, changing zoning, raising investors, doing all the due diligence, getting entitlement approvals, applying for financing, and signing the construction contract, then overseeing construction, financial reporting and payment to investors, hiring professional management, leasing, and refinancing or selling the completed project.

Elevation Drawings: *This is your first look at what your building will look like*

This is one of the most exciting experiences you will have as a developer—when you get your first glimpse of what the completed building will look like. No, not after it's been built; when you see your first elevation drawings and have a "That's it!" moment. An elevation drawing by your architect will be your first chance to see the building's facade from the front and side. You want to bring elevation drawings to your first city site plan review meeting. To get an idea of the building's look, review photos or conceptual design drawings of other similar buildings. Better yet, walk through town and take photos of buildings that have the right look. Then have your architect produce two to four initial elevation drawings of the front of the building for you. You might have to go through this four or five times before you find an elevation design you really get excited about.

Energy Star Rating: *This prestigious rating will save your money*

According to the Environmental Protection Agency (EPA), the average commercial building wastes 30% of the energy it consumes. Having your newly developed building Energy Star–rated is not only prestigious, but also smart, as it saves a lot of money. To get an Energy Star rating, a building must meet strict energy performance standards mandated by the EPA: the building has to have an annual score of 75 or higher, which indicates that it performs better than 75% of similar buildings nationwide. Start with having the building designed to save energy and purchase energy-saving HVAC and other systems. Save water and reuse wastewater. Put in an *energy management system* (see Encyclopedia Topic F, Repositioning) that installs energy-saving-measure controls and monitors them. With this system, common area lighting, heating, and cooling systems go to sleep at times of low usage. Encourage residents to save energy as well.

Entitlement Process: *Miss getting just one entitlement approved and your development project is done for*

Working with government and regulatory agencies to get all the entitlements approved is one of the most difficult jobs a developer has. Entitlements are approvals for building plans, environmental concerns, utilities, roads, landscaping, zoning variances, conditional use permitting, and

Time and Money Saving Tip

When investing in unentitled land, it is imperative that you assess accurately the risk of getting the property fully entitled. Before you execute the purchase and sale agreement on the land, consult with a local land use attorney to identify any inherent entitlement problems. Ideally, you want to have all entitlements

Development

fire department authorization. Often, a project can need 10 or more. Having just one of them not get approved and you will not be able to pull a building permit. Be sure to get the entitlement process started as soon as you can, as it can take between 4 and 12 months to obtain all of them. Most construction lenders do not want to start working on your construction loan until the property is fully entitled.

approved prior to closing on the land. To mitigate the risk of not being able to obtain all entitlements, choose the best local professionals who are respected by the city planning department and other regulatory agencies. These professionals should include your architect, contractor, structural engineer, civil engineer, traffic consultant, and land use attorney.

Furniture, Fixtures, and Equipment (FF&E): *These items can usually be financed with your loan*

Be sure to include FF&E in your construction budget. These are items that are not attached, and can be removed from the property. They include security equipment and furniture for the lobby and common areas. They also can include apartment furnishings, cabinets, desks, and even snow removal equipment.

Time and Money Saving Tip

If your construction financing is maxed out and you do not have room to finance FF&E items, or your lender will not finance them, you can likely lease them with off-balance-sheet financing. You can likely get a 10-year lease with very low payments and write 100% of the payments off.

Most construction lenders will allow you to include in your loan FF&E items that the building will need to operate. If you have preleased much of the property prior to construction, your construction lender may also allow you to finance an allowance for FF&E items for tenants when you are building to suit for them.

Hard Costs: *These include all construction costs except the cost of the land, professional services, loan expenses, and closing costs*

Hard costs refer to all construction-related expenses including storm and sewer work, bringing in utilities, grading the site, pouring the foundation, building the structure, electrical, plumbing, HVAC, landscaping, and paving the parking lot, roads, and walkways. Also included are fixtures that are built in and not movable.

Hydrologists: *These experts can help with flooding, erosion, and high-groundwater issues*

As part of your due diligence as a developer, you might need to hire a hydrologist who is trained to recognize land conditions that are prone to leading to flooding, landslides, erosion, high-groundwater tables, well-water quality, and failing septic leach fields, as well as flood plain, storm surge, and stormwater issues. A hydrologist can also advise you on how to mitigate these problems and recommend ways to contour the land or raise structures to solve flood plain issues. They are talented at helping you work with FEMA to take a property or part of it out of a flood plain.

Impact Fees: *These are fees charged per unit or by the square foot for construction*

Impact fees are really annoying and are viewed by many developers as a tax. When putting your construction budget together, don't forget to include impact fees, as they can be expensive. These are one-time fees assessed by municipalities on property developments to cover the cost of the new building's impact on the existing infrastructure for roads, water, wastewater, storm water, public safety, parks, schools, and more. The fee is usually charged per unit on apartment buildings and hotels, and per square foot on most other commercial property types. In Miami, multifamily impact fees in 2019 were $6,860 per unit. For a 60-unit complex, this would total $411,600. Not small change!

Land Assemblage: *If you can pull this off, you could make a fortune*
One way to use your brilliant mind and greatly increase the value of a group of land parcels is to create a land assemblage so you can build a larger commercial development or a *planned unit development (PUD)* (see later in this Topic). A land assemblage involves buying adjoining land parcels from different owners at a good price and combining them into one large parcel that will be worth a great deal more per acre once it is rezoned. For example: you buy four 100-acre parcels that are close to the city limits from different owners for a million dollars each. You then spend several years getting the 400 acres annexed to the city and rezoned for a planned community. Once that's been accomplished, you have 40 commercial lots to sell that have a combined value of $20 million. Smart, huh?

Land Use Attorney: *This is one expert you cannot do without*
A local respected land use attorney who has a diplomatic approach to working with planning staff and governing officials will pay dividends in saving you time and money. A skilled land use attorney often knows the zoning laws, building ordinances, construction permitting process, and land ordinances better than the city officials do. They can also be a powerful tool in getting all the entitlements approved more efficiently. Most of all, they can help work out conflicts in an objective manner with officials who often tend to be more subjective.

LEED Certification: *This is the most highly recognized green certification in America*
Building green as a developer will not only make your development more prestigious, but will also help your project win more favorable acceptance with municipalities. LEED certification is undoubtedly the most recognizable green certification in America and has three levels of certification: Silver, Gold, and Platinum. Which level your building attains is based on how many points it earns for energy use, efficient lighting and HVAC systems, water conservation, air quality, the location of the building, and the use of sustainable materials during construction. In most cases, green buildings attain higher rents than nongreen buildings, likely due to the lower utility costs for tenants.

Lump Sum Construction Contract: *This type of construction contract cannot be beat*
As a developer, if you can pull off doing a lump sum construction contract with a general contractor, you will sleep so much better at night! The benefit of such a contract is that the total construction costs are negotiated for a set price according to your budget. You will not only make your lender happy, but save a lot of hassle. This puts the risk of future price increases squarely on the shoulders of the contractor. This can be favorable for you as long you take the time to choose each item carefully and have your selections reviewed by your architect. The leading benefit of the lump sum project is

that the whole construction process is much easier to manage, as it is simplified and both parties get to avoid tracking or disputing costs.

A major drawback to lump sum contracts is that if the contractor has underestimated the cost, they might try to cut cost by lowering quality or making change orders more expensive than they reasonably should be. Therefore, it is imperative that you only work with general contractors with a stellar reputation. Construction lenders prefer lump sum contracts since they tend to keep construction costs on budget. Construction draws are paid on a set schedule, such as the first of every month, based on the percentage of work completed.

Modular Construction: You won't have to worry about bad weather if you are building this way

If you are building a larger commercial structure and would like to avoid delays from weather and save on construction costs, ask your architect if they can design the project using commercial modular construction. This process has 60% or more of the building prefabricated to building codes in modules in a warehouse off-site. The components are then shipped in a flatbed truck to the site and assembled. Projects can be completed an average of 25% faster with 15% trimmed off the cost of labor. Money is also saved because buildings are occupied sooner, producing income much faster.

Some drawbacks are that in some cities, building inspectors are not up to speed with the modular construction process, causing delays. So be sure to have a planning meeting with your architect, general contractor, and all building inspectors to make sure the process is well understood and coordinated.

Time and Money Saving Tip

If you are building an apartment building costing $6,000,000 or more, consider doing a HUD 221 (d)4 Construction loan. These loans go up to 85% of cost and are *non-recourse loans* (see Encyclopedia Topic H Financing). Better yet, your very-low-rate construction loan rolls over seamlessly to a 40-year fixed-rate, fully amortizing permanent loan at the same low rate. On the downside, these loans require that your contractor pay Davis-Bacon wages, called prevailing wages, which are considerably higher than ordinary wages. There is a loophole for this, however: if you build with modular construction, any modules that are completed off-site are exempt from the prevailing wage requirement. Another negative is that the entire process can take 10 months or longer. But this time frame can still work out if you are just starting to get your entitlements approved.

Time and Money Saving Tip

All construction projects have unexpected changes that create change orders. If you choose to do a lump sum contract, consider putting in a clause that change orders will be handled on a cost-plus basis. This is the actual verifiable cost of the item being changed plus an agreed-upon percentage like 8–10%. Otherwise, the contractor can charge you whatever they want. Also consider rewarding the contractor for every day they finish early and penalizing them for every day they finish late (excluding delays caused by weather).

New Urbanism: *You might be a New Urbanist and not even know it if you construct a building where tenants can walk to everything*

New Urban design is a planning and development approach that tries to reduce traffic and build a sense of community by situating shopping, parks, schools, and other public spaces within walking distance of where people live and work. As a developer, you can get involved in being a New Urbanist by building or redeveloping an apartment or office building in an urban area already up and coming with boutique shops and eateries. Millennials and seniors will love living or working in the conveniently located building you create.

Off-Street-Parking Requirements: *Are you going to be able to meet the city parking space requirement with the land you just bought and want to build on?*

When planning ground-up construction, be sure to check with the municipality to find out how many parking spaces you must provide for off-street parking. The last thing you want is to find out you do not have enough land for the size of the building and required parking. Cities base their parking ratio requirements on spaces per unit or spaces per square footage. For example, the City of Omaha requires one space per hotel unit or an efficiency apartment and two spaces for a two-bedroom apartment. For an office property, one space for every 300 square feet is required; for a medical office, one space for every 200 square feet is required. Keep in mind that properties that have more spaces than the minimum required are generally worth more.

Opportunity Zones: *If you have cash sitting around subject to capital gains taxes, read on*

Would you like to do ground-up construction or a major rehab of an existing property and do you also happen to have a lot of cash subject to capital gains? If the answer is yes, then look into investing in an opportunity zone. There are hundreds of thousands of buildings and land parcels that qualify nationwide. The tax savings incentives are impressive. Opportunity zones were created by Congress to revitalize economically distressed communities using capital gains tax incentives instead of taxpayer money. Governors in every state have designated the locations of these zones. They must be in a census tract that has a poverty rate of at least 20% and the median income cannot exceed 80% of metro or state levels. The tax incentives have two parts: first, funds subject to capital gains tax can be used to fund the construction and are eligible to have taxes deferred; second, if you hold the completed property for 10 years, any capital gains generated from a sale are tax-free. Not bad!

Performance Bond: *If your contractor takes out a performance bond and goes out of business, the insurance company—not you—will be responsible for completing construction*

Consider protecting your investment by requiring that your general contractor provide a performance bond that guarantees that the construction will be completed. Keep in mind that almost all loans require the developer and key principals to sign a completion guarantee. This makes you personally liable to complete the construction should the contractor go out of business. A performance bond puts the responsibility of completing the construction squarely on an insurance company's shoulders. Performance bonds are issued by surety companies that will step in and pay to complete the construction according to the construction contract. Government projects and those financed by HUD require a performance bond. This will cost the contractor from 1% to 2% of the cost of construction, and this cost will be passed on to you. A general contractor has to be strong enough financially and have good credit and enough net worth and liquidity to qualify for a performance bond. It is not uncommon for small contractors to not qualify.

Planned Unit Development (PUD): *This has one of the largest payoffs of any development. Do you have the time and ingenuity to pull it off?*

If you want to plan something big with a huge payoff, consider putting together a planned unit development (PUD). This is not easy to accomplish, and will take a lot of time. But if you can pull it off, it is one of the most profitable undertakings a developer can take on. You will be taking a large agricultural parcel that is adjacent to a city, creating a master site plan, incorporating the entire parcel into the city, and then getting it rezoned to build a PUD. Planned unit developments are also known as planned communities. They are large tracts of land that contain residential housing, commercial shops, restaurants, parks, swimming pools, workout centers, bike and walking trails, and full-size grocery stores. Often, municipalities can be sold on PUD developments because they draw people to move there, which increases their tax base. PUDs are attractive to residents because of the vast open spaces that incorporate the natural landscape and the convenience of having everything they need near their front door. PUDs often get special zoning approval for setbacks, density, and height restrictions. Often PUDs are senior 55 and older communities.

Predevelopment—20 Steps: *This can take even longer than building the project*

The predevelopment stage of developing a commercial property is so extensive and time consuming that it can take as long or even longer than the construction phase. It averages six to eight months, but can take a year or longer. Chapter 9 reviews in detail all the steps involved. Predevelopment starts out with finding the right land parcel, creating a vision of the completed project, acquiring the land, having preliminary architectural drawings done, and meeting with city planning staff, and goes clear through getting all entitlements approved, construction financing approved, signing a construction contract, and pulling building permits.

Twenty Main Steps of Predevelopment (listed in the order they need to be accomplished)

1. Creating the vision and site selection
2. Initial feasibility research
3. Letter of intent to purchase land
4. Land purchase and sale agreement
5. Due diligence
6. Planning department application
7. Preparing entitlement documents
8. City preapplication review meeting
9. City plan review meeting
10. Public hearing
11. Planning department/city council approval
12. Entitlement approval
13. Investor money goes into escrow

14. Close escrow on the land
15. Full plans and specs designed
16. Apply for construction financing
17. Sign construction contract

18. Create final project budget
19. Construction loan approval
20. Pull building permits

Preliminary Drawings: *You will need these for your first city plan review meeting*

You will have your architect prepare preliminary drawings of your proposed development for your preliminary city plan review meeting. These drawings include a site plan, floor plans, elevation drawings, and a 3-D conceptual drawing. It is important for your architect, civil engineer, and structural engineer to attend this meeting to lend support to your project. If you are building in an urban setting, bring your traffic consultant too.

Pro Forma Rent Roll: *Create this first before you do your pro forma for income and expenses*

A pro forma rent roll shows the square footage and estimated rent for each unit or space for your proposed commercial building in a rent roll format. For multifamily buildings, be sure to show the number of bedrooms and bathrooms and square footage for each unit. If some units are superior for some reason, such as having a better view, identify those. Be sure to attach your rent comparables report supporting your proposed rents if you do not have a feasibility study. You will need to put together a pro forma rent roll before creating your income and expense pro forma for projecting your net operating income for your development project.

Punch List, End of Construction: *Don't make the final payment to your contractor until every item on all punch lists have been satisfied*

Be sure that your construction contract has a clause that withholds final payment to the general contractor until your architect has approved the completion of a final punch list of all items either needing completion or having been completed unsatisfactorily. Upon getting your temporary certificate of occupancy, city inspectors will provide you with the "First Punch List" of items that are not complete or not conforming to building codes. Usually the developer is given 30 days to complete these. Once all the items have been completed on the first punch list, a "Closing-Out Punch List" will be created, showing

Time and Money Saving Tip

Most boilerplate construction contracts mandate full payment less estimated funds held back to complete punch list items when construction is completed. Keep in mind that this might be in conflict with your construction loan documents. Banks often require 5–10% of total construction hard costs to be withheld until the work on the first punch list is completed. It is recommended that you put into the construction contract that you will be retaining twice the cost to remedy the items on the first punch list until: (1) these items are signed off on as completed by the municipality and (2) your architect signs off on the third punch list.

Development

any items that are still substandard. Once these are completed, you can get your certificate of occupancy. The third punch list is the "Architect's Punch List," which has items that are still substandard or in need of repair. Once the architect signs off on these, you can make the final payment to your contractor.

This will give your contractor an incentive to finish quickly any incomplete or substandard work before starting another project. To make this even stronger, hold back final payment until a certificate of occupancy is obtained.

Raw Land Development: *Raw land developers can double or even triple the land value*

Some developers specialize in increasing the value of raw land. Land on its own appreciates rather slowly unless it is some of the last to be developed within an urban growth boundary. Doing some grading, providing better access, installing drainage, and bringing in the utilities can more than double the value. Take this further and get the land rezoned and fully entitled for a development, and the value can be

Time and Money Saving Tip

The total price of the land is not anywhere near as important as the land price per unit or per buildable square foot. Look for a land parcel where the zoning allows for much greater density, or has minimal or no setbacks. Although the price per acre for these parcels is going to be more expensive, the cost of the land per unit or building square footage will be a lot less. This results in tremendous cost savings and, better yet, more gross rent potential.

tripled. The seller can often carry the financing for someone who is short on cash. Another alternative is to do a *joint venture* (see Encyclopedia Topic C, Raising Investor Partnerships) with the seller, where they contribute the land and you contribute your knowledge and predevelopment costs. You then become partners and share in the profits.

Schematic Design: *This is where the magic starts with you and your architect*

The schematic design is the first phase and most important and creative step in designing your development project with the architect. This is where the rough design is conceived, showing the size, shape, location, and floor layout of the building. You and your architect will also discuss a time frame for construction. Be sure to be well prepared for this first meeting. You need to know your vision of the completed project—how it needs to function and what it should look like.

Yes, bring in some photos of buildings you like. Equally important, have some idea of how much you can afford to spend on construction. A good commercial architect will have the skill to design something that will incorporate your vision and hopefully your budget. After you describe what you are trying to accomplish, the architect will start working on the schematic design. They will take your vision of the finished product and apply it to the land dimensions, zoning, building codes, ingress, egress, and aesthetics, and come up with an initial floor plan of the building showing all the rooms and where the doors and windows will be located. Plan to have many meetings with your architect to refine these drawings.

Setbacks: *This is as close to the property line that you can build on*

So you just found what you think is the right land parcel to build your commercial building on. Here's where the fun begins. When you find a land parcel that you are interested in purchasing, start out by going to the city's website. Look up the zoning for the tax lot or address of the property. Then get the property dimensions and setbacks. After that, you can play around with sketching rough designs of where the building will be located on the parcel.

A setback is the distance from the property line or road that the city or county requires the building to be built. This can vary based on building structure. Prior to working with your architect on the *schematic design* (see earlier in this Topic), the architect will have a civil engineer determine accurately where the property lines and easements are located.

Single Room Occupancy (SRO): *These single rooms designed for one person can be perfect for student housing!*

Single room occupancy refers to buildings that contain individual rooms for one person to live in. SROs are mostly in boardinghouses or low-income housing. But they can serve another purpose that is very profitable. If you are considering building student housing near a university or college, making your building all SROs might be the way to go. Many more serious and graduate students would prefer living alone, but cannot afford an apartment. SROs can have a private bathroom, a microwave, hot plate, and small refrigerator; usually, they are not allowed to have full kitchens. Some SRO buildings have shared kitchens. Student housing SROs are usually around 200 square feet, and are akin to efficiency apartments. They command some of the highest rent per square foot of all multifamily properties, just like micro apartments do. But they are much less expensive to build, with lower-quality amenities. Also, many cities do not charge expensive impact fees on SROs.

Time and Money Saving Tip

If you are short on space to build your commercial building because of setback regulations, rather than downsizing the building or looking for another land parcel, consider hiring a local land use attorney who specializes in zoning variances. They can make a strong case with the city as to why a setback variance request should be approved and even take it to a zoning appeals board if the city denies the variance.

Time and Money Saving Tip

With the COVID-19 economic crisis, many hotel or motel properties will be sold at a discount. Find one for sale near a college or university and convert it into student housing SROs. The building will already be configured perfectly: there is already a bathroom in each unit so all you have to do is add an efficiency kitchenette and remodel the space. Providing these units furnished with a futon and a desk that can double as a table is definitely a plus. Students will pay premium rents for these spaces.

Development

Site Plan: *This will tell city planners if your development meets zoning requirements and building codes*

I cannot stress enough how important it is to hire a good architect who has vast experience working with the city planning department and knowledge of current building codes where your development project is located. Your architect will work with civil and structural engineers to produce a site plan that will pass muster with the city. The site plan is the most important visual document you will be bringing to your preliminary planning meeting with the city. It shows both existing and proposed elements of the property and will represent your project to city planners better than anything. The planners will be able to let you know immediately if your project is laid out to meet zoning codes, building codes, and other regulations. Included will be: surrounding streets, land contour, the new building footprints, property lines, setback parameters, fences, easements, utility lines, drainage, driveways, parking lots, walkways, fire hydrants, and more.

Soft Costs: *These are any construction expenses that do not add a physical component to the land or building*

From the day you locate a property to build on, keep track of all your soft costs. You can get credit for them toward the down payment of your construction financing. Soft costs are any development costs that do not add a physical component to the land or building. They include legal fees, architectural fees, engineering fees, other professional fees, third-party report fees such as a feasibility study, permits, insurance, LEED Certification fees, security fees, building permit fees, planning department fees, and any other fees associated with *predevelopment* (see earlier in this Topic).

Specifications/Specs: *Specs define all the detail about the work to be done, materials to be used, and how installations are to be done*

Many cost overruns and change orders occur because the developer did not fully comprehend the construction specifications, known as specs, and ends up with something different than what they expected. Sometimes general contractors get confused about specs, too, but this is more of an exception. I cannot stress enough how important it is that, as the developer, you understand the specs. Specs detail very specifically all the work that needs to be done and

Time and Money Saving Tip

Prior to starting construction, have a meeting with the general contractor, the subcontractors, and your architect and engineers to go over the specs to make sure that everyone has the same understanding of what materials to use and how the work is to be done. After this meeting, you will likely have to make a few changes to the construction contract. It will cost you less to have these changes made at the beginning of the project than down the road during construction.

are listed in a document that goes along with the building plans. Specs include materials, finishes, and how everything is to be installed. They even go as far as having instructions for measuring the effectiveness and quality of installations. Specs can get very technical and are put together by your architect and engineers. Even experienced developers have to ask questions of their architect and contractor to make sure they are all on the same page regarding the specs. Make sure that the specs are updated as you make changes to the building plans. Be sure to include a copy of the specs in the construction contract to ensure that your general contractor agrees to follow them to the T.

Stabilized Value, Newly Constructed Properties: *The property will be worth more after it is stabilized*

Be aware that if you are building a commercial property to sell, it will be worth more after you fill it with tenants than on the day you get your occupancy permit. A construction appraisal will have two valuations: one for the value of the property on the day it is completed, and another based on the stabilized value when the property reaches market occupancy. The stabilized value is considerably higher because a commercial property is worth more when it is producing an income than when it is

---

Time and Money Saving Tip

In an up seller's market, if you are offered a great price for the property early on for when you get your certificate of occupancy, WAIT! If a potential buyer is willing to pay that much for it at that time and they still have to find tenants, you can imagine what the property will be worth when it is stabilized and full of great tenants. If you can wait a year or more after stabilization to sell, it will have history and be worth even more. Of course, this is not the case if the market is starting to go down.

---

vacant. In an up market the stabilized value is going to be higher, as you can usually get much higher rents than competing older properties and as more units or spaces are filled, you can likely raise the rents on the remaining ones even higher. In a down market, stabilized value will be lower, as you will likely have to lower starting rents and offer rental concessions, and rents on remaining units or spaces will remain flat until the market turns around again.

Subterranean Parking: *This underground parking is very expensive*

Subterranean parking simply refers to underground parking and can be from one to four floors. It is often the most expensive space per square foot to build due to excavation costs and having to build a concrete structure that is strong enough to support the entire weight of the building. It is most popular in urban developments, where there is just not enough available land for a parking lot or structure to meet city off-street-parking requirements. Be sure to check with a geotechnical soil expert on the height of the water table and seismic requirements to determine whether you can build subterranean parking on the site and whether you will need to blast through bedrock. If so, this can double the cost.

Transit-Oriented Development (TOD): *Public transportation is located within a half mile of these buildings*

A land parcel to build on that is near public transportation is much easier to lease and add value to. A transit-oriented development (TOD) is in an urban setting, located within a half mile of public transportation. By doing a TOD, you will not only achieve much higher rents, but be contributing toward lowering carbon emissions. This is a

Development

popular trend for mixed-use multifamily, office, and retail space today. This greatly reduces driving for residents since they can live, work, and shop in the same area. Many cities have lowered parking requirements for TODs. Some have eliminated the need for off-street parking completely. This results in not having to bear the cost of using valuable land for parking or building a parking structure, as well as avoiding the extreme cost of subterranean parking.

Urban Infill: *These lots are hard to find these days, but still represent great development opportunities*

These days, it's difficult to find a good urban infill lot to develop. In most cities the best affordable ones have already been developed. These land parcels are within the city urban growth boundaries and already have utilities on-site for water, sewer, electricity, and gas. During an up seller's market, finding a vacant lot for a good price is not easy. You might do better by demolishing an existing structure or repurposing a building that has character. There are still great opportunities for developing infill lots, but you have to create them. During a down buyer's market, if you can afford to hold and wait, there will be infill lots that are discounted. You will just need to wait until the market goes up again to start development. Look for a property that has high or unlimited density. Although it's going to be expensive, it could still make sense, if the cost per unit or square foot for your project is low enough. If you are looking to build a multifamily project, look for lots that already have mid-high-rise buildings located there so you can build up and take advantage of high-density zoning. Find a lot that is in a high-traffic location where you can build mixed-use, with commercial space on the first floor and apartments above.

Value Engineering

The very best way to lower the cost of commercial construction is to do value engineering. This examines all the components of the construction and finds ways to cut building costs. Value engineering is usually requested too late, after the developer gets their first bids in and realizes the cost is sky-high. The best time to do value engineering is at the beginning, by having your architect, along with civil and structural engineers, design the project more cost-effectively. They are good at that, but I have seen the best results when the architect and contractor work together.

Years ago, I was working on construction financing for a Class A, 96-unit, $15,000,000 multifamily project in Boise, Idaho. Based on the rents the project would generate and the cost to build, we could only provide a 64% of cost construction loan. The developer needed at least 75% of cost. The architect and general contractor put their heads together and made some changes. Instead of doing a stucco exterior finish, they went with hardy plank siding. Instead of building 12 buildings, they redesigned the project for eight, and made the units just slightly smaller. They brought in a structural engineer to design the building so it was lighter in weight to cut down the cost of steel rebar and concrete in the foundation. They redesigned the kitchens so each was the same and they got a subcontractor to give them a great bulk price. Because the construction cost was lowered by $1,860,000, we were able to do a 78% construction loan.

Walk Score: *Properties that have a high walk score get higher rents and are more valuable*

Like bike score, properties that have a higher walk score are considered more valuable and get higher rents. Walk score is based on data compiled by the research company Walk Score. It measures the distance from the subject property to schools and major shopping. If most daily errands do not require a car, the score is between 90 and 100 and rated "Walker's Paradise"; a score between 70 and 89 is rated "Very Walkable"; and between 50 and 69 "Somewhat Walkable." Locations that have a score below 50 mean a car is needed. If your property has a great walk score, be sure to post in your marketing and on the property's website.

Zoning Variance: *Be sure to hire a skilled land use attorney to help you get one of these*

Obtaining a zoning variance can more than double land value, and, better yet, allow a developer to build something of much greater value. A zoning variance is applied for with the city or local government when a developer wants to change the zoning of a land parcel to a different zoning classification. Zoning variances are actually waivers of the existing zoning and are not easy to get. For the best results, it really makes sense to hire a land use attorney who has experience working in your market. They are experts at making the case that the existing zoning renders the land useless and that similar parcels have the desired zoning. Most often there will be a public hearing, where your land use attorney can make a stronger case than you likely can. If the zoning board declines the request, your land use attorney has the skill set to appeal the decision to the city council or another higher governing body.

PART VII

Smart Strategies
for Financing

CHAPTER 10

Trade Secrets for Getting the Best Rate, Loan Fees, and Terms

The man on the phone was cool, calm, and definitely in charge, even though *he* was the one asking *me* for a loan. "Here's what you are going to do if you want this loan," he told me. "You are going to get back to me within two days with a better offer than my bank. If you take more than two days, I am taking the deal I already have. I will email you a complete loan package in one hour."

When I train a new loan officer, I always tell them to establish a friendship with the client first. I suggest they ask about their jobs, kids, and hobbies. But this guy was not going to do any small talk. He was an expert at negotiating the best rate and terms. Win-win was certainly not his style. On one hand, I really wanted to tell him to shove off. On the other, I rather admired the guy for stating exactly what he wanted and not wasting anyone's time. And what difference did it make anyway? With my 20-plus years of experience, I could hear my mind clicking out of neutral and going into high gear. I was not going to make much on this deal, but I was sure going to fight for it.

He told me he wanted a $24 million loan on a high-end apartment complex in the Nob Hill neighborhood of San Francisco. He had finished construction five months prior. Occupancy was at 92% and climbing, and he was looking for a 55% loan-to-value perm loan. He said that if I could give him a 3.85%, 10-year fixed mortgage, I would take the deal away from his bank, which had come in at 4.10%. And he added, "I don't want those ridiculous loan fees the bank is charging me. I want you to get rid of those. Can you do all this for me?" I told him, "No problem, I can do this if you and the property are as financially strong as you are telling me." And then I wondered how I was going to deliver, as rates had been going up that week.

Just as he had said, an hour after we hung up, he emailed me the loan submission package. I sat gasping for breath looking at the photos of one of the most beautiful mid-rise buildings I had ever seen. Entering the lobby, you would think you were in a Four Seasons Hotel. I could picture myself being on vacation in the handsomely furnished and landscaped courtyard with its heated swimming pool. But his personal financial statement was even more stunning. Worth over $140 million, he was not just qualified for my loan, he was fabulously overqualified.

I always request proof when a borrower tells me they already have a very low rate from another lender. Many are blowing smoke. In his email was a letter of interest from Wells Fargo, one of the largest banks in America, proving that the 4.10%, 10-year fixed-rate, half-point fee loan I had to beat was real. Neither *Fannie Mae*, *Freddie Mac*, nor any of my other most competitive sources of capital could compete.

But I had my secret weapon. I had access to the best-priced insurance money for low-leveraged loans over $10 million. I was able to offer the borrower the 3.85% rate with no loan fee he wanted. I emailed the borrower a letter of interest the morning after the day of our first conversation. Ah, I thought. I can relax now.

But a whole day went by and then two more and I did not hear from him. I started feeling queasy. I called him. He told me the bank had come down to 3.75% and removed its loan fee, and that he had already wired them the loan deposit. Are you kidding me? I would have to work for nothing to match that. All I'd accomplished was getting him a better deal at his bank.

During the late 1990s, LendingTree came out with a great commercial that said, "When banks compete, you win." That is still their motto today. The ad showed a young couple interviewing about 20 bankers in their home who were competing for their home mortgage. It was hilarious to see the roles reversed. Well, as you can see from the story I just told you, there is no better way to get the best rate and terms on your commercial loan than to have lenders compete for it.

This chapter contains inside information that many commercial lending professionals are going to be upset with me for disclosing. My purpose in doing so is simply to level the playing field for borrowers. Commercial real estate financing does not have the consumer protections that residential real estate has in the United States. This gives lenders an unfair advantage. This chapter covers how lenders set their rates and terms, how much they can bend, how to negotiate with them, how to get them to compete, and why you should have a non-recourse loan.

THE TRUTH ABOUT HOW COMMERCIAL LENDERS SET RATES, TERMS, AND LOAN FEES

Commercial lenders sell money, much in the same way a car dealer sells autos. What these industries have the most in common is that they can really skinny down the profit on a deal if they have a lot of inventory and are forced to compete. Both will lower the price for a financially strong customer and charge more to those who are just scraping by and could use a break. In both enterprises, there is a cost of goods.

For commercial banks, the cost of goods begins with their cost for funds, which is the amount they pay in interest on deposits plus what it costs to borrow money from the feds and other banks. They then add on to this their average expense for putting a loan on their books, plus all other expenses for employees, overhead, and taxes to come up with their break-even cost. They obviously need to exceed this number to make a profit. The number-one priority for commercial bank executives is to run the bank profitably, so that they can preserve their jobs and please shareholders. To do this they need to earn as much as they can on each loan.

Of course, all lenders and auto dealers would like to get their starting price. They start out by telling the customer with a tone of authority that this is their best price—as if it is written in stone. On your first attempt to get a better deal with a car dealer, they will tell you something like this, "We have only marked this up $400 over invoice." A lender will say, "Based on our cost of funds, we are already offering you our best rate." Both industries know that they need to start high and be prepared to go down.

And that is the most important thing for you to remember. Yes! EVERY commercial lender starts out with a higher price for rates and fees and knows if there is competition, they will need to come down

Are Interest Rates Really Tied to Something?

Borrowers are savvy these days and keep up on whether interest rates are going up or down. On March 15, 2020, the Federal Reserve announced that it was dropping interest rates to 0% as an emergency measure to counter the economic impact of the coronavirus. Our phones rang off the hook the following week with borrowers wondering if rates had bottomed out, or if they could get a 0% loan. This rate only applied to the interest rate banks pay to borrow money from the Feds, and had no relationship to long-term mortgages.

Almost all lenders will tell you that they determine their rates based on an index plus a margin (also called a spread), as if this is something set in concrete by the government. The indexes they use are the federal home loan bank rate, Treasury yields, the prime rate, or the *LIBOR* (*London Inter-Bank Rate*). As an example, to come up with a 10-year fixed rate a lender could use the 10-year Treasury yield as the index, which is at 2.25% on that day, then add a spread of 2.50%. Adding the two together they tell the borrower the rate is 4.75%.

This system is really a bunch of smoke and mirrors, since lenders can always add more to the spread to earn what they want; did I really say that? Don't get me wrong. Rates being quoted as going up and down based on what those indexes are doing often does reflect market interest rates. But because lenders can always add whatever they want to the spread, this method is really a manipulation. Lenders really love this system because it makes it so much easier to sell the rate they want if it appears that the rates are set to some regulated system. The truth is that lenders set rates to cover their actual interest rate floor (what it costs them for the money and operating expenses) and how much profit they want to make on top of that. They control this by adding to the index the highest spread the market will bear.

Securitized lenders for Fannie Mae and Freddie Mac set their rates daily to the corresponding Treasury yield in real time for the loan's fixed-rate term. To determine the spread, they start out by shopping many bond traders on Wall Street to get the best rate of interest in real time. This reflects what investors are willing to pay for these mortgage-backed security bonds and how much commission the bond trader tacks on. To determine the final spread the lender adds on to the bond trader's rate what they need to cover expenses and profit. So what ultimately determines the rate offered to the borrower is what the lender wants to earn and whether they can get it.

HOW MUCH CAN LENDERS BEND?

Getting More Than Your Fair Share of the Gravy

As mentioned, lenders set their interest rates, loan fees, and other loan expenses based on what it costs them for the money—their cost of funds and operating expenses. They then add to this their expected profit. This represents their actual floor rate (the lowest rate they can charge). They are absolutely not going to go below this number, which is proprietary so you will never know it. But as mentioned they always mark this up to come up with the rack rates they offer borrowers. Let's just call the amount above their actual floor rate their "gravy money." If you are going to land the best deal, you need to dip into some of this. As long as the lender doesn't have to go below their actual floor rate, and you meet their credit criteria, they can make you a sweet deal. You will not know how low they can go on rate and fees—you will have to push them hard to compete to have a chance of discovering this.

For debt fund lenders and securitized lenders Fannie Mae, Freddie Mac, HUD, and commercial mortgage-backed security (CMBS) funds, your job is to wrestle away some of the gravy money that is used to increase lender profits and pay commissions to their originators and executives. Don't feel bad. The lender is trying to get the best deal for themselves, so why shouldn't you?

ADVICE FROM AN INSIDER ON NEGOTIATING WITH LENDERS

So what exactly can you negotiate on with a commercial investment property lender? As you read on, I go through 10 major areas of loan expenses and provide some advice on what's negotiable and what's not, and how far you can push these expenses down. The following sections discuss interest rates and loan fees, third-party reports, lender attorney fees, ancillary lender expenses, rate lock deposits, fixed rate terms, amortization, prepayment penalties, recourse, and title and escrow fees.

Interest Rates and Loan Fees

This is the most important loan component for all borrowers. To understand how much you can bargain with lenders on rates and loan fees, let's start using the lender's language.

In the lending world, the interest rate, loan fees, and premiums earned on loans when they are sold are thought of in *basis points* (*bps*). One percentage point of interest equals 100 bps. Ten bps is 10/100th of one percent of interest rate. I have put interest rates and loan fees together because bps can be freely interchanged to raise or lower both to the advantage of either you or the lenders.

Lenders covet and protect each basis point as if their life depended on it. This makes it difficult to win more than 25 bps from the lender when negotiating to lower the rate. Getting your rate lowered a quarter of a percent might not seem like a whole lot to the borrower, but to the lender it is humungous—especially a lender that sells its loans on the *secondary market* (see Encyclopedia Topic H, Financing). A rate that is 10 bps higher will earn at least another percent of premium earnings on the loan. On a million-dollar loan, this is an additional $10,000. As a mortgage banker, most of my loans are sold on the secondary market; I have earned my income from thinking in bps that are earned from loan fees, and selling the mortgage.

Here is a way to explain what a loss of 10 bps means for a community bank: On a five-year fixed-rate million-dollar loan that has a 5.00% rate and 30-year amortization, getting the rate lowered 10 bps will save you about $61 per month on your payment, which is not going to get you very excited. But to a community bank that might do $250 million a year in commercial real estate loans, this 10 bps represents $250,000 of additional profit on their annual loan volume. This could cover the salaries of six low-level employees at $40,000 per year each. For a loan with a five-year term this 10 bps comes to $1,250,000.

Negotiating with Banks on Rate and Loan Fees

Commercial banks have risk-based interest rate pricing mandated by federal regulators. Loans that have lower loan to values, and financially stronger borrowers with great credit scores, get lower rates. If you don't meet those criteria you are not going to get the bank's lowest rate, but you can still bargain for the best rate for your credit profile. If the bank sets the rate too low on a loan, the Feds will force them to put up a loan loss reserve (money they can't lend out) to counter the inherent risk.

Most commercial real estate investment property borrowers still get their loans from banks. Having a banking relationship with their customers is the highest motivator for banks to lower their rates. Here's how banks set commercial real estate rates: If on a five-year fixed-rate mortgage their cost of funds is 75 bps, they will likely need another 100 bps to cover their cost of putting a loan on the books and operating expenses. This brings their break-even cost to 175 bps. Now we need to add to this a minimum profit of 175 bps. This puts the bank's actual interest rate floor at 3.50%. They might offer this to their best customers who have very large deposits with the bank that they can lend out at a profit, but they certainly are not going to offer it to the average Joe. During strong economic times when interest rates are low, they are likely going to raise this floor to a rack rate of 4.25%, and during bad times like after the COVID-19 crisis hit, this could be raised to 5.00%.

The very best borrowers that make large deposits with the bank might be able to get the rack rate lowered by 65 bps. But for most, getting the rate lowered by 25 to 35 bps is more likely. And then as mentioned the bank has its regulated risk-based pricing to adhere to. If you can't get them to lower the rate much, go after the loan fee. Banks love loan fees as they go right to the bottom line, so they will fight to keep this at a minimum of 50 bps, which is ½ of a point. But if they want the deal and you threaten to walk, you can likely get the entire fee removed. Remember that it is far more painful for them to lower your interest rate than to waive the loan fee, since most of their income comes from interest earned over many years.

Negotiating with Securitized Lenders on Rate and Loan Fees

For securitized lenders that represent Fannie Mae, Freddie Mac, and Ginnie Mae (for HUD loans), and commercial mortgage-backed securities (CMBS) funds, don't expect to negotiate a rate that is more than 35 bps lower than the initial rate offered. Getting the rate lowered by 20 bps is a good achievement; 35 bps is a great achievement. These lenders do not make anything from the interest on loan payments; interest income goes to the investors that buy the mortgage-backed security bonds. The lenders' only earnings come from the bps they charge and a small amount for servicing the loan.

These lenders have a minimum amount they need to earn on each loan after expenses before they walk away. The larger the loan, the more bps you can negotiate in your favor. This example shows why: Let's say you are offered a rate of 4.75% on a $1 million loan and the lender has a profit of 50 bps figured in of $50,000. You bargain with them to lower this to 4.40%, which is a reduction of 35 bps. Now when they sell the loan they will only be earning 15 bps, which is $15,000. They are not going to work for that. But a reduction of 20 bps and a rate of 4.60% will likely work as it leaves them a profit of $30,000. Now for a large loan of $10 million, they can easily reduce the rate by 35 bps because that remaining 15 bps of earnings is $150,000—not small potatoes.

Just as with banks, it is easier to negotiate down the loan fee for these lenders. It will cost them about 10 bps on a 10-year fixed-rate mortgage to remove a 1% fee, but on a $1 million loan, that takes $10,000 out of the lender's pocket and puts it in yours to be used toward closing costs.

Negotiating with Debt Fund Lenders on Rates and Loan Fees

Now let's take a look at how private debt fund lenders price the money they lend. These lenders, which mostly do bridge loans, have raised money from investors that is in a fund regulated by the SEC. They have an annual yield or profit that they need to earn above their cost, which is what they pay investors plus operating expenses. Their gross yield is a combination of interest rate and loan fees and these two can be interchanged to create the same gross earnings to the lender.

For example, when the lender charges the borrower 8% in interest plus a 2% loan fee for a loan that has a maturity of one year, their gross annual yield is 10%. It doesn't really matter if this is earned via the interest rate or the loan fee. Now they are going to toss 1% to their originator, who is solely commissioned, and executives to share. Then they'll pay their investors 5%, and it'll take another 1% to pay all company expenses. That leaves a net yield of 3% annually.

Now, can you negotiate a full percentage point of interest off and get them down to a net yield of 2%? Not likely! They will have to pass if they have a smaller annual loan volume of under $200,000,000. It may be possible to get a half-point reduction in either the rate or loan fee, but not both. But if the lender has a larger annual loan volume of $400,000,000 or more and there is too much cash just sitting in the fund not earning a dime—remember, they have to pay their investors every month—they could be motivated to come down a point. This could be 50 bps on the rate and 50 bps on the loan fee. At a 2% net yield, they are still earning $8 million annually on $400,000,000.

So be sure to look up how large the fund is on the lender's website. If it doesn't list it there, just ask them. They will love bragging about it.

Negotiating with Hard Money Lenders on Rate and Loan Fees

The good news is that because there is so much hard money to lend, rates and fees have come down over the years. These loans are really in demand, since the COVID-19 economic crisis has made it difficult for banks to lend. The loans average from 9.00% to 12.00%, with two to four points. Hard money lenders mostly do bridge loans with short maturities that average one to two years. Many have warehouse lines of credit that they lend from. Some raise their funds from private investors. They really do need to charge a minimum of 9.00% and two points. You are going to have to get six or more hard money lenders to compete to get one that will give you a better deal than that. Many try to get three points and this is where you can negotiate. Stick to two points.

Third-Party Reports

These consist of the appraisal, the environmental report, the seismic report, and the property condition report. A reputable lender will charge you actual expenses for these. Although the cost for these reports can go over $10,000, some lenders will give you a flat reduced cost of something like $2,400. What they are doing is putting most of the cost of the reports into the rate. For a large loan this might only increase the rate by 3 bps. Most lenders can afford to pay for these reports but will want you to put something down as a loan deposit toward them to start the loan. They do not want to be stuck with the entire bill should you back out. When there is stiff competition, ask the lender to credit your entire loan deposit covering the reports at closing. This way they are protected.

Lender Attorney Fees

Commercial banks do not charge you for their attorney fees unless you have a very unusual ownership structure or difficulty clearing the title and they need to consult their counsel. Fannie Mae, Freddie Mac, *HUD* (*US Department of Housing and Urban Development*), CMBS, and life companies all use real estate attorneys to review the ownership borrowing entities, clear the title report, and create customized loan documents for each loan. These attorneys charge from $400 per hour and up. The total cost for lender legal fees can be $6,500–18,000 or more.

It is important that you get the lender to give you a firm quote on lender legal fees when you apply. That way if it goes over this amount the lender will have to pay the difference. If you have a strong deal and have received written offers for financing that do not have lender legal fees, you can negotiate this out of the terms. Again, the lender will be increasing the rate by a small amount to pay for some or all of this expense, so ask them to eat it on this and not raise your rate. The one catch here is that, again, if the loan does not close, the lender will be out of pocket for the money they saved you on legal fees. This is why lenders are reluctant to offer a discount here. Since these lenders are represented by their attorneys, you will need to have one. Don't forget to put this in your budget.

Ancillary Lender Fees

These fees are the easiest to nego-tiate away, but lenders don't like to give them up. They cover underwrit-ing, processing, doc prep, and lender's site visit. If you are already paying the lender a loan fee, do you really need to pay these too? With the exception of the site visit fee when the lender has to travel out of state, ancillary lender fees are additional income to the lender.

> ### Time and Money Saving Tip
>
> Most lenders are straight shooters and will only charge you what it costs them for third-party reports and legal services. Some private and hard money lenders pick up some extra bucks here, though, so it's just good business to ask the lender to provide you with a copy of the invoices from all vendors.

Most often the lender will insist that these are not negotiable, but it's amazing how they suddenly disappear when deals become highly competitive. These fees can also be put into the rate, but this means you will still pay for them over time.

Rate Lock Deposits

On many commercial real estate investment property loans, the interest rate floats until the loan is approved or until documents are drawn. This is to protect the lender from any sudden fluctuations in the market affecting their cost of funds. However, some loan programs do allow the borrower to use a rate lock deposit to lock in the rate at application time. Of course, you also have the option to just let the rate float. Most lenders will require a refundable rate lock deposit of 1% of the loan amount to lock the rate. If required, this item is not negotiable. This deposit allows the lender to enter into an interest rate swap with US Treasury bond traders so that they can give the borrower a fixed rate that is not at risk for changing. You are only at risk of losing the rate lock deposit if you decide not to take the loan. In this event, if rates go down lower than the rate that was locked, it will cost the lender and they will pass this on to you by taking it out of your rate lock deposit.

I recommend that you always rate lock early just so you can sleep better at night without worrying about the rate going up prior to loan approval or closing. This is very important for loans that just have enough *debt service coverage ratio (DSCR)* for the property's income to qualify. Rising rates can make your loan amount go down, and if you don't have the cash to make up the difference it can kill your loan.

Fixed-Rate Terms

With all commercial lenders, the longer you fix the rate, the higher it will be. Smaller commercial banks most often cannot fix a commercial rate for more than five years, and that period is not negotiable. This is because they have to keep a certain amount of their deposits in reserves and they cannot lend the amount out. If this reserve gets low they have to

Time and Money Saving Tip

If you have the opportunity to rate lock your commercial loan at application and you are in an environment in which rates are going down, ask the lender to put you on a rate lock watch. You will need to check with them daily to see where rates are at; once they start going up again is usually the best time to rate lock.

borrow money from the feds or other banks at an adjustable rate. Sometime they are just borrowing the money overnight, so they have a daily adjustable rate. If rates go in the wrong direction many years later, they can be in the red. Therefore it is risky for them to fix a rate for more than five years. Many community banks prefer to offer a 10-year term and having the rate adjust two to three times during that term.

If you are planning on a long-term hold for your property you will want a long-term fixed mortgage. You are going to want to go with a large bank or a securitized loan program. Larger banks do not have reserve problems since they have an abundance of deposit money and do not have to borrow funds. They can fix a rate for up to 10 years. Fannie Mae and some life companies can fix the rate for 15, 20, or even 30 years. HUD can fix the rate for up to 35–40 years for new construction. Most other *securitized loan programs*, such as Freddie Mac and CMBS, can fix a rate for up to 10 years.

Amortization

The longer the amortization, the lower the monthly payment. Amortization represents a substantial risk to commercial banks. This is because the longer the amortization, the less money will be going toward principal every month. They prefer that you pay the loan off faster. Most community banks prefer to not amortize their loans for more than 20 years on office, retail, and industrial properties, and 25 years for multifamily properties. This can be negotiable for stronger borrowers. Larger banks that require higher borrower strength requirements can do a 25-year amortization for general commercial properties and a 30-year amortization for multifamily properties. Most securitized lenders have more stringent lending requirements, and will go up to a 30-year amortization for all commercial property types. Most commercial investment property owners want their mortgage payments to be as low as possible. To achieve this they need to get lenders to compete so that they can get the lowest rate and longest amortization. Other investors want to pay less interest over time and prefer shorter amortizations.

Prepayment Penalties

All commercial lenders have prepayment penalties, with the exception of federally chartered credit unions, which are not allowed to charge them. Prepayment penalties ensure that the lender will receive the yield it needs to earn over a duration that makes the loan profitable. Even hard money lenders need to earn a minimum of 6–12 months of interest to make the loan worth it and most charge prepayment penalties for these durations.

The general rule of thumb here is the lower the interest rate, the more severe the prepayment penalty will be. If you know you are going to keep the property and not need a cash-out refinance for the full term of the prepayment penalty you can accept a more severe prepayment penalty.

As far as negotiating these away, don't even try with a securitized lender such as Fannie Mae, Freddie Mac, or CMBS, which have *yield maintenance* or *defeasance prepayment penalties*. These loans are bundled with other loans with the same maturities and sold as real estate bonds on Wall Street. Investors are promised a rate of return for the duration of the prepayment penalty.

Community and regional banks need prepayment penalties to ensure that they can recover the cost of putting the loan on their books. They will need you to keep the loan for at least three to four years on a five-year fixed-rate mortgage to accomplish this. They have a declining prepayment penalty percentage, such as a 5, 4, 3, 2, 1 on a five-year fixed. This is something you can bargain on as long as the lender is not planning to sell the loan on the secondary market. If they do sell your loan, it will be worth more if it has a more severe prepayment penalty. Try changing the penalty to a 3, 2, 1, 0, 0. Most large banks, such as Wells Fargo, Bank of America, JPMorgan Chase, and US Bank, have yield maintenance prepayment penalties.

Lastly, try and stay away from loans that have a prepayment lockout (L/O) for one to four years. This gives you no options if you absolutely need to refinance or sell. Lenders selling their loans on the secondary market can earn an extra premium if they can sell you an L/O. They will not give you a choice, and just tell you that the prepayment penalty is something like this on a 10-year mortgage: L/O, L/O, L/O, 3, 3, 2, 2, 1, 1, 1. Threaten to walk away and they will likely drop the L/O.

Recourse

Recourse allows the lender to go after any of the borrower's personal assets if they foreclose on the property to make up a deficiency. If you take out a non-recourse loan the lender can only take the subject property back if there is a default and your personal assets are not at risk. There is very little room to bargain on making a recourse loan non-recourse. Commercial banks almost never offer non-recourse, but can do so for a very low loan-to-value loan. Fannie Mae, Freddie Mac, HUD, CMBS, life companies, debt fund lenders, and many bridge lenders offer non-recourse financing. Read more about non-recourse financing at the end of this chapter.

Title and Escrow Fees

These are not something you can negotiate with the lender since the borrower pays these. Escrow fees are similar from one title company to another, but the cost of title insurance can vary quite a bit. Most title companies are intermediaries and mark up these fees.

NINE INSIDER TIPS FOR GETTING THE BEST LOAN TERMS

1. Choose a Lender That Has a Lot of Its Own Money to Lend

Large banks and credit unions have much more money on deposit than they can lend out. If you are willing to offer them multiple deposit relationships, you can get the best deal on interest rates when negotiating with them. Large banks can also give you a better deal because they run a much lower percentage of expenses than small banks. In the banking world this is called an efficiency ratio. Whereas many small community banks run a 65% expense ratio, large banks' ratios can be as low as 40%.

Credit unions are nonprofit and have an unfair advantage over banks because they don't pay taxes. This keeps their operating expenses very low, and they can offer just about whatever rates, terms, or loan expenses necessary to win the deal. They have the room to offer no loan fees right out of the gate. But they are smart; they keep up on the rates their competitors are charging and usually offer rates just slightly lower. But boy, do they have the gravy money for you to tap into. Be sure to grab as much as you can to lower your rate and fees.

2. Choose a Community Bank If You Are Short on Net Worth, Cash, or Experience

For low-rate permanent mortgages, the best-quality lenders—including large national banks, regional banks, and most other commercial lenders—require the borrower to have property ownership experience with the subject property type.

They also require a net worth equal to the size of the loan and an amount of cash equal to a minimum of 10% of the loan or 12 months of loan payments for post-closing liquidity.

If you are light on net worth, cash, and experience, and it's not during a recession, smaller community banks and credit unions are the way to go. They will even allow you to manage the property yourself if you don't have experience. These institutions have some of the lowest financial standards for commercial investment property borrowers. In fact, they don't really have a set standard for minimum net worth or liquidity. But they do require good credit. A 680 credit score is bare bones and 720 or above is preferred. And they require good personal income—often with more than one source as shown on tax returns.

On the down side, small community banks and credit unions are usually the first to lower loan-to-values and eliminate cash-out refinances when a recession starts.

3. Use These Tricks to Increase Your Loan Size

To achieve the largest loan possible, you will need to find the lender that can give you the best terms on these three loan components: DSCR, amortization, and interest rate.

1. *Debt service coverage ratio*. It is simple math that the lower the DSCR required by the lender, the more you can borrow. For this example we are using two different lenders, each of which can lend up to 75% of the purchase price on a $1,000,000, 16-unit apartment building. Both lenders offer the same interest rate—4.75%—and the same amortization—30 years. The property's net operating income is $56,338.

   Lender A requires a 1.25 DSCR and can lend you a maximum of $720,000. Lender B requires a 1.20 DSCR and can lend you a maximum of $750,000. Lender B will win this deal by lending you $30,000 more just because they have a lower DSCR requirement.

2. *Amortization*. Having a longer amortization will lower your annual debt service and can qualify you for a larger loan. On a million dollar loan, if both lender A and B offer the same rate of 4.75% but lender A offers a 25-year amortization and lender B offers a 30-year amortization, your annual debt service will be lowered by $5,816 annually with lender B. This will qualify you to borrow more money.

3. *Interest rate*. Again, on a million-dollar loan, with both lenders offering a 30-year amortization, lender A offers a rate of 4.75% and you are able to negotiate the rate down with lender B to 4.25%. Going with lender B, your annual debt service will be lowered by $3,566, which will raise the property's DSCR, which will then qualify you for a larger loan.

4. Choose a Lender That Will Lock the Rate at Application

See if you can find a loan program with good rates that will allow you to lock the rate at the beginning at application. Rising rates can lower your loan amount or even kill your loan if you do not have enough cash to make up the difference.

Small banks and regional banks that can close quickly (in 45 days) can sometimes take the risk and lock your rate at application without a rate lock deposit. Tell your lender you won't sleep well if you don't lock the rate right away, and that you are looking for a loan without a rate lock deposit. Large banks that have an abundance of deposit money to lend can afford to lock a rate without a deposit. They prefer to collect one as insurance so that the borrower won't back out.

5. Don't Want a Prepayment Penalty or Loan Fee? Borrow from a Credit Union

If you are purchasing a property to reposition it and plan on selling it within a few years after completion, it will be best for you to have a loan without a prepayment penalty. Or if you do not know what your exit strategy is for the property and want to leave all of your options open, not having a prepayment penalty is a must. Most credit unions have excellent rates and terms and do not have prepayment penalties. They are also the most negotiable on removing their loan fee.

6. Use These Lenders If You Don't Show Much Income on Tax Returns

If you are a self-employed commercial investment property borrower and do not show much income on tax returns, you are not likely to qualify at a commercial bank or credit union. Both of these institutions do a *global ratio*, which requires you to have a minimum verified income on tax returns.

Don't worry! There are many high-quality, low-rate loan programs that do not require tax returns. Fannie Mae, Freddie Mac, HUD, and CMBS are all securitized loan providers that do not require tax returns. Although most debt fund lenders collect them, they mostly do so to make sure the borrower filed their taxes. But they do not require stellar personal income.

7. Use These Lenders If You Want the Longest Fixed-Rate Loan

For multifamily properties, Fannie Mae can lock your rate for up to 30 years; HUD can lock it for up to 35 years. For all commercial properties that need larger loans over $5 million, life companies can often lock a rate for 15–25 years. CMBS lenders can fix a rate for 10 years.

8. Go with an Adjustable Rate If You Plan on Selling the Property Within Two Years

Adjustable-rate mortgages that are tied to the LIBOR or prime rate can average a full percentage point lower or more in interest than longer-term fixed rates. It can be advisable to use them for a short-term hold when these rates are low. Usually these loan programs allow you to prepay the loan without a prepayment penalty, so if they do shoot up you can refinance without penalty. Better yet, if the adjustable rate starts going up, some programs will allow you to convert to a fixed rate program for a nominal cost.

9. You Can Negotiate the Very Best Deal on Very Large Loans

If you need to borrow $10,000,000 or more, most lenders can afford to skinny down on rate and loan fees and still earn a good return on the deal because of its size. Just as real estate brokers offer a lower commission on large deals, lenders are used to sharpening their pencils on them too. But you will have to let the lender know it has some competition to get the best results.

A SEVEN-STEP CUTTING-EDGE RECIPE FOR GETTING LENDERS TO COMPETE

So you might be wondering how I would know the best recipe for getting lenders to compete. It's just that for the past six years, my staff and I have been shopped to death. And I just had to figure out what it would take for us to compete or face an earlier retirement than I had planned on.

Just doing high-quality work no longer counts with borrowers. You have to produce better rates and terms than the competition or you're out. Even my best clients, for whom I'd funded four or more loans over several decades, were shopping me. It had become an epidemic! So I started questioning the best of the shoppers to find out what the heck they were doing. I learned to make sure that they were coming to me at the end of their shopping spree so that I'd just have to make sure to beat or match their best deal. And that's how I came up with this recipe that you can use to compete.

1. Get Each Lender Excited About Your Deal

Make a list of 12 lenders. You are going to contact 6 to begin with, and eventually all 12. Choose a variety of banks and credit unions near the subject property, some national lenders, and some securitized lenders. Ask commercial real estate brokers for recommendations. Go to Encyclopedia Topic I, Fifteen Top Commercial Loan Programs, to get some ideas.

The first time you talk with a lender you want to impress them with your professionalism and really get them excited about your deal. You will have made a list of all the positives about your deal and will pitch these, of course. To get the best results, email the lender your *executive loan summary* while you are talking to them. You are going to ask them what their best rates and terms are. Most likely they will give you a range of these and tell you that until they get in a complete loan submission package they cannot give you a firm quote. You are not going to ask them to compete at this stage. They will need a complete submission package to do this.

However, this is a perfect time to ask them what their requirements are to qualify for the loan you want. These are gone into in detail in Chapter 11 (see The Seven Preapprovals in Commercial Lending). You want to make sure you and the property qualify before you waste their time or yours. Even if you or the property do not qualify for their loan program, you will have at least gotten their ballpark rates and terms to compare with others. Go to the *commercial loan submission checklist* (Encyclopedia Topic H, Financing) and read off some of the items you will be emailing the lender. This should impress them. Then ask them if there is anything else they need from you to give you a firm quote.

2. Apply with the Best Commercial Mortgage Broker Too

This step should have the effect of doubling the number of lenders that are competing. A good commercial mortgage broker will also be able to educate you as to the types of loans you and the property qualify for. And if you do not qualify for some of the best loan programs, what it would take to qualify.

3. Become a Stronger Borrower if Necessary

If the commercial mortgage broker and some of the lenders you have spoken with in step 1 offer the best rates and terms but you as the borrower do not qualify, look into bringing in a partner who has the missing net worth, cash in the bank, or experience.

4. Get Firm Quotes from 6 to 10 Lenders and Compare

You are going to email exactly the same loan submission package to the commercial mortgage broker and each lender on your list. You just want to individualize each with a short introduction to each lender in the body of the email. The submission items will all be sent as attachments. This should not take you more than

5 or 10 minutes for each lender. Most of your time is going to be taken up with compiling the submission items.

Most bank and credit union lenders will want you to fill out one of their applications. You do not need to do this at this stage. Sending them your current personal financial statement (you can find a sample in Appendix A, and an Excel version on my website: https://apartmentloanstore.com) will give them what they need to know. You should start getting email or verbal quotes from lenders in two or three days.

Tell each lender that you are shopping to get the best deal. Don't worry, there is an immense amount of competition out there and all lenders are used to this. Also, why not tell them you are looking for a no-fee loan? This way some may go down to half a point right out of the gate so you can use this to compete. Don't forget all the little loan expenses I call ancillary expenses. Examples are the cost of underwriting, processing, and document preparation. The lenders need to compete on these too. Don't forget to ask them if they charge for lender legal expense, which could be an expensive item, and what their prepayment penalties are. Why not ask them to pay for your appraisal, environmental report, and property condition report? They will say no, but if you get one lender to pay for just the appraisal, or even more of these, then some of the other lenders will likely follow suit.

Make it clear to the mortgage broker that you need to get LOIs from direct lenders. The mortgage broker can issue you a written quote too, but it will have little or no weight when used to compete with direct lenders.

Make a chart and compare each offer based on interest rate, amortization, fixed rate term, loan fee, prepayment penalty, third party report expense, and ancillary loan expenses. Be sure to prioritize these in the order of the most important based on your exit strategy for the property.

5. Make Sure Each Top Lender Has Something to Beat

Now go to the top lenders that have given you the best rate and terms and give each of them something to beat that you got from another lender's offer. You certainly do not want to mention more than two lenders or that will make them mad. Remember, you did tell them in step 4 that you are shopping. But no lender wants to be massively shopped. This combined with what the mortgage broker is working on should produce the very best results.

6. Don't Stop Until You Achieve the Best Loan

If you have not succeeded after step 5 in getting a loan offer you like, and especially if some of your highest priorities have not been met, don't stop. Find more lenders to compete if you have the time.

7. Take Your Best Offer to Your Favorite Lender and Ask Them to Beat It or Match It

If you have a favorite lender or commercial mortgage broker that you have worked with before that has done outstanding work, ask them to beat or match your best offer. There is a lot to be said for working with someone you trust and get along well with.

WHY YOU SHOULD JOIN THE NON-RECOURSE LOAN CLUB

There isn't really a club. It is just that non-recourse lending is one of the best-kept secrets in the lending world, which an elite group of mostly wealthy developers and investors in commercial real estate reap the benefits of. In fact, these high-net-worth individuals have real estate attorneys, estate trust attorneys, and financial advisors who insist that these individuals get only non-recourse financing. Why? Because with a non-recourse loan, the borrower is not required to sign a personal guarantee. This has a rather large benefit. The borrower is not putting everything they own at risk if they default on the loan.

Just so you know, non-recourse loans are available to the average Joe in America too. You just need to have good credit, enough net worth, and the down payment. So why do so few of the middle class seem to know what a non-recourse loan is? It is not that the lenders that offer these try to keep them a secret. It's just that the majority of investment property lending is done by commercial banks that almost never offer non-recourse terms to their customers. Why? Because if they did they would be giving up their largest most powerful weapon—recourse.

Why Banks Love Recourse Loans

Recourse gives the lender an insurance policy. You give it to them when you sign a guarantee that legally makes them whole should they have to foreclose on the subject property and not be able to recover the full amount of their loss from selling the property. Making them whole means that the lender can use any of your personal assets to make up a deficiency should they sell the property for less than you owe them. This deficiency can include back mortgage payments, delinquent property taxes, real estate commissions, and expenses to manage and maintain the property while they are selling it. And let's not forget the bank's attorney and court fees.

A Bank Recourse Loan and the Real Estate Empire of Daniel G.

In 2005 Daniel G. was a 58-year-old recently retired and widowed schoolteacher living in Tulsa, Oklahoma. I met Daniel at a commercial real estate seminar where I was a guest speaker. Full of enthusiasm, he told me he was buying a run-down, mixed-use building in up-and-coming downtown Tulsa. His plan was to rehab it. With gray hair but looking fit and younger than his years, he was full of confidence when he came up to me and said, "You don't know this yet, but you're going to do a big loan for me." He went on to tell me that he had retired early so that he could work full time at his true passion—real estate investing. He wanted to leave a financial legacy for his kids.

The subject property was built in the 1940s and had a lot of character. It had 9,000 square feet of commercial space on the first level. This consisted of a rented real estate office and three unleased retail spaces. There were 36 one-bedroom, one-bath apartment units on the four floors above that were dated and only 60% occupied. Daniel planned to remodel these extensively and convert them to 2-bedroom, 1.5-bath units. Building the tenant improvements to suit for the three unoccupied retail spaces was also in his plan. To make this an even better deal, the city was offering a grant of $350,000 in urban renewal funds.

Daniel's offer of $2,850,000 was accepted. His budget included $720,000 for improvements. With closing costs, this brought the project cost up to $3,700,000. He put 35% down and I arranged a 24-month bridge loan for $2.4 million.

SO WHAT HAPPENED?

The Great Recession happened. Daniel completed the rehab brilliantly: on time and under budget. His development was a success. He had the apartment units 96% occupied and the commercial spaces 100% occupied—all with much higher rents, just as he had planned. This enabled him to arrange a $2.5 million perm loan with his local bank to pay off our temporary bridge loan in early 2007.

By October of 2009, downtown Tulsa was in a steep decline. First, the real estate office went out and then two of the three retail spaces closed their doors. Only a thrift store that was doing a booming business remained on the first level.

(continued)

(continued)

Most of the apartment units were full, but the rents had to be lowered to achieve this. Daniel received a notice of default letter from his bank. This confused him at first because he was current on payments. As he read on, he found that his NOI no longer covered the required 1.30 DSCR required in the loan docs, which put the loan in default. The bank had also had an appraisal done and the property had greatly dropped in value. Daniel was given 90 days to refinance elsewhere.

THE FORECLOSURE

In February of 2010 Daniel got a letter with his last mortgage payment check enclosed. The bank was starting foreclosure. They gave Daniel a 35-day notice to pay off the loan in full or the property would be sold at public auction to the highest bidder. Unfortunately, Daniel's loan documents mandated a nonjudicial foreclosure and had a power of sale clause. This meant that the bank could foreclose outside of the court system (legal in Oklahoma)—in other words, the lender did not have to file a lawsuit to foreclose. Then there was the guarantee that Daniel signed when he took out the loan. This allowed the bank to obtain a deficiency judgment should the bank sell the property for less than Daniel owed them.

THE DEFICIENCY JUDGMENT

Daniel says that being served with the deficiency judgment was very unpleasant. The bank did not seem to even try to get a fair price for the property. They sold it to the highest bidder for only $1.7 million. They were going after him for a deficiency of $746,000. There were liens filed against his two remaining rental homes and levies filed against his bank accounts. His car, along with his two antique Buicks, also had liens filed on them. How did they know about the Buicks? Oh, of course—they were listed on his personal financial statement. Because of advice from an attorney early on, Daniel had homesteaded his home, which made it exempt from the deficiency judgment. His retirement was also exempt.

What if Daniel had obtained a non-recourse loan? The answer is very simple. In the case of a default on the loan, all Daniel would have had to do if the property failed was to hand over the keys to the lender. Sure, this would still be painful. But his personal assets would not ever come into the equation.

CHAPTER 11

Taking Charge of Your Commercial Loan

"**I**s there anything you can do to help me?" Richard asked me in desperation. He went on, "Two months ago I got a letter of interest from the bank promising me a 75% loan to cost construction loan, and yesterday I got a commitment letter from them for 60%. That leaves me $600,000 short. I've been a customer of theirs for years and have never missed a loan payment. They told me that management was not excited about doing a 55 and older project, which they thought was too risky. They loved the deal when I applied. I have already pulled permits. I'm ready to break ground next week—my subs are ready to start. I don't want to lose them. How can they do this to me?"

It was October of 2014. Richard was the developer and general contractor for a 40-unit senior multifamily construction project in Coeur d'Alene, Idaho. "It's just that they can do this to you," I answered. "You have to understand that the bank will always protect itself when it comes to the regulators."

As a mortgage-banking firm, my company was a member of the Idaho Bankers Association. Banks often refer loans that they cannot do to us to save the deposit relationship, since we do not take deposits.

"I know this bank," I went on to say. "They have concentration problems with the FDIC regulators. Their ratio of commercial loans to their liquidity is too high. So, if they take any more on, they are only going to cherry-pick the best. The loan officer that you have been working with was likely not kept in the loop. They really don't want to do the loan now, but instead of denying you, they have approved a loan that they know is too small for you to accept."

Fortunately, I knew another bank that was flush with capital from deposits. It too had some concentration issues, but it could do the construction loan for the amount Richard needed as long as we could do a permanent loan. The construction loan closed 40 days later.

The purpose of this chapter is to encourage commercial loan borrowers to get involved in the loan process. This means not sitting back and waiting for a favorable outcome after you have been preapproved by a lender, but instead to get involved in learning the main underwriting guidelines to determine yourself if you qualify for the loan. This chapter addresses the five risks that commercial lenders dread, the seven preapprovals for a commercial real estate loan, the truth about commercial appraisals, why you should use a commercial loan broker, and more.

WHY YOU SHOULD TAKE A HANDS-ON APPROACH

So where did Richard go wrong? It wasn't that he did not qualify for the loan. In fact, if anything he was overqualified and a valued customer of the bank. He already owned two senior apartment complexes in the area, one of which he built. He had a stellar reputation as a contractor. He had excellent credit and more than enough net worth and cash. But surprisingly, this made no difference, because it was the bank that did not qualify for the loan and not him.

There is one thing Richard could have done and that is to get more involved in the loan process at the beginning by communicating to the loan officer three things:

1. Do you have everything from me that you need to preapprove this loan?
2. Has the person who is going to approve my loan reviewed my loan package?
3. Respectfully, if the loan does not get approved as proposed, I'm not going to take it. You will have wasted my time, your time, and the bank's time. And I will expect you to give me a full refund on my loan deposit.

Unfortunately, most commercial borrowers believe that they are going to get the loan that is proposed in their letter of interest, just as Richard did. After all, why would a bank officer do a bait and switch—offer more money at the beginning and then deliver a lot less? There is certainly no better recipe to make the customer mad as hell. I can tell you that this happens much more often than it should.

On the lender's side, it's complicated. Commercial underwriting guidelines have so many moving parts. They all have to line up correctly for the loan to close as proposed. There are loan officers who are experts at juggling the insane number of items involved, identifying problems early on and using mitigations to ensure a favorable outcome. The main purpose of this chapter is to help you become familiar with these items and understand what it is going to take for your loan to get approved.

For Richards's loan, the underwriting guidelines did indeed go up to 75% of cost, so the bank was not lying. But bank officers are not only loan professionals but salespersons. They get bonuses based on their loan volume, the size of their portfolio, and the retention and creation of deposits. If they cannot deliver the loan as promised, they are experts at explaining how this was no fault of theirs or the banks. "Yeah, right," is what most borrowers are thinking when this happens. And then if the customer has a time constraint, they often have to accept the inferior terms anyway.

It is not that bank officers want to mislead you. But many are overworked and do not always take the time to do all their due diligence up front—and, more importantly, to run the deal up the flagpole. The credit administrator who had to approve Richard's loan would have known at the beginning that the bank could not do it.

Borrowers are certainly not encouraged to get as involved in the commercial loan process as I am advocating in this chapter. It is not spoken, but it is understood that he who has the gold rules. Borrowers are expected

> **Time and Money Saving Tip**
>
> It is always best to find a lender that requires only one, or at the most two, signatures to approve a commercial loan. If there is a loan committee of four or more it seems that one member will always play devil's advocate and try to convince the others to offer less favorable terms. Ask the loan officer at the beginning how many people have to approve your loan. If there is a loan committee, make sure that all of the members review the loan submission package.

to bow to the higher authority of the lender and not create too many waves. I believe this thinking is a mistake.

Lenders cannot earn an income without borrowers, so in my thinking that puts borrowers on equal ground with lenders. And making waves, if done respectfully, is not only good for the borrower but for the lender as well. Both will be investing a lot of time and money during the average 45 days it takes to get the loan approved. Both need to work together to ensure that the loan doesn't crash and burn. It is not that I am suggesting that the borrower do a high-octane takeover of the loan process, just that they not assume that the loan officer has preapproved the loan correctly.

Most importantly, I'm suggesting that you take the time to make sure that you and the property are qualified for the loan you are applying for. You will need to ask the lender the right questions at the beginning to determine this. These qualifying questions are outlined for you in this chapter.

Once the loan is started, and throughout the loan process, be sure to check in with the lender often and ask if any problems have come up. Then brainstorm with them what can be done to resolve them. The 10 mitigations presented later in the chapter can help you shore up a weak area by making another area stronger. The goal is to get everything resolved prior to final underwriting, which is done right before loan approval. The worst time to address unresolved issues is during the loan approval phase. Unresolved issues can generate a list of conditions that need to be resolved prior to closing, or cause your loan to be denied.

THE TOP SIX RISKS COMMERCIAL LENDERS DREAD

The first thing to understand about bank executives is that most are not entrepreneurs; they have likely always been employees and abhor risk. Even private lenders and hard money lenders that are not regulated have higher standards for risk than you might think. Here are the top six risks that lenders dread:

1. *High loan-to-value ratio.* The number-one risk for any lender is the borrower not having enough skin in the game. Loans with a loan-to-value (LTV) ratio of 75% or above are considered higher risk. A loan that is made at an 80% LTV to a borrower with excellent credit is higher risk than a loan that is made at 65% to a borrower with poor credit. This is evident in the fact that hard money lenders that do not exceed a 65% LTV have very low default rates. And they can make loans to borrowers who have poor credit and are almost broke. These borrowers just have too much of their own money in the property to take the chance of losing it.

2. *Recessions.* Lenders dread recessions. Most commercial properties lose occupancy, have collection problems, and drop in value during a recession. Some borrowers become insolvent, having their businesses or investment properties run in the red. For banks this means that the loan is now out of compliance with federal regulators that will require the property to be reappraised. If the value has indeed gone down, and/or the borrower no longer qualifies, the bank will have to put up loss reserves (money they cannot lend out). The bank will have to either take additional collateral from the customer or get the loan off their books.

3. *Low net worth, cash, and income.* Borrowers who have built up a net worth equal to the size of the loan and have a good chunk of cash left over after the loan closes have the lowest risk. They maintain their properties better and can handle a downturn in the economy. If the borrower has a four-tenant office building and two go out of business, and they have no cash in the bank to weather this, the lender might get the property back. My clients who had plenty of cash put away for a rainy day made it through the great recession. Those that did not mostly failed. Having multiple sources of income lowers the lender's risk too.

4. *Poor borrower credit.* Having a credit score of 740 and above represents the lowest risk to a lender. A credit score of 680 represents a moderate risk. Having

revolving debt like credit cards whose total has used up over 50% of your total limit is unfavorable. Borrowers who are willing to pay 16% or more in credit card interest are viewed by lenders as being poor stewards of their own money. Also, having had a bankruptcy or foreclosure shows a lender that when the going gets tough, the borrower bails out.

5. *Poor historical operating history.* If you were buying a business, would you want to buy one at full price that had only been operating successfully for six months? Not likely! The same is true for a commercial investment property, which is also a business. Properties that have less than a year of successful operating history are considered risky. Lenders love properties that have two or even three years or more of financials that show the property is a winner.

6. *Having other businesses or investment properties that do not cash flow.* If just one of your businesses or investment properties shows that it is barely hanging on, that is a red flag for most lenders. And yes, most will check to see whether all of your enterprises are running profitably. The risk here is that the failing ones might take you and the lender's new loan down with them financially.

Time and Money Saving Tip

If you are buying a commercial investment property during a recession, it is even more important to determine economic occupancy (based on actual rents collected) at the beginning. Do you want to pay full price for a property that is having problems collecting rent from tenants? Your lender will compare historical *economic occupancy* with physical occupancy, so you should beat them to this. To check economic occupancy accurately, ask the seller for a *trailing 12-month (T-12) report*. This will show you income and expenses broken out month-by-month for the preceding 12 months. Then ask for a year of month-by-month rent rolls for the same time period. Then compare each month's income collected from the T-12 report to what's shown on the rent rolls for each month. What you are looking for is discrepancies that show poor rent collections. If there is a large discrepancy, you will need to collect bank statements for the property from the same time period, and really hone down actual rent collections

THE SEVEN PREAPPROVALS IN COMMERCIAL LENDING

Did you know that unlike residential loans, which have two preapprovals—the borrower's financial condition and the physical condition of the property—commercial loans have seven preapprovals? Yes, SEVEN! These are the quality of the borrower, property location, property income, occupancy, tenants, leases, and the property's physical condition. All it takes is for one of these not to qualify and your loan is going to sink. If this seems complicated to you, you are right. It is! Be sure to ask each lender what its underwriting criteria is for these seven items before you apply. Here are the seven prequalifications:

1. Borrower Quality

We used to have a saying at our firm prior to the Great Recession: "Anyone with 10% down, a 640 credit score, and a pulse could get a commercial loan from us." Low standards for borrower financial strength was one of the main causes of the Great Recession. Another was large mortgage companies, such as Countrywide, making loans to borrowers who clearly did not qualify and colluding with appraisers to raise property values to increase loan size. Very large banks, such as Goldman Sachs, made huge premiums by bundling these subprime loans and selling them as mortgage-backed securities with high credit ratings. They were in fact selling junk bonds. In those days, we used to have some appraisers ask us, "What do you need the appraisal to come in at?"

After the recession, borrower standards flipped to the other extreme. They are still very stringent today. Even hard money lenders want their borrowers to have some financial strength and will not allow the borrower to be stone broke after closing. Borrower quality has the following six components and is the number-one prequalification for commercial lenders today.

Credit Score

Ask the lender what its minimum acceptable credit score is. Standards range from "it doesn't matter" for high-cost hard money loans to a minimum credit score of 680–720 for high-quality perm or construction loans. If you have had a bankruptcy or a foreclosure in the past 10 years, ask what their underwriting guidelines are with those circumstances. If your credit report shows you were late with any mortgage payments, you better be prepared with a really good explanation.

Background Check

Today all lenders, even hard money lenders, pull a background check for all borrowers. If you've had a bankruptcy or foreclosure, have a criminal record, or are currently involved in litigation, it is best to tell the lender about it up front. If they ask you if you have had any of these derogatory items, and you find yourself hesitant to disclose the ones that no longer show up on your credit report, disclose them all. The lender will find out when they pull a background check. If you have a good explanation and the problem was far enough in the past, sometimes they can still make the loan. Almost all commercial loan applications have a checklist for these items, and if you fill any of them out incorrectly and the background check states otherwise, the lender will almost certainly think you lied and cancel your loan.

Quite a few of our clients have stated on the application that they did not have a criminal record, and then the background check showed they had a DUI. Some thought this was not a criminal offense, but it is. Or maybe a client did a short sale on a property and thought that because they settled with the lender all was okay. If you did a short sale on a property you owned and a foreclosure was started, that is considered a foreclosure. In this situation, if you indicated on your application that you have never had a foreclosure, just remember that not being truthful on a loan application is a federal crime.

Net Worth

Ask the lender what their minimum borrower net worth is. It can be very low for expensive hard money loans, but large national banks, many regional banks, securitized lenders such as Fannie Mae and Freddie Mac, life company lenders, and low-cost bridge lenders will need it to be equal to the size of the loan. Community banks and credit unions have lower net-worth requirements. If there are multiple borrowers, most lenders will allow you to add up the cumulative net worth of all borrowers to meet the net worth requirement. Be prepared that if you list stock you own in your company as an asset, most lenders will discount the value to the depreciated value of real estate and equipment. The business's goodwill is usually not valued.

Liquidity

Ask the lender how much cash you will need to qualify. For all loans you will need to have the down payment, closing costs, plus some post-closing funds. These funds will need to be in the bank or in publicly traded stock accounts and be verifiable.

If you are doing a refinance on a property, do not assume that the lender will allow you to take cash out to cover its liquidity requirement. With the exception of debt fund and hard money lenders, lenders will require you to have its cash requirement prior to applying for the loan. They want to know that you are a saver who has a rainy day fund. Community banks usually allow borrowers to take cash out from refinances to cover closing costs, and renovations, but they are hesitant to allow it for other purposes. Regional banks and large national banks, along with all *securitized loan* programs, usually allow borrowers to take cash out for any purpose.

You will need to estimate closing costs as accurately as possible. Commercial lenders are not required to give you a good-faith estimate of these costs, as residential lenders are. See the *closing cost checklist for commercial loans* (Encyclopedia Topic H, Financing). Ask your lender or commercial mortgage broker for something like a good-faith estimate that shows all loan expenses and its requirement for impounds for taxes and insurance at closing.

If you have multiple borrowers you can show total cash from all of them together to meet the liquidity requirement. If it turns out that you are short on meeting the lender's liquidity requirement, make plans to raise additional funds before applying for the loan.

Time and Money Saving Tip

Most lenders will not waste their time with you if you do not have enough cash for the down payment, closing costs, and post-closing liquidity. And they certainly don't like it when you tell them you need to raise the money. So be sure to have the funds deposited in your account at least two to three months prior to applying for the loan. With the exception of hard money lenders, most lenders will request two months of bank statements to verify available cash right after you apply for the loan. If they see that you just deposited the money, they will want to source the funds to make sure it was not a gift or a loan. Lenders will assume that gifts are really disguising loans. With the exception of hard money lenders, lenders do not like it when you borrow the down payment.

Experience

Most lenders will want you to have commercial property ownership experience. Getting your first commercial loan can be like joining an exclusive club. Surprisingly, most regional banks and national lenders are snooty and do not give you credit for experience if you own multiple residential investment properties. But most community banks will.

Ask the lender if you need to have experience owning the same type of commercial property that you want to purchase or if any type of commercial property ownership experience will do. Community banks and Freddie Mac do not generally require experience. Regional banks, national lenders, and Fannie Mae do require experience. Bridge lenders that lend on repositioning projects and construction lenders both want you to have experience, preferably with the same type of property.

Your Distance from the Property

If you live far away from the subject property or out of state, ask the lender how they feel about this. Most community banks and credit unions prefer that the borrower live fairly close to the property, but there are some that will make exceptions. If they're going to make you a commercial loan, most community banks will want to have all of your deposit relationships, and this is only possible if you live close to where they have a branch. Fannie Mae is strict about not allowing out-of-state ownership, since almost all of their defaults during the Great Recession were on these kinds of properties. Many national lenders, regional banks, and bridge lenders are okay with out-of-state ownership if you have local professional management.

2. Property Location

Ask the lender what its minimum population requirement for a property market is and if it lends where the subject property is located. Many low-cost national loan programs, like life companies, will only lend in metropolitan statistical areas (MSAs) of 250,000 or more. Freddie Mac has tier-based pricing on interest rates, with the lowest for properties in large primary markets. Small MSAs that do not employ many people in a wide variety of industries are considered a much higher risk. Community banks usually prefer to lend in their own backyards.

Lenders will also scrutinize the quality of the neighborhood and will not lend in a high-crime area. Many national bridge and hard money lenders will not lend in states that have strong usury laws that limit the amount of interest they can charge.

3. Property Income

Ask the lender what its minimum *debt service coverage ratio* (*DSCR*) is. Ask them how many months the property has to have attained this. If the property is in a great location where market occupancy is high, this can be as short as one month. At the beginning of a recession many lenders will raise their DSCR. This protects them if net operating income drops in the future due to rising vacancy, or rent collection problems.

4. Occupancy

Ask the lender what its minimum occupancy is. Most lenders consider a property to be distressed if occupancy is less than 85% for multifamily properties and 80% for all other commercial property types. An occupancy of 90% and above is preferred for most loan programs. Also ask the lender how much seasoning at the minimum occupancy is required. For example, for Fannie Mae multifamily loans, a minimum of 90% occupancy for 90 days is required. Many of the best lenders want to see their minimum occupancy percentage achieved for six months or even a year or more. Strong historical occupancy represents a much lower risk.

5. Tenant Quality

Go over the rent roll with your lender and ask them to review and make comments on your tenant quality. Tenant quality mostly pertains to office, retail, and industrial tenants. National tenants that have a credit rating are always the most preferred. Tenants that show good business credit plus have more than one location are also preferred.

Tenant mix is essential too. Too many mom-and-pop tenants can be a problem during a recession, as many do not have the cash put aside to weather a financial crisis like the COVID-19 one. Some lenders will only lend on a strip mall if it has a good anchor tenant, such as a grocery chain, or several national *credit tenants*. Many large movie theater chains are or have been in bankruptcy and are not expected to survive COVID-19, resulting in most lenders taking the rent they pay off the rent roll.

If the lender sees that there are rent-collection problems, they will find out which tenants are slow paying or no paying and take their rents off the rent roll or deny the loan if this makes the minimum occupancy or debt service coverage ratio too low.

6. Lease Quality

Have the lender review the rent roll and comment on the lease quality. For multi-family properties, too many month-to-month tenants present a problem for many lenders. For office, retail, and industrial properties, leases with less than two years remaining will be a problem for most lenders. You are not going to get a long-term fixed rate loan—for example, a 10-year fixed—if the average time remaining on all the leases is only three years.

7. Property Physical Condition

Most commercial lenders require the property to be in good physical condition for a permanent loan. Ask the lender what it requires for this. HUD multifamily loans require that a property be in excellent condition. With the exception of some hard money loans, underwriting will require a recent property condition report, and any immediate repairs will need to be made prior to closing or funds will be withheld from the loan in an escrow account so that the repairs can be made in the near future. Health and safety items will need to be cured prior to loan closing.

If the property needs extensive rehabilitation, in most cases the borrower will need to use a bridge loan, which is a temporary loan, to get the work done. Keep in mind that most community banks will fund rehab projects if the market is strong and the borrower has the right team of professionals to get the job done.

THE TRUTH ABOUT COMMERCIAL APPRAISALS AND WHY THEY SOMETIMES KILL DEALS

At my mortgage company, we have the advantage of being mortgage bankers that represent our source of funds directly and mortgage brokers that can bring our loans to just about anyone.

In 2015 I brokered a loan for a large apartment complex in Boise, Idaho, with a regional bank. This was a $10.5 million cash-out refinance. The borrower was going to use the cash to buy another property. This loan request was at the lender's maximum of 75% loan to value. The appraisal needed to come in at $14 million. I felt confident that the property was worth this because the borrower had been offered that amount unsolicited. He decided not to sell. In addition, there were sales comparables that supported this value. The bank used a local appraiser that came in with a very low value of $12.6 million. This lowered the loan amount by $1,050,000, and this was going to kill the deal. I tried to negotiate with the lender's appraisal review department by providing it four comparable sales that supported a $14 million dollar value. But they did not want to challenge the report. So we canceled that loan and I replaced it with a higher-rate Freddie Mac loan. We used a national appraisal firm whose appraisal came in at $14,150,000, and we hit a home run.

On another deal our firm had a borrower in Atlanta who was doing a cash-out refinance with a large bank. The borrower was confident that the property was worth at least $9 million. The bank appraisal came in at $7.4 million. The borrower applied for a Fannie Mae loan with us and our appraisal came in at $8.6 million a month and a half later. This was $1.2 million more than the bank's appraiser had put the value at for the same property.

How is this possible that in both deals commercial banks came in with appraisals with substantially lower values than national securitized lenders? Please read on.

Before the Great Recession, a banker or mortgage broker could actually talk to an appraiser to review comparable sales before engaging them. Together they would reach a comfort level as to what the property would appraise for and the lender would know it would not be wasting its time or its borrower's time. Since the recession, this has become taboo.

Today bank loan officers are not allowed to order appraisals, and for that matter they are discouraged from speaking directly to an appraiser. Larger banks have a separate department with employees that are not commissioned ordering and reviewing commercial appraisals. Smaller banks have a bank employee who works strictly on salary order the appraisal. Then another appraiser reviews the report for accuracy. Loan brokers who are 100% commissioned are also discouraged from communicating with appraisers. And as for borrowers, it has never been okay for them to discuss a property's value with an appraiser.

This arm's length requirement has a positive purpose, in that it leaves little chance that the lender can collude with the appraiser to influence the valuation. The negative is that a lender is not allowed to ballpark the value with the appraiser at the beginning of the process, so there is just too much room to skew the report in one direction or another. This can result in the appraisal lowering your loan amount or killing the loan entirely.

So why do different appraisers often come out with such vastly different values for the same properties? Although most appraisers are straight shooters and want their reports to be as accurate as possible, for many there is often a pull to please the lenders that hire them. Bankers that have been around a long time have seen cycles where commercial properties have climbed sky high during an up cycle and then dropped in value during a down cycle. Banks just don't like being the first of something, and the last thing they want is to make a loan during an up cycle and have cap rates go up suddenly. The lower the cap rate, the higher the value. In their minds, they could be making a 70% loan that a year later could be an 80% loan. As mentioned earlier in this chapter, the feds can make a banker's life miserable when this happens.

Appraisers know this, and in my opinion sometimes purposefully do not include many comparables with lower cap rates that have recently come down in their reports. This is why appraisals from commercial banks are typically the most conservative. Most appraisers have had their appraisals challenged by banks when the value comes in high, and they hate that.

At the other extreme, agency lenders that represent Fannie Mae and Freddie Mac, other securitized lenders such as CMBS brokers, and private fund lenders are more entrepreneurial, and work more often with national appraisal firms that give them much more liberal valuations. These lenders do not have federal regulators going through their files. Although this is not really proper, they will even sometimes go over comparable sales with the appraiser to make sure that the appraisal supports their loan. Many hard money lenders tend to lean on the conservative side and more often prefer lower valuations.

The bottom line is that commercial property appraisal is not an exact science. The commercial appraiser starts out with what I call a marker and brings in research that supports that value. In purchases, the sales price is the marker. How can an appraiser argue with what someone is willing to pay for the property? That is obviously the best indicator of value. So, appraisers most often bring in market research that supports that value. This is why appraisals on purchases usually come in at the purchase price. On refinances, the appraiser has to choose another marker, which is usually the cap rate of the subject property, which is based on its NOI.

The income approach of valuation in a commercial appraisal averages cap rates from recently sold properties and the subject property to determine a value. Since this approach is king with lenders, the appraiser uses the cap rate of the subject property as the marker and then tries to find comparable properties that have sold at a similar cap rate. In some markets, the appraiser has a lot of comparable properties to choose from, which can skew the valuation up or down.

So how can you be proactive to ensure that the appraisal does not kill your loan? The good news is that it is perfectly acceptable and even expected for you to discuss property value with the loan officer at the beginning. I suggest that you work with an experienced real estate broker to do an analysis of value based on comparable properties that have sold in the past year that support the value you need. Then share these with your loan officer. Ask the loan officer to share these with and get the opinion of the credit managers that will be approving your loan. This sets up an expectation for the value. Better yet, if they agree, they have the authority to argue for a better valuation with the appraiser should the appraiser's come in low.

Time and Money Saving Tip

The worst time to apply for a commercial mortgage is during the first three months after a recession has started. During this time, all lenders are going nuts as they are no longer grounded in assessing the risk level for borrowers and properties. They counter this by lowering LTVs and raising the *underwriting interest rate* (see Encyclopedia Topic H, Financing) and DSCR. After a month into the COVID-19 economic crisis, Fannie Mae, Freddie Mac, HUD, and many banks required a 6- to 12-month payment reserve escrow to cover any missed future mortgage payments on commercial loans. This gave them the cushion to mitigate much of the risk. Just be aware that during the beginning of a recession, underwriting guidelines can change every two weeks. This makes it very difficult to know that the loan you are getting quoted today can be delivered. After three to four months, the storm often calms down and loan guidelines become more consistent again.

WHY YOU SHOULD USE A COMMERCIAL LOAN BROKER

A good commercial mortgage broker will save you time through knowing the lenders that have the best rates and terms to meet your financing goals. They will also most likely be able to deliver a loan that gets approved as originally proposed better than you can do yourself. This is because their reputation relies on this. If you want to shop multiple lenders for the best rate and terms but do not want to take the time to talk to each lender and make sure you qualify for all seven prequalifications, this is another reason to engage a good experienced commercial loan broker. The main advantage is that they will know the main underwriting guidelines for all the lenders they represent, plus each lender's rates and terms. These brokers will not earn a dime if they do not get you and the property prequalified correctly and get your loan closed.

Most commercial mortgage brokers are experts at evaluating commercial properties for value and financing and will be pleased to review many properties that you are interested in buying.

They are also great at being a third-party representative of your interests with a lender if it turns out that you or the property do not qualify for the rates and terms originally quoted. If this happens and you threaten to never use the lender again, you are just one customer. If a mortgage broker threatens this, they are representing multitudes of future borrowers.

Do not use a residential mortgage broker who has shallow commercial experience, as they will likely be shooting in the dark. Remember, in residential lending only the quality of the borrower and the physical condition of the property are preapproval conditions.

And I recommend being skeptical about commercial mortgage brokers that advertise that they have hundreds of lenders. What they are selling is that they will get them all to compete against each other to get you the best deal. First, lenders hate it when mortgage brokers do this, and they will likely find out from other lenders or mortgage brokers that your loan is being shopped to death. Lenders will most often refuse to compete under these circumstances.

Second, most mortgage brokers just do not have hundreds of lenders, and if they did, it would be a detriment. This is because there is no way a loan broker can learn the underwriting guidelines of that many lenders, which is essential to doing quality work.

Third, can you imagine the time involved for a mortgage broker to answer the questions that a hundred lenders will have for them to quote the deal?

Fourth, the quality of the relationships you have as a mortgage broker with each lender is what is really important. This ensures that the lender is watching the mortgage broker's back by being extra careful to preapprove the deal correctly. The mortgage broker is doing the same for the lender by carefully screening deals and only bringing them ones that qualify.

TEN MITIGATIONS THAT CAN HELP YOU QUALIFY FOR YOUR COMMERCIAL LOAN

In commercial lending, a skillful loan officer or mortgage broker knows how to use mitigations to qualify a borrower who is weak in one area but strong in another. For example, a loan might require that a multifamily borrower have experience owning an apartment building. A borrower might never have owned one but might have experience owning six residential rental properties and have plenty of extra cash in the bank. In this case there would be two mitigations that would balance out the lack of multifamily ownership experience. Go through the following list of mitigations and pick out the ones you can use if needed.

1. *Having strong sponsorship.* Sponsors are the key principals (partners who will be on the loan) applying for the loan. If you lack financial strength, bringing on a partner with high net worth and liquidity who is willing to be on the loan can be better for a lender than anything else to make a marginal deal work.

2. *Having a high debt-service coverage ratio.* Properties that have an excessive amount of net operating income left over after loan payments are made is a huge plus for a lender. We are talking about a DSCR of 1.45 and above. This can be used as a mitigation for less borrower experience, the borrower being out of state, or a less favorable property location. This also helps make the property recession-proof for the lender if the NOI drops.

3. *Showing successful commercial property ownership experience.* Just as when making a loan on a business, lenders love it when the borrower has experience owning the same kind of commercial property that they are purchasing. It's even better if the borrower made it through the Great Recession through their ingenuity and is now faced with surviving the COVID-19 financial crisis. For borrowers who live in a state different from where the property is located and who have properties that are in less favorable locations, experience rules as a major mitigation.

4. *Having a great property in a good location.* The property's location is the second most important prequalification to a lender. If the property is located in a high-rent submarket in a larger MSA, this can be used as mitigation for most risks. During a recession more tenants in these locations can afford to pay the rent. Also, the lender knows that they can sell the property quickly if the property comes back to them after a default.

5. *Having a bulletproof executive loan summary.* The *executive loan summary* is really the borrower's business plan. This will be the lender's first impression of the property and of the experience and quality of the borrower. Ideally, you want this to highlight the strengths of the deal. But you should also point a finger at the weaknesses and how you plan to remedy them. Be sure to emphasize what you will be doing or are already doing to recession-proof the property.

6. *Having lower leverage.* As mentioned, having a loan request with an LTV of 75% or higher is the lender's greatest risk. The lender knows it is not going to get the property back if the borrower has a lot of equity in it. So needing a loan of 65%

or less can be used to mitigate lower net worth and liquidity, experience, and living in a state different from the one in which the property is located.

7. *Having great tenants and leases.* Your commercial property is only as good as the quality of your tenants and their leases. For multifamily properties, having the rent roll show that tenants have been there for years is a plus. Month-to-month tenancy is a minus. For retail, office, and industrial properties most lenders prefer that the tenants have more than one location, and the lender might pull a credit report on them. Having a good mix of national and local tenants makes a difference. Having 65% or more of the leases with five years or more remaining on the leases is a plus.

8. *Having a property that is in good physical condition.* Almost all lenders require a property condition report. If it is a refinance and the property is in good or excellent condition, this tells the lender that you are always putting money back into maintaining the property. This means you are not operating on a shoestring and therefore you represent a much lower risk to the lender. For buyers, choosing a property that is in great condition is a plus. If it is not, having a plan and the money to get everything upgraded and repaired greatly lowers the lender's risk.

9. *Having the best team to get you to the finish line.* Teaming with a top-notch professional off-site property management company and an experienced partner, contractor, or other professionals who have great reputations in the community will give your lender confidence that you plan on running the property with quality and excellence.

10. *Having good historical financials.* Lenders know that properties that have two—or better yet, three—years of good occupancy and NOI showing on financials will most likely perform well in the future.

VETTING YOUR LENDER AND/OR COMMERCIAL LOAN BROKER

Unlike residential lending, which is highly regulated, commercial real estate lending has little regulation and is a playground rife with opportunity for fraudulent lenders and mortgage brokers. You do not have to worry about banks, of course. Private debt fund and crowd funding lenders that are licensed by the SEC are considered safe too. It is really important that you check out the reputation of any lender or loan broker you have not used before. Some tips to avoid getting ripped off are presented in the sections that follow.

Avoid Up-Front Fees

Most lenders and commercial mortgage brokers are legitimate, hard-working, good people. But then there are the ones who make their living by taking up-front fees and never making loans. Up-front fees or due diligence fees are charged for evaluating the loan to see if it qualifies. The fee is usually $10,000–30,000 or more. Charging up-front fees in most cases is not illegal if the lender provides the borrower a disclosure in the letter of interest that states that they are getting paid for doing due diligence. But if they do not make loans at all, this is committing fraud. Unfortunately many shady lenders operate in a grey area, since they will make a loan every once in a great while, but 9 times out of 10 they do not.

One of my loan officers decided to try a new bridge lender in Texas on three separate loans at the same time. Because the lender was only charging $5,000 as a loan deposit, it seemed the lender was legitimate. The loan officer thought the fee was being collected for the appraisal and the lender's site visit. The lender turned out to be a mortgage broker who was pretending to be a lender and had discovered it was much easier to con people out of five grand than to do all the work on a loan. Our firm refunded this money to our clients because it was our fault that we did not adequately screen this source of financing.

It's best not to do business with lenders or mortgage brokers who charge a fee to evaluate your loan. This should be part of their job. All lenders take a loan deposit before starting the loan. But this should be for paying for the third party reports (the appraisal, environmental, or property condition report, for instance) or other out-of-pocket expenses, such as visiting the subject site.

And then you have the downright crooked lenders. One of my clients was a developer who owned a 204-unit, brand-new apartment complex that was in its final stages of construction. His private construction loan had gone six months beyond its maturity date and was being called due. He only needed a loan to finish the last 12 units. The borrower shopped me and found a lender on his own in Utah that offered him a letter of interest with unrealistically great terms. With this in hand he got his previous lender to give him a three-month extension on paying the construction loan off. The Utah lender kept asking for more money, took $90,000 in up-front fees in total, and never came through with the loan. After my client threatened to file a complaint with the state attorney general's office and the Better Business Bureau, the lender returned $30,000, but kept $60,000. But what was so much worse was that the borrower ran out of time, the hard money lender foreclosed, and he lost the property.

Avoid Loan-to-Own Lenders

These are predatory hard money lenders who make loans to borrowers that are financially distressed. Most often these borrowers have equity of 60% or more in their properties. Usually the properties have been poorly managed and have low occupancy. How this scheme works is that the lender makes the loan for six months to a year knowing that the borrower does not have enough time or money to remedy the situation. The lender's intention from the beginning is to foreclose on the property and make a windfall. These lenders can be identified by their outrageously high rates and fees, short-term maturities, and low LTVs.

How to Avoid Predatory Lenders

If you are using a lender for the first time, start by googling the company name of the lender, and then the name of the owner or main principals, using the terms "fraud," "complaints," or "reviews." These con artists can change the name of their loan company faster than the sun rises. You can also check with the Better Business Bureau or on Ripoffreport.com to see if the lender has any complaints. If there are no complaints online, then ask the lender for references from at least four more customers for whom they have closed loans.

If You Are a Victim of a Predatory Lender

If you are convinced that you have been scammed by a lender that will not refund your loan deposit, start out by threatening to report it for mortgage fraud to the attorney general's office in your state and to the FBI. Then tell them you are going to give them a bad review on Google and file a complaint on Ripoffreport.com and with the Better Business Bureau. That should get their attention.

Financing

Adjustable/Floating Rate Commercial Mortgage: *Sometimes it is better to have an adjustable rate*

We are taught that a fixed rate is better than a floating rate. But sometimes it is a better choice to choose the floating rate. If you are buying a commercial property and intend on fixing and flipping it, an adjustable rate that is close to a point lower than a longer-term fixed rate can be the way to go. Adjustable rate mortgages almost never have prepayment penalties, so you do not have to wait for one to expire to sell the property. Also, some lenders will give you an option to fix a floating rate when the timing is good for you. Many commercial loans start out with a fixed rate and then convert to an adjustable rate. Most community banks will fix the rate for a period of 3–5 years and then the interest rate will adjust one or two times over a 10-year term. Many regional banks offer mortgages that have a fixed rate for up to 10 years and an adjustable rate for the next 15–20 years. Construction and bridge loans are usually adjustable rate, interest-only mortgages with an interest rate that adjusts monthly.

Appraisal (Three Approaches to Commercial Appraisals): *The income approach in a commercial appraisal is king for most lenders*

Three Commercial Appraisal Approaches

1. **Income Capitalization Approach:** I am listing this approach first because it is the gold standard for lenders. This approach uses the capitalization rate (or cap rate as it is better known) to determine value. The appraiser starts out by calculating the cap rate on the subject property based on its net operating income (NOI). If this is a purchase, they divide the NOI by the purchase price to get the property's cap rate. Next, they average the cap rates from between four and six comparable properties that have sold in the past year with the subject property's cap rate to come up with a market cap rate. The other properties have to be of similar age, size, and quality. The market cap rate is then multiplied by the subject property's NOI to come up with a valuation.
2. **Sales Comparison Approach:** In this approach the appraiser compares the sales price of between four and eight properties of an age, size, and quality similar to

Financing

Financing

the subject property that have sold in the same market over the past year. Next the appraiser compares the square footage, quality of construction, and amenities of the comparable properties to the same characteristics of the subject property. The value of the subject property is then determined by rating each of these items as either "plus" or "minus" dollar amounts, based on how it compares to the comparable properties that have sold.

3. **Cost Approach:** This approach is based on what it would cost to build the property today. The land is first appraised separately and then the building's replacement value is determined by applying current cost per square foot to the building's type and quality of construction. This approach is mostly used for construction loans and seldom used for purchase and refinance lending.

The final valuation is usually an average of the sales comparable approach and the income approach. But some lenders require that the results of all three approaches be averaged.

Bad-Boy Carve-Outs: *Engage in one of these bad-boy practices and your non-recourse loan will become recourse*

Non-recourse (see later in this Topic) lenders appear to have a sense of humor in calling fraudulent or irresponsible borrowers "bad boys." What makes non-recourse loans so attractive to commercial real estate investors is that they do not require a personal guarantee. Thus, the lender cannot go after the borrowers personal assets if there is a default on the mortgage. However, most non-recourse loans have a bad-boy carve-out provision in the loan documents that will convert the loan to recourse—allowing the lender to go after the borrower personally—if any of the following occur:

1. The borrower is engaged in criminal activity on the property.
2. The borrower commits fraud by purposefully misrepresenting the property's financials or their personal financials when they are applying for the loan or when they are doing the annual financial reporting.

Time and Money Saving Tip

All smaller commercial banks have a maximum amount they can lend to one customer. If you are taking out a commercial investment property loan of $3,000,000 or more, ask them what the maximum amount is that they can lend to you. If your loan request exceeds their maximum, they will have to get another bank to participate on the loan. Banks are not required to tell you and seldom do if they are participating the mortgage with another lender. The problem is that now you have to get the approval of two or more banks. If another bank is providing the biggest share of the funds, they will want to be the lead bank. The problem is that the lead bank will be the major decision maker on your loan, which makes your bank an intermediary. Ask the bank if they have to participate the loan. If they are, then tell them you want them to be the lead bank. Large banks, such as Wells Fargo, have much more in deposits and can lend very large amounts (up to $50,000,000 or more) to one customer. They will sometimes participate on the loans of smaller banks.

3. The borrower continually does not pay property taxes on the subject property.
4. The borrower changes the insurance without lender approval and it no longer meets the lender's insurance requirements.
5. The borrower does not allow the lender or the lender's agent to inspect the property when given notice to do so.
6. The borrower has the single-asset entity (e.g., the LLC) that owns the property directly declare bankruptcy.
7. The borrower is in violation of the environmental indemnification.

Blanket Mortgage: *Better to avoid this and always have separate loans on each property*

If you have two or more commercial properties located near each other, you might be thinking about having one loan for all of them. This is a *blanket* mortgage. The main advantage is the savings on loan expenses from having only one mortgage. I have a client who refinanced six hotels with a blanket CMBS mortgage and saved over $130,000 on legal fees. The disadvantages of getting a blanket mortgage outweigh the advantages, though. For one, the lender is taking the collateral from all of the properties, which often results in overcollateralizing the loan. But the larger problem is that it is difficult to get one property released if you want to sell it or do a cash-out refinance on it. With blanket loans, the lender will often ask you to pay off more than one property's share of the mortgage if you want to sell just that one.

Commercial banks, credit unions, and CMBS lenders offer blanket mortgages. If you decide to go this route, be sure to have a release provision written into the loan documents that allows you to easily sell one property and pay down just that portion of the loan's principal balance. My advice is to avoid blanket mortgages and to always have separate loans for each property.

Bridge Loan: *These short-term loans are great if you have bad credit or are repositioning a property*

If you need to close quickly on purchasing a commercial property or are doing a rehab project, a bridge loan could be just right for you. These loans can sometimes close in a week. A bridge loan is a temporary, short-term loan of one to two years that allows the borrower to bridge the gap until they sell the property or refinance it with a quality perm loan. Bridge loans work exceptionally well when buying a property that does not cash flow and needs repositioning. It also comes in handy when the borrower does not qualify for

Time and Money Saving Tip

Repositioning projects that require bridge loans because of cosmetic and constructional changes and unstabilized occupancy usually take longer than expected to complete. Bridge lenders know this and many will only offer you a one-year term with several six-month options to extend. But here's the catch: they will charge you (usually a one-point fee) for each option. This puts a lot more money in their pocket. If this seems to you like a predatory practice, it is. Be sure to always find a bridge program that has a minimum of a two-year term; for some projects, three years quality permanent financing. In this case, they might need several years to improve their credit scores, net worth, and liquidity. Bridge lenders don't care that much about credit scores, but they do like to get their money back quickly. So make sure you have your exit strategy well planned out before talking with them. The downside is that bridge financing is expensive, with rates of 7–12% and loan fees of two to four points.

is even better. This way you can avoid paying these annoying extension fees. Oh, worse yet, the loan-to-own bridge lenders will make a one-year loan, knowing the project is going to take longer to stabilize, and then refuse to extend the loan when it matures. Their plan all along was to steal the property from you through foreclosure.

Capital Improvement Reserves/ Cap-X: *Be sure to add this to expenses when you are first analyzing income and expenses on a property you are buying*

When taking out a loan on a commercial property you are buying, it is important to understand that lenders add an estimate for capital improvement reserves, also called Cap-X, to the expenses. This will create a lower NOI than you have likely calculated. The result can be a lower loan amount if the *debt service coverage ratio (DSCR)* (see later in this Topic) drops too low to cover a loan of the size you are applying for. Lenders add this to expenses because appraisers do. When you own the property, you will be paying for capital expenses too, so it is wise to show them as expenses when you are first analyzing the income for a property. These apply to major building replacements, such as roofs, HVAC systems, hot water heaters, paving the parking lot, or any items that will last five years or more.

For apartment buildings, allow from $150–400 per unit per year based on age and condition for Cap-X. For office, retail, and industrial properties you'll use an estimated cost per square foot. The appraiser will recommend the amount based on the age and condition of the property. When you're first analyzing the deal and before the appraisal is ordered, ask your lender what amount they recommend you use for Cap-X.

Capital Stack: *This shows who gets paid first in a deal that has a sponsor, investors, and lenders*

Seems like everyone is talking about the capital stack these days. Lenders, investors, and owners of businesses and commercial real estate seem to mention it a lot. The capital stack shows sponsors, investors, and lenders where their risk level is for receiving payment in relation to each other. The top of the stack gets paid last and has the largest risk, and the bottom gets paid first and has the smallest risk.

In this example, I am using a stack of four layers, but there can be more. At the very top you have common equity, which is the sponsor or owners of the property. They have invested 5% of the cost of the project. They only get a return on the investment after the next stack down—preferred equity—gets paid. These are the investors that the sponsor has brought in. Then you have mezzanine, or secondary debt. They get paid ahead of the preferred equity group. And lastly, in the most secure position, you have senior, or first-position, debt. They get paid from cash flows first. Let's use a $10 million commercial property purchase for an example:

Capital Stack on a $10,000,000 Purchase

Title	Position	Percentage	Total Contribution
Sponsor/owner	Common equity	5%	$500,000
Investors	Preferred equity	20%	2,000,000
Mezzanine debt	Secondary debt	15%	1,500,000
Senior debt	First-position debt	60%	6,000,000
Total		100%	10,000,000

Cash-Out Refinancing: *How much cash can you take out on a refinance? The worst to best lenders to use*

After all, it's your money—you should be able to take it out of the property and use it! Let's say you bought a property for a great price, and after closing you want to refinance it based on a higher appraised value and take your cash out. Sorry, but you are going to have to wait for a year or more to do this. Maybe even two. Or, you have completed ground-up construction or rehabilitation of a commercial property. You might think you can just do a cash-out refinance based on the current appraisal and pull all your equity out to buy another property. This is not likely to happen either.

All lenders require seasoning on the ownership of a property before they will let you take the maximum cash out on a refinance based on the current appraised value. After two years of the property reaching stabilized occupancy (see Encyclopedia Topic B, Due Diligence), some lenders will lend you up to their maximum LTV based on the appraised value. Banks prefer three years of seasoning. Here is a list of lenders and their approach to taking cash out on a refinance, from the most conservative to the most liberal:

- *Community banks.* Most do not like cash-out refinances. They know that the real estate market has cycles, where periods of growth are followed by downturns. They feel much more secure knowing that you have all that equity just sitting in the property. They usually require two to three years of seasoning to get maximum cash out. For most, if they'll lend up to 75% LTV on a refinance, they'll reduce that to 65% with cash out. And when doing a perm loan to pay off a construction or rehab loan, they usually only want to pay off the balance of your existing loan.
- *Regional banks, large banks, and national banks.* If you have owned the property for three years or more, you can refinance at 75% of appraised value with cash out. If you've owned for less than two years, they will usually only lend you 80% of

what you paid for the property plus what you put into it or 75% of appraised value, whichever is less. If you have done construction or rehab, hopefully this will cover the payoff on your existing loan.

- *Credit unions.* After two years, most will lend you up to 90% of what you paid for the property plus what you put into it or 75% of appraised value, whichever is less.
- *Life companies.* After two years, they will usually lend you up to 90% with cash out based on what you paid for the property plus what you put into it or 70% of appraised value, whichever is less.
- *Fannie Mae multifamily.* For cash-out refinances you can borrow up to 75% of appraised value after two years of ownership. If you are refinancing a rehab or construction loan, you can borrow up to 80% of what you paid for the property plus what you put into it or 75% of the appraised value, whichever is less.
- *Freddie Mac multifamily.* This used to be one of the most liberal cash-out programs, where you could refinance up to 80% of appraised value with cash-out for any reason after a year of ownership. But with the event of the COVID-19 economic crisis, this dropped down to 75%. For perming new construction or rehabilitation loans, you can borrow up to 90% of cost.

Note that after a recession starts, most banks and credit unions eliminate cash-out refinances. This happened shortly after the COVID-19 economic crisis began. Fannie Mae and Freddie Mac multifamily were still doing cash out to 75% LTV and HUD to 80% LTV. Debt fund and hard money bridge lenders seemed to be okay with cash out up to 70% LTV.

Closing Cost Checklist (Commercial Loan): *You will likely need to compile a list of closing expenses yourself, as lenders are not required to give you one*

Did you know that commercial lenders and loan brokers are not required to give you a good faith estimate of closing costs on a commercial loan? The Federal Truth in Lending Act requires this on residential loans, but does not regulate this for commercial ones. So how are you supposed to know what your closing costs will be? You will need to take responsibility for this yourself. Use the list below, which lists most closing costs that are $50 or higher. Contact the lender and title company to get the actual amounts. It's not fun getting to the closing table to find out that you do not have enough down payment money to cover all the closing costs.

Here are some of the largest closing cost expenses:

- Payment in advance of interest on your new loan until the end of the closing month
- Payment of interest on your old loan when refinancing through the closing date
- Payment of property taxes through the end of the current tax season at closing
- From four months to a year of insurance payments to start an escrow account if your lender requires impounds for insurance
- A reserve amount to be put in an escrow account for property taxes and insurance if your lender collects this with the mortgage payment.

Financing

Closing Cost Checklist for Items $50 and Above

- Appraisal cost
- Environmental report cost
- Property condition report cost
- Seismic report cost (if needed)
- Lender's site visit cost
- Lender loan fee
- Loan broker fee
- Lender's legal expense
- Borrower's attorney fees
- Document prep fee
- Underwriting fee
- Processing fee
- Credit report fee
- Lender's title policy

- Owner's title policy
- Escrow expense
- Recording fees
- Survey expense
- Endorsements: title
- Prepayment of interest on new loan
- This year's property taxes due
- Insurance escrow/impounds
- Tax escrow/impounds
- Reconveyance fee
- Tax service fee
- Miscellaneous title fees

Commercial Construction and Bridge Loan Programs: *These are all adjustable-rate, interest-only loans*

Where to Get a Commercial Bridge or Construction Loan

- *Local community banks.* You've got to love them because they are short-term loans and have much lighter regulations. Construction and rehab loans start at $150,000 for owner-occupied loans and $250,000 for investment property. Community banks lend at prime rate plus 1.00–2.00%. These loans go to 75% of cost and have a 1.00% loan fee. This is the best place to get a loan if you have lower net worth, cash, and experience.
- *Credit unions.* They are new to commercial construction loans and many still do not do them. Plan on prime rate plus 1.00–1.50% and 75% of cost. Often the loan is set up as a credit line. Experience is a plus, as is having a net worth equal to the loan size. They usually charge a 1.00% loan fee.
- *HUD multifamily.* Most HUD (US Department of Housing and Urban Development) lenders prefer construction loans to be $5,000,000 and larger. These are for the construction of apartment buildings, senior housing, assisted living, and nursing homes. This is the best-quality construction financing in America, at 85% of cost. The construction loan rolls over seamlessly to a perm loan, which has a low, 40-year fixed rate and a 40-year amortization. The uncertainty of what your perm loan rate will be is eliminated, as both construction and perm loans have the same rate, which is determined when the rate is locked a month prior to the closing of the construction loan. Low interest rates are tied to the 10-year US Treasury yield. The downside is that the construction loan can take from eight months to a year to close and loan expenses are high. But if you have the time, ending up with a 40-year, fixed-rate, assumable perm loan makes it worth it.

- *National bank lenders.* These are capital divisions of the largest national banks, including JPMorgan Chase, Bank of America, Wells Fargo, Citigroup, and Capital One. They have the lowest rates, as low as the 30-day LIBOR plus 1.75% with a 1.00% loan fee. Construction loans start at $10,000,000. The downside is that they only lend in large markets to strong borrowers and prefer 70% loan to cost or less.
- *Private fund lenders.* These lenders will make construction and bridge loans to borrowers that do not qualify at a bank. Lower credit scores are okay, but borrowers do need to have some financial strength, experience, and a solid project in a strong market. Construction loans start at $10,000,000. They lend at the 30-day LIBOR plus 4.00–6.00% with a one-point fee.
- *Hard money lenders.* If you have poor credit and low net worth and cash but a solid project, a hard money commercial construction loan might be your only option. These loans are made at 9.00–12.00% with two to four points. Some can lend at 80% of cost or 75% of appraised value, whichever is less.

Note that at the beginning of recessions most lenders with the exception of HUD and debt fund lenders will not do ground-up commercial construction or major rehab until the real estate market cycle moves into the recovery or expansion stages.

Commercial Loan Submission Checklist: *Your executive loan summary should have a synopsis of most of the information on this list*

For the Property

- Executive loan summary
- Proximity to main highways and shopping
- Purchase and sale agreement
- Budget for planned property improvements
- Current rent roll
- Last two years of income and expense statements
- Trailing 12-month (T-12) report (see Appendix A)
- Exterior and interior photos
- Operating budget pro forma (see Appendix A)
- Copy of leases or rental contracts
- Management company resume

For the Borrowers

- Three-bureau credit report on all key principals
- Current personal financial statement for all key principals (see Appendix A)
- Schedule of real estate owned for borrowers (see Appendix A)
- Last three years' 1040 tax returns
- Resume or bio of key principals

Completion Guarantee (Construction Loans): *Almost all construction loans will require the borrowers to sign one of these*

If you are a developer or key principal on a construction loan, you had better take managing the construction costs seriously. This is because most construction lenders will require you to sign a completion guarantee—non-recourse lenders too. This a promise to complete the construction lien-free should there be a problem with cost overruns due to construction-related expenses or other outside expenses such as interest, insurance, and taxes. If not completed, the completion guarantee requires the guarantor to complete the construction at their own expense or allows the lender to complete it at the guarantor's expense. Completion guarantees become void when the certificate of occupancy is issued.

Construction Loan Submission Checklist: *If you do not have much financial strength or experience, be sure to include a stronger partner who is willing to be on the loan*

For the Property

- Executive loan summary
- Description of improvements to be built
- Description of the land with aerial photos
- Proximity to main highways and shopping
- Purchase and sale agreement on land
- Detailed construction budget
- Approved zoning and other entitlements
- List of hard and soft costs paid to date
- Feasibility study
- Site plan, floor plan, and elevation drawings.
- Operating pro forma for the first three years
- Resume of the general contractor and projects completed
- Copy of leases or intent to lease
- Management company resume

For the Borrowers

- Current three-bureau credit report on all key principals
- Current personal financial statement for all key principals
- Schedule of real estate owned
- Last three years of 1040 tax returns
- Resume or bio of key principals

Construction Rollover to Permanent Loan: *Why not get approved for your construction and perm loan at the same time?*

When taking out a commercial construction loan, wouldn't it be great to know the terms of your permanent loan too? Construction rollover to permanent loan programs do just that. They won't be able to tell you what your interest rate will be once the construction and lease-up are completed, but they can tell you the permanent loan terms.

Community and national banks can give you a letter of interest for both the construction and permanent loan at the beginning. If you are building multifamily, HUD offers the very best of these types of loans. The HUD 221(d)(4) construction loan seamlessly rolls over to a low, 40-year fixed-rate, 40-year amortization perm loan. And best

Financing

of all, the permanent loan will have the same interest rate as the construction loan. So once you start construction, you don't have to live with the uncertainty of what your permanent loan interest rate will be. The downside is that this loan can take from 8 to 12 months to fund, so start early.

Coterminous Loan: *All debt on your commercial property has to mature at the same time*

If you are taking out *mezzanine debt* (see later in this Topic), a second mortgage, or *supplemental financing* (see later in this Topic), your first mortgage lender will require that all the loans be coterminous. This means that they will all have the same maturity date as the senior debt has. Should the property need to be refinanced or sold, it is important that all loans can be paid off at the same time.

> **Time and Money Saving Tip**
>
> When working with a commercial mortgage broker, tell them you would like to pull your own credit report. This will not affect your credit score. The lender that the broker refers the loan to will pull your credit report for sure. If the mortgage broker pulls it too within the same 30-day time frame, your credit score will go down 5–15 points. If you are tight on making the cutoff for qualifying for the loan based on minimum credit score, having your score lowered may disqualify you.

Cumulative Loan to Value (CLTV): *This is the combined LTV of all loans on the property*

If you plan on adding on mezzanine debt or a second mortgage, you need to find out what your first-position lender's cumulative loan to value (CLTV) is. This is the maximum combined LTV of all your loans that they will allow.

Debt Service Coverage Ratio (DSCR): *You can use this to increase your loan amount*

DSCR is determined by dividing the annual NOI (gross income minus expenses) by the annual loan payments:

$$\text{Annual NOI/Annual debt service} = \text{DSCR}$$

All commercial loan programs constrain the maximum amount that can be borrowed by setting a minimum DSCR. Finding a loan that has a lower DSCR requirement of 1.20, or even 1.15, can greatly increase your loan size for expensive commercial properties in low cap-rate markets. In this situation, NOI is usually too low to support a 70–75% LTV. The only way to get 75% LTV might be if the lender goes down to a 1.15% DSCR. Most commercial lenders prefer to lower their risk by lending at a higher DSCR, of 1.25 or above. Although they might lend up to 75% LTV, if they constrain the loan by a DSCR of 1.30, their maximum LTV might really only be 65%.

A 1.25 DSCR means that there is an extra 25 cents of profit left for the borrower for every dollar of loan payment made. Most lenders prefer higher DSCRs because a larger amount of income is left over after loan payments are made.

During strong economic times DSCRs often drop, which means you can borrow more money. During recessions they go up, resulting in your being able to borrow less. This is to protect the lender from making a loan that is too large to be covered by decreasing NOI.

Debt Yield: *A lender's secret weapon to lower the loan amount*

Most commercial loan borrowers do not know what debt yield is. Often lenders that use it do not mention it. It might come up when they have to explain to you why they cannot lend an amount that you know the *debt service coverage ratio* (see earlier in this Topic) supports. Many lenders mislead borrowers by offering higher loan-to-values that they rarely lend at, by protecting themselves with debt yield. Debt yield is the property's annual net operating income divided by the loan amount:

$$\text{Annual Net Operating Income/Loan amount} = \text{Debt yield}$$

When a lender uses debt yield, they are really saying something like this: "We can lend you up to 75% LTV as long as the net operating income is 10% of the loan amount or more." In this case, they are constraining their maximum loan by a debt yield of 10%. Lenders that use it love their debt yield, because if they set it high enough, they do not have to worry about property values dropping. This is because their loan amount is not really based on loan to value. It is based on a percentage of the loan amount that the net operating income can afford to pay.

Many banks, CMBS lenders, life companies, and even private fund lenders use debt yield to lower their risk by lending less money. The higher the debt yield, the less money a lender will lend you. If a property has $100,000 in net operating income and the lender has an 8% debt yield, they can lend you $1,250,000. If they have a 10% debt yield, they can only lend you $1,000,000.

$$\text{Annual Net Operating Income/Loan amount} = \text{Debt yield}$$

$$\$100,000/1,250,000 \times 100 = 8\% \text{ Debt yield}$$

$$\$100,000/1,000,000 \times 100 = 10\% \text{ Debt yield}$$

Many lenders prefer to lend at debt yields closer to 9–10%. Be sure to ask all lenders you are interested in if they use debt yield, and if so, what it is. The more favorable loan programs will lend at a debt yield closer to 8%.

Declining Prepayment Penalty: *Most banks have a declining prepayment penalty*

The only way a commercial lender that portfolios their loans (keeps the loans and doesn't sell them), such as a community bank, can be sure that they will cover their cost to put the loan on their books is by having prepayment penalties. Most commercial lenders do have them. If you are not sure how long you are going to hold a commercial property and you want a longer-term fixed rate, a declining prepayment penalty is the most favorable. Most banks have declining prepayment penalties. On a 10-year fixed rate the prepayment penalty percentage could be 5, 4, 4, 3, 3, 2, 2, 1, 1, 0 over the loan term. In other words, if you decided to sell the property after the first five years you would have a 2% prepayment penalty. This is still a good chunk of money, but if the property has gone up enough in value it is likely worth it. Of course, if you keep the loan for the full 10 years, the prepayment penalty doesn't matter.

Defeasance Prepayment Penalty: *This prepayment penalty can pay a dividend if rates are going up when you prepay*

CMBS loans (see Encyclopedia Topic I, Commercial Loan Programs) often have a defeasance prepayment penalty. These loans are converted to bonds and sold as mortgage-backed securities on Wall Street. Defeasance substitutes the real estate collateral for a portfolio of US Treasury bonds. These bonds pay investors a guaranteed rate of return for the same duration as the maturity of the mortgage. As a borrower, defeasance will likely be an unaffordable prepayment penalty if Treasury yields go down when you want to prepay the loan. This creates a shortfall of earnings to the bondholder and this loss is passed on to the borrower, along with a 1% fee. What's truly amazing is that when the opposite happens—when you prepay when rates have gone up—you can possibly earn money. Now the bondholder can replace the existing Treasury bonds with higher paying ones and make a profit. Some lenders pass a portion of this windfall to the borrower. The bottom line is that unless you know you are going to keep the loan for the full term, defeasance is a very risky prepayment penalty. If you do decide to take a loan with a defeasance, you will likely have to wait until rates go up to prepay.

> ### Time and Money Saving Tip
>
> With the exception of federally chartered credit unions, just about all lenders have prepayment penalties, because if you prepay too early they might not make a profit. If your bank has a declining prepayment penalty, ask them if they are keeping the loan in their portfolio or selling it. If they are keeping the loan, you should be able to negotiate a better declining prepayment penalty. On a five-year fixed mortgage, if the prepayment penalty is 5, 4, 3, 2, 1, try to negotiate it to 3, 2, 1, 1, 0 or even 3, 2, 1, 0, 0. Often a bank can recover their cost on the loan and make a profit after three years. Lenders that sell their loans on the secondary market will earn more premium if they have a more severe prepayment penalty. But if they want the loan, you can bargain with them too.

Earn-Out Provision: *This can help you get the loan you want when the property does not qualify*

If your commercial property does not qualify for the quality lower-rate permanent loan you are interested in because of low occupancy, low debt service coverage, or required repairs, ask the lender if they'll put an earn-out provision into the loan. This is an agreement that provides a larger loan now by withholding loan funds until occupancy reaches the required level or repairs are completed. The downside is that most lenders will not release the withheld earn-out funds to the borrower until the higher

Financing

required occupancy is *verified* and repairs are completed and inspected. For the property improvements, you'll have to use your own money to get the work done and then get reimbursed by the lender.

Environmental Report (Required by Lenders): *Almost all lenders require these to ensure there are no environmental hazards on the property*

When checking out environmental concerns as part of your due diligence when buying a property, be sure to have your lender order the environmental report. It might not be able to use it if you order it. Almost all commercial lenders will require an environmental report to verify that there is no contamination on or near the property. They know that if, in a foreclosure, they get a property, with environmental problems, they may not only have difficulty selling it but will also be responsible for any litigation that may result from environmental hazards. If your loan is small and your lender requires a phase 1 report but you want a lower-cost option, ask them if you can take out environmental insurance on the property.

The Three Types of Environmental Reports

1. **Transaction Screen Report:** Banks will sometimes use this low-cost report for small loans of under a million dollars or for urban properties that they feel are unlikely to have environmental hazards. This report has a limited scope of review. The cost is about $450.
2. **Phase 1 Environmental Report:** Investigators will research all previous tenants of the property and look for evidence of contamination of the subject property and adjoining properties. The cost is between $2,500 and $3,000.
3. **Phase 2 Environmental Report:** If contamination is suspected in the phase 1 report, a phase 2 report will be needed. Tests will be conducted on surfaces, soil, air, and groundwater. The cost is about $6,000 to $7,500.

Equity Participation Loan: *Only use this type of financing as a last resort*

This is a loan where the lender has also contributed to the equity or down payment and has an ownership interest in the property. When the property is sold the lender/partner gets its original capital back plus a share of the proceeds from any appreciation due to a higher property value. Private lenders make these loans. It is typical for the lender to make a loan at 65% and then contribute 20% of the total capital required toward the down payment. They will then become 20% owners of the property. Property investors make most of their profit from appreciation, so it will always benefit the sponsor to obtain secondary financing instead of an equity participation loan. The second-position lender does not share in proceeds from the sale of the property.

Estoppel Certificate (Required by Lenders): *If you are financing an office, retail, or industrial property, be sure to get started on these certificates early*

Almost all lenders who make commercial investment real estate loans on office, retail, and industrial properties will require tenants to fill out and sign their estoppel certificates. With this document the tenant confirms the terms of their lease, including rent, security deposit, and any outside agreements they have with the landlord. They also confirm that they are not in default on their lease and state whether they have any claims against their landlord. Be aware that it is rare for a lender to allow a loan to close before all the tenants sign their estoppel certificates. Almost all commercial leases today require tenants to review and sign estoppels from buyers and lenders. Problems almost always seem to occur when there is a large number of tenants, in getting them all to review and sign the document in a timely fashion. National tenants usually have to have their attorneys review the estoppel before they sign, and this can take a month or longer. So be sure to get estoppel certificates to all tenants as early as possible.

Executive Loan Summary: *Use this great tool to sell the lender on you and the property*

Lenders and commercial mortgage brokers always appreciate reviewing an executive loan summary before they spend time reviewing a loan submission package. The purpose of this is threefold. The first is to give perspective lenders just enough information for them to determine if the deal is right for them. Why waste time with phone calls and meetings if the lender can read your loan summary and determine in a matter of minutes if the deal is in their wheelhouse? The second is to get the lender excited about doing the loan, and the third is to sell the lender on you and your team's ability to develop and or oversee the property as a business. The briefer the summary, the better. It's good if you can keep it to three pages at the most. Here are the seven things that need to be included:

> ### Time and Money Saving Tip
>
> When a commercial tenant receives an estoppel letter to sign, this is a signal to them that you are either refinancing or selling the property. If you are in the middle of lease negotiations with an existing tenant, they often will use this to their advantage to negotiate lower rent and better terms. So it is always best to negotiate leases that are coming due well ahead of refinancing or selling. Another option is to arrange a secret private sale whereby the listing agent does not advertise the property, but only works with trusted colleagues and investors they know.

Executive Loan Summary Items

1. *Description of the project.* Describe in no more than half a page the scope of the project, how much you want to borrow, the type of financing you are looking for, and what your exit strategy is.
2. *Description of the property and/or proposed construction.* Describe the property's location and what major highways and shopping are nearby. Give details about the size of the land parcel, when the property was built, number of units or spaces, square footage, and amenities.

3. *Use of proceeds.* Show how much you are paying for the property; all expenses, including costs for renovations or construction; projected closing costs; and the loan amount requested and how much you are putting down or your equity in the property and how much cash you want to take out in a refinance. Here is an example:

Use of Proceeds

Purchase		Refinance	
Cash out		Cash out	
Purchase price	$2,000,000	Payoff of first mortgage	$1,540,000
Renovations	350,000	Repairs	110,000
Closing costs	26,000	Closing costs	28,000
Total	2,376,000	Cash out to borrower	400,000
Cash in		Total	2,078,000
First mortgage	1,782,000	Cash in	
Down payment	594,000	New first mortgage	2,078,000
Total	2,376,000		

4. *NOI.* Mention the annual NOI and what you plan to do to raise rents and lower expenses
5. *Ownership structure.* List the sponsor or general partners and the limited partners. Mention how much of the property each will own.
6. *Key principals.* These are the people who will be responsible for the loan. List them individually with a brief bio that describes their commercial property ownership experience and their net worth and liquidity.
7. *Professional team members.* Include brief bios for the sponsor, your property manager, and any other professionals. If the property will be new construction or involve a major rehab, include bios for your general contractor and architect.

Time and Money Saving Tip

Usually negotiations with a lender on loan rates and terms start out with the lender telling the borrower what they are going to get, as if it is written in stone. Better for you to reverse this and start the conversation out by telling the lender what rate and terms you want and will accept. Be sure to let them know that they are competing for your business. Tell the lender how long you want to fix the rate for, the interest rate you have in mind, and the amortization, prepayment penalty, and loan fees that you are looking for. Be prepared to share an offer from another lender that has offered you something close to these terms. You will be surprised how often the lender will get back to you with an even better offer.

Fixed-Rate Commercial Mortgages: *If you want to fix your interest rate for 10 years or longer, use one of the lenders below*

Unlike most residential loans, in which interest rates can be fixed for 30 years, the average community bank commercial loan is fixed for 3–5 years with a 10-year term. It's just too risky for these banks to fix an interest rate for a longer period. If the money they have in deposits falls below a certain level, regulators will require them to borrow the difference. Banks always borrow on a short-term basis (as short as one day) and these loans have adjustable rates. So it is risky for them to fix rates long term. The following lenders have the longest fixed rates:

These Lenders Can Fix the Rate for 10 Years or Longer

Fannie Mae multifamily. Rates fixed for 5–30 years.

Freddie Mac multifamily. Rates fixed for 5–10 years.

HUD/FHA multifamily, senior housing, assisted senior living, independent senior living, nursing homes, and hospitals. Rates fixed for 35 years, fully amortizing.

Regional bank income property division. Rates fixed for 3–10 years.

Large banks. Rates fixed for 3–10 years.

CMBS. Rates fixed for 5 or 10 years.

Life companies. Rates fixed for 5–25 years.

Forbearance Agreement: *If you are faced with a possible foreclosure, see if you can do this first*

If you miss several loan payments or you go beyond the maturity date on your loan, the lender will likely give you a default letter telling you the principal balance is due and payable or it will start foreclosure. There is an alternative that benefits the borrower and lender. If you just need more time to refinance or sell the property, consider asking the lender if it will do a forbearance agreement with you. This is a legal document that gives you an agreed-upon amount of time to cure the default, usually between 3 and 12 months. Keep in mind that a foreclosure on your record can ruin your credit and will prevent you from obtaining a quality low-rate mortgage for many years to come.

During the first three months of the COVID-19 economic crisis, many commercial lenders helped commercial real estate borrowers with forbearance. Under the Coronavirus Aid, Relief, and Economic Security Act (also known as the CARES Act), the federal government authorized Fannie Mae, Freddie Mac, and HUD to offer forbearance that waived loan payments for 90 days as long as eviction proceedings were not started during that period.

The best thing about a forbearance agreement is that it will not show up on your credit or background check. The downside is that you do have to make up the missing payments at some point and if you default on the agreement anyway, it will become invalid. A forbearance agreement has you pay a forbearance fee, all payments in arrears, plus the lender's attorney costs and any other expenses it has for processing the agreement. The fee is usually the only item that can be negotiated. Some lenders will demand that you put up additional collateral in property before they will agree to a forbearance agreement. This is something you should refuse to do. Losing the subject property is punishment enough. I have had clients who have tried to negotiate the principal balance down when negotiating a forbearance agreement. I have not seen this work, but it may be possible. Unfortunately, the lender is usually holding all the cards.

Foreign National Loan: *There are lenders that will lend to foreign nationals, but they need to establish credit in the United States*

The majority of lenders in the United States, including banks, Fannie Mae, Freddie Mac, HUD, SBA (Small Business Administration), and life companies, will make a loan to a foreign national if they are legal permanent or nonpermanent US residents. CMBS lenders, private fund lenders, and hard money lenders can often make a loan to foreign nationals that do not have resident status. If you are a foreign national, be sure to establish credit in the United States. Most lenders will require this.

Global Ratio: *When applying for a commercial loan at a bank, ask them what their global ratio is*

Residential lenders require a debt-to-income ratio to qualify the borrower, and all commercial banks require a global ratio for business and commercial investment property loans. To compute this, the lender looks at the ratio between all cash in and cash out for the borrower. They take the borrower's annual cash taken in from businesses, investment properties, W-2 wages, and interest income and divide this by all cash out from personal and business debts. Here is an example:

$$\frac{\$120,000 \text{ annual personal and business income}}{\$100,000 \text{ annual personal and business debts}} = 1.20 \text{ global ratio}$$

Banks love their global ratios because they show the borrower's personal and business debt as it relates to their income for both in one number. Ask a bank what its global ratio is. Why does this matter? Because the lower the global ratio, the easier it is to qualify for financing. Bank global ratios range from 1.20 to 1.40.

Index: *This is what mortgage rates are set to*

Mortgage rates are set to an index plus a margin or spread. Popular indexes are US Treasury yields, the Federal Home Loan Bank Rate, the *LIBOR*, and prime and *swap rates* (see later in this Topic). Community banks often use the Federal Home Loan Bank rate as

Time and Money Saving Tip

When you are taking out a commercial mortgage, get the index the lender is using to determine the rate and what the margin is going to be on top of the index in writing in the LOI. In the example below, the margin should stay the same at 2.50%. Your rate is going to go up and down until locked based on the index changing over time. This way you can track where your rate is daily until you can lock it. Lenders do change margins over time and can be sneaky (see Chapter 10 for more on this) by adding more to them to increase their profit in the commitment letter. Be sure to hold your lender to the margin in the LOI.

an index. The index fluctuates with the market. A spread or margin is added to the index to come up with the rate for each business day. The margin is usually set, but can change over time. Here is an example for a 10-year fixed mortgage that bases its rate on the 10-year Treasury yield index:

10-year Treasury yield	1.96%
Margin	2.50%
Interest rate	4.46%

Interest-Only Mortgage: *If you want the most net cash flow, choose an interest-only permanent mortgage*

Sometimes what really matters is having the most net cash flow every month. When applying for permanent commercial financing, there is nothing that can achieve this better than an interest-only mortgage. The downside is that you will not be paying down your principal during the interest-only period. But to balance that, your property is likely going up in value, so your equity is growing.

An amortizing loan versus an interest-only loan. For a $1 million, 10-year fixed Freddie Mac multifamily mortgage with a rate of 4.75%, your monthly payments with a 30-year amortization will be $5,216. Your full-term interest-only monthly payments will be $3,958 with the same interest rate. This is a savings of $42 dollars a day, $1,258 per month, and $15,096 a year—or over 10 years, you will have put $150,960 more in your pocket. Fannie Mae, Freddie Mac, and CMBS offer some interest-only mortgages. Private debt funds, bridge loans, and hard money lenders usually offer full-term interest-only mortgages. Community banks do not offer interest-only mortgages, but regional bank investment property divisions do.

Key Principal: *A key principal qualifies for the loan and is responsible for it. Do you want to be one?*

Do you or any of your investors want to be a key principal on the mortgage? Well, someone has to take this one on: Key principals are the individuals that apply for and are responsible for the loan. It is their personal credit, net worth, liquidity, and experience that the lender uses to qualify the borrower. For recourse loans, key principals sign on the promissory note, deed of trust, and personal

Time and Money Saving Tip

If you are the sponsor and lack the experience and financial strength to qualify for a mortgage, don't get discouraged. You just need to bring in an investor who has commercial property ownership experience and is loaded to be a key principal on the loan with you. You are looking for a high-net-worth individual who is looking to diversify and invest some of their funds in investment real estate, but doesn't want the responsibility of being the sponsor or managing partner. You likely want to keep that control yourself. They will be much more willing to take on this role if you can arrange a *non-recourse loan* (see later in this Topic), in which case your investors will not have to personally guarantee the mortgage and put all their personal assets at risk.

Financing

guarantee. For non-recourse loans the managing partner signs everything. Lenders want key principals that have substantial financial strength and experience. Any sponsors or investors that are individually putting in most of the down payment will be required to be key principals by most lenders. This is because they know that investors who have the most skin in the game will take overseeing the success of the project the most seriously. If you are just investing in commercial property and do not want to be responsible for the loan, it's best if you own 20% or less. Otherwise, most lenders will require you to be a key principal.

Most lenders require the sponsor to be a key principal. This is especially the case if the sponsor wants to be the managing partner. As sponsor, if you lack the financial wherewithal or experience to qualify as a key principal on the loan, you will need to bring in one or more investors that can add the experience and financial strength needed. And they will have to agree to be key principals.

Land Acquisition Financing: *Banks have the best financing for land that has the potential to be developed*

Raw, unimproved, and unentitled land is not easy to finance. Fortunately, sellers will often carry the financing. It represents a substantial risk to a lender as it produces no income yet has expenses for taxes and some maintenance. The risk is greatest if the land is not zoned for commercial use. If you are planning to develop raw land, community banks have the best-quality financing, especially if the land is in their own backyard. They will understand and get excited about the land's potential for development much more than a lender that is located out of the area. Banks have the highest LTV for land at 65%, and can make the loan for three years—for stronger borrowers, up to five years. The loan is usually a monthly adjustable rate tied to prime rate with interest-only payments. Although most banks will want the rate to adjust monthly, see if you can negotiate with them to adjust the rate annually or fix the rate for up to three years. To qualify you will need to have good credit and the excess income from other sources to make the loan payments. A good business plan to develop the land will be a plus. Otherwise, there are some hard money lenders that do land loans at 50% LTV.

> ## Time and Money Saving Tip
>
> If you find a land parcel for sale that is just right for development and you would like to build on it but need to raise investors for the down payment, consider taking the seller on as a joint venture equity partner. If they have owned the land for three years or more lenders will give them current appraised value for it. This equity could be enough for a large portion or even all of your down payment on the project. The seller will need to subordinate their interest in the land to the lender. The land seller will own a percentage of the completed stabilized property plus a share of the proceeds from a sale. It is common to give the seller the same percentage of ownership as the value their land represents in the total project costs. Of course, this is negotiable.

Letter of Interest/Intent (LOI) (Lender): *Don't make the mistake of thinking this is a loan approval. It is only an indication of interest in making the loan by the lender*

This is a written offer for financing from a lender, which states the proposed interest rate and loan terms. It will state clearly that this is not a loan commitment. Quality lenders do not issue these without thoroughly analyzing the quality of the borrower and the property. If you are purchasing a commercial property, be sure to give a copy of the LOI to the seller. Often, LOIs promise more than loan commitments deliver. This is usually due to the loan officer not having analyzed the complete loan submission package or not having the LOI reviewed by whoever is going to approve the loan. See Chapter 11 on taking charge of your commercial loan.

> **Time and Money Saving Tip**
>
> Commercial mortgage brokers often issue letters of interest to borrowers. Although these can often accurately state the interest rate and loan terms, they are usually of little value. This is because as an intermediary, the broker has no authority to make the loan. So be sure to ask for a letter of interest written on the lender's letterhead. This has clout!

LIBOR (London Inter-Bank Offered Rate):
Rates tied to the LIBOR are used most often for short-term loans

The LIBOR is an index that many commercial loan programs use for their interest rates. Almost all mortgage rates are composed of an index plus a margin. The LIBOR is based on the value of the world's top and most stable five currencies—the US dollar, the euro, the British pound sterling, the Swiss franc, and the Japanese yen. Many adjustable rate commercial mortgages use the LIBOR as an index to determine their interest rates. Regional banks, private debt funds, and many bridge and construction lenders have their rates based on the LIBOR. In addition, most long-term fixed-rate lenders use it for the adjustable period of their loans.

> **Time and Money Saving Tip**
>
> Taking a short-term adjustable rate bridge or construction loan based on the LIBOR is considered safe for a year. But taking an adjustable rate perm loan that is based on the LIBOR can be risky. This is because the LIBOR has been known to steadily climb to unsafe levels. In January of 2004, the six-month LIBOR was at 1.21%. One year later, it hit 2.97%—an increase of 1.76%. Three years later, in January 2007, it climbed to 5.40%, an increase of 4.19%.

Loan Extension: *If you cannot pay off your loan at the bank when it matures, ask for an extension well in advance*

So, your bank loan on an apartment complex is maturing in three months. You have a buyer for the property so you certainly do not want to refinance it. But then the sale fails, and now your loan is maturing in two weeks. If you are faced with not being able to pay your loan by the balloon date, talk to the loan officer about getting an extension. This is an agreement whereby the lender gives you more time to pay it off. Without an extension, if you are even one day late on paying the loan off, you will be considered in default. This is much more serious than missing a loan payment, since your loan will be due and payable within an average of 30 days of missing the maturity date. Be sure to arrange enough time. Request a 60-day extension well in

Financing

advance of your maturity date. This is usually the maximum time allowed. I have seen commercial banks give two or three extensions totaling more than six months without an additional charge. As long as the borrower is in communication with the lender and has solid reasons for the delay, they can keep the bank regulators at bay. Hard money and private debt fund lenders usually charge exorbitant fees for each extension. Be sure to get the extension in writing, as this is a legal agreement.

Fannie Mae, Freddie Mac, CMBS, and HUD do not give extensions as a rule. These loans are sold as mortgage-backed security bonds and they have to give the investors their principal back once the loan matures. You might be able to buy about 30 days, but not much more. The only other alternative is to go through a costly *forbearance agreement* (see earlier in this Topic).

Lockout Prepayment Penalty: *Try to negotiate lockout prepayment penalties away*

A lockout prepayment penalty does exactly what it says: during the years there is a lockout you are not allowed to prepay the loan period. The lockout period is typically the first two to three years. You should never accept a lockout period on the loan longer than the first year. Lockouts are favorites of lenders that sell their loans on the secondary market. The more severe the prepayment penalty is, the more premium lenders can earn on the loan sale. When selling loans on the *secondary market* (see later in this Topic), I could earn an additional point if I could sell the borrower a prepayment penalty with a three-year lockout. Although the lender will tell you this is not negotiable, I assure you it is. The lender just has to lower their earnings a bit to get rid of it.

Market Size: *Primary, secondary, tertiary, and small markets—most of the best commercial loan programs only lend in primary and secondary markets*

No one really seems to agree on the maximum or minimum population a city has to have to be classified as a primary, secondary, or tertiary market. But in the commercial lending world, these classifications have a lot of impact. Primary markets are very large cities that are economically strong. Everyone agrees that New York, Los Angeles, Chicago, San Francisco, and Washington, DC belong in this group. It seems that the Dallas–Fort Worth metro area, with over seven million people, should be in this group too. But for some reason it is considered a secondary market.

Phoenix, Philadelphia, Seattle, Portland, Houston, San Antonio, San Diego, and San Jose, each with over one million residents, are considered secondary markets. Why do you need to know this? Because primary markets and secondary markets represent a much lower risk to lenders, and you should be able to negotiate a better deal if the property is located in one. Also, many of the country's best commercial loan programs, such as those offered by life companies and national banks, only lend in primary and secondary markets. Freddie Mac will roll out the red carpet and give you a 75% loan at a much lower interest rate in a primary market.

Tertiary markets are smaller population areas; usually under 500,000, but some experts say this should be under 250,000. These markets have smaller economies with little major industry and fewer jobs, and are considered higher risk by commercial lenders. Fannie Mae, Freddie Mac, HUD, CMBS lenders, and regional and community banks are happy to lend in these areas.

Lastly, you have small markets, which have populations under 250,000, and very small markets, with 100,000 or fewer. Community banks rule here. But Fannie Mae and HUD have no problem giving some of the lowest rate multifamily loans in these markets. Fannie will even go as low as a population of 10,000.

Mezzanine Debt: *This isn't really a loan, but an investment in the ownership of the property*

If you are looking to borrow up to 85% for a large transaction, you might be able to get there with mezzanine debt. Mezzanine debt is in second position after the first-position mortgage. Although many professionals refer to this as a mezzanine loan, it isn't really a loan. Most first-position mortgages do not allow secondary financing but some will allow mezzanine debt. This is because the mezzanine lender actually takes an ownership interest in the property to secure its investment. Mezzanine debt usually carries an average rate of 15% because of the high risk involved. This sounds really high, but because mezzanine debt usually only represents 10–15% of the *capital stack* (see earlier in this Topic), the rate is affordable when blended with the first mortgage. Mezzanine debt usually starts at $1,000,000 but can be lower, and it is most often issued by *private debt fund lenders* (see Encyclopedia Topic I, Commercial Loan Programs).

Mini-Perm Loan: *These are interim loans to bridge the gap between your construction and permanent loan*

If you are building an office, retail, industrial, or self-storage property that will take time to fill with tenants after completion, you might need a mini-perm loan. These temporary loans are usually written for two years and pay off your construction loan. This gives you time to put permanent financing on the property. All banks offer these and they can have either fixed or adjustable rate mortgages. Multifamily proper-ties usually achieve market occupancy quickly and rarely need mini-perm loans.

Multiple Residential Investment Property Loan: *You can finance from 5 to over 100 one- to four-unit residential rental properties with this*

Many commercial property owners own residential investment properties

> ### Time and Money Saving Tip
>
> Mini-perm loans can be expensive, with higher rates, loan fees, and closing expenses. To avoid having to use one on construction projects that have a long *absorption schedule* (see Encyclopedia Topic G, Development), consider getting your construction loan from a large bank, such as Wells Fargo, US Bank, or JPMorgan Chase.
>
> A large bank can write your construction loan for up to three years to give you plenty of time to fill it with good tenants after completion. Smaller banks are not usually able to do this and keep the regulators happy. But the ones that are financially strong can accomplish the same thing by giving you many extensions when your construction loan matures.

of one to four units as well. Figuring out a way to finance many of these can be diffi-cult. Because most banks mainly underwrite these loans to conform to standards set by Fannie Mae and Freddie Mac, they are limited in the number of properties that are owned by one owner they can lend to. Fortunately, there is a new alternative. You can take out a multiple residential CMBS loan. This is a blanket loan that allows for an unlimited number of residential properties. These loans require a minimum of five properties worth a minimum of $50,000 each. Loan amounts range from $500,000 to over $20,000,000. These loans have rates that average 1% higher than conforming residential loan rates (the best rates for an owner-occupied residence) and have fees of one to two points. You can fix the rate for either 5 or 10 years with a 30-year amortization. Best of all, these are *non-recourse loans* (see later in this Topic). CMBS loans are great for the self-employed that do not show much income on tax returns and cannot qualify at a bank. These loans do not require the submission of tax returns.

No Money Down Commercial Loan: *Sorry, but a 90% SBA loan is as good as it gets*

I thought about leaving this one blank as a joke. But because our firm gets requests for no money down loans so often, I'm including it. Sorry, but this loan does not exist. All legitimate lenders want borrowers to have some skin in the game. The only ones that advertise 100% commercial financing will take a deposit from you and then disappear. Even JV capital firms require the sponsor to have at least 10% of the equity from their own funds invested. HUD/FHA *multifamily loans* (see Encyclopedia Subject I, Commercial Loan Programs) can go up to 85%. SBA loans can go up to 90% LTV for owner-occupied commercial properties. For large commercial loans with strong borrowers, you can get a 70% first mortgage and include 15% mezzanine debt to get to 85% CLTV financing. And no lender will issue an 85% loan to someone that is going to be broke after closing.

Non-Recourse Loan: *It's just smart business to get one of these*

It's really just smart business to take out a non-recourse loan. A commercial investment property is a business and has similar risks. With a recourse loan the borrower has to sign a personal guarantee. Should the economy take a dive and you find yourself not being able to make mortgage payments, all of your personal assets could be at risk if there is a foreclosure.

A non-recourse loan does not have a personal guarantee. For that matter, the loan is not even made out to you, but instead to an ownership entity, such as an LLC. So if you default on the loan, it won't even affect your personal credit. All the lender can do is take the property back. Although this is painful, it is nothing compared to defaulting on a recourse loan. It that case, the lender can not only take the property, but can get a court judgment that allows it to go after you personally for any deficiency. And yes, they will tack on all late payments, attorney fees, and court costs.

Another great benefit of non-recourse lending is related to estate planning. All commercial loans have annual financial reporting requirements. With a recourse loan, after you pass on, your heirs will have to qualify under the same personal financial criteria as you did. If they do not show enough income on tax returns, the loan could be called due and payable. With a non-recourse loan, because the loan is made to the property, the property has to qualify after your death. As long as the net operating income can still support the minimum debt service coverage and the property is kept in good condition, your heirs will not be at risk of losing the loan.

Fannie Mae, Freddie Mac, and HUD multifamily are all non-recourse loans. CMBS loans, most life company loans, and private debt fund loans are also non-recourse.

Operating Budget Pro Forma: *Be sure to include this in your loan submission package*

Most lenders will require an operating budget or forecast of net operating income as part of underwriting requirements. This will usually be for two to three years following the closing of the loan. Using an Excel spreadsheet, simply show a month-by-month forecast of gross rental income and operating expenses. Be sure to show your net operating income going up over time. Use footnotes to explain rental increases and how you determined expenses. Lenders really do not like it when you do not *explain* how you determined these. You can find a sample of a seven-year operating budget pro forma (the Seven-Year Month-by-Month Budget and Summary Spreadsheet) in Appendix A and a downloadable Excel version on my website: https://apartmentloanstore.com.

Owner-Occupied Commercial Mortgage: *Borrow up to 90% with an SBA loan*

If you have a small business and are renting, think about buying a property to house your business. You can get a 90% SBA 7(a) loan and have the benefit of the real estate appreciating plus the tax savings from depreciation. In commercial lending, the term "owner occupied" refers to a commercial property that is occupied by the owner of a business who also owns the real estate. There are more owner-occupied properties in the United States than any other type of commercial property. These are community banks' favorite loans because the real estate supplies a surplus of collateral for all of the other loans that they make to a business. Banks prefer short-term variable rates, but for stronger borrowers these loans can be fixed on the real estate. SBA loans can lend up to 90% on new construction, rehab, purchase, or refinance of owner-occupied properties. It requires that the business occupy at least 51% of the property.

PACE Financing: *This gap financing can bring your total financing to 90% on green construction*

If you are planning on doing new construction or major rehab and building green and cutting the cost of energy and water, you should look into PACE financing. Actually, PACE financing isn't really a loan, since it is paid back through the subject property's property taxes. The funds have to be used as gap financing with your construction loan and can go up to 90% CLTV. PACE funds have to be paid back in 10–25 years, depending on the project. The downside is that you do not get the funds until you get your certificate of occupancy. PACE wants to make sure you complete the project before you get the money. So you have to have funds available to cover the deficit until the building is completed. Also, many lenders—especially banks—do not want you to leverage too high and will likely limit you to 80% CLTV, although private lenders may go to 85%. This is because having to pay back the PACE funding in the form of higher property taxes puts more stress on cash flow. Google "PACE financing" to find a fund in your area.

Poor-Credit Commercial Mortgages: *If you have poor credit, call a commercial mortgage broker to find the best loan for you*

If you have high credit card balances or low credit scores, or have experienced a bankruptcy or a foreclosure in the past 10 years, don't even try getting a commercial loan from a bank. Banks prefer credit scores of 720 and above. Occasionally they can go as low as 680, if you have a good explanation for derogatory marks that are four years or more behind you. As far as paying down credit card debt with the loan, forget it. Banks see high credit card debt as evidence that you manage your finances poorly. Why else would you pay over 16% interest?

Fortunately, there are plenty of commercial lending programs that will make loans to borrowers with unsavory credit. They will even allow you to pay off your credit card balances from loan proceeds. In exchange, they charge higher interest rates and fees. If your credit score is 540–660, commercial mortgage brokers have access to secondary market lenders that have rates priced 1.5–2% above bank rates. Rates are based on credit score. You can usually borrow 65–75% on these programs. (See Poor-Credit Secondary Market Loan in Encyclopedia Topic I, Commercial Loan Programs.) Otherwise, the only other choice for bad-credit borrowers is hard money. These lenders do not care about credit score as long as there is plenty of equity in the property. They have high rates—from 9% to 12% with two to four points. Most prefer lending at 65% or less.

Portfolio Loan: *You can negotiate a better deal if the lender is not planning to sell the loan*

You can often negotiate a better deal with a portfolio lender. A portfolio loan is held on the lender's books. It is lending its own money, and as long as it is exceeding its cost of funds plus cost to put a loan on the books, it can cut you a better deal. Lenders that sell their loans on the secondary market, such as regional banks, or securitized lenders such as Fannie Mae, Freddie Mac, HUD, and CMBS lenders, have more rigid guidelines to follow and more restrictions on profitability. All community bank loans are portfolio loans initially, but the bank may sell them off over time if it needs to raise capital. Credit unions only make portfolio loans and would never think about selling a loan. Ask your lender if it will be keeping your loan in its portfolio. If so, go for the jugular when negotiating rates and terms (see Chapter 10 on trade secrets of getting the best loan terms in the section Advice from an Insider on Negotiating with Lenders).

Private Debt Fund Lender: *These lenders are entrepreneurial and have lower requirements than a bank*

If you just need to get your commercial deal done and are getting the runaround from banks, try a *private debt fund lender* (see Encyclopedia Topic I, Commercial Loan Programs). They are entrepreneurial and if they like your deal will bend to finance it. They mostly do short-term loans, such as bridge and construction loans. But some can often give you a term of three to four years. They prefer larger primary and secondary markets (see earlier in this Topic under *market size*). They have higher rates than banks; usually the 30-day LIBOR plus 4–6%. Most loans are interest only. But if you have a strong deal and a good professional team, you can get your foot in the door with them.

Most of these lenders lend nationally; loans start at $3,000,000 and are non-recourse. The Securities and Exchange Commission (SEC) regulates them. Many larger debt fund lenders are publicly traded and raise money on Wall Street. Hedge fund managers run some of these. Most of the smaller ones raise funds from private *accredited investors* (see Encyclopedia Topic C, Raising Investor Partners).

Rate Lock and Rate-Lock Deposit: *It's really important that you lock the rate early*

See if you can find a loan program that will allow you to lock the rate at application. Smaller community banks do not charge a rate lock deposit, so press them to lock the rate at application. Some will want to wait until loan approval just to see where rates go. Commercial loans that rate lock at loan approval—or even worse, when loan documents are drawn—create a lot of uncertainty for borrowers and lenders. Both benefit equally when rates are locked early. Borrowers sleep better at night not having to worry about interest rates going up. Lenders worry less knowing that the rate will not climb high enough to kill the loan before it can be locked.

Many lenders require a refundable rate-lock deposit of 1% of the loan amount to lock the rate. If a deposit is required, this is not negotiable. The truth about regional and large banks that have an abundance of their own money to lend from deposits is that when they require a rate lock deposit they are really just collecting an additional deposit to make sure you do not back out of the loan. For banks that are borrowing on short-term variable rates, they need to collect a rate lock deposit to enter into a long-term interest rate swap (see *swap rates* further in this section) to guarantee you a long-term fixed rate. Just like with Fannie Mae, Freddie Mac, and HUD lenders, this deposit is the only way they can safely lock the rate, by entering into an interest rate swap with US Treasury bond traders. They can then give the borrower a fixed rate that is not at risk of changing. All lenders that collect this deposit will refund it at closing as long as you do not change your mind about taking the loan. All securitized lenders place a hedge to guarantee the rate, and should you not take the loan and rates go in the wrong direction, they will lose money and pass that loss on to you.

Rehab Loan (Best Programs): *This great selection has something for every rehab deal*

Community banks. Community banks love rehab deals and actually have the best rates and terms for them. For light rehab, these loans go up to 75% of cost and are priced as perm loans right out of the gate. For major rehab, they are more often priced like construction loans at prime plus 1–2%. This cost is much lower than what you'd pay using a bridge lender. You do need to have good credit and income showing on tax returns. Net worth and post-closing cash can be minimal.

Ready for Freddie. For multifamily properties, this is a low-rate, low-cost bridge rehab loan program that can lend in primary and secondary markets. Once the rehab is completed and the property is stabilized at 90% occupancy, the loan rolls over to a 5- to 10-year fixed Freddie Mac permanent loan. Check with Freddie lenders to find the ones that have this bridge loan program.

Financing

HUD 223(f) or 232 for multifamily and healthcare. These programs are for light rehab of apartment buildings, senior housing, assisted living, and nursing homes. If you are planning to keep a property for a long time after renovating it, this program cannot be beat. You can borrow up to 85% of the transaction costs for a purchase (this includes purchase price plus renovations and closing costs). The best part is that you end up with a very low, 35-year fixed-rate fully amortizing non-recourse loan. Renovations cannot be more than 15% of the appraised value after completion. No tax returns are needed. The disadvantage of this loan program is the six months-plus that it takes to close.

Soft money bridge loan. Bridge loans are made for commercial rehabilitation projects and prices have come down due to the large number of these lenders competing. The best of these programs lend at 75% of completed stabilized value, which can easily be 80% of cost. With terms of up to two years, these loans are priced at 7–9% and some lenders will allow you to fix the rate. The best news is you do not have to have perfect credit or a strong net worth, just a solid project in a good neighborhood with lots of potential and a good contractor.

Replacement Reserves: *This is an escrow account you contribute to monthly for repairs*

Replacement reserves—or the amount many securitized lenders collect monthly with the mortgage payment for future major repairs—are annoying for most borrowers. But why not think of this reserve as a forced rainy day fund? Let's face it, the lender owns more of the property then you do. It just wants to make sure that its asset is kept in good condition. Based on the age and physical condition of the property, replacement reserves run $150–400 per unit per year for multifamily properties and 15–40 cents per square foot per year for office, retail, and industrial properties.

Time and Money Saving Tip

If you are taking out a bridge loan for rehabbing a property and the property's income cannot make the loan payments, be sure to insist that the lender put the construction interest into a payment reserve and have it financed with all the other project costs. Many lenders will want you to make the loan payments from other sources of income or your savings. Even if they tell you they have a policy against financing a payment reserve, I have found them to bend if you tell them you will have to walk away.

Time and Money Saving Tip

Are replacement reserves negotiable? The lender will tell you no out of the gate, but with the exception of HUD loans, the answer is yes. If the LTV is at 65% or below and you have strong net worth and liquidity, you can often bargain with the lender to remove this requirement. You are showing them you have the means to take good care of the property even during an economic downturn. If this doesn't work, show the lender some pics of another commercial property you own that is being maintained in very good condition. This is evidence that you take great care of your properties and do not need to be mothered.

Financing

How do replacement reserves work? Let's say one month you replace a hot water heater and stripe the parking lot. You pay for these and then submit the receipt to the lender. About a month later you'll get reimbursed from your replacement reserve escrow account. Banks do not typically collect a replacement reserve. The lenders that do are Fannie Mae and Freddie Mac (on large loans of over $6,000,000), HUD, CMBS lenders, and life companies.

Second Mortgage/Subordinate Loan: *Most first-position mortgages won't allow a second mortgage*

Since the Great Recession, the number of commercial lenders willing to carry a second-position mortgage has gone way down. Often we get requests for financing from a buyer who has a seller willing to carry 10–15% in second position. But this is considered taboo these days. With the exception of private debt funds and hard money lenders, most first-position lenders will not allow secondary financing—including owner-carry seconds—on commercial loans.

This is for two reasons. One, it puts their investment more at risk if the borrower is highly leveraged. Two, they do not want the second mortgage to foreclose should there be a default on that loan. First-position lenders require an intercreditor agreement that prohibits the second mortgage from taking action against the borrower should they be in default. Commercial banks will sometimes allow a second if they make the loan. SBA loans permit a seller-carry second mortgage. And on large loans, Fannie Mae, Freddie Mac, CMBS lenders, and life companies will often allow *mezzanine debt* (see earlier in this Topic) behind their first mortgage, but this is not really a loan.

> ### Time and Money Saving Tip
>
> If you have a bank, credit union, life company, or securitized loan like Fannie Mae, and you are thinking about taking cash out by adding a second mortgage, STOP. Read your mortgage note and you will find that if you put any kind of second-position loan against the property, you will be in default. This is much more serious than skipping a few mortgage payments, and if your first-position lender finds out, your loan will most certainly be called due.
>
> Strange, but this is something you can get away with until you are caught. Title companies do not check first-position mortgage notes to make sure secondary financing is allowed, and will gladly record a second at any time. How a first-position lender finds out there is a second mortgage is when the second lienholder wants to be listed as co-insured on the casualty insurance policy, and all lenders are listed together.

Secondary Market: *Is your commercial loan being sold?*

When a commercial loan is first originated, the lender has a choice to either keep it in its portfolio (on its books) or sell it on the secondary market. Most of a mortgage payment goes toward interest for the first 16 years, so many lenders, especially banks, would never want to give this income up. But other lenders prefer to make a quick buck and sell the loan. Most commercial loans can be sold at a three to four point premium, so this is not small potatoes. And the guaranteed portion of an SBA loan backed by the high credit rating of the US government can be sold for up to 10 points profit. Now that's a whole sack of potatoes! Most commercial lenders opt to service the loans they sell. They can earn up to another point, but more importantly, take good care of the borrower so they will get another loan from them in the future.

Fannie Mae and Freddie Mac purchase a vast amount of multifamily loans on the secondary market. Fannie Mae, Freddie Mac, HUD, and CMBS loans are sold as mortgage-backed securities, which is also a form of the secondary market.

> **Time and Money Saving Tip**
>
> Ask your lender if it will be keeping the loan in its portfolio or selling it. They might not tell you so you might have to be a sleuth to find out. If the lender is selling it, and your loan is going to be at 65% LTV or lower, they will earn a higher premium.
>
> They can also earn more by raising your rate. This is an opportunity for you to negotiate a lower interest rate or loan fee. Why not put this money in your pocket.

Self-Directed IRA Commercial Loan: *Your IRA will have two sources of income when it's invested in commercial real estate*

Did you know that you can invest your IRA funds or a portion of them in commercial real estate? And if you are raising investors, that they can also invest their IRAs in the property you are buying? The loan has to be lower leverage (55–60% LTV) and non-recourse. Your IRA will own the property, not you. Most lenders prefer to do this with multifamily properties since they are lower risk. The main advantage is diversification, and the fact that your investment will have two sources of income: (1) from real estate operations, and (2) from appreciation when the property sells.

All expenses for the property have to be paid out of your IRA, and all real estate income has to be returned to your IRA. This income can then go on to earn income in the stock or bond market. One negative is that the income earned by the percentage of the real estate investment that is represented by the loan will be taxable. If you do this with a Roth IRA you have already paid the taxes so this is not an issue. To find lenders that make loans to self-directed IRAs, simply google "self-directed IRA commercial loan."

Springing Lock Box: *On CMBS loans, this gives the lender control of the property's money if you are in default*

Well, this doesn't sound very good, does it? This is a feature that commercial mortgage-backed security (CMBS) loans have to make them bulletproof for the lender.

Here's how a springing lock box works: All rents are deposited by renters into an account controlled by the lender. As long as there are no defaults on the mortgage, the funds are immediately swept into the owner's operating account for the property. If there is a default, the first account springs shut. Ouch! Now the lender has control of your money. The lender will pay the mortgage itself first and then dole out some money for the property's expenses. If you have a good reason for the default, once the default is cured the lock box will open again and you should be able to operate as before.

Why does a springing lock box exist? It is easier for lower net worth and liquidity borrowers to qualify for a CMBS loan because of this feature. Is this negotiable? The answer is yes, for higher net worth borrowers with plenty of cash.

Stated Income Commercial Loan: *There are many commercial loans that do not collect taxes or look at personal income. These are similar to a stated income loan*

There is really no such thing as a stated income commercial loan. I have included this just because borrowers ask about this, and some poor-credit lenders sell their loans under this heading. The term "stated income loan" comes from the days prior to the Great Recession when you could put whatever you wanted as your income on a subprime loan application, knowing the lender was not going to verify it. The good news is that there are plenty of commercial mortgage lenders that do not use personal income to qualify borrowers and do not collect tax returns. This is pretty close to a stated income mortgage. These lenders are Fannie Mae, Freddie Mac, and HUD for multifamily properties, and CMBS lenders for most other commercial property types.

Supplemental Financing: *Fannie and Freddie may be able to do a second mortgage for you after a year*

Both Fannie Mae and Freddie Mac will not allow a second mortgage from another lender at any time. But both have what they call supplemental financing for apartment properties. Starting 12 months after the loan has closed, they will give you a second *coterminous* (see earlier in this Topic) mortgage that goes up to 75% of the appraised value of the property. The great advantage is if you want to pull cash out of the property in the future but do not want to have to refinance your low-rate first mortgage, you can apply for a coterminous mortgage. The downside is that most Fannie and Freddie lenders will not make supplemental loans of under $500,000. So this type of loan usually only works for higher-value properties of $3,000,000 and above.

Swap Rate: *Some commercial lenders will quote you a rate tied to swap rates. So what is a swap rate?*

If you are applying for a long-term, fixed-rate commercial mortgage, ask your lender if it will be using swap rates to determine your interest rate. If this is during an environment where rates are going up, you could be in a great position to negotiate a better rate than quoted. I will explain this in a moment. Lenders that use swap rates do this to eliminate the uncertainty of issuing a fixed-rate mortgage today when rates might go up in the near future. Many large banks tie their commercial mortgage rates to swap rates. This is the safest way for them to lower their risk when offering long-term fixed rates when the profitability of lending their funds is based on floating rates.

In interest rate swaps, the lender is trading a variable rate for a fixed rate for a set duration—usually 3, 5, 7, or 10 years. The receiver (the lender) has to pay the payer a fee for changing the floating rate to a fixed rate. A lender will pass this fee on to the borrower in additional mortgage interest.

Here's an insider secret: Based on which direction rates go, the lender can make additional money on the rate they sell you. If you are taking out a loan at a time when rates are going up, the lender that is quoting a rate tied to swap rates will earn more on the rate than on the rack rates they quoted you. This is the right time for you to put some of this money in your pocket by negotiating a lower rate.

Tax and Insurance Escrow/Impound: *Do you really want to pay taxes and insurance payments in advance with your mortgage payments?*

Tax and insurance impounds are common in commercial lending. This eliminates the lender's risk of the borrower piling debt on the property by not paying the taxes when due or putting the property at risk by not insuring it. Lenders that sell their loans on the secondary market always require these impounds. This makes the loans easier to sell. If you want to control your money for taxes and insurance instead of the lender, community banks often do not require impounds. For all other lenders that do require them, if your loan is at 65% LTV or lower and you have plenty of liquidity, you can often negotiate to have this requirement removed. If you need to borrow more than this and have always paid your property taxes on time, then stand your ground and fight with the lender over this.

Third-Party Report: *Ask you lender to shop competitively for these*

"Third-party reports" in commercial real estate refer to the following reports: appraisal, feasibility study, environmental, property condition, wood-boring insects, and seismic. The borrower is responsible for paying for these. Lenders collect a deposit for these reports prior to starting the loan. Most lenders are honest and will charge you their actual cost, but sometimes at loan application they collect more for these reports than they were charged, sometimes by mistake. To be absolutely sure you are not over-paying, ask the lender for a copy of the vendor invoices prior to closing. To get the cost down, ask you lender to shop competitively for these reports. Some lenders have their favorite vendors and always try to engage them first.

Underwriting Interest Rate: *Is your lender stressing the rate?*

I have had borrowers who are good at crunching the numbers tell me they think I made a mistake and should be able to lend them more money. This usually occurs because the interest rate was stressed with a higher underwriting rate when calculating their maximum loan. Be sure to ask your lender what its underwriting rate is for your loan. This way you can determine if the NOI of the property will be sufficient for the size loan you want. Most commercial mortgages have an underwriting interest rate that is higher than the actual rate. This is known as "stressing the rate."

For example: If you get a 10-year fixed Fannie Mae loan with an actual rate of 4.75%, to qualify the property income the lender will underwrite to 5.25%. It is not unusual for a bank to stress the rate a full percentage point higher than where rates actually are. This often lowers the loan proceeds. Lenders do this because they are concerned that if rates go up and property values come down once the loan matures (the average maturity period is 10 years), the principal balance will be too high to be refinanced.

Upfront Fee: *You shouldn't have to pay a lender an upfront fee to evaluate your loan*

Be wary of lenders who charge you a nonrefundable due diligence fee at loan application to analyze the loan for financing. This is not standard practice. It is considered part of a lender's job to evaluate the borrower and the property for financing at the beginning. Many of these lenders make most or all of their income from these fees and seldom close loans. The cost can be $5,000–30,000 or more and is called an "upfront fee." Most do this legally because they have you sign a disclaimer stating that you are aware that you are paying for the lender's due diligence and you might not qualify for a loan. Well, it's very easy to come up with some reason why you do not qualify.

Often mortgage brokers that are pretending to be lenders engage in this practice. It is normal and expected for a lender to charge a refundable-at-closing loan deposit at application to cover the cost of the *third party reports* (earlier in this section) and its site visit. There are some legitimate lenders that charge upfront fees. Before deciding to move forward with a lender that is charging one, be sure to google "reviews" or "fraud" with the lender's company name. Or go to ripoffreport.com to see if it has had complaints. Do the same with the owner's and the originator's name.

Wraparound Mortgage: *The buyer's ownership of the property is not secure if the seller wraps their mortgage*

It sure can be tempting to have the seller of a commercial property sell you the property on an owner-carry and just continue to make their existing loan payments. This is called a wraparound mortgage. They most often occur when distressed properties are sold. Most of these sellers have had little motivation to manage and maintain the property. They are motived to do a wraparound because they can get a better price for the property this way. The buyer usually puts very little down.

Although common, a wraparound mortgage is not a legal way to finance a property. This is because the seller's lender will have a clause in the loan documents prohibiting this. The problem for the buyer is that the owner-carry second mortgage that is wrapping around the seller's mortgage is not recorded. This means that if the seller's lender finds out, the loan will be in default and it will call the loan due and payable. And you will be left out in the cold. Quite often the lender will find out when they do an inspection of the property or from insurance agents sending out notifications. If the lender does not find out, you can get away with it. At some future date you can buy the property legally with another loan.

Yield Maintenance Prepayment Penalty: *This is a good prepayment penalty if you know you are going to keep the loan until it matures*

So you are taking out a commercial loan and you are told that the prepayment penalty is yield maintenance. What is this, you ask the lender? After listening for five minutes, the lender seems as confused as you are. Why is it that no one, not even the lender, can give you an explanation of yield maintenance that lets you finally say to yourself, "Okay, I get it!"

If you decide to prepay your loan early before it matures, yield maintenance is a mathematical equation that is designed to give the lender the same return on its loan as if you made all the payments until the loan matured. If Treasury yields go down at the time you prepay the mortgage, the lender will realize a loss and pass this loss on to you as a steep prepayment penalty. If they go up enough, the lender can make money by replacing the investment with bonds that have a higher yield. If this happens it will charge you a 1% prepayment penalty fee. So this can be a pretty good prepayment

Financing

penalty if rates go up and you prepay during the second half of the loan maturing. Also, loans that have yield maintenance are usually a good deal lower in rate than declining prepayment penalty loans.

I have made many loans with yield maintenance. When rates have gone up under ideal circumstances borrowers who prepaid prior to their loan maturing loved this prepayment penalty. Borrowers who were caught at the other end and needed to prepay when rates went down hated their yield maintenance, and they hated me. So my advice is to not take a loan with yield maintenance unless you know you are going to keep the loan until maturity.

Simplified equation of yield maintenance is calculated:

Yield maintenance = Present value of remaining payments on the mortgage

× (Your interest rate–Current Treasury yield)

Note that the Treasury yield should be for the bonds of the same duration as your mortgage rate was tied to. So if you took out a 10-year fixed-rate loan, you should use the current 10-year Treasury yield.

Commercial Loan Programs

Listed here are some of the most popular commercial loan programs in the United States and their guidelines. Loan sizes range from $75,000 at a local credit union to $250,000,000 at a large bank capital division. Be sure to check the requirements for borrowers for the loan programs you are interested in to see if you qualify. For daily commercial mortgage rates you can visit my websites—for multifamily rates go to https://apartmentloanstore.com and for all other commercial property rates go to https://businessloanstore.com.

Commercial Mortgage-Backed Security (CMBS) Loans: *Get a low 10-year fixed at a lower rate than what most banks have for their five-year fixed loan programs*

These non-recourse loans have competitive 5- and 10-year fixed rates and can do a blanket loan to include multiple properties. Lenders close with their own funds and then sell the loans in securitized pools as mortgage-backed security bonds.

Acceptable Property Types: Multifamily, mixed use, senior housing, student housing, mobile home parks, self-storage, industrial, hotels, office, and retail.

Types of Loans: Permanent loans only

Program Guidelines and Requirements

- Loan size: $2,000,000–50,000,000
- LTV: 75% with cash out
- 25–30 year amortization
- Nonrecourse
- 5- or 10-year fixed rates/term
- Tax returns not required
- No global or debt to income ratio
- No ground-up construction
- Loan fee: 1%
- Primary and secondary markets preferred
- 675 minimum credit score
- Minimum net worth negotiable
- Post-closing cash negotiable

- 1.25–1.35 minimum DSCR
- Yield maintenance or defeasance prepayment penalty
- Occupancy required: 85%, or market occupancy
- Assumable with a 1% fee
- Interest-only available
- Rate lock at loan approval
- Refundable rate-lock deposit required

Community Banks: *If you don't have a high net worth or experience but have solid income, this is where you will qualify*

These are small banks that make loans in their own backyard. They have low requirements for net worth and liquidity, but require good income and credit. Most are not fond of cash-out refinancing.

> **Acceptable Property Types:** Multifamily, mixed use, senior housing, student housing, mobile home parks, self-storage, industrial, hotels, office, retail, business owner-occupied, and land
>
> **Types of Loans:** Permanent, construction, rehabilitation, mini-perm, and credit lines

Program Guidelines and Requirements

- Loan size: $150,000–$6,000,000
- LTV: 75%; 65% with cash out
- 25-year amortization
- Recourse
- 3–5 year fixed rates
- 10-year term
- Tax returns required
- Global ratio and debt to income ratio
- Loan fee: 1.00%
- Lend in local market
- 680 minimum credit score
- Minimum net worth: negotiable
- Post-closing cash: negotiable
- 1.25–1.40 minimum DSCR
- Declining prepayment penalty
- Occupancy required: 85%, or market occupancy
- Assumable: no
- Interest-only: no
- Rate lock at loan approval or documents
- Refundable rate-lock deposit: no

Credit Unions: *If you have strong personal income and don't want a prepayment penalty, this is the place to shop*

Credit unions make loans to members who live nearby. They are nonprofit and can be very competitive on rates and loan fees. They are known for not having prepayment penalties.

Acceptable Property Types: Multifamily, mixed use, senior housing, student housing, mobile home parks, self-storage, industrial, hotels, office, retail, business owner-occupied, and land

Types of Loans: Permanent, rehabilitation, construction, and credit lines

Program Guidelines and Requirements

- Loan size: $75,000–15,000,000
- LTV: 75%; 65% with cash out
- 25-year amortization
- Recourse
- 3–10 year fixed rates
- 10-year term
- Tax returns: required
- Global ratio: required
- Loan fee: 1.00%
- Most lend in local markets
- Borrower required to join the credit union
- 675 minimum credit score
- Minimum net worth: negotiable
- Post-closing cash: negotiable
- 1.25 minimum DSCR
- Usually no prepayment penalty
- Occupancy required: 85%
- Assumable: no
- Interest-only: no
- Rate lock at loan application
- Refundable rate-lock deposit: no

Crowdfunding Loans: *If you only have 10% to put down, this can work here. But be careful. These lenders will want a preferred return and most of the ownership*

These loans can fund quickly in two or three weeks and are easier to qualify for than bank loans. Crowdfunding platforms are lenders that allow investors to invest in larger properties by pooling their money with other investors. Investors choose the properties they want to invest in, so be wary; sometimes they change their mind prior to closing and the crowdfunder has to find a replacement.

Acceptable Property Types: Multifamily, mixed use, senior housing, student housing, self-storage, and industrial

Types of Loans: Short-term, bridge/rehabilitation, and construction

Program Guidelines and Requirements

- Loan size: $250,000–12,000,000
- LTV: 75–80%
- Up to 80% cost of construction
- Interest-only
- Recourse
- 1–3 year term
- Tax returns: required
- Loan fee: 2–3%
- 640 minimum credit score
- Minimum net worth: negotiable
- Post-closing cash: negotiable
- 1.00–1.25 minimum DSCR
- 6–12 months prepayment penalty
- Assumable: no
- Primary, secondary, and small markets
- Experience a plus

Fannie Mae Multifamily Loans: *These low-rate non-recourse loans can be fixed for up to 30 years*

Fannie Mae, short for Federal National Mortgage Association, is a government-sponsored enterprise (GSE) and has some of the lowest rates and best terms around for apartment properties of five units or more. Rates can be fixed from 5 to 30 years. Fannie Mae does not actually originate loans, but is a publicly traded corporation that guarantees and securitizes them to be sold as mortgage-backed security bonds. Authorized lenders close with their own funds and then sell the loans to Fannie Mae.

Acceptable Property Types: Multifamily, senior housing, student housing, and mobile home parks

Types of Loans: Permanent loans only

Program Guidelines and Requirements

- Loan size: $1,000,000—unlimited
- LTV: 80%, 75% with cash out
- 30-year amortization
- Non-recourse available
- 5–30 year fixed rates/term
- No tax returns
- No global or debt to income ratio
- No ground-up construction
- Loan fee: 0.50–1.00%

- 680 minimum credit score
- Lend in any size market
- Minimum net worth equal to loan amount
- Post-closing cash: 12 months' loan payments
- 1.25 minimum DSCR
- 35% commercial space allowed
- Yield maintenance prepayment penalty
- 90% occupancy required for 90 days
- Affordable housing programs
- Assumable with a 1.00% fee
- Interest-only available
- Rate lock at loan approval
- Refundable rate-lock deposit required

Freddie Mac Multifamily Loans: *Non-recourse, low rates, and full-term interest only*

Freddie Mac is a GSE that securitizes loans from their approved lenders. These are put into mortgage pools and sold to investors as mortgage-backed security bonds on Wall Street.

Acceptable Property Types: Multifamily, senior housing, and student housing

Types of Loans: Permanent loans only

Program Guidelines and Requirements

- Loan size: $1,000,000–50,000,000
- LTV: 75% with cash out
- 30-year amortization
- Non-recourse available
- 5- or 10-year fixed rates
- 5–20 year term
- No tax returns
- No global or debt-to-income ratio
- No ground-up construction
- Loan fee: 0.50–1.00%
- Higher rates for smaller markets
- 660 minimum credit score
- Minimum net worth equal to loan amount
- Post-closing cash: 12 months' loan payments
- 1.20–1.25 minimum DSCR
- 35% commercial space allowed
- Yield maintenance or declining prepayment penalty

- 90% occupancy required for 90 days
- Affordable housing programs
- Assumable with a 1% fee
- Interest-only available
- Rate lock at application

Hard Money Bridge and Construction Loans: *These are expensive loans, but do not require great credit and net worth; they are fast and for many projects they pencil*

Poor credit and low net worth are usually acceptable. These lenders can close very quickly. It's much better to use a hard money lender that gets their funding from a warehouse line of credit than from small private investors who can change their minds prior to closing.

> **Acceptable Property Types:** Multifamily, mixed use, senior housing, student housing, mobile home parks, self-storage, industrial, hotels, office, retail, business owner-occupied, and land
>
> **Types of Loans:** Construction, rehabilitation/bridge

Program Guidelines and Requirements
- Loan size: $750,000–25,000,000
- LTV: 65–75%
- Up to 75% of cost of construction
- Interest-only
- Recourse and non-recourse
- 1–2 year term
- Tax returns: not required
- Global ratio: no
- No minimum credit score
- Net worth requirement: minimal
- Post-closing cash: minimal
- 6–12 months prepayment penalty
- Post-closing cash: negotiable
- Debt service ratio: 1.00 or less
- Assumable: no

HUD/FHA Multifamily and Healthcare: *Being able to fix a low rate for 35 years makes this government loan program very attractive*

The US Department of Housing and Urban Development (HUD) guarantees loans made from its approved lenders that are sold as the highest rated mortgage-backed security bonds on Wall Street.

> **Acceptable Property Types:** Multifamily, mixed use, senior housing, senior healthcare, and hospitals

Commercial Loan Programs

Types of Loans: Permanent loans for refinance, acquisition, and rehabilitation; also construction rollover to permanent loans

Permanent Loan Guidelines and Requirements

- Loan size: $2,000,000–100,000,000 plus
- LTV: 85%; 80% with cash out
- 35-year amortization
- Non-recourse
- 35-year fixed rates
- 35-year term
- No tax returns
- No global or debt to income ratio
- 25% commercial space of total sf
- Loan fee: 1.5%
- HUD fee: 0.30%
- Mortgage insurance: 0.25–1.00%
- Prior similar property ownership experience needed
- Primary, secondary, and small markets okay
- Good credit required with no specific score
- No minimum net worth requirement
- Post-closing cash required not specified
- 1.176 minimum DSCR for market rents
- 1.15 minimum DSCR for affordable housing
- Declining prepayment penalty
- 90% occupancy required for 90 days
- Affordable housing programs
- Assumable with a 0.50% fee
- Interest-only not available
- Rate lock at loan approval with a ½-point refundable deposit
- Minimum six months for loan approval

Construction and Major Rehabilitation Guidelines and Requirements

- Loan size: $5,000,000–100,000,000 plus
- LTV: 85% of cost
- 40-year amortization
- Non-recourse
- 40-year fixed rates
- 40-year term
- No tax returns
- No global or debt to income ratio
- 25% commercial space of total sf
- Loan fee: 2.00%
- HUD fee: 0.70%

Commercial Loan Programs

- Mortgage insurance: 0.25–0.70%
- Prior development experience required
- Primary, secondary, and small markets okay
- Good credit required with no specific score
- No minimum net worth requirement
- Post-closing cash required not specified
- 1.176 minimum DSCR for market rents
- 1.15 minimum DSCR for affordable housing
- Declining prepayment penalty
- Affordable housing programs
- Assumable with a 0.50% fee
- Interest-only not available
- Rate lock at loan approval
- Minimum six months for loan approval
- Refundable rate-lock deposit required with a ½-point refundable deposit

Large Commercial Banks: *If you are a high-net-worth experienced borrower, have large deposits with the bank, and are competing, they will break the bank to give you the lowest rate*

These are banks such as Chase, Bank of America, Bank of the Ozarks, and Wells Fargo. They can lend very large amounts in larger cities nationally. They have higher net worth, liquidity, and experience requirements than regional banks. Because they have so much of their own money to lend they can be very competitive on rates and fees.

Acceptable Property Types: Multifamily, mixed use, senior housing, student housing, mobile home parks, self-storage, industrial, hotels, office, retail, business owner-occupied, and land

Types of Loans: Permanent, construction, rehabilitation, mini-perm, and credit lines

Program Guidelines and Requirements
- Loan size: $250,000–75,000,000
- LTV: 75%; 70% with cash out
- 25- or 30-year amortization
- Recourse
- 3-, 5-, 7-, 10-year fixed rates
- 10-year term
- Tax returns: required
- Global ratio: required
- Loan fee: 1%
- Primary, secondary, and small markets
- 700 minimum credit score

- Minimum net worth: equal to loan size
- Post-closing cash: 10–15% of loan amount
- 1.25–1.35 minimum DSCR
- Yield maintenance or declining prepayment penalty
- Occupancy required: 85%, or market occupancy
- Assumable: no
- Interest-only: no
- Rate lock at loan approval
- Refundable rate-lock deposit: no

Life Companies: *They prefer low LTVs, strong borrowers, and large cities. But they have the very lowest long-term fixed rates*

These large insurance companies have capital divisions that lend on commercial real estate. They prefer lending at 65% LTV or less, and have very low rates that can be locked for up to 25 years. They prefer large cities and financially strong, experienced borrowers. Life companies lend their own money, with many doing CMBS executions.

Acceptable Property Types: Multifamily, senior housing, student housing, mixed use, office, retail, industrial, and hotel

Types of Loans: Permanent, bridge, and construction loans

Program Guidelines and Requirements
- Loan size: $10,000,000–150,000,000 plus
- LTV: 70%
- 25–30 year amortization
- Non-recourse
- 5–25 year fixed rates
- 5–25 year term
- Tax returns required
- No global or debt-to-income ratio
- Strong borrower experience required
- Loan fee: 1%
- Primary and secondary markets
- 720 minimum credit score
- Minimum net worth equal to 1.5 times loan amount
- Post-closing cash: 20% of loan amount
- 1.25 minimum DSCR
- Yield maintenance prepayment penalty
- 90% occupancy required
- Assumable with a 1% fee
- Interest-only available
- Rate lock at loan approval
- Refundable rate-lock deposit required

Commercial Loan Programs

National Bank Capital Divisions: *Loan size is not a problem here—and they have the lowest construction loan rates for strong, experienced developers*

These subsidiaries of large banks such as JPMorgan Chase, Bank of America, Wells Fargo, and Citigroup have the best loan programs for stronger, experienced borrowers. Along with lending their own money, many can do Fannie Mae, HUD, and CMBS lending.

> **Acceptable Property Types:** Multifamily, mixed use, senior housing, student housing, mobile home parks, self-storage, industrial, office, and retail
>
> **Types of Loans:** Permanent, construction, and rehabilitation

Program Guidelines and Requirements

- Loan size: $10,000,000–250,000,000
- LTV: 70%
- 25- or 30-year amortization
- Recourse or non-recourse considered
- 5-, 7-, 10-year fixed rates
- 10-year term
- Tax returns required
- Global ratio and debt to income ratio: required
- Loan fee: 1%
- Primary markets preferred
- 720 minimum credit score
- Minimum net worth of twice the loan's size
- Post-closing cash: 25% of loan size
- 1.20–1.25 minimum DSCR
- Yield maintenance prepayment penalty
- Occupancy required: 90%
- Assumable: no
- Interest-only: no
- Rate lock at loan approval or documents
- Refundable rate-lock deposit: no

Poor-Credit Secondary Market Loans: *Yes, rates are high, but if you have bad credit get your project funded here and work on building a high credit score*

If your credit is less than perfect, these loan programs have much better rates and terms than hard money lenders. Commercial mortgage brokers specialize in these loans.

> **Acceptable Property Types:** Multifamily, mixed use, senior housing, student housing, self-storage, and industrial, hotels, office, and retail
>
> **Types of Loans:** Permanent and bridge loans

Program Guidelines and Requirements

- Loan size: $500,000–6,000,000
- LTV: 70% with cash out
- 25- or 30-year amortization
- Non-recourse
- 2–5 year term
- Tax returns: not required
- Loan fee: 1–2%
- Rates based on credit score
- 540 minimum credit score
- Minimum net worth: negotiable
- Post-closing cash: negotiable
- 1.25 minimum DSCR
- Declining prepayment penalty
- Assumable: no
- Primary and secondary markets

Private Debt Funds: *If you are getting turned down at banks and have a strong deal, this is the place to get your loan. They have simple make-sense underwriting*

These are private lenders that are regulated by the SEC. They pool money from investors and lend it at moderate to moderately high rates on commercial real estate. Loans are made more on the strength of the property than on the borrower. Commercial mortgage brokers specialize in these loans.

> **Acceptable Property Types:** Multifamily, mixed use, senior housing, student housing, self-storage, industrial, hotels, office, and retail
>
> **Types of Loans:** Construction, bridge/rehabilitation

Program Guidelines and Requirements

- Loan size: $3,000,000–75,000,000
- LTV: 75% with cash out
- Up to 80% cost of construction
- Interest-only
- Non-recourse
- 1–4 year term
- Tax returns: required
- Loan fee: 2–3%
- 640 minimum credit score
- Minimum net worth: negotiable
- Post-closing cash: negotiable
- 1.00–1.20 minimum DSCR

- 6–12 months prepayment penalty
- Assumable: no
- Primary and secondary markets

Regional Bank Income Property Divisions: *You can get a low 3-to-10-year fixed rate and lock the rate immediately at application*

These lenders are capital divisions of banks and lend in the larger cities in the states they are located in; some lend in neighboring states as well. They generally have lower rates than community banks, can fix a rate for up to 10 years, and can lend larger amounts. Many sell their loans on the secondary market. They have higher net worth and cash requirements than community banks, but some of the lowest rates.

Acceptable Property Types: Multifamily, mixed use, industrial, office, hospitality, and retail

Types of Loans: Permanent loans only

Program Guidelines and Requirements

- Loan size: $1,000,000–15,000,000
- LTV: 75% with cash out
- 30-year amortization multifamily
- 25-year amortization commercial
- Recourse
- 3-, 5-, 7-, 10-year fixed rates
- 25- or 30-year term
- Tax returns: required
- Global ratio: required
- Primary and secondary markets preferred
- Loan fee: 1%
- 680 minimum credit score
- Minimum net worth equal to loan amount
- Post-closing cash: 12 months' loan payments
- 1.20–1.25 minimum DSCR
- Declining prepayment penalty
- Occupancy required: 90%
- Assumable: yes, with a 1% fee
- Interest only: no
- Rate lock at application
- Refundable rate-lock deposit: yes

SBA for Hospitality, Self-Storage, and Owner-User: *Borrow up to 85% for self-storage and hotels*

Although the SBA (Small Business Administration) will go up to 90%, plan on 85% unless you can get a seller-carry second mortgage. These loans are easier to qualify for than most commercial loans.

Acceptable Property Types: Self-storage, hotels, and owner-occupied business properties

Types of Loans: Permanent and construction loans

Program Guidelines and Requirements

- Loan size: $125,000–12,000,000
- LTV: 85–90%
- 90% loan to cost for construction
- 25-year amortization for real estate
- Recourse
- Floating rates or 10-year fixed with SBA 504
- Tax returns are required
- Global and debt to income ratio required
- Ground-up construction okay
- SBA guarantee fee: 3.00–3.50%
- Experience preferred
- 675 minimum credit score
- Minimum net worth negotiable
- Post-closing cash negotiable
- 1.10–1.20 minimum DSCR
- Declining prepayment penalty
- Occupancy required: negotiable
- Assumable: yes
- Interest-only: no
- Rate lock at loan approval
- Lends nationally in any size market

PART VIII

Smart Strategies for Managing and Leasing

CHAPTER 12

Smart Strategies for Managing and Leasing

This chapter goes over the nuts and bolts of managing and leasing and helps you answer these questions: Is it better for you to self-manage or hire professional management? Should you choose a larger or smaller management company? What are the methods property managers use to steal from you? What are the questions you should ask when screening management companies? How do leasing objectives differ between landlords and tenants? What are your leasing objectives? What are some of the mistakes you should avoid when leasing?

SELF-MANAGEMENT VERSUS PROFESSIONAL MANAGEMENT

I have clients that rave about their property management companies. These commercial investment property owners team up with their property managers. They seem to almost finish each other's sentences. You would think they were best friends.

Yes, there are exceptionally good property management companies out there that pride themselves on quality and excellence. They have killer maintenance and accounting software that is state of the art. They even have online portals for owners that make everything transparent. Say it's 1:30 in the morning and you want to know if unit 16 has been rented yet, or if building B has been scheduled for painting, or if the range has been replaced in unit 28. You can check for yourself in minutes. Fees range from 4% for office properties to 10% of gross rents for small multifamily properties under 24 units. See *property management fees* (Topic J, Managing and Leasing). These top-notch property managers often put in 55 hours per week or more and some have heart palpitations.

But the majority of my clients complain about their property management companies performing poorly. They say they just do not seem to care about running the property profitably. That they make endless excuses for not staying within the budget after agreeing to run things lean and mean. That they are lazy about getting vacancies rent ready. That they seldom get multiple bids on major repairs. That the cost for these repairs ends up being much more than they were told. That financial reporting is often chaotic—and worse yet, downright confusing. That rent rolls are not updated until requested, and financial reports have entries that cannot be explained.

Many of my colleagues and referral sources are real estate brokers that own property management companies. Boy, do they give me an earful. This does not seem like a fun job. One of my favorite property managers told me about the time they had the unpleasant job of going out to a large apartment complex after a call from a hysterical tenant. They got there just in time to stop a neighboring tenant from sacrificing a lamb in the front yard for a religious holiday. They tried to explain that the children next door would be traumatized if they carried this out. The offending tenant argued that in America you are allowed to practice your religion without interference, then asked where the rule was in writing to forbid this.

Not that I want to take sides, but property managers are the busiest people I know and my experience is that most are honest. Are they really going to risk their property management and real estate license by stealing from property owners? Some do! You will get to read about 11 ways property managers can rip you off a little later in this chapter. Property management employees are some of the lowest-paid professionals in America, earning on average less than $28,000 per year. One thing that is obvious: property management is not a cost-effective business. There is just too much to do in too little time for the pay. Maybe this is why so many have to take shortcuts.

Property managers are on the phone a lot—screening tenants, supervising vendors, and talking with owners. They are responsible for making vacant spaces ready to rent. Sometimes this means negotiating on tenant improvements, overseeing all new floor and window coverings, or even reconfiguring dividing walls. Property managers are the ones who get to harass slow-paying and no-paying tenants by sending them threatening notices. And God forbid, sometimes they have to go to court to evict them. They are responsible for all repairs and maintenance, including landscaping and snow removal. And often they have to mother employees and vendors to get jobs done. And let's not forget negotiating leases, paying all the bills, and monthly financial reporting to owners. For a complete list, see *management duties for commercial property managers* (Topic J, Managing and Leasing).

A Problem with Toilets

In 2003 I had just financed a 28-unit apartment complex in Louisville, Kentucky, for a sweet elderly lady who had purchased it. Two months after we closed she called me in hysterics, saying she did not know what to do. She was on her second property management company: could I recommend another? The first one she'd fired and the second one had just quit.

She told me there was a problem with the toilets. When someone flushed, the material sometimes went into another apartment's toilet along with the smell of raw sewage instead of into the sewer system. The first management company just could not figure out how to fix the problem and stopped returning the owner's calls. The second management company was a small mom-and-pop. They had their own in-house maintenance man. He said the problem was just too smelly to deal with and quit.

I called a local management company that was owned by a real estate broker I worked with to take the property on. They called a sewer-line contractor. It turned out that the cast iron horizontal sewage line running under the cement slab foundation was corroded in many places. The methane gas had nowhere to go but up and that's what was causing the problem. The faulty sewer lines were replaced and the problem was solved.

So Should You Self-Manage?

To put more money in your pocket, I can understand why you might be tempted to get your property manager to lower their fee from 7% to 6%. But on a 24-unit multifamily property in which all the units rent for $1,000, that 1% equals $240 per month. Do you really want to take that out of the property manager's pocket and push them toward taking shortcuts? But we really should look at owning and managing your property yourself, saving the 7% off-site management fee. That could save you $20,160 per year. That's not exactly small change.

If you want to take on the job of managing your property, don't forget that it can be a 20 hour a week job. It can also be a troublesome one—don't forget the problem with toilets story. If you have the ingenuity to buy a commercial property, isn't there a more productive, more profitable use of your time?

Seven Essential Property Management Skills

If you are going to self-manage your commercial property, the following are the top skills needed. Do you possess these?

1. *Customer service.* Do you have the ability to treat each tenant with respect and to make them feel special? They are your customers. Being a good listener and making each tenant feel as if you care about them and getting their issues resolved is important. Say a potential tenant just does not like the gray industrial-grade carpeting in an office space. They want you to pay to replace it with beige carpet. You might tell them that grey is not your favorite color either and offer to split the cost with them.

2. *Problem solving.* So a retail space has a leaky roof and it is ruining merchandise. Your maintenance guy has replaced a section of the roof, but now the water is dripping in another place eight feet away and also dripping on the tenant below. It's your responsibility to get this problem solved. Will you be relentless in doing so?

3. *Mothering tenants, employees, and vendors.* Are you good at supervising? So you have left many messages for an apartment tenant saying that they cannot store an extra refrigerator on their deck.

Time and Money Saving Tip

During tough economic times, investment property owners who self-manage and get deeply involved in communicating with tenants and controlling rental income and expenses can make a huge difference in their effectiveness in riding out the storm.

During the Great Recession and the coronavirus recession, my clients who self-managed their investment properties and those who aggressively managed their property managers fared much better with rent collections, controlling income and expenses, and filling vacancies. The property owners who had professional management and took a duck-and-cover approach, choosing not to get actively involved, did not fare as well.

In the early stages of the coronavirus recession in April of 2020, Ann, one of my multifamily clients, was self-managing a 46-unit Class C complex in a blue-collar neighborhood in Springfield, Oregon. Twelve percent of her tenants did not pay all the rent that month. A lightbulb went off in her head and she thought, "I'm going to find out if my renters are okay." She caringly communicated with each tenant to see how the pandemic was affecting them and their ability to pay the rent. She knew and cared about these people, and they knew her. Seventy-six percent of the tenants were making ends meet. They were either working at home, students with loans, or had a retirement income. The remaining 24% had either lost their jobs or were on reduced wages. Ann made arrangements with this group to accept partial payments—anything

They ignore you. So you send them a written notice telling them they are in violation of their lease and have a week to cure the problem or you will be starting eviction. Or the vendor you are renting the laundry equipment from has not repaired the two broken washing machines out of the four you have and it's been over a week and you have called the company many times. Your tenants are complaining. You threaten to cancel the contract with the vendor, report them to the Better Business Bureau, and give them an unfavorable rating online.

> the tenants could afford. Some just needed to wait until their unemployment checks came in. Ann, who had a Fannie Mae loan, then applied for *forbearance* (see Topic H, Financing), which would allow her to not make loan payments for 90 days without being in default. In exchange, Ann would not be allowed to start eviction proceedings on any tenants during this time period. Smartly, she attacked her rent collection problem from both ends.

4. *Financial management and budgeting.* You have a budget for all expenses and are going over on some. So you find ways to lower them. You also plan to raise some rents, which will help you to hit your target numbers.

5. *Multitasking.* In one day you have to meet with three contractors to get bids for resurfacing the parking lot, showing a space to a new tenant, and giving written and verbal notice to all tenants that an appraiser will be walking through their spaces. You also need to get payroll done and get caught up on accounting entries.

6. *Negotiating.* A high-quality tenant wants you to pay for major leasehold improvements but does not want their rent increased to the level it needs to be to pay for it. They also want their rent waived for the first three months of occupancy and tell you another landlord has offered this deal. With the two months it will take for the improvements, this will give you five months without any rent on the space. Can you work out something that is fair to both parties?

7. *Marketing.* It's competitive out there. You have several empty spaces and are not getting a good response on Craigslist. As a commercial property manager it is your responsibility to do marketing. Do you have a knack for this?

IS A LARGER OR SMALLER MANAGEMENT COMPANY BETTER?

If you are going to purchase an apartment complex with more than 8 units or a multitenant commercial property and you live beyond driving distance of the property, you will be better off hiring a professional management company that is located within an hour's drive of the property. These firms make it possible for you to have a life and will be able to be Johnny-on-the-spot faster than you can be.

It is a rule of thumb for multifamily properties that it is just not cost effective for a commercial property management company to manage fewer than 24 units, which results in higher fees for these smaller properties. There are national and regional management companies that manage 30,000 units or more for hundreds of clients. They are often in a position of doing the best job just because economies of scale permit them to hire more help. They usually have the latest software that makes accounting and maintenance very efficient. But they are picky. Don't be surprised if you find them screening you. These firms prefer Class A, B, and great-condition C multifamily properties of 60 units or more. One of the best benefits is that these large companies almost never steal from property owners. There are just fewer opportunities to do so. The downside is that you'll end up working with many different staff members and the continuity of major projects can be less efficient.

Many of my clients swear that their small mom-and-pop management companies that manage under 3,000 units give them service that far exceeds that of the large companies. Most of these smaller firms are owned by commercial real estate brokers who are sharp on keeping up on market rents and are the best at keeping your rents at the top of the market. And when you are ready to sell your property they are the best at selling it. After all, they know it inside out.

MANAGING YOUR PROPERTY MANAGER

Remember that property management is an overworked, underpaid, and underappreciated industry. It seems like many companies only have time to give topnotch service to owners that bug them. So you will get astoundingly better results if you are willing to manage your property manager. Think of it as having a partner and co-managing your business with them.

Unless you own a *triple net lease* property, there is no commercial property that is truly a passive investment whose owner just has to sit back and get paid. Sorry for the cliché, but it is the squeaky wheel that gets the grease.

Time and Money Saving Tip

When shopping for a property management company for a commercial property you are purchasing, ask them to make a budget for expenses and explain how they came up with those numbers. This will likely give you a more accurate estimate of expenses. Why not go with the company that is willing to run the property more lean and mean?

Be that squeaky wheel. Be sure to email or call your property manager once a week.

Do this early in the morning to put your property on their plate first. Remember that they work for you. Ask for their opinions about how you can add more to the bottom line. Then give them your ideas. Set goals with them for marketing and occupancy. Hold them to these goals. Make sure they have someone showing vacant units on weekends. Get excited with them about perspective tenants and how best to negotiate a lease with them. Get involved with reviewing bids from vendors and subcontractors, and especially with lease negotiations and resolving issues with problem tenants.

It will cost you if your manager takes shortcuts on these items. Some office, retail, and industrial property tenants that go into default on their leases are experts at stalling eviction. Their attorneys can stall the process for a year or more. Your involvement can cut this time in half. Make a list of what the management company is excelling

Time and Money Saving Tip

Make an agreement with your property manager to run the costs for major repairs by you before hiring the work out. And tell them if you are not satisfied with the estimates that you have the right to hire whomever you like.

at and compliment them on it. Make another list for areas for improvement and communicate these respectfully to them.

Dr. McConnell's Story

"What do you mean, you are going to recommend canceling the loan?" I asked my underwriter.

He replied, "I just went out to see the property and it's a mess. The parking lot is full of cracks, and the striping is worn off. And there are many health and safety violations. Several of the balconies are sagging; there are railings on staircases that are broken. In fact, one stairway to the second floor is leaning dangerously. And then there are four burned-out units from over a year ago and they still haven't been repaired.

"The property manager said the insurance money came in, but the owner used it to pay personal bills. She said the owner never comes to see the property and refuses to fix anything. This is not someone we want to make a loan to."

This was a refinance on a 90-unit apartment building in Oklahoma City, Oklahoma. The owner lived in San Diego. This was not the first time I had come across an out-of-state owner not managing their property manager.

(continued)

(*continued*)

But this just did not add up to me. I knew from doing two previous loans for Dr. McConnell that he often put his own money into keeping his apartment buildings in good condition. Being a slumlord and keeping a property in dangerous condition was not his style. When I checked with him, it turned out he had been given false reports and invoices for the work being done. But not visiting the property often because he lived out of state gave him some accountability for the property's poor condition.

Something unsavory was going on with Nancy the property manager. She was doing both off-site and on-site management and lived on the property.

This is one rule you do not want to break. Never have off-site and on-site management done by the same person. There is no system of checks and balances if you do that.

The rent rolls we got from Nancy showed the property at 94% physical occupancy. But the actual amount of rental income being deposited into the operating bank account showed that the property was running at 74% economic occupancy. When we asked for month-by-month income and expense statements and rent rolls going back two years she kept putting us off, saying her computer was broken.

And then there were the burned-out units. The insurance agent said that the claim had been settled and provided us with a copy of a notarized sworn statement signed by Nancy on a Lloyd's of London insurance claim loss form. It showed $144,000 due the property after subtracting for depreciation and a $10,000 deductible. It was dated 10 months earlier. Nancy had told Dr. McConnell that the claim was never settled. But she'd told my loan underwriter that the owner had used the insurance money for personal bills. Now we had her!

The insurance money had been paid to the property and Nancy had stolen all of it. Further investigation showed that she was stealing the rent money from nine units. She told those renters that she was the owner and they paid with cash or money orders made out to her. On top of that she was making payments to a maintenance contractor who never did the work. Well, you guessed it! Nancy owned the maintenance company.

Nancy had stolen over $300,000 from the property. She was arrested and released on $25,000 bail. My client, for some reason, decided to drop the charges. But the city held Nancy responsible for not maintaining the living conditions in a safe condition and indicted her for this.

ELEVEN WAYS PROPERTY MANAGERS CAN RIP YOU OFF (AND I'M SURE THERE ARE MORE)

As mentioned, in my experience most commercial property managers are honest. Some might push the envelope and engage in some questionable but legal practices to increase their profits. It would be much better if they informed you if they were inflating the cost of work done by vendors or getting kickbacks from them. Actual theft occurs when a property manager uses schemes to siphon off a little cash here and there. This is downright embezzlement and it is a crime. Here are 11 of the most popular ways property managers rip off property owners:

1. *Embezzlement.* This is the most serious, and unfortunately most common, form of property management theft. Embezzlement is an art. It takes a very creative, entrepreneurially minded individual who gets a high from figuring out ways to get something for nothing to do this. Most are smart and difficult to catch. There are over 20 methods. Here are nine of the most common:

   1. *Stealing cash payments.* A tenant pays the rent in cash and the property manager keeps the money. They then show the unit as vacant on the books.

   2. *Skimming rents from a few tenants.* The property manager has a few tenants deposit their rent in a bank account that neither the tenants nor the owner know is controlled by the property manager. These units show up as vacancies on the rent roll.

   3. *Falsifying the rent roll.* The property manager steals several months' rent or more by indicating that a tenant moved out earlier than they did. The property manager then falsifies the rent roll to show the unit as vacant and funnels the stolen funds into an account they control.

   4. *Showing paying tenants as delinquent.* Accounts receivable show tenants as being behind on rent when they actually paid on time. Eventually the "delinquent" rent is shown as bad debt. Again, the funds are funneled into a bank account controlled by the property manager.

   5. *Making payments to a shell company for services not rendered.* The property owner does not know that the property manager owns the business in question.

   6. *Being in collusion with a third party vendor.* The vendor bills the management company for a service or product that was never provided to the property. The vendor retains half and gives the other half to the property manager.

   7. *Cooking the books.* Accounting software is manipulated to eliminate rent payments or show false payments for expenses to legitimate accounts. The funds are then funneled into a bank account controlled by the property manager so that accounts payable and accounts receivable match.

8. *Raising rents and stealing the increase.* The rent roll is not updated to show the increase and the excess funds are then syphoned off to the property manager.

9. *Running a Ponzi scheme.* Funds from other properties are funneled into the property's operating account to hide theft when the owner realizes that the operating account is low and cash in does not match up to cash out.

Remedy: Embezzlement is a statutory offence and punishable by a lengthy jail sentence. If the offender is really good at what they're doing, it will take a forensic investigation of the accounting software to uncover it.

Require that all rent payments be made by auto payment or on the property's website. Make sure that you have online access to the property's operating accounting software and bank account and monitor both of these weekly. Watch out for unreasonable delays in the deposit of rental income. Look for unrealistically high expenses or an unexplained drop in net operating income, as well as less gross rent being deposited in the bank than shown by occupancy on the rent roll.

Look out for expenses that always exceed budgeted amounts. Be wary of property managers that will not commit to setting a budget for expenses. Set a limit on how much a property manager can spend without your approval. If there are a lot of expenses just under that limit, be suspicious.

Check vendor invoices monthly. Be wary of vendors that have a post box address instead of a street address on their invoices. Look out for many payments made to one vendor. Occasionally call third party vendors and question them about the work they performed. Chances are they will not know if theft has occurred, but they will tell you if they never did the work. Check with the secretary of state's corporation division online and find out who owns the vendor's company. If it is the property manager, then you need to dig deeper to search for fraud.

Be wary of property managers who get defensive or evasive when you ask them about discrepancies in accounting statements, such as when accounts payable are not in balance with accounts receivable.

2. *Vendor kickbacks.* The property manager colludes with a vendor to bill a higher amount than the actual cost of services. The vendor then cuts a check back to the property manager for the difference or does free work for them. This is a grey area and is very difficult to detect. It is almost never found to be illegal.

Remedy: Occasionally get a quote from vendors for a similar job for a make-believe property and see if they quote you a lot less. Better yet, get involved with getting quotes from vendors—especially on expensive work.

3. *Stealing security and cleaning deposit money.* This is actually stealing from your tenants and involves overcharging them for cleaning fees or damage and then pocketing the difference—or billing the tenant for damage they did not do and keeping their damage deposit. In both cases the deposit is shown as refunded on the books.

   Remedy: If the property manager makes a habit of this, tenants will give bad online reviews or file a claim in small claims court. If this is a reoccurring practice, you should be suspicious.

4. *Charging a fee above actual costs for vendors.* This is an acceptable practice if disclosed to the property owner. Some management companies charge a fee of 10% or more for arranging for work to be done outside of their payroll when requested by the owner.

   Remedy: Ask your property manager if they are marking up services preformed by their staff or third party vendors. If they have not told you about this practice, tell them this is not okay with you since you were not notified of the practice.

5. *Buying hardware, equipment, or supplies and returning them.* The property manager simply buys items for the property and then returns them for cash, which they pocket.

   Remedy: This is very difficult to detect. Watch out for supplies being purchased frequently, and if the outlays seem high, be suspicious.

6. *Stealing laundry and vending machine money.* Taking a portion of this money is not difficult.

   Remedy: Purchase or lease vending machines that take only credit or debit cards or have laundry and vending equipment owned by third party vendors that give you a cut.

7. *Comingling funds.* A property manager pays your bills out of their company account and then gets reimbursed from your property operating account. This is a system that is ripe for skimming. Or they put security and cleaning deposits in their property management business account. They can then more easily steal money from the tenants without your being able to monitor the transactions.

   Remedy: All property income should only be deposited in a segregated property operating account that the property owner also signs on. All expenses for the property should only be paid out of this account. Tenants' security deposits and cleaning deposits should always be kept in a separate account or in a client trust account. The property owner needs to have online access to these accounts and closely monitor them.

8. *Stealing your tenants.* Sometimes property managers are offered a bonus if they can fill one of your competitor's new apartment complexes quickly. Offering your tenants a *rent concession* to move to a nicer, newer property is stealing your tenants, but not illegal.

   Remedy: If you notice that many of your tenants have left around the same time, do some investigative work. Always get tenant phone numbers from the property manager. Tell them that you want to check with the tenants every so often to see if they are being well taken care of. Phone the tenants that have left and ask they why they moved. Most likely they will be honest and tell you they were offered a better deal by your property manager.

9. *Filling your property with poor-quality tenants.* Some property managers are just plain lazy and do not screen tenants for credit and background adequately. Or they offer rent concessions that are not needed but help them fill vacancies quickly and easily, such as paying only half of the first month's rent when the tenant signs a year's lease. This can cost you a lot of money in poor rent collections and property damage.

   Remedy: Get your property manager to agree to get your authorization for any rent concessions if they feel they are necessary. In addition, get them to email you a copy of the tenant files showing signed leases and a copy of the tenants' credit and background reports, along with notes on rental references that were checked.

10. *Buying supplies for their personal use.* When shopping for supplies for your property at a store like Costco, the property manager buys many items for their personal use.

    Remedy: Ask the property manager to turn in copies of their receipts for supplies. If they are overbuying legitimate items or purchasing items that are not for the property it will be easily detected. Be suspicious if they keep telling you that they lost receipts.

11. *Stealing from a petty cash fund.* When the office petty cash fund keeps dwindling with no explanation, this is a sign that the office employee is helping themselves. Often they will claim they used it for a legitimate expense but forgot to write it down.

    Remedy: Get the property manager to agree to account for all cash expenditures and to provide you with copies of receipts.

In conclusion, the best way to prevent property management theft is to have online portal access to the accounting system and to question the property manager about entries that you do not understand. You should also look at their reconciliations with bank statements. This way they know you are looking at their books continually. Be sure to do weekly backups of the accounting to your personal computer and the cloud. Let the management company know that you will be conducting periodic audits.

> **Time and Money Saving Tip**
>
> Choose a property management company that has a fidelity bond protecting the property owner against theft of money or property by their employees. Most of the larger management companies carry this insurance. The bond will only cover losses when a police report is filed.

TWELVE SCREENING QUESTIONS TO ASK WHEN CHOOSING A PROPERTY MANAGEMENT COMPANY

These days, the best property managers want to market their software technology for serving tenants, their expertise in performing maintenance, and their transparency in property accounting to attract clients. Be sure to meet in person with the manager or owner of the management companies you are interested in. Then put them on the spot by asking them these 12 questions:

1. *What property types do you specialize in and how many units do you manage?* Does the management company have extensive experience in your property type? What asset class do they like? How many units do they manage? Many property management companies specialize only in apartment buildings, others only in office, retail, or industrial. And some manage every commercial property type. Many of the national firms will only take on larger Class A and B and excellent-condition C properties.

2. *What are your qualifications? Are you licensed and/or accredited?* Most states require the owners of property management companies to be licensed real estate brokers, but some states do not require any licensing. There are various accreditations. Being a certified property manager (CPM) from the Institute of Real Estate Management is the most highly regarded accreditation, and it is not easy to qualify. Review the bios of owners and top staff to see that they have education, training, and accreditation. Ask them for four references from satisfied clients.

3. *What are your fees?* Ideally you want to choose a company that just charges you a fair percentage of gross rental income and doesn't nickel-and-dime you. Some charge a standard monthly fee per unit, others a flat fee plus a percentage. It is standard for office, retail, and industrial properties to charge between a half

and a full month's rent when leasing a unit. Some multifamily management companies that specialize in small complexes of 12 and under also charge this. Ask them if they mark up any third party services, and if so by how much.

4. *What services do you provide?* These should include marketing, tenant quality control, tenant relationships, market rent research, leasing, accounting, maintenance, and construction. For a full description of these services, see *Management Duties for Commercial Property Managers* (Encyclopedia Topic J, Managing and Leasing).

5. *What accounting services do you offer?* Ask what is included in monthly reports. The best management companies have a portal on their website that you can go to that offers full transparency 24/7 for accounting, including rent rolls, profit and loss statements, accounts payable, accounts receivable, and bank reconciliation accounting.

6. *How do you manage budgeting during good times and during a recession?* This is a really important one. What is their procedure for budgeting rental increases, expenses, repairs, and capital improvements? They should provide you with an annual budget pro forma. Do they monitor the budget monthly and inform you of any changes or explain why adjustments need to be made? In the event of a recession, what actions do they take in terms of lowering rents, lowering expenses, and offering concessions to keep the property running profitably?

7. *What is your maintenance program?* How do they monitor repairs and routine maintenance as well as preventive maintenance? Do they have an online portal for this? What software, if any, do they use to track repairs and routine maintenance? Do they use their own maintenance staff or use vendors? Do they get bids from vendors and contractors and communicate these to you? Do they ever get kickbacks from them? I know the last is a touchy question, but if they don't take kickbacks they will be proud to answer it.

8. *How do you handle rent and/or CAM (common area maintenance) charge collections?* Ideally you want to have rent collection set up so that tenants can make payments online at a tenant portal on your property's website. Another good option is autodraft from the tenant's checking account.

9. *Do you offer a biannual market rent analysis?* They should provide an analysis of the rents of your competitors and update you on market occupancy and absorption rates.

10. *What is your purchasing process?* Do they competitively shop insurance, maintenance supplies, and equipment? Or do they mostly do business with companies they have a relationship with?

11. *How good are you at tenant relations?* What tactics do they use for negotiating leases and lease renewals? What is their process for handling tenant maintenance requests and complaints? How do they communicate with tenants? Do

they have a portal on the property website that tenants can go to? How quickly do they respond?

12. *How good are you at marketing?* Why are they the best at marketing? What do they do to improve the image of your property when marketing it? Do they use a marketing plan, and if so, what are the components? Do they provide a website for your property? Does it have software that automatically posts vacancies to the website? Do they post vacancies to popular real estate listing websites such as Craigslist, LoopNet, Apartments.com, HotPads, and Zillow? What type of rental concessions do they typically use and under what circumstances do they use them?

LEASING BASICS

Have you thought about how diametrically opposed leasing objectives are for landlords and tenants? Understanding the tenant's side can really help you with lease negotiations. When you start negotiating a lease with a tenant, will you know what all of your leasing objectives are? This section mostly pertains to leasing office, retail, and industrial space.

Objectives of Landlords and Tenants

As the property owner, you are in a position to call most of the shots when negotiating leases. After all, your attorney will be drawing up the lease. But let's face it. Tenants and landlords have many opposing objectives, which can make lease negotiations difficult.

Tenants want to start paying rent the day they open for business, whenever that happens. If a buildout is being done they can't possibly know the exact date they will occupy the premises. If they can negotiate three months' free rent, that is even better. Often they will tell you that someone else has offered this deal to them.

On the other hand, landlords also want the rent to start on opening day, but no later than a predetermined commencement date written in the lease. Landlords prefer longer-term leases, as it makes their properties more valuable and easier to finance. Unless it's a dynamite high-traffic location, tenants more often prefer shorter-term leases with many options for renewals. That way if their business grows they can move to a larger space. If it doesn't they can exercise an option to stay longer. Landlords don't get excited about lease options. There's really no benefit for them.

If it's a high-quality, in-demand property landlords prefer triple net leases, where the tenant pays a prorated share of the cost for all of the property's maintenance, taxes, and insurance. Tenants much prefer gross leases, where the property owner pays for all of that. Landlords are often willing to pay for leasehold improvements for a tenant who signs a long-term lease and will usually only increase the rent modestly on such a tenant. But they rarely mind paying for leasehold improvements when they can borrow the money from a low-rate line of credit and then charge an astronomically high amount of rent. Higher rents increase their property's value. But if the cost of improvements has to come out of the landlord's pocket in cash, they more often prefer that the tenant pony this up. Tenants almost always prefer it when the landlord pays for tenant improvements, since with the short amortization a bank will give them (not longer than the lease term), it is usually not cost effective for them to borrow the money. Tenants prefer annual rent escalations to be based on the consumer price index (CPI) when inflation is flat. Landlords prefer a set increase: for example, 3% per year or the annual increase in the CPI, whichever is higher.

Knowing Your Ideal Lease Objectives

The number-one value of a commercial property is not its brick-and-mortar but the historical strength of its net operating income (NOI). You can buy commercial properties for 65 cents on the dollar if they have low occupancy and low NOI; if they are vacant, less than 50 cents on the dollar.

For office, retail, and industrial properties, the quality of the tenants and leases are equally important, especially when these properties are put up for sale or refinanced. Having mostly mom-and-pop tenants renting by the month or leases that run out in less than two years lowers the property's value and makes the property more difficult to finance. When selling, having an anchor tenant's lease running out in five years or less lowers the property value.

Whether you're dealing with a 4-page apartment rental agreement or a 90-page commercial property lease, it is essential that you know what your objectives are before negotiating leases with your tenants. Balancing these with what is realistically attainable in the market is essential. A real estate broker who knows the market and the competition can help you to determine your leasing objectives. A good real estate attorney will assist you in incorporating these into a lease.

Twelve Top Commercial Leasing Objectives Landlords Should Know Before Negotiations

1. *What does your ideal tenant mix look like?* Is there too much duplication of the same products or services by tenants on your property? Do you need to mix in some national tenants? Is the intended use of a potential tenant in harmony with that of your other tenants? Do you need to change out some tenants?

2. *What is your minimum acceptable rent?* How much do you think you can get for the space and for rent escalations? Be sure to conduct a market rent analysis to determine how high to set your rents. Then balance this with your financial expectations to make sure that you are not leasing the space with low rents that will cause your NOI to suffer. If this is a tenant's market with an abundance of available space to rent, will you be offering any free rent?

3. *How long is your ideal lease term and option to renew?* If you are going to want a 10-year fixed loan in the near future, lenders will not want to fix the rate for much longer than the average of the maturity of your lease terms. If you are planning on selling the property in the next few years, having longer remaining lease terms will make the property's value higher. What options to renew will you offer?

4. *What type of lease will this be?* Will you want a gross lease, double net lease, triple net lease, absolute triple net lease, or a percentage lease?

5. *How much will the security deposit be?* Check with the laws in your state, as many states limit this.

6. *Who will pay for common area expenses?* These expenses include maintenance and utilities for outdoor areas, lobbies, shared conference rooms, restrooms, parking lots, and the like.

7. *Will you have an expense stop?* This is the maximum amount of operating expenses a landlord will pay annually; any amounts above the expense stop are paid by the tenant.

8. *What will your policy be for tenant improvements?* You can make the lease as is or pay for a portion or all of the improvements in exchange for a longer lease or higher rent payments.

9. *What will your policy be for subleasing?* Will you allow subleasing? If so, what standards will you require the replacement tenant to meet?

10. *What will your policy be on tenant signage?* Most cities have signage laws that limit the size of signs for businesses. But what parameters will you have as to the type of sign and placement?

11. *What will your parking policy be?* Most municipalities mandate the minimum number of parking spaces a commercial property has to have based on the types of tenants on the property. For example, more spaces are required for restaurants than for a tax preparer's office. How will you regulate parking in the lease? How many spaces will each tenant be allowed for their employees, customers, or clients? Will you be charging for parking?

12. *Will you require financial reporting on request?* The best commercial financing often requires tenant financials.

Fourteen Mistakes Landlords Make When Leasing Commercial Property

1. *Not knowing market rents.* Setting your rents too high based on a whim can cause your property to not be competitive and your vacancies to not be filled. You need to know what market rents are to determine how much rent to charge. If you are purchasing a multifamily property, you can just go to your competitors' websites. For office, retail, and industrial properties, be sure to have a market rent analysis done by a commercial real estate broker.

2. *Not calculating your break-even point.* This is not an area to take a shortcut on. Sometimes commercial property owners do not crunch the numbers and do not know they are operating at close to or below their break-even point. If this is the case, the only way to pull the NOI up to a safe level will be to discount rents or offer concessions on vacant units. Often commercial properties with occupancy problems are running the property using cash-flow instead of accrual accounting; the latter is based on net profit. The property could be running at a loss and the owner would not know it until it's too late.

3. *Not checking the tenant's financial strength and potential for bankruptcy.* Financially strong tenants with excellent personal and business credit, cash assets, and good income seldom file for Chapter 11 bankruptcy. Those that do file for bankruptcy can legally occupy the space rent free for an undetermined amount of time. You can guard against this risk just by screening tenants adequately. You should ask for the last three years of company tax returns and a current profit and loss statement and balance sheet. Asking for their most recent business plan will tell you about the company's future growth plans.

4. *Having weak conditions for the tenant's transfer rights.* These refer to a tenant's rights to have their lease assumed when selling their business. The lease needs to have big teeth to protect you from the tenant selling their business to an operator who is much less qualified than they are.

5. *Having a weak approval clause for tenant use.* This refers to the type of services or products a tenant can offer. Tenants prefer to leave this clause as open as possible so they can add new services or products in the future. This can cause conflict with other tenants due to duplication. The tenant use clause needs to be written tightly to allow for specific uses only and include a provision that adding another use will need the landlord's written permission.

6. *Not having a clause in the lease mandating tenant financials.* Many lenders require business financials from tenants when approving financing for a commercial property. Not having a strong clause in your lease for this could prevent you from getting the best-quality financing. The clause should specify the period of time for which the tenant has to provide financials. Thirty days is reasonable.

7. *Not having a clause in the lease mandating move-in and move-out inspections.* In an addendum to the lease, the landlord and tenant should certify that the premises were in good condition at move-in. Or identify items that need upgrading or repair. This is the only way to legally use a tenant's deposit to repair damage when the tenant leaves. All states have laws that protect tenants' damage and security deposits. They all require that the landlord allow for normal wear and tear.

8. *Not collecting the maximum security deposit.* All states regulate what the maximum amount for a security deposit can be. I recommend that you collect the maximum amount. Tenants that can come up with a larger amount are more likely to be strong financially and less likely to cause damage.

9. *Allowing too much time for a tenant to start paying rent.* Be sure to put a commencement date for when rent will start in the lease. Tenants will often try to negotiate free rent for two to four months. If it takes the tenant three months to complete their tenant improvements and then you give them three months' free rent, that is six months without any rent. Only offer free rent if this is a stellar tenant signing a long-term lease and you can afford it.

10. *Accepting partial payments after filing for eviction.* Most states will consider this to be evidence that you are working out a plan to reinstate the tenant and nullify the eviction.

11. *Pursuing rent collections when a tenant has filed for bankruptcy.* Under US bankruptcy laws, you are not allowed to pursue a tenant for back or current rent. Only the bankruptcy court can determine how or whether the rent will be paid.

12. *Signing too many short-term leases.* Having too many short-term leases of three years or less will make your commercial property less stable financially and more difficult to finance.

13. *Not negotiating all lease terms at once.* Don't let the tenant keep coming back with more and more items to be negotiated. This can lead to lease negotiations breaking down. Better to have an initial meeting with each side's professionals to go over the intent to lease. Most negotiations should take place during this meeting. Have a second meeting to approve the completed lease and finalize any negotiations. After that, the tenant needs to agree that the lease is acceptable and written correctly.

14. *Letting tenants know the property is for sale.* This can be used against you by tenants that have renewals coming up or are in negotiations with you to rent space. They will know that you need the new lease signed and can delay the process, resulting in your having to reduce their rents. I have seen this happen many times.

Managing and Leasing

Absolute Triple Net Lease: *This lease gets the tenant to pay for absolutely everything*

In a triple net lease, the tenant pays a prorated share of the building's maintenance, taxes, insurance, and common area maintenance (CAM). It doesn't get much better than that, does it? Actually, there is something better—an absolute triple net lease! Here, on top of all of that they pay for in a triple net lease, the tenant also pays a pro rata share of all structural repairs, or capital improvements, for the property. To pull this off, it takes the very best location, a national tenant, and a 15- to 25-year lease.

Americans with Disabilities Act (ADA) Compliance: *The landlord is legally liable if the tenant's space is not ADA compliant*

Be aware that if you are leasing to a new tenant that is doing tenant improvements, the landlord is equally liable if the changes do not meet ADA compliance regulations for the disabled. This is the case whether you or the tenant are paying for the improvements. Requirements include the installation of ramps, widening doors, the installation of grab bars in restroom stalls, access to an elevator, wider curb cuts, wheelchair accessible paths, and more. So it makes sense for the landlord to get involved at the beginning to make sure that the plans are checked out by the city for ADA compliance and that the installations made are compliant.

Assignment of Lease Clause: *As landlord, make sure that you put into the assignment of lease clause exactly what it will take for a replacement tenant to qualify*

You own a strip mall and carefully screen your tenants before leasing to them. One day your tenant notifies you that they are selling their pet store and want to assign their lease to another party. You ask about the qualifications of the replacement tenant. You are told they are great people who have never had a business before. Now how are you going to handle this?

Most office, retail, and industrial leases have an assignment of lease clause. This gives the option of assigning the lease to another party if the tenant sells their business. Although assigning the lease will not release the tenant from being liable for the lease, it is important that the property owner have stringent qualifications in the lease for approving the replacement tenant. Most assignment of lease clauses just state that the landlord needs to approve the replacement tenant. To save a lot of headaches, be sure to write into the clause the requirements the new tenant will need to meet. Hopefully the tenant will go back, read this clause, and use it to prequalify any party that wants to buy their business. If they don't and they bring you an undesirable replacement tenant, you can tell them that the qualifications are in the lease.

Audit Rights for Landlords: *If you have a percentage lease, make sure that it gives you the right to audit the tenant's financials*

This refers to *percentage leases* (see later in this Topic), where the landlord receives a base rent plus a percentage of the tenant's gross revenue. Most percentage leases give the landlord the right to audit the tenant's business financials to ensure that the tenant is not underreporting income. You will need to use an independent accountant to do the audit. It is always best not to give notice to the tenant too much before the audit date. You don't want them cleaning up the books. Thirty days' notice is best; you shouldn't give more than 60 days' notice.

Audit Rights for Tenants: *Don't allow a tenant to exercise their audit rights against you if they are behind in the rent*

With a *net lease* (later in this Topic), the tenant has the right to audit the landlord's charges for their share of taxes, insurance, and maintenance expenses. Usually the tenant covers the cost of the audit, but some leases state that if the landlord's statements are determined to be inaccurate by an independent accountant, the landlord pays. As landlord, be wary of a tenant that is behind on rent and calls for an audit. This can be a stalling strategy. Be sure to insist that the tenant get caught up on the rent before you allow them to audit you.

Base Rent: *Be sure to know what base rent per square foot is going for in your market before negotiating base rent*

This refers to the rent per square foot. On a triple net lease, all common area maintenance charges, taxes, and insurance are charges in addition to base rent. On a percentage lease, the percentage is charged on top of base rent and CAM charges.

As the landlord, think about how you are going to counter the guerilla tactics that real estate brokers representing tenants are famous for. These tactics include advising them to offer 15% less than the property owner is asking for base rent and to never mention that they are interested in a longer-term lease (they are advised to start out with a letter of intent for a 3-year term with options, then agree to sign a longer lease of 5–10 years in exchange for lower base rent).

As the property owner, be sure to know what market rents are for a property of your type and quality. Consult with a property manager or real estate broker to determine how good your location is and how much space is available at what price at your competitors' properties. This way you will be prepared to negotiate the base rent.

Buildout: *If you as the landlord are paying for the buildout or a portion of it, be sure to state the maximum you are willing to spend*

This refers to the construction for tenant improvements that will be made for a new tenant. As the property owner, be sure to have your attorney put an exhibit in the

Managing and Leasing

lease that defines everything about the buildout: the scope of the work, the quality of the materials, the qualifications for who will be doing the construction, and who will be paying for the work. If you as landlord are paying for all or a portion, be sure to put in the maximum amount per square foot that you are willing to spend.

Common Area Maintenance (CAM) Fees: *Be sure to show these on your books as additional revenue*

On net leases, a pro rata share of these fees are paid by tenants to landlords to cover operating expenses for common areas. Common areas are bathrooms, lobbies, elevators, parking lots, and any other shared spaces. CAM fees can be either fixed, where they stay the same, or variable, where they're based on the fluctuation of actual expenses. As the property owner or manager, be wary of tenants who try to cut out certain CAM charges when negotiating a lease with you. It is not fair to your other tenants if you cut a special deal for them. Also be sure to show CAM fees collected as additional revenue in your accounting.

Credit/Investment Grade Tenant: *Your chances of getting struck by lightning are higher than a credit tenant with an AA+ rating defaulting on their lease*

If you can land a credit tenant with a high credit rating for a single-tenant property, you should have nothing to do except collect the rent. You will not even need a management company. These tenants almost always sign a *triple net lease* (Managing and Leasing Subjects) and sometimes even sign an *absolute triple net lease* (see earlier in this Topic). A credit tenant can be a national chain or government entity that has a good Standard and Poor's, Moody's, or Fitch credit rating of between BBB– and AAA. Some of the tenants that have the highest credit ratings are the US government at AA+, Walmart at AA, and 7-Eleven at AA–. Credit tenants usually have very high customer counts, so try to mix one or two in if you have a strip mall.

Creditworthy Tenant: *Checking the tenant out will pay dividends over time*

A creditworthy tenant is the kind of tenant you want all your tenants to be. Make sure to take the time to screen your tenants for the following six items to determine if they are creditworthy:

1. *Check their Dun & Bradstreet business credit rating.* A score of 80–100 is very low risk, 50–79 moderate risk, and 0–49 high risk.
2. *Check their rental history.* Many of my clients tell me that good reviews from previous landlords means the most.
3. *Pull personal credit reports for all signers and guarantors of the lease.* You're looking for credit scores of 680 plus good history of making payments. If they have a history of bankruptcy or foreclosure, this tells you that if the going gets tough, they might bail out.
4. *Do a background check on all signers and guarantors.* This is likely even more important than the credit check. Renting to someone who has a criminal history can be dangerous.

5. *Review their financials.* This might seem over the top, but you can and should verify the financial strength of the business. Collect three years of the business's tax returns plus a year-to-date profit and loss statement and a current balance sheet. A business that shows some cash in the bank and not much bad debt on accounts payable is even better.

6. *See if they have more than one location.* Finding tenants that have more than one location lowers the risk of default. This is a sign that a tenant is successful and if they get off to a slow start at your property they have other income to fall back on.

Double Net Lease: *The tenant may opt for a double net lease in exchange for lower base rent*

Here the tenant pays the base rent plus a pro rata share of taxes and insurance. The property owner pays for all maintenance and repair on the building's exterior and the cost of maintaining common areas.

Effective Rent: *Take the time to calculate the actual rent you will be getting over the lease term*

Be sure to see what your effective rent will be before finalizing lease negotiations with a tenant. This is the gross amount payable by the tenant during the full term of the lease less any rent concessions, such as free rent, tenant improvements you are paying for, and leasing commissions. You then get to see what the actual monthly rent is averaging after the giveaways. Here's the thing: It's so easy to make a decision to give a tenant a lot of breaks to entice them to sign a lease. But doing this without knowing what the effective rent will be on the space is risky. Calculating the effective rent will tell you if you can afford these giveaways.

Escalation Clause (Rent): *Choose a rental increase that you can count on*

This clause pertains to annual rent increases as stated in the lease. A landlord needs to know ahead of time what those increases are going to be so they can count on them. There are three types of rent escalations:

1. **Stepped Increases**: These are based on an increase in rent per square foot annually.
2. **Fixed Increases**: These are based on an increased percentage, such as 2–3% each year.
3. **Variable Increases:** These are tied to the consumer price index (CPI), which models annual inflation. Tenants usually prefer this type of increase during times of low inflation.

Talk to a good real estate broker and commercial real estate attorney and get an idea of how much you can raise the rent per square foot each year. Then play around with these methods to determine which is best for you. Another alternative is to do a combination of fixed and variable increases. An example would be an increase of 3% or the CPI increase, whichever is higher.

Estoppel Letter (Lease Clause): *This is where the tenant certifies what their lease terms are and that the lease is in good standing*

For office, retail, and industrial properties, your commercial lease should have a requirement that the tenant has to provide an estoppel letter or certificate upon request. This is a statement that is signed by the tenant for the benefit of another party—usually a buyer of the property or a lender. The estoppel has the tenant certify the lease terms, any defaults by the tenant or landlord, promises or unfulfilled commitments made by the landlord, and when the last rent payment was made. The main purpose of the estoppel is to provide proof that the lease is cash flowing and in good standing. After all, the buyer is purchasing the income from the property along with the real estate. And a lender needs to know that the property is collecting the rents showing on the rent roll. When you are selling the property, make sure that all of the commitments you have made to the tenant have been fulfilled and that you have disclosed to the buyer or lender ahead of time if the tenant is in default. These things will come out when the tenant signs the estoppel.

> ### Time and Money Saving Tip
>
> Not getting tenant estoppel certificates in is one of the main reasons why commercial real estate purchases are delayed or fail. National tenants can take two months or longer to get these filled out, reviewed by their attorneys, and signed. A lender will not allow a loan to close until all of the estoppel certificates are in. I have had many loans delayed waiting for these. Put into the lease that estoppels have to be returned within 30 days. Better yet, make it a default if the tenant takes more than 45 days to return the estoppel. Be sure to start requesting estoppels as early as possible.

Eviction Process: *Don't try to lock out a nonpaying multifamily tenant, but you can likely do this for an office, retail, or industrial tenant if this is a remedy in the lease*

Multifamily properties. Evicting a multifamily tenant can be a complicated process and take three months or longer if the tenant has a long-term lease and stalls the process. Some of my clients who own apartment buildings keep all of their tenants on month-to-month rental contracts. In most states this makes the eviction process much faster. The landlord has to go through due process and cannot lock the tenant out. If the tenant refuses to leave after the notice to vacate has expired, the landlord will have to file a lawsuit to have the tenant removed. In many states, this is done much faster and less expensively in small claims court. Often the tenant does not show up for the court case and the judge makes a default judgement of guilt against the tenant. The court will usually give the tenant up to a month to move out. The landlord has to hire the sheriff's department to forcibly remove the tenant if they still will not leave.

Office, retail, and industrial properties. Commercial tenants do not have the same rights as multifamily tenants do. In most states if locking out the tenant is a remedy in the lease, it can be enforced. Tenants still have to be given written notice of the default and a chance to cure it by a certain date. If they fail to do so the landlord can file a complaint with the court and a summons is served to the tenant. The tenant can then explain in court why they are not in default. If the court rules against the tenant they are often given a short time—as little as a week—to vacate the space. If they still will not move out, the landlord has the right to remove and sell the items left by the tenant. In some states they have to give the tenant notice before doing this.

Expense Stop and Fully Serviced Leases: *Put an expense stop in your gross leases to protect your NOI, should operating expenses skyrocket*

For office, retail, and industrial properties, if you are signing a gross lease with a tenant where the landlord pays all the expenses, it is smart to put an expense stop in the lease. This caps operating expenses at a defined amount and specifies that if expenses go over that amount annually then the tenant will pay a pro rata share of the difference.

If this practice continues for the remaining lease term, this in effect turns the lease from a gross lease to what's called a "fully serviced lease." You are still giving the tenant a break in the first year since they only have to pay the base rent. In one year you could get hit by unforeseen expenses, such as major insurance claims resulting in increased premiums, a sudden increase in taxes, or an abundance of expensive repairs. If your expenses skyrocket and your net operating income (NOI) falls below the debt service coverage ratio mandated in your loan documents, your loan could be called.

First Right of Refusal: *This is something that benefits tenants, not landlords*

This gives the tenant the right to any additional space you have available should you have an offer to lease the space from a new tenant. It can also give the tenant the first right to purchase the building should you have an offer to buy it. If it is an offer you are willing to accept, you have to give the existing tenant the right to occupy the space or purchase the property under the same terms as what was offered by the other tenant or buyer. First rights of refusal are not something landlords put into leases. You will come across them occasionally in the tenant's letter of intent (LOI). Tenants' attorneys put this clause into the lease when reviewing it. Many landlords view this clause as harmless. There is little benefit to a landlord who allows this, so be cautious before you agree to it. It could throw a wrench into a future transaction where you have a highly qualified tenant or buyer.

Furniture, Fixtures, and Equipment (FF&E) (Commercial Lease): *Be prepared to sign a lien waiver on your tenant's FF&E if they have a bank loan*

The majority of business tenants will need to finance FF&E costs with their bank. Almost all commercial leases have a lien against the tenant's FF&E. Lenders will require that the landlord subordinate their lien on FF&E to the lender. This is accomplished by the landlord signing the lender's lien waiver document. This is something you don't have much say in. If you do not subordinate, the tenant will not be able to finance the items they need to run their business and they will not be able to rent the space. The downside is if the tenant defaults on the loan the bank can take equipment back, such as built-in fixtures like cabinets, display cases, lighting, and equipment, such as an HVAC system that is attached to the roof.

General Vacancy and Credit Loss: *If you are buying a property, be sure to allow something for general vacancy and credit loss in your annual budget*

As a commercial property owner or manager, it important to anticipate a future down market that negatively affects vacancy and to plan for some tenants not paying the rent. It always amazes me how few buyers of commercial properties think about doing this. I guess it is like getting married; you don't think about having marital problems someday.

When doing an operating pro forma for the annual budget, be conservative and allow something for general vacancy and credit loss. Project the property's annual vacancy at 5% or at market vacancy, whichever is higher. To be more conservative, prepare for a recession by putting in 10–12% vacancy and 10% credit loss. Then plan to allow for a projected credit loss by lowering your rent collection figure by 5–10% annually, depending on the quality of your tenants. Here is an example not reflecting a possible recession:

Gross annual rents	$356,500
Less vacancy (5%)	–17,825
Less credit loss (3%)	–10,695
Adjusted annual rents	$327,980

Go Dark Clause (Lease): *This allows the tenant to close up shop for good but still pay you the rent until their lease term expires*

This is a clause in a commercial lease that allows the tenant to stop operating and still pay rent and honor all the other covenants in the lease. In 2017 Macy's went dark on 68 stores due to massive competition from online retailers. Large empty spaces can really hurt shopping malls and office buildings. As the property owner, if you have a go dark clause in your leases always put in the right to lease the space to a new tenant. The old tenant will have to continue to pay the rent until their lease expires or the new tenant moves in, whichever is first.

Gross/Full Service Lease: *Charging top of the market rents is expected with a gross lease*

A gross lease is one in which the landlord pays for all the operational expenses of the property and the tenant just pays their base rent. There is an expectation that the base rent will be on the high side since the tenant will not be paying a portion of the landlord's expenses for taxes, insurance, and maintenance. Net leases tend to have lower base rents than gross leases. Be sure to include the future projected expenses for operating the property in the base rent on a gross lease.

Managing and Leasing

Managing and Leasing

Lease-Up Fee (Leasing Commission):

Be prepared to pay a fee to a real estate broker who is leasing a space for you

This usually refers to a onetime fee charged by commercial real estate brokers for finding a commercial tenant for an office, retail, or industrial property. But a management company can also charge this. The fee is usually a month's rent. This is usually fair compensation because the broker usually places the listing on MLS and online listing services, such as LoopNet, and might have to split the fee with another agent. It can be negotiated lower for higher rent transactions. Some multifamily management companies charge from a half to a full month's rent when they find a new tenant for smaller properties of 24 units or under. For large apartment properties, charging this fee is not the norm.

Letter of Intent (LOI) to Lease: *Be sure to know all of your leasing objectives before reviewing a letter of intent to lease from a tenant (see Chapter 12)*

Time and Money Saving Tip

If a commercial real estate broker is representing a tenant who is interested in leasing from you, be aware that the broker has to earn their keep. They will most certainly ask for a lot more than is reasonable at the beginning and assume you will come down a lot.

For example, say the going rate for your Class B retail space is $35 per square foot with $20 per square foot in tenant improvement allowances and three months of free rent. Brokers will start out asking for $30 per square foot in rent, $30 per square foot in tenant allowances, and six months of free rent. Be sure that you take the time to calculate the *effective rent* (earlier in this Topic) and know what your minimum acceptable rent is for each space before you start negotiations, and that if your property drops below 85% occupancy you will still be running profitably after debt service with the space rented at this rate.

This is a non-legally binding letter stating the main terms of a commercial lease. It is usually prepared by the tenant, especially if they have a real estate broker representing them. Once signed by both parties, it represents a deep interest in committing to a lease under its stated terms. Once the initial terms have been agreed upon, the property owner has a draft lease prepared for further negotiations. Although there are often over 40 clauses in a commercial lease, here are the main terms that go into an LOI to lease:

Lessee's name

Security deposit

Lessor's name

Use of space

Property name and address

Subleasing

Description of space to be leased

Assignment of lease when selling business

Lease term

Leasehold improvements

Options /renewal

Rental increases

Rent

State to be governed clause

Expenses and CAM charges

Nonbinding clause

Time and Money Saving Tip

If a tenant showing an interest in leasing a commercial space does not have a broker representing them, it is more likely they will not have an LOI to lease prepared. As the property owner, you likely already have your leasing objectives. So it is in your best interests to start out the leasing negotiations by preparing the LOI to lease yourself. That way you can present to the tenant what the lease terms will be as if they are written in stone.

Management Duties for Commercial Property Managers: When hiring a management company, make sure that these 10 items are covered in the contract

1. *Branding and marketing management.* Larger commercial properties should be professionally branded. Once you have your logo and website designed, your management company should use the site and social media to attract new, quality tenants. Tenant profiles for the type of tenant you want to attract should be created, and designing a marketing campaign with time frames is essential. Also, positive online reviews should be solicited. For multifamily properties, the property website should be used for keeping vacancies and unit rents up to date, showing floor plans for each unit type, and posting attractive photos of the building and units.

2. *Tenant quality control management.* Screening tenants for credit, completing background searches, and obtaining references from previous landlords are important. The rental application should have a clause that gives permission to pull credit reports and a background check for all lease signers and guarantors. The application should be shown to one of the three credit bureaus—Equifax, Experian, or TransUnion—and a fee submitted to pull a credit report. A tri-merge report for all three bureaus is best and can be purchased from any of them for an extra charge. For a background check, the management company can contact lexisnexis.custhelp .com or truthfinder.com. To check a business's credit, they can go to dnb.com. They should be sure to look the business up on the Better Business Bureau website too.

3. *Tenant relationship management.* This is about letting your tenants know you care about them. This can pay off big-time in five-star tenant reviews on your property's website. Keeping them happy entails having a portal on the website where you can communicate with them. The property's website should include a forum where notices of work to be done are posted and suggestions are solicited from tenants. The company should check with tenants periodically to see what can be done to improve their experience at the property. Having a tenant lunch or creating a fun event for them are examples of things that could be considered. The company

Managing and Leasing

should also be responsible for the negative side of tenant relationship management, including enforcing the default clauses of leases and evicting tenants if necessary.

4. *Market rent analysis and competition research management.* Your management company should be doing market research on your competitors in the market to determine if your rents have room to be increased and if your property's condition and amenities are competitive.

5. *Lease management.* The company should be responsible for the following areas of lease management: reviewing leases and setting up a leasing plan with goals, meeting with new and existing tenants to negotiate leases, meeting with a commercial real estate attorney to draft leases based on specific criteria, and obtaining estoppels from tenants when needed.

6. *Accounting management and budgeting.* The company should be handling the following areas of accounting management: having the property website set up so tenants can make payments on it, setting up a bookkeeping and accounting system, overseeing the collection of rents, establishing and maintaining budgets, and finding ways to raise rents and reduce expenses.

   The company should also be responsible for financial reporting for the property owner, including monthly rent rolls, expense ledger, accounts payable, accounts receivable, monthly profit and loss, balance sheet, and bank reconciliation report. Property owners should have access through an online portal to the manager's accounting software along with online access to the operating bank account. The property manager should also be responsible for paying all bills, including the mortgage payment, and making distributions to the owner and partners.

7. *Maintenance management.* The management company should have an online portal where management staff and maintenance workers can communicate. They should be reviewing the physical structure, parking lot, and outdoor areas periodically; implementing a system for preventive maintenance and monitoring ongoing work for maintenance, repair, and replacements; and supervising all vendors that handle repair and maintenance. They also should oversee making vacant units ready to rent.

8. *Personnel management.* The company should be responsible for supervising employees, maintenance, and security staff.

9. *Purchasing management.* The company should be responsible for purchasing maintenance and cleaning supplies, equipment, furnishings, and insurance.

10. *Construction management.* The company should be managing the bidding process, awarding construction contracts, and scheduling and overseeing the work of subcontractors doing remodeling and new construction.

Modified Net Lease: *Do this if you want to give the tenant a major break on their first year's rent*

If you want to give a tenant a major break in their first year to get them off to a great start, consider doing a modified gross lease. The first year they would only pay the base rent, and starting in the second year they would convert to a net lease where they pay a pro rata share of the building's expenses.

Net Lease: *Protect against the uncertainty of increasing taxes, insurance, and maintenance by having your tenants pay these with a net lease*

With a net lease the tenant gets lower base rent in exchange for paying some of the operational expenses, such as taxes, insurance, and CAM expenses for utilities, trash, and janitorial. Net leases can be single net, double net, or triple net. Net lease properties tend to run more profitably and are lower risk. This is because the burden of increases in expenses is passed on to the tenants. Net leases are used most often with stand-alone buildings, and for office, retail, and industrial properties.

Off-Site Management Fees: *Be wary of property managers that nickel-and-dime you*

For multifamily properties of 12 units and under, be prepared to pay 10% of gross rental income; for properties of 13–36 units, 8%. Above 36 units, fees range from 6% to 8% of gross rents. For office, retail, and industrial properties off-site fees range from 4% to 8% and there is usually a fee of a half to full month's rent to find a tenant. Some multifamily property managers charge up to a full month's rent for filling a vacancy (common only on small properties). You should try and negotiate this away, or not pay more than a half month's rent.

Be wary of property managers that nickel-and-dime you. Some charge $50 per month for a unit that is vacant, along with a new account set-up fee and a lease renewal fee. A fee for eviction is customary.

On-Site Management Cost: *It's great to have boots on the ground to show vacant units and take care of tenant repair requests*

Multifamily and self-storage properties often have on-site managers that live on the property. Their salary, which ranges from $28,000–45,000 annually, most often includes a unit to live in, which is part of their wages. On-site managers show units to new tenants, make units ready to rent, and handle light maintenance on the property.

Operating Expense Caps: *Which method will you use to cap expenses in an expense stop?*

This refers to the methods by which expenses are capped before the landlord charges the tenant for a pro rata share of the overage in an *expense stop* (see earlier in this Topic).

Three Ways of Capping Expenses

1. **Year-to-Year Cap:** Expenses are capped at the previous year's amount. Any amount over this is shared pro rata with the tenant.
2. **Partial Cap on Controllable Expenses:** Only operating expenses that are under the property owner's control—such as repairs, maintenance, and administrative costs—are capped. Taxes, insurance, and utilities are not capped. This is the best of all worlds for the landlord.
3. **Percentage Cap:** The cap increases each year by an agreed percentage and is not based on actual increases in expenses.

Option Clauses (Leases): *Lease options only benefit the tenant*

Options in commercial leases really do not benefit the landlord. They leave all options open for the tenant. For the property owner, a lease option is often a disadvantage. If it's an up market and there is a shortage of this type of space available, when the lease expires they can often get more rent with a new tenant. If it's a down market and the lease expires, the existing tenant will likely continue to pay above-market rent so they don't have to go through the expense of moving.

Most tenants prefer to have one or two options to extend the lease. They might need to move to a larger space but then they might not. It is far better for the landlord to have a long-term lease without options. If they need to sell the property, long-term leases represent income security to a buyer. Also the buyer is going to want to attract a new tenant with higher rent when the lease expires.

I have a client right now that is interested in buying a 9,600-square-foot single-tenant retail building in a small market that is occupied by Goodwill. Great tenant, and priced at $850,000 at a 9 cap. What a buy! The listing broker is bragging that the tenant has two years remaining on their lease with two five-year options. This tenant has a good credit rating, and thrift stores do well during recessions. But I cannot even make a loan on this deal. I can only take into consideration the two-year lease. Lease options mean nothing to a lender. In two years if the tenant does not renew the option, the building is 100% vacant. In a small town, who else will rent this space?

> ## Time and Money Saving Tip
>
> If you are going to allow your tenant options, be sure to put into their lease that they have to give you six months' notice to exercise the option. If they leave, it can take you six months to find another tenant, and another three months for tenant improvements to be completed before you can start the new rent.

Percentage Lease: *Why not make a percentage of the tenant's excess profit by charging a percentage of it in additional rent?*

With a percentage lease, the tenant pays a base rent and a percentage rent. This is used almost exclusively in retail shopping malls, and the percentage averages 7%. These tenants are usually on triple net leases. When the tenant's sales hits a predetermined monthly amount, called a "breakpoint," anything above that amount is subject to the percentage rent. The landlord starts by determining the minimum amount of base rent they need for the space. Let's say the base rent is $3,500 per month. To determine the breakpoint you divide $3,500 by 7%, which comes to $50,000 a month in sales. Any gross revenue above $50,000 per month is subject to the 7% percentage rent.

As landlord, keep in mind that tenants are scared of percentage rent and would prefer to keep the breakpoint where percentage rent kicks in as high as possible. To give the tenant a feeling of well-being and also to protect yourself in case the tenant's sales crash, this is what works best:

Raise both the base rent and the breakpoint. Using the example above, raise the base rent from $3,500 to $4,500. When you divide $4,500 by 7% you get a breakpoint of

$64,285. For the tenant, that means they have to sell $14,285 per month more before they have to start paying the percentage rent. For the landlord, this means they are getting $1,000 more in guaranteed rent per month regardless of how the tenant runs their business. In both examples, the tenant is being charged 7% of their gross sales monthly in total rent so this is a win-win.

Property Management Contract (Protections for the Property Owner): *Although you will be provided with a boilerplate management contract, you can make changes*

Here are some of the most important things to watch out for or put into a property management contract:

1. *Fees.* Ideally, you want to just pay a percentage of the rent. Many management companies like to accessorize with fees for vacant units. Charging extra for finding tenants is standard for office, retail, and industrial properties, but is only the norm on smaller multifamily properties of 12 units and under. Of course, it is reasonable to pay extra for extras that are time consuming, such as evictions and overseeing construction. Ask the property manager to add to the contract that they will not be marking up the services of third party contractors.
2. *Services.* See *management duties for commercial property managers* (earlier in this Topic) and make sure that all of those items are listed as services provided.
3. *Contract duration.* Your lender will want to see a contract for a minimum of a year, which is also usually the property manager's minimum.
4. *Termination clause.* Just in case you choose a terrible management company, you want to be able to get out quick with 30 days' notice for any reason. Management companies prefer 90 days' notice. This is understandable, as it can take more than 30 days for them to complete projects and turn the property and financials over to you or to another management company. Have it in writing that they cannot charge you a penalty if you end the contract early. You want to just pay them for their last month of work. I have seen management contracts that require the property owner to pay what would be their earnings for the remaining period of the contract if they cancel early. Never agree to do this. Put into the agreement that upon termination, they need to provide you with all leases, financials, and other property documents within 30 days.
5. *Hold harmless clause.* This protects the management company from being liable for anything except their own negligence. They will require that you indemnify them for everything else. Your greatest risk with this is that they hire an employee or vendor that is incompetent. Be sure to put into the contract a requirement that they have to screen all employees and vendors.
6. *Reserve fund.* This is something management companies really do need in order to cover unexpected expenses and emergencies. Funds from rents will all be going out each month for expenses and owner distributions. A full or even a half month's expenses is likely enough for this fund. If the property needs a lot of repair, then adjust this accordingly. Make sure this is an amount you can afford. If it is not, tell them you will add to it later when needed.

7. *Finding tenants.* Most management companies have it in the contract that the owner cannot find tenants. Unless you absolutely do not want to find tenants, it can be in your interest to write into the contract that you can also do this—and also that you have the right to review tenant files to see evidence that the management company is screening tenants adequately.

8. *Insurance.* The management agreement will list the amount of coverage you need to have for various types of insurance. They will also want you to cover them. This is standard. Make sure you have it in writing that they will competitively shop for insurance that meet your lender's requirements for insurance. Some management companies get kickbacks from insurance agents, so put into the contract that you need to review at least three bids. Commercial property insurance is very competitive.

> **Time and Money Saving Tip**
>
> If you have more than one commercial property, see if you can get a multiple property insurance policy for casualty and liability. Many of my clients have saved a lot of money doing this. If you buy this directly from a major carrier, such as Allstate, State Farm, or American Family (or others), you will really save. Keep in mind that although independent insurance agents represent a wide range of insurance companies, they are intermediaries. A direct carrier can be more competitive by cutting out the commission to the independent agent. If you only own one commercial property, see if your property manager can get you a deal because of the volume they represent on insurance. Again, get at least three bids.

Property Management Software: *Be sure that your property is being managed by the latest software*

Whether you are using a management company or self-managing, it is essential these days to use the latest commercial property management software. These are Web-based systems that have portals for property owners, property managers, tenants, and maintenance staff to access information and communicate. Importantly, tenants can pay their rent online or set up an automatic draft there. On the financial side, the software creates reports on accounts payable, accounts receivable, rent rolls, profit and loss statements, bank ledgers, and bank reconciliation. You should have online visibility for occupied, soon to be vacated, and vacant units. The system can capture tenant files and lease information. A tenant can make a repair request and even attach a photo. Three of the top property management software packages are AppFolio, Yardi Breeze, and SimplifyEm.

Rent Abatement: *This is the tenant saying, "Give me free rent please"*

Often when office, retail, or industrial tenants are negotiating a new lease they will request rent abatement (to not pay rent) for three months or longer for the following reasons:

- To cover the time they need to relocate and move to the new space. This is a reasonable request, but I recommend you split the difference. They might have three months or more remaining on their lease at their current location.
- To cover the time it will take to install leasehold improvements (LIs). This one is reasonable, but be sure to put in a commencement date when the rent absolutely has to start—who knows when the tenant improvements will be completed?
- To help them get off to a great start by not having rent for the first three to six months. Yes, this "Just give me free rent" is how real estate brokers that represent tenants earn their keep. Often they'll tell you that they were offered this by someone else and if you don't match it.... This one only makes sense if you will be getting good rent for the space or it has been hard to lease.

Rent Concessions: *These can be a double-edged sword. Use them carefully and sparingly*

Rent concessions are a discount on rent or a rebate offered to a tenant to entice them into moving in quickly. They should only be used in a sluggish rental market and hopefully used temporarily. If they are ongoing, they will greatly lower the property's annual NOI, which will ultimately lower the property's value. Lenders will often annualize ongoing concessions and take that income off the rent roll. This can result in a smaller loan.

Here are some popular rent concessions: for multifamily properties, lower rent for the first three months; get your 12th month rent-free when you sign a year's lease; free cable TV and Internet for six months; a big-screen TV. For office, retail, and industrial properties, get one to three months' free rent; a lower security deposit; paying for tenant improvements; and paying the tenant's real estate broker fee.

The one time that rent concessions make sense is after a property is newly constructed or rehabbed and the lease-up is going slowly due to a down market cycle. Rent concessions can be a double-edged sword: they may solve an immediate problem but then cause another one in the future. An example of this is when a seller has under-market occupancy and quickly fills the property to increase occupancy, only to start having rent collection problems.

Rent per Square Foot: *It's good to start thinking in rent per square foot if you have an office, retail, or industrial property.*

For multifamily and self-storage properties, rent is simply a quote per unit per month. For office, retail, and industrial properties, real estate brokers and property managers quote rent as a price per square foot. This is actually per square foot per year. So for a 2,600-square-foot retail space, the rent might be quoted at $14 per square foot. This is 2,600 × $14 = $36,400 annual rent. Or, divided by 12 equals $3,033 per month. If you are new to this, it is important to start thinking in price per square foot and then have your calculator handy to figure out the monthly rent.

Request for Proposal (RFP) (Leases): *This is a tenant asking you for your best lease terms*

This is a request from a tenant to a landlord for a written proposal for the very best lease terms they can offer and a request for a copy of their standard lease. Commercial real estate brokers that represent strong national tenants often request this. Just be aware that they are most likely getting offers from multiple properties in your market and may use them to have the properties compete against each other. It is smart business to ask the tenant's representative what offers they have received so far. If this is a tenant you really want, then they will be worth competing for.

Time and Money Saving Tip

If you have just purchased an office, retail, or industrial property, be sure to check to confirm that each space has been measured accurately. These days well-informed tenants have their space professionally measured. Measurements provided by the landlord are often inaccurate if dividing walls are at an angle. If a tenant can prove that their space is actually 130 square feet smaller than they were told, at $16 per square foot they will save $2,080 annually, or $10,400 over five years, by contesting this.

Security Deposits: *Larger security deposits equate to financially stronger tenants*

Multifamily property security deposits. It is standard when renting multifamily properties for the tenant to put down a month's rent and a second month's rent as a security deposit. Certainly do not accept less than that or you will be attracting a less financially secure tenant. My multifamily clients that ask for first month's rent plus one and a half month's rent security deposit never have a problem with those tenants paying the rent or damaging the property. And be sure not to call any of the deposit "last month's rent," because in most states those funds can only be used to cover the last month's rent.

Office, retail, and industrial property security deposits. For office, retail, and industrial properties, it is better to collect the first month's rent plus two month's rent for the security deposit. Again, if the tenant has the capacity to come up with this larger amount at the signing of the lease that's going to sit there for 5–10 years, they are more likely to be financially strong. Also, in the future if the tenant is on the verge of going out of business and stops paying rent, it can take you three months or longer to evict them if you have to go through the court system. Then the additional security deposit will come in handy.

Single Net Lease: *Can you get your tenants to pay the building's real estate taxes?*

In addition to their base rent, the tenant pays a pro rata share of the property's real estate taxes. A single net lease is rarely used.

Sublease Clause (Leases): *If you don't have a sublease clause in the lease, your tenant may be able to sublease to anyone*

It's important that your commercial leases have a sublease clause that is very specific as to under what conditions the tenant can sublease. In most states, the tenant can sublease to whomever they want if there is no sublease clause. Be sure to require that the replacement tenant use the space for the same purpose or get approval from the landlord for another use. Have it written into the sublease clause that you have to approve the replacement tenant's financials, credit, and experience.

Subordination, Non-Disturbance, and Attornment Agreement (SNDA): *It's imperative to have an SNDA clause in your leases (for office, retail and industrial properties).*

Without signing an SNDA, the tenant is in a position superior to the landlord's lender should the property be foreclosed upon. The tenant could move out or dig their heels in and stay if they are in default. After all, the lease is between them and the landlord, not between them and the landlord's lender. When a tenant signs a lease with an SNDA, they are agreeing that their lease will remain in full force should the landlord's lender foreclose on the property.

The SNDA benefits the lender, the tenant, and the landlord. Let's say the property is foreclosed upon and sold by the lender, and the buyer wants to demolish the building so they can use it for another purpose. The tenant would just be out without an SNDA. Most commercial real estate lenders require tenants to sign their SNDAs. This ensures that the lease is still active and gives them control over the tenant if they foreclose on the property. The last thing they want if they foreclose is have a property to sell without good leases and tenants. As far as the landlord goes, they are not likely to get a quality mortgage without the tenants agreeing to sign SNDAs. So it is important to have a clause in the lease that requires tenants to sign an SNDA.

> **Subordination:** In this clause the tenant agrees to have their interest in the lease and rights to occupy the space subordinate or junior to the interest of the landlord's lender. Why would they agree to this? Because of the non-disturbance clause described next.

> **Non-disturbance:** In exchange for subordinating their interest to the lender and recognizing a buyer of the property as their landlord, they are given the rights to occupy the space under the terms of their lease if the property is foreclosed on and eventually sold. This is as long as they are not in default on the lease.

> **Attornment:** Whether a new owner of the property acquires it through a purchase or a foreclosure sale, the tenant agrees to accept the new owner as their landlord and agrees to pay the rent to them and follow the covenants of the lease.

Tenant Allowance (TA)/Tenant Improvement Allowance (TIA): *It's best to only give a tenant allowance to new, financially strong, creditworthy tenants*

This is an agreement in the lease where the property owner agrees to pay for all or a portion of a new tenant's buildout for leasehold and tenant improvements. It is negotiated as a certain dollar amount per square foot, which protects the landlord from cost overruns. It can cover anything from light remodeling to construction. It is typical for the allowance to include floor coverings, construction materials and labor, design and architectural drawings, professional fees, and building permits. Signage, furniture, and fixtures are not usually included.

As landlord, it is always best to contribute to TAs for stronger, high-credit tenants signing longer leases. These tenants can afford to pay for work done and then be reimbursed progressively as the work is completed and inspected. If the tenant needs the TA upfront from you to do the work, they may be financially strapped and not be the right tenant.

Tenant Improvements (TI)/ Leasehold Improvements (LI): *Be careful when tenant improvements alter a space so that its future use is limited*

Tenant improvements, also called leasehold improvements, include most items needed to complete a new tenant's buildout. These include paint, floor, and window coverings, HVAC, plumbing, electrical, and interior walls. It's negotiable who pays for TIs. The landlord typically only pays the entire cost for TIs for strong-credit or creditworthy tenants signing long-term leases. Landlords get much higher rents in exchange. The right TIs can be a good investment for the future. Make sure if the tenant is altering the space in a way that makes the space unusable for most future tenants that they are signing a long lease and pay for most or all of the TIs. An example of this would be a buildout for a dental office in a shopping center when the space was originally built for retail.

Time and Money Saving Tip

If the tenant is paying for leasehold improvements, most will use a bank loan. Make sure your commercial lease has a strong leasehold financing clause. Without this, if the tenant goes out of business you can be caught in a quagmire of litigation with both the tenant and the lender. Often the lender will want to take security in what they call "the tenant's leasehold interests." This can be a broad range of items, including fixed items like HVAC units or even the right to sell all the leasehold improvements to another tenant. It is essential to make clear to the tenant in the early stages of lease negotiations and in the lease that the lender can only take security in their trade fixtures that are removable. Encourage them to collateralize the loan with other sources like their inventory. If they are getting an SBA loan, the loan does not have to be fully collateralized.

Tenant Mix: *It's really worth it to take your time with putting the right tenant mix together*

This really is important for the owners of retail and some flex light-industrial properties. When looking for new tenants, decide ahead of time what type is going to fit best with your existing tenants. You don't want to over-duplicate the products or services of your other tenants. Do you need to attract a tenant that has a huge following to act as your anchor tenant? Sometimes adding a very popular restaurant chain or national tenant can have the same effect as having an anchor tenant by drawing many shoppers that will patronize other businesses close by.

Tenant Relocation Clause: *It's going to cost you a bundle if you have to move a tenant*

This clause gives the landlord the right to move a tenant to another space should they need to combine the space with a space next door to make room for a larger tenant. This clause is found mostly in shopping centers and light-industrial property leases. Why would a tenant agree to this? Well, most tenants will not.

To entice the tenant to allow this clause in their lease, it will be costly when you move them. Here are a few guidelines for what the landlord will likely need to agree on:

- To only move them one time during their lease term
- To pay for all LIs and to build out the space to the quality and specifications of the tenant's original space
- To move them to a similar sized space
- To compensate them for moving costs and lost income during the move

Now you have to decide if moving them is worth it!

Term of Lease: *Is it better for you to have tenants sign a long- or short-term lease?*

Advantage of long-term leases for landlords. If you own a multifamily property and want to get some of the best-quality financing from Fannie Mae or Freddie Mac, it's best to have all tenants on annual leases. These lenders are concerned that many monthly tenants will move out at the same time. Community banks are okay with month-to-month tenancy as long as the property has a good occupancy history. For office, retail, and industrial properties, most lenders will require the remaining term of your leases to average at least 70% of the fixed rate term you desire on the loan.

For example, say you have 10 tenants that have remaining lease terms averaging 7 years. You can likely qualify for a 10-year fixed rate mortgage. If you want to sell it, the property will be worth more if the majority of the leases have 5 years or more remaining on leases and anchor tenants have 10 years or more remaining.

Advantages of short-term leases for landlords. For multifamily properties, in most states it is faster to evict a tenant on a month-to-month tenancy than on an annual lease. Also with lease terms of six months, you can raise rents more frequently. For office, retail, and industrial properties, the main benefit in keeping leases as short as three years is that you can raise rents based on what the market will bear much more frequently. Also if you need to make room for a larger national tenant that will draw like an anchor, you can kick out two to four smaller tenants when their lease terms run out.

Triple Net Lease: *Sit back and relax, as the property owner has little to do*

Triple net leases are often signed by investment grade tenants that are getting favorable base rent in exchange for also paying a prorated share of the property's taxes, insurance, and maintenance. Structural repairs like roof replacement are not included. Many large indoor shopping malls have triple net leases as well as Class A and B office properties.

Managing and Leasing

Stand-alone credit tenant triple net lease properties have almost nothing for the property owner to do, so there is really no need for professional management. But be prepared for lengthy, complicated lease negotiations. For national credit tenants it can take six months or longer to get a lease signed. I financed a Walgreens once and it took over two years to negotiate the lease. These tenants are sophisticated and have tough attorneys. But the good news is that they want to sign long-term leases, most often as long as 25 years.

Turnkey: *This implies that there is nothing much to do*

This usually refers to investment grade tenant, triple net lease properties for sale. In this case, turnkey implies that there is nothing for the property owner to do. The tenant maintains the building and pays for maintenance, taxes, and insurance. The property owner just collects the rent.

A turnkey lease is an office, retail, or industrial space that is configured perfectly for many tenants. And if it is not, the landlord will take care of all the tenant improvements at their cost, except for FF&Es. If you are the landlord providing a turnkey lease, you should be able to get a premium in rent.

Useable Square Footage Versus Rentable Square Footage: *Can you get your tenants to pay not only for their own space, but for common areas, restrooms, stairways and walkways?*

To maximize your income on a multitenant commercial property, it makes sense to have the tenants pay not only for the space they occupy, but for all the space in common areas. *Triple net leases* (see earlier in this Topic) take advantage of this concept.

Useable square footage refers to just the space the tenant occupies. Rentable square footage refers to the tenant's own space plus all shared areas, including common areas such as indoor and outdoor meeting spaces, lobbies, shared restrooms, hallways, and stairwells. The amount of space a tenant is paying for in rentable square footage above their own space is called their "load factor." Tenants are advised to keep this below 15%. Landlords just want to make sure that the entire square footage of the building is being paid for by tenants.

Appendix A

The forms in this appendix are samples only, as the originals are in Excel format and editable versions cannot be printed in a book. To find the downloadable Excel versions on my website, just go to https://apartmentloanstore.com and click on "Loan Forms & Tools" at the top right.

Commercial Property Purchase or Finance Evaluator: Take the annual totals from the seven-year month-by-month budget summary spreadsheet and plug them into this spreadsheet. This will calculate your annual CCR and IRR over time.

04-07-2020

APARTMENT PURCHASE OR FINANCE EVALUATOR

Note: Enter property information in the YELLOW fields

	29	Units	Cap Rate	6.62%

Property Address:	1235 Colonial Blvd, Seattle WA 12345		
INVESTMENT PRO FORMA			
Price or Value:	5,250,000	Land	1,050,000
Loans:	3,675,000	Improvements	4,260,000
Down Payment or Equity:	1,575,000	Property/Taxes	70,000
Capital and Closing Cost:	91,875	LTV	70.00%
Renovations	60,000	DSCR	1.56
Investment Amount:	1,726,875		

INVESTMENT RETURNS	
Purchase Price Per Unit	$181,034
Capitalization Rate	6.62%
Cash on Cash Return Year 1	7.18%
Average Cash on Cash Return	7.83%
Seven (7) Year Pre-Tax IRR	14.03%

Loan:	Loan Amount	Int Only	Term In Years	Payments Per Year	Due In	Interest Rate	Prin & Int Payment	Annual Debt Service	Loan Closing Escrow Costs
Existing/New 1st Mortgage	3,675,000	n	30	12	10	4.500%	18,620.69	223,448	78,750

SCHEDULED RENT ROLL			
# of Units	Type	Monthly Rent/ bed	Total
20	1 br	$ 800.00	$ 16,000.00
3	2br/1bath	$ 800.00	$ 2,400.00
3	2br/2bath	$ 1,000.00	$ 3,000.00
2	studio	$ 700.00	$ 1,400.00
1	office	$ 500.00	$ 500.00
Total 29		$ 3,800.00	$ 45,600.00

ANNUAL OPERATING INCOME	$	% of EGI	Per SF
Gross Scheduled Income	$ 547,200.00	100.3%	$18,869
Other Income (utility)	$ 28,153.00	5.2%	$971
Gross Operating Income	$ 575,353.00	105.5%	$19,840
Vacancy Factor	$ 28,767.65	5.0%	($992)
Rent Concessions	$ 1,200.00		
Effective Gross Income	$ 545,385.35		$18,806
Real Estate Taxes	$ 70,000.00	12.8%	$2,414
Insurance	$ 18,000.00	3.3%	$621
Electricity & Gas	$ 34,000.00	6.2%	$1,172
Advertising & Admin	$ 1,500.00	0.3%	$52
Management	$ 27,269.27	5.0%	$940
On-site Manager	$ 3,600.00	0.7%	$124
Maintenance/Repairs	$ 14,000.00	2.6%	$483
Landscape Maint.	$ 16,000.00	0.6%	$552
Turning Expenses	$ 2,500.00	0.5%	$86
Garbage	$ 1,200.00	0.2%	$41
Supplies	$ 50.00	0.0%	$2
0	$ -	0.0%	$0
Telephone	$ 500.00	0.1%	$17
Sewer/Water	$ 2,000.00	0.4%	$69
	$ -	0.0%	$0
Reserves	$ 7,250.00	3.0%	$250
	$ -	0.0%	$0
	$ -	0.0%	$0
Total Operating Expense	$ 197,869.27	36.28%	$6,823
Net Operating Income	$ 347,516.08	60.4%	$11,983
Annual Debt Service	$ 223,448.22	38.8%	$7,705
Cash Flow Before Taxes	$ 124,067.86	7.2%	$4,278

INVESTMENT ASSUMPTIONS	
Income Growth	3.0%
Expense Growth	3.0%
Land Value % of Purchase Price	0%
SF of NRA	29
Years of Investment	7
Investor's Tax Bracket:	30%
Federal Capital Gains Tax	15%
State Capital Gains Tax	9%
Depreciation Recapture Rate	25%
Straight-Line Deprecation Apartments	27.5
Notes:	
Appreciation	3.0%

ANALYSIS

1st Mortgage — Encumbrances

1st Mortgage	Beginning Balance	Int Only	Remaining Term	Payments Per Year	Due In	Interest Rate	Prin & Int Payment	Annual Debt Service
Interest only (Y/N)	3,675,000	n	30	12	10	4.50%	18,621	223,448

	Year 1	Year 2	Year 3	Year 4	Year 5	Year 6	Year 7
Interest	N	N	N	N	N	N	N
2nd & 3rd Mortgage — Interest	3,615,714	3,553,704	3,488,846	3,421,008	3,350,053	3,275,839	3,198,216
Principal Reduction	164,162	161,439	158,590	155,610	152,494	149,234	145,825
	0	0	0	0	0	0	0
	59,286	62,010	64,858	67,838	70,954	74,214	77,623

Taxable Income

Income Growth 3.0% · Expense Growth 4.0%

	Year 1	Year 2	Year 3	Year 4	Year 5	Year 6	Year 7
	0.0%	4.0%	3.0% / 4.0%	3.0% / 4.0%	3.0% / 4.0%	3.0% / 4.0%	3.0% / 4.0%
Effective Gross Income	545,385	545,385	561,747	578,599	595,957	613,836	632,251
-Operating Expense	197,869	205,784	214,015	222,576	231,479	240,738	250,368
Net Operating Income	347,516	339,601	347,732	356,023	364,478	373,098	381,883
-Interest	164,162	161,439	158,590	155,610	152,494	149,234	145,825
-Depreciation	154,909	154,909	154,909	154,909	154,909	154,909	154,909
Taxable Income	28,445	23,254	34,233	45,504	57,075	68,955	81,149

Cash Flows

	Year 1	Year 2	Year 3	Year 4	Year 5	Year 6	Year 7
Net Operating Income	347,516	339,601	347,732	356,023	364,478	373,098	381,883
-Annual Debt Service	223,448	223,448	223,448	223,448	223,448	223,448	223,448
-Funded Reserves							
Cash Flow Before Taxes	124,068	116,153	124,283	132,575	141,030	149,650	158,435
Net Return Before Taxes	7.18%	6.73%	7.20%	7.68%	8.17%	8.67%	9.17%
Tax Liability	8,533	6,976	10,270	13,651	17,123	20,686	24,345
Cash Flow After Taxes	115,535	109,177	114,013	118,924	123,907	128,964	134,090
Net Return After Taxes	6.69%	6.32%	6.60%	6.89%	7.18%	7.47%	7.76%

Analysis of Sale Proceeds

Original Basis	5,401,875
+Capital Improvements	20,000
+Costs of Sale	531,490
Sub-Total	5,953,365
-Depreciation	1,084,364
-Partial Sales	0
AB at Sale	4,869,001
Sale Price	6,643,625
-AB	4,869,001
Gain	1,774,624
Capital Gains Tax	24.00%
Tax Liability & Recapture	436,753

Sale Proceeds

Sale Price	6,643,625
-Costs of Sale	531,490
-Mortgage	3,198,216
Gross Proceeds	2,913,919
-Tax on Proceeds	436,753
Net Proceeds	2,477,166

Factors

Gross Rent Multiplier (GRM)	9.59
Cap Rate	6.62%
Cash on Cash Return after Tax	6.69%
IRR After Tax	11.30%

The information contained herein has been obtained from sources deemed to be reliable but not guaranteed by Broker. Any projections, assumptions, opinions, or estimates are used for example only and do not represent current or future performance of the property. Any prospective buyer is advised to seek advice from competent tax, financial, and/or legal advisors. State and local taxes are not figured in the worksheet.

Apartment Quick Analysis Calculator: When you find a property you are interested in buying, just fill in the sales price and net operating income, and this spreadsheet will calculate a range of values based on cap rates and gross rent multiplier (GRM).

Apartment Quick Analysis Spreadsheet

Note: Enter property information in the YELLOW fields

Operating Financials

Income

	Monthly	Annual
Rents	$ 15,657	$ 187,883
Other Income	$ —	$ —
Total Rents	$ 15,657	**187,883**
Less Vacancy 5.0%	$ (783)	$ (9,394)

Adjusted Rental Income

	Monthly	Annual
	14,874	**178,489**

Expenses

	Monthly	Annual
Operating Expenses 0%	$ 5,922	$ 71,067
Management $ 250 Per Unit/Annum	$ —	$ —
Capital Reserves	$ 188	$ 2,250
Total Expense	$ 6,110	**73,317**

Net Operating Income

	$ 8,764	$ 105,172

Number of Units	9
Purchase Price	$ 2,000,000.00
Down Payment	$ 500,000.00
Loan Size	$ 1,500,000.00
Cost per Unit	$ 222,222.22

PI Reserve	$ 136,805.03

Cap Rate at above price	5.26%

Value Based on Cap Rate		Value Based on GRM	
5.0%	$ 2,103,437.00	15	$ 2,818,245
5.5%	$ 1,912,215.45	14	$ 2,630,362
6.0%	$ 1,752,864.17	13	$ 2,442,479
6.5%	$ 1,618,028.46	12	$ 2,254,596
7.0%	$ 1,502,455.00	10	$ 1,878,830

Loan Details

Loan Amount	$ 1,500,000.00
Loan to Value	75%
Interest Rate	4.50%
Term	360
Monthly Payment	$ 7,600.28

Debt Service Cash Ratio (DSCR)	1.15

Commercial Quick Analysis Calculator: This performs the same analysis as the apartment quick analysis spreadsheet, but for general commercial properties.

Commercial Quick Analysis Spreadsheet

Note: Enter property information in the YELLOW fields

Operating Financials

Income

	Monthly	Annual
Rents	$ 19,167	$ 230,000
Other Income	$ 125	$ 1,500
Tenant Expense Reimbursement	$ 1,000	$ 12,000
Total Rents	$ 20,292	$ 243,500
Less Vacancy	$ (958)	$ (11,500)

5.0%

Adjusted Rental Income	$ 19,333	$ 232,000

Expenses

	Monthly	Annual
Operating Expenses	$ 4,500	$ 54,000
Management	$ 1,150	$ 13,800
Capital Reserves	$ 1,094	$ 13,125
Total Expense	$ 6,744	$ 80,925

6%
$0.75 Per Square Ft

Net Operating Income	$ 12,590	$ 151,075

Purchase Price	$ 2,000,000.00
Downpayment	$ 500,000.00
Loan Size	$ 1,500,000.00

Number of Units	12
Square Footage	17,500.00
Cost per Sq Ft	$ 114.29
Annual Rent per Sq Ft	$ 13.14
Monthly Rent per Sq Ft	$ 1.10
Cost per Unit	$ 166,666.67

Cap Rate at above price	7.55%

Value Based on Cap Rate

		Value Based on GRM	
6.0%	$ 2,517,916.67	12	$ 2,922,000
6.5%	$ 2,324,230.77	11	$ 2,678,500
7.0%	$ 2,158,214.29	10	$ 2,435,000
7.5%	$ 2,014,333.33	9	$ 2,191,500
8.0%	$ 1,888,437.50	8	$ 1,948,000

Loan Details

Loan Amount	$ 1,500,000.00
Loan to Value	75%
Interest Rate	4.50%
Term	360
Monthly Payment	$ 7,600.28

Debt Service Cash Ratio (DSCR)	1.66

Commercial Rent Roll: Use this rent roll for office, retail, and industrial properties. It includes space square footage, lease dates, type of lease, and more.

Business Loan Store

COMMERCIAL RENT ROLL CERTIFICATION

Subject Property Address: _____ City _____ State _____ ZIP _____

Borrower (print name): _____

Add'l Borrower (print name): _____

TENANT	UNIT NO.	SQ FT. PER UNIT	MONTHLY RENT	LEASE START DATE	LEASE END DATE	Lease Type: NN, NNN, or MG	Section 8 or Subsidized (yes or no)	Tax and Insurance	CAM	Escalation Date	Comments
Total		0	$ -				0	$ -	$ -		

(*) Lease Type **NN** = Double Net; **NNN** = Triple Net; **MG** = Modified Gross

The undersigned certify(ies) that all information provided in this rent roll is true, accurate, and complete in all respects.

_____ _____ _____ _____
Borrower's or Authorized Agent's / Seller's Signature Date Borrower's or Authorized Agent's / Seller's Signature Date

_____ _____ _____ _____
Borrower's or Authorized Agent's / Seller's Signature Date Borrower's or Authorized Agent's / Seller's Signature Date

Multifamily Rent Roll: This rent roll form has unit configuration, beginning and ending dates for rental contracts, Section 8 tenancy, and more.

Multifamily Rent Roll   Number of Units   20

Apt #	Tenant Name	Beds/Baths	Sq Feet	Current Rent	Section 8	Section 8 Pays	Renter Pays	Lease Start Date	Lease Expiration
1	Joan Baker	3/2	850	$ 1,350.00	Y	$ 1,100.00	$ 250.00		Dec 2020
2	John Smith	2/2	750	$ 1,200.00	N	$ -	$ 1,200.00		Mar 2021
3	David Klein	2/1	650	$ 1,150.00	N	$ -	$ 1,150.00		Apr 2021
4									
5									
6									
7									
8									
9									
10									
11									
12									
13									
14									
15									
16									
17									
18									
19									
20									

Total Rents	$ 3,700.00	$ 1,100.00	$ 2,600.00

Personal Financial Statement: This is a statement of your assets, liabilities, and net worth. Lenders and sellers will want to review this.

Sample Assets and Liabilities Statement:

Assets:		Liabilities	
Cash in Bank	$ 125,000.00	Credit Card Debt	$ 26,000.00
Cash in Savings	$ 35,000.00	Personal Loans	$ 12,000.00
Stocks and Bonds	$ 75,000.00	Vehicle Loans	$ 25,000.00
Life Insurance Surrender Value	$ 5,000.00	Home Mortgage: 256 Elm St Seattle	$ 180,000.00
Notes Receivable	$ 8,000.00	Mortgage 1: 125 Oak St Seattle	$ 450,000.00
Vehicles	$ 28,000.00	Mortgage 2: 225 Oak St Seattle	$ 285,000.00
Household Items	$ 25,000.00	**Mortgage 3: 325 Oak St Seattle**	**$ 310,000.00**
Business Interests	$ 30,000.00	Mortgage 4: 425 Oak St Seattle	$ 265,000.00
Other Assets	$ 25,000.00	Mortgage 5: 525 Oak St Seattle	**$ 643,000.00**
		Mortgage 6: 625 Oak St Seattle	**$ 276,000.00**
Real Estate			
Primary Home: 256 Elm St Seattle	$ 850,000.00	**Total Liabilities**	**$ 2,472,000.00**
Rental 1: 125 Oak St Seattle	$ 835,000.00		
Rental 2: 225 Oak St Seattle	$ 275,000.00		
Rental 3: 325 Oak St Seattle	**$ 375,000.00**	**Net Worth**	**$ 2,279,000.00**
Rental 4: 425 Oak St Seattle	$ 850,000.00		
Rental 5: 525 Oak St Seattle	$ 835,000.00		
Rental 6: 625 Oak St Seattle	$ 375,000.00		
Total Assets	**$ 4,751,000.00**		

Repositioning Pro Forma: Use this pro forma worksheet to project cash flows for repositioning projects over time.

7 YEAR REPOSITIONING MORTGAGE DATA AND INSTRUCTIONS

Mortgage 1	
Loan Amount	$ 1,500,000.00
Interest Rate	4.00%
Amortization Period	360
Monthly Payment	$ 7,161.23

Mortgage 2	
Loan Amount	$ 1,000,000.00
Interest Rate	5.00%
Amortization Period	360
Monthly Payment	$ 5,368.22

INSTRUCTIONS

Fill in the yellow fields for the following:

Mortgage Details

Rents for Year 1
Rents for Year 2

Income other than Rents in the **Budget Year 1** Tab
Expense in Budget Year 1 Tab
Beginning Cash in Budget Year 1 Tab
Monthly Cash Injection in Budget Year 1 Tab
Monthly Renovation Cost in Budget Year 1 Tab
Monthly Owner Draw in Budget Year 1 Tab

Monthly Cash Injection in Budget Year 2 through Year 7 Tabs
Monthly Renovation Cost in Budget Year 2 through Year 7 Tabs
Monthly Owner Draw in Budget Year 2 through Year 7 Tabs

Adjust the monthly Expense Percent Increase in the Year 2 Tab
Adjust the monthly Income and Expense Increase in the Year 3 through Year 7 Tab

The rest of the numbers will self-populate according to embedded formulas
Value Summary Tab allows you to enter Cap Rates for valuation purposes

FIRST YEAR REPOSITIONING PRO FORMA RENTAL INCOME

Unit	Month 1	Month 2	Month 3	Month 4	Month 5	Month 6	Month 7	Month 8	Month 9	Month 10	Month 11	Month 12	Total
1	$ 960.00			$ 1,200.00	$ 1,200.00	$ 1,200.00	$ 1,200.00	$ 1,200.00	$ 1,200.00	$ 1,200.00	$ 1,200.00	$ 1,200.00	$ 11,760.00
2	$ 960.00			$ 1,200.00	$ 1,200.00	$ 1,200.00	$ 1,200.00	$ 1,200.00	$ 1,200.00	$ 1,200.00	$ 1,200.00	$ 1,200.00	$ 11,760.00
3	$ 960.00			$ 1,200.00	$ 1,200.00	$ 1,200.00	$ 1,200.00	$ 1,200.00	$ 1,200.00	$ 1,200.00	$ 1,200.00	$ 1,200.00	$ 11,760.00
4	$ 960.00	$ 960.00	$ 960.00	$ 960.00	$ 960.00	$ 960.00	$ 960.00	$ 960.00			$ 1,200.00	$ 1,200.00	$ 10,080.00
5	$ 960.00	$ 960.00	$ 960.00	$ 960.00	$ 960.00	$ 960.00	$ 960.00	$ 960.00			$ 1,200.00	$ 1,200.00	$ 10,080.00
6	$ 960.00	$ 960.00	$ 960.00	$ 960.00	$ 960.00	$ 960.00	$ 960.00	$ 960.00			$ 1,200.00	$ 1,200.00	$ 10,080.00
7	$ 960.00	$ 960.00	$ 960.00	$ 960.00	$ 960.00	$ 960.00	$ 960.00	$ 960.00			$ 1,200.00	$ 1,200.00	$ 10,080.00
8	$ 960.00	$ 960.00	$ 960.00	$ 960.00	$ 960.00	$ 960.00	$ 960.00	$ 960.00	$ 960.00	$ 960.00	$ 960.00	$ 960.00	$ 11,520.00
9	$ 960.00	$ 960.00	$ 960.00	$ 960.00	$ 960.00	$ 960.00	$ 960.00	$ 960.00	$ 960.00	$ 960.00	$ 960.00	$ 960.00	$ 11,520.00
10	$ 960.00	$ 960.00	$ 960.00	$ 960.00	$ 960.00	$ 960.00	$ 960.00	$ 960.00	$ 960.00	$ 960.00	$ 960.00	$ 960.00	$ 11,520.00
11	$ 1,150.00	$ 1,150.00	$ 1,150.00	$ 1,150.00	$ 1,150.00	$ 1,150.00	$ 1,150.00	$ 1,150.00	$ 1,150.00			$ 1,350.00	$ 11,710.00
12	$ 1,150.00	$ 1,150.00	$ 1,150.00	$ 1,150.00	$ 1,150.00	$ 1,150.00	$ 1,150.00	$ 1,150.00	$ 1,150.00			$ 1,350.00	$ 11,710.00
13	$ 1,150.00	$ 1,150.00	$ 1,150.00	$ 1,150.00	$ 1,150.00	$ 1,150.00	$ 1,150.00	$ 1,150.00	$ 1,150.00			$ 1,350.00	$ 11,710.00
14	$ 1,150.00	$ 1,150.00	$ 1,150.00			$ 1,350.00	$ 1,350.00	$ 1,350.00	$ 1,350.00	$ 1,350.00	$ 1,350.00	$ 1,350.00	$ 12,900.00
15	$ 1,150.00	$ 1,150.00	$ 1,150.00			$ 1,350.00	$ 1,350.00	$ 1,350.00	$ 1,350.00	$ 1,350.00	$ 1,350.00	$ 1,350.00	$ 12,900.00
16	$ 1,150.00	$ 1,150.00	$ 1,150.00			$ 1,350.00	$ 1,350.00	$ 1,350.00	$ 1,350.00	$ 1,350.00	$ 1,350.00	$ 1,350.00	$ 12,900.00
17	$ 1,150.00	$ 1,150.00	$ 1,150.00			$ 1,350.00	$ 1,350.00	$ 1,350.00	$ 1,350.00	$ 1,350.00	$ 1,350.00	$ 1,350.00	$ 12,900.00
18	$ 1,150.00	$ 1,150.00	$ 1,150.00	$ 1,150.00			$ 1,350.00	$ 1,350.00	$ 1,350.00	$ 1,350.00	$ 1,350.00	$ 1,350.00	$ 12,700.00
19	$ 1,150.00	$ 1,150.00	$ 1,150.00	$ 1,150.00			$ 1,350.00	$ 1,350.00	$ 1,350.00	$ 1,350.00	$ 1,350.00	$ 1,350.00	$ 12,700.00
20	$ 1,150.00	$ 1,150.00	$ 1,150.00	$ 1,150.00			$ 1,350.00	$ 1,350.00	$ 1,350.00	$ 1,350.00	$ 1,350.00	$ 1,350.00	$ 12,700.00
21	$ 1,150.00	$ 1,150.00	$ 1,150.00	$ 1,150.00			$ 1,350.00	$ 1,350.00	$ 1,350.00	$ 1,350.00	$ 1,350.00	$ 1,350.00	$ 12,700.00
22	$ 1,150.00	$ 1,150.00	$ 1,150.00	$ 1,150.00			$ 1,350.00	$ 1,350.00	$ 1,350.00	$ 1,350.00	$ 1,350.00	$ 1,350.00	$ 12,700.00
23	$ 850.00	$ 850.00	$ 850.00	$ 850.00	$ 850.00			$ 1,100.00	$ 1,100.00	$ 1,100.00	$ 1,100.00	$ 1,100.00	$ 9,750.00
24	$ 850.00	$ 850.00	$ 850.00	$ 850.00	$ 850.00			$ 1,100.00	$ 1,100.00	$ 1,100.00	$ 1,100.00	$ 1,100.00	$ 9,750.00
25	$ 850.00	$ 850.00	$ 850.00	$ 850.00	$ 850.00			$ 1,100.00	$ 1,100.00	$ 1,100.00	$ 1,100.00	$ 1,100.00	$ 9,750.00
26	$ 850.00	$ 850.00	$ 850.00	$ 850.00	$ 850.00			$ 1,100.00	$ 1,100.00	$ 1,100.00	$ 1,100.00	$ 1,100.00	$ 9,750.00
27	$ 850.00	$ 850.00	$ 850.00	$ 850.00	$ 850.00			$ 1,100.00	$ 1,100.00	$ 1,100.00	$ 1,100.00	$ 1,100.00	$ 9,750.00
28	$ 1,250.00	$ 1,250.00	$ 1,250.00	$ 1,250.00	$ 1,250.00	$ 1,250.00			$ 1,400.00	$ 1,400.00	$ 1,400.00	$ 1,400.00	$ 13,100.00
29	$ 1,250.00	$ 1,250.00	$ 1,250.00	$ 1,250.00	$ 1,250.00	$ 1,250.00			$ 1,400.00	$ 1,400.00	$ 1,400.00	$ 1,400.00	$ 13,100.00
30	$ 1,250.00	$ 1,250.00	$ 1,250.00	$ 1,250.00	$ 1,250.00	$ 1,250.00			$ 1,400.00	$ 1,400.00	$ 1,400.00	$ 1,400.00	$ 13,100.00

31	$ 1,250.00	$ 1,250.00	$ 1,250.00	$ 1,250.00	$ 1,250.00	$ 1,250.00			$ 1,400.00	$ 1,400.00	$ 1,400.00	$ 1,400.00	$ 13,100.00
32													$ -
33													$ -
34													$ -
35													$ -
36													$ -
37													$ -
38													$ -
39													$ -
40													$ -
41													$ -
42													$ -
43													$ -
44													$ -
45													$ -
46													$ -
47													$ -
48													$ -
49													$ -
50													$ -
Monthly Rent	$ 32,650.00	$ 29,200.00	$ 29,200.00	$ 28,200.00	$ 22,450.00	$ 23,600.00	$ 25,350.00	$ 30,850.00	$ 32,610.00	$ 32,610.00	$ 37,410.00	$ 37,410.00	$ 361,540.00

SECOND YEAR REPOSITIONING PRO FORMA RENTAL INCOME

Unit	Month 13	Month 14	Month 15	Month 16	Month 17	Month 18	Month 19	Month 20	Month 21	Month 22	Month 23	Month 24	Total
1	$1,200.00	$1,200.00	$1,200.00	$1,200.00	$1,200.00	$1,200.00	$1,200.00	$1,200.00	$1,200.00	$1,200.00	$1,200.00	$1,200.00	$14,400.00
2	$1,200.00	$1,200.00	$1,200.00	$1,200.00	$1,200.00	$1,200.00	$1,200.00	$1,200.00	$1,200.00	$1,200.00	$1,200.00	$1,200.00	$14,400.00
3	$1,200.00	$1,200.00	$1,200.00	$1,200.00	$1,200.00	$1,200.00	$1,200.00	$1,200.00	$1,200.00	$1,200.00	$1,200.00	$1,200.00	$14,400.00
4	$1,200.00	$1,200.00	$1,200.00	$1,200.00	$1,200.00	$1,200.00	$1,200.00	$1,200.00	$1,200.00	$1,200.00	$1,200.00	$1,200.00	$14,400.00
5	$1,200.00	$1,200.00	$1,200.00	$1,200.00	$1,200.00	$1,200.00	$1,200.00	$1,200.00	$1,200.00	$1,200.00	$1,200.00	$1,200.00	$14,400.00
6	$1,200.00	$1,200.00	$1,200.00	$1,200.00	$1,200.00	$1,200.00	$1,200.00	$1,200.00	$1,200.00	$1,200.00	$1,200.00	$1,200.00	$14,400.00
7	$1,200.00	$1,200.00	$1,200.00	$1,200.00	$1,200.00	$1,200.00	$1,200.00	$1,200.00	$1,200.00	$1,200.00	$1,200.00	$1,200.00	$14,400.00
8	$960.00			$1,200.00	$1,200.00	$1,200.00	$1,200.00	$1,200.00	$1,200.00	$1,200.00	$1,200.00	$1,200.00	$11,760.00
9	$960.00			$1,200.00	$1,200.00	$1,200.00	$1,200.00	$1,200.00	$1,200.00	$1,200.00	$1,200.00	$1,200.00	$11,760.00
10	$960.00	$960.00	$960.00			$1,200.00	$1,200.00	$1,200.00	$1,200.00	$1,200.00	$1,200.00	$1,200.00	$11,280.00
11	$960.00	$960.00	$960.00			$1,200.00	$1,200.00	$1,200.00	$1,200.00	$1,200.00	$1,200.00	$1,200.00	$11,280.00
12	$960.00	$960.00	$960.00	$960.00	$960.00			$1,200.00	$1,200.00	$1,200.00	$1,200.00	$1,200.00	$10,800.00
13	$960.00	$960.00	$960.00	$960.00	$960.00			$1,200.00	$1,200.00	$1,200.00	$1,200.00	$1,200.00	$10,800.00
14	$1,350.00	$1,350.00	$1,350.00	$1,350.00	$1,350.00	$1,350.00	$1,350.00	$1,350.00	$1,350.00	$1,350.00	$1,350.00	$1,350.00	$16,200.00
15	$1,350.00	$1,350.00	$1,350.00	$1,350.00	$1,350.00	$1,350.00	$1,350.00	$1,350.00	$1,350.00	$1,350.00	$1,350.00	$1,350.00	$16,200.00
16	$1,350.00	$1,350.00	$1,350.00	$1,350.00	$1,350.00	$1,350.00	$1,350.00	$1,350.00	$1,350.00	$1,350.00	$1,350.00	$1,350.00	$16,200.00
17	$1,350.00	$1,350.00	$1,350.00	$1,350.00	$1,350.00	$1,350.00	$1,350.00	$1,350.00	$1,350.00	$1,350.00	$1,350.00	$1,350.00	$16,200.00
18	$1,350.00	$1,350.00	$1,350.00	$1,350.00	$1,350.00	$1,350.00	$1,350.00	$1,350.00	$1,350.00	$1,350.00	$1,350.00	$1,350.00	$16,200.00
19	$1,350.00	$1,350.00	$1,350.00	$1,350.00	$1,350.00	$1,350.00	$1,350.00	$1,350.00	$1,350.00	$1,350.00	$1,350.00	$1,350.00	$16,200.00
20	$1,350.00	$1,350.00	$1,350.00	$1,350.00	$1,350.00	$1,350.00	$1,350.00	$1,350.00	$1,350.00	$1,350.00	$1,350.00	$1,350.00	$16,200.00
21	$1,350.00	$1,350.00	$1,350.00	$1,350.00	$1,350.00	$1,350.00	$1,350.00	$1,350.00	$1,350.00	$1,350.00	$1,350.00	$1,350.00	$16,200.00
22	$1,350.00	$1,350.00	$1,350.00	$1,350.00	$1,350.00	$1,350.00	$1,350.00	$1,350.00	$1,350.00	$1,350.00	$1,350.00	$1,350.00	$16,200.00
23	$1,100.00	$1,100.00	$1,100.00	$1,100.00	$1,100.00	$1,100.00	$1,100.00	$1,100.00	$1,100.00	$1,100.00	$1,100.00	$1,100.00	$13,200.00
24	$1,100.00	$1,100.00	$1,100.00	$1,100.00	$1,100.00	$1,100.00	$1,100.00	$1,100.00	$1,100.00	$1,100.00	$1,100.00	$1,100.00	$13,200.00
25	$1,100.00	$1,100.00	$1,100.00	$1,100.00	$1,100.00	$1,100.00	$1,100.00	$1,100.00	$1,100.00	$1,100.00	$1,100.00	$1,100.00	$13,200.00
26	$1,100.00	$1,100.00	$1,100.00	$1,100.00	$1,100.00	$1,100.00	$1,100.00	$1,100.00	$1,100.00	$1,100.00	$1,100.00	$1,100.00	$13,200.00

27	$ 1,100.00	$ 1,100.00	$ 1,100.00	$ 1,100.00	$ 1,100.00	$ 1,100.00	$ 1,100.00	$ 1,100.00	$ 1,100.00	$ 1,100.00	$ 1,100.00	$ 1,100.00	$ 13,200.00
28	$ 1,400.00	$ 1,400.00	$ 1,400.00	$ 1,400.00	$ 1,400.00	$ 1,400.00	$ 1,400.00	$ 1,400.00	$ 1,400.00	$ 1,400.00	$ 1,400.00	$ 1,400.00	$ 16,800.00
29	$ 1,400.00	$ 1,400.00	$ 1,400.00	$ 1,400.00	$ 1,400.00	$ 1,400.00	$ 1,400.00	$ 1,400.00	$ 1,400.00	$ 1,400.00	$ 1,400.00	$ 1,400.00	$ 16,800.00
30	$ 1,400.00	$ 1,400.00	$ 1,400.00	$ 1,400.00	$ 1,400.00	$ 1,400.00	$ 1,400.00	$ 1,400.00	$ 1,400.00	$ 1,400.00	$ 1,400.00	$ 1,400.00	$ 16,800.00
31	$ 1,400.00	$ 1,400.00	$ 1,400.00	$ 1,400.00	$ 1,400.00	$ 1,400.00	$ 1,400.00	$ 1,400.00	$ 1,400.00	$ 1,400.00	$ 1,400.00	$ 1,400.00	$ 16,800.00
32													$ -
33													$ -
34													$ -
35													$ -
36													$ -
37													$ -
38													$ -
39													$ -
40													$ -
41													$ -
42													$ -
43													$ -
44													$ -
45													$ -
46													$ -
47													$ -
48													$ -
49													$ -
50													$ -
Monthly Rent	$ 37,410.00	$ 35,490.00	$ 35,490.00	$ 35,970.00	$ 35,970.00	$ 36,450.00	$ 36,450.00	$ 38,850.00	$ 38,850.00	$ 38,850.00	$ 38,850.00	$ 38,850.00	$ 447,480.00

FIRST YEAR PRO FORMA BUDGET

Income	Month 1	Month 2	Month 3	Month 4	Month 5	Month 6	Month 7	Month 8	Month 9	Month 10	Month 11	Month 12	Total
Gross Potential Rent	$ 32,650.00	$ 29,200.00	$ 29,200.00	$ 28,200.00	$ 22,450.00	$ 23,600.00	$ 25,350.00	$ 30,850.00	$ 32,610.00	$ 32,610.00	$ 37,410.00	$ 37,410.00	$ 361,540.00
Vacancy	$ (2,500.00)	$ (2,500.00)	$ (1,500.00)	$ (2,500.00)	$ (1,500.00)	$ (1,500.00)	$ (500.00)	$ (500.00)	$ (500.00)	$ (500.00)	$ (500.00)	$ (500.00)	$ (15,000.00)
Concessions	$ (1,200.00)	$ (1,200.00)	$ (1,200.00)	$ (1,200.00)	$ (1,200.00)	$ (1,200.00)	$ (1,200.00)	$ -	$ -	$ -	$ -	$ -	$ (8,400.00)
Bad Debt	$ (500.00)	$ (500.00)	$ (500.00)	$ (500.00)	$ (500.00)	$ (500.00)	$ (500.00)	$ (500.00)	$ (500.00)	$ (500.00)	$ (500.00)	$ (500.00)	$ (6,000.00)
Other Income	$ -	$ -	$ -	$ -	$ -	$ -	$ -	$ -	$ -	$ -	$ -	$ -	$ -
Other Income	$ -	$ -	$ -	$ -	$ -	$ -	$ -	$ -	$ -	$ -	$ -	$ -	$ -
Laundry Income	$ 100.00	$ 100.00	$ 100.00	$ 100.00	$ 100.00	$ 100.00	$ 100.00	$ 100.00	$ 100.00	$ 100.00	$ 100.00	$ 100.00	$ 1,200.00
Parking Income	$ 180.00	$ 180.00	$ 180.00	$ 180.00	$ 180.00	$ 180.00	$ 180.00	$ 180.00	$ 180.00	$ 180.00	$ 180.00	$ 180.00	$ 2,160.00
Utility Reimbursement	$ 400.00	$ 400.00	$ 400.00	$ 400.00	$ 400.00	$ 400.00	$ 400.00	$ 400.00	$ 400.00	$ 400.00	$ 400.00	$ 400.00	$ 4,800.00
Other Income	$ -	$ -	$ -	$ -	$ -	$ -	$ -	$ -	$ -	$ -	$ -	$ -	$ -
Other Income	$ 50.00	$ 50.00	$ 50.00	$ 50.00	$ 50.00	$ 50.00	$ 50.00	$ 50.00	$ 50.00	$ 50.00	$ 50.00	$ 50.00	$ 600.00
Commercial Income	$ 100.00	$ 100.00	$ 100.00	$ 100.00	$ 100.00	$ 100.00	$ 100.00	$ 100.00	$ 100.00	$ 100.00	$ 100.00	$ 100.00	$ 1,200.00
Commercial Income	$ 100.00	$ 100.00	$ 100.00	$ 100.00	$ 100.00	$ 100.00	$ 100.00	$ 100.00	$ 100.00	$ 100.00	$ 100.00	$ 100.00	$ 1,200.00
Commercial Vacancy	$ (50.00)	$ (50.00)	$ (50.00)	$ (50.00)	$ (50.00)	$ (50.00)	$ (50.00)	$ (50.00)	$ (50.00)	$ (50.00)	$ (50.00)	$ (50.00)	$ (600.00)
Total Income	$ 29,330.00	$ 25,880.00	$ 26,880.00	$ 24,880.00	$ 20,130.00	$ 21,280.00	$ 24,030.00	$ 30,730.00	$ 32,490.00	$ 32,490.00	$ 37,290.00	$ 37,290.00	$ 342,700.00

Expenses	Month 1	Month 2	Month 3	Month 4	Month 5	Month 6	Month 7	Month 8	Month 9	Month 10	Month 11	Month 12	Total
Real Estate Taxes	$ 3,000.00	$ 3,000.00	$ 3,000.00	$ 3,000.00	$ 3,000.00	$ 3,000.00	$ 3,000.00	$ 3,000.00	$ 3,000.00	$ 3,000.00	$ 3,000.00	$ 3,000.00	$ 36,000.00
Other Taxes	$ 85.00	$ 85.00	$ 85.00	$ 85.00	$ 85.00	$ 85.00	$ 85.00	$ 85.00	$ 85.00	$ 85.00	$ 85.00	$ 85.00	$ 1,020.00
Insurance	$ 620.00	$ 620.00	$ 620.00	$ 620.00	$ 620.00	$ 620.00	$ 620.00	$ 620.00	$ 620.00	$ 620.00	$ 620.00	$ 620.00	$ 7,440.00
Fuel / Gas	$ 100.00	$ 100.00	$ 100.00	$ 100.00	$ 100.00	$ 100.00	$ 100.00	$ 100.00	$ 100.00	$ 100.00	$ 100.00	$ 100.00	$ 1,200.00
Electricity	$ 850.00	$ 850.00	$ 850.00	$ 850.00	$ 850.00	$ 850.00	$ 850.00	$ 850.00	$ 850.00	$ 850.00	$ 850.00	$ 850.00	$ 10,200.00
Trash Removal	$ 180.00	$ 180.00	$ 180.00	$ 180.00	$ 180.00	$ 180.00	$ 180.00	$ 180.00	$ 180.00	$ 180.00	$ 180.00	$ 180.00	$ 2,160.00
Water and Sewer	$ 780.00	$ 780.00	$ 780.00	$ 780.00	$ 780.00	$ 780.00	$ 780.00	$ 780.00	$ 780.00	$ 780.00	$ 780.00	$ 780.00	$ 9,360.00
Bldg Maint and Repair	$ 680.00	$ 680.00	$ 680.00	$ 680.00	$ 680.00	$ 680.00	$ 680.00	$ 680.00	$ 680.00	$ 680.00	$ 680.00	$ 680.00	$ 8,160.00
Cleaning/Turnover	$ 150.00	$ 150.00	$ 150.00	$ 150.00	$ 150.00	$ 150.00	$ 150.00	$ 150.00	$ 150.00	$ 150.00	$ 150.00	$ 150.00	$ 1,800.00
Landscape	$ 380.00	$ 380.00	$ 380.00	$ 380.00	$ 380.00	$ 380.00	$ 380.00	$ 380.00	$ 380.00	$ 380.00	$ 380.00	$ 380.00	$ 4,560.00
Management Fee	$ 1,200.00	$ 1,200.00	$ 1,200.00	$ 1,200.00	$ 1,200.00	$ 1,200.00	$ 1,200.00	$ 1,200.00	$ 1,200.00	$ 1,200.00	$ 1,200.00	$ 1,200.00	$ 14,400.00
Office Salary	$ 450.00	$ 450.00	$ 450.00	$ 450.00	$ 450.00	$ 450.00	$ 450.00	$ 450.00	$ 450.00	$ 450.00	$ 450.00	$ 450.00	$ 5,400.00
Maintenance Salary	$ 380.00	$ 380.00	$ 380.00	$ 380.00	$ 380.00	$ 380.00	$ 380.00	$ 380.00	$ 380.00	$ 380.00	$ 380.00	$ 380.00	$ 4,560.00
Security	$ 150.00	$ 150.00	$ 150.00	$ 150.00	$ 150.00	$ 150.00	$ 150.00	$ 150.00	$ 150.00	$ 150.00	$ 150.00	$ 150.00	$ 1,800.00
Payroll Taxes & Benefits	$ 100.00	$ 100.00	$ 100.00	$ 100.00	$ 100.00	$ 100.00	$ 100.00	$ 100.00	$ 100.00	$ 100.00	$ 100.00	$ 100.00	$ 1,200.00
Apt. Allowance	$ 750.00	$ 750.00	$ 750.00	$ 750.00	$ 750.00	$ 750.00	$ 750.00	$ 750.00	$ 750.00	$ 750.00	$ 750.00	$ 750.00	$ 9,000.00
Marketing	$ 120.00	$ 120.00	$ 120.00	$ 120.00	$ 120.00	$ 120.00	$ 120.00	$ 120.00	$ 120.00	$ 120.00	$ 120.00	$ 120.00	$ 1,440.00
Professional Fees	$ 86.00	$ 86.00	$ 86.00	$ 86.00	$ 86.00	$ 86.00	$ 86.00	$ 86.00	$ 86.00	$ 86.00	$ 86.00	$ 86.00	$ 1,032.00
Office Expenses	$ 54.00	$ 54.00	$ 54.00	$ 54.00	$ 54.00	$ 54.00	$ 54.00	$ 54.00	$ 54.00	$ 54.00	$ 54.00	$ 54.00	$ 648.00
Miscellaneous Expenses	$ 320.00	$ 320.00	$ 320.00	$ 320.00	$ 320.00	$ 320.00	$ 320.00	$ 320.00	$ 320.00	$ 320.00	$ 320.00	$ 320.00	$ 3,840.00
Total Expenses	$ 10,435.00	$ 10,435.00	$ 10,435.00	$ 10,435.00	$ 10,435.00	$ 10,435.00	$ 10,435.00	$ 10,435.00	$ 10,435.00	$ 10,435.00	$ 10,435.00	$ 10,435.00	$ 125,220.00

NOI	$18,895.00	$15,445.00	$16,445.00	$14,445.00	$9,695.00	$10,845.00	$13,595.00	$20,295.00	$22,055.00	$26,855.00	$26,855.00	$217,480.00
Mortgage 1 Payment	$7,161.23	$7,161.23	$7,161.23	$7,161.23	$7,161.23	$7,161.23	$7,161.23	$7,161.23	$7,161.23	$7,161.23	$7,161.23	$85,934.75
Mortgage 2 Payment	$5,368.22	$5,368.22	$5,368.22	$5,368.22	$5,368.22	$5,368.22	$5,368.22	$5,368.22	$5,368.22	$5,368.22	$5,368.22	$64,418.59
Operating Cash Flow	$6,365.55	$2,915.55	$3,915.55	$1,915.55	($2,834.45)	($1,684.45)	$1,065.55	$7,765.55	$9,525.55	$14,325.55	$14,325.55	$67,126.65
Month Beginning Cash	$50,000	$81,266	$79,081	$77,897	$69,712	$71,778	$74,993	$60,959	$68,624	$57,476	$61,701	
Month Cash Injection	**25,000**	**25,000**	**15,000**	**25,000**	**25,000**	**25,000**	**10,000**	**5,000**	**5,000**	**$ -**		**$185,000.00**
Available Cash	$81,366	$109,181	$97,997	$104,812	$91,878	$95,093	$101,059	$78,724	$83,150	$77,576	$71,801	$76,027
Less Renovation Cost	$ -	$30,000	$20,000	$35,000	$20,000	$20,000	$40,000	$10,000	$20,000	$20,000	$10,000	$245,000.00
Less Owner Draw	$100	$100	$100	$100	$100	$100	$100	$100	$100	$100	$100	$1,200.00
Month-End Cash	$81,266	$79,081	$77,897	$69,712	$71,778	$74,993	$60,959	$68,624	$63,050	$57,476	$61,701	$55,927

SECOND YEAR PRO FORMA BUDGET

Expense Increase %   3.00%

Income	Month 13	Month 14	Month 15	Month 16	Month 17	Month 18	Month 19	Month 20	Month 21	Month 22	Month 23	Month 24	Total
Gross Potential Rent	$ 37,410.00	$ 35,490.00	$ 35,490.00	$ 35,970.00	$ 35,970.00	$ 36,450.00	$ 36,450.00	$ 38,850.00	$ 38,850.00	$ 38,850.00	$ 38,850.00	$ 38,850.00	$ 447,480.00
Vacancy	$ (2,500.00)	$ (2,500.00)	$ (2,500.00)	$ (2,500.00)	$ (2,500.00)	$ (2,500.00)	$ (2,500.00)	$ (2,500.00)	$ (2,500.00)	$ (2,500.00)	$ (2,500.00)	$ (2,500.00)	$ (30,000.00)
Concessions	$ -	$ -	$ -	$ -	$ -	$ -	$ -	$ -	$ -	$ -	$ -	$ -	$ -
Bad Debt	$ (500.00)	$ (500.00)	$ (500.00)	$ (500.00)	$ (500.00)	$ (500.00)	$ (500.00)	$ (500.00)	$ (500.00)	$ (500.00)	$ (500.00)	$ (500.00)	$ (6,000.00)
Other Income	$ -	$ -	$ -	$ -	$ -	$ -	$ -	$ -	$ -	$ -	$ -	$ -	$ -
Other Income	$ -	$ -	$ -	$ -	$ -	$ -	$ -	$ -	$ -	$ -	$ -	$ -	$ -
Laundry Income	$ 100.00	$ 100.00	$ 100.00	$ 100.00	$ 100.00	$ 100.00	$ 100.00	$ 100.00	$ 100.00	$ 100.00	$ 100.00	$ 100.00	$ 1,200.00
Parking Income	$ 180.00	$ 180.00	$ 180.00	$ 180.00	$ 180.00	$ 180.00	$ 180.00	$ 180.00	$ 180.00	$ 180.00	$ 180.00	$ 180.00	$ 2,160.00
Utility Reimbursement	$ 400.00	$ 400.00	$ 400.00	$ 400.00	$ 400.00	$ 400.00	$ 400.00	$ 400.00	$ 400.00	$ 400.00	$ 400.00	$ 400.00	$ 4,800.00
Other Income	$ -	$ -	$ -	$ -	$ -	$ -	$ -	$ -	$ -	$ -	$ -	$ -	$ -
Other Income	$ 50.00	$ 50.00	$ 50.00	$ 50.00	$ 50.00	$ 50.00	$ 50.00	$ 50.00	$ 50.00	$ 50.00	$ 50.00	$ 50.00	$ 600.00
Commercial Income	$ 100.00	$ 100.00	$ 100.00	$ 100.00	$ 100.00	$ 100.00	$ 100.00	$ 100.00	$ 100.00	$ 100.00	$ 100.00	$ 100.00	$ 1,200.00
Commercial Income	$ 100.00	$ 100.00	$ 100.00	$ 100.00	$ 100.00	$ 100.00	$ 100.00	$ 100.00	$ 100.00	$ 100.00	$ 100.00	$ 100.00	$ 1,200.00
Commercial Vacancy	$ (50.00)	$ (50.00)	$ (50.00)	$ (50.00)	$ (50.00)	$ (50.00)	$ (50.00)	$ (50.00)	$ (50.00)	$ (50.00)	$ (50.00)	$ (50.00)	$ (600.00)
Total Income	$ 35,290.00	$ 33,370.00	$ 33,370.00	$ 33,850.00	$ 33,850.00	$ 34,330.00	$ 34,330.00	$ 36,730.00	$ 36,730.00	$ 36,730.00	$ 36,730.00	$ 36,730.00	$ 422,040.00

Expenses	Month 13	Month 14	Month 15	Month 16	Month 17	Month 18	Month 19	Month 20	Month 21	Month 22	Month 23	Month 24	Total
Real Estate Taxes	$ 3,090.00	$ 3,090.00	$ 3,090.00	$ 3,090.00	$ 3,090.00	$ 3,090.00	$ 3,090.00	$ 3,090.00	$ 3,090.00	$ 3,090.00	$ 3,090.00	$ 3,090.00	$ 37,080.00
Other Taxes	$ 87.55	$ 87.55	$ 87.55	$ 87.55	$ 87.55	$ 87.55	$ 87.55	$ 87.55	$ 87.55	$ 87.55	$ 87.55	$ 87.55	$ 1,050.60
Insurance	$ 638.60	$ 638.60	$ 638.60	$ 638.60	$ 638.60	$ 638.60	$ 638.60	$ 638.60	$ 638.60	$ 638.60	$ 638.60	$ 638.60	$ 7,663.20
Fuel/Gas	$ 103.00	$ 103.00	$ 103.00	$ 103.00	$ 103.00	$ 103.00	$ 103.00	$ 103.00	$ 103.00	$ 103.00	$ 103.00	$ 103.00	$ 1,236.00
Electricity	$ 875.50	$ 875.50	$ 875.50	$ 875.50	$ 875.50	$ 875.50	$ 875.50	$ 875.50	$ 875.50	$ 875.50	$ 875.50	$ 875.50	$ 10,506.00
Trash Removal	$ 185.40	$ 185.40	$ 185.40	$ 185.40	$ 185.40	$ 185.40	$ 185.40	$ 185.40	$ 185.40	$ 185.40	$ 185.40	$ 185.40	$ 2,224.80
Water and Sewer	$ 803.40	$ 803.40	$ 803.40	$ 803.40	$ 803.40	$ 803.40	$ 803.40	$ 803.40	$ 803.40	$ 803.40	$ 803.40	$ 803.40	$ 9,640.80
Bldg Maint and Repair	$ 700.40	$ 700.40	$ 700.40	$ 700.40	$ 700.40	$ 700.40	$ 700.40	$ 700.40	$ 700.40	$ 700.40	$ 700.40	$ 700.40	$ 8,404.80
Cleaning/Turnover	$ 154.50	$ 154.50	$ 154.50	$ 154.50	$ 154.50	$ 154.50	$ 154.50	$ 154.50	$ 154.50	$ 154.50	$ 154.50	$ 154.50	$ 1,854.00
Landscape	$ 391.40	$ 391.40	$ 391.40	$ 391.40	$ 391.40	$ 391.40	$ 391.40	$ 391.40	$ 391.40	$ 391.40	$ 391.40	$ 391.40	$ 4,696.80
Management Fee	$ 1,236.00	$ 1,236.00	$ 1,236.00	$ 1,236.00	$ 1,236.00	$ 1,236.00	$ 1,236.00	$ 1,236.00	$ 1,236.00	$ 1,236.00	$ 1,236.00	$ 1,236.00	$ 14,832.00
Office Salary	$ 463.50	$ 463.50	$ 463.50	$ 463.50	$ 463.50	$ 463.50	$ 463.50	$ 463.50	$ 463.50	$ 463.50	$ 463.50	$ 463.50	$ 5,562.00
Maintenance Salary	$ 391.40	$ 391.40	$ 391.40	$ 391.40	$ 391.40	$ 391.40	$ 391.40	$ 391.40	$ 391.40	$ 391.40	$ 391.40	$ 391.40	$ 4,696.80
Security Salary	$ 154.50	$ 154.50	$ 154.50	$ 154.50	$ 154.50	$ 154.50	$ 154.50	$ 154.50	$ 154.50	$ 154.50	$ 154.50	$ 154.50	$ 1,854.00
Payroll Taxes & Benefits	$ 103.00	$ 103.00	$ 103.00	$ 103.00	$ 103.00	$ 103.00	$ 103.00	$ 103.00	$ 103.00	$ 103.00	$ 103.00	$ 103.00	$ 1,236.00
Apt. Allowance	$ 772.50	$ 772.50	$ 772.50	$ 772.50	$ 772.50	$ 772.50	$ 772.50	$ 772.50	$ 772.50	$ 772.50	$ 772.50	$ 772.50	$ 9,270.00
Marketing	$ 123.60	$ 123.60	$ 123.60	$ 123.60	$ 123.60	$ 123.60	$ 123.60	$ 123.60	$ 123.60	$ 123.60	$ 123.60	$ 123.60	$ 1,483.20
Professional Fees	$ 88.58	$ 88.58	$ 88.58	$ 88.58	$ 88.58	$ 88.58	$ 88.58	$ 88.58	$ 88.58	$ 88.58	$ 88.58	$ 88.58	$ 1,062.96
Office Expenses	$ 55.62	$ 55.62	$ 55.62	$ 55.62	$ 55.62	$ 55.62	$ 55.62	$ 55.62	$ 55.62	$ 55.62	$ 55.62	$ 55.62	$ 667.44
Miscellaneous Expenses	$ 329.60	$ 329.60	$ 329.60	$ 329.60	$ 329.60	$ 329.60	$ 329.60	$ 329.60	$ 329.60	$ 329.60	$ 329.60	$ 329.60	$ 3,955.20
Total Expenses	$ 10,748.05	$ 10,748.05	$ 10,748.05	$ 10,748.05	$ 10,748.05	$ 10,748.05	$ 10,748.05	$ 10,748.05	$ 10,748.05	$ 10,748.05	$ 10,748.05	$ 10,748.05	$ 128,976.60

													Total
NOI	$24,541.95	$22,621.95	$22,621.95	$23,101.95	$23,101.95	$23,581.95	$23,581.95	$25,981.95	$25,981.95	$25,981.95	$25,981.95	$25,981.95	$293,063.40
Mortgage 1 Payment	$7,161.23	$7,161.23	$7,161.23	$7,161.23	$7,161.23	$7,161.23	$7,161.23	$7,161.23	$7,161.23	$7,161.23	$7,161.23	$7,161.23	$85,934.75
Mortgage 2 Payment	$5,368.22	$5,368.22	$5,368.22	$5,368.22	$5,368.22	$5,368.22	$5,368.22	$5,368.22	$5,368.22	$5,368.22	$5,368.22	$5,368.22	$64,418.59
Operating Cash Flow	$12,012.50	$10,092.50	$10,092.50	$10,572.50	$10,572.50	$11,052.50	$11,052.50	$13,452.50	$13,452.50	$13,452.50	$13,452.50	$13,452.50	$142,710.05
Month Beginning Cash	$55,927	$92,939	$98,032	$103,124	$103,697	$119,269	$135,322	$131,374	$154,827	$173,279	$191,732	$205,184	
Month Cash Injection	$25,000	$25,000	$15,000	$25,000	$25,000	$25,000	$25,000	$10,000	$5,000	$5,000	$ -	$ -	$185,000.00
Available Cash	$92,939	$128,032	$123,124	$138,697	$139,269	$155,322	$171,374	$154,827	$173,279	$191,732	$205,184	$218,637	
Less Renovation Cost	$ -	$30,000	$20,000	$35,000	$20,000	$20,000	$40,000						$165,000.00
Less Owner Draw	$100	$100	$100	$100	$100	$100	$100	$100	$100	$100	$100	$100	$1,200.00
Month-End Cash	$92,939	$98,032	$103,124	$103,697	$119,269	$135,322	$131,374	$154,827	$173,279	$191,732	$205,184	$218,637	

INVESTMENT INCOME VALUE SUMMARY

	Income	Expense	Net Income
Year 1	$ 342,700.00	$ 125,220.00	$ 217,480.00
Year 2	$ 422,040.00	$ 128,976.60	$ 293,063.40
Year 3	$ 462,798.00	$ 132,845.90	$ 329,952.10
Year 4	$ 485,937.90	$ 136,831.27	$ 349,106.63
Year 5	$ 510,267.87	$ 140,936.21	$ 369,331.66
Year 6	$ 535,781.26	$ 145,164.30	$ 390,616.96
Year 7	$ 562,570.33	$ 149,519.23	$ 413,051.10

Cap Rate	Income-Based Value						
	Year 1	Year 2	Year 3	Year 4	Year 5	Year 6	Year 7
4.00%	$ 5,437,000	$ 7,326,585	$ 8,248,803	$ 8,727,666	$ 9,233,291	$ 9,765,424	$ 10,326,277
4.50%	$ 4,832,889	$ 6,512,520	$ 7,332,269	$ 7,757,925	$ 8,207,370	$ 8,680,377	$ 9,178,913
5.00%	$ 4,349,600	$ 5,861,268	$ 6,599,042	$ 6,982,133	$ 7,386,633	$ 7,812,339	$ 8,261,022
5.50%	$ 3,954,182	$ 5,328,425	$ 5,999,129	$ 6,347,393	$ 6,715,121	$ 7,102,127	$ 7,510,020
6.00%	$ 3,624,667	$ 4,884,390	$ 5,499,202	$ 5,818,444	$ 6,155,528	$ 6,510,283	$ 6,884,185
6.50%	$ 3,345,846	$ 4,508,668	$ 5,076,186	$ 5,370,871	$ 5,682,025	$ 6,009,492	$ 6,354,632
7.00%	$ 3,106,857	$ 4,186,620	$ 4,713,601	$ 4,987,238	$ 5,276,167	$ 5,580,242	$ 5,900,730
7.50%	$ 2,899,733	$ 3,907,512	$ 4,399,361	$ 4,654,755	$ 4,924,422	$ 5,208,226	$ 5,507,348
8.00%	$ 2,718,500	$ 3,663,293	$ 4,124,401	$ 4,363,833	$ 4,616,646	$ 4,882,712	$ 5,163,139
8.50%	$ 2,558,588	$ 3,447,805	$ 3,881,789	$ 4,107,137	$ 4,345,078	$ 4,595,494	$ 4,859,425
9.00%	$ 2,416,444	$ 3,256,260	$ 3,666,134	$ 3,878,963	$ 4,103,685	$ 4,340,188	$ 4,589,457
9.50%	$ 2,289,263	$ 3,084,878	$ 3,473,180	$ 3,674,807	$ 3,887,702	$ 4,111,758	$ 4,347,906
10.00%	$ 2,174,800	$ 2,930,634	$ 3,299,521	$ 3,491,066	$ 3,693,317	$ 3,906,170	$ 4,130,511

	Year 1	Year 2	Year 3	Year 4	Year 5	Year 6	Year 7	
Owner Draw	$ 1,200	$ 1,200	$ 120,000	$ 225,000	$ 230,000	$ 245,000	$ 260,000	$ 1,082,400
Owner Cash Injection	$ 185,000	$ 185,000	$ 1,000	$ 4,000	$ 3,000	$ 2,000	$ 3,000	$ 383,000
					Owner Net Cash Position			$ 699,400
Less Renovation Cost	$ 245,000	$ 165,000	$ 170,000	$ 10,000	$ 20,000	$ 5,000	$ 3,000	$ 618,000
					Net Cash After Renovation			$ 81,400

Schedule of Real Estate Owned Spreadsheet: This gets attached to your personal financial statement and gives lenders everything they need to know about the properties you own.

Schedule of Real Estate Owned Short Form

Address	City	State	Zip	# Units	Current Value	Current Mortgage	Rent	Mortgage Payment	Taxes and Insurance	Operating Expenses
1234 Colonial Ave	Seattle	WA	98115	15	$ 200,000.00	$ 140,000.00	$ 1,800.00	$ 790.00	$ 2,400.00	$ 1,400.00
						$ 200,000.00	$ 140,000.00	$ 1,800.00	$ 790.00	$ 2,400.00	$ 1,400.00

Net Equity	$ 60,000.00

Seven-Year Month-by-Month Budget and Summary Spreadsheet: Use this spreadsheet to project how a commercial property will do over time.

FIRST YEAR PRO FORMA BUDGET

Income	Month 1	Month 2	Month 3	Month 4	Month 5	Month 6	Month 7	Month 8	Month 9	Month 10	Month 11	Month 12	Total
Gross Potential Rent	$ 36,000.00	$ 36,000.00	$ 37,000.00	$ 37,000.00	$ 38,000.00	$ 38,000.00	$ 39,000.00	$ 39,000.00	$ 39,000.00	$ 39,000.00	$ 39,000.00	$ 39,000.00	$ 456,000.00
Vacancy	$ (2,500.00)	$ (2,500.00)	$ (1,500.00)	$ (2,500.00)	$ (1,500.00)	$ (1,500.00)	$ (500.00)	$ (500.00)	$ (500.00)	$ (500.00)	$ (500.00)	$ (500.00)	$ (15,000.00)
Concessions	$ (1,200.00)	$ (1,200.00)	$ (1,200.00)	$ (1,200.00)	$ (1,200.00)	$ (1,200.00)	$ (1,200.00)	$ -	$ -	$ -	$ -	$ -	$ (8,400.00)
Bad Debt	$ (500.00)	$ (500.00)	$ (500.00)	$ (500.00)	$ (500.00)	$ (500.00)	$ (500.00)	$ (500.00)	$ (500.00)	$ (500.00)	$ (500.00)	$ (500.00)	$ (6,000.00)
Other Income	$ -	$ -	$ -	$ -	$ -	$ -	$ -	$ -	$ -	$ -	$ -	$ -	$ -
Other Income	$ -	$ -	$ -	$ -	$ -	$ -	$ -	$ -	$ -	$ -	$ -	$ -	$ -
Laundry Income	$ 100.00	$ 100.00	$ 100.00	$ 100.00	$ 100.00	$ 100.00	$ 100.00	$ 100.00	$ 100.00	$ 100.00	$ 100.00	$ 100.00	$ 1,200.00
Parking Income	$ 180.00	$ 180.00	$ 180.00	$ 180.00	$ 180.00	$ 180.00	$ 180.00	$ 180.00	$ 180.00	$ 180.00	$ 180.00	$ 180.00	$ 2,160.00
Utility Reimbursement	$ 400.00	$ 400.00	$ 400.00	$ 400.00	$ 400.00	$ 400.00	$ 400.00	$ 400.00	$ 400.00	$ 400.00	$ 400.00	$ 400.00	$ 4,800.00
Other Income	$ -	$ -	$ -	$ -	$ -	$ -	$ -	$ -	$ -	$ -	$ -	$ -	$ -
Other Income	$ 50.00	$ 50.00	$ 50.00	$ 50.00	$ 50.00	$ 50.00	$ 50.00	$ 50.00	$ 50.00	$ 50.00	$ 50.00	$ 50.00	$ 600.00
Commercial Income	$ 100.00	$ 100.00	$ 100.00	$ 100.00	$ 100.00	$ 100.00	$ 100.00	$ 100.00	$ 100.00	$ 100.00	$ 100.00	$ 100.00	$ 1,200.00
Commercial Income	$ 100.00	$ 100.00	$ 100.00	$ 100.00	$ 100.00	$ 100.00	$ 100.00	$ 100.00	$ 100.00	$ 100.00	$ 100.00	$ 100.00	$ 1,200.00
Commercial Vacancy	$ (50.00)	$ (50.00)	$ (50.00)	$ (50.00)	$ (50.00)	$ (50.00)	$ (50.00)	$ (50.00)	$ (50.00)	$ (50.00)	$ (50.00)	$ (50.00)	$ (600.00)
Total Income	$ 32,680.00	$ 32,680.00	$ 34,680.00	$ 33,680.00	$ 35,680.00	$ 35,680.00	$ 37,680.00	$ 38,880.00	$ 38,880.00	$ 38,880.00	$ 38,880.00	$ 38,880.00	$ 437,160.00

Expenses	Month 1	Month 2	Month 3	Month 4	Month 5	Month 6	Month 7	Month 8	Month 9	Month 10	Month 11	Month 12	Total
Real Estate Taxes	$ 3,000.00	$ 3,000.00	$ 3,000.00	$ 3,000.00	$ 3,000.00	$ 3,000.00	$ 3,000.00	$ 3,000.00	$ 3,000.00	$ 3,000.00	$ 3,000.00	$ 3,000.00	$ 36,000.00
Other Taxes	$ 85.00	$ 85.00	$ 85.00	$ 85.00	$ 85.00	$ 85.00	$ 85.00	$ 85.00	$ 85.00	$ 85.00	$ 85.00	$ 85.00	$ 1,020.00
Insurance	$ 620.00	$ 620.00	$ 620.00	$ 620.00	$ 620.00	$ 620.00	$ 620.00	$ 620.00	$ 620.00	$ 620.00	$ 620.00	$ 620.00	$ 7,440.00
Fuel/Gas	$ 100.00	$ 100.00	$ 100.00	$ 100.00	$ 100.00	$ 100.00	$ 100.00	$ 100.00	$ 100.00	$ 100.00	$ 100.00	$ 100.00	$ 1,200.00
Electricity	$ 850.00	$ 850.00	$ 850.00	$ 850.00	$ 850.00	$ 850.00	$ 850.00	$ 850.00	$ 850.00	$ 850.00	$ 850.00	$ 850.00	$ 10,200.00
Trash Removal	$ 180.00	$ 180.00	$ 180.00	$ 180.00	$ 180.00	$ 180.00	$ 180.00	$ 180.00	$ 180.00	$ 180.00	$ 180.00	$ 180.00	$ 2,160.00
Water and Sewer	$ 780.00	$ 780.00	$ 780.00	$ 780.00	$ 780.00	$ 780.00	$ 780.00	$ 780.00	$ 780.00	$ 780.00	$ 780.00	$ 780.00	$ 9,360.00
Bldg Maint and Repair	$ 680.00	$ 680.00	$ 680.00	$ 680.00	$ 680.00	$ 680.00	$ 680.00	$ 680.00	$ 680.00	$ 680.00	$ 680.00	$ 680.00	$ 8,160.00
Cleaning/ Turnover	$ 150.00	$ 150.00	$ 150.00	$ 150.00	$ 150.00	$ 150.00	$ 150.00	$ 150.00	$ 150.00	$ 150.00	$ 150.00	$ 150.00	$ 1,800.00
Landscape	$ 380.00	$ 380.00	$ 380.00	$ 380.00	$ 380.00	$ 380.00	$ 380.00	$ 380.00	$ 380.00	$ 380.00	$ 380.00	$ 380.00	$ 4,560.00
Management Fee	$ 1,200.00	$ 1,200.00	$ 1,200.00	$ 1,200.00	$ 1,200.00	$ 1,200.00	$ 1,200.00	$ 1,200.00	$ 1,200.00	$ 1,200.00	$ 1,200.00	$ 1,200.00	$ 14,400.00
Office Salary	$ 450.00	$ 450.00	$ 450.00	$ 450.00	$ 450.00	$ 450.00	$ 450.00	$ 450.00	$ 450.00	$ 450.00	$ 450.00	$ 450.00	$ 5,400.00
Maintenance Salary	$ 380.00	$ 380.00	$ 380.00	$ 380.00	$ 380.00	$ 380.00	$ 380.00	$ 380.00	$ 380.00	$ 380.00	$ 380.00	$ 380.00	$ 4,560.00
Security	$ 150.00	$ 150.00	$ 150.00	$ 150.00	$ 150.00	$ 150.00	$ 150.00	$ 150.00	$ 150.00	$ 150.00	$ 150.00	$ 150.00	$ 1,800.00
Payroll Taxes & Benefits	$ 100.00	$ 100.00	$ 100.00	$ 100.00	$ 100.00	$ 100.00	$ 100.00	$ 100.00	$ 100.00	$ 100.00	$ 100.00	$ 100.00	$ 1,200.00
Apt. Allowance	$ 750.00	$ 750.00	$ 750.00	$ 750.00	$ 750.00	$ 750.00	$ 750.00	$ 750.00	$ 750.00	$ 750.00	$ 750.00	$ 750.00	$ 9,000.00
Marketing	$ 120.00	$ 120.00	$ 120.00	$ 120.00	$ 120.00	$ 120.00	$ 120.00	$ 120.00	$ 120.00	$ 120.00	$ 120.00	$ 120.00	$ 1,440.00
Professional Fees	$ 86.00	$ 86.00	$ 86.00	$ 86.00	$ 86.00	$ 86.00	$ 86.00	$ 86.00	$ 86.00	$ 86.00	$ 86.00	$ 86.00	$ 1,032.00
Office Expenses	$ 54.00	$ 54.00	$ 54.00	$ 54.00	$ 54.00	$ 54.00	$ 54.00	$ 54.00	$ 54.00	$ 54.00	$ 54.00	$ 54.00	$ 648.00
Miscellaneous Expenses	$ 320.00	$ 320.00	$ 320.00	$ 320.00	$ 320.00	$ 320.00	$ 320.00	$ 320.00	$ 320.00	$ 320.00	$ 320.00	$ 320.00	$ 3,840.00
Total Expenses	$ 10,435.00	$ 10,435.00	$ 10,435.00	$ 10,435.00	$ 10,435.00	$ 10,435.00	$ 10,435.00	$ 10,435.00	$ 10,435.00	$ 10,435.00	$ 10,435.00	$ 10,435.00	$ 125,220.00
NOI	$ 22,245.00	$ 22,245.00	$ 24,245.00	$ 23,245.00	$ 25,245.00	$ 25,245.00	$ 27,245.00	$ 28,445.00	$ 28,445.00	$ 28,445.00	$ 28,445.00	$ 28,445.00	$ 311,940.00

SECOND YEAR PRO FORMA BUDGET			Rent Increase %		5.00%	Expense Increase %		3.00%				

Income	Month 13	Month 14	Month 15	Month 16	Month 17	Month 18	Month 19	Month 20	Month 21	Month 22	Month 23	Month 24	Total
Gross Potential Rent	$ 40,950.00	$ 40,950.00	$ 40,950.00	$ 40,950.00	$ 40,950.00	$ 40,950.00	$ 40,950.00	$ 40,950.00	$ 40,950.00	$ 40,950.00	$ 40,950.00	$ 40,950.00	$ 491,400.00
Vacancy	$ (2,625.00)	$ (2,625.00)	$ (2,625.00)	$ (2,625.00)	$ (2,625.00)	$ (2,625.00)	$ (2,625.00)	$ (2,625.00)	$ (2,625.00)	$ (2,625.00)	$ (2,625.00)	$ (2,625.00)	$ (31,500.00)
Concessions	$ -	$ -	$ -	$ -	$ -	$ -	$ -	$ -	$ -	$ -	$ -	$ -	$ -
Bad Debt	$ (525.00)	$ (525.00)	$ (525.00)	$ (525.00)	$ (525.00)	$ (525.00)	$ (525.00)	$ (525.00)	$ (525.00)	$ (525.00)	$ (525.00)	$ (525.00)	$ (6,300.00)
Other Income	$ -	$ -	$ -	$ -	$ -	$ -	$ -	$ -	$ -	$ -	$ -	$ -	$ -
Other Income	$ -	$ -	$ -	$ -	$ -	$ -	$ -	$ -	$ -	$ -	$ -	$ -	$ -
Laundry Income	$ 105.00	$ 105.00	$ 105.00	$ 105.00	$ 105.00	$ 105.00	$ 105.00	$ 105.00	$ 105.00	$ 105.00	$ 105.00	$ 105.00	$ 1,260.00
Parking Income	$ 189.00	$ 189.00	$ 189.00	$ 189.00	$ 189.00	$ 189.00	$ 189.00	$ 189.00	$ 189.00	$ 189.00	$ 189.00	$ 189.00	$ 2,268.00
Utility Reimbursement	$ 420.00	$ 420.00	$ 420.00	$ 420.00	$ 420.00	$ 420.00	$ 420.00	$ 420.00	$ 420.00	$ 420.00	$ 420.00	$ 420.00	$ 5,040.00
Other Income	$ -	$ -	$ -	$ -	$ -	$ -	$ -	$ -	$ -	$ -	$ -	$ -	$ -
Other Income	$ 52.50	$ 52.50	$ 52.50	$ 52.50	$ 52.50	$ 52.50	$ 52.50	$ 52.50	$ 52.50	$ 52.50	$ 52.50	$ 52.50	$ 630.00
Commercial Income	$ 105.00	$ 105.00	$ 105.00	$ 105.00	$ 105.00	$ 105.00	$ 105.00	$ 105.00	$ 105.00	$ 105.00	$ 105.00	$ 105.00	$ 1,260.00
Commercial Income	$ 105.00	$ 105.00	$ 105.00	$ 105.00	$ 105.00	$ 105.00	$ 105.00	$ 105.00	$ 105.00	$ 105.00	$ 105.00	$ 105.00	$ 1,260.00
Commercial Vacancy	$ (52.50)	$ (52.50)	$ (52.50)	$ (52.50)	$ (52.50)	$ (52.50)	$ (52.50)	$ (52.50)	$ (52.50)	$ (52.50)	$ (52.50)	$ (52.50)	$ (630.00)
Total Income	$ 38,724.00	$ 38,724.00	$ 38,724.00	$ 38,724.00	$ 38,724.00	$ 38,724.00	$ 38,724.00	$ 38,724.00	$ 38,724.00	$ 38,724.00	$ 38,724.00	$ 38,724.00	$ 464,688.00

Expenses	Month 13	Month 14	Month 15	Month 16	Month 17	Month 18	Month 19	Month 20	Month 21	Month 22	Month 23	Month 24	Total
Real Estate Taxes	$ 3,090.00	$ 3,090.00	$ 3,090.00	$ 3,090.00	$ 3,090.00	$ 3,090.00	$ 3,090.00	$ 3,090.00	$ 3,090.00	$ 3,090.00	$ 3,090.00	$ 3,090.00	$ 37,080.00
Other Taxes	$ 87.55	$ 87.55	$ 87.55	$ 87.55	$ 87.55	$ 87.55	$ 87.55	$ 87.55	$ 87.55	$ 87.55	$ 87.55	$ 87.55	$ 1,050.60
Insurance	$ 638.60	$ 638.60	$ 638.60	$ 638.60	$ 638.60	$ 638.60	$ 638.60	$ 638.60	$ 638.60	$ 638.60	$ 638.60	$ 638.60	$ 7,663.20
Fuel/Gas	$ 103.00	$ 103.00	$ 103.00	$ 103.00	$ 103.00	$ 103.00	$ 103.00	$ 103.00	$ 103.00	$ 103.00	$ 103.00	$ 103.00	$ 1,236.00
Electricity	$ 87.50	$ 87.50	$ 87.50	$ 87.50	$ 87.50	$ 87.50	$ 87.50	$ 87.50	$ 87.50	$ 87.50	$ 87.50	$ 87.50	$ 10,506.00
Trash Removal	$ 185.40	$ 185.40	$ 185.40	$ 185.40	$ 185.40	$ 185.40	$ 185.40	$ 185.40	$ 185.40	$ 185.40	$ 185.40	$ 185.40	$ 2,224.80
Water and Sewer	$ 803.40	$ 803.40	$ 803.40	$ 803.40	$ 803.40	$ 803.40	$ 803.40	$ 803.40	$ 803.40	$ 803.40	$ 803.40	$ 803.40	$ 9,640.80
Bldg Maint and Repair	$ 700.40	$ 700.40	$ 700.40	$ 700.40	$ 700.40	$ 700.40	$ 700.40	$ 700.40	$ 700.40	$ 700.40	$ 700.40	$ 700.40	$ 8,404.80
Cleaning/ Turnover	$ 154.50	$ 154.50	$ 154.50	$ 154.50	$ 154.50	$ 154.50	$ 154.50	$ 154.50	$ 154.50	$ 154.50	$ 154.50	$ 154.50	$ 1,854.00
Landscape	$ 391.40	$ 391.40	$ 391.40	$ 391.40	$ 391.40	$ 391.40	$ 391.40	$ 391.40	$ 391.40	$ 391.40	$ 391.40	$ 391.40	$ 4,696.80
Management Fee	$ 1,236.00	$ 1,236.00	$ 1,236.00	$ 1,236.00	$ 1,236.00	$ 1,236.00	$ 1,236.00	$ 1,236.00	$ 1,236.00	$ 1,236.00	$ 1,236.00	$ 1,236.00	$ 14,832.00
Office Salary	$ 463.50	$ 463.50	$ 463.50	$ 463.50	$ 463.50	$ 463.50	$ 463.50	$ 463.50	$ 463.50	$ 463.50	$ 463.50	$ 463.50	$ 5,562.00
Maintenance Salary	$ 391.40	$ 391.40	$ 391.40	$ 391.40	$ 391.40	$ 391.40	$ 391.40	$ 391.40	$ 391.40	$ 391.40	$ 391.40	$ 391.40	$ 4,696.80
Security Salary	$ 154.50	$ 154.50	$ 154.50	$ 154.50	$ 154.50	$ 154.50	$ 154.50	$ 154.50	$ 154.50	$ 154.50	$ 154.50	$ 154.50	$ 1,854.00
Payroll Taxes & Benefits	$ 103.00	$ 103.00	$ 103.00	$ 103.00	$ 103.00	$ 103.00	$ 103.00	$ 103.00	$ 103.00	$ 103.00	$ 103.00	$ 103.00	$ 1,236.00
Apt. Allowance	$ 772.50	$ 772.50	$ 772.50	$ 772.50	$ 772.50	$ 772.50	$ 772.50	$ 772.50	$ 772.50	$ 772.50	$ 772.50	$ 772.50	$ 9,270.00
Marketing	$ 123.60	$ 123.60	$ 123.60	$ 123.60	$ 123.60	$ 123.60	$ 123.60	$ 123.60	$ 123.60	$ 123.60	$ 123.60	$ 123.60	$ 1,483.20
Professional Fees	$ 88.58	$ 88.58	$ 88.58	$ 88.58	$ 88.58	$ 88.58	$ 88.58	$ 88.58	$ 88.58	$ 88.58	$ 88.58	$ 88.58	$ 1,062.96
Office Expenses	$ 55.62	$ 55.62	$ 55.62	$ 55.62	$ 55.62	$ 55.62	$ 55.62	$ 55.62	$ 55.62	$ 55.62	$ 55.62	$ 55.62	$ 667.44
Miscellaneous Expenses	$ 329.60	$ 329.60	$ 329.60	$ 329.60	$ 329.60	$ 329.60	$ 329.60	$ 329.60	$ 329.60	$ 329.60	$ 329.60	$ 329.60	$ 3,955.20
Total Expenses	$ 10,748.05	$ 10,748.05	$ 10,748.05	$ 10,748.05	$ 10,748.05	$ 10,748.05	$ 10,748.05	$ 10,748.05	$ 10,748.05	$ 10,748.05	$ 10,748.05	$ 10,748.05	$ 128,976.60
NOI	$ 27,975.95	$ 27,975.95	$ 27,975.95	$ 27,975.95	$ 27,975.95	$ 27,975.95	$ 27,975.95	$ 27,975.95	$ 27,975.95	$ 27,975.95	$ 27,975.95	$ 27,975.95	$ 335,711.40

INVESTMENT INCOME VALUE SUMMARY

	Income	Expense	Net Income
Year 1	$ 437,160.00	$ 125,220.00	$ 311,940.00
Year 2	$ 464,688.00	$ 128,976.60	$ 335,711.40
Year 3	$ 487,922.40	$ 132,845.90	$ 355,076.50
Year 4	$ 512,318.52	$ 136,831.27	$ 375,487.25
Year 5	$ 537,969.17	$ 140,936.21	$ 397,032.96
Year 6	$ 564,867.63	$ 145,164.30	$ 419,703.33
Year 7	$ 593,111.02	$ 149,519.23	$ 443,591.79

Cap Rate	Income-Based Value						
	Year 1	Year 2	Year 3	Year 4	Year 5	Year 6	Year 7
4.00%	$ 7,798,500	$ 8,392,785	$ 8,876,913	$ 9,387,181	$ 9,925,824	$ 10,492,583	$ 11,089,795
4.50%	$ 6,932,000	$ 7,460,253	$ 7,890,589	$ 8,344,161	$ 8,822,955	$ 9,326,741	$ 9,857,595
5.00%	$ 6,238,800	$ 6,714,228	$ 7,101,530	$ 7,509,745	$ 7,940,659	$ 8,394,067	$ 8,871,836
5.50%	$ 5,671,636	$ 6,103,844	$ 6,455,936	$ 6,827,041	$ 7,218,781	$ 7,630,970	$ 8,065,305
6.00%	$ 5,199,000	$ 5,595,190	$ 5,917,942	$ 6,258,121	$ 6,617,216	$ 6,995,056	$ 7,393,196
6.50%	$ 4,799,077	$ 5,164,791	$ 5,462,715	$ 5,776,727	$ 6,108,199	$ 6,456,974	$ 6,824,489
7.00%	$ 4,456,286	$ 4,795,877	$ 5,072,521	$ 5,364,104	$ 5,671,899	$ 5,995,762	$ 6,337,026
7.50%	$ 4,159,200	$ 4,476,152	$ 4,734,353	$ 5,006,497	$ 5,293,773	$ 5,596,044	$ 5,914,557
8.00%	$ 3,899,250	$ 4,196,393	$ 4,438,456	$ 4,693,591	$ 4,962,912	$ 5,246,292	$ 5,544,897
8.50%	$ 3,669,882	$ 3,949,546	$ 4,177,371	$ 4,417,497	$ 4,670,976	$ 4,937,686	$ 5,218,727
9.00%	$ 3,466,000	$ 3,730,127	$ 3,945,294	$ 4,172,081	$ 4,411,477	$ 4,663,370	$ 4,928,798
9.50%	$ 3,283,579	$ 3,533,804	$ 3,737,647	$ 3,952,497	$ 4,179,294	$ 4,417,930	$ 4,669,387
10.00%	$ 3,119,400	$ 3,357,114	$ 3,550,765	$ 3,754,872	$ 3,970,330	$ 4,197,033	$ 4,435,918

Trailing 12-Month Report (T-12): This spreadsheet shows the most current trailing 12 months of income and expenses in a month-by-month format. Most lenders require this, and it's a great tool for your due diligence.

TRAILING 12-MONTH P&L – T12

Income	Month 1	Month 2	Month 3	Month 4	Month 5	Month 6	Month 7	Month 8	Month 9	Month 10	Month 11	Month 12	Total
Gross Potential Rent													$ -
Vacancy													$ -
Collection Loss													$ -
Concessions													$ -
Other Income													$ -
Laundry Income													$ -
Parking Income													$ -
Utility Reimbursement													$ -
Total Income	$ -	$ -	$ -	$ -	$ -	$ -	$ -	$ -	$ -	$ -	$ -	$ -	$ -

Expenses	Month 1	Month 2	Month 3	Month 4	Month 5	Month 6	Month 7	Month 8	Month 9	Month 10	Month 11	Month 12	Total
Real Estate Taxes													$ -
Other Taxes													$ -
Insurance													$ -
Fuel/Gas													$ -
Electricity													$ -
Trash Removal													$ -
Water and Sewer													$ -
Bldg Maint and Repair													$ -
Cleaning/Turnover													$ -
Landscape													$ -

Expenses	Month 1	Month 2	Month 3	Month 4	Month 5	Month 6	Month 7	Month 8	Month 9	Month 10	Month 11	Month 12	Total
Management Fee													$ -
Office Salary													$ -
Maintenance Salary													$ -
Security													$ -
Payroll Taxes & Benefits													$ -
Apt. Allowance													$ -
Marketing													$ -
Professional Fees													$ -
Office Expenses													$ -
Miscellaneous Expenses													$ -
Total Expenses	$ -	$ -	$ -	$ -	$ -	$ -	$ -	$ -	$ -	$ -	$ -	$ -	$ -

| NOI | $ - | $ - | $ - | $ - | $ - | $ - | $ - | $ - | $ - | $ - | $ - | $ - | $ - |

Acknowledgments

This book would not be what it is without my editorial team at John Wiley & Sons: executive editor Richard Narramore, whose brilliant mind guided this work to be a hybrid between an encyclopedia and a how-to book—we called it our invention; developmental editor Vicki Adang, whose encouragement was unrelenting—early on, she told me, "You'll be spending a lot of time at the computer this summer, but it's going to be an invaluable book for so many people"; the professionalism of production editor Jayalakshmi Erkathil Thevarkandi; and the expertise of editorial assistant Victoria Anllo; in addition, the copyediting team at Cape Cod Compositors, who made my words sing.

My gratitude goes to Robert Powell, Nancy Lemas, and Rod Massimo, commercial real estate brokers and coaches, for the discussions we had that made the buying and selling chapters much more impactful, and to Tim Marshall, for his guidance on the art of 1031 exchanges. Many thanks to my commercial lending colleagues Kevin Geraci, Troy Willis, Fred Barrow, and Gregg Gregory for their input on the financing chapters.

I'd like to make special note of developer and client, Roy Carver, who assisted me in conveying accurately all the steps in developing a commercial property. Thanks to Fred Passmore, for creating commercial property analysis spreadsheets for this book. I'd also like to extend a special thanks to Peter Harris, commercial real estate coach, for the years we collaborated on the success of multitudes of new commercial real estate investors. The knowledge gleaned contributed greatly to the chapters on raising investor partners, repositioning, and management and leasing.

About the Author

Terry Painter is the president and founder of Apartment Loan Store and Business Loan Store—two mortgage-banking firms that have closed over four billion dollars in commercial loans nationally. He is a member of the Oregon Bankers Association, the Mortgage Bankers Association, and the *Forbes* Real Estate Council, where he is a contributing writer. Terry lives in Portland, Oregon, and the Dominican Republic.

For updates and additional tips on commercial real estate investment and financing, visit:

https://theencyclopediaofcommercialrealestateadvice.com

If you would like to have Terry Painter speak to your real estate group, you can contact him at:

terry@TheEncyclopediaOfCommercialRealEstateAdvice.com

For information on commercial loan products and daily interest rates, please visit:

https://apartmentloanstore.com
https://businessloanstore.com

Index